EARLY MUSLIM ARCHITECTURE

VOLUME I · PART II

EARLY MUSLIM ARCHITECTURE

BY

K. A. C. CRESWELL, C.B.E.

Second Edition ~~in two parts~~

VOLUME I PART II

UMAYYADS

A.D. 622–750

WITH A CONTRIBUTION ON
THE MOSAICS OF THE DOME
OF THE ROCK IN JERUSALEM
AND OF THE
GREAT MOSQUE IN DAMASCUS
By MARGUERITE
GAUTIER-VAN BERCHEM

HACKER ART BOOKS, NEW YORK, 1979

Volume One, first published
Oxford University Press, Oxford 1932
Revised second edition
Oxford University Press, Oxford 1969

Volume Two
Oxford University Press, Oxford 1940

This reprint of the revised edition 1969
for Volume One, and 1940 for Volume Two
has been authorized by
the Clarendon Press Oxford.

Reprinted by Hacker Art Books, Inc.
New York 1979

Library of Congress Catalogue Card Number 75-11057
ISBN 0-87817-176-2

Printed in the United States of America

TABLE OF CONTENTS

VOLUME I PART II

XI

THE AQṢĀ MOSQUE AT JERUSALEM[1]

The Second Aqṣā Mosque (al-Walīd)—The third Aqṣā Mosque (al-Manṣūr)—The Fourth Aqṣā Mosque (al-Mahdī)—The Fifth Aqṣā Mosque (aẓ-Ẓāhir)—The form of aẓ-Ẓāhir's mosque—Further discoveries—Reconstruction of al-Mahdī's mosque—The Umayyad Aqṣā Mosque—Hamilton's vital discovery—Details of the remains of al-Walīd's work.

THE SECOND AQṢĀ MOSQUE AT JERUSALEM.[2] We have seen above (pp. 32–4) that although no Arabic author says that ʿUmar built a mosque at Jerusalem, there is every reason for believing the statements of some early Christian sources that he actually did so, for the mean structure which he erected, apparently out of the ruins of the Stoa of Herod, was seen and described by Arculf.

When was this mean structure replaced? If we are to believe some of the Arabic authors who deal with this question, it was ʿAbd al-Malik who was the first to build an Aqṣā Mosque worthy of the name. These authors are Muqaddasī (985),[3] the author of the *First Muthīr* (1351),[4] and Mujīr ad-Dīn (1496);[5] but a discordant note is struck by Eutychius (939),[6] Ibn al-Athīr,[7] Bar Hebraeus,[8] and Ibn aṭ-Ṭiqṭaqā,[9] who attribute it to al-Walīd.

Fortunately we now possess a better authority than any of the above, the earliest of whom wrote over two centuries after the event. I am referring to the contemporary Aphrodito papyri,[10] the official correspondence of Qurra ibn Sharīk, Governor of Egypt from 90 to 96 H. (709–14), with Basilius, the Prefect (διοικητής) of the District of Aphrodito in Upper Egypt. No. 1403 reads:

ʻConcerning labourers and skilled workmen for Jerusalem.

ʻIn the name of God, Qurra, &c. . . . The maintenance of the labourers and skilled workmen for the mosque of Jerusalem (μασγίδα Ιεροσολύμων) and the palace of the Amīr al-Mu'minīn.'

ʻDocket: (Date.) Brought by Abū Ḥassān the courier; concerning labourers (?) and skilled workmen for Jerusalem.'[11]

No. 1414 contains the following:

ʻFor the cost of oil and salt for the maintenance of labourers employed on the mosque of Jerusalem and the palace of the Amīr al-Mu'minīn, 3 persons for 12 months. . . .'[12]

No. 1435 contains the following:

ʻEpeiph—same [14th] Indiction [25 July/24 Aug. 715], for work at the mosque of Jerusalem . . . ibn Yazīd, 1 labourer for 6 months, with ½s. for provisions on the journey, 4½s.

And farther on:

ʻHathyr 20, 14 Indiction [16 Nov./15 Dec. 715], for a shift (?) for the construction of the mosque of Jerusalem . . . ibn Yazīd the superintendent, in the present 14th Ind., year 97, 3 labourers with supplies in money for 12 months, viz. 7½s. each including ½s. each for provisions [on the journey]. 22½s.'[13]

And another reads:

ʻPhaopi 6, collected by the same for [supplies?] for labourers on the mosque of Jerusalem, ⅝ labourer for 12 months. . . .'[14]

[1] In the first edition of my *E.M.A.*, this chapter on the Aqṣā Mosque was placed in Vol. II, because at that time the oldest part that could be reconstructed was the Aqṣā Mosque of al-Mahdī. But as we can now prove the existence in the present structure of part of the Aqṣā Mosque of al-Walīd, it has been necessary to put it back (with the necessary additions) so as to come after the Great Mosque of Damascus. If the question is asked: why give all these details about the mosque at later periods? the answer must be that it is only by a process of subtraction that one can arrive at, and single out, the part that belongs to the earliest period.

[2] For the first Aqṣā Mosque, see above, pp. 32–4.

[3] P. 168; Le Strange's transl., *P.P.T.S.*, III (γ), p. 41; Ranking's transl., pp. 275–6.

[4] Le Strange's text, in the *J.R.A.S.*, N.S., XIX, p. 303; transl., p. 285; copied verbatim by Shams ad-Dīn as-Suyūṭī (1470).

[5] Pp. 240–42 (copied verbatim from the *First Muthīr*); Sauvaire's transl., pp. 48–51. He adds, however, that the eastern part fell down during the reign of al-Walīd and was re-built by him; p. 242; transl., p. 52.

[6] Pococke's ed., II, p. 373; Cheikho's ed., II, p. 42, ll. 2–3.

[7] V, p. 5.

[8] *Dynasties*, Bedjan's text, p. 201; transl., Budge's p. 129.

[9] Derenbourg's ed., p. 173; Amar's transl., p. 203.

[10] Discovered at Kōm Ishgauh (30 miles north of Sohāg) in 1901.

[11] Bell (H. I.), *Greek Papyri in the British Museum*, IV, pp. 75–6; and *Translations of the Greek Aphrodito Papyri*, *Der Islam*, II, p. 383. This dispatch of workmen from Egypt to Jerusalem was not an innovation, for we learn from Leontius of Neapolis (wrote A. D. 645) that Modestus, about A. D. 629, sent thousands of Egyptians to Jerusalem to assist in the rebuilding of churches which had been destroyed by the Persians in 614; see his *Life of John, Archbishop of Alexandria*, Gelzer's ed., p. 37, and notes on pp. 137–8.

[12] *Der Islam*, III, p. 137.

[13] *Ibid.*, IV, pp. 93 and 95.

[14] *Der Islam*, XVII, p. 6.

Thus there can no longer be any doubt that it was al-Walīd and not 'Abd al-Malik who built the second Aqṣā Mosque.[1] And this puts a certain statement of al-'Umarī in a new light.

'The Khalif al-Walīd used it [the postal service] for transporting from Constantinople to Damascus, mosaic, that is to say the tesserae of gilt glass wherewith to face the walls of the Great Mosque at Damascus, and to Mekka, Madīna, and Jerusalem; nothing is left of it now [740 H. = 1340] except what there is at Damascus in the ṣaḥn, a remnant at Mekka . . . and a remnant in the Qubbat aṣ-Ṣakhra; all the rest has disappeared.'[2]

al-'Umarī has jumped to the conclusion that the mosaics which his source (not specified) states were sent to Jerusalem were for the Qubbat aṣ-Ṣakhra, which had been finished fourteen years before al-Walīd's accession. I believe that they were intended for the mosque which, according to the Aphrodito papyri, he was building there, in other words the second Aqṣā Mosque, hitherto erroneously attributed to 'Abd al-Malik.

THE THIRD AQṢĀ MOSQUE. How long did al-Walīd's structure last? The *First Muthīr* (1351) gives the answer as follows: 'when the Khalif Abū Ja'far al-Manṣūr came [to Jerusalem] both the eastern and 'the western portions of the mosque had fallen down. Then it was reported to him: "O Commander '" of the Faithful, verily the eastern part of the mosque and the western part also fell down at the time of '" the earthquake in the year 130 (Sept. 747–Aug. 748);[3] now, therefore, do thou give orders to rebuild '" the same and raise it again." And he replied: "I have no money", but he ordered the plates of silver 'and of gold that overlaid the gates to be stripped off and they coined therefrom dīnārs and dirhems, 'which moneys were expended on the rebuilding of the Mosque until it was completed.'[4]

Le Strange suggests that this took place in 154 H. (771), for in that year al-Manṣūr visited Jerusalem and prayed in the mosque.[5] But I find that he had already visited Jerusalem in 141 H. (758/9) according to Mas'ūdī.[6] As the people of Jerusalem doubtless took the earliest opportunity to appeal on behalf of the mosque, I suggest that this is the more probable date.

THE FOURTH AQṢĀ MOSQUE. According to the *First Muthīr* another earthquake[7] took place a few years later.[8] This must be the earthquake 'in the days of the 'Abbāsids', mentioned by Muqaddasī, which he says 'threw down the sanctuary [*mughaṭṭa* = the covered portion; see above, p. 27, n. 13] 'except the part around the miḥrāb. Now when the Khalīf heard of this, he was informed that not all the 'sums in the Treasury would suffice to restore it to its former state. So he wrote to the Governors of the 'Provinces and the other Commanders, directing that each should undertake the building of an arcade '(*riwāq*). So they rebuilt it stronger and more massive in construction than it had been; and the more 'ancient portion remained, even like a beauty spot, in the midst [of the new]. This portion extends as 'far as the limit of the marble columns, for beyond, where the columns are built up (*mushaiyada*), the 'later part commences.'[9]

According to the author of the *Muthīr*, it was the Khalif al-Mahdī who was responsible for this work. He adds the following information: 'And the Khalif said that the mosque had been [of old] too

[1] Or that at least part (i.e. the final part) of the work was due to al-Walīd as H. I. Bell suggests; *The Aphrodito Papyri*, in the *Journal of Hellenic Studies*, XXVIII, p. 116.

[2] *Ta'rīf*, p. 185, ll. 7 ff.; quoted by van Berchem, *C.I.A.—Jérusalem*, II, p. 242, n. 1.

[3] The earthquake of this year is also mentioned by Theophanes, I, pp. 662–3 (under A. M. 6248 = 748), Dionysius of Tell Maḥrē, Chabot's text, p. 47; transl., p. 42 (under year 1059 = 747/8); Severus ibn al-Muqaffa', Evetts' ed., in the *Patrologia Orientalis*, V, pp. 139–40 (apparently under A.D. 750); Agapius of Manbij, *Kitāb al-'Unwān*, Vasiliev's ed., *ibid.*, VIII, p. 521; Elias of Nisibis, Delaporte's transl., p. 105 (under 131 H. = 748/9); Cedrenus, II, p. 7 (under 6th year of Constantine Copronymus = A. D. 746/7); Zonaras, III, p. 268; and Michael the Syrian, Chabot's text, II, p. 510; transl., II, p. 466.

This footnote is exactly as it appeared in my first edition, yet Sauvaget (in *La Mosquée omeyyade de Médine*, p. 188) has the nerve to write: 'Pour lui la mosquée d'al-Walīd a été renversée par un tremblement de terre en 130 = 747–48 *mais il note lui même (p. 120) que cet accident n'est connu que par un auteur tardif dont le témoignage ne peut être reçu sans un recoupement par un texte plus autorisé.*' The lines in italics are *not* to be found in my book, they have been invented by Sauvaget. Moreover, according to Sauvaget the only authority I cite is Dionysius of Tell Maḥrē (d. 847), whereas I cite eight authors, beginning with Theophanes (d. 818).

[4] Le Strange's text, *loc. cit.*, p. 304; transl., pp. 286–7; and his *Palestine*, pp. 92–3; copied verbatim by Shams ad-Dīn as-Suyūṭī and Mujīr ad-Dīn, p. 250; Sauvaire's transl., p. 59.

[5] *Op. cit.*, p. 93. al-Manṣūr's visit in 154 H. is recorded by Ṭabarī, III, p. 372; Elias of Nisibis, transl., p. 110; and Ibn al-Athīr, IV, p. 467.

[6] VI, p. 212; and Elias of Nisibis, transl., p. 108.

[7] I cannot help feeling that this second earthquake may be a duplication of the same event, for the former is well documented (note 3) *but not the second.*

[8] *Loc. cit.*, p. 304; transl., p. 287; Mujīr ad-Dīn, p. 250; transl., pp. 59–60.

[9] P. 168; Le Strange's transl., *P.P.T.S.*, III (γ), pp. 41–2; and in his *Palestine*, p. 98; Ranking's transl., p. 276.

narrow, and of too great length—and [for this reason] it had not been much used by the people—so now they should curtail it in length (*ṭūlihi*) and increase it in breadth (*'arḍihi*).'[1] There is a curious error here, for although the text is clear we shall see that al-Mahdī reduced its width and increased its depth. As for the year, Le Strange suggests 163 H. (780),[2] for in that year, according to Ṭabarī,[3] he went to Jerusalem and prayed in the Aqṣā Mosque.

Here is the only description which we possess of this mosque, that of Muqaddasī: 'The covered 'portion (*mughaṭṭa*) of the mosque has twenty-six doors. The door opposite the miḥrāb, called the '*Bāb an-Nuḥās al-a'ẓam*, is plated with gilded brass (*ṣufr*) and is so heavy that only a man strong of 'shoulder and arm can open one half. To the right hand of it are seven large doors, the centre one of 'which is covered with gilt plates; and on the left the same. And on the eastern side are eleven doors, 'unornamented. Over the fifteen is a portico (*riwāq*) supported on marble pillars, which was erected 'by 'Abd Allāh ibn Ṭāhir [Governor of Syria 205–7 H. = 820–22]. In the court of the mosque on the 'right-hand side [i.e. along the west side of the Temple Area] are porticoes (*arwiqa*) supported by 'marble columns (*'amūd*) and piers (*usṭuwāna*); and at the back [i.e. on the north side of the Temple 'Area] are porticoes (*arwiqa*) vaulted in stone. Over the centre part of the covered portion is a mighty 'gable roof (*jamal*) over which rises a beautiful dome. The roofs (*suqūf*) everywhere, with the ex-'ception of that of the halls on the farther side of the court, are sheathed with lead. . . .'[4]

What was this mosque like? Let us leave this question for a moment and follow the history of the building.

THE FIFTH AQṢĀ MOSQUE. A great earthquake on 15 Muḥarram 425 (10th Dec. 1033)[5] damaged the Aqṣā Mosque, and necessitated its rebuilding by the Fāṭimid Khalif aẓ-Ẓāhir in 426 H. (1035). This mosque was seen by Nāṣir-i-Khusrau in A. D. 1045; according to him it measured 420 cubits from north to south and 150 from east to west.[6] The former measurement is manifestly absurd for it would bring the façade up to the Dome of the Rock, and Le Strange, the only author who has attempted to reconstruct the Aqṣā Mosque of this time, proposes to emend the figure to 120.[7] But it is waste of time attempting to tinker with Nāṣir's description. For example, he says that there were 280 columns, which we shall see is equally absurd.

The Aqṣā Mosque in its present form (Fig. 445) has generally been regarded as mainly due to the Crusaders and Saladin, but that is a great mistake. It is true that parts to east and west of the nave are obviously Crusaders' work, and that the miḥrāb is due to Saladin, but a great deal of aẓ-Ẓāhir's work remains! Our knowledge of the structure has been enormously increased during the last forty years, first by the details laid bare by the late Kemāl ad-Dīn, the very competent Turkish architect who was employed by the Supreme Muslim Council in 1924–7, to repair the mosque; and secondly by the continuous observations made by members of the Department of Antiquities during the works executed under the direction of Maḥmūd Pasha Aḥmad in 1938–42.[8]

1 Arabic text in the *J.R.A.S.*, N.S., XIX, p. 304; transl., p. 287; Le Strange, *op. cit.*, p. 93; repeated by Shams ad-Dīn as-Suyūṭī; and Mujīr ad-Dīn, p. 250; transl., p. 60.

2 *Palestine*, p. 93.

3 III, p. 500.

4 P. 168; transl. by Le Strange, *P.P.T.S.*, III (γ), p. 42; and in nis *Palestine*, pp. 98–9; Ranking's transl., pp. 276–7.

5 Le Strange (*Palestine*, p. 103) says 'the earthquakes of the years 407 H. or 425 H.', but we have seen (above, pp. 94–6) that there is no reason for believing that there was any earthquake in 407 H. As for that of 425 H., it was the earthquake which destroyed Ramla (see above, p. 182) and also damaged the southern and eastern outer wall of the Temple Area, for its repair a year later by the Khalif aẓ-Ẓāhir is recorded by an inscription on two of the crenellations near the south-east corner; de Vogüé, *Temple de Jérusalem*, p. 77; Le Strange, *P.E.F., Q.St.*, 1888, pp. 279–80; and his *Palestine*, p. 101; and van Berchem, *C.I.A.—Jérusalem*, II, pp. 15–18.

6 Schefer's ed., p. 25; transl., pp. 79–80; Le Strange's transl., in the *P.P.T.S.*, IV (α), pp. 37–8; and his *Palestine*, pp. 105–106.

7 *Op. cit.*, p. 104.

8 No records were ever published of the facts about the structure revealed during the works of Kemāl ad-Dīn, except those that I was able to make, through happening to be in Jerusalem part of the time, measuring and photographing in the Dome of the Rock.

So some years later, when I heard that very extensive works were about to be undertaken on the Aqṣā Mosque under the direction of Maḥmūd Pasha Aḥmad, I was determined to do all I could to avoid the loss of priceless archaeological information. I therefore went to Jerusalem in February 1938 with a letter from Sir Walter Smart of our Embassy in Cairo to General Sir Arthur Wauchope, High Commissioner, Palestine. After I had explained the cause of my anxiety he passed me on to Mr. Kirkbride, who passed me on to the Supreme Muslim Council. There I was most successful, for it was agreed that representatives of the Department of Antiquities would be allowed to be present throughout the duration of the works, to take photographs, to make drawings and take whatever measurements they wished. They were also to be allowed to make small 'sondages' provided it did not interfere with the work. This agreement was faithfully kept, and the wealth of information thereby obtained has been admirably presented, with real forensic skill, by R. W. Hamilton in *The Structural History of the Aqsa Mosque*, Oxford, 1949.

(1) Kemāl ad-Dīn stripped the plaster from the north face and spandrels of the northern dome-bearing arch, and exposed a splendid decoration in glass mosaic, consisting of great scrolls of acanthus[1] surmounted by two lines of Kufic inscription, just below the ceiling, in the name of the Fāṭimid Khalif aẓ-Ẓāhir.[2] This inscription is somewhat similar to but not the same as that dated 426 H. (1035) seen by ʿAlī of Herāt in 1173.[3] This proves that this great dome-bearing arch cannot be later than 1035.

(2) He partly stripped the lead covering from the lower rim of the wooden dome. This lower rim or 'lip' is turned out slightly, so as to throw off rain-water and snow. It is maintained in this position by a series of projecting beams or consoles, as in the Dome of the Rock (above, Fig. 33), which are set in the drum like the spokes of a wheel. They project about 75 cm. and hold up the lip. They were entirely covered by a lead casing, and were re-cased after the works were finished. I was fortunate enough to see them exposed; most of them were very badly worm-eaten but a few, which had escaped more or less, were carved on their under side with early Fāṭimid ornament (Fig. 120, facing p. 272, in Vol. II, 1st ed.). This proves that the drum of the dome cannot be later than aẓ-Ẓāhir, and therefore the four dome-bearing arches also, and not merely the one below the inscription.

(3) All the arches of the mosque are braced by ties, consisting of two beams laid parallel, with bracing pieces between like the rungs of a ladder. Nailed to the lower side of each pair is a plank with remarkable painted decoration. This decorated part, as well as the sides of the beams, had been covered by a deal casing, shaped like a trough and painted yellow. The casing of some ten or twelve ties was removed and their painted decoration exposed. One tie, next to the south wall and to the west of the miḥrāb, bore similar decoration and across it ran a band of eleventh-century Kufic. At least some arches near the dome must therefore be due to aẓ-Ẓāhir.

(4) The first tie next the dome on either side of the central aisle was stripped also; similar painted decoration was revealed on the under side of each. These two arches must therefore be the work of aẓ-Ẓāhir also. The rest are of exactly the same form, so there can be little doubt that the two arcades which form the wide central aisle are also the work of aẓ-Ẓāhir.[4]

Now let us look at the plan (Fig. 446, facing p. 379). We observe that a row of great round columns still exists intact to the east of the nave arcade for, although three have been encased in piers, their great capitals are still visible but, whereas the nave measures 11·80 m. wide from centre to centre of the columns, this side aisle is 7·10 m. only. If we go one aisle farther east (width 6·60 only) we find that only one great column has survived. But more of the part on slenderer columns to the east and west of the dome has been preserved.

It will be observed that the northern and southern dome-bearing arches are continued to east and west so as to carry the thrust through to the side walls, thus creating a sort of T-plan on paper but not in reality, for all the aisle arcades are carried right through to the qibla wall. It is therefore quite different from the T-plan of the Great Mosque at Qairawān.

Thus it is clear that a large part of the present mosque (before the works of 1938–42) is the work of aẓ-Ẓāhir or earlier, viz. the arcades of the central aisle, the four arches under the dome and the drum up to its top edge, an arcade to the east of the nave arcades, the arcades to the left of the eastern dome-bearing arch, and the two corresponding arcades on the opposite side with their tie-beams.

Sauvaget (*Mosquée*, p. 188) admits that 'les conditions dans lesquelles j'ai dû consulter ce livre (my *E.M.A.*, II, pp. 119–26) ne m'ont pas permis de faire mieux que survoler ces pages' (presumably he saw it in a bookseller's shop), yet by merely looking at my Fig. 119 he feels able to decide that the wide central aisle, which we know is due to the Fāṭimid Khalif aẓ-Ẓāhir in 426 H. (1035), was Umayyad, likewise the dome, although it cannot be due to al-Walīd, because transverse arcades had to be added subsequently to his structure to take its thrust. He goes even farther. He even asserts that the marble columns to right and left of the dome 'ne peuvent être antérieures à la restauration fatimide' (*Mosquée*, p. 101, n. 2). All this after merely glancing at Fig. 119 in my second volume (1st ed.).

[1] There were a number of bare patches, chiefly in the gold background, but they have since been restored.

[2] This inscription has been published by Wiet, in van Berchem, *C.I.A.—Jérusalem*, II, pp. 452–3; and in his *Répertoire d'épigraphie arabe*, VII, p. 7.

[3] Bodleian MS., fol. 36 *b*; passage printed by Le Strange, in the *P.E.F.*, *Q.St.*, 1888, p. 280; transl. in his *Palestine*, p. 102, van Berchem, *op. cit.*, II, pp. 381–92; and Wiet, *op. cit.*, VII, pp. 6–7.

[4] ʿAlī of Herāt, speaking of the inscription which he saw, says: 'This inscription, as well as the aisles, are all done over with mosaics of gold, and these the Franks have not touched or in any way damaged'; Bodl. MS., fol. 38 *b*; Le Strange, *op. cit.*, p. 102.

THE FORM OF AZ-ẒĀHIR'S MOSQUE. The northern limit of aẓ-Ẓāhir's mosque must have been the same as to-day for the three central doorways, on account of their mouldings (Fig. 121, in Vol. II, 1st ed.), must date from the eighth century at the latest. This disposes of the fantastic figure of 420 cubits from north to south, given by Nāṣir-i-Khusrau, which, as I have said, would bring the front right up to the Dome of the Rock. My general conclusions may be summarized as follows:

(1) Quite a large part of the present Aqṣā Mosque is the work of the Fāṭimid Khalif aẓ-Ẓāhir.

(2) His mosque consisted of a series of seven aisles formed by arcades running perpendicular to the qibla wall, of which all except the two on either side of the centre consisted of eleven arches.

(3) The central aisle was nearly double the width of the rest (11·80 against 6·50 m.); it had a clerestorey, and was covered by a great gable roof, beyond which rose a great wooden dome.

(4) The transverse dome-bearing arches were carried through to the side walls on account of their thrust.[1] The side aisles were covered by gable roofs at a lower level than the great gable and parallel to it. The width of this mosque cannot be fixed with certainty, but it is obvious that Nāṣir's figure of 280 for the number of columns is absurd, for it would imply at least twenty-five aisles, involving a width of about 170 m., which is impossible, for he himself says that there was a clear space of 200 cubits between the south-east corner of the Ḥaram ash-Sharīf and the east side of the mosque.[2] I am inclined to believe that aẓ-Ẓahīr's mosque was no wider than the present building, that is to say that it consisted of seven aisles only.

FURTHER DISCOVERIES. During the works carried out between 1938 and 1942 the whole of the two arcades flanking the east side of the nave were taken down and replaced by new ones. It was then discovered:

(i) that the great columns of the nave and to the east of it were not columns at all, but were round piers 85 cm. in diameter, built in courses of stone, there being two semicircular blocks in each course,[3] and

(ii) that the two northern wall-piers in which these two arcades terminated were not bonded into the north wall, and

(iii) that the position and springing of an earlier arcade was revealed by two superimposed stones, 72 cm. wide, which curved out slightly from the wall, and of which the axis did not correspond with that of the arcades which had been demolished, but was displaced towards the east. The same feature was observed at the northern end of the western arcade, except that it was displaced towards the west. The same condition was revealed at the opposite end of the nave, the abutment of earlier arcades being found, displaced outwards in both cases, so that the previous nave must have been about 72 cm. wider, i.e. 11·40 instead of 10·68 m.[4]

Hamilton emphasizes that there was no indication that the mosaic decoration of aẓ-Ẓāhir had ever extended to meet the lines of these earlier arcades,[5] in other words it is clear that his decoration was executed in connexion with the arcades just demolished.

This proves that the dome-bearing arches are older than aẓ-Ẓāhir, and consequently the transverse arcades which take the thrust. We can now say, from the history of the mosque, that these earlier arcades must belong to the work of al-Mahdī, and likewise the great dome-bearing arches against which they abut.

But this is not all. Excavations beneath the floor showed that the foundation blocks of the supports of al-Mahdī's mosque were only about 62–65 cm. square. I say 'supports' because Muqaddasī, as we have seen, says that they were *mushaiyada* (= built up); they were therefore either columns built in courses or, according to Hamilton,[6] rectangular masonry piers like those used by him to carry his transverse arches to the east of the dome (Plate 63). Eight bases in a row were found, and are marked

[1] We shall see that these transverse arcades as well as the dome-bearing arches are actually earlier than aẓ-Ẓāhir, and were merely incorporated by him in his reconstruction.

[2] Schefer's text, p. 25; Le Strange's transl., IV (*a*), p. 36; and his *Palestine*, p. 105. The distance between the east side of the Ḥaram ash-Sharīf and the so-called 'Mosque of 'Umar' is roughly 120 m.

[3] Hamilton, *Quarterly of the Dept. of Antiquities*, XIII, pp. 103–20; and his *Structural History of the Aqsa Mosque*, pp. 1–3.

[4] Hamilton, *Structural History*, p. 8.

[5] *Ibid.*, p. 9.

[6] *Ibid.*, pp. 62–3 and 71.

e to *l* on Hamilton's fig. 30. They averaged 4·20 m. from centre to centre, so that there must have been twelve arches north of the dome and sixteen in the other arcades which went right through to the qibla wall.[1]

Reconstruction of al-Mahdī's Mosque. *c.* 163 H. (780). Let us now turn back to Muqaddasī's description of al-Mahdī's mosque. No one can fail to be struck by the resemblance of the main features of his mosque to the salient features of aẓ-Ẓāhir's structure, e.g. the great central doorway with smaller ones to right and left, the mighty gable roof over the central aisle with a beautiful dome rising above it, the roofs covered with sheets of lead, &c.

But there is more than this. We have already seen that in aẓ-Ẓāhir's mosque the columns were of two sizes, the large ones in the nave and to the east of it averaging 85 cm. in diameter, and that these were not columns at all but were built in courses of stone. In al-Mahdī's mosque likewise, most of the supports, although not some 85 cm. in diameter as in aẓ-Ẓāhir's mosque, were nevertheless piers built in courses. This at once recalls the words of Muqaddasī in speaking of al-Mahdī's mosque: 'the 'more ancient portion remained, even like a beauty spot, in the midst [of the new]. This portion ex-'tends as far as the limit of the marble columns, for beyond, *where the columns are built up*, the later 'part commences.' Why did al-Mahdī adopt built up piers? Presumably because the shortage of money (we have seen that this was acute) rendered the use of marble columns out of the question.

Thus the mosque of al-Mahdī like that of aẓ-Ẓāhir was partly on marble columns and partly on piers, and the central aisle was covered by a mighty gable roof, over which rose a magnificent dome. But we have seen above that the central aisle of al-Mahdī's mosque was about 72 cm. wider than aẓ-Ẓāhir's, being about 11·40 m. instead of 10·68.[2]

Taking all these points into consideration, the obvious conclusion seems to be that aẓ-Ẓāhir respected the plan of al-Mahdī, except that he made two new arcades for the central aisle and reduced its width by about 72 cm., and whereas al-Mahdī's two arcades sprang directly from the north wall and the northern dome-bearing piers, aẓ-Ẓāhir's two arcades ended to the north against a wall pier applied to the north wall, and to the south against a column.[3] al-Mahdī's arches were 72 cm. wide and his central aisle 11·40 m. in width, consequently the width of his mosque must have been 12·12 m. for the central aisle (from centre to centre of the piers), plus 6·5 × 14 for the fourteen side aisles, corresponding to the fourteen lesser doors = 103·12 m. The length from south to north, measured along the main axis, being 69·60 m.,[4] inside measurement, we have a proportion of almost exactly 3 : 2 (should be 69·60 × 103·40), a favourite ratio in 'Abbāsid architecture, e.g. in al-Manṣūr's work at Baghdād, and at Ukhaiḍir, and in the following century at Sāmarrā. Fifteen aisles would mean adding four aisles on either side of the present mosque. Is it not a curious coincidence that in the little annexe to the east, the so-called 'Mosque of 'Umar', there are just four bays, their average width being not quite 6·75 m.? The east side of this annexe, therefore, corresponds to the east side of the mosque of al-Mahdī, if reconstructed as suggested above, and the wall piers on the south side of this annexe are approximately on the axis of the wall-piers required by my theory (Fig. 445).

The Umayyad Aqṣā Mosque. It follows from the account of Muqaddasī that part of an earlier mosque, with arcades running from north to south and resting on marble columns, survived in the mosque of al-Mahdī. Such arcades still exist to the east and west of the domed part.

When the dome was inserted by al-Mahdī it was naturally necessary to provide abutment to east and west by transverse arcades running through to the side walls, and consisting of a series of arches resting on independent supports placed on either side of the corresponding column of the longitudinal arcades, the older arcades being 'nipped' between the new transverse arches.

1 Hamilton, *op. cit.*, pp. 56 and 60.

2 al-Ma'mūn presented this mosque with a fine door, which survived aẓ-Ẓāhir's reconstruction and was seen by Nāṣir-i-Khusrau, for he says: 'Among these gates is one of brass, most finely wrought and beautiful; so that one would say it was of gold; inlaid with silver and chased. The name of the Khalif al-Ma'mūn is upon it, and they say that al-Ma'mūn sent it from Baghdād'; Schefer's text, pp. 25, ll. 23–5; transl., p. 81; Le Strange's transl., *P.P.T.S.*, IV (*a*), p. 38; and his *Palestine*, p. 107.

3 Hamilton, *op. cit.*, p. 8.

4 The depth of the present Aqṣā Mosque is 69·45 m. measured within on the east side, and 69·80 m. on the west side according to Dikijian's plan in Hamilton's *Structural History of the Aqsa Mosque*.

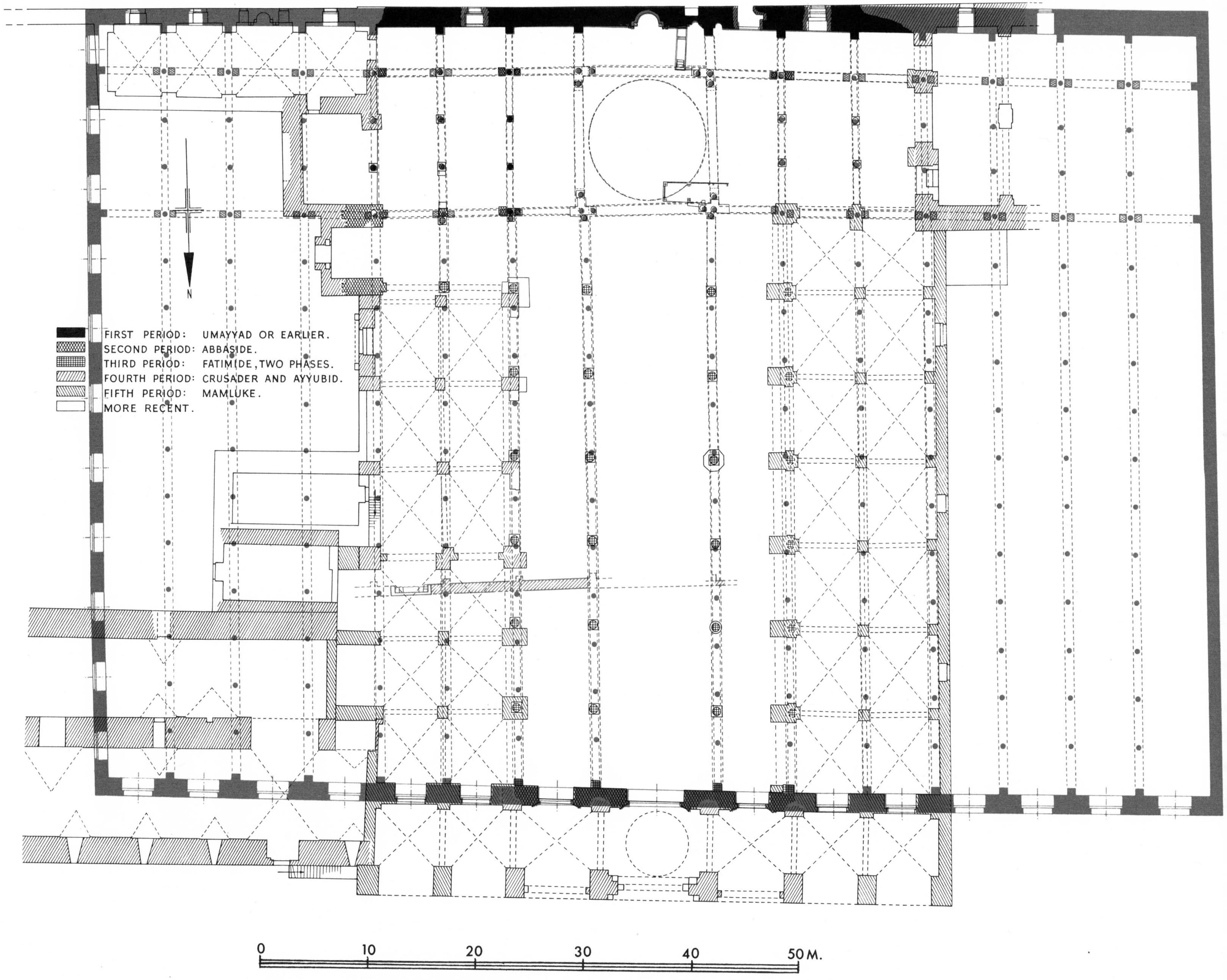

FIG. 446. JERUSALEM: The Aqṣā Mosque. Scale 1 : 300

HAMILTON'S VITAL DISCOVERY. During the works of 1938–42, when the plaster was stripped off, Hamilton was able to confirm this, for he found that the masonry of the spandrels of the transverse arches was not bonded into the masonry of the spandrels of the first longitudinal arcade to the east of the dome.[1] This is not the case with the second arcade, for here the transverse arches spring from the same support as the arches to north and south, so he concludes that it had suffered more from the earthquake and been re-built by al-Mahdī. It is impossible to overrate the importance of this discovery, for it proves that the transverse arches, and the two dome-bearing arches of which they take the thrust, are later than al-Walīd's work, and consequently that al-Walīd's mosque cannot have had a great dome.

Will it be believed that this vital and absolutely decisive discovery is completely ignored by Stern, in his article on the Aqṣā Mosque,[2] because he wants to believe that al-Walīd's structure had a wide central aisle, ending in a great dome? He does not discuss Hamilton's discovery or dispute its significance, he *simply ignores it*, and consequently arrives at impossible and untenable conclusions in his analysis of the mosque.

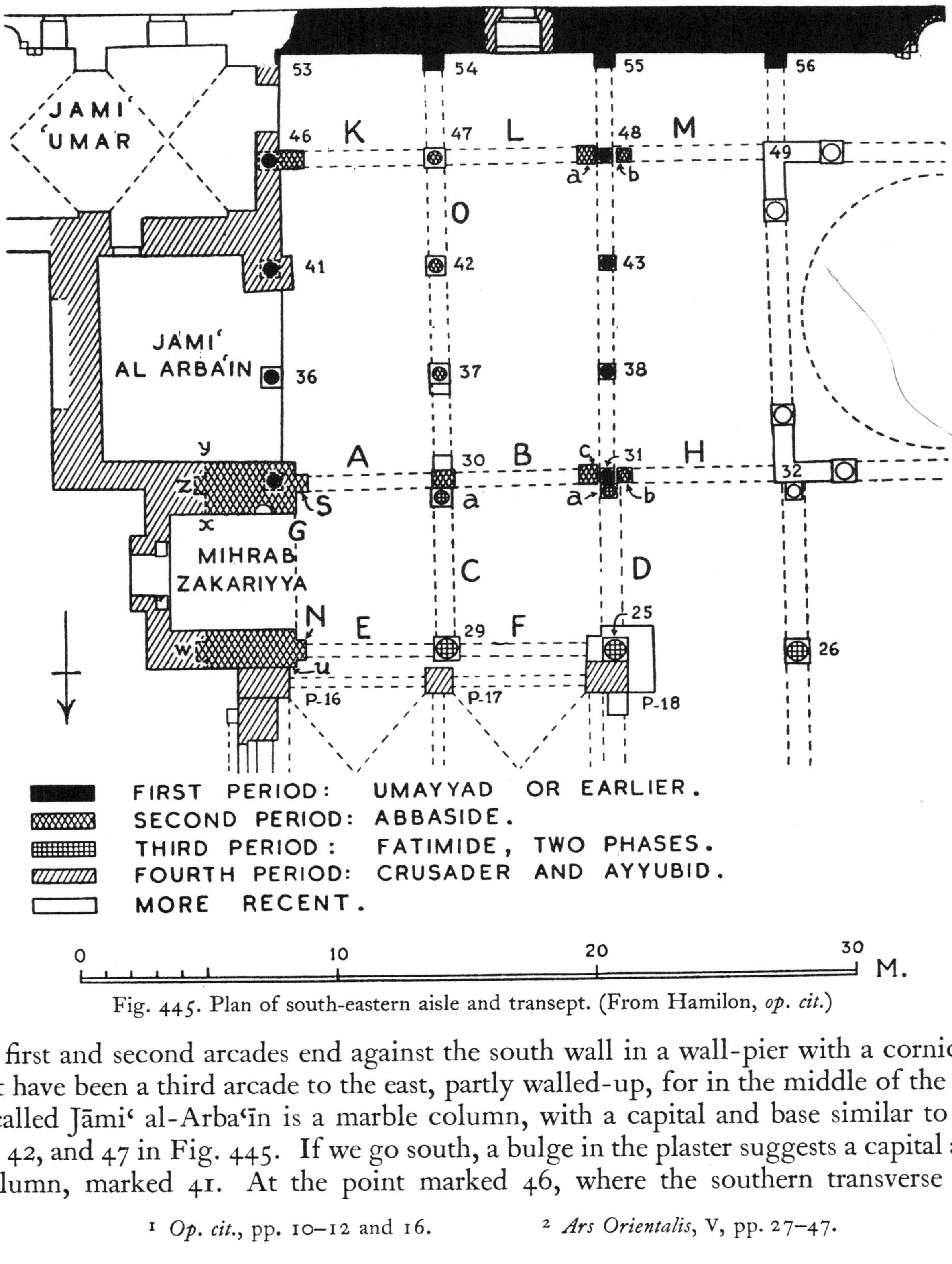

Fig. 445. Plan of south-eastern aisle and transept. (From Hamilon, *op. cit.*)

Both the first and second arcades end against the south wall in a wall-pier with a cornice moulding. There must have been a third arcade to the east, partly walled-up, for in the middle of the opening into the room called Jāmiʿ al-Arbaʿīn is a marble column, with a capital and base similar to the columns marked 37, 42, and 47 in Fig. 445. If we go south, a bulge in the plaster suggests a capital and therefore another column, marked 41. At the point marked 46, where the southern transverse arcade abuts

[1] *Op. cit.*, pp. 10–12 and 16. [2] *Ars Orientalis*, V, pp. 27–47.

against the side of the Jāmi' al-'Umar, the tip of a capital can actually be seen in the southern re-entrant angle, projecting at a level corresponding to that of the other capitals.

This establishes the existence of at least three aisles to the east of the dome, and the little arches above the third and partly walled-up one can be seen, as Hamilton points out, from the roof of the Jāmi' al-Arba'īn.[1] He also points out that two of these upper openings are blocked up internally by arches K and A of the transverse arcades of al-Mahdī, and consequently must belong to the earliest period. Unfortunately it is not possible to say how many more aisles there were, but I must point out once more that if they were roughly 6·70 m. apart, like the first three, they would correspond exactly with the wall-piers in the Jāmi' al-'Umar. In Egypt the foundations of arcades are generally continuous, e.g. in the Mosque of 'Amr,[2] but this is not the case in Palestine, or at least in the Aqṣā Mosque, where each column, as we have seen, has its own foundation. Consequently excavations made to the north of the 'Mosque of Omar' have been inconclusive and have not revealed three lines of foundations running N.–S., for such foundations were not part of Palestinian building principles.

Details of the Remains of al-Walīd's work. Here are some details of the first arcade (the second is an exact copy of it), authentic work of al-Walīd. The columns are of dark variegated marble, with varying types of Byzantine capitals, but the bases are uniform; the latter are all partially concealed by the floor, because the Umayyad floor was lower than the present one.

Diameter of columns, *c.* 50 cm.; height of columns and capitals 5 m.; springing of stilted and slightly pointed arches begins at 7·23 m.; height of apex, 9·20 m. Above the three main arches are five arched openings with their sills 9·80 m. from the floor; height of openings about 2 m.; height of ceiling about 12·40 m. The axis of the first, third, and fifth opening corresponds with the axis of the arch below, the second and fourth with the column (Plate 63). The arches are tied together above the capitals with wooden tie-beams as elsewhere, and wooden ties traverse the length of the walls at the level of the sills and also above the crowns of the openings above. The thickness of the walls, excluding the plaster, is about 61 cm. A number of discoveries were made when a long trench was cut across the central aisle (Trench A on plan). First of all it revealed a mortar bedding 10 cm. thick about 80 cm. below the present floor, on which the impressions of a marble pavement were sufficiently clear for the width of the missing slabs to be measured; a few fragments of gray marble were still in position.[3] This pavement did not extend to the present north wall, but stopped against *an earlier north wall*, in some cases one course high, which was exposed and traced across the three eastern aisles for over 18 m. It was exactly 1 m. thick, and built of fair-sized blocks of white limestone; some of the headers went right through the wall. Its south face had a marble panelling, for its coating of white plaster showed the marks of the slabs, one of which must have been 72 cm. long and at least 35 cm. high. Its south face, at its eastern extremity, was 18·00 m. distant from the inner face of the present north wall, and at its western extremity about 19·75 m.[4] Consequently the earlier mosque was only from 51·45 to 50·05 m. deep, but its width cannot be fixed. When this wall was followed eastwards into the third aisle, the sill of a large doorway was exposed, exactly in the centre of the aisle; it was fitted with sockets for door pivots on either side. It was too late to follow this wall across the central aisle, because a new pavement had been laid there.

Another important point: this wall was provided with pilasters, 62 m. wide[5] and 6·80 cm. apart from entre to centre, which align with the arcades to the east of the dome, as shown in Fig. 446 (red overlay).

Stern can only have read Hamilton's book in patches, for he does not seem to be aware that the Umayyad Aqṣā was from 18 to 20 m. shorter from north to south than the present building. He even says: 'La mosquée omeyyade a dû posséder une nef centrale de même larguer et de même longeur que l'Aqṣā abbaside',[6] and he speaks of the three northern doors as follows: 'Elles sont pour nous, avec la corniche sous la coupole les seules restes en place de la mosquée omeyyade.'[7] How does he explain the wall just mentioned, from 18 to 20 m. south of the present north wall? By the same technique he adopted regarding Hamilton's vital discovery mentioned above, viz. by saying nothing whatever about it.

[1] *Op. cit.*, p. 15 and pl. XI, 1–2.
[2] *E.M.A.*, II, 1st ed., pp. 189–90 and Fig. 168.
[3] *Op. cit.*, p. 54.
[4] *Op. cit.*, pp. 56–7. The present Aqṣā Mosque is 69·45 m. deep along its eastern side, and 69·80 along the western.
[5] *Ibid.*, p. 58.
[6] *Loc. cit.*, pp. 34–5.
[7] *Ibid.*, p. 36.

XII

MINYA[1]

The series of excavations—The Enclosure—The Walls—The Gateway Tower—The Ramp—The Mosque—The State-Rooms—The successive symmetrical subdivision into three—The room with the central row of columns—The Throne-Room—The five-roomed *bayt*—The west side—The north side—The court—The date—The cresting—Bibliography.

THE SERIES OF EXCAVATIONS. The site, before excavation, consisted of a low mound with formless ruined walls, about 1,200 m. west of the German Hospice at Ṭābgha, and about 230 m. from the northern end of Lake Tiberias. It takes its name from a Khān about 330 m. to the north, known as Khirbet al-Minya.

The excavations were begun by Mader in February and March 1932. He laid bare the greater part of the west wall, but the corner towers and the intermediate towers were only partly exposed. The entrance tower, however, was completely cleared down to the floor, which was found at a depth of 8 m., and many large carved blocks, as well as decorated pieces of the fallen dome including large pieces of glass mosaic, were found on the floor among the débris.[2] He came to the conclusion, under reserve, that the enclosure wall and its towers were Roman, and probably the work of Trajan or Hadrian, A. D. 98–138.

Schneider, in March and April 1936, carried out further excavations by making a trial trench 2 m. wide right through the enclosure from the entrance to the west side. He found that a passage, about 12 m. long and 7 m. wide, led from the entrance into a central court paved with basalt slabs. He also made a trench along the middle part of the west wall and found two five-room groups each consisting of a central room, 5·8 m. wide and 11 m. deep and apparently vaulted,[3] flanked by a pair of smaller rooms; in other words two groups of rooms exactly like the five-room group later discovered on the south side.[4] I must emphasize that the remains of the partition wall between each pair of lateral rooms is clearly shown on his plan in three cases out of four. This typical group, which it is now usual to call a *bayt*, is so exactly what we would expect, that it is very surprising to find that Puttrich-Reignard in his last report says that a trial trench made along the eastern outer wall of this group, and continued nearly as far as the middle, 'proved that the shape of plan assumed by Schneider must be carefully tested again'.[5] There, unfortunately, the matter rests, awaiting the complete clearance of an area only 33 m. wide and 12 deep.

Alt had no difficulty in showing that Mader's attribution was completely untenable. He asks: 'Why 'should the Romans in that early period of their rule over Palestine have been induced to place a 'garrison for which a building of this size was necessary, at a point on the route of so little strategic 'importance, and at so great a distance from the boundaries of the Empire. In addition the comparison 'of the architectural remains of the structure in Minya only partly investigated by Mader, with the 'hitherto known type of Roman frontier forts has its limits; above all the artistic design of the entrance 'appears scarcely in keeping with the rules of military expediency, to which the construction of the 'entrance should have conformed, had it been intended to build a fort. So one may have doubts re-'garding the attempts of interpretation and dating put forward by Mader with all due reserve, and must 'wish that they will be controlled by means of further excavations.

'This wish has now been fulfilled; Schneider, commissioned by the Görresgesellschaft in Mader's 'place, has again undertaken the task in 1936, and, by freeing the structural remains within the great 'walled rectangle, has brought things to the point, that the plan of the original building has now been 'completely and once for all obtained. From that it appears that Mader's proposed interpretation and 'dating cannot be upheld. Already the ceramic finds, which, in the oldest layer we are dealing with, 'consist only of a few characteristic potsherds of smooth monochrome ware, speak against the attribu-'tion of the building to the early Roman period, and are attributed by Schneider rather to the fourth or

1 For Bibliography, see p. 389.

2 *Journ. Palestine Oriental Socy.*, XIII, pp. 213–18; and *Oriens Christianus*, dritte Serie, VI, pp. 254–5.

3 The fallen vault of the central hall of the southern *bayt* has since been seen by Grabar; *Sondages à Khirbet el-Minyeh, Israel Exploration Journal*, X, p. 229.

4 *Oriens Christianus*, dritte Serie, XI, p. 102 and Abb. 1; and *Ein frühislamischer Bau am See Genesareth*, p. 11.

5 *Die Palastanlage von Chirbet el Minie*, Appendix, p. [3].

'fifth century A. D. Above all, however, the form and arrangement of the inner structures, only now 'brought to light does not correspond to what one would have expected if it was a question of a Roman 'frontier fort, especially of such a late period.'[1]

On account of the two *bayts* partly excavated on the western side, which we must bear in mind was the only part of the interior then exposed,[2] Alt assumed that the rest of the interior must have been bare or nearly so, as at Hatra, and he came to the conclusion that it was a Ghassānid[3] building. This is unthinkable from the geographical point of view, for the Ghassānids were the guardians of the eastern frontier of Syria in late Roman times, not the western.

A great step forward was made by the excavations of Puttrich-Reignard in March–July 1937. I visited the site with Kühnel on 15th February, just before the beginning of this campaign,[4] and suggested that as the central part most probably consisted of an open court, the best way to begin would be to start next the entrance and make a trench along the inner side of the wall, as the partition walls exposed in this way would show how the rooms next to it were divided up. And, being convinced that it was an Umayyad palace, I added: 'When you start work along the inner side of the south wall and find the miḥrāb, send me a telegram.' Work was begun at the south-east corner and a fortnight later I received a telegram reading 'miḥrāb found'.

Work was continued in the spring of 1938 and again from 28th October 1938 to 10th May 1939, and we may now say that the palace has been completely excavated except the central part of the west side.

THE ENCLOSURE consists of an irregular rectangle which faces the four cardinal points. The sides, without the towers, measure 66·40 m. (north), 73 m. (east), 67 m. (south), and 72·3 m. (west),[5] average just under 70 m., the standard size of an Umayyad palace. There is a round tower, 4·10 m. in diameter at each corner (Fig. 448), and a half-round tower 4 m. in diameter in the centre of the north, west, and south faces. On the east side, about 3·70 m. north of the centre, is the gateway salient about 16·5 m. wide.

THE WALLS, which are about 1·40 m. thick, are still preserved in some places to a height of 4·50 m., although the north wall has been pillaged almost down to its basalt socle. They rest on rough stone foundations which vary in depth, according to the nature of the subsoil. Resting on this foundation is a socle of well-dressed basalt blocks, 40 cm. high. Above that the wall consists of very carefully executed masonry in courses 55 cm. in height, of which the stretchers average a metre in length. The headers are only about 30 cm. wide, but they are very deep, varying from 70 cm. to 1 m.[6] (Plate 64 *b*). Even the partition walls are of good masonry. The walls were crowned with stepped and undercut crenellations, 1·22 m. wide and 1·10 m. high. No less than four such blocks were found during the excavations.[7]

THE GATEWAY TOWER (Plate 64 *c*) consisted of a square domed chamber, formed by two nearly half-round towers joined by the open arch which formed the entrance. The eastern part had been destroyed, probably in the great earthquake of A. D. 747, and then rebuilt centuries later in a diminished form when the ground had risen some 2 m. The inner sill of this new gateway was found to consist of a broken marble block with an inscription of al-Walīd upside down.[8] The original appearance, however, can still be established without difficulty, for the white plaster floor in front of the outer side still shows the outer border of the old gateway in negative. On the north and south sides of this vestibule are great semicircular niches, of which the semi-domed hoods exhibit rosettes in circles (Plate 64 *d*). The northern niche had been entirely blocked up in the second period, the southern to the extent of half (Plate 64 *e* and *f*). From this open vestibule we pass into the interior by a door 3·75 m. wide which is in alignment with the wall of the enclosure; its sill is of bluish-white marble. As for the jambs of the

[1] *Zeitschr. des Deutschen Palästina-Vereins*, LIX, pp. 214–15.
[2] See Schneider's plan in *Oriens Christianus*, dritte Serie, XI, fig. 1 on p. 103.
[3] For the Ghassānids, see below, pp. 625–6 and 636–7.
[4] I also visited it on 11th Feb. 1938, and on 29th Feb. 1939.
[5] *Ein frühislamischer Bau*, p. 7.
[6] *Ibid.*, p. 8.
[7] Two were found on the ground in the hall with a central row of columns (Plate 67 *e*). Another was found by Schneider on the west side and another came to light on the north side, see *Ein frühislamischer Bau*, p. 8 and fig. 1; and *Die Palastanlage von Chirbet el Minje*, p. 12 and Abb. 8; also Schneider, *Ḫirbet el-Minje* in *Annales Archéologiques de Syrie*, II, p. 31.
[8] See Kühnel, in Puttrich-Reignard, *Palastanlage*, pp. 7–8.

outer arch of this vestibule, which apparently was not closed by a door, only a few blocks remained, some coffered, some with looped circles (Fig. 447). The carved blocks and vaulting stones which were found among the débris in the vestibule permit a more or less certain reconstruction of the dome, which was certainly open at the top, as is shown by the carving of the richly decorated cornice stones Nearly all the blocks of the cornice moulding at the base of the dome have been preserved (Plate 65 *i-j*). The frieze below this cornice exhibits an undulating acanthus stalk. The rest of the blocks of richly carved white limestone which formed the decoration of the dome can be arranged in eight semicircles (Fig. 447). In the dome were also set the variously formed rosette-stones (Fig. 447 and Plate 65 *a-b*), the arrangement of which in the dome can likewise still be fixed. That part of the dome which was not carved was coated with glass mosaic, the colours being light green, light and dark blue, red, gold, and silver.[1]

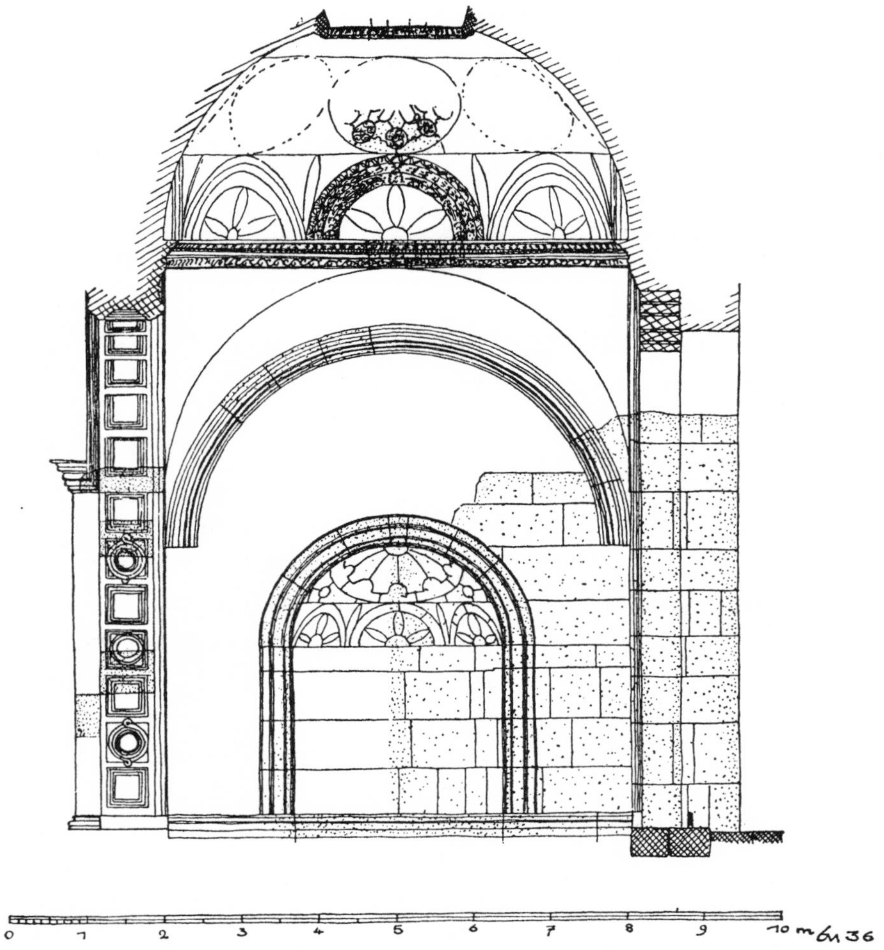

Fig. 447. Minya: Section (restored) through entrance (from Schneider, *Ein frühislamischer Bau*).

The Ramp. From this vestibule a passage about 7 m. wide and 12 m. long leads into the central court (Plate 66 *b*). On the left side of this passage, at a distance of about 4 m. from the entrance, is the beginning of a gentle ramp which turns to the left on reaching the end of the passage (Plate 66 *c*). The exposure of this ramp, which was quite obviously planned afterwards, cleared up existing uncertainties concerning the group of rooms between the entrance passage and the mosque. There had apparently been three parallel rooms here of equal length, each with a door at the western end. After the ramp had been made the door of the northern room was walled up, the middle one alone remained open, and the southern one disappeared, except for a still visible jamb. As for the room itself it now consists of the underside of the ramp after it turns east. This has involved heavily reinforcing the north–south walls of this part and the disappearance of the two rooms owing to the removal of their southern wall.

The Mosque. In the south-eastern corner of the enclosure, occupying nearly all the space between the entrance and the south wall, is the palace mosque (Plates 66 *e-f* and 67 *a-c*) measuring 13·10 m. in width and 19·42 m. in depth, a proportion of almost exactly 2 : 3. Its eastern and southern sides are formed by the walls of the enclosure, which here stand to a height of 2 m., whereas the west wall is only about 1·20 m. high throughout and the north wall has almost entirely disappeared. The latter must have formed one side of a narrow passage which ended in a little door in the south-east corner of the central court. Another doorway 1·38 m. wide, on the west side 87 cm. from the south wall, forms a connecting link with the state-rooms of the palace, and a third doorway on the east side enabled Muslims living near the palace to enter the mosque directly from outside, exactly as at Qaṣr al-Ḥayr ash-Sharqī (below, Fig. 576). The excavators remark that the stones of the door jambs (Plate 67 *c*) so clearly form part of the outer wall that not the least doubt can exist that this doorway belongs to the original building.[2]

The most important part, the miḥrāb in the exact centre of the south wall, is still preserved two courses

[1] Schneider, *Ein frühislamischer Bau*, pp. 8–11; and *Ḫirbet el-Minje* in *Annales Archéologiques de Syrie*, II, pp. 31–3.
[2] *Die Palastanlage*, p. 9.

high above the basalt foundations, and it clearly forms one with the southern wall of the enclosure. It is 1·62 m. in width and 1·12 in depth, and on both sides of it are the usual recesses 18–19 cm. deep for the flanking colonnettes (Plate 67*b*).[1] 'In the floor of the mosque at regular intervals were three rows 'of well-set basalt and limestone slabs which, contrary to earlier assumptions,[2] must be regarded, not 'as guide-stones for an unfinished pavement, but certainly as pier foundations, in spite of the fact 'that the middle one of each row is in a direct line with the miḥrāb' (Plates 67*a* and *c*).[3] Schneider remarks that this most unusual feature occurs in the Great Mosque at Baʿalbek which, although undated, is usually regarded as old,[4] and he adds, 'as well as in the little mosque attributed to Omar, at al-Khānzīre in the Ḥaurān' (*Z.D.P.V.*, XLIX (1926), p. 10)'.[5] I have verified this and found that his statement will not stand. Steuernagel's plan (Abb. 97) shows a mosque 13 m. wide and 19 m. deep, with an arcade of three arches on two columns in front of the miḥrāb, which is only about 85 cm. off centre. But two other examples may be cited besides Baʿalbek, viz. the contemporary mosque at Jabal Says (below, p. 476 and Fig. 538), and the little Makutanī Mosque at Kilwa.[6]

One of the wall piers of the northern arcade still exists on the west wall. On the north side of the passage already referred to on the north side of the mosque are two rooms which open for their entire width on to the passage. Their north–south walls have been reinforced, presumably to take two vaults to support the under side of the last part of the ramp already mentioned.

THE STATE-ROOMS. To the west of the mosque are the state-rooms, which occupy an area 42·20 m. wide and 19·42 m. deep and consequently take up the greater part of the south side. Their north wall is in an exact line with the north wall of the mosque. They must have been intended for ceremonial purposes for the decoration was of great magnificence. They comprise a three-aisled hall in the centre, which I shall call the Throne-Room, a hall to the east with a central row of columns, and a group of five rooms to the west. *Only the Throne-Room can be entered from the court*, with which it is connected by three doors. It has three doors on the east side, opening into the hall with a central row of columns, and likewise three doors on the west opening into the five-room complex. Of these doors the middle one is always the widest.

THE SUCCESSIVE SYMMETRICAL SUBDIVISION INTO THREE. If we take the area occupied by the state-rooms we observe that it is divided into three by a wide central and two narrower flanking rectangles. These again, or at least two of them, the Throne-Room and the five-room group, are again subdivided into three in exactly the same way—a wider central and two narrower side parts. We shall meet with this same principle at Mshattā where, however, it is carried farther (pp. 581-2 and Fig. 635).

THE ROOM WITH THE CENTRAL ROW OF COLUMNS. Between the mosque and the Throne-Room is a long room measuring 12 m. in width and 20 m. in depth. On the west side three doors opened, as we have seen, into the Throne-Room. Especial care appears to have been devoted to the central one, of which the moulded door post (Plate 68*a*) was excavated in the immediate neighbourhood. Another door 1·38 m. wide, on the east side next the south wall, gave access to the mosque. This hall was divided in a north–south direction by a row of columns (Plate 67*e*). Of the three supports which originally existed, a pedestal and a marble base were found *in situ*. Of the southern support only the foundation socket was still in position.[7] The arches (or architraves) carried by these columns rested on pilasters which still project from the north and south walls. No columns were found, but several marble capitals and bases were found in the débris. They were of pre-Muslim date, in which connexion Puttrich-Reignard remarks that in case Minya is of early Muslim origin this need cause no surprise, for it was the custom to use such things, almost without exception, from older buildings. The floor of this room was obviously in an unfinished state. It consisted entirely of a *pavement of stone cubes embedded in mortar*.[8] Nothing can be said as to the nature of the roofing.

1 *Die Palastanlage*, p. 8. The crevice which runs through the middle of it is one of the many evidences of earthquake damage which can be observed at Minya. It has one unusual feature—a sill 25 cm. high, of which I know only one other example, Mshattā, where the sill is 35 cm. high (Plate 115 *b*).

2 *Ein frühislamischer Bau*, p. 29.

3 *Die Palastanlage*, p. 9.

4 For this mosque see Reuther, in T. Wiegand, *Baalbek*, III, pp. 100–103 and Abb. 112–14.

5 *Oriens Christianus*, dritte Serie, XIII, p. 123.

6 Chittick, *Notes on Kilwa*, *Tanganyika Notes and Records*, No. 53, p. 190 and fig. 4.

7 *Die Palastanlage*, p. 11.

8 *Ibid.*, p. 11.

The Throne-Room, a triple-aisled basilical hall 20 m. square, dominates the south side of the palace. Its south wall is still 2 m. high but on the other sides the walls have been robbed down to the lowest course, so that the three entrances on the north and east sides can only be recognized as recesses in the wall. Of the six supports of the two arcades (or colonnades) only one base exists—the middle one in the east row, still *in situ*, but the position of the rest can be fixed from the basalt foundations of the floor. Here also the arches (or architraves) were supported to north and south by pilasters (Plate 67 *e*). The roof must have been a wooden one covered with tiles, for a number of flat and half-round tiles, similar to those found at Mafjar[1] were lying on the floor.

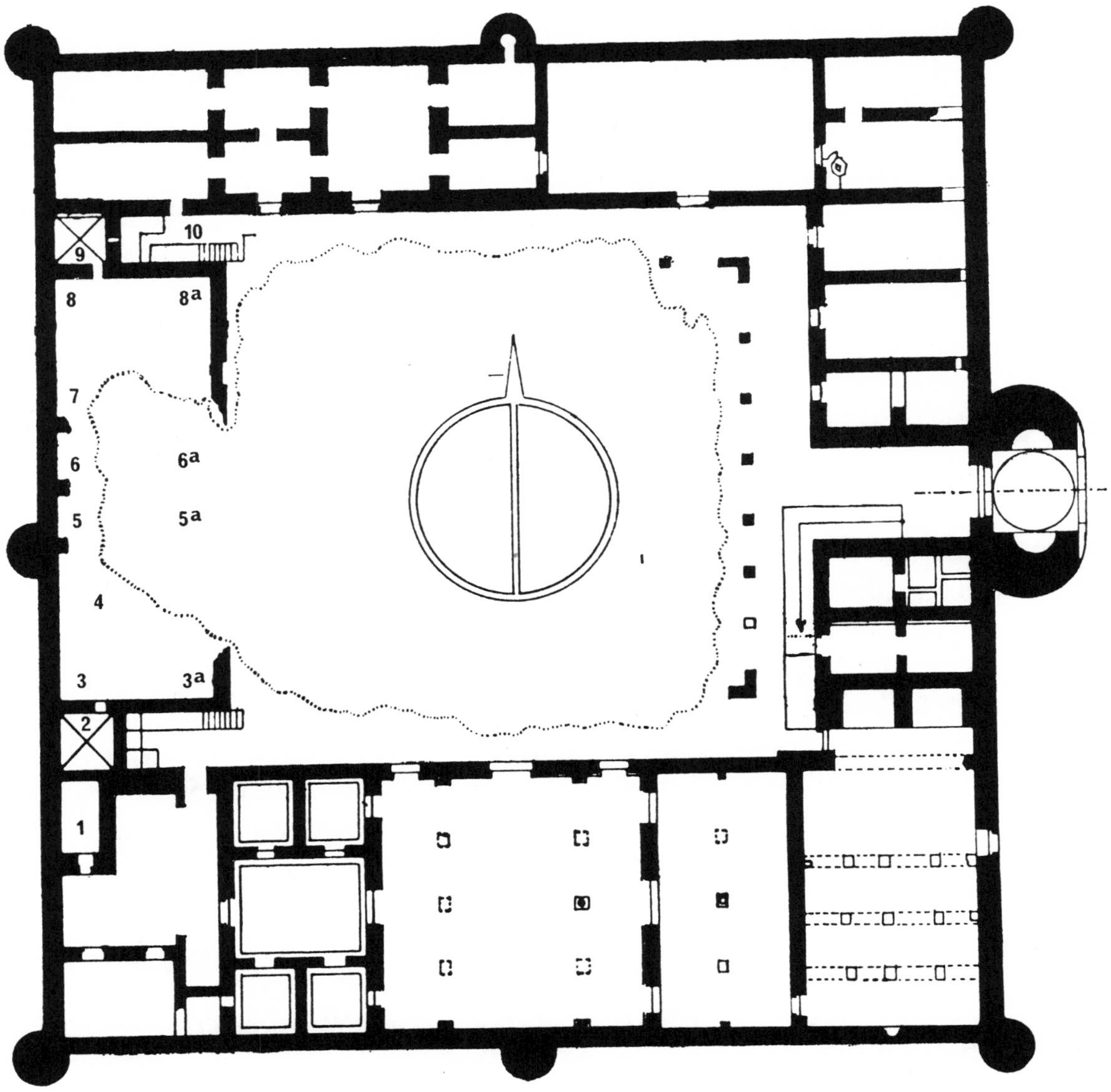

Fig. 448. Minya: Plan.

It is clear that the decoration must have been very rich, although very little of it is left to-day. A few intact slabs of marble on the floor and the negative imprint of many others show that there was a marble pavement. Of the original marble dado only traces have been preserved near the floor, but the fact that the south wall is pitted (Plate 67 *f*) to a height of 2 m. shows that this marble dado must have been at least 2 m. high.[2] Large and small fragments of ornamented marble slabs were also found on the floor of the Throne-Room which, like the remainder of the paving slabs, belonged to older buildings and had been re-employed. Whether they were used as decoration remains uncertain. These presumably are the marble slabs with crosses seen by Schneider.[3] Above it the walls must have been covered with mosaic, for thousands of little cubes of glass and stone cover the floor. The following colours occur: yellow, yellow-green, bright green, grass green, dark green, olive-green, blue-green, gray, light blue, dark blue, violet, brick red, and black, also transparent glass cubes with gold leaf laid upon them. The

[1] *Ibid.*, p. 12.

[2] These slabs have doubtless been looted by passing traders to be sold in Damascus, just as has happened in modern times at Quṣayr ʿAmra, according to Musil (below, p. 395, n. 10).

[3] *Ḫirbet el-Minje*, in *Annales Archéologiques*, II, p. 40.

following colours occurred in the stone cubes: black, white, dark red, light red, grey, and yellow; also a number of stone cubes, with a bright-red coating.[1] Puttrich-Reignard compares this rich decoration with that of the Dome of the Rock, and he adds that during a visit to Jerusalem he was enabled to examine the mosaics then being restored and verify that the glass cubes in size, shape, tint, and substance fully agree in every respect with those of Minya.[2]

THE FIVE-ROOMED *Bayt* is the same in size and shape as the room with a central row of columns on the far side of the Throne-Room. Its north and west walls are still preserved to a height of two or three courses (Plate 68 *b*), whereas only one course remains on the south and west. In plan it closely resembles similar groups of rooms at Mshattā and Qaṣr aṭ-Ṭūba which it is now usual to call *bayts*. It can be entered from the Throne-Room by the three western doors of the latter, and on the western side of it are two more doors opening into rooms in the south-western corner, which the excavators believe were intended for servants (Plate 68 *c*).[3] The four side rooms are each connected with the central room by one door.

The floor mosaics of all four rooms were in a remarkable state of preservation which, as Puttrich-Reignard remarks, gave them the appearance of real state-rooms. In the south-east room, in fact, the mosaics had been specially protected by a layer of clay 15 cm. thick which must have been put there by the mosaicist to protect his work until the completion of the building. Hence its remarkable preservation, whereas the floors of the other rooms were more or less damaged and covered with a thin layer of lime, the removal of which needed much care. In the small rooms the only colours used are black, white, bright red, dark red, and golden-brown, but in the pavement of the great central room the palette is enriched by the addition of yellow, and light- and dark-green glass cubes (Plate 69).[4]

In the little south-eastern room the middle field resembles a plaited mat; it is framed by a border of alternating rhomboids and circles. The pattern in the south-western room, which has remained completely undamaged, is quite different and much more complicated. Here is Puttrich-Reignard's excellent description: 'An ingenious interlacing band system surrounds the middle field, which is divided 'into rectangles surrounded by an endless plaited band. The squares are filled by various individual 'motifs. Great skill and technical knowledge are shown at the crossing points of the plaited bands 'which, at the intersections, become knotted and unknotted in a most easy manner. The band motif 'is so far without parallel. It consists of two bands of different colours, which interlace in endless 'alternation. In many turns one band winds round the other which serves as a stick, and then itself takes 'the place of the other as a stick, round which the other winds. This scheme is not even broken at the 'corners; the bands, however, become knotted and unknotted in such a complicated way that the eye 'has difficulty in following their course.[5]

'Far more beautiful, and in its way much more worthy of notice, is the pavement of the great central 'room, which spreads over a surface of 7×10 m. Except for a few damaged places which can be re-'paired without difficulty, it has remained uninjured and without unevenness. In contrast to the other 'floors, we also find glass cubes employed here, of which yellow, light and dark green tints give to the 'floor quite a special charm and an intense play of light. The size of the mosaic stones has been adapted 'to the glass cubes of 1 cm. each way, which must have been imported. These are of the same kind as 'those used in the Throne-Room. The mosaic master could not have been more successful in the 'arrangement of the colours, and it shows how with a simple and uniform geometrical pattern an un-'usually lively effect can be obtained.

'Comparison with a carpet is nowhere so justified as it is with this pavement. Border and middle 'field are in the right proportion. The middle field is spread over with a carefully constructed network 'continually repeating itself, the base motif of which is the lozenge. In the direction of length there 'are three lozenges with their points in contact, one over the other; in the direction of breadth four 'lying side by side. The lozenges are surrounded by an endless lotus band and each contains five 'smaller lozenge-like surfaces, which in their turn are formed of an endless interlacing band. The 'little lozenges contain small coloured *kelīm*-like fillings or swastikas seen in perspective, frequently 'consisting entirely of glass mosaics.

[1] *Die Palastanlage*, p. 13.
[2] *Ibid.*, pp. 13–14.
[3] *Ibid.*, pp. 10–11 and 14.
[4] *Ibid.*, pp. 14–15.
[5] *Ibid.*, p. 15.

'The surrounding borders are formed of several friezes of varying widths with bands of chevrons, 'stripes with white points on a red field, four rows of twists and crenellated patterns. On the east side 'the ground is limited by a broad strip with squares linked together and filled with *kelīm* motifs.'[1]

The mosaics of the sills of the doorways, which are very well preserved in places, consist of zigzag bands, twists, and various bands of geometrical ornament.

According to Puttrich-Reignard the walls of the five-room group appear to have been without decoration,[2] but it is difficult to believe that the efforts of the architect to obtain such a rich interior could have been confined to the floor.

Here again the roofing question is a problem. Puttrich-Reignard suggests that it must have been of wood, as the stones (or bricks) of a falling vault would have damaged the mosaics.[3]

The West Side. The centre of this side, according to Schneider, was occupied by two great *līwān*-halls, 5·80 m. broad and 11 m. deep, each flanked by a pair of small rooms, in other words, two typical *bayts*, the existence of which has been questioned by Puttrich-Reignard.[4] There the question must rest until this area, which only measures 33×11 m. has been completely excavated.

However, Grabar and three collaborators carried out brief excavations here from 19th July to the 10th August 1960.[4] In the northern *bayt* they found that the vault of the southern lateral rooms had collapsed *en bloc*.[5] They excavated below it until they reached the floor, which was decorated with mosaic. About one square metre was laid bare, which sufficed to show that it was of the same type (entrelacs and plant motifs) as the others on the south side, stones of seven different colours being employed.[6]

They found that there were not two lateral rooms but one only, 3·50 m. wide divided into two parts, 6·50 m. and 5·50 m. long, not by a wall but by two pilasters which must have carried an arch supporting the tunnel vault. In the wall which separates the central hall from the southern lateral rooms they found a doorway, 1·65 m. wide and 4 m. high, with a semicircular arch still in position.[7]

Between the southern side of this complex and the south-western corner group is an oblong room with walls still over 2 m. high, which opens into the latter by a small door, whereas its east end is completely open to the courtyard. A staircase, of which nine steps are still preserved, starts in the courtyard and runs up in an east–west direction against the south side of the complex. Behind the west wall of this room is a small rectangular room, with a dome on spherical triangle pendentives and a mosaic floor, which can only be entered from the south side of the complex. Sauvaget has suggested that we have here an Umayyad *ḥammām* of which (4) is the hall for undressing and repose, (3^a) the warm room, (3) the hot room, (2) the furnace, (1) the boiler room, and the space open to the sky in the south-western corner—the court of service (depot for fuel, access to the furnace, &c.).[8] But he stipulates for a slight modification of the positions of the doorways shown in Schneider's plan. Grabar, however, after three weeks of excavation (unfortunately not completed) in this part of the palace, says: 'L'hypothèse de Sauvaget que l'on trouverait un bain dans le coin sud-ouest du palais n'est, pour l'instant, pas à retenir'.[9] In the corresponding place on the north side of the complex is another small room, this time definitely square with the remains of a mosaic floor and with a small door opening into the northern side of the complex.[10] In front of this is another oblong room with a staircase, 1·40 m. wide, running up against the north side of the complex (Plate 68 *d*).

The North Side. Here the enclosure walls for the greater part are preserved to a height of more than 2 m. The western half was occupied by another five-room group, the central and western parts of which each had a door opening into the courtyard. The north-eastern room had a door opening into a latrine in the hollow middle tower (Plate 68 *f* and Fig. 448) just like those of Mshattā and Qaṣr Bāyir (Fig. 687). This group was flanked to the east by a great hall, the same in size and shape as the room with the central row of columns, and to the west by two narrow rooms each about 11 m. long. Both were connected by

1 *Ibid.*, pp. 16–17.
2 *Ibid.*, p. 17.
3 This has actually happened to the mosaic floors at Mafjar; see below, p. 569.
4 *Die fünfte Grabungskampagne*, p. 5.
5 *Sondages*, *Israel Exploration Journal*, X, pp. 226–43.
6 *Ibid.*, p. 230.
7 *Ibid.*, p. 234.
8 *Ibid.*, p. 235.
9 *Journal Asiatique*, CCXXXI, p. 37.
10 *Israel Exploration Journal*, X, p. 226, n. 2.
11 *Ein frühislamischer Bau*, pp. 11–12 and Abb. 4.

doors with the western rooms of the five-room group, and the southern one had a door into the staircase-room as well.

Between the north-eastern corner and the entrance passage are five oblong parallel rooms of which the two northernmost are connected with each other and the second has a door opening into the great hall; of the three remaining ones each has a door into the courtyard. The room next the entrance passage is divided into two so that the last three rooms look almost like a *bayt*. Puttrich-Reignard says that these rooms were certainly intended for soldiers and guards, and that a great quantity of unglazed pottery, weapons, and other implements belonging to the building period of the palace came to light, as well as a gold dinār of 89 H. (708).[1]

THE COURT. During the fifth campaign, which ended on 10th May 1939, a broad trench made on the east side of the court showed that it was surrounded by an arcaded cloister. Of the eight bases of the supports on the east side seven were found *in situ* and the first socle-base of the northern row of supports, which was needed for the proof, was likewise found *in situ* (Fig. 448).[2]

THE DATE. All are agreed that Minya, Mshattā, and Qaṣr aṭ-Ṭūba belong to one group and to-day, as Schneider admits, they are almost universally regarded as Umayyad,[3] nevertheless he and Alt[4] prefer to place them all in the sixth to seventh century and insist that they must have been built by the Ghassānids. This as regards Mshattā and Qaṣr aṭ-Ṭūba has been answered on pp. 636–7; in the case of Minya the proposal is absurd for geographical reasons, as remarked above, for the Ghassānids formed a sort of buffer state protecting the eastern frontier of Syria in Late Roman times, not the western.

The proposal to attribute Minya to al-Walīd I is supported by the inscription of al-Walīd on the broken marble slab which had been used as a sill when the gateway was rebuilt centuries later at a higher level and in a diminished form. Schneider accepts all the architectural fragments—cornices, vaulting stones, rosettes, &c., found amongst the débris on the floor of the old gateway, as belonging to the original structure, yet he actually refuses to believe that this inscription also belonged to the old gateway *because it is of marble*, whereas the gateway and walls are of limestone. He must have forgotten that the original sill of the inner gateway, which is still in position, is mentioned in his own report as being of bluish-white marble![5]

The only coins found in the palace were three gold dinārs of the Umayyad period, as follows:

(1) of 89 H. (708) in one of the rooms to the north of the entrance;[6]
(2) of 98 H. (716/17) in the mortar joints of the pavement of the hall with a central row of supports;[7] and
(3) of 116 H. (735) on the floor on the east side of the same hall.[8]

The above coins fall in the reigns of the Khalifs al-Walīd, Sulaymān, and Hishām respectively.

We have also seen that a big block of marble with a building inscription of al-Walīd was found built in as a sill, upside down, in the re-made part of the entrance.

From these coins, from the style of the five-room *bayts*, and from the style of the latrine in the middle tower on the north side,[9] we are justified in regarding the palace as Umayyad, and there can be no reasonable doubt that the inscription built into the re-made part of the entrance belonged to the original structure. This being so, to what part of al-Walīd's reign must we attribute it? The mosque has a concave miḥrāb and we have seen that the concave (*mujawwaf*) miḥrāb first appears in the Mosque of Madīna as rebuilt by al-Walīd in 88–90 H. (707–9) (above, pp. 147–8), the second in the Mosque of 'Amr as rebuilt by Qurra ibn Sharīk in 92–3 H. (710–12) (above, p. 149), and the third in the Great Mosque of Damascus, built by al-Walīd between 86 and 96 H. (705–15). We may therefore place our palace between 712 and the death of al-Walīd in 715.

1 *Die Palastanlage*, Appendix, p. [4].
2 *Ibid.*, p. [5].
3 *Oriens Christianus*, dritte Serie, XIII, pp. 124–5.
4 *Z.D.P.V.*, LIX, p. 224.
5 'Das 3·75 m. breite Westportal liegt im Zuge der Ostmauer, seine Türflügel öffneten sich nach dem Hofe zu. Die Schwelle besteht aus einem blauweißen Marmorstein'; *Ein frühislamischer Bau*, p. 10.
6 Puttrich-Reignard, *Die fünfte Grabungskampagne*, p. [4].
7 Puttrich-Reignard, *Die Palastanlage*, p. 12.
8 *Ibid.*
9 Compare the latrines at Mshattā and Qaṣr Bāyir, pp. 583 and 643.

The Cresting. Stepped crenellations are typical of Assyria and ancient Persia. We meet with them at Khorsābād in the palace of Sargon (721–705 B. C.),[1] at Persepolis in the palace of Darius (521 B. C.),[2] at Susa in the palace of Artaxerxes II (405–359 B. C.),[3] and, just before Islam, we find them carved on the rock face above the līwān of Ṭāq-i-Bustān (A. D. 590–628).[4] But in all these examples the steps have

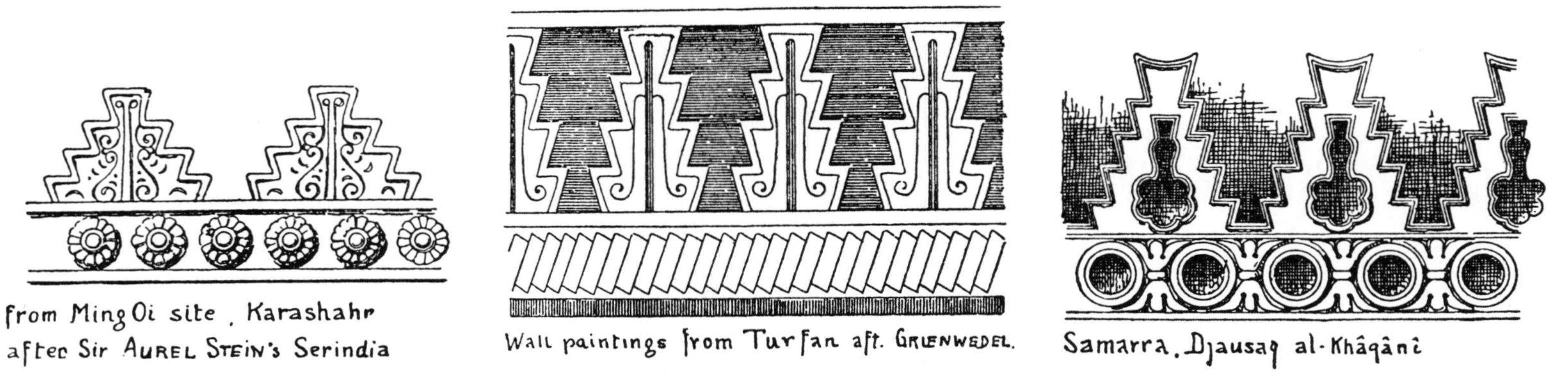

Fig. 449. Types of cresting from Ming Oi, Turfān, and the Jausaq al-Khāqānī at Sāmarrā. (From Herzfeld, *Paiquli.*)

vertical faces. Undercutting, apparently, is first found in Eastern Turkistān, judging from the examples collected by Herzfeld, e.g. Ming Oi and Turfān (Fig. 449). It then appears in the façade of a palace, depicted on a late Sasanian silver dish in the Hermitage at Leningrad.

It first appears in Islam in al-Walīd's palace at Minya on Lake Tiberias.

BIBLIOGRAPHY

1931 Mader, A. E. Die Ausgrabungen der Görresgesellschaft am See Genesareth. *Oriens Christianus*, dritte Serie, VI, pp. 254–5.

1932 Mader, A. E. Die Ausgrabung eines römischen Kastells auf Chirbet Minje an der Via Maris am See Genezareth. *Forschungen und Fortschritte*, VIII, pp. 229–30.

1933 Mader, A. E. Die Ausgrabung eines römischen Kastells auf *Chirbet el-Minje* an der Via Maris bei eṭ-Ṭābgha am See Gennesareth. *Journal of the Palestine Oriental Society*, XIII, pp. 209–18 and pl. XV.

1936 Schneider, A. M. Die Grabung der Görresgesellschaft auf Chirbet Minje am See Genesareth. *Oriens Christianus*, dritte Serie, XI, pp. 102–5, with 3 figs.

— Alt, A. Ein Ghassanidenschloß am See Genezareth. *Zeitschr. des Deutschen Palästina-Vereins*, LIX, pp. 214–26 and Abb. 8–9.

1937 Puttrich-Reignard, Oswin. Die dritte Grabung auf Chirbet el Minje bei Tabgha am See Genezareth in Palästina. *Das heilige Land*, LXXXI, pp. 117–22, with 1 fig. and 4 plates.

— Puttrich-Reignard, Oswin. Bericht über die Frühjahrsgrabung 1937 auf Chirbet el-minje bei Tabgha am See Genezareth in Palästina. *Oriens Christianus*, dritte Serie, XII, pp. 269–72, with 1 fig.

— Schneider, A. M., and O. Puttrich-Reignard. Ein frühislamischer Bau am See Genesareth. Zwei Berichte über die Grabungen auf Chirbet el-Minje. Bachem, Köln, 1937. (*Palästina-Hefte des Deutschen Vereins vom Heiligen Lande*, Heft 15.)

1938 Puttrich-Reignard (Oswin). Die Ergebnisse der dritten und vierten Ausgrabungskampagne auf Chirbet el Minje bei Tabgha am See Genezareth. *Berichte aus den Preussischen Kunstsammlungen*, LIX, pp. 80–84, with 4 illus.

— Puttrich-Reignard (Oswin). Deutsche Ausgrabungen in Tabgha am See Genezareth in Palästina. *Zeitschr. d. Deutschen Morgenländischen Gesellschaft*, XCII, Appendix, pp. 24–8, with 1 fig.

1938 Schneider, A. M. Bemerkungen zum neuen Bericht über die Grabungen in chirbet el-minje. *Oriens Christianus*, dritte serie, XIII, pp. 122–6.

1939 Puttrich-Reignard (Oswin). Die Palastanlage von Chirbet el Minje. Ein Vorbericht über die Ergebnisse der im Frühjahr und Herbst 1937 und im Frühjahr 1938 durchgeführten dritten und vierten Grabungskampagne auf Chirbet el Minje bei Tabgha am See Genezareth in Palästina. (Unpaged appendix: Die fünfte Grabungskampagne auf Chirbet el Minje (28. Oktober 1938 bis 10. Mai 1939).) *Palästina-Hefte des Deutschen Vereins vom Heiligen Lande*, Heft 17–20/1939.

— Sauvaget (J.), Remarques sur les monuments omeyyades. *Journal Asiatique*, CCXXXI, pp. 36–7.

— P[icard], C. H., Le Palais de Chirbet el Minje. *Revue Archéologique*, 6me sér., XIV, p. 85.

1937–41 Anon. Excavations in Palestine. *Quarterly of the Department of Antiquities*, VI, pp. 215–17; VIII, pp. 159–60; and IX, pp. 209–10.

1941 Schneider, A. M. Die Bauinschrift von chirbet el-minje. *Oriens Christianus*, XXXVI, pp. 115–17.

1946 Stern (Henri). Notes sur l'architecture des châteaux omeyyades. *Ars Islamica*, XI–XII, p. 73 and figs. 3–4.

1952 Schneider, A. M. Ḫirbet el-Minje am See Genesareth. *Les Annales Archéologiques de Syrie*, II, pp. 23–45, with 26 illus.; synopsis in Arabic, pp. ١٣٩—١٤٨.

1958 Creswell, K. A. C. A Short Account of Early Muslim Architecture, pp. 82–4 and fig. 16.

1960 Grabar, O., J. Perrot, B. Ravani, and Myriam Rosen. Sondages à Khirbet el-Minyeh. *Israel Exploration Journal.* X, pp. 226–43, pls. 27–30 and 8 figs.

— Shapiro and Avi-Yonah. Israel: Ancient Mosaics, plate 32 (coloured).

[1] Perrot and Chipiez, *History of Art in Chaldea and Assyria*, I, fig. 106.

[2] Dieulafoy, *L'Art antique de la Perse*, III, fig. 111; and Perrot and Chipiez, *History of Art in Persia*, fig. 66.

[3] *Ibid.*, figs. 62, 68, and 178.

[4] Herzfeld, *Am Tor von Asien*, Taf. XXXIII.

XIII

QUṢAYR 'AMRA

QUṢAYR 'AMRA:—Discovered by Musil—Detailed description—Material—The well—Purpose of the building—The decoration: the famous fresco paintings—The date: brilliant deductions of Nöldeke, Littmann, and van Berchem—The headgear of the Persian king—The *raison d'être* of Quṣayr 'Amra: Half-Bedawī life of the later Umayyad Khalifs—Inspiration of the fresco paintings—Nationality of the artists—The question of the lawfulness of painting in early Islam.—BIBLIOGRAPHY.

THE FLOOR MOSAICS, by CHRISTEL KESSLER

THE ZODIAC OF QUṢAYR 'AMRA, by the late FRITZ SAXL.

THE ASTRONOMICAL SIGNIFICANCE OF THE ZODIAC OF QUṢAYR 'AMRA, by the late ARTHUR BEER.

ARCHITECTURAL ORIGINS:—Similar baths at 'Abda and Ruḥayba—The hypocausts—The plan of the audience hall—The pointed arch: Qaṣr Ibn Wardān, &c. The low springing of the transverse arches—The vaulting system of the audience hall—Examples in the Ḥaurān—Hatra—Ṭāq-i Īwān—Qaṣr Kharāna—Conclusions—Result of analysis.

QUṢAYR 'AMRA[1]

QUṢAYR 'AMRA—the 'little palace of 'Amra'—was discovered by the late Alois Musil in June 1898. During his earlier travels he had heard from the Bedawīn of the existence, in a dangerous part of the desert, of a little palace decorated with paintings. He first reached it on 8th June 1898, but scarcely had he set foot within it than a cry of alarm was raised and he and his guides had to leave in haste.[2] On 10th July 1900, under cover of a raid made by the Banū Ṣakhr against the Ruwala, he visited it a second time, and stayed there three days measuring and photographing.[3] In 1901 he visited it for the third time accompanied by the painter Mielich, and stayed there from 26th May to 9th June.

Musil points out that there are a few references to Quṣayr 'Amra in travel literature, as follows: (1) Ḥājjī Muḥammad in the second half of the seventeenth century calls it 'Emri and couples it with Azraq.[4] (2) Ḥājjī Khalīfa, about the same date, also mentions 'Amra in connexion with Azraq.[5] (3) Seetzen heard of it from a travelling merchant,[6] likewise Burckhardt,[7] who visited it about 1810–12. Grey Hill had also heard of it and its paintings.[8]

Quṣayr 'Amra (Plates 70–76) stands on the southern edge of the bed of the Wādī Buṭm in the desert due east of the northern end of the Dead Sea, and about fifty miles east of 'Ammān,[9] or more precisely

[1] For Bibliography, see pp. 414–15.

[2] *Sitzungsberichte*, CXLIV, Abh. VII, pp. 20–21.

[3] *Ibid.*, pp. 26–44 and figs. 12–20.

[4] *Itinéraire de Constantinople à la Mecque, extrait de l'ouvrage turc intitulé: Kitab menassik el-Hadj de el-Hadj Mehemmed Edib Ben Mehemmed, Derviche* [Constantinople, 1232 H.]. Traduit par Bianchi, *Recueil de Voyages et Mémoires*, II, p. 124.

[5] *Jihān Numā*, Latin translation by Norberg, II, pp. 209 and 226–7.

[6] *Beyträge zur Geographie Arabiens*, in *Monatliche Correspondenz zur Beförderung der Erd- und Himmels-Kunde*, XVIII (1808), pp. 384–5: 'Das Gebäude, welches man eigentlich el Kassr Amarâ nennt, hat ein Kuppeldach, worauf inwendig Gasellen, Füchse, Hasen und andere Thiere mit bunten Farben gemalt seyn sollen. Säulen findet man da nicht.'

[7] *Travels in Syria*, pp. 665–6. His description is amazingly accurate and detailed:

'On the western side of the Szauan, nearer to the Wady Serhhan than to the Hudrush, is a castle called Kaszr Amera, and at a quarter of an hour from it, on the foot of a hill, the ruins of a village. Between the Kaszr and the village is a low ground where the rain water collects, and forms a small lake in winter half an hour in length. Before the castle is a well more than thirty feet deep, walled in by large stones, but without water. Over the well are four white marble columns, which support a vaulted roof or Kubbe, such as are often seen at wells in these countries. The castle is built of white square stones, which seem not to have been cemented together. Its dimensions are thirty-six or forty feet from W. to E. and twenty-five from S. to N. The entrance door, which is only about three feet high, is on the S. side, and leads into an apartment half the size of the whole building. In the middle of the western wall of this apartment is another door, as low as the former, leading to a second apartment of the same size as the former, except that one corner is partitioned off to form a third chamber. Each of the two latter have a window in the western wall. The roof [*sic*] of the apartments are vaulted below, and flat above. The walls which divide the apartments are two yards in thickness; in the two first rooms there is a stone pavement, in the small room the Arabs have taken up the pavement to dig for treasures; but they found nothing underneath, except small pieces of planks and some rusty iron. The ceiling of all the three apartments is chalked over, and looks quite new. In the small room it is painted all over with serpents, hares, gazelles, mares, and birds; there are neither human figures nor trees amongst the paintings. The colour of the paintings is red, green, and yellow, and they look as bright and well preserved, as if they had been done a short time ago. There are no kinds of niches, bas-reliefs, or inscriptions in the walls.' It will be noted that Burckhardt has turned the building round from north to south.

[8] *A Journey East of the Jordan*, in *P.E.F.*, *Q.St.*, 1896, p. 34: '. . . to the east a low wâdy leading, our Sheikhs said, to "Amr", which they describe as a ruin with pictures on the wall (perhaps a church), and beyond to Azrek; . . .'

[9] The itinerary runs—'Ammān, Muwaqqar, Qaṣr Kharāna, Quṣayr 'Amra; another twelve miles or so east is Azraq. The Wādī Buṭm runs into the Wādī Sirḥān; it owes its name to several turpentine trees growing on its banks, some of which are large enough to shelter one from the sun. They are an astonishing sight here, but it must be remembered that this wādī is full of water in the spring, nevertheless, as Jaussen and Savignac remark: '. . . il fallait être bédouin pour venir placer ici une maison de campagne!'; *Les Châteaux arabes*, p. 8.

36° 33′ E. of Greenwich and 31° 48′ N. (see Plate 70 and map on p. 404). It is a building of moderate size and has been well defined by van Berchem as a 'pavillon de chasse doublé d'un bain'.[1] It is composed in fact of two principal elements: (1) a rectangular audience hall, A, measuring roughly 8½ × 7½ m., with an alcove, B, opening on the south side, flanked by two rooms, C and C′, apsidal in form and without windows, and (2) a bath, consisting of three little rooms, D, E, and F, the first tunnel-vaulted, the second cross-vaulted, and the third covered by a dome (Fig. 450). On the east side of the latter is a tunnel-vaulted passage, G, at present blocked up, leading to an unroofed enclosure, H, apparently later[2] and probably never finished.

The exterior corresponds exactly with the interior and no attempt has been made to conceal the extrados of the vaults by raising the exterior walls or otherwise.

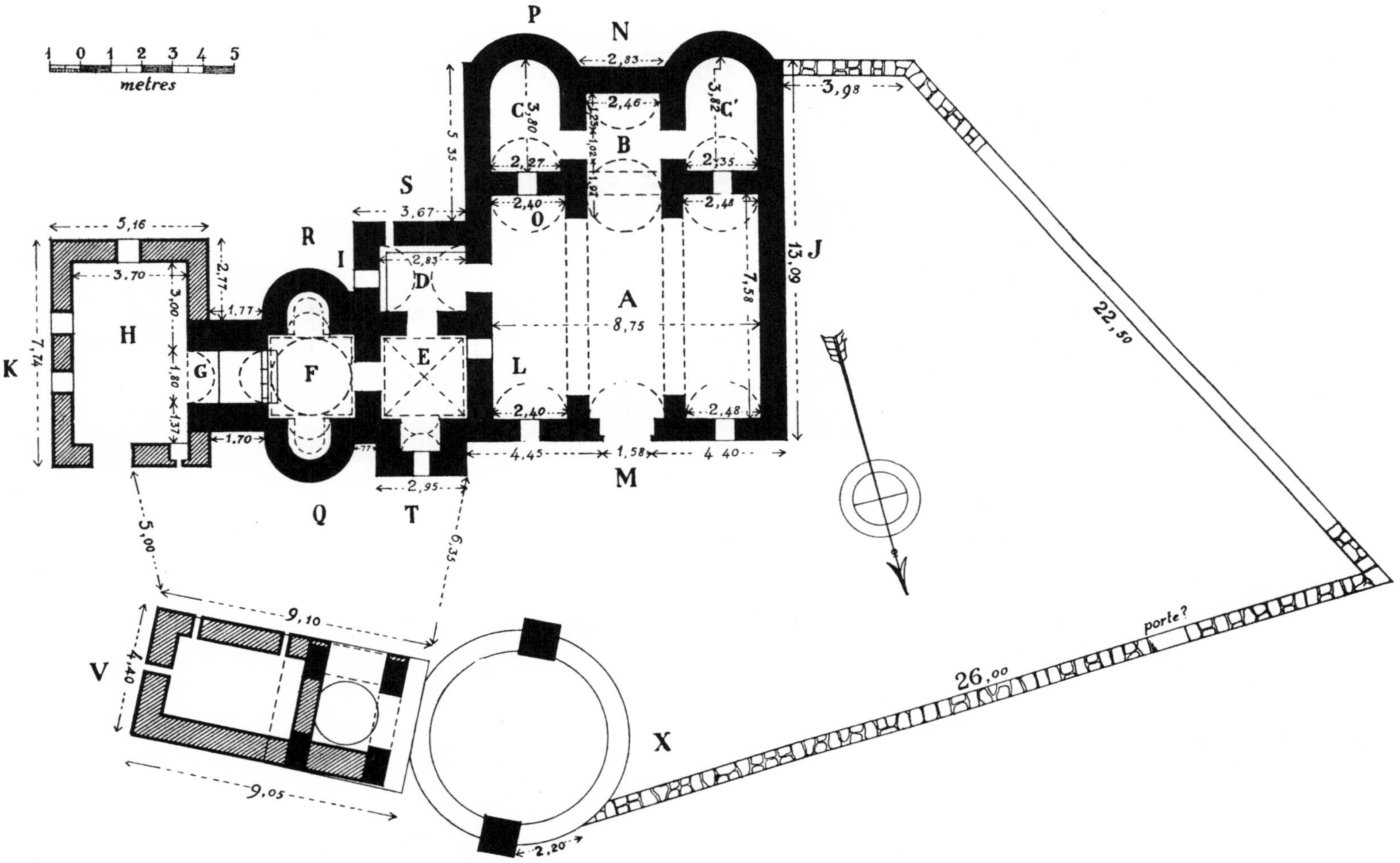

Fig. 450. Quṣayr 'Amra: Plan. (From Jaussen and Savignac, *op. cit.*)

Detailed Description. One enters by a doorway, M, in the centre of the north façade of the main building (Plate 70 *a* and 71 *b*). The first thing to strike one is the curious vaulting system, the nearly square interior being divided by two transverse arches into three bays of almost equal width, on which rest three tunnel-vaults (Plate 71 *c*). These three vaults are pierced on each side by a row of four holes irregularly spaced, which have been formed during the construction by inserting clay pipes about 10–12 cm. in diameter. The transverse arches spring from four low pilasters (*c.* 1 m. above the present ground level), and are chiefly remarkable in that they are slightly pointed—one of the earliest examples of this feature in Muslim architecture. Jaussen and Savignac were the first to call attention to this fact,[3] their measurements giving 6·18 m. for the span above the piers and 3·39 for the rise, i.e. 30 cm. more than it would be if they were semicircular, as they are shown by Musil.[4] They have, therefore, been struck from two centres not quite 63 cm. or one-tenth of the span apart (Plate 71 *d*).[5] There is a set-back of about 5 cm. at the springing, no doubt intended for the centering.

1 *Journal des Savants*, 1900, p. 406.

2 It breaks bond with the rest of the structure; see Jaussen and Savignac, *Les Châteaux arabes*, pp. 78, n., and 84, and pl. XXXVIII_2, where the break in bond can be seen.

3 *Op. cit.*, pp. 78 n. and 80. Dieulafoy (*Art in Spain*, p. 39) cites this building, quite wrongly, as containing an example of the horse-shoe arch.

4 *Ḳuṣejr 'Amra*, Taf. IX.

5 I have verified this, with a pair of compasses, on a wide-angle photograph taken in the axis of the arch.

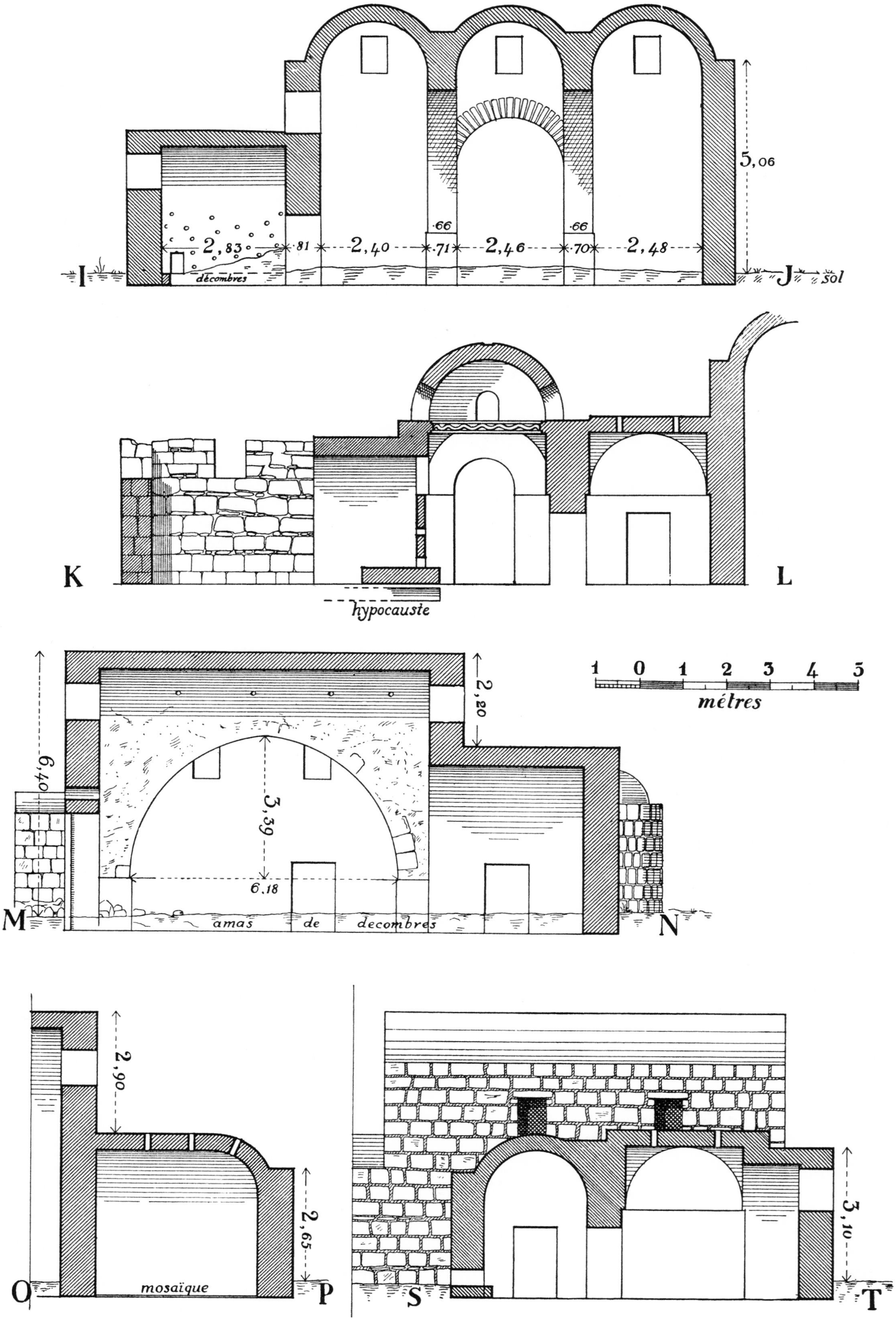

FIG. 451. QUṢAYR 'AMRA: Sections. (From Jaussen and Savignac, *op. cit.*)

At the back of the central bay is an alcove, B, which, although square-ended, resembles an apse; it is covered by a tunnel-vault, the crown of which is only about 3½ m. above the ground level, instead of nearly 6 m. like the transverse vaults. The sides of this recess are flush with the inner sides of the pilasters of the central nave. There is a window, placed as high as possible, at each end of the three tunnel-vaults of the main hall, and two high up in the eastern wall, making eight in all. These windows are all rectangular and average 1 m. in height and 65 cm. in width; in spite of their small size the hall is adequately lit. The framework of these windows, as Jaussen and Savignac point out,[1] has not been the object of any special care; they are not splayed and do not possess any grooves at the sides to receive a wooden frame. A block of hard white limestone serves as a lintel. There do not appear to have been any means of closing them, and Jaussen and Savignac add that it is doubtless for that reason that there are no windows on the west side, for it is against this side that the winter rains must generally beat.

A small door to right and left of the alcove opens into the little flanking chambers C and C′; they are slightly lower than the alcove and are each roofed with a tunnel-vault terminating in a semidome over the apsidal part. They lack windows and receive their light, such as it is, by the door and from four little holes pierced in the centre line of the vault, of the same construction as those in the three tunnel-vaults. These two chambers were obviously meant for repose, the main hall being intended for official receptions.

Musil[2] and Jaussen and Savignac[3] found that these little rooms had been paved with mosaic representing conventionalized foliage. This pavement was found at a depth of 30–40 cm. below the present surface, which is composed of gravel, sand, &c., and it was taken as the ground level in all their sections, reproduced here.

Let us now return to the main hall. A door 1·40 m. in height (but which must really measure about 1·70 m. from the true ground level) leads into the little tunnel-vaulted[4] room D (2·83 × 2·30 m.), which is lit by a window on the east side placed high up under the vault. In the south wall, near the south-east corner and at the ground level, is a small opening 32 cm. wide and 43 high.[5] At the foot of the east and south walls was a little plastered bench 30 cm. high and 22 wide. The walls here are pitted with holes evidently intended for the attachment of a coating of marble or stucco. Musil excavated the débris in this and the two following rooms, and found piers 70 cm. high which must have supported the original floor, the space between these piers serving for the passage of heated air from the furnace. The hypocausts in the Baths of Caracalla are constructed in this way (see below, pp. 440–41).

On the north side of D is a door 1·70 m. high and 1·06 wide leading into a cross-vaulted room E, 2·83 m. square, on the north side of which is a little tunnel-vaulted alcove 1·25 × 1·22 m. with a window at the back. The vault, like that of D, is pierced with a number of holes. Here again the lower part of the walls was evidently decorated with a coating of some sort. At about 2 m. above the floor the walls overhang about 12 cm., and in each corner beneath this projection are four clay water-pipes about 7 cm. in diameter, leading from the roof. The water was conducted along the roof in cemented channels.

A door similar to the last leads from E into F, a room quite different from any of the preceding. It consists of a central square practically identical in size to E, with a deep apsidal recess to north and south. The latter are covered by tunnel-vaults, terminating in semidomes as in C and C′, the crowns of which are 85 cm. below the base of the dome. The central part is covered by a dome nearly if not quite hemispherical (Plates 75 *b-c* and 76 *a*).[6] It rests on spherical-triangle pendentives, and between the top edge of the latter and the base of the dome is a cornice of cut stone, 30 cm. high, decorated with a triple chevron.

The dome is pierced with four windows which open immediately above the cornice; they average 53 cm. in width, 65 in height internally and 85 externally. The arches of these windows and the dome also are built of small flat slabs of limestone embedded in good mortar. The dome itself is 47 cm. thick; a little square socket at its summit indicates that it must once have been decorated with a finial.

[1] *Op. cit.*, pp. 78 n. and 80.

[2] *Kuṣejr ʿAmra*, pp. 65 and 87.

[3] *Op. cit.*, p. 81.

[4] Musil (*Sitzungsberichte*, folding plate at end), makes the axis of this vault run from north to south, instead of from east to west. This error, however, has been corrected in his *Kuṣejr ʿAmra*, Taf. XII.

[5] I do not know the purpose of this opening. Herzfeld speaks of it as being intended for the discharge of water; *Encyclopaedia of Islām*, I, p. 337.

[6] Jaussen and Savignac say 'légèrement surhaussée', and give its internal diameter as 2·60 m., and its height as 1·40, i.e. 10 cm. more than it would be if hemispherical; *op. cit.*, p. 82.

The walls of this chamber are also pitted with holes, evidently meant to hold a coating of some sort or other; the upper part overhangs as in the last room, and in each corner is a water-pipe in connexion with the channels on the roof. A little masonry seat runs round the two alcoves. Jaussen and Savignac were able to distinguish several remains of masonry channels (hypocausts ?), 30 cm. wide, under the débris which covered the ground.[1] These conduits must once have been covered by the pavement. They believe that the floor of room E was constructed in the same way.[2]

On the east side of F is a tunnel-vaulted passage 1·80 m. in width, now separated from it by a thin wall of bad masonry, which had a window a metre high in its upper part.[3] At its foot in F is a ledge forming

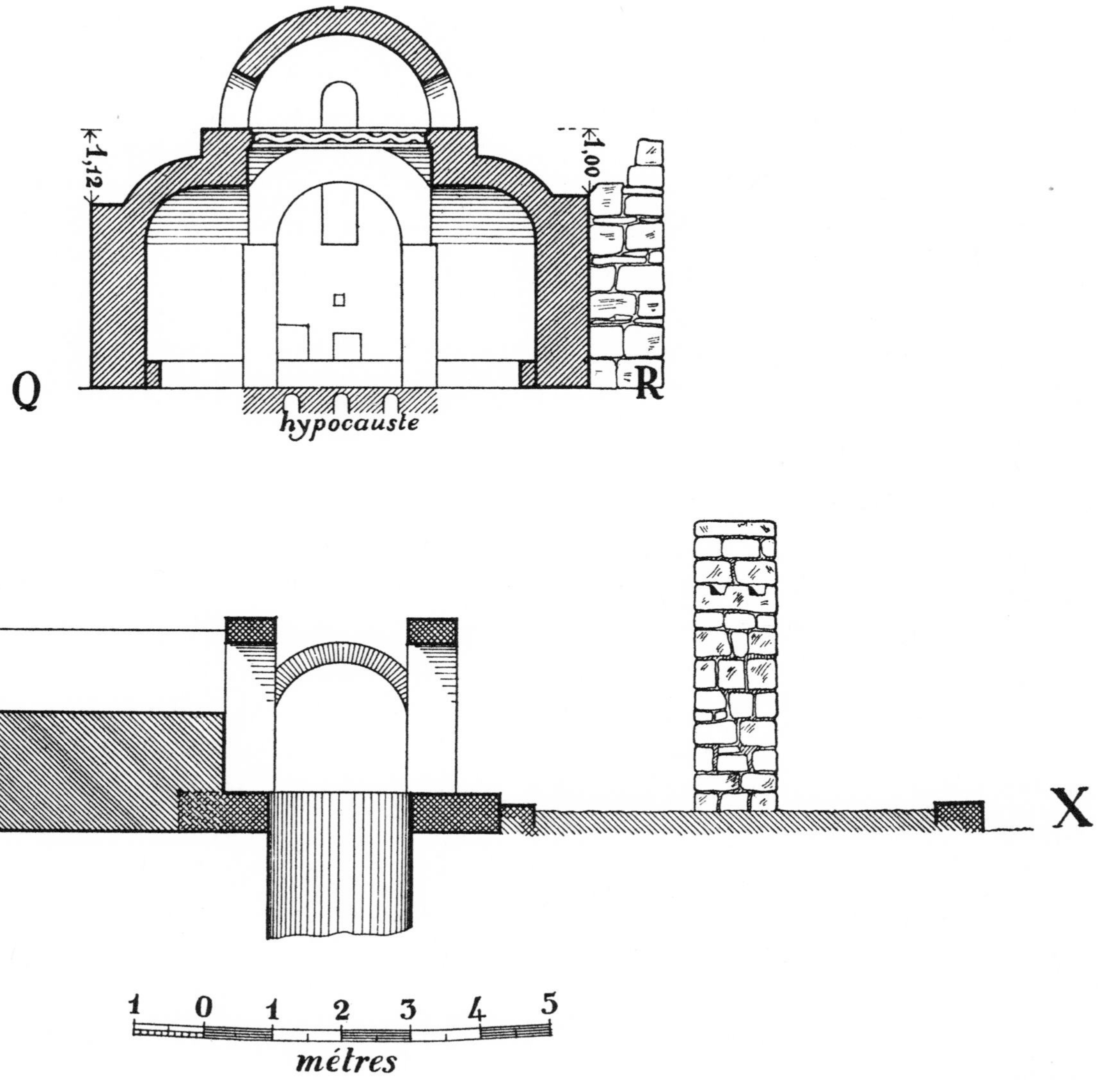

FIG. 452. QUṢAYR ʻAMRA, *Calidarium* and well. (From Jaussen and Savignac, *op. cit.*)

a seat 41 cm. high and 38 deep. At the far end of this passage, partly above and partly below ground level, is what appears to have been the furnace.[4]

The unroofed enclosure H (Plate 70 *b* to right), which measures 6·17×3·70 m., is of rougher masonry than the rest of the structure and, as we have seen above (p. 391, n. 2), is probably a later addition. The entrance is in the north side, but only one jamb of it remains. There were to have been three windows, one in the south side and two in the east, but the walls only rise three courses above their sills, and Jaussen and Savignac believe, from the absence of débris, that they were never completed.[5] The presence of windows, however, shows that H was intended to have been roofed.

MATERIAL. The walls, which vary in thickness from 80 to 84 cm., are constructed of hard reddish limestone from the neighbouring hills; there are a number of blocks 40 cm. in height, most of which are in the north façade (Plate 71 *a–b*), but the average is not more than 32–33 cm. The courses, therefore,

[1] *Op. cit.*, p. 83. Musil, on the other hand, says that he found piers here, 70 cm. high, as in the two other rooms; *Ḳuṣejr ʻAmra*, p. 87.

[2] *Op. cit.*, p. 82.

[3] The upper part no longer exists.

[4] This is Kropf's view also, in Musil's *Ḳuṣejr ʻAmra*, p. 188.

[5] *Op. cit.*, p. 84.

are very irregular and do not correspond at the corners; on the west side it has even been necessary to add a course to equalize the height. Most of the stones have not been cut, but merely shaped with a hammer; they are seldom long and frequently nearly square, and the innumerable irregularities are compensated for by chips of stone and a liberal amount of mortar, exactly as is done to-day in Cairo when native workmen construct a house of the poorer sort under the supervision of a native builder. The only dressed masonry occurs in the two transverse arches of the main hall, and the size of the voussoirs where exposed by a fall of plaster is 20 cm. broad by 39 deep. Basalt has been used for the lintel and jambs of the doorway M, likewise for the relieving arch; this basalt, according to Musil, came from al-ʻUwaynid, about 12 km. to the east.[1]

The vaults are constructed of flat stones embedded in mortar, the radial arrangement being maintained by chips of stone wedged between the outer ends; each vault has been covered by a coating of excellent mortar which has almost everywhere resisted the destructive action of centuries.

THE WELL. At a distance of 5 or 6 m. to the north is a well[2] and reservoir V, and alongside it a low circle of masonry, 5·80 m. in diameter, just emerging from the ground (Plate 70 *c* to left). Two piers of masonry are set opposite each other in this circle, one standing, the other overturned. Jaussen and Savignac suggest, with reason,[3] that these two posts were destined to support a beam forming part of the mechanism of a *sāqiya*, and that the circle of masonry was merely intended to mark the area in which the beast of burden walked round and round.

At a few minutes walk to the south-east of Quṣayr ʻAmra are the remains of a similar structure.[4]

At the south-west corner of the audience hall are the remains of a wall, 58 cm. thick, which goes towards the west for 3·98 m., then north-west for 22·50 m., and then nearly east for 26 m., ending against a circle of masonry belonging to the *sāqiya* which serves the well X (Fig. 450). It is impossible to say how high the wall was originally; as for its purpose it appears to have been intended to protect the little palace from an overflow of the *wādī* after a sudden rainfall, hence its pointed form upstream.

PURPOSE OF THE BUILDING. A comparison with two little bath-houses at ʻAbda and Ruḥayba (see below, pp. 440–41) south of Beersheba suffices to show that the annexe on the east side of the main hall A was a bath-house. The first room D, with its two benches, and an outlet for the water only but no pipes, must have served as the *apodyterium*, the second room E, with its water-pipes and hypocausts under the floor, was the *tepidarium*, and the domed chamber next the furnace the *calidarium*. Musil's suggestion that the passage G was the original entrance, subsequently closed,[5] is untenable as Herzfeld has pointed out,[6] for the normal sequence of the bath-rooms, which necessarily commences with the *apodyterium* and ends with the *calidarium*, excludes such an hypothesis. The entrance to the bath must always have been from A. Nevertheless, there is one feature which puzzles me; why is the tunnel-vault leading out of the *calidarium* built as though it were intended to be left open, and then closed by a thin wall of bad masonry? At ʻAbda (see below, p. 440) and at Ḥammām aṣ-Ṣarakh (see below, p. 501) the corresponding closing wall, which surely must have existed, has gone without leaving any trace, and apparently in the bath at Jabal Says also.[7]

THE DECORATION: THE FAMOUS FRESCO PAINTINGS. The little rooms flanking the alcove possessed mosaic floors, which were in good condition when Musil saw them.[8] The other rooms were formerly paved with marble slabs about 3 cm. thick, remains of which still existed at the time of Musil's visits.[9] The lower part of the walls of the main hall and the three rooms of the bath are unplastered, but holes chiselled in the exposed masonry indicate that there was once a marble dado.[10] Above this the walls are plastered and decorated with the now famous paintings, the importance of which may be realized when

1 *Arabia Petraea*, I, p. 226.

2 Burckhardt, who saw Quṣayr ʻAmra about 1810–1812, says: 'Over the well are four white marble columns, which support a vaulted roof or Kubbe, such as are often seen at wells in these countries'; see above, p. 390, n. 7.

3 *Op. cit.*, pp. 84–5.

4 Musil, *Arabia Petraea*, I, p. 222 and fig. 98; Jaussen and Savignac, *op. cit.*, p. 85, fig. 16, and pl. XXXVIII$_5$.

5 *Ḳuṣejr ʻAmra*, p. 63.

6 See his article *ʻAmra*, in the *Encyclopaedia of Islām*, I, p. 337.

7 De Vogüé, *Syrie centrale*, fig. 28.

8 *Ḳuṣejr ʻAmra*, p. 65.

9 *Ibid.*, pp. 64–5.

10 *Ibid*, p. 64. At the time of his second visit the eastern wall of the main hall still retained its panelling, which measured 80 cm. above the débris; *Sitzungsberichte*, p. 28. Musil says that he was informed by his Bedawīn companions that the beautiful, well-polished, dark marble slabs had been taken away by travelling traders and sold, probably in Damascus; *Ḳuṣejr ʻAmra*, p. 89.

one remembers that 'no such extensive decoration in fresco is known to have survived in any other secular building, or indeed in any building earlier than the Romanesque period'.[1] The colours are directly applied to a mortar facing about 3 cm. in thickness, and, according to the Austrian chemists, Pollak and Wenzel,[2] are to be regarded as fresco and not as tempera, for no traces of size were found. The range of colours is limited to blue, deep brown, light brown, dull yellow, and bluish-green, obtained as follows:

Bright blue—natural ultramarine.
Deep brown—a red, apparently produced from oxide of iron, overlaid with a thin coat of ultramarine.
Light brown—ochreous compositions containing iron.
Dull yellow—the same, mixed with chalk.
Bluish-green—yellow which has received a light coating of ultramarine.

The paintings in the audience hall have suffered far more than those in the small rooms; nearly all in fact are too faded or too blackened by smoke to give a useful result if photographed. We are therefore almost entirely dependent on the paintings of Mielich for our knowledge of them, which is all the more to be regretted in that those paintings of his which can be checked, viz. those of the three rooms of the bath, are seen to be travesties of the originals. This, of course, is due to the fact that his paintings are not copies completed on the spot, but reconstructions worked up months later in his studio from his tracings, notes, copies of the colours, and from two or three fragments which were detached and taken away.[3] I propose to describe these paintings in the following order: alcove, walls, soffits of arches, vaults.

The Alcove. The walls of the alcove B, from above the place formerly occupied by the marble dado to about half their height, were painted to imitate hanging drapery. At the back of the alcove was a throned monarch with a nimbus under a baldachin,[4] resting on two spirally decorated columns, on the arched front edge of which was painted a Kufic inscription in white on a blue background,[5] invoking a blessing on some person whose name no longer remains.[6] To the right of the throne was a man standing and apparently waving a *flabellum*; to the left another standing figure, almost destroyed. The monarch, doubtless the one for whom the building was erected, rests his feet on a foot-stool, beneath which is another scene with waterfowl and a boat.[7] There can be no doubt that this alcove, directly opposite the entrance, was intended for the throne recess. Strzygowski suggests that a curtain hung here,[8] which was drawn back at the time of audience, but I cannot help thinking that such a practice, which would have been in perfect keeping with the elaborate ceremonial of the Sasanian,[9] 'Abbāsid,[10]

1 Dalton, *Byzantine Art*, p. 281.

2 *Ḳuṣejr 'Amra*, pp. 200–202.

3 See the remarks of Müller, the editor, in *Ḳuṣejr 'Amra*, pp. iv–vii, and of Wickhoff, *ibid.*, p. 203; also van Berchem, *Journal des Savants*, 1909, p. 308. The fragments taken away are reproduced in facimile in *Ḳuṣejr 'Amra*, Taf. XVI and XXIII.

4 Musil, *Sitzungsberichte*, p. 34; *Ḳuṣejr 'Amra*, p. 209, Taf. VIII and XV (reproduced by Strzygowski, *Amra und seine Malereien*, in the *Zeitschrift für bildende Kunst*, n.F., XVIII, Abb. 1; Diez, *Kunst der islamischen Völker*, Abb. 28; Arnold, *Painting in Islam*, pl. LVII *b*); Musil, *Arabia Petraea*, I, p. 286; Brünnow, *W.Z.K.M.*, XXI, p. 277; and Jaussen and Savignac, *op. cit.*, pl. XL.

5 Painted inscriptions are very rare and I can only cite six others: (1) on the walls of the little palace known as Qaṣr Kharāna, is a *graffito* of 92 H. (710): see below, pp. 447–8; (2) house at Madīna (Upper Egypt), discovered by Somers Clarke in 1900: six lines written with a *qalam* in simple Kufic—'and Mālik son of Kathīr has written [it] in Rajab of the year 117 (Aug. 735)'; see the *C.I.A.—Égypte*, I, pp. 693–7; (3) Church at Sebaiṭa in the Negeb; (4) the Pīr-i-'Alamdār at Dāmghān, built 417 H. (1026); see Pope, *The Painted Inscription on the interior of the Pir-i-'Alamdār*, *Bull. of the American Inst. for Persian Art and Archaeology*, IV, pp. 139–41, with 2 illus.; (5) sarcophagus of the Qā'id Munjib al-Qāhirī al-Āmirī, discovered in the Cemetery of 'Abbāsīya and now in the Museum of Muslim Art (No. 11710): fine inscription in Kufic running round the interior; the title al-Āmirī fixes the date between 495 and 524 H. (1101–30); see Wiet, *Répertoire*, VIII, p. 164; and (6) Mashhad of Sayyida Ruqayya, Cairo: inscription round the base of the dome, dated Dhu'l-Qa'da 527 (Sept. 1133); see my *Muslim Architecture of Egypt*, I, p. 250 and pl. 86 *c*.

6 Musil, *Ḳuṣejr 'Amra*, figs. 131–2. For a carefully measured copy of what remains of this inscription see Jaussen and Savignac, pl. LVI and pp. 96–7, where they point out that their tracing renders impossible certain readings which have been suggested, and especially that proposed by Karabacek, *Ḳuṣejr 'Amra*, pp. 213–16, a reading already criticized by Nöldeke, *Z.D.M.G.*, LXI, p. 224; Becker, *Zeitschrift für Assyriologie*, XX, pp. 361–4; and van Berchem, *Journal des Savants*, 1909, pp. 363–4.

7 The part with the boat was taken away; a coloured facsimile of it is given on Musil's Taf. XVI.

8 *Amra und seine Malereien*, *loc. cit.*, p. 217.

9 Ibn Hishām and Ṭabarī give an account of the audience granted to Nu'mān ibn al-Mundhir of Ḥīra, by Chosroes at Ctesiphon. They say that the Sasanian crown was like a great cask of gold studded with enormous rubies, emeralds, pearls, &c., and of such enormous weight that, no neck being able to bear it, it was suspended from the great vault (*ṭāq*) by a golden chain. The Persian king was concealed by a curtain until he had taken his place on the throne and put his head inside the crown; the curtain was then drawn back. They add that whoever saw him for the first time fell on his knees in awe; see Ibn Hishām, Wüstenfeld's ed., I, p. 42, ll. 2–8; transl. in Browne, *Literary History of Persia*, I, pp. 128–9 (see also p. 179) and by Guillaume, *Life of Muhammad*, p. 30; Ṭabarī, Prima Series, pp. 946–7; transl. in Nöldeke, *Sasaniden*, pp. 221–2; ath-Tha'ālibī, Zotenberg's

[Footnotes 9 and 10 continued on opposite page

and Fāṭimid courts,[1] was scarcely likely at the court of the Umayyads, so dominated by Bedawīn ideas of equality. The tunnel-vault above was divided on each side into a series of panels, formed by round arches resting on columns, decorated with spiral zigzag bands; in each stood a half-nude woman in front of a curtain, above which appeared the head of a second. Practically nothing of this remains. The apex of the vault was filled with tendrils growing out of a vase.

The Walls. The west bay of the south wall, according to Musil,[2] was occupied by the figure of a woman, now almost completely destroyed, above which to the right was the word NIKH—Victory.[3] This figure, as has already been pointed out, must surely have a direct connexion with the famous picture of the defeated enemies of Islam alongside, at the south end of the west wall. On the west wall was a great painting,[4] or rather a series of three paintings, the first of which (Plate 71 *e*) consisted[5] of six richly dressed figures; three are placed in the foreground with their right hands open in sign of homage or submission, and three placed between and behind them, their costumes being partly concealed by the figures in the foreground. Above the first four were fragments of superscriptions in Arabic and Greek; it is on the interpretation of these superscriptions that the dating of the building rests, so we shall return to this picture again (see below, pp. 400–401). To the right is a lattice-work screen which surrounds two sides of a bath, out of which steps a nude life-sized woman; another woman is visible at the far end and the heads of several more appear over the screen. The third scene consists of a group of athletes, each wearing a loin-cloth, apparently practising gymnastic exercises. There are only the faintest traces of paintings on the north wall,[6] but sufficient remains on the east wall to show that its whole surface, up to the tops of the windows, was occupied by a hunting scene,[7] for it is just possible to discern a pack of dogs in pursuit. The east bay of the south wall contains what Jaussen and Savignac[8] believe to be a continuation of the previous hunting scene, for one can see an antelope stretched out on the ground, whilst a man is disembowelling another.[9] Above, to the right of the window under the vault, are traces of a woman with the word ΠΟΙΗC[IC]—Poesy—painted alongside.[10] Facing her on the other side of the window are the remains of two figures symbolizing history and philosophy, as is indicated by the words ICTOPI[A][11] and CKΨH (*εκέψις*). In the bay above the alcove, Musil[12] shows the remains of four heads, but it is impossible to distinguish anything now.

The Transverse Arches. The decoration on the soffits of the transverse arches is better preserved than any we have discussed hitherto. On the southern half of the eastern arch (Plate 71 *c*) is a seated musician playing a long-handled stringed instrument.[13] Above him and reaching to the apex of the arch is a woman, wearing nothing but a tight-fitting skirt, with her arms above her head.[14] The part above her hands had gone even when Musil saw it, but I suggest that she is holding up a portrait medallion, as at Palmyra, where very similar narrow slip compositions (Fig. 456, facing p. 446) occur

edition and translation, pp. 699–700; and Christensen, *L'Empire des Sassanides*, in the *Mém. de l'Acad. Roy. des Sciences et des Lettres de Danemark*, 7me série, Sect. des Lettres, I^{1}, p. 102.

10 See the account of the reception of the envoy of the Fāṭimid Khalif al-ʿAzīz billāh at the ʿAbbāsid court in A. D. 980. The Khalif was concealed by a curtain which was presently drawn aside revealing him seated on a high throne surrounded by a hundred guards with drawn swords, all magnificently dressed; Quṭb ad-Dīn, Wüstenfeld's ed., *Chroniken der Stadt Mekka*, III, pp. 168–9; quoted by Arnold, *Caliphate*, pp. 66–67.

1 See the account of the reception of Hugh of Caesarea and Godefroy Fulcher by the last Fāṭimid Khalif al-ʿĀḍid in 1167. Arrived at the throne room, the Wazīr ungirded his sword and prostrated himself three times; a heavy curtain, embroidered with gold and pearls, was then drawn aside, revealing the Khalif seated on a golden throne; William of Tyre, *Historia*, Bk. XIX, cap. 19–20; in the *Recueil des hist. des croisades, B : Occidentaux*, I, pp. 911–13; and Schlumberger, *Campagnes du roi Amaury Ier*, pp. 118–25.

2 *Sitzungsberichte*, p. 31; *Ḳuṣejr ʿAmra*, pp. 210–11 and Taf. XXV.

3 Tracing in Jaussen and Savignac, pl. LV$_5$. I was unable to distinguish this word.

4 Musil, *Sitzungsberichte*, pp. 29–30; *Ḳuṣejr ʿAmra*, p. 211, fig. 134 and Taf. XXVI (reproduced by Strzygowski, *Amra und seine Malereien*, *loc. cit.*, *Abb.* 2; by Brockelmann, in *Der Islam* (Pflugk-Harttung, *Weltgeschichte*, Band: *Orient*), pp. 180–81; by Mann, *Der Islam einst und jetzt*, Abb. 31–2; and Diez, *Kunst der islamischen Völker*, Abb. 27); Brünnow, *W.Z.K.M.*, XXI, pp. 275–6; and Arnold, *op. cit.*, pl. LVII *a*.

5 It has since suffered so much that it is almost impossible to distinguish anything now; see Jaussen and Savignac, p. 89 and pl. XXXIX$_2$.

6 Musil, *Sitzungsberichte*, pp. 31, 33, and 35; *Ḳuṣejr ʿAmra*, pp. 210–11 and Taf. XXI, XXVII, and XXXII; and Brünnow, pp. 276–7.

7 Musil, *Sitzungsberichte*, p. 36; *Ḳuṣejr ʿAmra*, p. 211 and Taf. XXX and XXXI; and Brünnow, p. 275.

8 *Op. cit.*, p. 92.

9 Musil, *Ḳuṣejr ʿAmra*, p. 211 and Taf. XXIX (reproduced by Strzygowski, *Amra und seine Malereien*, *loc. cit.*, Abb. 6); Brünnow, p. 276.

10 Tracing in Jaussen and Savignac, pl. LV$_7$.

11 Tracing in Jaussen and Savignac, pl. LV$_6$.

12 *Ḳuṣejr ʿAmra*, Taf. XIX.

13 Musil, *Ḳuṣejr ʿAmra*, p. 210 and Taf. XXIII and XXIV; *Arabia Petraea*, I, pp. 282, 286, and fig. 124; Brünnow, p. 278; and Jaussen and Savignac, p. 90 and pl. XL$_2$.

14 Musil, *Sitzungsberichte*, pp. 34–5; *Ḳuṣejr ʿAmra*, p. 210 and Taf. XXIV and XXVIII (inset); Jaussen and Savignac, p. 90 and pl. XXXVIII.

in a rock-tomb known as al-Maghārat al-Jadīda.[1] A similar figure decorates the corresponding part of the northern half of the arch, below which is the figure of a man standing and apparently waving a streamer of some light fabric.[2] On the southern half of the western arch is a nude dancer making sinuous and undulating movements with her arms and body (Plate 71 *c*). Above was part of the skirt of a figure (now gone), which according to Mielich's painting (Taf. XXIV) must have been identical with that on the other arch.

The Three Vaults. The western vault has now lost all its decoration,[3] but the two halves of the central one are divided, by means of ornamental bands decorated with red and blue medallions, into two rows of eight rectangular frames, each containing an inner frame formed by a gable resting on two columns; these frames contained figures, some of which were seated.[4] Two triangular spaces are formed above each pediment, and each is occupied by a bird which Jaussen and Savignac propose to identify as the *qaṭā*, a kind of grey partridge (? sand-grouse) found in the desert. The eastern vault was divided up into the same number of frames, in this case square, each containing the personification of a trade—carpentry, stone-cutting, brick-laying, &c.[5] Those on the east side are the best preserved.

Rooms flanking Alcove. In the centre of the north wall of room C is a vase with a broad, round foot, a bulbous body, and a broad, flat top like a tray. The vine scrolls which cover the wall spring, not from the mouth of this vase, but from its foot.[6] The walls and vaults of both rooms, C and C′, are covered with vine scrolls.[7]

The Apodyterium (room D) contains the best preserved paintings in the building. Over the lintel of the door leading from the main hall is a comparatively well preserved painting which fills the whole tympanum of the vault. Slightly to the right of the centre is a Cupid with wings spread, holding out his hands over two figures lying on the ground, and appearing, as Jaussen and Savignac (p. 91) express it, to 'écarter dans le même mouvement un autre personnage dont le buste apparaît à sa droite dans le haut'. The latter figure is that of a woman resting on her elbow, who appears to be gazing on the reclining figures. Musil took the object on the ground for a corpse wrapped in a winding-sheet,[8] and Mielich's painting is a travesty of the original,[9] but Savignac's excellent photograph (Plate 72 *c*) shows sufficiently clearly that there are two bodies lying side by side, although their heads can no longer be distinguished. Above them, near the left elbow of the Cupid, appears to be the top of a palm tree.

The centre of the corresponding tympanum is occupied by a window. The space to the left (north) is occupied by a woman, nude or nearly so, sitting with her chin resting on her hand (good) and looking towards a man (faded) on the other side of the window, who looks at her over his shoulder.[10] (Plate 72 *a* and *b*).

The tunnel-vault is divided up by bands, decorated with leaves, into seventeen lozenges, the outer points of which touch the edges, thereby forming twelve triangles. These lozenges and triangles are each filled by one figure, either a man, a woman, an animal, or a bird, generally accompanied by a little plant.[11] On the south side (Plate 73 *b*), going from left to right, we observe:

[1] For this tomb, see below, p. 407, n. 3.

[2] Jaussen and Savignac, p. 90 and pl. XL_3.

[3] At the time of Musil's second visit it apparently still retained traces of its decoration; *Sitzungsberichte*, pp. 30–31.

[4] *Sitzungsberichte*, pp. 32–3; *Ḳuṣejr ʿAmra*, pp. 200–210 and Taf. IX, XX, and XXII; Brünnow, *loc. cit.*, p. 274; and Jaussen and Savignac, p. 89.

[5] Musil, *Sitzungsberichte*, pp. 36–8 and fig. 14; *Ḳuṣejr ʿAmra*, pp. 209 and 211 and Taf. XI, XXVIII, and XXX (reproduced by Brockelmann, *Der Islam*, illustrations on pp. 176–7); *Arabia Petraea*, I, pp. 280–82; and Jaussen and Savignac, p. 90 and pls. XLI (reproduced by Migeon, *Revue Biblique*, N.S., XI, fig. 6) and XLII.

[6] See Jaussen and Savignac, pp. 90–91 and pl. XLIII. I did not enter this room as the floor was occupied by a number of desiccated corpses, presumably of Bedawīn, very neatly and carefully wrapped up in winding-sheets.

[7] For room C, see Musil, Taf. XI. Brünnow, p. 278, remarks that these vine scrolls recall those on the façade of Mshattā.

[8] *Sitzungsberichte*, p. 39. I conclude that this is why Karabacek (*Ḳuṣejr ʿAmra*, p. 232) and Nöldeke (*loc. cit.*, p. 223) were led to take the Cupid for Isrāfīl, the Angel of Death.

[9] Compare Musil, Taf. XXXIII (reproduced by Strzygowski, *Amra und seine Malereien, loc. cit.*, Abb. 4; Dalton, *Byzantine Art*, fig. 171; and Diez, *Kunst der islamischen Völker*, Abb. 30) with Jaussen and Savignac's pl. XLV (reproduced by Migeon, *Revue Biblique*, N.S., XI, fig. 5).

[10] Musil, *Sitzungsberichte*, p. 39; *Ḳuṣejr ʿAmra*, p. 212 and Taf. XXXV (reproduced by Strzygowski, *Amra und seine Malereien, loc. cit.*, Abb. 5; by Brockelmann, *Der Islam*, illustration on p. 182; and by Diez, *Kunst der islamischen Völker*, Abb. 29); Musil, *Arabia Petraea*, I, p. 280; Brünnow, p. 278; and Jaussen and Savignac, pp. 91–2 and pls. XLVI and XLVII_1.

[11] Musil, *Sitzungsberichte*, pp. 39–41 and figs. 15–17; *Ḳuṣejr ʿAmra*, p. 212 and Taf. XXXIV (reproduced by Strzygowski, *ʿAmra und seine Malereien, loc. cit.*, Abb. 3; Brockelmann, *Der Islam*, illustration on p. 179; Dalton, *Byzantine Art*, fig. 170; Migeon, *Revue Biblique*, N.S., XI, plate to face p. 393; Diez, *Kunst der islamischen Völker*, Abb. 29; and Pijoán, *History of Art*, II, fig. 310); Karabacek, in *Ḳuṣejr ʿAmra*, p. 232; Musil, *Arabia Petraea*, I, pp. 280–282 and figs. 121–3; Jaussen and Savignac, pp. 92–4 and pls. XLVIII (reproduced by Glück and Diez, *Kunst des Islam*, Abb. 143), XLIX and L, also XLVII_2.

Row 1 (triangles)—(*a*) A small animal with its tail turned up over its back, (*b*) a snake coiled up ready to strike, and (*c*) a small animal like a cat, watching its prey.

Row 2—(*a*) A stork with very long legs and neck, (*b*) a wild ass, (*c*) a deer (?) scratching its neck with its left hind leg, and (*d*) a crested bird, perhaps the bustard (*ḥabārā*) of this region, as Jaussen and Savignac suggest.

Row 3—(*a*) Monkey or bear, sitting on a foot-stool and playing a stringed instrument; Jaussen and Savignac suggest the *rabāba* still in use amongst the Arabs, (*b*) a monkey standing on its hind legs and clapping its fore-paws, like Arabs at a *fantasia*, (*c*) man in a short tunic, apparently combing his hair.

Row 4—(*a*) Another stork, (*b*) gazelle, (*c*) trotting camel, (*d*) crane (?).

Apex of Vault. The three lozenges were occupied by three busts. The face of that to the left (my Plate 75 *a*) has almost disappeared, but the costume can still be made out; in the next the face is still distinguishable, but the costume has faded; the third is that of a man, white-haired according to Mielich, with a sceptre or lance in his right hand. Wickhoff suggests that these three heads are intended to represent the three ages of man.[1]

On the north side (Plate 73 *a*) we have:[2]

Row 1—Disappeared.

Row 2[3]—(*a*) Stork, (*b*) gazelle (?), (*c*) another gazelle, (*d*) destroyed.

Row 3—(*a*) Man in Roman tunic playing a flute, (*b*) female dancer wearing a long white skirt with a broad red border, above it a sleeveless tunic gathered in at the waist with a white girdle; the lower edge of the tunic whirls out away from the skirt, (*c*) very badly damaged, but apparently a man standing.

Row 4—(*a*) Heron (?), (*b*) an animal (Jaussen and Savignac suggest a wild ass), (*c*) a similar animal in a different attitude, (*d*) a swan (?).

The Tepidarium. On the west, south, and east sides the tympanum of the cross-vault is occupied by pictures, as follows. West side—women bathing, now almost entirely destroyed.[4] South side (Plate 74 *a* and *c*)[5]—to the left a half-reclining woman, in the centre a figure holding in its[6] arms a little child, the head and right arm of which are visible above the shoulder. To the right again, at the door, another woman enters holding in her left hand an object which Jaussen and Savignac believe to be a cradle of the type used by the Bedawīn. All the figures are entirely nude, which suggests the idea of a hot bath. The object carried may, however, be a leather water-skin. East wall[7]—to the left a nude woman leans forward with arms outstretched holding a baby which she passes to another person whose head only can be distinguished.

On the north side the tympanum is cut into by the vault of a little alcove; what remains of the tympanum is decorated with vine tendrils, which form loops round bunches of grapes.[8] The alcove itself is decorated in a similar way (Plate 74 *b*), but the loops are much larger and each contains a figure, either of a man, a lion, a bear, a hare, or a panther.[9]

The vault is decorated with plants and foliage of which a little is visible on Plate 74 *b*.

The Calidarium (Plates 75 *b–d* and 76).[10] The dome resembling the vault of heaven was evidently intended to be painted as such, for the chief constellations of the northern hemisphere are depicted there together with the signs of the Zodiac. In the centre was the Great Bear and the Little Bear separated by the tail of the Dragon. To the right, a person with arms extended was recognized by Jaussen

1 In Musil, *op. cit.*, pp. 206 and 212.

2 Musil, p. 212 and Taf. XXXIV; and Jaussen and Savignac, pp. 92–3 and pl. L (reproduced by Migeon, *loc. cit.*, XI, fig. 7).

3 Jaussen and Savignac, pp. 93–4. Their numbering has gone wrong here; they omit the row of triangles at the bottom edge, count row 2 as 'ligne 1', and continue on to 'ligne 4' which, being really line 5, does not exist, as may be seen on examining their pl. XLIX$_1$.

4 Musil, *Sitzungsberichte*, p. 42; *Ḳuṣejr ʿAmra*, p. 212 and Taf. XXXVI; also Wickhoff's remarks, *ibid.*, p. 205.

5 See also Musil, *Sitzungsberichte*, p. 42; *Ḳuṣejr ʿAmra*, p. 212 and Taf. XXXVII (reproduced by Brockelmann, *Der Islam*, illustration on p. 183); Wickhoff, *ibid.*, p. 205; and Jaussen and Savignac, pl. LI.

6 Wickhoff (in Musil, p. 212) takes this figure for that of a woman, likewise Brünnow, p. 279; Jaussen and Savignac, however (p. 94), take it for that of a man.

7 Musil, *Sitzungsberichte*, pp. 42–3; *Ḳuṣejr ʿAmra*, p. 212 and Taf. XXXVIII; Wickhoff's, *ibid.*, p. 205; Jaussen and Savignac, p. 94 and pl. LII.

8 Musil, *Sitzungsberichte*, p. 43 and fig. 18; *Ḳuṣejr ʿAmra*, p. 212 and Taf. XXXIX; Jaussen and Savignac, p. 94 and pl. XLIX$_2$.

9 See also Jaussen and Savignac, pl. LIII. Brünnow (p. 279) compares the treatment to that of the façade of Mshattā.

10 See also Musil, *Sitzungsberichte*, p. 43 and figs. 19–20 (photographs); *Ḳuṣejr ʿAmra*, p. 212 and Taf. XL–XLI; his *Arabia Petraea*, I, p. 276 and figs. 118–20; and Jaussen and Savignac, pl. LIV.

and Savignac as Andromeda, with Cassiopeia at her feet. The reader, however, is referred to the brilliant studies of this zodiac, by the late F. Saxl and the late Arthur Beer, on pp. 424–40.

The Date : brilliant deductions of Nöldeke, Littmann, and van Berchem. The true period of the building was certainly grasped by Musil, as may be seen from his learned chapter on the history of the region,[1] but the matter was unfortunately taken out of his hands by the Vienna Academy, under whose auspices *Kuṣejr ‘Amra* was published, and the chapter on the date entrusted to Karabacek. The actual dating is based, as stated above (p. 397), on the interpretation of the fragments of bilingual superscriptions still preserved above the group of figures at the south end of the west wall (Plate 71 *e*). These inscriptions consist of four Greek and four Arabic words, forming four doublets above the first four personages from the left in the group of six personages there represented. The Greek letters average 3½ cm. in height.[2] Karabacek, to whom the epigraphy was entrusted, read the word above the first figure as [ΚΑΙ]CΑΡ / ق[صر], after which by a series of *tours de force*, which included reading a Greek name backwards to get Theodora, he arrived at the conclusion that the building was due to the ‘Abbāsid prince, Aḥmad, in the ninth century.[3] Nothing could be more improbable as van Berchem has pointed out, for the Syrian desert, the favourite residence of several Umayyad Khalifs (see below, pp. 402–6), was completely neglected by the ‘Abbāsids, who ruined the Bedawī policy of the dynasty they had supplanted and made Mesopotamia their home. Nor is it likely that an ‘Abbāsid prince, even if he had built a little palace in the Belqā, the home of his deadliest enemies, would have painted the Byzantine Empress Theodora on its walls![4]

We owe the true solution to Nöldeke.[5] Beginning from the left, he read [ΚΑΙ]CΑΡ / ق[صر] as Karabacek had done,[6] but in the case of the third figure, by combining the two mutilated words, he was able to read ΧΟCΔΡΟΙC.[7] He points out that Χοσδρόης for Χοσρόης occurs in Malalas and the Paschal Chronicle; as for ι instead of η, he remarks that that need cause no astonishment at the period in question. On the head of this figure, moreover, is a crown with the same ornaments as appear on the coins of the later Sasanians, e.g. the coins of Khusrau II (A. D. 590–628).[8] After that he quickly convinced himself that the Arabic inscription over the fourth figure was *Najāshī*. This reading, generally accepted, has now been rendered certain by the discovery, made by Jaussen and Savignac in 1909, of the corresponding Greek word above—Ν, then Ι and Γ and the half of an Ο = ΝΙΓΟ[C]. They add that it would not be impossible to take the second letter for Η linked with Γ thus—ΗΓ of which the bar has disappeared.[9] Nöldeke showed his results to Littmann, who then read the inscription[10] over the second figure as ΡΟΔΟΡΙΚ^{C} / [ل]ودريق or ΡΟΔΟΡΙΚ$^{\text{O[C]}}$. The four personages thus designated are of course the Byzantine Emperor, the Visigothic King of Spain, the Sasanian Emperor, and the Negus of Abyssinia, that is to say, sovereigns whom the rising Arab power had either entirely overcome, or robbed of part of their territory. The Negus of Abyssinia comes under this description, for the Arabs had taken Dahlak from him. Nöldeke explains the youthful appearance of the Persian king by the fact that the last ‘Chosroes’, Yazdagird III, was very young when he ascended the throne.[11]

The Byzantine Emperor is clad in his imperial robes with a tiara on his head, the Sasanian Emperor,

[1] See van Berchem, *Journal des Savants*, 1909, p. 307; also Nöldeke, *Z.D.M.G.*, LXI, p. 225; and Herzfeld, *Encyclopaedia of Islām*, I, p. 338.

[2] Jaussen and Savignac, *op. cit.*, p. 97.

[3] *Kuṣejr ‘Amra*, pp. 213 ff. This theory had already been put forward by Karabacek in the *Neue Freie Presse*, of 29th May 1902, pp. 28–9; and in the *Almanach der Kaiserl. Akad. der Wissenschaften*, LII (1902), pp. 352–5.

[4] Nöldeke, *Z.D.M.G.*, LXI, p. 224; Brünnow, pp. 280–81; van Berchem, *loc. cit.*, pp. 364–5; and Moritz, *M.F.O.B.*, III, p. 428.

[5] *Loc. cit.*, pp. 222–8. Accepted by Brünnow, *loc. cit.*, pp. 280–81; Becker, *Zeitschrift für Assyriologie*, XX, pp. 363–70 (reprinted in his *Islamstudien*, pp. 294–9); and van Berchem, *loc. cit.*, pp. 365–7.

[6] *Loc. cit.*, p. 224. This fragment (photograph in *Kuṣejr ‘Amra*, fig. 135) is now in the Staatliche Museen, Berlin.

[7] *Ibid.*, pp. 224–5. Jaussen and Savignac traced and measured the Greek characters and found them to be 3½ cm. high; *op. cit.*, p. 97 and pl. LV$_4$. Of the corresponding Arabic characters all but the *Kāf* had disappeared.

[8] See Strzygowski, *Mschatta*, *Jahrbuch der Königlich Preuszischen Kunstsammlungen*, XXV, pp. 322–3.

[9] *Op. cit.*, p. 98 and pl. LV$_4$ (tracing).

[10] Now destroyed.

[11] *Neue Freie Presse*, 28th March 1907, p. 3; *Z.D.M.G.*, LXI, pp. 224–5; Brünnow, pp. 280–281; Becker, *Zeitschrift für Assyriologie*, XX, pp. 365–9 (reprinted in his *Islamstudien*, pp. 296–9); and van Berchem, *loc. cit.*, p. 366.

beardless, with thick curly hair, wears a purple cloak and purple shoes and the Sasanian crown on his head, and the Negus is wearing a light-coloured garment with a dark-coloured stole.

Generally speaking the names Kaisar, Chosroes, and Najashi being *titles* always remained well known, but Rōdorīk, who came to power in A. D. 710, was killed in the battle of the Guadalete on 19th July of the following year,[1] and soon after was only known to the learned. From this Nöldeke and Becker conclude that the painting in which he is depicted must have been executed not very long after his death in 711, and in any case not later than the fall of the Umayyads (A. D. 750).

Can the date be fixed still more closely? Van Berchem has brilliantly attempted to do so.[2] He points out that the six personages in the group form a composition obeying definite rules, three being in the foreground and three intercalated between and behind them, as shown in the diagram. Of these the first four are identified by inscriptions as follows:

No. 1. Kaisar (the Byzantine Emperor).
2. Rōdorīk (the Visigothic King of Spain).
3. Chosroes (the Emperor of Persia).
4. Negus (the King of Abyssinia).

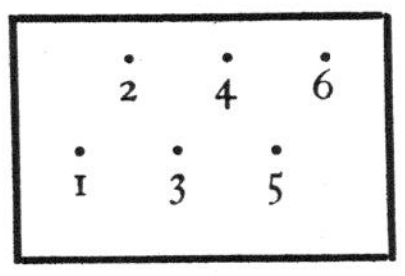

From this he deduces (1) that the personages in the foreground are sovereigns of great empires, whilst those in the background represent the rulers of simple kingdoms, and (2) that in each row, the arrangement of the three personages from left to right corresponds to their geographical situation from west to east. If these conclusions are correct then No. 5 cannot represent the last Ghassānid; it must be intended for a great sovereign of Asia residing to the east of Persia. Similarly No. 6 cannot be the Muqauqis of Egypt, but rather a ruler of the second order residing to the east of Abyssinia.

Now it was at the beginning of the eighth century that Qutayba recommenced against the Turkish races of Central Asia the campaign which had been abandoned during the civil war between 'Alī and Mu'āwiya, and two notable victories were gained, one in 707 between Merv and Bukhārā, the other in 712 under the walls of Samarqand. He points out that the Emperor of China at this time was regarded as the suzerain of all Central Asia, and it was he whom all the rulers of Turkish race called to their aid against the Arabs. No. 5, therefore, may be intended for the Emperor of China, in which case No. 6 could represent one of the Turkish kings involved in the campaigns of Qutayba, or the Hindu King Dāhir,[3] killed in Sind in 712. Van Berchem continues: 'If one reflects on these curious synchronisms; 'if one bears in mind that all these victories, which carried the fortune of the Umayyads to its highest 'point, followed each other, one after the other, during the reign of Walīd I; that the latter was a great 'builder and resided in the Belqā it becomes very tempting to attribute 'Amra to 'him, in which case this picture would be a monument of his victories. The Kaisar would be one of 'the feeble Byzantine Emperors defeated by al-Walīd's general Maslama in Asia Minor, the painting 'of Chosroes would represent not Yazdagird himself, but one of his descendants[4] who attempted at the 'end of the seventh century to restore the Sasanian dynasty, a matter on which Chinese documents have 'thrown some light.' As for the Negus we lack precise information. If these hypotheses are accepted and the picture symbolizes the victories of al-Walīd I, then there can be no doubt that he is the author of the building, which in that case must be placed between 711 (battle of the Guadalete), or 712 (victory at Samarqand), and 715 the year of his death.[5]

1 For this date, see above, p. 142.
2 *Journal des Savants*, 1909, pp. 367–70.
3 For Dāhir, see Cousens (H.), *Antiquities of Sind*, pp. 14–24.
4 Yazdagird III, the last real ruler of the Sasanian dynasty, was defeated by the Arabs at the battle of Nihāvand in 642; he escaped, but was murdered in 651 or 652 by a man with whom he had taken refuge. His son Pērōz III, although a refugee in the mountains of Tukhāristān, called himself King of Persia and was recognized as such by the Emperor of China. When China became suzerain of Central Asia after her victories over the Western Turks between 645 and 658 she laid claim to Persia also. On account of what to-day would be called his nuisance value, she gave a sort of investiture to Pērōz, who resided at Tsiling (probably Zaranj in Sīstān, according to Yule, Chavannes, and Huart). Attacked by the Arabs, Pērōz was soon driven out and fled to China, being received by the Emperor in 674. He died a few years later, leaving a son Ni-nie-che (Narses?). The latter went to Tukhāristān and remained there more than twenty years, but was finally compelled to abandon his vain hopes; about 707 he decided to return to China and died there shortly after his arrival; see Marquart, *Ērānšahr* (*Abh. der Kgl. Gesell. der Wiss. zu Göttingen*, n.F., III, No. 2), pp. 68–9; Chavannes, *Documents sur les Tou-kiue occidentaux*, pp. 172–3, 256–8, and 302; Yule, *Cathay and the Way Thither*, 2nd ed., I, pp. 96–9; also Huart, *La Perse antique*, pp. 166–7.
5 Van Berchem's brilliant suggestion has already received the adherence of Herzfeld, *Encyclopaedia of Islām*, I, pp. 338–9; in the *Orientalistische Literaturzeitung*, XXII, cols. 254–6; and his *Malereien von Samarra*, pp. 5–6; Migeon, *Revue Biblique*, N.S., XI, p. 399; Diez, *Kunst der islamischen Völker*, p. 27; and Arnold,

THE HEADGEAR OF THE PERSIAN KING. In all discussions of the famous picture of the Enemies of Islam, reference is generally made to the headgear of the Persian King, and to the crescent and star above it, but I do not remember ever having seen any comment on the distinctly shown pair of horns growing out of it on either side. Each Sasanian king had a crown of his own, all similar but differing in detail, but no Persian king is ever shown, on his coinage or elsewhere, with anything like the horns in Quṣayr ʿAmra. This may easily be verified, thanks to Erdmann, who has made an exhaustive study of the subject.[1] I have long tried to find something similar, but without success until recently, when I came across Shinnie's article on Nubian churches, in which is published a wall painting in the church, at ʿAbd al-Gadir, near Wādī Ḥalfa, which, according to an inscription alongside, depicts the Eparch (Governor) of Nubia.[2] He is shown holding a model of the church of which, presumably, he was the founder. Above his dome-like head-dress, which bears a 'seal of Solomon', is a spike terminating in a crescent, and from below two horns curve upwards and inwards. Shinnie refers to it as 'the horned headdress which seems to have been the mark of Nubian royalty'. Impossible to imagine anything closer to Quṣayr ʿAmra, but before we can make use of it we must try to fix the date. The nearest Shinnie can suggest is the ninth to eleventh century, which is too late for our purpose. It occurred to me that the distinctive design on the Governor's gown—looped circles with a double-headed bird in each[3]—might enable an expert in textiles to suggest a date. So I asked Mr. Wingfield-Digby of the Victoria and Albert Museum. He replied that he could not put it farther back than the ninth century, which unfortunately is also too late for our purpose.

FIG. 453. The Eparch of Nubia. (From Shinnie, *Medieval Nubia*.)

What can these two horns mean? They at once recall the story of Alexander's visit to the sanctuary of Jupiter Amon, where he was initiated and returned with the skin of a goat on his back and the head with its horns on his head. Several statues show him with the horns, which led to his being known to the Arabs as Iskander Dhu'l-Qarnain 'Alexander of the two horns'.

Later on in Muslim times, Persian kings called themselves Iskandar Thānī—the Second Alexander—but as far as I know specific examples of this are late. But the representation at Quṣayr ʿAmra of Kisrā already with two horns would seem to suggest that the Umayyads had already in some way linked the Persian King with Iskandar Dhu'l-Qarnain.

THE *RAISON D'ÊTRE* OF QUṢAYR ʿAMRA. We have seen above (pp. 16 and 64) that the armies of the Conquest were composed of coarse Bedawīn, chiefly from the heart of eastern Arabia, and that these tribes found it difficult to drop their former mode of existence. From time to time they felt the attrac-

Painting in Islam, p. 30. A recent writer (Wittek, in *Der Islam*, XIV, pp. 402–6), believing the fifth figure to represent a woman, has suggested that it may be intended for the Khātūn, or Queen, of Bukhārā, who is mentioned in the accounts of the Arab conquests in Central Asia (Yaʿqūbī, *Taʾrīkh*, II, p. 281; Balādhurī, pp. 410–11, Murgotten's transl., II, pp. 172–3; Ṭabarī, II, p. 169; and Narshakhī, pp. 7–8, 32, and 36–42), but the matter is so involved with details which are obviously legendary, that it is not even possible to say whether the Khātūn, who is said to have submitted in A.D. 683, really took part in the rebellion of 705 as Narshakhī states (Wittek, *loc. cit.*, p. 405). Gibb (*The Arab Conquests in Central Asia*, p. 19) inclines to the belief that 'the germ of the native version is probably to be found in a confusion of the Arab conquests with the later war between Bukhārā and Wardāna, whose echoes are heard in Qutayba's invasions thirty years after'. He has since pointed out (*Der Islam*, XX, pp. 196–7) that the Khātūn was no longer ruling at the time of Qutayba's expeditions in 706–9, for the Arabic historians all speak of a Bukhār Khudā, or Prince of Bukhārā, at this time, and he is inclined to support van Berchem's suggestion that the fifth figure may represent the Emperor of China. See also Herzfeld, '*Die Könige der Erde*', *Der Islam*, XXI, pp. 233–6 (a reply to Wittek); revised in his *Archaeologische Mitteilungen aus Iran*, V, pp. 149–52.

[1] See *Die Entwicklung der sāsānidischen Krone*, *Ars Islamica*, XV–XVI, pp. 87–121, with 43 illus. on 4 plates and 65 figs. See also *Die sasanidische Krone an der Fassade von Mschatta*, *Forschungen und Fortschritte*, XXVIII, pp. 242–5, with 13 figs.

[2] P. L. Shinnie, *Nubian Churches*, *Archaeology*, IX, p. 58 and fig. 7; and his *Medieval Nubia* (*Museum Pamphlet No. 2*), Khartoum, 1954, pp. 11–13 and fig. 5.

[3] Shinnie calls them double-headed Byzantine eagles and regards them 'as evidence of the persistence of Byzantine traditions'.

tion of the camel and the longing to drink camel's milk. The Prophet himself was not exempt from this yearning, for he prayed God to preserve him from it. For his nation he only feared the diet of milk, saying 'the passion for milk will lead you to abandon the centres of settlement and return to the nomad life'.[1] Hatred of the narrow enclosures of cities and of a settled life characterized the Arab conquerors on every front, whether in Mesopotamia, Syria, or Egypt. Hence the adoption of Jābiya,[2] the old camp-city of the Ghassānid Phylarchs south of Damascus,[3] as the centre of the Arab Government, after the conquest of Syria.[4] It was at Jābiya, which had become the great military base of the country, that 'Umar convened the famous congress at which was settled the future administration of Syria.[5] Here it was that 'Abd al-Malik, many years later, proclaimed the candidature of his two sons.[6]

Half-Bedawī life of the later Umayyad Khalifs. As for the Umayyad Khalifs, their instincts were likewise nomad; although Mu'āwiya the founder of the dynasty made Damascus his capital and resided there, his successors visited it only when state ceremonial compelled their presence.[7] At other times, 'by a kind of atavism of the Bedawin *ḥîra*', as van Berchem has expressed it,[8] they preferred the *bādiya*, or spring pasturage, when the desert is covered with green after the winter rains.

The oasis of Dūmat al-Jandal and the splendid Syro-Roman city of Damascus merely reminded them, in the words of the poet Akhṭal, of the pallor and rigours of the fevers caught by them in the gardens of the Ghūṭa.[9] Jāḥiẓ (d. A. D. 869) expresses the same feeling when he says: 'Beware of the *rīf* (cultivated land), it is death, and a quick death to approach it';[10] likewise the Bedawī poet Ibn Mayāda when he said to Walīd II, 'the proximity of springs does not suit us; mosquitoes and fevers devour us'.[11] And so each Umayyad Khalif, the members of his family, and the principal men of state, each possessed their camping ground.[12] These encampments, at first no doubt of tents, gradually increasing in luxury,[13] developed into a standing camp, and later on buildings of a permanent nature came to be erected. In some cases they even occupied Byzantine forts such as Qasṭal[14] and Azraq (see p. 405 n.17), forming part of the great Roman block-house line which ran from the Gulf of 'Aqaba to Damascus and from Damascus to Palmyra. Thus from *bādiya* developed *ḥīra*, an agglomeration of buildings half mobile, half permanent.

Mu'āwiya's successor Yazīd (60–64 H. = 680–83) was the son of a Bedawī woman; he loved wine and dancing and lived and died at Huwwārīn,[15] about twelve miles north-west of Qaryatain,[16] on the road from Damascus to Ḥomṣ via Quṭaiyifa and Qāra. Marwān I (64–5 H. = 684–5) lived amongst the Bedawīn, especially with the tribe of Kalb.[17] 'Abd al-Malik resided, according to the season, at Damascus, Ṣinnabra (the ancient Σενναβρις, south of Lake Tiberias, according to Lammens), Ba'albek, and Jābiya.[18] Walīd I also moved about a great deal, but his various places of residence always seem to

1 Lammens, *La Bâdia et la Ḥîra sous les Omaiyades*, in the *M.F.O.B.*, IV, pp. 91–2, quoting Ibn Ḥanbal, *Musnad*, II, p. 176, l. 1, and IV, p. 155.

2 John of Ephesus, IV, 22, calls it 'the *ḥīrthā* (military camp) of Arethas (= Ḥārith) the son of Gabala'.

3 At the foot of Tell al-Jābiya, about fifteen miles south-east of Kuneitra, and about fifty miles from Damascus (SSW.). For its identification, see Brünnow, in the *Mitth. und Nachr. der D. P. V.*, 1896, pp. 17–20; and Dussaud and Macler, *Mission dans les régions désertiques de la Syrie moyenne*, in the *Nouvelles Archives des Missions scientifiques*, X, pp. 42–8.

4 Nöldeke, *Die Ghassânischen Fürsten aus dem Hause Gafna's* (*Abh. der Kgl. Preuss. Akad. der Wissenschaften*, 1887), pp. 47–8 of the offprint.

5 Lammens, *La Syrie*, I, p. 57, and in the *B.I.F.A.O.*, XXXVI, p. 42; see also *L'Avènement des Marwānides*, in *Mélanges de l'Université S.-Joseph*, XII, pp. 77–9. 'Ce n'était pas à proprement parler une ville "mais une agglomération autour des constructions royales" (Dussaud). Ces constructions devaient être assez primitives. Les poètes, panégyristes grandiloquents des Ġassānides, ne les ont jamais célébrés en qualité de bâtisseurs. L'agglomération se composait surtout de tentes, de haras et de parcs à troupeaux. L'ensemble se rattache à ce que nous avons appelé le type des *bādia*. Ce caractère explique l'insignificance des ruines qu'y ont trouvées les archéologues . . .'; p. 77.

6 *B.I.F.A.O.*, XXVI, p. 43, n. 3.

7 Musil, *Kuṣejr 'Amra*, p. 161; Lammens, *La Syrie*, I, pp. 91–2.

8 *Journal des Savants*, 1909, p. 307.

9 *Diwān*, p. 121, l. 1, and p. 203, l. 4, cited by Lammens, *La Bâdia, loc. cit.*, IV, p. 94. Al-Ghūṭa, 'the Garden Land', is the great belt of orchards, seven or eight miles broad, which sweeps round the south side of Damascus.

10 *Ḥayawān*, IV, p. 88, l. 3, cited by Lammens, *La Bâdia*, p. 96.

11 *Ibid.*, p. 95, quoting the *Kitāb al-Aghānī*, II, p. 109, l. 4.

12 *Ibid.*, pp. 100–101.

13 Lammens, *ibid.*, p. 102, quoting the *Kitāb al-Aghānī*, II, pp. 35–36.

14 Occupied by Walīd II and Prince 'Abbās; see below, p. 406.

15 Akhṭal, *Diwān*, Ṣālḥanī's ed., p. 289; Ṭabarī, II, p. 203, l. 14 and p. 427, ll. 19–20; Mas'ūdī, *Prairies*, V, pp. 126–7, and his *Tanbīh*, p. 306, Carra de Vaux's transl., p. 397; the *Kitāb al-Aghānī* (Būlāq, 1285 H.), XII, p. 88; Yāqūt, *Mu'jam*, II, p. 355; Musil, *Kuṣejr 'Amra*, p. 152; Lammens, *Études sur le règne du Calife Omaiyade Mo'âwia I*, *M.F.O.B.*, III, pp. 245–8; *L'Avènement des Marwānides*, *ibid.*, XII, pp. 61–2; and Musil, *Palmyrena*, p. 281.

16 Yāqūt, *Mu'jam*, III, p. 170, and the *Marāṣid*, II, p. 61 (quoted by Le Strange, *Palestine under the Moslems*, p. 79), erroneously treat them as one and the same place.

17 Musil, *op. cit.*, pp. 152–3.

18 *Ibid.*, p. 154; quoting the anonymous Chronicle edited by Ahlwardt (Leipzig, 1883) which says (p. 200) that he passed the winter at Ṣinnabra and when it was over settled at Jābiya. Later on he entered Damascus and stopped at the monastery called Dayr Murrān until the heat was oppressive, when he went to Ba'albek. He stayed there until the winds of winter became

have been on the edge of the desert. He used to move to Khunāṣira al-Aḥass,[1] as al-Bakrī puts it 'when good rains brought on the *rabīʿ* there'.[2] We also hear of him residing at Qaryatain[3] and Usays,[4] which Yāqūt says was a watering place for caravans to the east of Damascus, and which Musil identifies with Tell Seis, 105 km. south-east of Damascus.[5] At the foot of the 'tell'—a volcanic crater—there

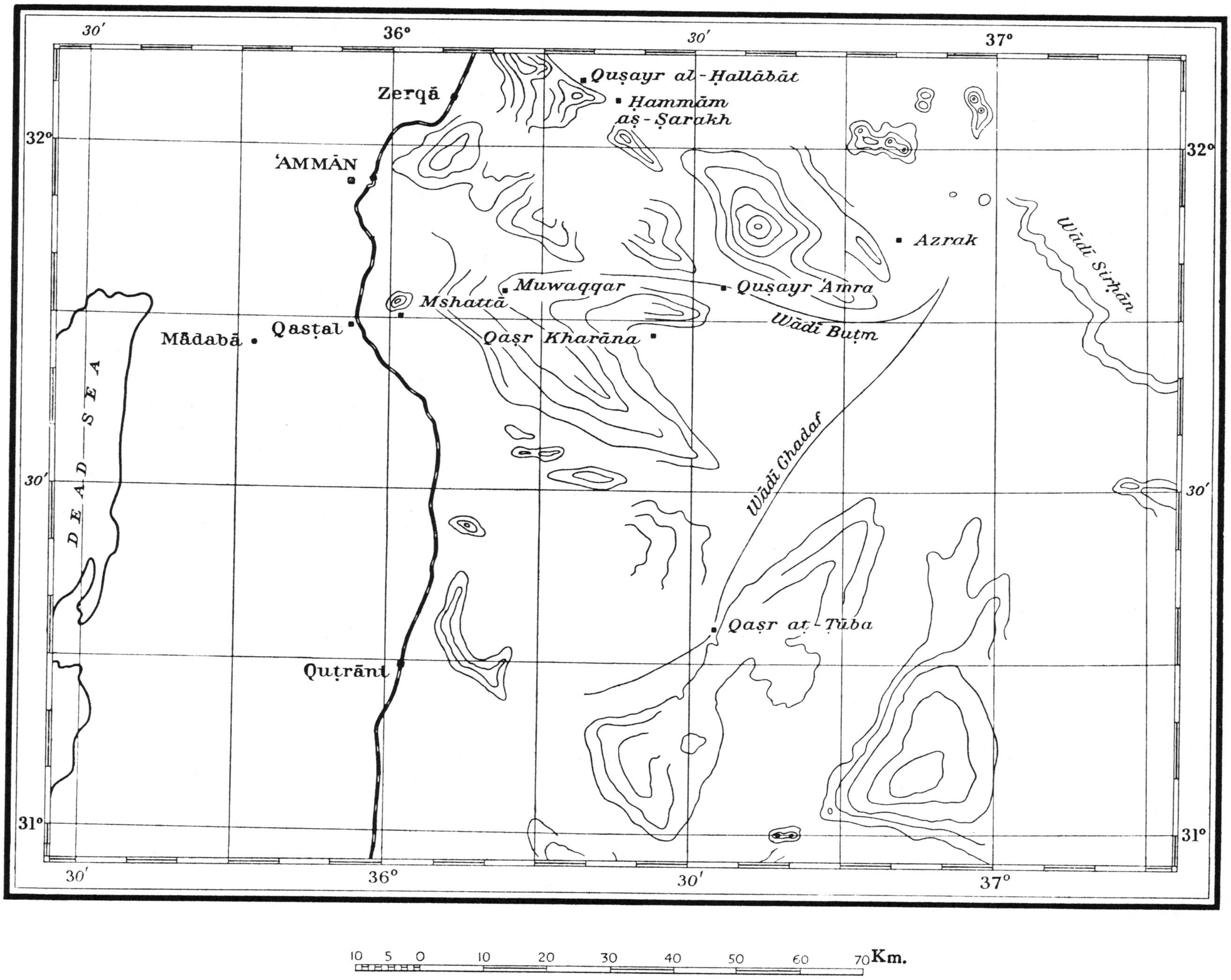

FIG. 454. Map of the Belqā (Transjordan).[6]

is a lake in winter and, to the south of it, a *qaṣr*, a small camp mosque and a *ḥammām* with audience hall attached recently excavated by Dr. Brisch (see below, pp. 472–7).

His son and successor Sulaymān (96–9 H. = 715–17), who was brought up in the desert,[7] founded Ramla and held his court there.[8] ʿUmar II (99–101 H. = 717–20), who devoted his whole time to

severe, when he returned to Damascus, leaving again for Ṣinnabra if the cold became too great.

[1] Khunāṣira, the classical Anasartha (Musil, *Palmyrena*, p. 204, n. 58) was the capital of this region, according to Yāqūt, who says 'it is very small and is now ruined except some part of it'; *Muʿjam*, I, p. 151, ll. 15 and 17–18. It corresponds to the modern village of Khanāṣir, on the edge of the desert at the south-east end of the Jabal al-Ḥaṣṣ, 55 km. south-east of Aleppo. There are a few classical remains there, for which see Butler, *Architecture and other Arts*, pp. 300–301 and 307–8.

[2] Wüstenfeld's ed., II, p. 318, ll. 3–4, and p. 319, ll. 3–4.

[3] *Kitāb al-Aghānī*, XII, pp. 32–3.

[4] Yāqūt, *Muʿjam*, I, p. 272.

[5] *Palmyrena*, p. 282.

[6] This map, which I owe to the kindness of Squadron-Leader Soden of the Royal Air Force, ʿAmmān, shows the position of the monuments marked according to the latest and most accurate information.

[7] Ibn Qutayba, *Kitāb al-Maʿārif*, p. 183, quoted by Nöldeke, *Z.D.M.G.*, LXI, p. 227. He only visited Damascus for his coronation; Lammens, in the *B.I.F.A.O.*, XXVI, p. 27, n. 2.

[8] See Chap. XVII.

agriculture,[1] also chose Khunāṣira as his favourite place of residence, as we learn from Iṣṭakhrī, when speaking of Khunāṣira—'lying over against Qinnasrīn [twenty miles north-east of Ma'arrat an-Nu'mān] on the desert side and at its edge and border. The Khalif 'Umar ibn 'Abd al-'Azīz used to live there.'[2] He died and was buried at Dayr Sim'ān, not far away.[3] Yazīd II (101–5 H. = 720–24), son of 'Ātika, the daughter of Yazīd I, and therefore the great grandson of a Bedawī woman, appears to have been a thorough Bedawī in disposition, and liked to spend his time at Muwaqqar[4] (between Mshattā and Qaṣr Kharāna, see map) amusing himself with poets, singers, dancers and musicians,[5] and also at Bayt Rās (east of lake Tiberias).[6] He had a greater passion for the *ḥarīm* than any of his predecessors; the influence of his favourite concubine Ḥabāba and the singer Sallāma was supreme at court, and his love for the former was so great that when she died he only survived her a few days.[7]

His successor Hishām (105–25 H. = 724–43) was living at Zaytūna when he was made Khalif.[8] Of Zaytūna, Yāqūt says: 'this is a place in the Syrian desert where the Khalif Hishām lived before he built Ruṣāfa.'[9] We shall see (below, pp. 512–14) that it must be identified with Qaṣr al-Ḥair al-Gharbī. Later on he lived at Ruṣāfat-Hishām. Ṭabarī says: 'Hishām used to live at Ruṣāfa which was in the 'administrative district of Qinnasrīn. Aḥmed ibn Zuhayr ibn Ḥarb has related to me from 'Alī ibn 'Muḥammad, saying: The Khalifs and their sons used to flee from the plague. They would therefore 'go to live in the desert away from the people. When Hishām wanted to live at Ruṣāfa someone said to 'him: Do not go, for Khalifs do not catch the plague, no Khalif was ever seen with the plague. But 'Hishām replied: Do you wish to make an experiment with me? So he went to live at Ruṣāfa which is 'in the desert, and built two *qaṣrs* there. [The town itself of] Ruṣāfa is a Rūmī town, built by the *Rūm*.'[10] Musil remarks:[11] 'From the sources we learn that ar-Ruṣāfa meant not only the town but the outlying neighbourhood' (i.e. the Desert of Ruṣāfa). Here he lived until his death. Ya'qūbī says that he also had a palace at Quṭaiyifa.[12] Theophanes says that he began to build palaces and lay out plantations, parks, and fountains,[13] and Qaṣr al-Ḥayr ash-Sharqī (see Chap. XIX) must be one of them.

His dissolute successor Walīd II (125–6 H. = 743–4) had lived in the desert for twenty years before he became Khalif,[14] and it is expressly stated that even when he was Khalif he never set foot in a town.[15] He himself in his verses speaks of the desert as the scene of his feasts.[16] Ṭabarī speaks of his going to Azraq[17] (c. twelve miles east of Quṣayr 'Amra), and of his staying at 'the water of al-Aghdaf', sometimes called al-Ghadaf in the *Kitāb al-Aghānī*,[18] for which reason Musil identifies it with the Wādī

---

[1] Musil, *Ḳuṣejr 'Amra*, p. 154.

[2] Ya'qūbī, *Ta'rīkh*, II, p. 368; Iṣṭakhrī, p. 61; Ibn Ḥauqal, p. 119; Mas'ūdī, *Prairies*, V, p. 434; Yāqūt, *op. cit.*, I, p. 151, ll. 15 and 17–18; Abu'l-Fidā', ed. of Reinaud and de Slane, p. 232; Le Strange, *op. cit.*, p. 485.

[3] Ṭabarī-Zotenberg, IV, p. 249; Mas'ūdī, *Prairies*, V, p. 416; Yāqūt, *op. cit.*, II, p. 671; and the *Marāṣid*, I, p. 432; quoted by Le Strange, *op. cit.*, pp. 433–4; Ibn 'Adhārī, I, p. 34; Fagnan's transl., I, p. 45; Ibn aṭ-Ṭiqtaqā, Derenbourg's ed., p. 177; Amar's transl., p. 208; Abu'l-Fidā', *Ta'rīkh*, Reiske's ed., I, p. 440; Ibn Baṭṭūṭa, I, p. 145; Mujīr ad-Dīn, p. 250, transl., p. 59. See also a recent attempt by Janine and Dominique Sourdel to fix the position of Dayr Sim'ān in *Les Annales Archéologiques de Syrie*, III, pp. 83–8.

[4] Musil (*Palmyrena*, p. 283) says that Muwaqqar was destroyed by the Khalif Abu'l-'Abbās [as-Saffāḥ], 132–6 H. (750–54).

[5] Musil, *op. cit.*, pp. 155 and 156; quoting Yāqūt, *Mu'jam*, IV, p. 687, ll. 1–2. Other sources cited by Lammens, *La Bâdia, loc. cit.*, p. 103, n. 2.

[6] *Kitāb al-Aghānī*, XIII, p. 165, l. 4.

[7] Mas'ūdī, *Prairies*, V, pp. 446–53; Muir, *Caliphate* (Weir's ed.), p. 381.

[8] Ṭabarī, II, p. 1467, ll. 1–3; Mas'ūdī, *Tanbīh*, transl., p. 416; Yāqūt, *op. cit.*, II, p. 784; Bar Hebraeus, Bedjan's ed., p. 208, Budge's transl. p. 134; as-Suyūṭī, *Khalifs*, Jarrett's transl., p. 251; Le Strange, *Palestine under the Moslems*, p. 522; and Musil, *Palmyrena*, pp. 277–8. Yāqūt, quoting Ibn Butlān who passed through Ruṣāfa in 1049, says: 'Hishām reconstructed and inhabited Ruṣāfa; he took refuge there from the gnats on the banks of the Euphrates.'

[9] *Op. cit.*, II, p. 965.

[10] II, p. 1737, l. 16–p. 1738, l. 5.

[11] *Palmyrena*, p. 278.

[12] *Geography*, p. 325; Wiet's transl., p. 172.

[13] Under year 6216 = A.D. 725; Bonn ed., p. 620; de Boor's ed., p. 403: ἤρξατο κτίζειν κατὰ χώραν καὶ πόλιν παλάτια, καὶ κατασπορὰς ποιεῖν καὶ παραδείσους, καὶ ὕδατα ἐκβάλλειν; quoted by Musil, *op. cit.*, p. 156 and note 327.

[14] *Kitāb al-Aghānī*, VI, p. 104, ll. 27–8: 'Hishām was displeased with al-Walīd (II) and his associates, so he [i.e. al-Walīd] went away [from Ruṣāfa] having with him a party of his associates and clients, and stayed at Abraq between the territory of the (tribe of) Balqain and Fazāra and a water called al-Aghdaf'; see also Ya'qūbī, *Ta'rīkh*, II, p. 394; Ṭabarī, II, pp. 1743 and 1795; *Aghānī*, II, p. 79. Musil seems to suggest that this event took place in the first half of A.D. 735; *Ḳuṣejr 'Amra*, p. 160, and his *Palmyrena*, p. 277.

[15] al-'Iqd (ed. of 1302 H.), II, p. 351 below, quoted by Nöldeke Z.D.M.G., LXI, p. 226; and de Goeje, *Fragmenta Historicorum Arabicorum*, p. 130, last line.

[16] Nöldeke, *Z.D.M.G.*, LXI, p. 226, quoting the *Kitāb al-Aghānī*, VI, p. 121, l. 22 f., and p. 136, last line–p. 137, l. 1.

[17] II, p. 1743, quoted by Musil, *Ḳuṣejr 'Amra*, p. 156 and note 333, with other sources. Azraq is a Roman fort of the time of Diocletian and Maximian (dedication on stone in court), reconstructed by Malik Mu'aẓẓam 'Īsa in 634 (1236/7); see Dussaud and Macler, *Mission dans les régions désertiques de la Syrie moyenne*, pp. 30–31, 268–9, and 337, and pls. V–VI; Musil, *Sitzungsberichte*, CXLIV, pp. 2–4; Jaussen and Savignac, *Mission archéologique en Arabie*, III, pp. 12–13 and pl. IV; Musil, *Arabia Deserta*, p. 339 and figs. 74–5; and Wiet, *Répertoire d'épigraphie arabe*, XI, pp. 74–5.

[18] II, p. 79.

Ghadaf on which Qaṣr aṭ-Ṭūba stands.[1] Severus ibn al-Muqaffa' says of him: 'Since, however, his 'people hated him, he began to build a city named after himself in the desert, for he gave his name to it; 'but the water was fifteen miles distant from it. He collected workmen from all quarters, and built 'that city by means of forced labour. . . .'[2] He also occupied Qasṭal[3] and Zīza.[4] He led a careless, unrestrained life, and poets, singers, and dancers came from all sides to his court; when one pleased him particularly he would give him a large sum of money, sometimes even he would impulsively doff his rich garments and present them also.[5] He was indifferent in religious matters, possessed many wives and concubines, was a great lover of wine, and frequently got drunk[6] to the scandal of Islam. At the time he was murdered he was staying at the Qaṣr al-Bakhrā' on the edge of the desert about fifteen miles south-west of Palmyra.[7]

At about the same time (in 126 H. = 744/5) 'Abbās, the son of Walīd I and therefore cousin of Walīd II, lived at Qasṭal, and his brother Yazīd (not the Khalif) lived in a palace which lay only a few miles farther away in the desert,[8] which palace, as Musil says, can only be Mshattā (about five miles east of Qasṭal).

After the murder of Walīd II, the Khalifate passed to his cousin Yazīd III (son of Walīd I), who had to promise that he would live in Damascus and 'lay neither stone on stone nor brick on brick'.[9] He died after a reign of four months, and can scarcely be said to have been succeeded by his brother Ibrāhīm, for no general homage was paid to the latter, and Marwān II seized the Khalifate a few months later. Damascus was neglected once more, for the new Khalif took up his residence at Ḥarrān in Northern Mesopotamia.[10] Michael the Syrian mentions this fact and adds that the Syrians complained that he did not live amongst them. A little farther on he speaks of Marwān returning to Ḥarrān, which he had made his capital.[11] Six years later the Umayyad Khalifate came to an end, and with it the period of Arab ascendancy.

Hence we may say, with Gertrude Bell, that these desert residences 'are a logical outcome of the 'period of cultural transition during which they arose, the difficult and distasteful passage from nomadic 'to settled life; they attest the abiding call of the open wilderness, to which the poets and chroniclers 'of the first century after the Hijrah are faithful witnesses. To the Arab the desert is more than a habita-'tion; it is the guardian of traditions older and more deeply rooted than Islâm; of traditions which are 'sacred to his race; of his purest speech, and of his finest chivalry. It is for him the natural theatre of 'his actions, and there is no other stage on which he can play out his part. To this day I have heard 'the Beduin speak of themselves as the Ahl al-Ba'îr, the People of the Camel, just as they spoke of 'themselves in the early centuries as Ahl al-Ḍar', People of the Udder. The authority of the Prophet 'was powerless to stay the current of his race. . . . and the Umayyad Khalifs returned to the habits of 'their forefathers. . . . They escaped to the bâdiyah, the spring pasturage in the rolling steppes, where 'the tents of the Ṣukhûr still cover the plain when the winter rains are past; they transported their courts 'to the ḥîrah, the palace camp.'[12]

INSPIRATION OF THE FRESCO PAINTINGS. The paintings of Quṣayr 'Amra clearly belong, not to the hieratic art of Byzantium, but to the late Hellenistic art of Syria, and bear eloquent witness to its vitality.

[1] *Op. cit.*, pp. 156–7. Nöldeke agrees, *loc. cit.*, p. 226. 'Al-Walīd received news whilst he was in Aghdaf and Aghdaf is a town in 'Ammān'—Ṭabarī, II, p. 1795, l. 11; see also Ibn al-Athīr, V, p. 215, l. 16: 'Whilst he was in Aghdaf in 'Ammān.'

[2] The above is Evetts' translation in the *Patrologia Orientalis*, V, p. 114.

[3] *Kitāb al-Aghānī*, VI, pp. 113, l. 8; quoted by Lammens, *La Bâdia*, *loc. cit.*, p. 103.

[4] Ṭabarī, II, 1754, ll. 10–11; 'When al-Walīd [II] was Crown Prince he used to give food to pilgrims in a place called Zīza for three days.'

[5] *Kitāb al-Aghānī*, XII, p. 81; quoted by Musil, *op. cit.*, p. 157; also Mas'ūdī, *Prairies*, VI, p. 9. See also the *Kitāb al-Aghānī*, VI, p. 36, last line–p. 137, l. 1.

[6] Wellhausen, *Das arabische Reich*, pp. 356–7; and Musil, *op. cit.*, pp. 157–8.

[7] Mas'ūdī, *Prairies*, VI, p. 1, and his *Tanbīh*, transl., p. 419, also Musil, *op. cit.*, p. 162, and sources cited. See also Ibn 'Abd Rabbihi, *al-'Iqd* (Būlāq, 1302 H.), II, p. 351. For the remains here see Musil, *Palmyrena*, pp. 142–3, 234, 285–7, 290–97 and figs. 38–9. Michael the Syrian (Chabot's ed., II, pp. 463–4; transl., II, p. 502) on two occasions speaks of Walīd II being in the desert.

[8] Ṭabarī, II, p. 1784, ll. 7–9; quoted by Musil, *op. cit.*, p. 160. Musil points out that it cannot be Zīza, where pilgrims and caravans were maintained up to a period of three days at the expense of al-Walīd II, or Muwaqqar which belonged to the Khalif himself.

[9] Ibn al-Athīr, V, p. 220, l. 12; quoted by Musil, *op. cit.*, p. 163. See also Ibn aṭ-Ṭiqṭaqā, Derenbourg's ed., p. 183; Amar's transl., p. 216; and as-Suyūṭī, *Khalifs*, Jarrett's transl., pp. 257–8.

[10] Ṭabarī-Zotenberg, IV, p. 322; Mas'ūdī, *Prairies*, VI, pp. 46–7; and his *Tanbīh*, transl., p. 420; Bar Hebraeus, *Dynasties*, Bedjan's ed., p. 212; Budge's transl., p.137; and Abu'l-Fidā', *Ta'rīkh*, Reiske's ed., I, pp. 468.

[11] Chabot's ed., II, p. 464; transl., II, p. 505. See also Dionysius of Tell Maḥrē, Chabot's text, p. 46; transl., pp. 41–2.

[12] *Ukhaiḍir*, p. 55.

Not only have we the four personifications of Poesy, History, Philosophy, and Victory (labelled in Greek), the Three Ages of Man, and a winged Cupid, but the very modelling of the figures, e.g. the treatment of the standing woman in the bathroom scene (Plate 74 *c*), especially her shoulder, and the man with the helmet in Plate 75 *d* bear this out. The same remarks apply to the lozenge diaper on the vault of room D, which recalls a favourite treatment of mosaic pavements, e.g. at Mādabā, less than fifty miles away, the mosaic pavement discovered at Jerusalem in 1892 near the so-called Church of St. Stephen,[1] a mosaic pavement on the Mount of Olives, and another, more recently excavated by the American expedition to Antioch (Fig. 455, facing p. 446).[2] I have already suggested that the female figures, with their arms above their heads, painted on the transverse arches of the main hall, were probably holding portrait busts as at Palmyra. I would now call attention to the resemblance between the costume of the dancing girl in the lozenge diaper on the vault of the *Apodyterium* (Plate 73 *a*) and the costume of the figures (winged Victories standing on celestial spheres) in a tomb at Palmyra,[3] below illustrated (Fig. 456, facing p. 446). At Palmyra the eye is apt to be confused by the flowing ends of the girdle, but a closer examination shows that the costume is identical in both cases, a long under-skirt, very full and reaching almost to the feet, an over-garment reaching to the knees only, fastened close to the waist, full above, sleeveless, and gathered together by a brooch on either side of the neck (a Greek *chiton* in fact), so that the point of the shoulder is exposed.

That the paintings of Quṣayr ʿAmra are derived from the Hellenistic art of Syria has been recognized by practically every writer who has discussed them. Thus Brünnow says: 'That these paintings belong 'to the Greek cycle of art is clear without further discussion, they even exhibit direct relationships with 'the antique as in the little picture on Taf. XXXIII'[4] (with the winged Cupid, see Plate 72 *c*);—Strzygowski: '. . . they are derived from the late Hellenistic art of Syria in Roman times', and 'In ʿAmra the Hellenistic tradition of Syria predominates':[5]—van Berchem, after discussing the architectural characteristics of ʿAmra, speaks of the paintings as by 'their style likewise Syrian';[6]—Diehl: '. . . they also spring from Hellenistic iconography, and testify clearly to the influence which Byzance 'exercised at this time on Arab art';[7]—Herzfeld: 'Both in form and contents the syro-hellenistic 'tradition is predominant. Certain features, especially the epic style and perhaps the type of some of the 'female figures, seem to be derived from old oriental art, while the aquatic scenes and the chase with 'nets remind us of the art of the Sāsānid period. Other elements, such as the architecture of the back-'grounds and niches with their spiral columns, give a definitely Byzantine impression; while the laurel-'garlands and draperies recall western classical art';[8]—Dalton: 'They show us how absolutely the art 'of the early Mohammedan period depended upon the Hellenistic art of Syria and Mesopotamia. In 'the second place they prove how tenacious of life and of its old traditions the Hellenistic art of Hither 'Asia really was. The survival of a classical spirit in certain MSS. and other works of art in the tenth 'and eleventh centuries appears much less abnormal now that we have before us these frescoes dated in 'the middle of the eighth century, works so purely Hellenistic in style that competent observers at 'first considered them to be some three centuries earlier than they are. Here, as in Constantinople, the 'old genre scenes retained their popularity, and at once found favour with the luxurious princes of the

1 *Revue Biblique*, 1892, fig. on p. 118 (see also p. 259); and *P.E.F.*, *Q.St.*, 1892, pp. 190–92 with illus.

2 *Ibid.*, 1895, p. 86. See also the fresco in the 'Casa stabbiana' in the Museum at Naples illustrated by Grüneisen, *Les Caractéristics de l'Art copte*, fig. 61.

3 For this tomb, known as al-Maghārat al-Jadīda, see Strzygowski, *Orient oder Rom*, pp. 11–32, Taf. I and Abb. 1–4; Farmakowski, *Painting at Palmyra* (in Russian), in the *Bulletin of the Russian Archaeological Institute at Constantinople*, VIII, pp. 172–98 and pls. XXI–XXVII; P. von Kokowzoff, *New Aramaean Inscriptions at Palmyra*, *ibid.*, VIII, pp. 302–29 and pl. XXXVI; Cumont, *Études syriennes*, p. 65 and fig. 29; Ahmed Djemal Pascha, *Alte Denkmäler aus Syrien*, Taf. 68; Chabot, *Choix d'inscriptions de Palmyre*, pp. 96–105, and pls. XIV_2, XV, XVII_2, and XVIII; and Karl Gröber, *Palästina, Arabien und Syrien*, Taf. 243 (excellent). These paintings have recently been reproduced in colour by Kraeling, *Color Photographs of the Paintings in the Tomb of the Three Brothers at Palmyra*, in *Les Annales Archéologiques de Syrie*, XI–XII, pp. 13–18, with 42 illus. (40 coloured) on 16 plates. Five inscriptions still exist on the entrance of this tomb, ranging in date from A.D. 160 to 242, so, as Chabot points out (p. 101): '. . . we have therefore in these paintings . . . authentic specimens of Greek art in Syria at the beginning of the third century, before it could be influenced by Byzantine conceptions.'

4 *W.Z.K.M.*, XXI, p. 282.

5 *Byzantinische Zeitschrift*, XVI, p. 734. Stryzgowski, I should add, appears to have changed his former opinion, for we read in a more recent work (*Origin of Christian Church Art*, p. 119) that 'the decoration of the main hall in the small castle of Quseir ʿAmra is executed entirely in the Iranian spirit, and shows the persistence of this ancient tradition in Umayyad times', and twenty pages farther on, 'the ornamentation of the Baths [i.e. rooms D, E, and F] in this desert palace is rather Indo-hellenistic in style, with the exception of a diaper enclosing animal figures on one of the barrel-vaults' [room E].

6 *Journal des Savants*, 1909, p. 402.

7 *Manuel d'art byzantin*, p. 320.

8 *Encyclopaedia of Islām*, I, p. 338.

'conquering faith';[1]—Migeon: 'It is the same [i.e. of Syrian inspiration] with an important part of 'the painted decoration, of an inspiration frequently quite Classical, with those nude figures which are 'related to Oriental Hellenism, and, as has been well pointed out by Strzygowski, to that great artistic 'centre Antioch, the metropolis of Syria, where antiquity and Christianity were able to endure side by 'side without mixing. On the contrary, the decorative ornament has a character more frankly Mesopo-'tamian, as is also indicated by those hunting scenes, the taste for which was always so keen in Baby-'lonian and Iranian civilization, and the accurate observation of the movement and attitudes of animals';[2] —Diez: 'The painted decoration of ʻAmra shows us how long the Hellenistic tradition remained in 'activity, and of what charmingly gifted creations it was still capable at the beginning of the eighth 'century. The ʻAmra series of paintings is the last great creation of a secular character that Hellenistic 'art has left us. The happy sensuality of the antique here flares up once more for the last time';[3]—Glück and Diez: '. . . expressed in vigorous Hellenistic fashion';[4]—Dalton: 'The audience-hall and 'bath-rooms . . . are covered with frescoes partly late-Hellenistic, partly late Sasanian in style, the 'former predominating';[5]—Herzfeld: 'The greater part of the paintings of Quṣair ʻAmra is actually 'created out of pure Syrian-Hellenistic tradition';[6]—and Arnold: '. . . the first example of painting 'in the Muhammadan period is one of the last creations of profane art surviving from the Hellenistic 'age'.[7]

There is, however, one trace of Persian influence, and that is the inspiration behind the painting depicting the Enemies of Islam. This, as Herzfeld has shown,[8] must have been derived from a Persian prototype in which the Kings of the Earth do homage to Chosroes on his throne. Such a picture existed and is referred to by Yāqūt as follows: 'At Qarmīsīn [i.e. Kirmānshāhān, or Kirmānshāh] is the '*dukkān*[9] where the Kings of the Earth, amongst them Faghfūr[10]—the King of China, Khāqān—the 'King of the Turks, Dāhir—the King of Sind, and Kaisar—the King of Rūm, are convoked by Kisrā 'Aparwīz.' Mustawfī, who also speaks of it, adds; 'to kiss his hand'.[11] Herzfeld also points out that the arrangement, whereby the relative rank of the figures at Quṣayr ʻAmra is indicated by their arrangement in two rows, is characteristically Persian, likewise the position of the right hand of the three figures in the foreground, which is the attitude of homage in Sasanian sculpture.

Grabar on the other hand regards this painting as '. . . an attempt to adapt the Sasanian artistic theme 'of the "Kings of the Earth" gathered to pay homage to their overlord, to the concept of the "Family 'of Kings". This latter concept was altered so as to imply that the Umayyad dynasty was the descendant 'and heir of the dynasties it had defeated.'[12]

Granted that the composition has been taken from a Persian source, Grabar's theory that it has an *allegoric* significance cannot be accepted, for the name of Rodorik, written above the second figure, is decisive and gives it definite *historical* significance. And as Rodorik was defeated under al-Walīd, the picture must be intended to celebrate one of his victories, which is confirmed by the figure of a woman labelled NIKH—Victory placed immediately to the left of it. Moreover, it must have been executed during his reign, for no Eastern potentate would think of celebrating the victories of a predecessor.

Secondly, if the painting represents a sort of Family of Kings and not defeated enemies, why is it depicted to the left of the alcove with the ruler on a throne, instead of to the right?

And how could the painting represent a 'Family of Kings', as Grabar would have it, when one of them (Rodorik) had been killed in battle by the Umayyads, another (Kaisar) was on the worst possible terms with them, and another (Kisrā), the last descendant of the Sasanian Kings, had died whilst a refugee in China?

[1] *Byzantine Art and Archaeology*, p. 279.
[2] *Revue Biblique*, N.S., XI, pp. 397–8.
[3] *Kunst der islamischen Völker*, p. 24.
[4] *Die Kunst des Islam*, p. 24.
[5] *Treasure of the Oxus*, 2nd ed., p. lxxii.
[6] *Die Malereien von Samarra*, p. 5.
[7] *Painting in Islam*, p. 30.
[8] *Die Malereien von Samarra*, pp. 5–6. Also in the *Orientalistische Literaturzeitung*, XXII, p. 254; *Der Islam*, XII, p. 136; *Jahrbuch der Preuszischen Kunstsammlungen*, XLII. p. 133; and *Der Islam*, XXI, pp. 233–6; revised in his *Archaeologische Mitt. aus Iran*, V, pp. 149–52.
[9] Barbier de Meynard (*Dict. géographique de la Perse*, p. 438) translates this word as 'plate-forme'.
[10] Corruption of the Persian *Bagaputhra* = son of God.
[11] Yāqūt, *Muʻjam*, IV, p. 70, ll. 1–3 ; Mustawfī, *Nuzhat al-Qulūb*, Le Strange's ed., p. 108; transl., p. 106; Herzfeld, *Malereien von Samarra*, p. 6.
[12] *The Painting of the Six Kings at Quṣayr ʻAmrah*, in *Ars Orientalis*, I, pp. 185–7.

We can readily admit that the inspiration of this painting is Persian.[1] But it must be emphasized that, of the total surface decorated with paintings at Quṣayr ʿAmra, this picture occupies less than a twentieth part; moreover it is only Persian in inspiration, and not in execution, so that the Persian element in the whole decoration is less than a fortieth part, perhaps about 2 per cent.

NATIONALITY OF THE ARTISTS. Brünnow[2] and Becker[3] have pointed out that the Arabic inscriptions have obviously been executed by one accustomed to write Arabic, whereas the letters of the Greek inscriptions, according to the observations of Mielich,[4] have first been outlined in a darker colour and filled in afterwards. They therefore conclude that the artists knew Arabic better than Greek, but not perfectly, as is indicated by the fact that they have written Kisrā as they heard it pronounced (كسرا) and not as it should be written (كسرى). Becker also points out that the use of the title ΚΑΙϹΑΡ for the Byzantine Emperor is not taken from Byzantine practice and would not have been employed by a Greek, for it is merely a transliteration of the Arabic *qaiṣar*.[5]

One can even go further and say that a Greek would not have understood the term, as is evident from the fact that Procopius, writing in the second half of the sixth century, says: 'Chosroes was indignant that the envoys had not been sent him by Kaisar', and then feels bound to add, by way of explanation: 'for thus the Persians call the King (Βασιλευς) of the Romans'.[6] In Byzantine practice, as from Anastasius (491–518), the Greek Emperor is always called *αἰώνιος Αὔγουστος Αὐτοκράτωρ* instead of the earlier Caesar semper Augustus.[7] Then the title Αὐτοκράτωρ was gradually displaced by *βασιλευς*, this change became definite under Heraclius in 629, and this title was henceforth adopted by them.[8] Brünnow and Becker come to the conclusion that the artists knew Arabic but not Greek, and that they were either Syrians or Aramaeans, a conclusion which is all the more striking in that it is precisely the conclusion to which Mlle van Berchem has been led regarding the craftsmen who executed the mosaics of the Dome of the Rock (see above, pp. 141–2).

And in this connexion I would call attention to another significant fact: the artists of the Palmyrene school, to which we have seen that some of the paintings at Quṣayr ʿAmra are closely related, were apparently of the same stock, judging from the name of the only artist that has come down to us—Ilasamsos (= the sun is God)—who executed the now famous painting at aṣ-Ṣāliḥīya (Dura-Europos) on the Euphrates, about 140 miles east of Palmyra.[9]

THE QUESTION OF THE LAWFULNESS OF PAINTING IN EARLY ISLAM.[10] The paintings of Quṣayr ʿAmra raise, in an imperative fashion, the question of the lawfulness or otherwise of painting in Islam.

1 Dalton does so in his *East Christian Art*, p. 231, n. 2; and his *Treasure of the Oxus*, 2nd ed., p. lxxii.

2 *W.Z.K.M.*, XXI, p. 282.

3 *Zeitschrift für Assyriologie*, XX, pp. 362–4. See also Arnold, *Painting in Islam*, p. 57.

4 In Musil's *Kuṣejr ʿAmra*, pp. 196 and 198.

5 *Loc. cit.*, p. 363.

6 *Wars*, II, xxi, 9.

7 Letter of 24. xi. 51 from Dr. A. Grohmann.

8 See Bréhier, *L'Origine des titres impériaux à Byzance*, *Byzantinische Zeitschrift*, XV, pp. 161–78; Bury, *The Constitution of the Later Roman Empire*, p. 20; his *History of the Later Roman Empire*, I, p. 16; and his *Selected Essays*, edited by Temperley, p. 109; also the remarks of Stein, in the *Byzantinische Zeitschrift*, XXIX, p. 353.

9 These paintings, of which Prof. Sarre caught a fleeting glimpse in 1898 (*Archäologische Reise*, II, p. 392), were rediscovered by Capt. Murphy in 1920, and photographed and published by Prof. Breasted. See Sarre, in Sarre and Herzfeld, *Archäologische Reise*, II, p. 392; Breasted, *Peintures de l'époque romaine dans le désert de Syrie*, in *Syria*, III, pp. 177–213, with five coloured plates and five in black and white; in the *Comptes rendus de l'Acad. des Inscriptions*, 1922, pp. 240–41; and *Les Fresques d'époque romaine relevées par M. Breasted à Es-Sâlihîye* (reprinted from *Syria*), in *Les Travaux archéologiques en Syrie de 1920 à 1922*, pp. 48–54; his *Oriental Forerunners of Byzantine Painting*, pp. 52–61 and 75–102 and pls. VIII–XIX; and Cumont, *Rapport sur une mission à Sâlihîyeh sur l'Euphrate*, *Comptes rendus*, 1923, pp. 23–31. Cumont has shown that they must have been executed in the last years of the first century A.D.; see his *Fouilles de Ṣâlihîyeh sur l'Euphrate*, in *Syria*, IV, pp. 47–50.

10 BIBLIOGRAPHY: — 1721, Bourguignon d'Anville, *Mémoire où il est question de la Peinture des Turcs & des Persans. . . Le Nouveau Mercure*, April, 1721, pp. 25–52; — 1787, Toderini (G.), *Letteratura turchesca*, III, pp. 45–74; French transl., III, 47–78; German transl., II, pp. 193–209; — 1859, Lavoix (H.), *Les Peintres musulmans*, *Revue de l'Orient, de l'Algérie, et des colonies*, N.S., IX, pp. 353–69; — 1862, Montaut (H.), *De la représentation des figures animées chez les musulmans*, *Mém. de l'Institut égyptien*, I, pp. 61–5; — 1869, Pharaon (F.), *La Peinture et la Sculpture chez les musulmans*, *Gazette des Beaux-Arts*, 2me période, I, pp. 422–6; Viardot (L.), *Quelques notes sur la peinture et la sculpture chez les musulmans*, *ibid.*, pp. 556–9; — 1875, Lavoix (H.), *ibid.*, XII, pp. 97–113, 312–21, and 423–37; Lane-Poole (S.), *Academy*, VIII, pp. 233 and 250–51; X, p. 364; — 1876, Barbier de Meynard, *Les Peintres arabes*, *Revue critique*, N.S., I, pp. 333–5; Karabacek (J.), *Ueber das angebliche Bilderverbot des Islâm*, *Kunst und Gewerbe*, X, pp. 281–3, 289–91, 297–9, 307–8, 315–17, and 332–3; — 1893, Gayet, *L'Art arabe*, pp. 55–60; — 1895, Nahuys (M. de), *Les Images chez les Arabes*, *Annales de l'Acad. d'archéologie de Belgique*, XLVIII, pp. 229–34; — 1896, Chauvin (V.), *La Défense des images chez les musulmans*, *ibid.*, XLIX, pp. 403–30; — 1902, Karabacek (J. von), in the *Almanach der Kaiserl. Akad. der Wissenschaften, Wien*, LII, pp. 356–7; — 1903, Juynboll (Th. W.), *Handleiding tot de kennis van de mohammedaansche wet*, pp. 157–8; German transl., *Handbuch des islamischen Gesetzes*, pp. 166–7; — 1904, Muḥammad ʿAbduh, *aṣ-Ṣuwar wat-Tamāthil wa fawāʾiduha wa ḥukmuhā*, *al-Manār*, VIII, p. 35 (reprinted in

Even at the present day the belief is very widely held that all forms of painting are forbidden by explicit passages in the Qurān, but this is a popular error for no such passages exist, as Orientalists have frequently pointed out.[1]

Azraqī (d. A. D. 858), author of the earliest extant history of Mekka, tells us that Muhammad, after his triumphal entry into that city in Ramaḍān 8 (Dec. 629–Jan. 630), went inside the Kaʿba and ordered the pictures in it to be obliterated, but put his hand over a picture of Mary with Jesus seated on her lap, and said: ʻ Rub out all the pictures except these under my hands ʼ; and Azraqī goes on to say that this picture remained until the Kaʿba was destroyed in 63 H. (see above, pp. 2–3).

We have also seen (above, pp. 22–3) that Saʿd ibn Abī Waqqāṣ and his Arabs at the capture of al-Madā'in, or Ctesiphon, used the great Īwān for the Friday prayer, and were not disturbed by the paintings decorating it, one of which represented the siege of Antioch by Khusrau Anūshirwān (A. D. 540). Zakī Ḥasan tries to explain away this fact partly by the lack of time, the troops being so anxious to give thanks for their great victory that they did not stop to obliterate them, and partly by saying that ʻ victorious armies do not always act according to religious principles ʼ.[2] But he has to admit that these paintings were allowed to remain for two and a half centuries at least, for they were seen by al-Buḥturī, who died in A. D. 897 (see above p. 23, n.). An early example of Muslim painting may be mentioned; at-Tanūkhī (10th cent.) says that the palace of al-Baidā' at Baṣra, built by ʿUbayd Allāh the son of Ziyād ibn Abīhi, was decorated with wall paintings.[3] Then again we are told that the rigid Khalif ʿUmar used a censer with human figures on it, which he had brought from Syria, to perfume the Mosque of Madīna, and that it was only in A. D. 785 that a Governor of Madīna had these figures erased.[4] This hardening of opinion towards the end of the eighth century is in perfect keeping with the evidence given below. We have also seen that Muʿāwiya and ʿAbd al-Malik struck coins with their own effigy (above, p. 131).

Recently Zakī Ḥasan[5] has sought to explain the undisputed existence of painting under the Umayyad Khalifs by saying that ʻ they did not keep the straight and narrow way in matters of religion ʼ, except

1925 by Muḥammad Rashīd Riḍa, *Ta'rīkh Muḥammad ʿAbduh*, II, pp. 499–501); — 1906, van Berchem, *Journal des Savants*, p. 418; — 1907, Snouck Hurgronje (C.), *Ḳuṣejr ʿAmra und das Bilderverbot*, *Z.D.M.G.*, LXI, pp. 186–91; reprinted in his *Verspreide geschriften*, II, pp. 449–56; — 1909, van Berchem, *Journal des Savants*, pp. 134–5 and 370–72; — 1910, Bréhier, *Les Origines de l'art musulman*, *Revue des Idées*, VII, pp. 196–8; and Horovitz (J.), *Die Beschreibung eines Gemäldes bei Mutanabbi*, *Der Islam*, I, pp. 385–8; — 1911, ʿAbd al-ʿAzīz Shāwīsh, *at-Taṣwīr wa Ittikhādh aṣ-Ṣuwar*, *al-Hidāya*, II, pp. 487–91; Becker (C. H.), *Christliche Polemik und islamische Dogmenbildung*, *Zeitschrift für Assyriologie*, XXVI, pp. 191–5; reprinted in his *Islamstudien*, I, pp. 445–9; and van Berchem, in Sarre and Herzfeld, *Archäologische Reise*, I, pp. 36–8 (apropos of the Talisman Gate at Baghdād); — 1914, Bulley (M. H.), *Ancient and Medieval Art*, pp. 265–6; — 1915, Lammens (H.), *L'Attitude de l'Islam primitif en face des arts figurés*, *Journal Asiatique*, 11me série, VI, pp. 239–79; reprinted in his *Études sur le siècle des Omayyades*, pp. 351–89; — 1919, Enani (A.), *Beurteilung der Bilderfrage im Islam nach der Ansicht eines Muslim*, in the *Mitteilungen des Seminars für orientalische Sprachen zu Berlin*, II. Abt., pp. 1–40; — 1920, Goldziher (I.), *Zum islamischen Bilderverbot*, *Z.D.M.G.*, LXXIV, p. 288; — 1921, Massignon (L.), *Les Méthodes de réalisation artistique des peuples de l'Islam*, *Syria*, II, pp. 47–53; — 1925, Wensinck (A. J.), *The Second Commandment*, *Mededeelingen der Koninklijke Akad. van Wetenschappen*, Afd. Letterkunde, Deel LIX, Ser. A, no 6; — 1927, Herzfeld (E.), *Die Malereien von Samarra*, pp. 1–3; and Migeon (G.), *Manuel d'art musulman*, 2me éd., I, pp. 101–3; — 1928, Arnold (T. W.), *Painting in Islam*, pp. 1–40; and Wensinck, article *Ṣūra*, in the *Encyclopaedia of Islām*, IV, pp. 561–3; — 1930, Aly Bahgat and F. Massoul, *La Céramique musulmane de l'Égypte*, pp. 38–39; — 1931, Aḥmad Mousa, *Zur Geschichte der islâmischen Buchmalerei in Aegypten*, pp. 15–16; — 1932, Creswell (K. A. C.), *Early Muslim Architecture*, 1st ed., pp. 269–71; and Marçais (G.), *La Question des images dans l'art musulman*, *Byzantion*, VII, pp. 161–83; and Wiet, in Hautecœur and Wiet, *Les Mosquées du Caire*, pp. 167–83; — 1933, Fernández (G.), *La Alhambra*, 2nd ed., pp. 190–92; — 1935, Lamm (C. J.), *The Spirit of Moslem Art*, *Bull. of the Faculty of Letters, Egyptian University*, III(1), pp. 3–5; — 1942, Zakī M. Ḥasan, in his notes to Aḥmad Taymūr Pasha, *Painting, Sculpture and the reproduction of living forms among the Arabs* [in Arabic], pp. 119–39; — 1946, Creswell (K. A. C.), *The Lawfulness of Painting in Early Islam*, *Ars Islamica*, XI–XII, pp. 159–66; — 1952, Anon., *De la prohibition de la forme humaine et animale dans l'art islamique*, *Cahiers d'Art*, XXVII, pp. 297–301, with 13 illus.; — 1956, Zakī M. Ḥasan, *The Attitude of Islam towards Figurative Painting*, *The Islamic Review*, XLIV, no. 7, pp. 24–9, with 1 illus.; and Vasiliev (A. A.), *The Iconoclastic Edict of the Caliph Yazid II*, A.D. 721, *Dumbarton Oaks Papers*, IX–X, pp. 23–47; — 1957, Grabar (André), *L'Interdiction des images et l'art du Palais à Byzance et dans Islam ancien*, *Comptes rendus de l'Acad. des Inscriptions et Belles-Lettres*, 1957, pp. 393–401, — 1960, Paret (Rudi), *Textebelege zum islamischen Bilderverbot*, in the *Hubert Schrade Festschrift*, pp. 36–48.

1 The first to point out that the prohibition against painting comes, not from the Qurān but from the *Ḥadīth*, was Lavoix in 1859, in the *Revue de l'Orient*, N.S., IX, pp. 353–4. He was followed by Pharaon, *Gazette des Beaux-Arts*, 2me période, I, pp. 443–4; Lavoix, *ibid.*, XII, pp. 98–9; Karabacek, *loc. cit.*, p. 291; de Nahuys, *Annales de l'Acad. d'archéologie de Belgique*, XLVIII, pp. 229 and 233; Chauvin, *ibid.*, XLIX, pp. 405–6; Lammens, *Journal Asiatique*, 11me série, VI, pp. 242–3; Kühnel, *Miniaturmalerei*, p. 1; Migeon, *op. cit.*, I, pp. 101–2; Arnold, *Painting in Islam*, pp. 4 ff.; Aḥmad Mousa, *op. cit.*, p. 16; etc.

2 *Op. cit.*, p. 124.

3 *al-Faraj baʿd ash-Shidda* (Cairo, 1903), p. 110, ll. 5-6; repeated by Yāqūt, *Muʿjam*, I, p. 792, l. 21–p. 793, l. 4. ʿUbayd Allāh was killed at the battle of the river Khāzīr, near Mosul, in 67 H. (686); Zettersteén's article ʻ*Ubaid Allāh b. Ziyād*, in the *Encyclopaedia of Islām*, IV, p. 985.

4 Ibn Rusta, p. 66, ll. 15–19; quoted by Enani, *op. cit.*, p. 25, and Arnold, *op. cit.*, pp. 8–9.

5 *Loc. cit.*, p. 127.

'Umar ibn 'Abd al-'Azīz who, on one occasion, actually is recorded to have objected to a picture in a bath. He had it obliterated and exclaimed: 'If only I could find out who painted it, I would have him severely beaten.'[1] I suggest that this painting was most probably pornographic, as was often the case in *ḥammāms*,[2] and that this was the real cause of 'Umar's anger, for we have just seen that he had no objection to a censer with human figures on it which was used to perfume the Mosque of Madīna.

Yet in spite of the silence of the Qurān, the Traditions (*Ḥadīth*)[3] are uniformly hostile to all representations of living forms.[4] Arnold, one of the latest scholars to discuss this question, believed that this hostility dates almost from the time of Muhammad, and holds that the paintings of Quṣayr 'Amra were executed in defiance of it.[5] Now although later Khalifs and Sultans certainly did defy the prohibition on many occasions, there appears to be good reason for believing that this prohibition had not yet been formulated at the time when the frescoes of Quṣayr 'Amra were executed. When did the change take place? A valuable clue is provided, curiously enough, by the Patrology. Our first witness is John, Patriarch of Damascus[6] and the great opponent of the Iconoclasts, who, in the words of Becker, 'represents the whole world of thought of the Eastern church at that time'. He did not live secluded in some distant monastery, but occupied a prominent place in the court life of the later Umayyad period, although he retired to a monastery shortly before his death. He belonged to an old Damascus family, the Banū Sarjūn, which had played an important part in the state administration under 'Abd al-Malik and even earlier. His active life must be placed roughly between A.D. 700 and 750,[7] so he was a contemporary of Quṣayr 'Amra.

As Becker has pointed out, John knew the doctrines of Islam well, his quotations from the Qurān in Greek are sometimes almost literal translations of the original, and he even gives the actual names of the Sūras cited.[8]

But although he was a violent opponent of the Iconoclastic movement and wrote his treatises 'against those who depreciate the holy images'[9] under the strong emotion caused by the Edict of 726, and although he wrote against Islam, he never refers to the Muslims as being guilty in this respect, but only to the Christians and Jews, whereas it would have been the first thing he would have seized on to reproach them with, had they held such opinions. But Theodore Abū Qurra, Bishop of Ḥarrān,[10] who was a contemporary of Hārūn ar-Rashīd and al-Ma'mūn and the first Father of the Church to write in Arabic, although he took most of his ideas from the writings of John, differs from him in this respect, for he includes the Muslims amongst the people opposed to painting. He does not actually refer to them as Muslims, but merely says: 'Those who assert that he who paints anything living, will be compelled on the Day of Resurrection, to breathe into it a soul.'[11] Although the Muslims are not

1 Ibn al-Jawzī, *Manāqib 'Umar ibn 'Abd al-'Azīz*, Becker's ed., p. 80; quoted by Enani, *op. cit.*, p. 33, and Arnold, *op. cit.*, pp. 46–7.

2 al-Ghuzūlī, *Maṭāli' al-Budūr* (Cairo, 1300 H.), II, p. 8; and Ibn al-Hajj, *Madkhal* (Cairo, 1348 H.), II, pp. 178–9.

3 The *Ḥadīth* are traditions concerning the actions and sayings of Muhammad, which circulated orally until they were collected, sifted, accepted or rejected, systematized and written down for the first time in the ninth century by Bukhārī, Muslim, Abū Dā'ūd, Mālik ibn Anas, Ibn Sa'd, Aḥmad Ibn Ḥanbal, Ibn Hishām, etc., each tradition being accompanied by its *isnād*, or chain of oral descent (e.g. So-and-so heard it from his father, who heard it from So-and-so, who knew the blessed Prophet). As early as the middle of the ninth century the number of *Ḥadīth* in circulation was enormous, the majority being false or suspect, for Bukhārī, who died in A.D. 870, only accepted 7,000 out of 600,000 which he had heard; see Nicholson, *Literary History of the Arabs*, p. 146.

4 Snouck Hurgronje, *Z.D.M.G.*, LXI, pp. 186–91; van Berchem, *loc. cit.*, p. 371; Lammens, *loc. cit.*, p. 249; Enani, *Beurteilung der Bilderfrage im Islam*, *loc. cit.*, pp. 1–40; Arnold, *op. cit.*, pp. 5–19, 31, and 38–40; etc. For a complete list of references to this question in the early collections of *Ḥadīth*, see Wensinck, *A Handbook of Early Muhammadan Tradition*, p. 108. Snouck Hurgronje has shown that Karabaček's contention, that paintings are permissible in the entrance hall of a building (*Kuṣejr 'Amra*, p. 229, and n. 69 on p. 237), is due to a misunderstanding of the text of al-'Asqalānī. See also Becker in the *Zeitschrift für Assyriologie*, XX, pp. 373–5; reprinted in his *Islamstudien*, I, pp. 300–304.

5 *Painting in Islam*, pp. 4–9 and 19.

6 He died *c.* A. D. 750. For his life and works see Perrier, *Jean Damascène: sa vie et ses écrits* (Strasbourg, 1863); Langen (J.), *Johannes von Damaskus* (Gotha, 1879); Lupton (J. H.), *Saint John of Damascus* (London, 1882); Ermoni (V.), *Saint Jean Damascène* (Paris, 1904); and Becker, *Christliche Polemik und islamische Dogmenbildung*, *Zeitschrift für Assyriologie*, XXVI, pp. 177–87; reprinted in his *Islamstudien*, I, pp. 434–43. His three treatises 'against those who depreciate the holy images' were written between 726 and 737.

7 *Christliche Polemik*, *loc. cit.*, XXVI, pp. 177–8; reprinted in his *Islamstudien*, p. 434.

8 *Ibid.*, pp. 179–80; *Islamstudien*, p. 436. This suffices to show that Zakī Ḥasan's remarks that Abū Qurra 'could judge the Muslims by what he read in their books, and not only by what they practised' (*loc. cit.*, p. 180), applies equally well to John.

9 Λογος πρωτος (—δευτερος—τριτος) απολογητικος προς τους διαβαλλοντας τας ἁγιας εἰκονας, in Migne, *Patrologia, Series Græca*, XCIV, cols. 1231–1420, and three smaller treatises in XCV, cols. 309–86, and XCVI, cols. 1347–62.

10 For his life, see Constantin Bacha, *Un Traité des œuvres arabes de Théodore Abou-Kurra*, Tripoli, 1905, pp. 3–7. His works have been published at Beyrut in 1904, and by G. Graf, *Die arabischen Schriften des Theodor Abû Qurra*, Paderborn, 1910; and the part that concerns us by Arendzen, *Theodori Abu Kurra de Cultu imaginem Libellus* (Bonner Dissertation, 1897).

11 Arendzen, *op. cit.*, pp. 18–19; and Graf, *op. cit.*, pp. 297–8.

actually named, the almost literal citation of the Muslim *ḥadīth*[1] proves that they are meant and, in addition, that the *ḥadīth* in question was already in circulation amongst the Muslims in the time of Abū Qurra. Thus the movement may be placed towards the end of the eighth century.

This fact is of considerable importance to students of Byzantine art, for it renders untenable the theory, put forward by Diehl[2] and Dalton,[3] that the Iconoclastic movement,[4] which took definite form in the Edict of the Emperor Leo the Isaurian[5] in 726, was partly due to defeats inflicted on the image-worshipping Byzantine army by an army of men hostile to all forms of human representation. This theory has been accepted by Wiet who, after citing the decree of the Khalif Yazīd (see below), goes on to quote Michael the Syrian to the effect that 'l'empereur des Grecs, Léon, ordonna *lui aussi, à l'exemple du roi des arabes*, d'arracher les images des parois, et il fit abattre les images qui étaient dans les églises et les maisons, celles des saints aussi bien que celles des empereurs ou d'autres'.

'Michel le Syrien', adds Wiet, 'est logique avec la tradition de l'Église. On sait qu'au deuxième concile de Nicée, tenu en 787, les évêques qui condamnèrent les iconoclastes estimèrent que les mesures prises contre les images l'avaient été à l'imitation des musulmans.'[6]

What was this decree of Yazīd? According to Theophanes (d. 818) 'a Jew of Latakia, coming in haste to Yazīd, promised him a reign of forty years over the Arabs if he destroyed the holy ikons which were adored in the churches of the Christians in all his Empire. But in this same year Yazīd died before most of the people had even had time to hear about his Satanic order'.[7] The execution of this order had already begun in Egypt[8] when Yazīd died (26th Jan. 724), and his successor Hishām revoked it on his accession.

As for the famous Council of Nicaea of 787, Michael the Syrian, who wrote in the second half of the twelfth century, does not tell the whole story. The true facts may be learnt by referring to an original document, viz.: the actual Proceedings of the Council in question, which may be consulted by turning to the great work of Mansi. There we read that at the reopening of the fifth session (4th Oct. 787), Tarasius remarked that the accusers of the Christians had, in their destruction of images 'imitated the Jews, Pagans, Samaritans, Manichaeans, and Phantasiasti (or Theopaschites)'.[9]

[1] From Bukhārī, Juynboll's ed., II, p. 41, and IV, p. 106: 'On the Day of Judgment the punishment of hell will be meted out to the painter, and he will be called upon to breathe life into the forms that he has fashioned; but he cannot breathe life into anything'; see Arnold, *Painting in Islam*, p. 5.

[2] *Manuel d'art byzantin*, p. 336.

[3] *Byzantine Art and Archaeology*, p. 13, and *East Christian Art*, p. 15.

[4] For an account of this movement see: — Paparrigopoulo (C.), *Histoire de la Civilisation hellénique*, pp. 184–203; Heferle (J. von), *A History of the Councils of the Church*, Clark's transl., V, pp. 370 ff.; Schwarzlose (Karl), *Der Bilderstreit*, Gotha, 1890; Lombard (A.), *Études d'histoire byzantine*, pp. 105–28; Bréhier (L.), *La Querelle des images*, Paris, 1904; Diehl (Ch.), *Manuel d'art byzantin*, pp. 334–9; 2me éd., I, pp. 360–65; Dalton (O. M.), *Byzantine Art*, pp. 13–16; Diehl (C.), *Leo III and the Isaurian Dynasty*, in the *Cambridge Medieval History*, IV, pp. 5–11; Leclercq (H.), article *Images*, in Cabrol and Leclercq, *Dictionnaire d'archéologie chrétienne*, VII, cols. 232–302; Ostrogorski (G.), *Studien zur Geschichte des byzantinischen Bilderstreits*, Breslau, 1929; Ostrogorski, *Les Débuts de la querelle des images*, in *Mélanges Charles Diehl*, I, pp. 235–55; Vasiliev (A. A.), *Histoire de l'Empire byzantin*, French transl., I, pp. 333–51; and Diehl and Marçais, *Historie du Moyen Âge*, III, pp. 259–78.

[5] As a result of recent research it now seems probable that Leo was of North Syrian and not of Isaurian origin; see Vasiliev, *Histoire de l'Empire byzantin*, French transl., I, pp. 311–12.

[6] Pauty, *Bois sculptés d'églises coptes*, Wiet's introduction, pp. 3–4; and Wiet, in Hanotaux, *Histoire de la Nation égyptienne, IV: L'Égypte arabe*, pp. 55–6.

[7] De Boor's ed., p. 401. He places this event in the Year of the World 6215 (= A. D. 724). Dionysius of Tell Maḥrē (d. A.D. 845) places it in the year of the Greeks 1035 (= 723–4); Chabot's ed., p. 19, and transl., p. 17. Michael the Syrian (Chabot's ed., II, p. 457; transl., II, p. 489) and Bar Hebraeus (*Chronography*, Bedjan's text, p. 118; Budge's transl., p. 109) also mention it but without giving a date. Maqrīzī (*Khiṭaṭ*, I, p. 302, l. 31; Casanova's transl., *M.I.F.A.O.*, III, p. 165) says that it took place in 104 H. (June 723–June 724). I must add, however, that doubts have been expressed regarding the authenticity of this story, e.g. by Wellhausen (*Das arabische Reich und sein Sturz*, pp. 202–203) and Musil (*Kuṣejr ʻAmra*, p. 155). It is true that Ṭabarī, as Wellhausen points out, merely states that a Jew had prophesied that Yazīd would reign forty years, and that Eutychius and Buṭrus ibn ar-Rāhib know nothing of the matter. But the silence is not complete, for other writers, equally early, speak of it, e.g. the Arabic historian al-Kindī (d. 961), and three ecclesiastical historians, Dionysius of Tell Maḥrē, quoted above, the anonymous Syriac chronicle of the year A. D. 846, published and translated by Brooks in the *Z.D.M.G.*, LI, p. 584; and Severus ibn al-Muqaffaʻ, Bishop of Ashmūnain in the tenth century; see al-Kindī, Guest's ed., pp. 71–2; and Severus ibn al-Muqaffaʻ, Evetts' ed., *Patrologia Orientalis*, V, pp. 72–3 (or Seybold's ed., p. 153, l. 7): quoted by Lammens, *loc. cit.*, p. 278. The objections of Wellhausen and Musil are therefore invalid. Moreover, on reading the proceedings of the Council of Nicaea, I have come across a contemporary witness, the Bishop of Messina who, at the fifth session, stated that he was a boy in Syria when the Khalif (σύμβουλος) of the Saracens threw down the images; Mansi, *Sacrorum Conciliorum nova et amplissima Collectio* (Florence, 1769), XIII, col. 200.

[8] It is to this order that Quibell attributes the mutilation of the paintings and sculptures found during his excavations at the Monastery of Apa Jeremias at Saqqāra; see his *Excavations at Saqqara (1908–9, 1909–10)*, p. iv. Crowfoot found that the figure subjects in the floor mosaics of the churches at Jerash had been mutilated before the final destruction of the city by an earthquake, probably that of 747; see *Churches at Jerash* (*British School of Archaeology at Jerusalem, Supp. Papers*, 3), p. 4; there can be little doubt that this was done in compliance with the same decree.

[9] Mansi, *op. cit.*, XIII, col. 196.

Whereupon the monk John, representative of the Eastern Patriarchate, asked permission to correct these erroneous ideas and to clear up the real origin of the attack on images, apparently speaking, like the Bishop of Messina (see end of note 7 on last page) from first hand knowledge of the facts.[1] This is what he said:

> After 'Umar's death [9th Feb. 720] Ezid (Yazīd II), a frivolous and unstable man, succeeded him. There lived at Tiberias a leader of the lawless Jews, a magician and a fortune-teller and a tool of soul-destroying demons, named Tessarakontapechys [= 40 cubits high].... On learning of the frivolity of the ruler Ezid, he approached him and began to utter prophecies . . . saying: 'You will live long and reign for thirty years if you follow my advice.... Give order immediately, without any delay or postponement, that an encyclical letter be issued throughout your empire to the effect that every representational (εἰκονικήν) painting, whether on tablets or in wall-mosaics or on sacred vessels and altar coverings, and all such objects as are found in all Christian churches, be destroyed and finally abolished, and so also all representations of any kind whatever that adorn and embellish the market places of cities' . . . The impious tyrant, yielding to his advice, sent [officials] and most frivolously destroyed the holy ikons and all other representations in the whole province under his rule and, thanks to the Jewish magician, thus ruthlessly robbed the churches of God under his sway of all ornaments, before the evil came into this land. As the Christians fled lest they should [have to] overthrow the holy images with their own hands, the Amirs who were sent for this purpose pressed into service abominable Jews and wretched Arabs; and thus they burnt the venerable ikons, and either smeared or scraped the ecclesiastical buildings.
>
> On hearing this the pseudo-Bishop of Nicolia and his followers imitated the lawless Jews and impious Arabs and outraged the churches of God.... When, after doing this, the Khalif (Σύμβουλος) Ezid died no more than 2½ years later [25 Sha'bān 105 = 27th Jan. 724],[2] the images were restored to their pristine position and honour. His son Οὔλιδος (= al-Walīd—should be Hishām), filled with indignation, ordered the magician to be ignominiously put to a parricide's death as a due reward for his false prophecy.[3]

Thus this act of Yazīd was in no way inspired by the doctrine of Islam at that period; on the contrary it would never have taken place had it not been for the vain promises of a fortune-teller,[4] and it was promptly revoked by his successor.

How did the feeling arise? It has been suggested that it arose through the inherent temperamental dislike of the Semite for human representations in sculpture and painting,[5] an anti-naturalistic reaction in fact. This undoubtedly helped, but the internal evidence points to a direct Jewish influence; Lammens points out that the *Ḥadīth* bearing on the question in many cases show Jewish inspiration. Take, for example, the sayings: 'The angels will not enter a house containing a bell, a picture or a dog', and 'At the end of the world when 'Īsā appears he will break the cross and kill the pigs'.[6] Bells were unknown in the time of Muhammad, and the *semantron* did not inspire the Arabs with any antipathy. Nor did they before Islam experience any special repugnance for pigs. The name Khinzīr is met with, and the flesh of the wild boar appeared at feasts. The sayings cited above can only be explained as due to Talmudic influence.[7] Again it is remarkable that the earliest recorded instance of hostility to images and painting appears to have been inspired by Jewish influence, viz. the iconoclasm of Yazīd II, cited above. A Christian influence, springing from the iconoclastic movement which broke out in A. D. 726, is therefore unlikely, likewise a spontaneous Muslim impulse.

This Jewish influence was doubtless due to the internal effect of Jews who had been converted to Islam, like the famous Yemenite Jew Ka'b al-Aḥbār, who was called Rabbi Ka'b on account of his wealth of theological and especially Biblical knowledge. Ka'b entered Jerusalem with 'Umar, was converted to Islam in A. D. 638 and died in 652 or 654. He is frequently cited as an authority for *Ḥadīth* and 'Abd Allāh ibn al-'Abbās, one of the earliest expositors of the Qurān, was a pupil of his, likewise Abū Huraira. Another famous Jew convert was Wahb ibn Munabbih. These two men were the great authorities among the early Muslims on all points of ancient history.[8]

Finally, as a predisposing psychological basis for the hostility to painting, there was the feeling, so common amongst primitive peoples, that the maker of an image or a painting in some way transfers part of the personality of the subject to the image or painting, and in so doing acquires magical powers

1 The importance of this cannot be overrated, for all the works of the Iconoclasts, the Imperial decrees, and the acts of the iconoclastic councils of 753–4 and 815 were destroyed when their adversaries triumphed.

2 This gives the end of July 721 for the date of Yazīd's act.

3 Mansi, *op. cit.*, XIII, cols. 198 and 200.

4 Let us remember that this was a period when 'individuals' as Diehl says 'put faith in the prophecies of wizards, and Leo III himself, like Leontius or Philippicus, had been met in the way by one who had said to him: "Thou shalt be King"'; *Cambridge Medieval History*, IV, p. 6.

5 Viardot, *Gazette des Beaux-Arts*, 2me période, I, pp. 556–9; Barbier de Maynard, *Revue critique*, N.S., I, pp. 333–5, &c.

6 Lammens, *loc. cit.*, pp. 276–7.

7 Lammens, *loc. cit.*, pp. 276–9.

8 See Le Strange, *Palestine under the Moslems*, p. 142; and Schmitz's article *Ka'b al-Aḥbār*, in the *Encyclopaedia of Islām*, II, pp. 582–3.

over the person reproduced.[1] This feeling, which is still prevalent in some parts of the world, was once very widely spread. The practice of making wax images of the person to be bewitched, and thrusting pins through them, was known to the Egyptians,[2] Greeks, and Romans, and was widely spread in medieval Europe, e.g. John of Nottingham's attempt to bring about the death of Edward II in 1324, and the similar attempt of Agnes Sampson on the life of James VI of Scotland in 1589;[3] also the League's attempt to kill Henry III of France.[4] A similar attempt on the life of Muhammad is related by Jannābī and ʿAlī al-Ḥalabī.[5]

My conclusion therefore is that the prohibition against painting did not exist in early Islam, but that it grew up gradually, partly as a result of the inherent temperamental dislike of Semitic races for representational art, partly because of the influence of important Jewish converts, and partly because of the fear of magic. It also follows that Muslim influence on the Edict of Milan is excluded.

BIBLIOGRAPHY OF QUṢAYR ʿAMRA

d. 1657 Ḥājjī Khalīfa, Jihān Numā, transl. into Latin by Norberg, 1818, II, pp. 209 and 226–7.

1682 Ḥājjī Muḥammad Adīb ibn Muḥammad, Intinéraire de Constantinople à la Mecque, extrait de l'ouvrage turc intitulé: *Kitāb menassik al-Hajj*, Constantinople, 1232 H. (1816/17), p. 68; translated by Bianchi in *Recueil de voyages et mémoires publié par la Société de Géographie*, II, p. 124 [p. 44 of the *tirage à part*].

1808 Seetzen (U. J.), Beyträge zur Geographie Arabiens. *Monatliche Correspondenz zur Beförderung der Erd- und Himmels-Kunde* (Gotha), XVIII, pp. 384–5.

1822 Burckhardt (J. L.), Travels in Syria, pp. 665–6.

1847 Ritter, Erdkunde, XIII, pp. 397–8.

1896 Grey Hill, A Journey East of the Jordan. *P.E.F., Q.St.*, 1896, p. 34.

1902 Musil (A.), Ḳuṣejr ʿAmra. *Sitzungsber. der Philos.-hist. Classe der Kaiserl. Akad. der Wissenschaften, Wien*, CXLIV, Abh. vii, pp. 1–4, 20, 26–44 and 47–51, figs. 12–22, and folding plate. [Referred to as *Sitzungsberichte*.]

— Anon. Schloss Amra auf der Halbinsel Sinai. *Das heilige Land*, XLVI, pp. 180–82.

— Clermont-Ganneau, in the *Journal des Savants*, 1902, pp. 281–4 (Review).

— Karabacek (J.), Ueber die Auffindung eines Khalifenschlosses in der nordarabischen Wüste. *Neue Freie Presse*, No. 13563 (29th May), pp. 26–9.

— Karabacek (Joseph von), Über die Auffindung eines Chalifenschlosses in der nordarabischen Wüste. *Almanach der Kaiserl. Akad. der Wissenschaften*, LII, pp. 339–61.

— H. Die Auffindung des Khalifenschlosses Amra in der nordarabischen Wüste. *Deutsche Bauzeitung*, XXXVI, pp. 337–9.

1905 Musil (A.), in the *Anzeiger der Phil.-hist. Klasse der Kaiserl. Akad. der Wissenschaften, Wien*, No. XII, pp. 40–46.

1907 Musil (A.), Ḳuṣejr ʿAmra (Wien, 1907), pp. 42, 57–65, 81, 87–92, 96, and 187–238, figs. 39, 44–8, 72–4, 134, and Taf. I–XLI. [Referred to as *Ḳuṣejr ʿAmra*.]

— Migeon (G.), Manuel de l'art musulman, II—Les Arts plastiques, pp. 4–5; 2ᵐᵉ éd. (1927), I, pp. 106, 229, and 230.

1907 Musil (A.), Arabia Petraea, I, pp. 222–33 and figs. 96–105, pp. 276–89 and figs. 118–24.

— Nöldeke (T.), Ein Wüstenschloss, in the *Neue Freie Presse*, No. 15301 (28th March), 1907.

— Hurgronje (C. S.), Ḳuṣejr ʿAmra und das Bilderverbot. *Z.D.M.G.*, LXI, pp. 186–91.

— Nöldeke (T.), in the *Z.D.M.G.*, LXI, pp. 222–33. [A review of *K. ʿA.*]

— Brünnow (R.), in the *W.Z.K.M.*, XXI, pp. 268–83. [A review of *Ḳ. ʿA.*]

— Becker (C. H.), in the *Münchener Neueste Nachrichten* (28th May), 1907.

— Brünnow (R.), in the *Kölnische Zeitung*, No. 771 (24th July).

— Brentano (H.), Ḳuṣejr ʿAmra. *Deutsche Rundschau*, CXXXI (June, 1907), pp. 427–35. [A review of *Ḳ. ʿA.*]

— Becker (C. H.), Das Wiener Quṣair ʿAmra-Werk. *Zeitschrift für Assyriologie*, XX, pp. 355–79; reprinted in his *Islamstudien* (1924), pp. 287–307.

— Strzygowski (J.), Amra und seine Malereien. *Zeitschr. für bildende Kunst*, n. F., XVIII, pp. 213–18, with 6 illus.

— Strzygowski (J.), in the *Byzantinische Zeitschrift*, XVI, pp. 733–4. [Review of *Ḳ. ʿA.*]

— Strzygowski (J.), ʿAmra als Bauwerk. *Zeitschr. fuer Geschichte der Architectur*, I, pp. 57–64, with 3 illus.

1908 Moritz (B.), Ausflüge in der Arabia Petraea. *M.F.O.B.*, III, pp. 424–5 and 427–33, and Taf. VI.

1909 Berchem (M. van), Au pays de Moab et d'Edom. *Journal des Savants*, 1909, pp. 301–9, 363–72, 401–2, and 406–8.

— Butler (H. C.), Ancient Architecture in Syria, Sect. A: Southern Syria, pp. 78, 80, and xx–xxiv, *passim*.

— Bréhier (L.), Les Origines de l'Art musulman d'après des découvertes récentes. *Revue des Idées*, VII_1, pp. 195–6 and 198.

1910 Brockelmann (C.), Der Islam (in Pflugk-Harttung, *Weltgeschichte*, Band *Orient*), illus. on pp. 176–7 and 179–83, and plate facing p. 136 (all from Musil's *Ḳuṣejr ʿAmra*).

— Diehl (C.), Manuel d'art byzantin, p. 320; 2ᵐᵉ éd., p. 345.

[1] See Sébillot, *Les Portraits*, in the *Revue des Traditions populaires*, I, pp. 349–54, and *Les Statues*, *ibid.*, II, pp. 11–23; Chauvin, *loc. cit.*, pp. 423 ff.; Doutté, *Merrâkech*, pp. 136–8; his *Magie et religion dans l'Afrique du Nord*, pp. 16–17; and Frazer (J. G.), *Golden Bough*, I, pp. 148–9; 2nd ed., I, pp. 10–18 and 295–7.

[2] A small model of a man made of wax, papyrus, and hair, which was intended to be burned slowly in a fire whilst incantations were recited, in order to produce some evil effect upon the person whom it represented, was obtained in Egypt by Budge in 1895. It is now in the British Museum, No. 37,918; see Budge, *By Nile and Tigris*, II, p. 347; and his *Guide to the Third and Fourth Egyptian Rooms*, p. 20.

[3] See the Rev. Montagu Summers's introduction to his translation of the *Malleus Maleficarum*, pp. xix–xx and xxii. The wax dolls used were called ʻMommetsʼ.

[4] See Pierre de l'Étoile, *Véritable Fatalité de Saint Cloud*, in Duchat (J. Le) and D. Godefroy, *Journal des choses mémorables advenues durant le régne de Henry III* (Cologne-Bruxelles, 1720), art. 8.

[5] Chauvin, *loc. cit.*, pp. 425–6.

1910 Herzfeld (Ernst), in *Der Islam*, I, pp. 106–8.

— Herzfeld (E.), 'Amra. Article in the *Encyclopaedia of Islām*, I, pp. 336–9.

— Lammens (H.), La Bâdia et la Ḥîra. *M.F.O.B.*, IV, p. 107 and pl. I.

1911 Dalton (O. M.), Byzantine Art and Archaeology, pp. 68–9, 257, n. 1, 260–61, 278–82, and 646, n. 3, and figs. 170–71.

— Rhodokanakis (N.), Wort- und Sachforschung im Arabischen. *Wörter und Sachen*, III, p. 120.

1912 Strzygowski (J.), Der grosse hellenistische Kunstkreis in Innern Asiens. *Zeitschrift für Assyriologie*, XXVII, pp. 139–46, with 1 plate.

1913 Dieulafoy (M.), Art in Spain and Portugal, pp. 31, 39, 71, 89, 202, and fig. 68.

1914 Bell (G. L.), Palace and Mosque at Ukhaiḍir, pp. 111–12.

— Mann (Traugott), Der Islam einst und jetzt. *Monographien zur Weltgeschichte*, Bd. 32, Abb. 31–2.

— Migeon (G.), Qesejir Amra. *Revue Biblique*, N.S., XI, pp. 392–401, with 1 plate and 7 illus.

1915 Diez (Ernst), Die Kunst der islamischen Völker, pp. 24–8 and Abb. 24–30.

1916 Moritz (B.), Bilder aus Palästina, Nord-Arabien und dem Sinai, p. 5 and Abb. 29–32.

— Woltmann (Alfred), Die Malerei des Mittelalters. Neu bearbeitet von M. Bernath, pp. 285–6.

1918 Creswell (K. A. C.), The Vaulting System of the Hindola Maḥal at Mandu. *J.R.I.B.A.*, Third Series, XXV, pp. 242–3 and fig. 10; reprinted (with additions) in the *Indian Antiquary*, XLVII, p. 6 and pl. II D.

1919 Herzfeld (E.), Archäologische Parerga, IV: Die Gemälde: Die Könige der Erde, in the *Orientalistische Literaturzeitung*, XXII, cols. 254–6.

— Strzygowski (J.), Ursprung der christlichen Kirchenkunst, pp. 102, 104, 115, and 118; transl. of Dalton and Braunholtz, pp. 119, 122, 135, and 139.

1920 Woermann (Karl), Geschichte der Kunst (2te Aufl.), II, pp. 378–9 and Abb. 318.

1921 Herzfeld (E.), Mshattâ, Ḥîra und Bâdiya. *Jahrbuch der Preuszischen Kunstsammlungen*, XLII, p. 133.

— Herzfeld (E.), in *Der Islam*, XII, p. 136.

1922 Jaussen and Savignac, Mission archéologique en Arabie, III—Les Châteaux arabes de Qeṣeir 'Amra, Ḥarâneh et Ṭûba, pp. 7–8, 9–10, 78–100, 108–14, 126, figs. 16–18 and pls. XXXV–XLIII and XLV–LVII.

1923 Ahlenstiel-Engel (E.), Arabische Kunst, pp. 9 and 16, with plan.

— Dussaud (R.) in *Syria*, IV, p. 257. [A review of Jaussen and Savignac's work.]

1924 Woermann (Karl), Geschichte der Kunst aller Zeiten und Völker, II, pp. 378–9 and Abb. 318.

1925 Dalton (O. M.), East Christian Art, pp. 40, n. 2, 166, 231, n. 2, 250, 252, and 261–2.

— Glück (H.), and E. Diez, Die Kunst des Islam, pp. 23–4 and 533, and Abb. 142–3.

— Wittek (P.), Eine türkische Fürstin auf dem Wandgemälde von Ḳuṣajr 'Amra. *Der Islam*, XIV, pp. 402–6.

1926 Butler (A. J.), Islamic Pottery, pp. 22 and 117.

— Dalton (O. M.), The Treasure of the Oxus, 2nd ed. (only), pp. lxxii–lxxiii.

1927 Herzfeld (E.), Die Malereien von Samarra, pp. 4–7.

— Musil (A.), Arabia Deserta, A Topographical Itinerary (*American Geographical Society. Oriental Exploration and Studies*, No. 2), pp. 343–7 and figs. 80–81.

1927 Pijoán (J.), History of Art, II, p. 207 and fig. 310.

1928 Arnold (Sir Thomas W.), Painting in Islam, pp. 12, 19, 29–30, 57, 124–5, and pl. LVII.

— Ritter (H.), in *Der Islam*, XVII, p. 141. [A notice of Jaussen and Savignac's work.]

1929 Kühnel (Ernst), Kunst des Orients, Abb. 40.

— Kühnel (E.), in Springer's *Handbuch der Kunstgeschichte*, VI, pp. 377–8, 382–3 and Taf. VIII (coloured).

— Munthe (Gustaf), Islams konst, pp. 47–9, with 2 illus.

1930 Strzygowski (J.), Asiens bildende Kunst, pp. 403 and 645–7, and Abb. 422 and 580.

— Wiet (G.), Répertoire chronologique d'Épigraphie arabe, I, pp. 20–21.

1931 Hartner (W.), article Minṭaḳa, in the *Encyclopaedia of Islām*, III, p. 501.

1932 Gibb (H. A. R.), Zu Der Islam XIV 402–6. *Der Islam*, XX, pp. 196–7.

— Terrasse (H.), L'Art hispano-mauresque, pp. 23–4.

1933 Herzfeld (Ernst), Die Könige der Erde. *Der Islam*, XXI, pp. 233–6. Revised in his *Archaeologische Mitteilungen aus Iran*, V, pp. 149–52.

— Klüber (H. von), in *Die Sterne*, XIII, pp. 37–8. [A review of Saxl and Beer's contribution.]

— Pauty (Edmond), Les Hammams du Caire, pp. 17–21 and fig. 2; pp. 45–7 and fig. 18.

— Panofsky (Erwin), and Fritz Saxl, Classical Mythology in Mediaeval Art. *Metropolitan Museum Studies*, IV, pp. 228–80

— Weber (J.), in the *Vierteljahrsschrift der Astronomischen Gesellschaft*, LXVIII, pp. 72–3. [A review of Saxl and Beer's contribution.]

1934 Lorey (E. de), in *Ars Islamica*, I, pp. 32–7 and figs. 15–16.

1936 Strzyowski (J.), L'Ancien art chrétien de Syrie, pp. 71–2 and fig. 42.

1939 Sauvaget (J.), Remarques sur les monuments omeyyades. *Journal Asiatique*, CCXXXI, pp. 13–16 and fig. 1.

1943 Écochard (Michel), and Claude Le Cœur, Les Bains de Damas, II, pp. 126–7.

[1947] Marçais (Georges), L'Art de l'Islam, pp. 27 and 31, and fig. 3.

1949 Pijoán (José), Summa Artis, XII—Arte islámico, pp. 31–4, figs. 41–5 and lám. 1.

1951 Mahmoud (H. E.), The Umayyad Desert Palaces. Their historical importance and purposes. *The Islamic Review*, XXXIX, No. 7, pp. 8–11, with 3 illus.

1952 Glueck (Nelson), The other side of the Jordan, pp. 39–40 and fig. 13.

1954 Grabar (Oleg), The Painting of the Six Kings at Quṣayr 'Amrah. *Ars Orientalis*, I, 'Notes', pp. 185–7.

1955 Littmann (Enno), Mauḳauḳis im Gemälde von Ḳuṣair 'Amra. *Zeitschr. der Deutschen Morgenländischen Gesell.*, CV, pp. 287–8, with 1 plate.

1959 Harding (G. Lankester), The Antiquities of Jordan, pp. 154–7, fig. 9 and pl. 21.

— Sauvaget (Jean), La Mosquée omeyyade de Médine, pp. 126–7 and fig. 15.

1962 Ettinghausen (Richard), Arab Painting, pp. 29–33, coloured illus. on p. 31, and illus. on pp. 190–91.

1965 Kessler (Christel), Die beiden Mosaikböden in Quṣayr 'Amra, in *Studies . . . in Honour of K. A. C. Creswell*, pp. 105–31, with 11 illus.

THE FLOOR MOSAICS OF QUṢAYR ʻAMRA

By Christel Kessler

THE MOSAIC PAVEMENTS lie in the small rooms C and C′ which flank the central recess of the hall.[1] They are in a fairly good condition.[2]

The Material. Jaussen and Savignac's definition as 'glass mosaics' is only partly true. Most of the tesserae are cut from natural stone, only a few double strands of glass cubes are inserted.[3] The percentage of glass therefore is comparatively small. To the colours of the natural stone material, which is restricted here to hues in white, yellow, red-brown, and black, the glass adds a bright yellow and green (a colour rarely occurring in stone) and that in two tones: a blue-green and a yellow-green (in Figs. 458 and 460 the double strands combining yellow-green and blue-green are indicated by a simple line, those combining yellow-green and yellow by a dotted line within the interlacing bands).

The stone tesserae average 7 mm. square, so the floors would be classed as 'fine' works after the categories of M. Avi-Yonah.[4] A small quantity of larger cubes, *c.* 1 cm.,² occurs also, but only in subordinate places like the neutral zones between patterns and walls and in the lines separating the different border designs. The glass cubes are smaller and of rather irregular shape, they seem to be re-used material.

The Patterns. The 'stylized foliage' seen by Jaussen and Savignac[5] exists, but it is far from representing the characteristic decoration of the floors. The foliage elements are few and occupy places of secondary importance. They occur in the upper end of the apses, which are practically unlit. The apse of room C is filled with two simple vine-scrolls issuing from an amphora; they end in a grape and from each scroll two feathery vine leaves branch off. In the apse of room C′ the interlacing motif contains in its central circle a plant representing a leaf or a fruit. This same room shows, furthermore, a border design, which might be called foliage, i.e. the band of lotus flowers with their calices turned alternately in opposite directions.[6]

All other patterns are abstract geometrical. Of minor interest are the static designs among them, i.e. the patterns combining squares and elongated hexagons, which are used for such unobtrusive places as the thresholds.[7] The main stress lies on a more dynamic type; the curvilinear design, in which the effect of motion is enhanced by the device of interlacing. All-over patterns of this type are spread, carpet-like, over the great rectangles under the vaults. These fields of interlacings are the device which determines the character of the Quṣayr ʻAmra floors.

All designs—representational or geometrical—are taken from the pre-Islamic pattern repertory for floor mosaic decoration. However, a new spirit is at work as we shall see below (pp. 421–2), and this manifests itself in the principal motif, i.e. the interlacing networks. While the amphora-vine scroll motif, the bands of lotus flowers, guilloche, and stepped crenellation are taken over from pre-Islamic tradition without any alteration, the interlacing all-over patterns are developed further, they alone manifest a step beyond tradition and will therefore be the object of a more detailed study.

Analysis of the Interlacing Fields. *The pattern of room C.* It is composed of two superimposed networks of identical shape (see Figs. 457 and 458). Each forms an independent unit and is developed as

[1] They must have been excavated after April 1957 (when Prof. Dubler had found the floors still covered with débris) and before November 1957 (i.e. the date of a letter in the files of the Jordan Department of Antiquities, which mentions the clearing of the castle), see *Studies in Islamic Art and Architecture in Honour of Professor K. A. C. Creswell*, London, 1965, p. 106.

[2] Description of the condition, *ibid.*, pp. 106–7. The horizontal hatchings in Figs. 457 and 460 indicate damages cemented over; the fragment extracted by Mr. Mielich (Musil, *op. cit.*, p. 96), which is now in the Islamic Section of the former Kaiser Friedrich Museum in Berlin, is inserted in its original position within the largest damaged spot. The vertical hatchings indicate unrepaired damages (state of 1961).

[3] The introduction of glass tesserae into a pavement of natural stone cubes is not a general practice, it is, however, known since ancient times. Glass was used in order to enrich the restricted colour scale of the natural stones, and that was especially the case in Hellenistic times, when mosaic art was understood as an imitation of painting. Dots or strokes of glass tesserae stressed the effect of a facial expression, of a crown, jewel, weapon, or gown. In subordinate places, such as borders, it was not found or only exceptionally.

[4] *Mosaic Pavements in Palestine*, *Q.D.A.P.*, III, p. 72.

[5] *Op. cit.*, p. 81.

[6] It may be mentioned here that it is not certain whether this design is derived from a plant form. Doro Levi has studied its history and has come to the conclusion that it has rather developed from the ancient wave band motif, in which the negative forms of the pattern are of a calix-like shape (*Antioch Mosaic Pavements*, 1947, pp. 453 ff.).

[7] *Studies in Honour of Prof. Creswell*, figs. 7 and 8.

follows: tangent circles of equally large size are outlined with bands (five mosaic strands thick) and interlocked by means of an overlapping small circle; at the points of intersection the bands are interlacing. This device inevitably produces a kind of secondary form, for the bands—instead of describing a circle—are now closing round the space between the circles, thus describing an annular form with four

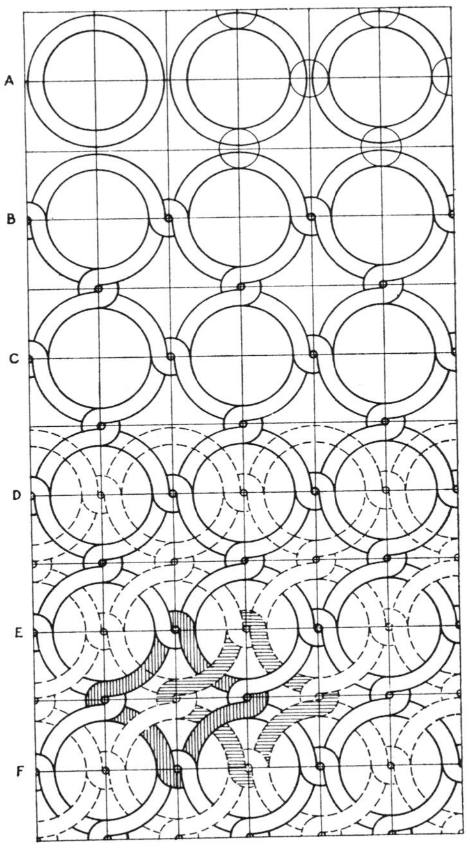

Fig. 457. Pattern analysis of Room C.

Fig. 458. Room C.

concave quarter circles (in Fig. 457, E–F hatched). However, the basic geometric unit of the design—the full circle—continues to be the figure which determines the pattern.

In the combination the second network was displaced horizontally for half a pattern unit, with the result that the small circles came to lie in the centre of the other network's corresponding large circles. In this new pattern the two networks are not distinguished in function, i.e. as far as the texture of the field is concerned; at the borders, however, the difference becomes manifest and we see that one is acting as the basic and the other as the filling design. For at the borders the endless repetition ('der unendliche Rapport') of the pattern is terminated in each network after a different fashion: the bands of the basic network transform themselves into straight lines forming a kind of frame, whereas the bands of the filling network start and end abruptly in the corners and break at the sides in two rectangular turns; at the ends they seem to bind into the ' frame ' thus creating the impression that the filling network weaves through the pattern in a longitudinal direction.

The pattern of room C′. Here the basic geometric units are circles and squares set on edge (see Fig. 460, A–C). They are placed alternately and are interlaced after the same method that we have noticed in the

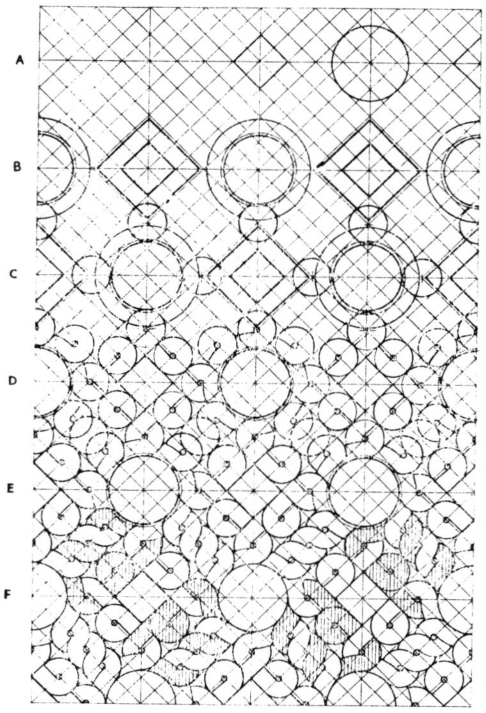

Fig. 459. Pattern analysis of Room C′.

Fig. 460. Room C′.

other pattern. In contrast to room C the density of the interlacing here is not produced by an interwoven second network, but by enriching one single network with additional looping: four loops are added round each circle and square (Fig. 459, D) and another small circle is introduced (in D–E marked with a dotted line), in order to produce between the circles a continuous guilloche strand in the diagonal (E–F).

Here too the device of interlacing has created a secondary form which, however, is more complicated (marked by hatchings in E–F).

Stylistic characteristics common to both patterns. 1—Linear geometry; 2—The role of the secondary form; 3—The termination of the infinite design.

1. The patterns are purely geometrical—no figural or representational elements participate; they are *linear* geometry, i.e. it is not the geometric field that is stressed, but the outline of such fields and their linear enrichment. Wherever the basic design leaves open a field of classical shape—circular or square—its visual importance is eliminated. The elimination is achieved in room C by interweaving a second network, as we saw. In room C′ the circular and square fields are small and tend to be more a kind of nucleus round which the design proper is developed in abundant looping and twisting; in addition to that they are filled with unobtrusive diapers and circles, which assimilate them to their interlacing surrounding.[1] The line clearly dominates.

2. The inserted glass strands trace the secondary forms and not the outlines of the circles and squares, thus attention is attracted to forms which seem to have nothing in common with the basic geometric figures. Whether this effect was intended or was a chance result of the glittering material and contrasting colours of the glass cannot be decided; important, however, is that this effect was accepted.

3. The patterns, being strictly geometrical, could be infinitely extended in each direction and each given space. However, in the floors of Quṣayr ʻAmra no use is made of this possibility—on the contrary, the patterns are organically terminated at the borders. They are brought to an end at a definite point in the rhythm of the design, i.e. at the loops which link the basic pattern units. At this point—and only there—the bands leave the infinite repetition and arrange themselves to form a frame, after which they return into the texture of the design.

This organic termination is stressed by additional features: in room C the filling network starts, ends, and breaks at the frame; in C′ the density of the design is attenuated at the borders by omitting a series of small loops. There can be no doubt that it was the full intention of the mosaic master of Quṣayr ʻAmra to transform the endless geometrical pattern into a kind of large defined motif.

A pattern defined thus is restricted in its adaptability to a given space. The mosaicist has shown some skill in dealing with this problem, as his solution in room C′ proves. Since the interlacings were conceived as defined motifs, they demanded a kind of framing. This was easily done by means of a guilloche border in room C. In the interlacings of room C′, however, the last linking loop before the end of the space, i.e. the last possibility of organically terminating the pattern, would have fallen too close to the wall; he therefore interrupted the pattern at the last loop but one. The result was a restricted field and a broader zone with space for three decorative borders to pass round.

This solution is as successful as it could be, yet the difficulty in adapting the defined pattern to the given space could not be mastered fully. We notice that in both the rooms a zone without decoration remains at the end opposite the apse. The gap is filled in C′ with six to nine rows of large black tesserae and in C with seventeen to nineteen rows of large white tesserae,[2] into which some simple lozenges are introduced as fillings.

STYLISTIC CONSIDERATIONS. The attribution of Quṣayr ʻAmra to al-Walīd I is based on the historical interpretation of one of the paintings. The mosaics have so far not yet entered the discussion. With their excavation a challenge is given to investigate whether their style confirms or opposes the accepted dating. We must ask, can the conspicuous concentration on geometrical all-over patterns of interlacings be taken as characteristic for al-Walīd's time?

The origin of the patterns. The answer leads back into the history of floor-mosaic pattern. As a matter of fact interlacings are found in late Roman and Byzantine pavements. They appear as all-over patterns, larger concentric motifs, and small single motifs filling geoemtric compartments. The historical sequence of their development is not clear, since dated floors are rare.[3]

[1] See *Studies in Honour of Prof. Creswell*, fig. 2.

[2] *Ibid.*, figs. 9 and 10.

[3] There is, however, a series of well datable pavements in the churches of Gerasa ranging from *c.* A.D. 365 to 565, in which interlacings occur (see below, p. 420, n. 6 and 7 and p. 421, n. 1 and n. 2). The very large number of floors excavated by the Princeton University in Antioch on the Orontes did not yield an absolute dating by inscription before the end of the fourth century A.D. i.e. in the Kaoussie Church, dated A.D. 387, and that seems to be a single instance. For the few cases of dated or datable pavements see the comparative chronology in Doro Levi, *Antioch Mosaic Pavements*, 1947, pp. 625–6. The inventory of Avi-Yonah of *Mosaic Pavements of Palestine* (*Q.D.A.P.*, II, 1932, pp. 136–81; III, 1933, pp. 26–47 and 49–73; IV, 1935, pp. 187–93) in which 588 floors are registered, contains only eight cases with an absolute dating by inscription, and these cover only the relatively short period from A.D. 516 to 601 (*Q.D.A.P.*, III, p. 71).

Doro Levi, who has gathered exhaustive comparative material in connexion with his studies of the Antioch mosaic pavements, has come to the conclusion that 'at the present state of our knowledge it is not possible to decide whether the adoption of the motif as filling element was the first step towards its growth, preceding its use as a continuous motif for borders or for all-over pattern, or whether it presupposes the existence of such continuous patterns'.[1]

Without taking up the discussion about the historical sequence of the different forms, we may, however, state in a general way the different stages of the development of interlacing all-over patterns.

The classical antique type of all-over pattern—a combination and interlocking of geometrical compartments—was of a static order. Starting in the first centuries A.D. a growing interest in linear geometry gradually dissolved this order by first accentuating and then interlacing the outlines of these compartments. In these early stages the line in its simple form was not yet considered as having aesthetic value; the outlines, therefore, were given a decoration; mostly classical border designs like guirlands, wave-bands, rainbow pattern, guilloche and lotus-flower calices. Among the earliest interlacing all-over patterns thus created was the single network of circles; it is found e.g. in a pavement of Hadrian's Villa in Tivoli (second century A.D.),[2] in Djem in Tunisia (second to fourth century A.D.)[3] and in the mosaics of the vaults of Sta. Costanza in Rome (A.D. 324–6).[4] When in some other patterns an outlining with simple bands is found—i.e. with bands of five parallel strands, the two outer ones black, the three inner ones coloured, as in Quṣayr ʻAmra—it will be seen that their role remains subordinate to the classical pattern conception, i.e. the geometrical compartments and their representational filling motifs alone are important.

The decisive change takes place in the sixth century when patterns appear, in which the compartments have lost importance while the line dominates.[5]

All-over patterns related to those of Quṣayr ʻAmra are found in Gerasa and Antioch on the Orontes. A network of tangent circles and squares decorates the apsidial end of the north aisle in the Church of Procopius in Gerasa, which is dated A.D. 526/7.[6] Its geometrical structure is only slightly different from the basic pattern of room C′; the squares are not connected to the circles at their points but at the lateral middle, and circles and squares alternate in a diagonal direction. The same pattern—this time parallel to the sides—appears again in Gerasa shortly after, i.e. in the middle of the sixth century, in the Mortuary Church.[7] Antioch provides an even closer correspondence to Quṣayr ʻAmra; the basic single network of circles occurs there in two spacious pavements. One can be dated on archaeological evidence in the first half of the sixth century; it lies in the upper level of the 'Phoenix Villa'.[8] The other one, being very similar, may be ascribed to the same century.[9]

In contrast to the second- to fourth-century interlacings mentioned above, the compartments have become small and their decoration is unobtrusive; the interlace is consistently built up of undecorated bands composed of five parallel running mosaic strands, which enhance the linear effect.[10]

It is obvious that during the sixth century A.D. the aesthetic value of the simple line had reached full appreciation. Besides these all-over patterns[11] interlacing border designs and small motifs are found in

[1] *Op. cit.*, p. 460: for the all-over interlacings in general see pp. 457 ff.

[2] E. Blake, *Roman Mosaics of the Second Century in Italy*, *Memoirs of the American Academy in Rome*, XIII (1936), pl. 12².

[3] P. Gauckler, *Inventaire des mosaïques de la Gaule et de l'Afrique*, tome 2, 1910, no. 71, d.

[4] W. F. Volbach, *Frühchristliche Kunst* (München, 1958), fig. 31.

[5] E.g. in the Church of Suhmātā, datable A.D. 555 (*Q.D.A.P.*, III, p. 101, pl. XXVII); the static pattern of overlapping circles is transformed into a dense interlace; here, without the usual straight framing band. The same design as border in Tell Ḥassān (*Q.D.A.P.*, V, pl. LII).

[6] F. M. Biebel, *Mosaics*, in Carl H. Kraeling, *Gerasa, City of Decapolis*, 1938, pp. 338–40, pl. LXXXII, a.

[7] *Ibid.*, p. 336, pl. LXXVII, c.

[8] D. Levi, *op. cit.*, p. 351–2, assumes on account of coin finds as *terminus post quem* the year A.D. 518 and as *terminus ante quem* the date of the earthquake of A.D. 526; see *ibid.*, pls. LXXXIII, b and CXXXV, a and c.

[9] It was excavated south of the 'Mosaic with the Biblical Inscription', see *ibid.*, p. CXXX, d.

[10] In this connexion the mosaic pavement of the Church of the Nativity in Bethlehem should be mentioned. A large network of interlaced tangent circles occurs there in which the compartments have practically disappeared (*Q.D.A.P.*, V, pl. XLIV). Through a radical change in the proportions of the design they have been reduced to a dot, and the pattern appears as a dense interlace of secondary forms. Doro Levi (*op. cit.*, p. 466, n. 260) regards these pavements as belonging to the restoration of Justinian after the Samaritan uprising in the year A.D. 529. This dating is the most acceptable to our approach.

[11] Avi-Yonah mentions in his *Mosaic Pavements of Palestine* thirteen more examples of the simple network of tangent circles under the symbol 'J 1' (*Q.D.A.P.*, II, p. 141 and III, p. 59). Of these only two are dated, and these belong to the sixth century (no. 20, A.D. 5..) and the first year of the seventh century (no. 11, A.D. 601). Of the network of squares and circles he gives four more examples, under 'J 2' (*Q.D.A.P.*, II, p. 141 and III, p. 59) of which two, however, are border designs only.

greater frequency and richer complication.[1] In addition, large medallions of concentric interlacings were created.[2] Interlace has become a device of equal importance to other conventional forms of decoration.

The sixth-century all-over patterns of interlace from Gerasa[3] and Antioch represent the basic geometrical layout of the Quṣayr ʿAmra patterns. In other words, the Quṣayr ʿAmra interlacings are rooted in the mosaic pattern tradition of Byzantine Syria (based in its turn on static classical conceptions), but they have gone beyond this tradition. In what respect?

ACTION AND COUNTERACTION OF TRADITIONAL AND NEW CONCEPTIONS. 1. While interlacing design played a subordinate role in late antique decorative pavements and rose to a certain equality during the sixth century A.D., it has now moved into the centre of the main field, and with this into the centre of the aesthetic interest of the time. The interlacing all-over pattern has taken the place which was previously held by figural or other representational motifs. (The amphora with the vine scrolls—one of the principal motifs of early Byzantine art—is shifted to the dark upper end of an apse and seems to be used there only on account of its adaptability to the curved space given.)[4]

But while this revaluation manifests a new spirit, a traditional conception must still have been in the mind of the designer. According to classical principles of decoration the main motif—then figural or representational—was a unit created for and defined within the space available. This, I believe, must have been the unconscious background of the fact that the mosaicist of Quṣayr ʿAmra felt bound to transform the endless geometric pattern into a kind of large defined motif.

A similarly emphasized definition of complicated interlacings is found in two fields in the pavements of Khirbat al-Mafjar,[5] for which palace an Umayyad dating has been established.[6]

2. As another reminiscence may be regarded the fact that the heightening effect of the glass was restricted to the motifs only.[7] Glass does not occur in the borders; we find it, however, at the mouth of the amphora and in the fruit (or leaf) and, as we saw, to the greatest extent in the principal motifs, the interlacing fields. The shining bright strands are distributed there in an elaborately irregular way—a kind of balanced disorder (compare Fig. 458 and Fig. 460)—thus insinuating animation into the motifs' rigid regularity.

3. A step beyond traditional usage is obviously the increased density of the design. This is achieved not as in the sixth century by reducing a single network's compartments in size and their filling motifs in importance, but by richer looping and twisting (in room C′)[8] or by interweaving a second network (in room C).[9] In both cases the enrichment of the design results from adding different linear movements to the traditional outlining of compartments. A similar richer and freer development of all-over patterns is again met with in the Umayyad Khirbat al-Mafjar.[10]

1 E.g. in Gerasa in the Church of Procopius of A.D. 526 (Kraeling, *op. cit.*, pls. LXXX and LXXXIII, a and b), the Church of St. George, A.D. 529–30 (*ibid.*, pl. LXXII, a), the Synagogue Church, A.D. 530–1 (*ibid.*, pl. LXVI, a) and the Church of St. Cosmas and Damian, A.D. 533 (*ibid.*, pl. LXXIII).

2 In Gerasa in the Church of Procopius, north aisle (*ibid.*, pl. LXXXI, a and b) and south aisle (*ibid.*, pl. LXXXIII, a); in the Nativity Church in Bethlehem, two smaller and two larger motifs in the nave (*Q.D.A.P.*, V, pl. XLIV); a similar large motif in the early Byzantine church of Tell Ḥassān, first half of sixth century (*Q.D.A.P.*, V, pl. LI, 2).

3 Quṣayr ʿAmra lies only *c.* 80 km. south-south-east of Gerasa, and the churches must have been in use during the time of its construction, for it was only some years after the suggested date of Quṣayr ʿAmra that their pavements suffered iconoclastic mutilations. J. W. Crowfoot holds the Khalif ʿUmar II responsible for this deed (*Early Churches of Palestine*, p. 162). He relies for that on Father de Vaux's studies of the mosaics of Maʿin (*Revue Biblique*, 1938, p. 257), who interprets the date of the restoration inscription, ΧΙΔ, as 614 after the era of Boṣrā, which corresponds to A.D. 719/20, and quotes passages from Muqaddasī and Ibn al-Jawzī in order to illustrate ʿUmar II's iconoclastic ideas. ʿUmar ibn ʿabd al-ʿAzīz was Khalif from Sept./Oct. A.D. 717 to Feb. 720. Creswell, however, dates this event to the reign of Yazīd II, see above, p. 413.

4 It offers indeed a better solution than the apse motif in room C′. There an interlacing design, which was originally created for a rectangular space, has been fitted into the apsidial curve by amputating two loops, and the design does not penetrate into the corners

5 I.e. the fields 4 and 9, where two networks are interwoven (Hamilton, *op. cit.*, pl. LXXX.) For further comparison of the Quṣayr ʿAmra interlacings with those of Mafjar and Minya see *Studies in Honour of Prof. Creswell*, pp. 122–8.

6 See below, pp. 574–6.

7 The insertion of glass strands into the interlacing is peculiar to the Quṣayr ʿAmra mosaics only. Glass tesserae are found in Minya (see above pp. 385–6) in the largest floor; however, they do not emphasize the linear movement, but small rhomboid fields.

8 It is true that the pattern of C′, with four instead of three twists of the guilloche, is found in a pavement of a monastery at Zabābida, south of Nazareth (*Q.D.A.P.*, III, p. 46, no. 329, pl. XVIII, 2), unfortunately undated; but its larger scale and rough filling decoration do not produce the density and linear clarity which are achieved in our pattern and which indicate a later stage.

9 On smaller surfaces a few attempts at duplication had already been made in the sixth century, e.g. in the intercolumnar spaces in the Procopius Church at Gerasa (Biebel, *op. cit.*, pl. LXXX, c), in a border in the Church of the Multiplying of the Loaves at Tabgha (dated by D. Levi, *op. cit.*, pp. 466–7, n. 260, to the sixth century rather than to the middle or end of fourth century according to Schneider).

10 Hamilton, *op. cit.*, p. 332, 'the horror vacui assuaged not by

4. Action and counteraction of new and old conceptions can furthermore be witnessed in the role the secondary forms play in Quṣayr 'Amra. Strands of glass tesserae with brilliant surface and brighter colours make some of them stand out in the pattern.[1] This affects the basic layout of the design: each time the eye meets with one of those outstanding secondary forms it is attracted to follow up their peculiarly winding course which runs utterly contrary to the traditional order of circles and squares.

Thus the secondary form does no longer figure as a mere by-product of the device of interlacing—it has become a factor which counteracts the traditional ratio of the pattern: a fluctuation of the design is produced—a to-and-fro between forms emerging and forms dissolving—which did not exist previously, but which is characteristic of later Islamic interlace.[2]

5. One strange feature of the interlacing texture must be discussed, since it is most revealing for the understanding of the progress in the pattern development.

As a general rule interlacing bands pass alternately over and under each other (o – o – o – o –). This regular weave is observed in all networks of whatever design and period—but not in Quṣayr 'Amra's room C. There the rhythm is o – o o – – o – o o – –. How is this striking deviation to be explained?

With the help of the analysis, Fig. 457, we can verify that the irregularity in the final pattern occurs only when the two networks are combined. The basic single network is interlacing regularly o – o –, and the superimposed second network too has retained—within its own texture—the regular rhythm. It is clear that the irregular weave in the combination is inevitable as long as the regular weave in the individual networks is retained.

The fact that the mosaicist of Quṣayr 'Amra insisted on not dissolving the regular weave of the individual networks for the sake of regularity in the combined pattern shows how much ancient tradition was still present in his mind, viz. his craft: the single network of tangent circles with its established regular weave was, as we saw (p. 420), one of the most frequent patterns in pre-Islamic times. The mosaicist, therefore, was not creating a new design, but was creating a new variation of an older pattern which was more in keeping with the taste of his time, and in this sense more 'modern'.

The only other example of this peculiarity is found in another palace of al-Walīd, i.e. in Khirbat al-Minya.[3] It shows the same irregularity and the same distinction between basic and filling network at the borders. However, it has not yet risen to full appreciation, but decorates the small space of a threshold only; moreover, it lacks the precision of movements and proportions. On the whole the pavements of Minya indicate a less advanced progress towards linear geometry, and it is just possible to regard the appearance of our pattern there as an earlier attempt at producing a denser interlace by this kind of duplication.

It is interesting to notice that the knowledge of the origin of the design has later been lost when transposed into another material. The designer of the stucco window grilles of Qaṣr al-Ḥayr al-Gharbī,[4] a palace of al-Walīd's brother Hishām, has used the same combination of two networks of tangent circles, but for him the pattern was nothing more than a geometric formula: a distinction between basic and filling network exists no longer and both are combined in a regular interlacing rhythm.[5]

These stylistic considerations have shown that no advance was made in the field of representational art (the fresco paintings prove that also), whereas the abstract linear patterns were elaborated and brought

insertion of filling motifs but by looping and tightening the interlace. Behind the wormlike writhings which resulted there was a prosaic structure of squares and circles.'

[1] Different colour combinations within the bands did already occur in ancient patterns, yet the difference remained unobtrusive and never led to a similar contrasting of forms, which do not emphasize the basic layout of the design. These secondary forms originate from necessity when the interlace is basically built on tracing outlines of geometric compartments. Nils Åberg describes the networks as 'a puzzle-like fusion of mutually free motifs, only held together by interlace' (*The Occident and Orient in the Art of the Seventh Century*, I *Kungl. Vitterhets Historie och Antikvitets Akademiens Handlingar*, del. 56: 1, 1943, p. 43).

[2] The later Islamic interlacing patterns, however, are free inventions of the designers and no longer conceived on the basis of the classical pattern composition of compartments; therefore no such 'mutually free small motifs' exist. The fluctuation of the design is then a to-and-fro between the different possibilities of grouping the design units, e.g. the star and polygon shapes, produced by the rectilinear interlace in Mamlūk patterns.

[3] See *Studies in Honour of Prof. Creswell*, fig. 11; and above, Pl. 68*b*, at the right-hand bottom corner.

[4] *Annales Archéologiques de Syrie*, I, 1951, pl. 20$_{(1)}$. This is a restoration of the grille in the National Museum at Damascus. It contains only a few small original fragments, but fortunately one slightly larger coherent piece reveals the original rhythm of interlacing. Its regular weave is not always rendered properly in the restored parts.

[5] The same is true for a marble grille of the Umayyad Mosque at Cordova, see *E.M.A.* II, 1st ed. pl. 28, c to left.

to greater prominence. It was no longer nature in its different forms which stimulated the artistic production, as in Hellenistic times, but rather the abstract world of linear geometry, in which the decorative arts of later Islamic centuries excelled, especially in Syria and Egypt. The basic forms of our patterns, however, had already been developed in early Byzantine Syria, i.e. a period during which the pagan emphasis on nature was being abandoned.

The style of the Quṣayr ʻAmra floors reveals nothing that would contradict the dating to al-Walīd I; on the contrary it illustrates very well the aesthetic attitude of Syrian artists *circa* eighty years after the Muslim conquest of Syria.

THE ZODIAC OF QUṢAYR ʿAMRA

By THE LATE FRITZ SAXL[1]

THE REPRODUCTION OF THE CUPOLA of Quṣayr ʿAmra with its representation of the constellations, published by Musil more than twenty years ago, has received little attention. The reason for this may lie in the fact that the reproduction was too inadequate to permit more detailed study. If, however, one attempts to use the new photographs of the cupola, made by Mr. Creswell, and to reconstruct the fresco from its fragments by a comparison of its representation of the constellations with others dating from Antiquity and the early Middle Ages, one recognizes without difficulty that this cupola painting is a document of fundamental importance for cultural history.

We know from monuments and literary sources that, in the East as well as in the West, there have been since ancient times representations of the heavens on ceilings, as, for example, the Egyptian paintings on the ceiling of the tomb of Seti I,[2] the circular sculpture of Roman times at Denderah,[3] the Athribis tomb of the same period,[4] etc. In the old Egyptian period the representations are in rows, while those at Denderah, obviously under Greco-Roman influence, are already round. All these representations show the map of the heavens projected upon a plane. It would, however, seem highly probable from literary sources that there were also *cupolas* with such paintings of the constellations.[5] In such cases the possibility for making scientifically correct representations of the starry heavens was greater than in transpositions of the painting on a plane surface. But of these cupola paintings there is, so far as we know, only a single example extant, the fresco from the dome of Quṣayr ʿAmra.

The fresco of Quṣayr ʿAmra is the only painting based upon that achievement, which is perhaps the most important of Greek astronomy: the exact reproduction of the stars on a spherical surface, i.e. on a globe. Thus it deserves, to a certain extent, to be placed beside that most famous astronomical monument of antiquity, the Farnese Atlas.[6]

Moreover, there has not been preserved either in the West or, so far as we know, in the Near East any other monumental representation of a scientific kind which could be compared with that of Quṣayr ʿAmra. No astronomical manuscripts are known of the earliest Islamic period. From Byzantium we have an illuminated copy of Ptolemy, but this is from the second decade of the ninth century and contains only a few illustrations.[7] Similarly, all that has been preserved in the western world is later and, for the most part, illustrated in an entirely unscientific manner, if by 'scientific' we mean what a man like Hipparchus or Ptolemy meant by it. Moreover, from this standpoint the fresco occupies a position of particular importance. We are enabled to deduce from it the degree of scientific accuracy which may be attributed to the thought and feelings of a fresco painter in the service of a prince, at this medieval period in the East.

Finally, this painting must be of particular significance to the historian of culture in so far as it originated on the boundary between the Mediterranean Basin and the Near East; that is, in a cultural orbit in which exchanges between East and West took place; exchanges which, on the one hand, contributed to the development of a high Islamic culture; on the other hand, conditioned the formation of a mixed culture between Arabia and South Italy and between Arabia and Spain,[8] which, from the point of view of the natural sciences, so vitally fertilized the western culture of the Middle Ages. It will be seen that there are links connecting Quṣayr ʿAmra with the Arabic globes of the thirteenth century and further with the astral configurations of the western medieval age which were based upon these globes.

[1] Translated from the German by Mrs. Ruth Wind.

[2] Cf. Alexander Pogo, *The Astronomical Ceiling-decoration in the Tomb of Senmut*, in *Isis*, XIV (1930), pp. 300–325.

[3] Franz Boll, *Sphaera*, Leipzig, 1903, p. 232.

[4] Flinders Petrie, *Athribis*, London, 1908.

[5] Ath-Thaʿālibī reports: 'Above this throne there was a vault of gold and lapis-lazuli, on which the signs of the Zodiac and of the seven Climates were reproduced.' For parallel references in classical literature see my treatise: *Frühes Christentum und spätes Heidentum*, in the *Jahrbuch f. Kunstgeschichte*, 1923, p. 111, n. 104. That the Greeks already adorned their *bathrooms* with *cosmological* representations, exactly as the painter of Quṣayr ʿAmra did, we learn from Johannes Gazaeus in his *Ἔκφρασις τοῦ κοσμικοῦ πίνακος τοῦ ὄντος ἐν τῷ χειμερίῳ λουτρῷ* (see Paul Friedländer, *Johannes v. Gaza und Paulus Silentiarius*, Leipzig, 1912, pp. 111 and 135).

[6] Georg Thiele, *Antike Himmelsbilder*, Berlin, 1898, pp. 19 ff.

[7] Cf. Franz Boll, *Beiträge zur Überlieferungsgeschichte der griechischen Astrologie und Astronomie; Sitzungsberichte der Bayerischen Akad. d. Wissenschaften, Philos.-philol. u. hist. Kl.*, 1899, pp. 110 ff.; Albert Rehm, *Eratosthenis Catasterismorum fragmenta Vaticana*, Progr. Ansbach, 1899, pp. 1 ff.

[8] Charles H. Haskins, *Studies in the History of Mediaeval Science*, Cambridge, Mass., 1924, pp. 3 ff., *passim*.

Fig. 461. The Twins.

Fig. 462. Orion.

Fig. 463. Ketos.

Fig. 464. The Dolphin.

THE ASTRONOMICAL REPRESENTATIONS OF QUṢAYR ʿAMRA COMPARED WITH CLASSICAL AND MEDIEVAL EXAMPLES

One certainly cannot consider the fresco merely as a product of scholarship. Rather is it both scientific and 'decorative' in the same sense as, for instance, the Farnese Atlas.

It is all the more striking that the geometric outline in which the various figures are placed presents a strictly scientific system. This system is in fact rather complicated. In the centre of the cupola is the celestial pole. However, the twelve radii, drawn at a distance of thirty degrees from one another, do not begin at this pole, but at the pole of the apparent path of the sun, the ecliptic, in which lie the twelve signs of the zodiac, separated from one another by those radii. There are also a number of declination-circles, whose centre lies in the northern pole of the heavens.

This system of co-ordinates was, of course, originally contrived to allow the exact placing of stellar positions in the picture. It seems somewhat peculiar to find such a system in a dome painting, for who should control here, with square and ruler, astronomical observations which had been made of the heavens? This seems to us the first hint that the painting was obviously taken from a foreign source and transferred to the wall with more or less understanding, and certainly executed by a man who not only was no astronomer, but also could seldom have observed the heavens. For he who looked into the starry cupola of Quṣayr ʿAmra saw the stars not as they appear in the heavens, but with a transposition from left to right. He saw them there as they are reproduced on the *outer surface of a globe of the heavens* or on the page of a book, not as they appear to the observer who stands within the celestial globe.

The second point which seems to prove that in Quṣayr ʿAmra the page of a book was transferred to a cupola is that constellations were reproduced which were no longer within the northern hemisphere but had already passed into the southern heavens. Since the painter took the north pole to be in the zenith of the dome, and since the dome is hemispherical, only the constellations of the northern hemisphere should appear there. The base of the dome in Quṣayr ʿAmra does not represent the horizon, and the stars reproduced are not constellations which at a certain time, and from a certain terrestrial point, appear simultaneously above the horizon on the celestial sphere. On the contrary, in the dome of Quṣayr ʿAmra, the celestial equator lies considerably above the base of the cupola. Thus, the southern tropic has a larger diameter than the equator.

To the modern mind, trained as it is to think perspectively, this procedure is difficult to understand. But this representation of the heavens, which simply placed the constellations row after row in concentric circles—with the celestial north pole as centre—was customary in the late classical and medieval manuscript traditions of the western world. The peculiarity is only that the painter of Quṣayr ʿAmra, faced with the task of reproducing the heavens, not on a plane, but on the inner surface of a sphere, nevertheless chose this model of a flat surface.

His procedure revenged itself on him; for, in his transfer of the plane-drawing to the dome, as he neared the apex of the cupola, the difficulty arose of finding a place on the much smaller space of the curved surface for all the figures of the plane. It was probably on account of this difficulty that in painting the Perseus group there was no place for one of the figures—Cassiopeia: Andromeda is incorrectly represented as hovering just above Cepheus' head instead of over that of the mother.

On comparing the various figures of our fresco with the usual stellar representations of the Greco-Roman period, one is astounded by the extreme similarity of the two. Orion's crook (Fig. 462) and the naked Twins (Fig. 461),[1] standing parallel and seen half from the back, are as like Greco-Roman models as is Ketos (Fig. 463) or the gracefully moving Dolphin (Fig. 464). Half-destroyed fragments of the drawing, as, for instance, that above the outstretched arm of Hercules (Fig. 465), become explicable when compared with the pictures of the Farnese Atlas: the painter tried here, too, to reproduce a form similar to that used by the sculptor of the globe, who attempted to give the connexion of Testudo and Lyra.

[1] In the following figures F = Farnese Globe (Georg Thiele, *Antike Himmelsbilder*, Berlin, 1898, pp. 19 ff.).
Gr. 1 = Codex Vat. Graec. 1087 } (see Franz Boll, *Beiträge zur Überlieferungsgeschichte d. griech. Astrologie und Astronomie.*)
Gr. 2 = Codex Vat. Graec. 1291 }
V = Codex Vossianus 79·4° (Georg Thiele, *op. cit.*).
C = Late Carolingian Ivory (A. Goldschmidt, *Elfenbeinskulpturen*, Bd. I, Nr. 156 and 157).
Q = Quṣayr ʿAmra.
D = Dresden Globe (Drechsler, *Der arabische Himmelsglobus angefertigt zu Maragha*, Dresden, 1873).
L = London Globe (Dorn, *Description of an Arabic Celestial Globe*, in the *Transactions of the Royal Asiatic Society*, 1829, II, pp. 371–92).

Fig. 465. Hercules.

Fig. 466. Part of Coma Berenices.

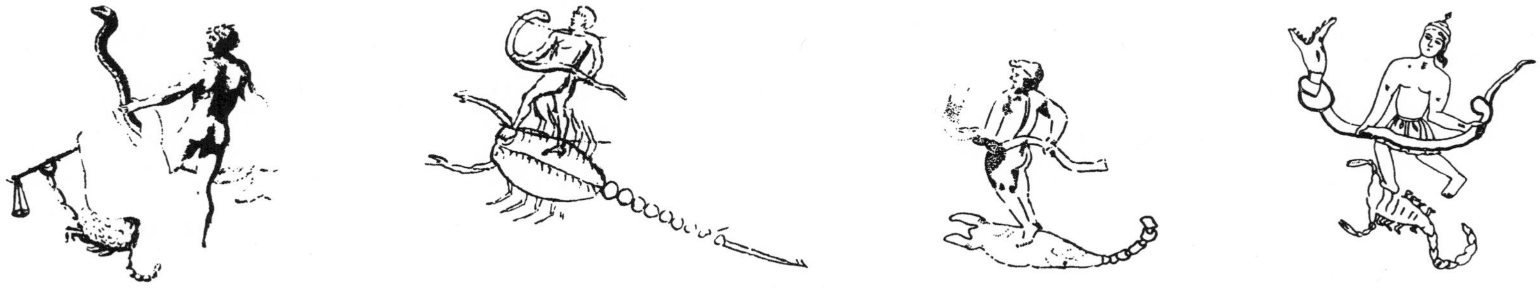

Fig. 467. Serpentarius.

Fig. 468. Aquila.

Fig. 469. Cygnus.

THE ASTRONOMICAL REPRESENTATIONS OF QUṢAYR ʿAMRA COMPARED WITH CLASSICAL AND MEDIEVAL EXAMPLES

By means of an astronomical error and various peculiarities of our picture we are enabled to go beyond such general comparisons and to refer to a specific group of Greek manuscripts which the artist of Quṣayr ʻAmra must have known. One of the most striking astrothetical errors of the fresco is that Hercules appears, not between Bootes and Ophiuthos, but after them. In Codex Vat. graec. 1087 (fifteenth century) is a Greek map of the heavens which has exactly the same error. The sources for some of its examples, however, are preserved in a Ptolemy manuscript of the beginning of the ninth century, which is also to be found in the Vatican Library (Codex Vat. gr. 1291), and a comparison of original and copy shows that the copyist usually did his work with care. We may then assume that our error already existed in the Greek maps of the heavens in the early Middle Ages (probably already in late antiquity).[1]

In the same late manuscript we find the explanation of a peculiar formation (an explanation which the author for a long time was unable to find). A figure appears above the tail of Leo which looks like a large conventionalized leaf (Fig. 466). There is nothing similar at the corresponding place on the Farnese Globe, nor is there anything of the sort in the Latin manuscripts of the Middle Ages or on the later Arabic globes. In the Greek Ptolemy, however, there appears just over Leo the design of a leaf: it is a part of the constellation of Berenice's hair, which Ptolemy describes as an ivy leaf and places above the tail of Leo.

If one now compares the remaining figures of our fresco with these two affiliated Greek manuscripts, further parallels appear. As in the manuscripts, so, too, in Quṣayr ʻAmra, Canis Minor stands with lifted tail by the foot of the Twins (Fig. 461), and the relation of Lepus to Orion is also very similar in both (Fig. 462). As in the Greek map of the heavens, so also in Quṣayr ʻAmra, Serpentarius (Fig. 467) stands with both legs on Scorpion—on the Farnese Globe only one leg rests on the zodiacal sign—and Hercules (Fig. 465) is lifting a club, while on the Farnese Globe, as in the older tradition, he is represented only as a kneeling man without attributes.

This similarity between the Greek manuscripts and the Arabic fresco is repeated in the constellation of Aquila (Fig. 468). The usual representation of Aquila is full-face; he is represented thus not only on the classical globe, but also in the majority of the medieval astrological manuscripts. But, on our fresco and in the Greek manuscript, Aquila is presented in profile. In addition, the representations of Cygnus (Fig. 469) are similar in even the smallest details. Were it still possible to doubt that there is a direct connexion between our fresco and the manuscripts of the Vatican, it would be answered by the figure of Aquarius (Fig. 470). The remaining fragments show a figure holding an urn upside-down with the left hand, with a piece of a garment on a level with the right shoulder. In the Greek manuscript of the fifteenth century we invariably find the upheld urn, the right hand lifted and behind it the fluttering garment. This differs from Quṣayr ʻAmra; but, in the Ptolemy manuscript of the ninth century, we find the figure which makes it possible to reconstruct the Quṣayr ʻAmra fragment. Aquarius empties the urn with one hand, the other hand is lifted and from it hangs the garment, of which a fragment still remains on the dome. If the remains of the fresco become thus explicable from these manuscripts, it is no longer possible to doubt that the stellar pictures preserved in the two manuscripts of the Vatican must have been related to the source used by the painter of the dome.

So much for the basic Greek character of the work. But to what extent is it medieval?

Generally speaking, there are three figures which differ from those known to us in the Greek map of the stars, but which thoroughly coincide with those of the later Oriental globes.[2] They are the figures of Cepheus (Fig. 471), Bootes (Fig. 472), and Orion (Fig. 462).

In the fresco Cepheus is represented *kneeling* and with uplifted arms, but on the Farnese Globe, as well as in our Greek manuscripts, as standing and with arms outspread. If, on the other hand, one considers the figure on the famous Dresden Globe of 1279,[3] Cepheus is found to have the same position as in the fresco, although in this representation the head, with its peculiarly formed hair, is still reminiscent of the figure on the Farnese Globe.

[1] These correspondences of the map in the fifteenth-century manuscript with the fresco of Quṣayr ʻAmra point also to the fact that the copyist of the manuscript worked carefully.

[2] E. L. Stevenson, *Terrestrial and Celestial Globes*, New Haven, 1921: cf. also Saxl, *Verzeichnis astrol. u. mythol. ill. Hss. des lat. Mittelalters, II.* (*National-Bibliothek in Wien*), in the *Sitzungsberichte d. Heidelberger Akad. d. Wissenschaften, Phil.-hist. Kl.*, Jahrg. 1925/6, 2. Abh., Heidelberg, 1927, pp. 180 f. (Cod. Vind. 2563, 2583*.)

[3] Drechsler, *op. cit.*

Fig. 470. Aquarius.

Fig. 471. Cepheus.

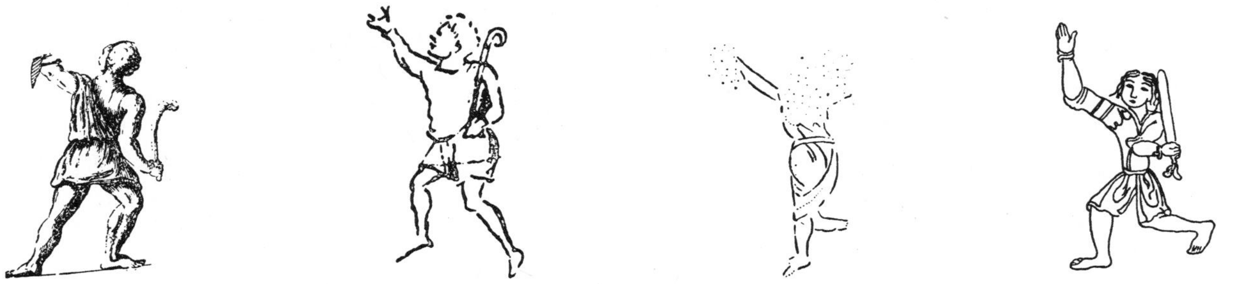

Fig. 472. Bootes.

Fig. 473. Sagittarius.

The Bootes in Quṣayr ʿAmra has one leg raised; in the Greek representation he appears with both feet on the ground, whereas on the Dresden Globe he is represented as in Quṣayr ʿAmra.

In the Greek representation Orion stands (cf. Cod. Vat.) or kneels (Farnese Globe). In Quṣayr ʿAmra and on the Dresden Globe he is shown with one leg bent and Lepus is placed beneath this leg.

These correspondences are certainly not accidental. The classically rounded motifs of motion are transformed into severe and inorganic rigidity. Quṣayr ʿAmra is clearly a connecting link between the classical style and that of the late Middle Ages in the East.

This interesting and important phenomenon of the slow recoining of forms, of the orientalization of the Greek plastic feeling, is perhaps best observable in the figure of Sagittarius (Fig. 473). He is represented in such a way that he does not shoot in the direction in which he is going, but backwards.

This position, since it is also to be found on a late Carolingian ivory relief of the tenth century and in Occidental manuscripts,[1] is by no means an invention of our painter. The peculiarity of the figure is only that the garment which flutters from his shoulders, and which is traceable to genuine classical sources (in the manuscript of the Vatican it is represented as a skin), does not flutter backwards but, illogically, in the direction in which he is going (to the right). The section of the shoulders with the bow and the fluttering garment corresponds to *one* Greek picture, the lower part of the body is arranged in accordance with *another* classical tradition in the opposite direction; so that Sagittarius shoots backward while his garment flutters forward.

Thus considered, the constellations in the dome of Quṣayr ʿAmra form a highly instructive document for the early medieval astronomy of the East. Into a system of strictly scientific origin, figures are introduced unscientifically and inexactly. The order of the stars is represented as anti-clockwise in relation to reality. The single figures, however, must have been copied almost exactly from a Greek manuscript; changes of form show the orientalization of the types at an early stage, and prove also that it was not a classical Greek manuscript which served as a model, but one already somewhat changed, which elsewhere, at a later date, led to the rise of the 'Arabic' types of constellations. It is not simply that the painter used his model with artistic freedom; rather he copied a scientific model without understanding it; for he certainly possessed a leaning towards exact science as well as the artistic ability to reproduce with accuracy.

Thus far—but only thus far—the fresco is related to the western astronomical manuscripts of the early Middle Ages. For the authors of the latter also copied, with intended accuracy but with actual errors from their models, the classical pictures of the stars, and they, too, executed their copies from astronomical models without any actual observation of the heavens.

However, the essential difference between East and West is that the manuscripts which the Latin medievalists copied consisted of those handbooks which Roman scholars had, in their turn, copied for their own use from the mass of scientific—and therefore Greek—material. These astronomical handbooks were already in a half-popular mythological, half-scientific astronomical style. The East, on the other hand—and this again is shown very clearly by the reconstruction of Quṣayr ʿAmra—copied directly from the scientific Greek models.

And although the provincial painter of Quṣayr ʿAmra may have copied his model with little understanding, he, nevertheless, lived in a province in which Sebōkht, a few decades earlier, had written his scholarly text-books of astronomy, based upon Greek sources.[2] There is the same difference between the astronomical cupola of Quṣayr ʿAmra and the astronomical manuscripts of the early Middle Ages as between the works of a Sebōkht and those of a Bede. Sebōkht writes in order to acquire, and to propagate, astronomical knowledge; Bede wishes to save a part of the literary heritage from ancient Rome for the new civilization of the West in order to give them the cultural background, which will enable them to understand the Christian doctrines. For him culture is not an end in itself, but a pedagogically religious task.

It was, however, fifty years after the painting of Quṣayr ʿAmra that the great astronomical researches

[1] This form becomes typical in the East later on.

[2] Anton Baumstark, *Geschichte der syrischen Literatur*, Bonn, 1922, pp. 246 f.

were made in the Arabic language. In fact, the pictures of our fresco are in content not yet under eastern influence. Hercules has not yet, as later in the Arabic manuscripts,[1] a scythe in his hand, but still retains the club. Andromeda is represented without the fish over the upper part of her body, etc. The cupola of Quṣayr ʿAmra is *Greek in the late classical sense of the term*. And it is only because the later medieval art and science of the East is based on this very phase that we find *also* later in the East those changes from the classical period which are already to be seen in Quṣayr ʿAmra. Thus we can clearly recognize in what manner the representation of the constellations in the dome of Quṣayr ʿAmra is to be considered as a connecting link between the late classical period and Islam.

[1] Paris, Bibl. Nat., MS. Arabe 5036 (ʿAbd ar-Raḥmān aṣ-Ṣūfī), reproduced in E. Blochet, *Les Enluminures des mss. orienteaux* Paris, 1926, pl. 39.

THE ASTRONOMICAL SIGNIFICANCE OF THE ZODIAC OF QUṢAYR ʿAMRA

BY THE LATE ARTHUR BEER

(1) *Basis of the Problem.* The most important tasks presented to the astronomer by a study of the cupola fresco in Quṣayr ʿAmra are:

(i) Discovery of the errors in representation in so far as they are related to the astronomically fixed positions of the stellar constellations; (ii) Interpretation of the curves and circles and discussion of the systems of co-ordinates used; (iii) Attempt to derive the date of the work from the positions of the stars.

Since the photograph made by Mr. Creswell (Plate 76 *a*) of the interior of the dome (with a Zeiss Double Protar, *f* 18·5 cm.; height above the ground, 1·60–1·65 m.) was not taken from a quite central position there resulted a distortion of size within the various figures as well as in the systems of circles. However, it was possible to eliminate these perspective distortions by means of an aerotopograph.[1] The reconstruction of the figures in Plate 76 *b* is based on the perspectively readjusted photograph so obtained.

(2) *Chart of comparison and stellar positions.* In order to make as complete an astronomical criticism as possible of the dome fresco, it was necessary to have an exact representation of the heavens as they must have appeared to an observer at Quṣayr ʿAmra in the year A. D. 700 (cf. pp. 400–401).

It might have seemed plausible to draw this actual picture of the heavens in the same projection which the photograph of the cupola presented. However, the study of the fresco made it clear that the painter had not been bound by the heavens as they really were, but had rather used models based on the northern heavens. Were the former the case, he would have had to include the southern heavens, down to a declination of almost minus 60 degrees (−58·2°), whereas, in reality, he barely took the constellations down to minus 40 degrees.[2] But had he portrayed the actual heavens, the result—on the inner surface of the hemisphere—would have been of even more distorted proportions than it now is; for on the surface of such a dome, with the celestial pole as the central point, there is just place for the northern heavens down to the equator; thus, it would have been useless to compare the photograph of the dome with a reconstruction of the heavens in spherical perspective.

Instead of this, there was needed a celestial chart with the usual means of orientation and including all auxiliary circles and facts for determining:

(i) The exact equatorial co-ordinates of the stars (Right Ascension R, Declination D); (ii) the exact ecliptical co-ordinates of the stars (Longitude L, Latitude B); (iii) that part of the heavens visible above the horizon in Quṣayr ʿAmra, so constructed as to serve for the various hours and days of the year; (iv) the stellar figures which are to be drawn in conventional forms based on those in representations of the same period as those of Quṣayr ʿAmra.

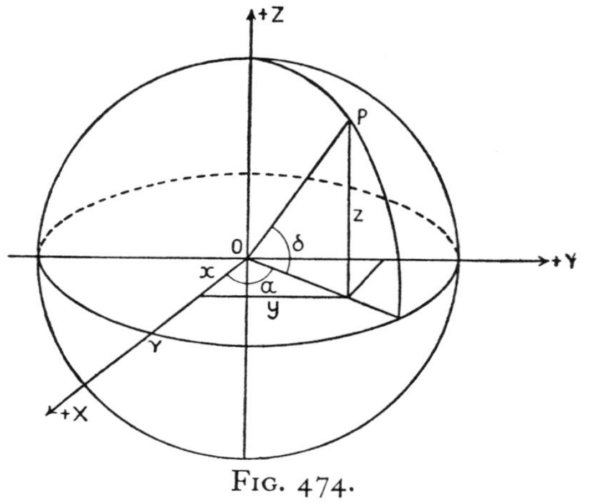

FIG. 474.

Although the method of projection to be chosen was indifferent for the purposes enumerated, it was nevertheless preferable to choose one which would not accentuate the unsatisfactory features (to a certain extent unavoidable) of the scale drawing, and, particularly, one which did not compress the polar region too greatly. The choice was: equidistant representation of the circles of declination, which are to be taken up to about minus 70 degrees; the north pole in the centre as in the fresco; the hour-circles from 40 minutes to 40 minutes in Right Ascension, radiating in straight lines; laterally, corresponding to the 'obliquity' of the ecliptic, the pole of the ecliptic, and, through this, the curves for the circles of ecliptic longitude. The result is reproduced in the drawing (Fig. 477).

The theoretical basis is as follows:

Let P be a point of the celestial sphere (Fig. 474). A rectangular system of co-ordinates is so placed that the XY-plane coincides with the plane of the Equator, the Z-axis pointing towards the celestial north pole. Further, let the

[1] The system of R. Hugershoff was used by courtesy of the 'Hamburger Luftbild G.m.b.H.' in the aerodrome, Hamburg.

[2] This is, however, only valid as a general statement; at certain points one could believe the fresco to be the copy of an almost North European picture of the heavens, but there are also constellations represented there which can first be seen in the Mediterranean or even farther to the south, as, for instance, the 'Corona austrina', the entire 'Vela', the 'Ara' (more than −55° declination), etc. It is therefore clear that the section of the horizon reproduced there combines constellations which are not all visible from the same spot.

$+X$-axis lie in the direction of the point ♈, i.e. the vernal equinox. Then, the angle δ expresses the declination and α the right ascension of the star P, and therefore the rectangular co-ordinates of P will be:

$$(1)\quad x = \cos\delta . \cos\alpha;\ y = \cos\delta . \sin\alpha;\ z = \sin\delta.$$

All points whose co-ordinates satisfy this equation (1) and for which δ and α include all values between $-90° \leqq \delta \leqq +90°$ or $0° \leqq \alpha \leqq 360°$ fill the surface of the whole sphere, which is therefore represented by the equations of (1).

We are concerned with the horizon of Quṣayr 'Amra, where the geographical latitude ϕ is $31°\ 50'$: the plane E of this horizon (Fig. 475) is perpendicular to the direction of the Zenith S of Quṣayr 'Amra and passes through our point of observation O in the centre of the sphere (in Fig. 475, therefore, it passes perpendicularly on the plane of the paper through E). The line which it traces on the sphere, i.e. the line of the horizon, is to be found: Since the plane passes through the X-axis, the equation of E will be free from X and is:

$$(2)\quad \ldots z = y . \tan(90 - \phi).$$

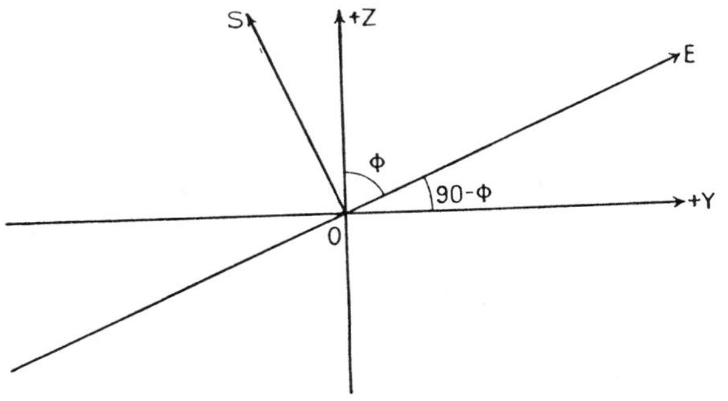

FIG. 475.

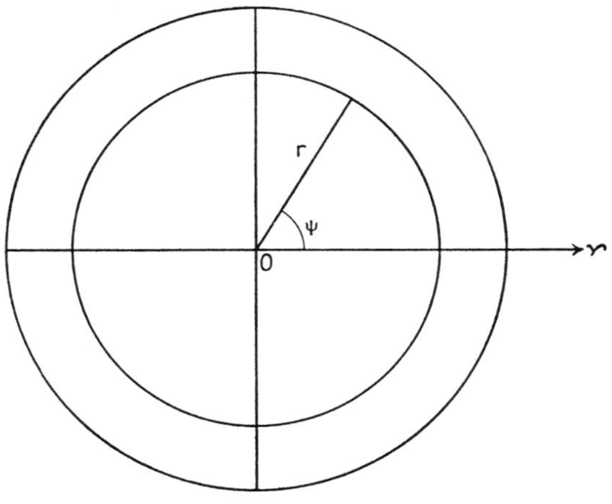

FIG. 476.

Therefore the line of the horizon must satisfy the equations (1) and (2). If the second and third equations of (1) are unified with (2) we have:

$$(3)\quad \sin\alpha = \tan\delta . \tan\phi$$

as equation of the line of the horizon. How does this affect our projection? In Fig. 476 it may be seen that: the polar angle ψ is equal to the right ascension α and the radius vector r is equal to the complementary angle of the declination δ, that is:

$$(4)\quad r = 90° - \delta;\ \psi = \alpha.$$

Whereby: $0° \leqq \psi \leqq 360°$ and $0° \leqq r \leqq 180°$ (for the north pole we have $\delta = +90°$, therefore $r = 0°$; for the equator $\delta = 0°$, therefore $r = 90°$; for the south pole $\delta = -90°$, therefore $r = 180°$). There, if (3) is transformed through unification with (4), there results the desired projection of the horizon:

$$(5)\quad \tan r = \tan\phi/\sin\psi.$$

Now the drawing was reckoned by points, proceeding from 10 to 10 degrees. Since the geographical latitude of Quṣayr 'Amra is 31·8°, $\tan\phi = 0{\cdot}620$. The r-values correspond to one another in the single quadrants, symmetrically or supplementarily.

By means of the same equation (5) we also get immediately the line of the ecliptic on our chart. For this results from just such a cut on the sphere by a plane, except that this plane is inclined not to $(90° - \phi)$ but to the 'obliquity of the ecliptic' ϵ to the $X\Upsilon$-plane, i.e. the equator. Thus, in equation (5) it is only necessary to replace ϕ by $(90° - \epsilon)$, whereby there results:

$$(6)\quad \ldots \tan r = \cot\epsilon/\sin\psi.$$

In the year A. D. 700 we have $\epsilon = 23°\ 36{\cdot}6'$, therefore $\cot\epsilon = 2{\cdot}288$.

The curves of the ecliptical longitude from 30 to 30 degrees can be found analogously, by the cut of a complex of planes with the sphere, whereby the single planes are determined first by the pole of the ecliptic ($\alpha = 270°$, $\delta = 66{\cdot}5°$) and, each in turn, by a straight line going from the centre of the sphere to a point of the ecliptic, the angular distance of which, counted from the ♈-line of nodes, is $30\,n$ degrees, where $n = 1, 2, \ldots 12$. The orientation of the horizon of Quṣayr 'Amra chosen on the chart (Fig. 477) is made clear by the facts written on the outer edge: that part of the heavens which lies within the horizon-oval was to be seen in Quṣayr 'Amra at the date of the winter solstice, at midnight on December 21, A. D. 700—the ecliptic is then exactly between its two nodes above the horizon, the ♈-point is just disappearing in the west, the ♎-point just appearing in the east. The same image of the heavens was visible on September 23 at noon, on March 21 at 6 o'clock in the evening, and on June 21 at 6 o'clock in the morning.

It was now necessary to place the stars in this basic network. In order to get as close a connexion as possible between the figures of Quṣayr 'Amra and their models, all stars visible above the horizon of Quṣayr 'Amra in A. D. 700, for which ephemerides were available,[1] were used. On the whole, 291 exact positions could be thus reckoned. But these

[1] Neugebauer, P. V., *Tafeln zur astronomischen Chronologie, I.: Sterntafeln*, Leipzig, 1912.

proved in many cases insufficient, so that 119 further positions were included, by means of alignments between the neighbouring stars (these latter positions are marked in Fig. 477 and Fig. 479 by the signs ● and ○). Finally about 400 stellar positions were so obtained. All stars of the third magnitude or brighter ($\leqq$ 3·0 m.) are included, and in about 100 cases those of lesser magnitude.

(3) *Discussion of the reconstructed picture of the heavens*. In the reproduction in Fig. 477 all facts have been included which are necessary for an astronomical reconstruction of the network. Thus, the various stars can be related to the ecliptic system as well as to that of the equator. Longitude, declination, and right ascension are made clear. The horizon and its uttermost limits are included. The various constellations are given in their abbreviations; the stars themselves are marked with their designation according to Bayer or Flamsteed. The figure itself contains the necessary explanation of the circles, polar-points, etc.

Of the 71 constellations (according to the modern method of division), which must have been visible in Quṣayr ʿAmra at that time, there are only 37, entire or in more or less large fragments, to be recognized in the fresco. Now there is no pictorial reproduction to be found in contemporary representations for the following 23 out of the 34 constellations lacking in the fresco:

Antlia (Ant), Caelium (Cae), Camelopardalis (Cam), Canis Venaticorum (CVn), Columba (Col), Crux (Cru), Doradus (Dor), Fornax (For), Grus (Gru), Horologium (Hor), Indus (Ind), Lacerta (Lac), Leo Minor (LMi), Lynx (Lyn), Microscopicum (Mic), Monoceros (Mon), Norma (Nor), Phoenix (Phe), Sculptor (Scl), Scutum (Sct), Telescopium (Tel), Triangulum (Tri), Vulpecula (Vul).

For the remaining 11 constellations, however, which are lacking in the fresco, such a representation was to be expected. Thus, they were probably lost by the partial destruction of the ceiling. These are:

Aries (Ari), Cepheus (Cep), Canis Major (CMa), Corona Borealis (CrB), Equulei (Equ), Libra (Lib), Lupus (Lup), Pegasus (Peg), Perseus (Per), Piscis Austrinus (PsA), Sagitta (Sge).

The reproduction given in Fig. 478 was gained by emphasizing in the theoretical chart those sections which correspond to the remaining parts of the fresco. The system of circles corresponds to the results of §§ 4 and 5; the values found there are included in the drawing.

Variations of the Quṣayr ʿAmra fresco (Plate 76 *b*) from the actual image of the heavens (Fig. 478) may be divided into two groups: those which concern the figures themselves, and those which affect the relative position to one another.

The most obvious variations within the figures in Quṣayr ʿAmra from those representations chosen for comparison[1] and our reconstruction in Fig. 478 are as follows:

And. In Quṣayr ʿAmra the body of the figure is turned in the opposite direction to that in which it is looking. Moreover, left and right are interchanged. Cf. § 4. (Andromeda.)

Aqr. Body itself held erect instead of slanting in the belt of the ecliptic. Cf. § 4. (Aquarius.)

Aql. The second wing is obviously not drawn (cf. Cod. Vat. gr. 1291). (Aquila.)

Arg. The size of the ship, particularly of the sail, is much too small. (Argo.)

Aur. In Cod. 1036, Geber, Paris, Bibl. de l'Arsenal, the designations of the stars 8 and 9 are interchanged, as compared with the description of Ptolemy.[2] (Auriga.)

Boo. Cf. § 4. (Bootes.)

Cas. The position of the body is more upright in Cod. 1036; in Quṣayr ʿAmra it has perhaps been adapted to the seat of the throne. Cf. § 4. The interpretation of this figure as Cas is uncertain. It has been so designated provisionally here, whereas in the study of Professor Saxl (above, p. 426) this figure was definitely considered as Cep. At any rate, one of the two figures is lacking and since the figure given is next to Dra in the fresco, it would be plausible to assume that it is Cep. Moreover, the fragment of the painting might allow one to deduce a masculine figure (Cep) rather than a feminine one (Cas). The reason nevertheless for assuming here that the figure is Cas has its basis only in the astronomical determination of the outlines of the figure. According to Ptolemy[2] the stellar field, ϵ Cep-λ Cep, fills a high tiara, which is as little to be reconciled with the fresco fragments as the position of the stars γ and κ. (Cassiopeia.)

Cen. A part of the Centaur's cloak blows backward into the region of Corvus. (Centaurus.)

CMi. Cf. § 4. (Canis Minor.)

[1] Paris, Bibl. de l'Arsenal, MS. 1036, s. XIII (Geber); Paris, Bibl. Nat., MS. Arabe 5036 (Sûfi); Dorn, B., *Description of an Arabic Celestial Globe*, in *Transactions of the Royal Asiatic Society*, London, 1830, II, pp. 371–92; Paris, Bibl. Nat., Kufic Planisphere in bronze, (s. XI); Drechsler, Adolph, *Der arabische Himmels-Globus angefertigt 1279 zu Maragha, von Muhammed bin Muwayid Elardhi*, Dresden, 1873; *Orbis Caelestis Tabūla / Ex marmore antiquō / in Aedibūs Farnes: / Romae*, in *M. Manilii Astronomicon ex rec. . . . R. Bentleii*, Londini, 1739, post p. xvi; Planisphere, from Cod. Vat. graec. 1087; Saxl, Fritz, *Verzeichnis astrologischer und mythologischer ill. Hss. des lat. MA. I., II.*, in *Sitzungsber. der Heidelberger Akad. d. Wiss.*, 1915 and 1925/6; Thiele (Georg), *Antike Himmelsbilder*, Berlin, 1898.

[2] *Des Claudius Ptolemäus' Handbuch der Astronomie*, II. Band, ed. K. Manitius, Leipzig, 1913.

Cnc. In the picture of Cancer right and left are interchanged. Its claw ought to be open in the direction of Leo's head. (There remains little available apart from the position of θ Cnc.) Cf. § 4. (Cancer.)

Com. In Quṣayr 'Amra the figure of the leaf shows signs of being held by Vir. This would correspond to the charts in the *Description of an Arabic Celestical Globe* and *Der arabische Himmels-Globus . . .* (see n. 1 on p. 434) (Coma Berenices).

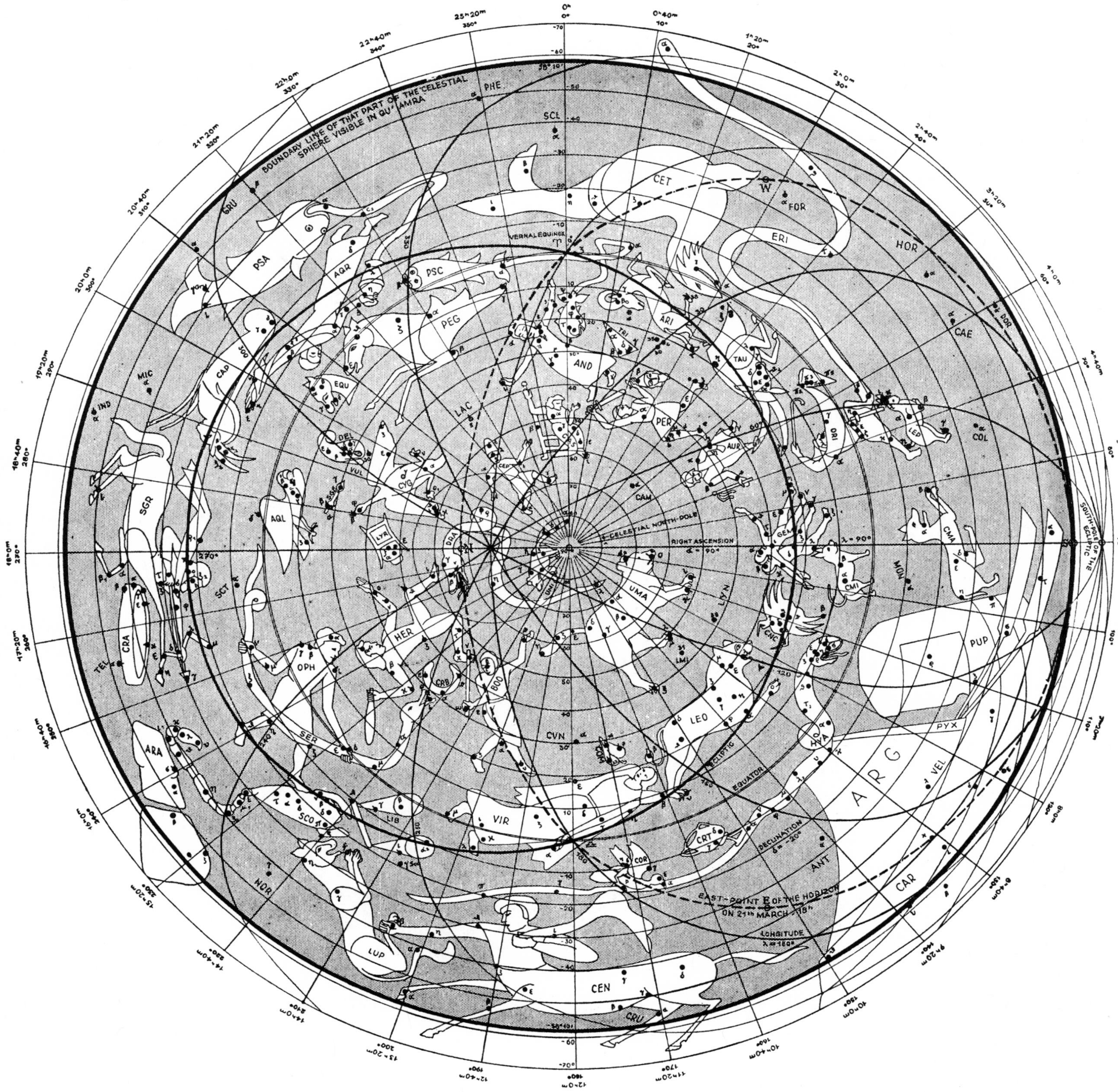

FIG. 477. A theoretical chart of that part of the celestial sphere visible in A.D. 700 at Quṣayr 'Amra.

CrA. The picture in Quṣayr 'Amra shows the crown seen from the side, elsewhere it generally appears as seen from above. Cf. § 4. (Corona Austr.)

Cor. Right and left interchanged. (Corvus.)

Dra. The knots in the body of the dragon, which appear in all other sources, are obviously lacking in Quṣayr 'Amra. (Draco.)

Gem. In the position of the feet, left and right are interchanged as compared with Ptolemy (see n. 2 on p. 434). Cf. § 4. (Gemini.)

Her. Left and right interchanged. Cf. § 4. (Hercules.)

Hya. Hydra's head is much too far in the south. It ought to be raised far above the equator. (The painter obviously wanted to bring the Hydra into correct connexion with the sail of Arg which is much too small.) Here, too, the knots in the body are lacking, although Ptolemy (see n. 2 on p. 434) suggests them in his description. Cf. § 4. (Hydra.)

Leo. Cf. § 4. (Leo.)

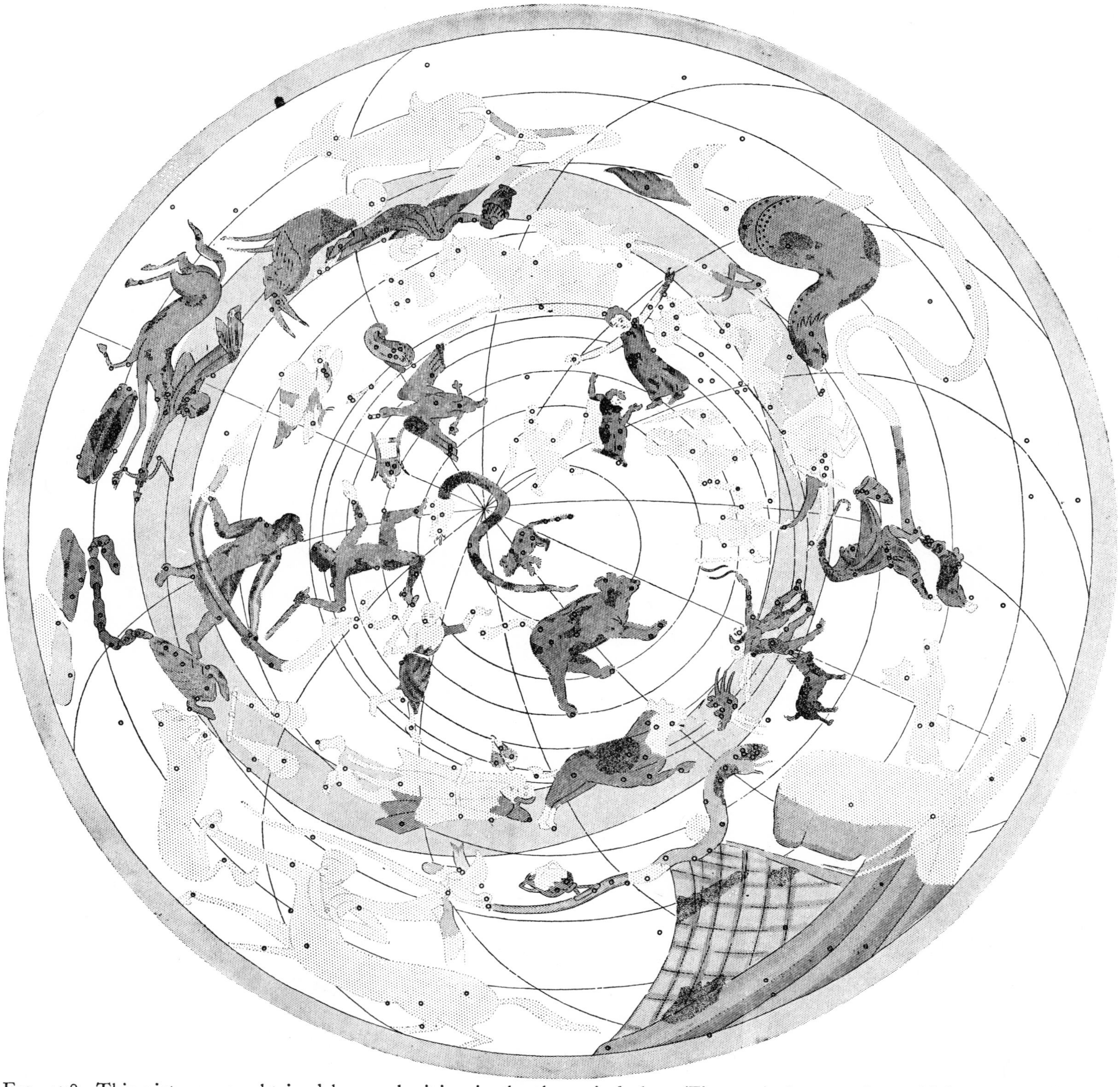

FIG. 478. This picture was obtained by emphasizing in the theoretical chart (Fig. 477) those sections which correspond to the remaining parts of the fresco.

Lyr. Cf. § 4. (Lyra.)

Oph. Different position of the body. In Quṣayr 'Amra, seen from the back, legs interchanged. Moreover, according to the position of the stars, Oph ought to have only one leg on Sco, while the other should reach backward to the line Club of Hercules—Tail of Scorpius! There is also variation from Cod. 1036 (see p. 434, note 1). In Quṣayr 'Amra Serpens is in front of the body of Oph! Cf. § 4. (Ophiuchus.)

Ori. Incorrectly drawn: different position of the legs (also another form of the fur, etc.); in order that the star κ Ori should reach the knee an entirely different position of the body is required. Cf. § 4. (Orion.)

Psc. Line is knotted. Cf. § 4. (Pisces.)

Sco. Cf. § 4. (Scorpius.)

Ser. In Quṣayr 'Amra Serpens is much drawn out. Cf. § 4. (Serpens.)

Sgr. The upper part of the body is correct from the point of view of a stellar chart, whereas the entire lower part of the body is turned, with an exchange of right and left. The horse must be turned around the line $L_{10} = 270°$ that Sgr may have $L = 285°$ instead of $255°$. (Sagittarius.)

Tau. Cf. § 4. (Taurus.)

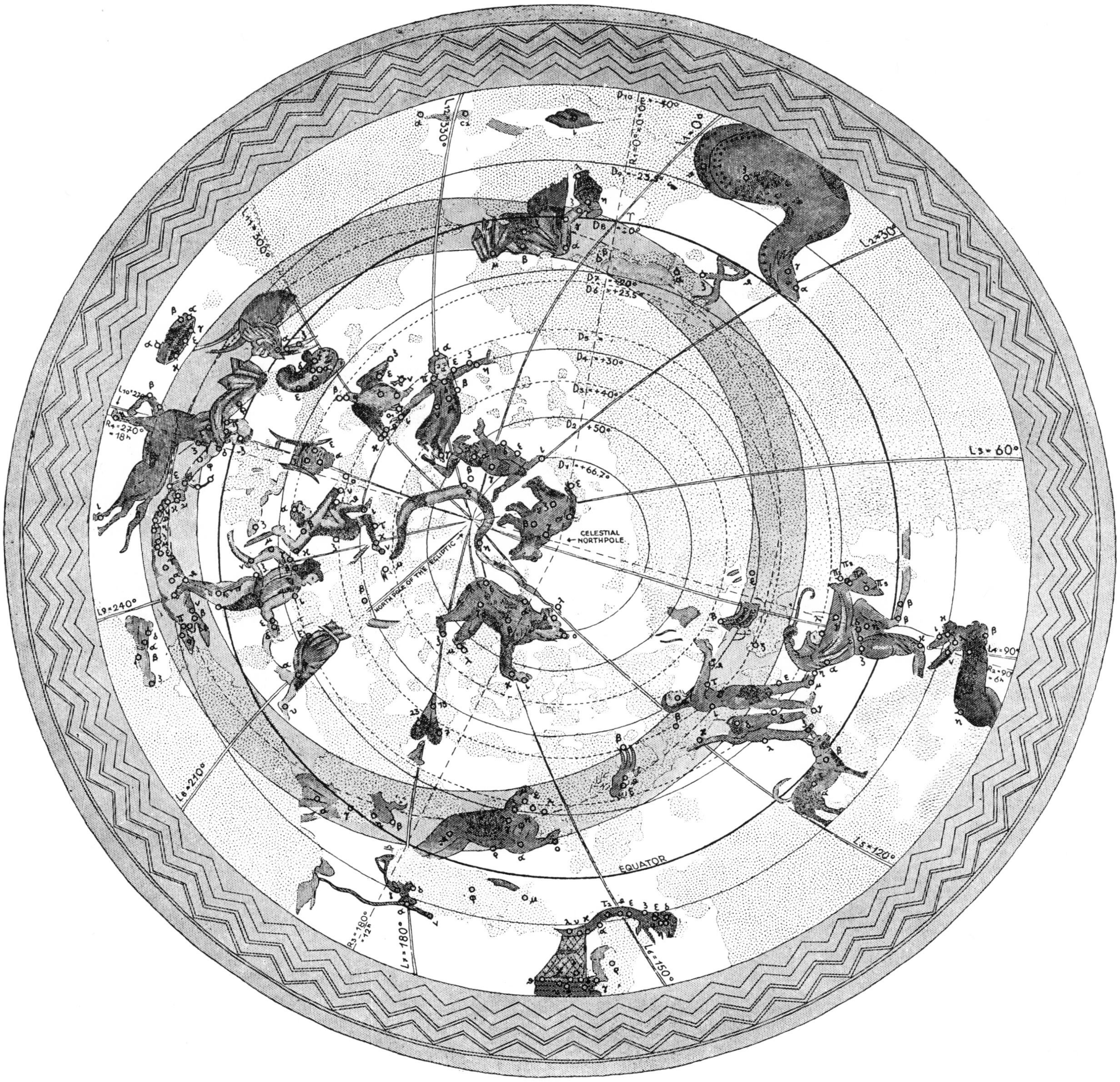

FIG. 479. Interpretation of the systems of circles and restoration of the missing co-ordinates.

UMa. The tail of Ursus is turned downward (it seems certain that it was never contained in the gap of the painting above the body) instead of being held horizontally as is necessary in order to include the stars η, ζ, ϵ. The hind paws, too, are incorrectly shortened. (Ursa Major.)

UMi. Left and right interchanged and the position turned. Cf. § 4. (Ursa Minor.)

Vir. Cf. § 4. (Virgo.)

(4) *Interpretation of the ecliptical system.* The stars of Fig. 477 were introduced into the reconstructed Quṣayr ʿAmra photograph (i.e. Plate 76), taking care to adapt them to the situation of the figures, as far as possible. There resulted Fig. 479. Naturally, a certain freedom was unavoidable. Thus, for

instance, in Her the stars had to be fitted into the picture with 'anatomic correctness' and without regard for those Ptolemaic designations of left and right, which are interchanged (cf. § 3), &c.

In order to identify the 12 curves of longitude *L* 1, *L* 2 . . . *L* 12, which are drawn at distances of 30 degrees from one another, we shall try to compare the constellations in Fig. 478 and Fig. 479 starting, at the vernal equinox ♈ and going along the ecliptical zone.[1] In Fig. 479 the curve $L\,1 = 0°$ passes not far from the star β Psc. In Fig. 478 (the calculated chart), however, β Psc lies exactly on $L = 330°$. Thus, there is already here, in Psc a longitudinal difference: L_o (observed) minus L_c (computed = +30°).

Ari. The next sign of the zodiac stretches into L_c from *c.* 10–30°. Aries is missing in Quṣayr ʻAmra because of the destruction of the fresco at this point.

Tau. In Quṣayr ʻAmra from 60°–90° instead of from 30°–60°, therefore the difference $\Delta L = +30°$ remains here too.

Gem, Cnc, Leo are in like manner pushed about 30° ahead.

Vir. Beginning here, the effort of the painter to compress the space becomes clear. He shortens Vir from $L_c = (155–200°)$ to $L_o = (180–215°)$, that is, by about 10°.

Lib. The picture is lacking because of a gap.

Sco. Should extend between 220° and 250°: in Quṣayr ʻAmra the body begins at 235° (that is +15 ahead). But it becomes much too long even though the tail with the sting is again greatly shortened (so much that there is no place left for some of the Ptolemaic stars of the joints of the body); thus Scorpius reaches to nearly 260°.

Sgr. Order is restored, of course, only in so far as the upper part of the body is concerned (see § 3).

Cap. Also of correct position in longitude. (Capricornus.)

Aqr. Begins suddenly at 335° instead of 305°; with λ Aqr it reaches to about 355° instead of 325°, that is the longitudinal system has jumped ahead again by 30°, and that is just the difference which was noticed in the case of β Psc (see above) which is now directly adjoining.

Thus it becomes clear that the entire fresco, with the exception of the narrow sectors at about $L = 240°–300°$ and at $L = 0°–30°$, is greatly changed in position and figure. This change affects, of course, the latitude as well as the declination. Since the 'window-sections' were seemingly left out in part (§ 6), the painter had difficulty in including all of the figures, which led to omissions as well as to distortions. The most essential of these errors are contained in the following list (whereby *L* and *D* refer to the co-ordinates of the original fresco in Fig. 479).

And. The longitudinal axes of the figures must be turned about −60° into the longitudinal circle $L = 0°$.
Aql. $L+20°$. Cf. Her.
Aqr. $L-30°$.
Boo. Cf. Her.
Cas. Turn the axis on +90°; $L+30°$!
CMi. $L+15°$, $D+10°$.
Cnc. $L-30°$.
CrA. $L-15°$ (this false position of CrA in Quṣayr ʻAmra corresponds to the partial distortion of Sgr (§ 3)!).
Cyg. $D+15°$. (Cygnus.)
Del. $D+10°$. (Delphinus.)
Dra. The head of the dragon which ought to lie between the foot of Her and UMa is about 30° behind in *L* in Quṣayr ʻAmra.
Gem. $L-30°$.
Her. Turn the longitudinal axis about −20°. The correct sequence (see, for instance, Drechsler, *op. cit.*) is: Boo-Her-Oph, whereas in Quṣayr ʻAmra it is Boo-Oph-Her! —Oph, however, should have been placed slanting downward, instead of standing upright on Sco. Then *L* at Aql would have been pushed over the necessary +20°, and between Boo and Her there would have been the space necessary for CrB and the head of Hya, instead of Oph now falsely placed there.
Hya. *D* of the head +15°!
Leo. $L-30°$.
Lyr. Turn axis through −45°; $D+10°$.
Oph. $L+15°$; $D-10°$; (ν Oph).—Cf. Her.
Ori. $D-10°$.

[1] In order to find the circle of the ecliptic one would naturally look for the ♈-point (i. e. Aries-point), that is the point where, according to definition, the three circles $D\,8 = 0$ (equator), $B = 0$ (ecliptic), and $L\,1 = 0$ (circle of longitude 0) intersect. In other words, the ecliptic ought to pass through the two points of intersection of the equator and the zero-circle of longitude, which lie diametrically on the sphere. But in the fresco of Quṣayr ʻAmra only the more southern of the two limiting circles of latitude of the ecliptic belt pass through these two 'solstices-points', and not the middle line of the belt. So it would seem that the painter had no understanding of the meaning of this belt of the ecliptic, which ought to limit the irregularities of the planets and the moon on either side. Instead of tracing the belt of the ecliptic at a width of 8 or 10 degrees on either side of the ecliptic, the painter—perhaps in order to save space—drew it at its full width on the northern side of the ecliptic.

Psc. $L-30°$.
Sco. $L-10°$.
Ser. Distortion in position in connexion with Oph.
Tau. $L-30°$.
UMi. Turn$+30°$ around an axis connecting the snout with the joint of body and tail; interchange right and left! (Thereby the standing-basis of UMi is only slightly inclined toward the backline of UMa, whereas in Quṣayr ʻAmra it is perpendicular to it!)
Vir. $L-15°$.

(5) *Interpretation of the equatorial system.* The circles of declination are visible in the fresco in unequal degrees of clearness—partly sharp, partly washed out—so that one might at first assume that the genuine circles of declination were mixed with auxiliary lines or with a basically designed network which was inadequately erased afterwards. This impression is increased by the irregularity of the distances between these circles.

After many attempts,[1] the only possible solution seemed to me to be the relation of the positions of the circles to the positions of the neighbouring stars. The necessary facts can be derived from Fig. 479.

*D*1 = 66·7°. This *D*-circle is clearly the polar-circle about the ecliptic-pole. By taking the mean of the declinations and by combining the positions of neighbouring stars there resulted: (*D*) = 63·9° (by means of ι Cas, Ecl.-Pole, κ Dra, β Dra, δ UMa, o UMa).

*D*2 = 50°. There results (*D*) = 49·8° (by means of γ And, α Cas, ξ UMa, γ UMa, κ UMa, o UMa, λ UMa).

*D*3 = 40°. There results (*D*) = 40·9° (by means of γ And, ν And, χ Her, ξ UMa, ν Her, μ UMa, α CVn, λ UMa, 23 Com, κ UMa, ι UMa, β Tau, o UMa, ϵ Tau, θ Gem, η And, δ Cas, θ Cyg).

*D*4 = 30°. There results (*D*) = 31·9° (by means of ϵ Tau, θ Gem, α Gem, 15 Com, β Boo, ι Cyg, ι And, δ And, η And).

D 5 = xxx. This circle obviously does not belong to the final system. It is also the least clear in drawing; possibly it belongs to an original design, mentioned above. There resulted, by the way, something like (*D*) = 27° (with great distribution of the single values of ζ Tau, β Gem, 15 Com, 23 Com, ϵ And, α And, αOph, β Boo, ζ Her).

D 6 = 23·5°. There results (*D*) = 23·8° (by means of ϵ Gem, ζ Gem, θ Cnc, ϵ Cnc, μ Leo, 15 Com, 23 Com, α Her). 'Northern Tropic.'

D 7 = 20°. This results essentially from η Gem, ζ Gem, λ Gem. The use of γ Leo, ζ Leo, ϵ Boo, α Boo, μ Oph, γ Oph, because of the systematic displacement of declination of these stars towards the north, must be left out of consideration. Nevertheless, since, with so few available fixed points, the value of this circle could only be insufficiently fixed, the above value *D* 7 = 20° receives sufficient support from the neighbouring circles *D* 6 and *D* 8.

D 8 = 0°. The numerical determination of the equator resulted from the ten fixed points in Psc, Ori, CMi, Hya, Leo, Vir, Oph, Aql, Cap, Aqr, for which (in accordance with Fig. 478) we have D_c = 0. The mean of the distances (Pole—place of constellation) in Fig. 479 gave the equator-circle there marked.

D 9 = −23·5°. There results (*D*) = −18·7° (by means of κ Lep, α Cet, δ Cet, γ Crt, ρ Sco, α Sco, τ Sco, κ Sco, ζ Cet, γ Cet). 'Southern Tropic.'

D 10 = −40°. There results (*D*) = −39·9° (by means of γ Cet, ζ Cet, β Lep, λ Lep, η Lep, α Lep, γ Vel, ρ Pup, α Ara, ζ Ara, ι Sgr, η Sgr, α Tel, η CrA, α Psc, c_2 Aqr). It is, however, necessary to remember the great scattering of the positions found for this circle by means of connexion with the above stars. But since in the fresco of Quṣayr ʻAmra the permanent section of the horizon is seen absolutely without relation to reality (see p. 432, n. 2) the divergent values of these limiting declinations become comprehensible.

(6) *Cause of distortions in the Cupola and estimation of the date.* If one considers the space around 300° between Cap and Aqr—where in § 5 the most striking longitudinal distortion was noticed—it is seen that just at this place a window was pierced in the dome. It is possible that in order to include his inventory of figures, in any case, the painter placed the whole figure of Aqr on the farther side of the window, thus keeping the entire figure together, although, in order to regain a part of the space so lost, it was necessary to place the figure in an unusual and astronomically false position. The same is true for another window opening: Taurus ought to be between 30° and 60°, but, since the horns are at 90°, it obviously began at 60°. This beginning, however, should lie near to the longitudinal circle which passes through the mouth of Cetus, and that would be at 30°! Thus it seems that the space between 30° and 60° was left empty and that there has been no pictorial loss, as was feared, by the destruction of the surface at this point, but rather that the painting was distorted to avoid the window opening!

It must be clear from the preceding discussions that it would be unreasonable to try to date the

[1] Very valuable suggestions were made by Dr. W. Hartner, China-Institut, Frankfurt a/M., who attempted to take into account the real dimensions of the dome; but the available facts proved insufficient.

painting from an astronomical comparison of stellar positions. There is no space for a detailed discussion of the various attempts made for this purpose (e.g. positions of ♈-points, of α UMi, of $L = 90$, of $D = 0$, etc.). Nevertheless, the relative position of equator and ecliptic allow us to make a rough estimation of the date. A comparison of Fig. 477 and Fig. 479, especially in regard to the position of the point of intersection ♈, shows a change caused by the 'Precision' which leads back to a date between A.D. 500 and 1000, that is, a term in no period contradictory to the date historically deduced, A.D. 712–15. Since (cf. § 3 and § 4) it is impossible to control the exact date with astronomical methods, the date based upon historical research (*c.* A.D. 700) was taken as basis in this work.

ARCHITECTURAL ORIGINS

SIMILAR BATHS AT ʿABDA AND RUḤAYBA. Excluding the audience hall, the bath-houses at Quṣayr ʿAmra and Ḥammām aṣ-Ṣarakh closely follow a local type of which two pre-Muslim examples have been preserved, viz. at ʿAbda and Ruḥayba.[1] The former (Fig. 480) has been described by Musil[2] who visited it in 1898, and by Vincent[3] who examined it in 1904. The doorway X leads into a room which apparently had no other exit; Y, on the contrary, leads into a regular sequence of bathrooms, of which the first must be the *apodyterium*, B the *tepidarium*, and M the *calidarium*. The roof of the first room has fallen, but B still retains its tunnel-vault; M was covered by a dome of which only the lower part remains. Vincent restores it as a conical structure, on the analogy of the still intact dome at Ruḥayba.[4] Its most interesting feature, however, is the primitive manner in which it is set across the corners of the square (see below, p. 457). The same vertical grooves for pipes, which we have noticed in the walls of the *tepidarium* and *calidarium* at Quṣayr ʿAmra and Ḥammām aṣ-Ṣarakh, are found here also (Figs. 480–81). On the far side of the domed chamber is a tunnel-vaulted passage, D, exactly as at Quṣayr ʿAmra.

The bath at Ruḥayba,[5] known locally as Qubbat al-Bīr (Fig. 481), bears a still closer resemblance to that at Quṣayr ʿAmra. Not only are there the same number of chambers—three—but the sequence followed in the method of roofing is the same, viz. a tunnel-vault for the *apodyterium*, a cross-vault for the *tepidarium*, and a dome for the *calidarium*. Musil found a similar bath near the Roman post of al-Ḥoṣob in the Wādī al-ʿAraba.[6]

These two baths, according to Jaussen and Savignac, date from the Christian period, before the Arab conquest which sowed destruction in all the towns of the Negeb, and as the greater part of the tombstones that have been dug up in the cemeteries of Khalaṣa, Ruḥayba, and Sebaiṭa date from the second part of the sixth century, they place these baths in the same period also.[7]

At Quṣayr ʿAmra and Ḥammām aṣ-Ṣarakh, however, there is one novelty, viz. the combination of a bath-house with a hall of audience, a combination which, as Herzfeld has pointed out,[8] is not found in the pre-Muslim baths of Syria, and he asks whether this arrangement was an innovation brought from elsewhere. I think the answer is that the baths which he mentions, e.g. at Sarjillā, Bābisqā, Andarīn, Boṣrā, and Brād, were in towns, close to residences, whereas Quṣayr ʿAmra and Ḥammām aṣ-Ṣarakh are built in the open desert, so that the provision of an audience hall, in which the Khalif could hold his desert court, was quite natural.[9]

THE HYPOCAUSTS of Quṣayr ʿAmra described above are constructed on exactly the same principle as in the Baths of Caracalla (A.D. 212–16). This is how Dr. Ashby describes the latter:

'From 3 to 4 feet below the pavement of the baths, on a bed of concrete, were laid the ordinary Roman tiles (2 feet square and averaging 1¾ inches thick). On this floor were built small piers, 2 feet high, of smaller tiles, 8 inches square.

[1] ʿAbda is about thirty miles south of Beersheba, and Ruḥayba about twenty-two miles south-east of the same place. This region to-day is almost a desert.

[2] *Kuṣejr ʿAmra*, pp. 67–8 and figs. 57–9.

[3] *Revue Biblique*, N.S., I, pp. 423–4; plan, elevation, and details on p. 422; and Musil, *Arabia Petraea*, II_2, p. 106 and figs. 66–8. See also Jaussen and Savignac, *Mission archéologique en Arabie, III: Les Châteaux arabes*, p. 112.

[4] See Musil, *Kuṣejr ʿAmra*, p. 67 and fig. 50; and his *Arabia Petraea*, II_2, fig. 47.

[5] Described by Musil, *Arabia Petraea*, II_2, pp. 79–82 and figs. 46–53; and his *Kuṣejr ʿAmra*, p. 67 and figs. 49–56; see also Jaussen, Savignac, and Vincent, *Revue Biblique*, N.S., I, pl. III (6); *Les Châteaux arabes*, p. 112; and Herzfeld, *Encyclopaedia of Islām*, I, p. 337. This little building was noted by Viscount Castlereagh in 1842; *Journey to Damascus*, II, p. 76.

[6] *Kuṣejr ʿAmra*, p. 68.

[7] *Les Châteaux arabes*, p. 112.

[8] *Mshattâ, Ḥîra und Bâdiya, loc. cit.*, p. 133.

[9] Jaussen and Savignac have expressed themselves to the same effect; *Les Châteaux arabes*, p. 112.

These piers carried a concrete floor about 12 inches in thickness, on which was floated first a layer of pounded tufa and potsherds, and then a thin course of marble cement in which the mosaics were embedded or on which marble slabs were laid. The furnaces, stoked and lighted from the inner courts, were at a lower level than the hypocaust floor, and the smoke and heated air passed under the floor. . . .'[1]

The Plan of the Audience Hall. Strzygowski, basing himself on Musil's plan, compares the audience hall to a three-aisled church with apse and flanking rooms.[2] This impression, which the plan

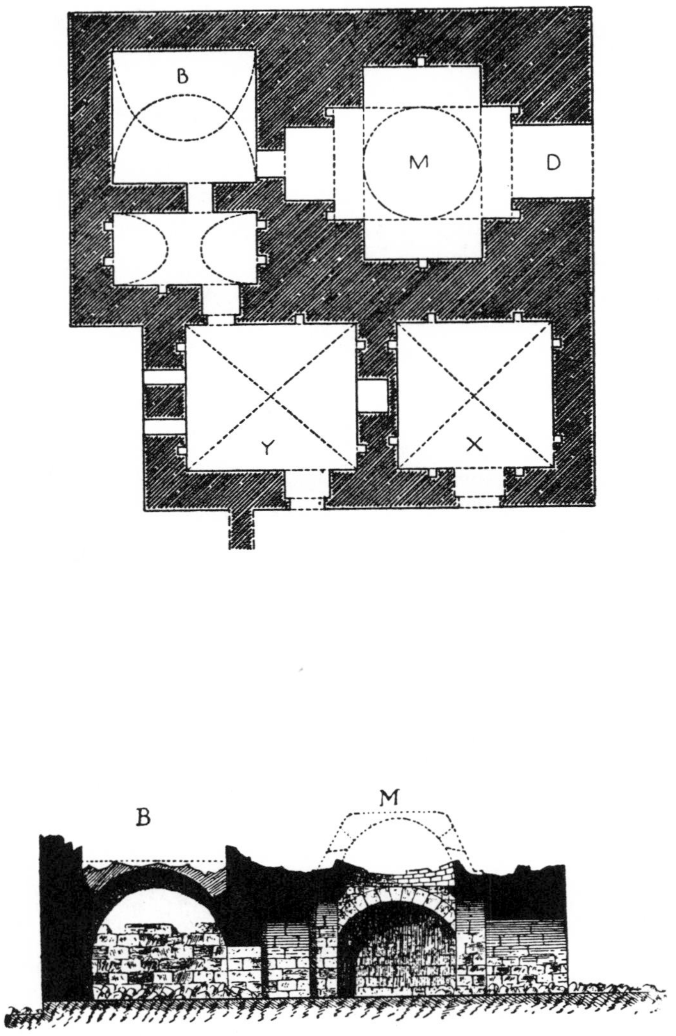

Fig. 480. 'Abda: Bath. Plan (from Musil) and section (from Vincent).

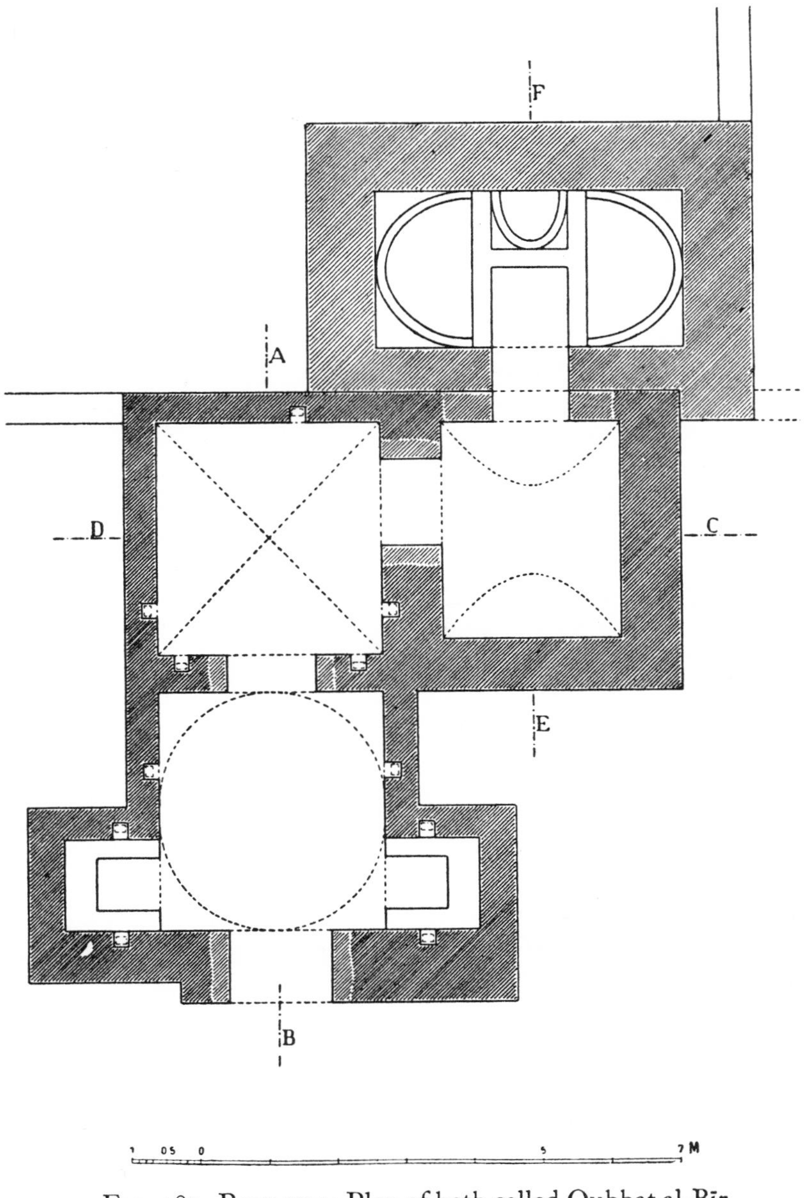

Fig. 481. Ruhayba: Plan of bath called Qubbat al-Bīr. (From Musil, *Kuṣejr 'Amra*.)

certainly gives, is erroneous, for one does not get any impression whatever of three aisles when standing in the hall. The effect produced is that of a clear interior, nearly square, without aisles, the triple division being confined to the vaulting above one's head.

The Pointed Arch. Pointed arches are arches in which the two halves are struck from a different centre. The less the separation of these two centres, the less the acuteness of the arch, all trace of a point vanishing when these two centres become one (the semicircular arch).[3]

1 Anderson and Spiers, *The Architecture of Ancient Rome*, Ashby's ed., p. 106 and pl. XVIII. This closely corresponds to the instructions given by Vitruvius, Bk. V, c. x, sect. 2: 'First the surface of the ground should be laid with tiles a foot and a half square, sloping towards the furnace . . .; thus the heat of the fire will more readily spread under the hanging flooring. Upon them, pillars made of eight-inch bricks are built, and set at such a distance apart that two-foot tiles may be used to cover them. These pillars should be two feet in height, laid with clay mixed with hair, and covered on top with the two-foot tiles which support the floor.' For an example of this arrangement in the Stabian Baths at Pompeii see Morgan's translation of Vitruvius, plate facing p. 157. Another example, at Lydney Park, Gloucestershire, has been published by Wheeler in *Reports of the Research Committee of the Society of Antiquaries*, No. IX, pl. XVI B.

2 *Amra und seine Malereien, loc. cit.*, pp. 213–14; and his *Amra als Bauwerk*, in the *Zeitschrift fuer Geschichte der Architektur*, I, p. 59.

3 As a matter of fact, all perceptible trace of a point vanishes when the separation of the centres is reduced to less than a twelfth of the span or nearly so.

I have found that one of the first questions to be asked by those whose interest in Muslim architecture has been aroused is: 'What is the origin of the pointed arch; did it come from the East?' Its occurrence at Quṣayr 'Amra and Ḥammām aṣ-Ṣarakh is proof of the priority of the East, for no European examples are known until the end of the eleventh or the beginning of the twelfth centuries.[1]

Qaṣr Ibn Wardān, etc. But according to the late H. C. Butler, who was architect to the Princeton University Archaeological Expedition to Syria in 1904–5, there is a still earlier Eastern example in the church at Qaṣr Ibn Wardān in north-east Syria, built between A. D. 561 and 564.[2] He says:

'It is especially worthy of notice that many of the arches in this building are not semi-circular, but are two-centred, and consequently bluntly pointed. The arch of the apse and the four great arches that carried the dome are all struck from two points, 30 cm. on either side of the actual centre [i.e. they are 60 cm. apart]. The arches of the triforium are likewise two-centred, and the arches of the lower arcade are both pointed and stilted, as may be seen from my photographs and from those of Baron von Oppenheim.'[3]

He also says that:

'Almost all of the great tunnel vaults were slightly pointed. The tunnel vault of the east and west halls on the ground floor [his Illus. 35], the corresponding vaults above them, the vault of the southern apsis on the upper floor, as may be seen in Dr. von Oppenheim's photograph [*Jahrbuch der Königl. Preusz. Kunstsammlungen*, Band 25, Heft 4, Abb. 22], were all struck from two centres; the upper vaults were more pointed than the lower.'[4]

Butler's plan shows the span of the apse arch as 4·70 m., and of those under the dome as 6·66. I have quoted him verbatim, for his statement has been flatly contradicted by Herzfeld, who says:

'Likewise no pointed arch is to be found in Qaṣr Ibn Wardān in Euphratesia. Neither do the photographs of Butler nor those of von Oppenheim, nor those which I bought in Aleppo show any pointed arch in the building. The four arches which carry the dome are a little foreshortened perspectively in all photographs, they do not appear as plain semicircles but as slightly stilted ellipses. The difference between the rise and the half-span of these ellipses amounts to scarcely a quarter of the difference which, in the drawing, is shown as the pointedness (*stich*) of the arch in front elevation. In the drawing there appears a wedge of bricks at the apex of the arch, as is necessary in the case of pointed arches, since the bricks are set from two centres. In the photograph that is *not* the case, rather are the bricks normal and radiating as if set from the centre of a semicircle. The dome-bearing arches of Qaṣr Ibn Wardān are therefore stilted semicircles. As regards the arches over the sets of columns at the sides of the domed part, the photographs leave no shadow of doubt that we have to do with plain semicircular arches, as in all the other arches of the building. Qaṣr Ibn Wardān has no pointed arch, and consequently the existence of a pointed arch in the monumental architecture of pre-Islamic times cannot be demonstrated up to the present.'[5]

[1] The earliest pointed arches in Europe appear to be those of the nave and presbytery in the Abbey of Cluny, the construction of which lasted from 1089 to 1130 (Rivoira, *Lombardic Architecture*, II, pp. 104–6). In England, two rude wall-arches of pointed form are found in Gloucester Cathedral (1089–1100), in a radiating chapel on the south side of the apse (*ibid.*, II, pp. 217–20) and in the wall-arches of the groined vault in the south-east apse (F. Bond, *Gothic Architecture in England*, p. 266); but free-standing pointed arches are not found until some years later, e.g. Durham Cathedral (1128–33), in the transverse arches of the nave vault (Bond, *op. cit.*, p. 266 and illustration on p. 8), in the pier arcades at Malmesbury, which may date from before 1139 (Bond, however, thinks they are twenty years later, *op. cit.*, p. 266), and in the pier arcades at Fountains Abbey (1147–50) (Bond, *ibid.*).

I cannot help thinking that Palermo may have been the link between Syria and the rest of Europe, as has already been suggested by Georg Jacob, (*Die Wanderung des Spitz- und Hufeisenbogens*, in Grote's *Beiträge zur Kenntnis des Orients*, p. 56), for the pointed arch is the only one used there, e.g. in San Giovanni degli Eremiti (1132); the Cappella Palatina (1132–43); the bridge known as the Ponte dell'Ammiraglio, built by the Admiral Giorgios of Antioch; La Favara (*fauwāra*) Palace (1153); the church of San Cataldo, finished before 1161; the Ziza Palace, begun 1166, etc. There can be little doubt that this series, which starts suddenly in 1132, after a gap of centuries, must have been based on the style in use by the Muslim rulers of the island before the Norman conquest in 1072.

[2] Qaṣr Ibn Wardān lies far out in the desert, about fifty-four miles north-east of Ḥomṣ, from which it is best approached. The ruins consist of a palace, church, and barracks, all in the same style, of which the former is dated Indiction 13, of the 876th year = Nov. 564, and the latter apparently 873 (= 561); see Prentice, *Greek and Latin Inscriptions, Sect. B: Northern Syria*, pp. 38–41. The first description of the ruins was given by Mordtmann in 1884 (*Archäologisch-epigraphische Mittheilungen aus Oesterreich*, VIII, pp. 191–2); this was followed by Østrup in 1893 (*Historisk-topografiske bidrag til kendskabet til den syriske Ørken*, in the *Mém. de l'Acad. Roy. des Sciences et des Lettres de Danemark, Lettres*, 6me sér., Vol. IV, pp. 87–9; translated into German by Hartmann, in the *Z.D.P.V.*, XXIII, pp. 104–6). Von Oppenheim also visited it in 1889 (*Zeitschr. der Gesell. für Erdkunde zu Berlin*, XXXVI, p. 78), and some of the photographs which he took were published by Strzygowski in his *Kleinasien ein Neuland der Kunstgeschichte*, Abb. 91 and 93–9, together with an archaeological study. See also his *Mschatta*, in the *Jahrbuch der Kgl. Preusz. Kunstsammlungen*, 1904, pp. 237–42 and Abb. 21–3; *Amida*, pp. 292–3 and Abb. 240; and *L'Ancien art chrétien de Syrie*, pp. 49–50 and figs. 26–7. Butler published his thorough description in 1908, in his *Ancient Architecture in Syria, Sect. B: Northern Syria*, pp. 26–45, Illus. 24–40 and pls. I–VII; see also his *Early Churches in Syria*, pp. 168–9 and Illus. 178–9. Herzfeld has discussed this building in his *Mshattâ, Ḥîra und Bâdiya*, in the *Jahrb. der Kgl. Preusz. Kunstsammlungen*, XLII (1921), pp. 122–3, and Taf. 2 *a*.

[3] *Ancient Architecture in Syria, Sect. B: Northern Syria*, p. 32.

[4] *Ibid.*, pp. 38–9.

[5] *Archäologische Reise im Euphrat- und Tigris-Gebiet*, II, p. 92, note 1. See also his *Mshattâ, Ḥîra und Bâdiya, loc. cit.*, pp. 122–3.

In another place he says that 'not a single pointed arch can be shown to exist in any pre-Islamic building in the whole East';[1] and again: 'As an architectural principle the pointed arch is completely foreign to the pre-Islamic period. Even in the latest monuments of classical architecture it remains unknown.'[2]

Now although it is certainly correct to say that a wedge of bricks is a necessity at the crown of a pointed arch, if the latter has a pronounced point, the necessity diminishes as the degree of acuteness becomes less and less. If the arches are as described by Butler, i.e. span 6·66 m., struck from two centres placed 60 cm. apart, the pointedness becomes almost imperceptible, and could be compensated for, when setting the bricks, by a slight increase in the thickness of the mortar at the median joint. This is precisely what Butler's drawing (his Plate III) shows when examined under a magnifying glass. As for the photographs, all those published are too small and too smudgy to confirm or confute this point.[3] I must point out, however, that Littmann, in reviewing Herzfeld's work, supports Butler's opinion that the arches referred to were pointed.[4]

However, here is an absolutely frontal photograph (Fig. 552, facing p. 468), which I took in the early nineteen-thirties, with the camera carefully levelled. It shows (i) a slightly pointed arch and (ii) a wedge of bricks at its apex. Butler, therefore, is vindicated.

In addition to this, it is significant that the separation of the two centres, which Butler gives as 60 cm., is practically the same as that found at Quṣayr ʿAmra, where the arches are on much the same scale (6·18 m. as against 4·70 and 6·66 m.). At Ḥammām aṣ-Ṣarakh the pointed arch is also used, as is clearly shown in my photographs (Plate 83 *a–c* and *e*). Against this we have the fact, admitted by Herzfeld, that the pointed arch is absolutely unknown in Sasanian architecture.[5] Even if we omit Qaṣr Ibn Wardān, the pointed arches of Quṣayr ʿAmra and Ḥammām aṣ-Ṣarakh justify us in saying that this feature is of Syrian origin. And this view is confirmed by the fact that the very evolution of the pointed arch, i.e. the gradual separation of the two centres, can be observed there. At Ḥammām aṣ-Ṣarakh, for example, the separation of the centres increases to nearly a sixth of the span, and at Mshattā (in the vaults) to a fifth, a ratio which becomes fairly constant henceforth. At Ramla, for example, the arches of the so-called 'Cistern of St. Helena' have this profile. (This is the *quint-point* arch of the Gothic architects.)

Thus we have:

		Date.	*Separation of centres.*
Qaṣr Ibn Wardān .	Church, arches under dome, and apse arch	A.D. 561–4	$\frac{1}{11}$ of span
Damascus . . .	Great Mosque, arched frame at north end of transept	„ 705–15	$\frac{1}{10}$ „
Quṣayr ʿAmra . .	Audience hall, transverse arches	„ 712–15	$\frac{1}{10}$ „
Boṣrā . . .	So-called ʿUmar Mosque	„ 720–21	$\frac{1}{10}$ „
Ḥammām aṣ-Ṣarakh .	*Calidarium* of bath	„ 725–30 (?)	$\frac{1}{7}-\frac{1}{6}$ „

The series continues as follows:

		Date.	*Separation of centres.*	*Remarks.*
Qaṣr al-Ḥayr .	Great Mosque	110 H. (728/9)		Very slightly pointed
Mafjir . .	*Sirdāb* and portico of forecourt	(739–43)	$\frac{1}{8}$ to $\frac{1}{6}$ of span	
Mshattā . .	Section of vaults	A.D. 744	$\frac{1}{5}$ of span	
Qaṣr aṭ-Ṭūba .	„ „	„ „	About the same	
Raqqa . .	Baghdād Gate[6]	155 H. (772) or later		Four centred arch
Ukhaiḍir .	Vault of entrance hall	Last quarter, eighth century	$\frac{1}{7}-\frac{1}{6}$ and stilted	
Ramla . .	Arches of cistern	172 H. (789)	$\frac{1}{7}-\frac{1}{5}$ of span	
Fusṭāṭ . .	Mosque of ʿAmr, windows of SW. wall	211 H. (827)		Slightly pointed
Sāmarrā . .	Bāb al-ʿĀmma	221 H. (836)		Four centred arch
Fusṭāṭ . .	Nilometer	247 H. (861/2)	$\frac{1}{3}$ of span	

1 *Op. cit.*, II, p. 333, note 2.

2 *Der Islam*, I, p. 111, also p. 112.

3 One, however, taken by Thévenet and published by Herzfeld in his *Mshattâ*, Taf. 2 *a*, shows one of the dome-bearing arches very clearly; it appears to me to be pointed!

4 *Deutsche Literaturzeitung*, 1921, cols. 101–2.

5 'Es gibt also in der sasanidischen Baukunst kein Beispiel eines Spitzbogens'; *Archäologische Reise*, II, pp. 91–2.

6 For this monument and the following, see *E.M.A.*, 1st ed., Vol. II.

		Date.	Separation of centres.	Remarks.
Qairawān	Great Mosque, arches lining transept under dome	248 H. (862)	$\frac{1}{7}$ of span	Pointed, with slight return
„	Jāmiʿ Tlēta Bībān	252 H. (866)		Pointed horse-shoe arch
„	Great Mosque, portico of sanctuary	261 H. (875)		„ „
Cairo	Mosque of Ibn Ṭūlūn	263–5 H. (876–9)	Irregular, about $\frac{1}{4}$ of span and stilted	

Thus the first seven examples of this feature all occur in Syria, and, in view of this fact, the views of Rhodokanakis,[1] Dussaud,[2] Diehl,[3] and Herzfeld[4] that the pointed arch is of Persian origin must be given up. As for Strzygowski's claim[5] that it was known in Egypt in the first century of Islam, the dates which he suggests for his two examples—the Mosque of ʿAmr and the Nilometer—will not stand for a moment.

The Low Springing of the Transverse Arches. This also is a thoroughly local feature, good examples of which may be seen in a church at Ṭafḥā,[6] the fort of Quṣayr al-Ḥallābāt,[7] at Ṣamma (see below, Fig. 576), in the east church at Umm al-Jimāl,[8] in the palace at Boṣrā,[9] in a villa at Jemerrīn,[10] in a church and house at Lubbēn in the Lejā,[11] etc.

The Vaulting System of the Audience Hall.[12] Architecturally the most remarkable feature of Quṣayr ʿAmra is its vaulting system, in which the roof being carried on fixed points well apart, the wall between them becomes merely a curtain wall, which may be pierced at will and lateral lighting obtained, as in Gothic vaulting. With a simple tunnel-vault running from one end of a hall to the other adequate lateral lighting becomes difficult, owing to the necessity of meeting the continuous thrust of the vault. I shall therefore attempt to trace this somewhat unusual solution to its earliest type, a type in which this potentiality for lateral lighting is not realized, and in which the arches, placed seldom more than six or seven feet apart, are roofed with stone slabs and never vaulted. This primitive type can be traced back to the beginning of the Christian era, when it is found in Nabataean tombs[13] still existing in the Jabal Ḥaurān (the country lying south-east of Damascus).

Examples in the Ḥaurān. The architecture of the Ḥaurān, as might be expected, was governed by local conditions. The only rock in the entire region is black basalt, except at its southernmost extremity, where limestone appears as a building stone in the ruins of Quṣayr al-Ḥallābāt.[14] The country does not produce any timber, and this quite material necessity became the mother of invention and led

[1] 'Rein persisch ist aber der Spitzbogen'; *W.Z.K.M.*, XIX, p. 294. See also p. 295.

[2] *Les Arabes en Syrie avant l'Islam*, pp. 45 and 51.

[3] 'Un trait d'architecture perse'; *Manuel d'art byzantin*, p. 48.

[4] '. . . es ist kein Zweifel mehr, dass im 'Irāq der Spitzbogen geboren wurde, nur wesentlich später'; *Archäologische Reise*, II, p. 67.

[5] *Mschatta*, in the *Jahrb. der Kgl. Preusz. Kunstsammlungen*, XXV, pp. 246–7. The oldest part of the Mosque of ʿAmr dates from 212 H. (827), and the Nilometer from 247 H. (861/2); see Vol. II, first ed.

[6] Butler (H. C.), *Architecture and Other Arts*, illus. on pp. 409 and 410; and his *Early Churches in Syria*, p. 22 and Illus. 18.

[7] Butler (H. C.), *Ancient Architecture in Syria*, *Sect. A: Southern Syria*, Pl. VI.

[8] *Ibid.*, Illus. 152.

[9] *Ibid.*, pl. XI.

[10] *Ibid.*, Illus. 268.

[11] *Ibid.*, Illus. 361 and 363.

[12] The theory set forth here was first published in 1918 in my *Vaulting System of the Hindola Maḥal at Māndū*, in the *J.R.I.B.A.*, Vol. XXV, Third Series, pp. 237–45; reprinted, with additions, in the *Indian Antiquary*, XLVII, pp. 169–77. It appears to have been accepted by Monneret, *Les Couvents près de Sohâg* (Milan, 1926), pp. 77–9, who adds an interesting example from a cistern at Delos, published by Plassart in the *Bulletin de Correspondance hellénique*, XL (1916), pp. 240–41 and fig. 40.

[13] The Nabataeans, who were once thought to have been Aramaeans on account of their language (Quatremère, *Journal Asiatique*, XV (1835), pp. 209–40), have been shown by Nöldeke (*Z.D.M.G.*, XVII, pp. 703–8) and others to have been true Arabs who made use of Aramaic for literary purposes—all their inscriptions are in Aramaic—because Arabic had not at the time developed into a literary language. Our knowledge of them may be said to date from the Hellenic period, when we hear of Antigonus sending his general Athenaeus against them in 312 B.C., previous to which we know practically nothing about them. At this time they were nomads, without agriculture; nevertheless they were great traders. The first ruler (*τύραννος*) of whom we hear is Aretas (= Ḥāritat), with whom Jason the High Priest in vain sought refuge in 169 B.C. (2 Macc. v. 8). The Nabataeans profited by the fall of the empire of the Ptolemies and the Seleucids, and their kingdom may be said to date from Erotimus, *c.* 110–100 B.C. In 84 B.C. the Nabataean king Aretas III took Damascus from Antiochus XII; it was recovered by Herod in 23 B.C., but it again changed hands nineteen years later, being taken by Aretas IV in 4 B.C. In A.D. 106 the Nabataean kingdom, which now comprised Boṣrā (the capital of the Ḥaurān) and Petra, was converted into a Roman province (*Provincia Arabia*) by Cornelius Palma, the Roman Governor of Syria; see E. Schürer, *Geschichte des jüdischen Volkes im Zeitalter Jesu Christi*, 3te and 4te Aufl., I, pp. 726–44; Macpherson's transl. (Clark's *Foreign Theological Library*, Vol. XLIII), pp. 345–62; Musil, *Kuṣejr ʿAmra*, pp. 128–9; Kammerer (A.), *Pétra et la Nabatène*, Chaps. I–XIV; and Honigmann's art. *Nabataeans*, in the *Encyc. of Islām*, III, pp. 801–2.

[14] Butler (H. C.), *Ancient Architecture in Syria*, *Sect. A: Southern Syria*, pp. 63–4.

to the discovery of new constructive methods. Thus the arch, the sole means of covering wide spaces, became the principal element of construction and a series of parallel arches supporting ceiling slabs served to cover most of the halls (Fig. 469).[1]

The architecture of this region is divided by Butler into five groups: (1) The Prehistoric—a rough megalithic style without any indication of date, (2) the Nabataean, (3) the Roman, (4) the Christian, and (5) the Muhammadan. The first historical period is the Nabataean, of which the earliest monument that can be accurately dated is placed by him *c.* 60 B.C. It may, of course, have begun somewhat earlier, and it lasted until A.D. 106, the date at which the Roman period commenced. The Roman and Christian periods have much reduced the Nabataean remains, but many scattered details of very characteristic ornament and numerous inscriptions in Nabataean script remain.

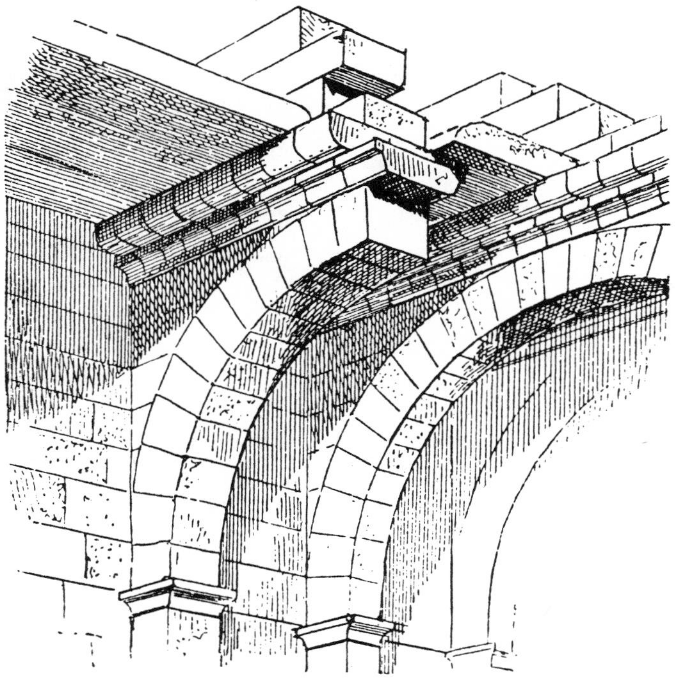

FIG. 482. Roofing system used in the Ḥaurān. (From de Vogüé, *Syrie centrale*.)

Butler, like de Vogüé, emphasizes the fact that the architecture 'was the most truly lithic that the world had seen; it was entirely of stone, sometimes even to the doors and window shutters'.[2] It offers a marked contrast to that of Northern Syria in plans, principles of construction, and ornamental details—in all those things that go to make up style.[3] For the roofing of all narrow apartments stone slabs were employed; when the width did not exceed nine feet the space was reduced by corbels to about six feet, and slabs slightly over that length were placed across. The wall was always carried up above the corbels to weight them and keep them in place. When broader spaces were to be roofed, an arch was thrown across, the haunches of the arch were filled up level with the side walls, and long slabs were laid from these side walls to the central line of support thus provided. Corbelling was used at the same time to reduce the strain on the cross slabs. In roofing a space that was very long as well as over nine feet in width, two or more transverse arches were used, giving a series of transverse supports all down the hall. The Druses of the Ḥaurān build their houses in this fashion at the present day.

Tombs were wholly or partially excavated in the ground and paved, walled, and roofed with stone. One of the earliest found is described and illustrated by Butler. It is roofed with arches which support slabs (Fig. 483) and eight stelae with Nabataean inscriptions were found in it. Some examples of this form of roofing were published by de Vogüé over fifty years ago.

The Ḥaurān in recent years has been thoroughly re-examined by the Princeton Expedition, which has described and published many new buildings roofed in this way. Confining myself to those which are dated, I have compiled the following list:

A.D. 345. UMM AL-JIMĀL: Church of Julianos.[4]

371. " : Praetorium.[5]

412. QAṢR AL-BĀ'IQ, near the western border of the southern Ḥaurān. A Greek inscription states that it was built in the reign of the Emperor Arcadius under the *dux* Phil. Pelagios.[6]

430–31. AL-MAJDAL: a small house with this system of vaulting on the ground floor.[7]

508 (?). AL-UMTĀ'ĪYA: Church No. 1. An inscription gives a date which may possibly be equivalent to A.D. 508.[8]

515. ZOR'A (or (Ezra'): Church of St. George, dated 410 of the Era of Boṣrā (= A.D. 515).[9]

1 De Vogüé, *Syrie centrale*, I, p. 6.
2 Butler, *op. cit.*, p. 68.
3 Butler (H. C.), *Architecture and Other Arts*, p. 310.
4 Butler, *Ancient Architecture in Syria, Sect. A: Southern Syria*, pp. 173–6.
5 *Ibid.*, pp. 160–66.
6 *Ibid.*, pp. 80–83.
7 *Ibid.*, pp. 120–22.
8 *Ibid.*, p. 92.
9 De Vogüé, *op. cit.*, pp. 61–2 and pl. 21.

A.D. 529. QUṢAYR AL-ḤALLĀBĀT: Fortress, room next entrance.[1] This example is specially important, for it is only a stone's throw from the mosque described below, and about three miles from Ḥammām aṣ-Ṣarakh. Its dimensions compared with the latter are 8·45×7·20 m. against 8·95×7·90 m.

578. AL-HAIYĀT: House of Flavios Seos—a Latin-Nabataean name.[2]

624–5. SAMA: Monastery of St. George.[3]

Let us now stop a moment to examine the exact *raison d'être* of this roofing system. The Ḥaurān being a country of stone, the people naturally had a predilection for the lintel, and used it wherever possible. Where, however, this was not possible they used the arch, and it may well be asked, why did they not make the arch continuous, and thus form a tunnel-vault? I think the answer must be that, as they were not acquainted with the Mesopotamian method of building a vault without centering (by using flat bricks in rings sloping backwards at a considerable angle against a head wall), any tunnel-vault built by them would have required considerable timber for centering—a serious matter. By building a series of separate arches, however, the same piece of centering could be used over and over again, as soon as one arch had set, thus reducing the timber required to an absolute minimum, and their favourite lintel system could then be used for the final covering.

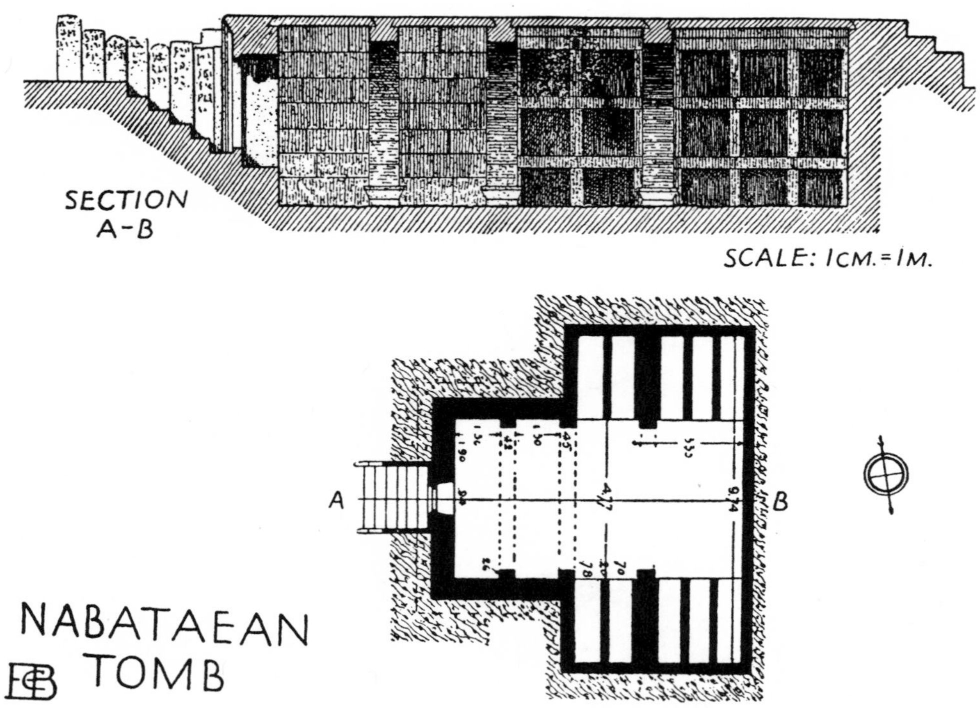

FIG. 483. Nabataean Tomb. (From Butler, *Ancient Architecture in Syria*.)

In all these early buildings, however, the fact that the roof is borne on points of support spaced at regular intervals permits the piercing of the side walls for lateral lighting. Yet out of the large number of examples—some thirty or forty—described by de Vogüé and Butler, there are not many in which this opportunity has been utilized, and even in these cases it has only been made use of in a timid and halting manner, small square windows pierced at irregular intervals, and not in each bay, being all that the builders attempted.

HATRA. This system must have been known in Mesopotamia at a fairly early date, since it is found in the Palace of Hatra, or al-Ḥaḍr (Fig. 484, facing),[4] built about fifty miles south of Moṣul by the Parthians, whose dynasty came to an end in A.D. 226.

ṬĀQ-i ĪWĀN. It was left to the keen architectural insight of the Persians to realize its potentialities fully and to carry it to its final development. They were responsible for two innovations: (1) they were the first to use tunnel-vaults to connect the transverse arches, thus making it possible to place them farther apart, and (2) they pierced windows in each of the curtain walls between these arches and thus obtained excellent lateral lighting, so that when Dieulafoy saw the ruins of the earliest existing building of this type he was irresistibly reminded of a Gothic cathedral. The building in question, known as Ṭāq-i Īwān, or Kūt Gāpān (Figs. 485–6, facing), stands at Karkh, known in Syriac as Karkhā de Lādan, a town founded by Shāpūr II (A.D. 309–79). Dieulafoy was the first to survey and describe it about seventy-five years ago[5] although Rawlinson had seen it as early as 1838.[6]

[1] Butler, *op. cit.*, pp. 71–4, Illus. 55, and pl. VI.

[2] Butler, *op. cit.*, pp. 362–3.

[3] *Ibid.*, pp. 83–6.

[4] Andrae (W.), *Hatra.* (*Wissenschaftliche Veröffentlichungen der Deutschen Orient-Gesellschaft*, Nos. 9 and 21). It occurs in Room 15; see his Abb. 228.

[5] *L'Art antique de la Perse*, V, pp. 79–87, pls. VII–IX and figs. 55, 56, and 58–62. See also Gayet, *L'Art persan*, pp. 116–20, with 4 figs.; R. Phené Spiers, *Sassanian Architecture*, *J.R.I.B.A.*, VII, New Series, pl 66, expanded in his *Architecture: East and West*, pp. 82–3 and fig. 37; Herzfeld, *Iranische Felsreliefs*, pp.

[*Footnotes 5 and 6 continued on opposite page*

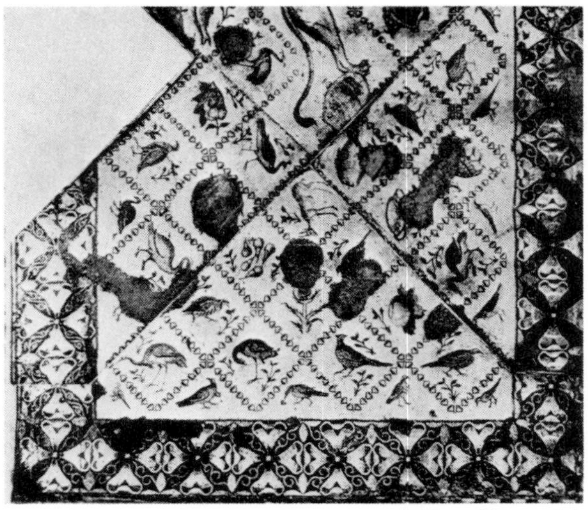

Baltimore Museum of Art

FIG. 455. ANTIOCH: Mosaic pavement excavated by the American Expedition

FIG. 484. HATRA: Remains of transverse arches in room of main palace. (From Andrae, *Die Ruinen von Hatra*)

FIG. 456. PALMYRA: Painting in tomb known as Maghārat al-Jadīda. (From Chabot, *Choix d'inscriptions de Palmyre*)

FIG. 486. ṬĀQ-I ĪWĀN: Side of Great Hall. (From Dieulafoy, *op. cit.*)

FIG. 485. ṬĀQ-I ĪWĀN: Great Hall, showing remains of transverse arches. (From Dieulafoy, *L'Art antique de la Perse*)

It is raised on a sub-basement connected with an immense rectangular enclosure, to which it probably formed a monumental gateway. In its present state it consists of a gallery about 50 m. long by 9 m. broad which originally formed one of the arms of a long hall, the centre of which was occupied by a dome. Each arm was spanned by transverse arches (*arcs-doubleaux*) brought up level and joined by tunnel-vaults (*formerets*). Fig. 487 shows Dieulafoy's restoration and Fig. 488 explains the vaulting system in detail. The curvature of the transverse arches was found to correspond to a radius equal to half the width of the hall, hence semicircular arches are shown in the restoration. If we bear in mind the restrictions imposed by longitudinal lighting, the very great step forward here taken will be realized. Herzfeld has recently suggested that it may be 'of about 490 A.D.'[1]

Fig. 487. Khark. Ṭāq-i Īwān, reconstruction. (From Dieulafoy, *L'Art Antique de la Perse.*)

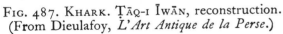

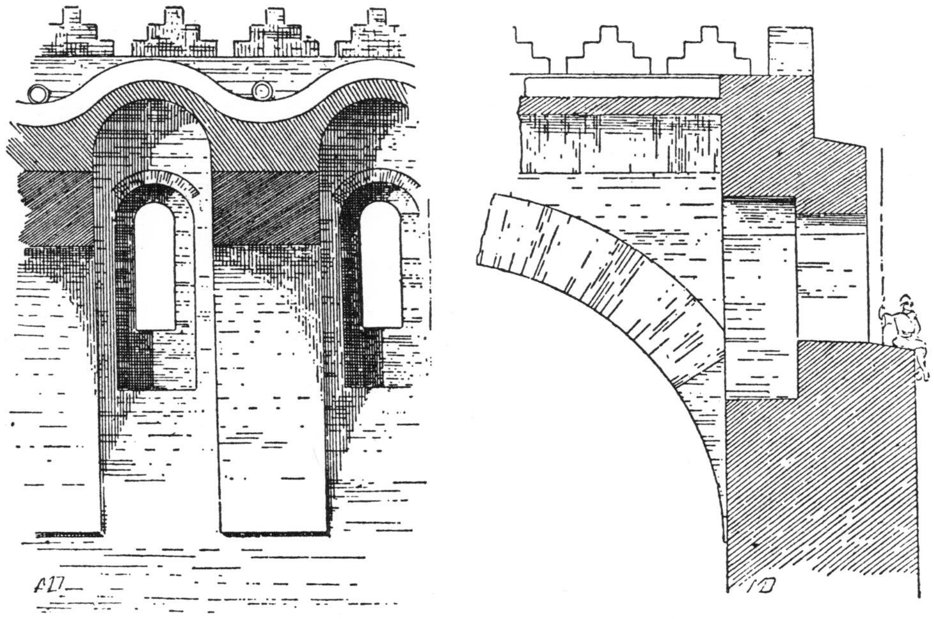

Fig. 488. Ṭāq-i Īwān: Details of vaulting system. (From Dieulafoy, *op. cit.*)

Qaṣr Kharāna. We now come to Qaṣr Kharāna,[2] a building which every writer who has expressed an opinion regarding its date, with the exception of van Berchem,[3] has regarded as Muhammadan. Our vaulting system occurs in three halls on the upper floor (Fig. 489, facing p. 454). A *terminus ad quem* is fortunately provided by the preservation on its walls of the last three lines of an Arabic inscription painted in black, which was copied by Moritz, as follows: '... and 'Abd al-Malik the son of 'Ubayd

130–31; Dieulafoy, *Art in Spain and Portugal*, pp. 13–14, and figs. 29–30; G. L. Bell, *Ukhaiḍir*, pp. 95–6 and fig. 20; Glück and Diez, *Kunst des Islam*, pp. 14 and 529 and Abb. 127 *a*; Reuther, in Pope, *Survey of Persian Art*, pp. 506–7 and fig. 135; and Herzfeld, *Damascus: Studies in Architecture*, *Ars Islamica*, X, p. 52.

6 *J.R.G.S.*, Vol. IX, p. 71.

1 *Loc. cit.*

2 For Qaṣr Kharāna, see Gray Hill, *P.E.F.*, *Q.St.*, 1896, pp. 33–5, with 3 illus.; Musil, *Sitzungsberichte*, CXLIV, pp. 18–19 and 26 and fig. 11; his *Kuṣejr 'Amra*, pp. 38–40, 99–100, and figs. 36–7 and 82–6; and his *Arabia Petraea*, I, pp. 290–93 and figs. 129–35; Brünnow, in the *W.Z.K.M.*, XXI, pp. 283–6 and 296; Moritz, *Ausflüge in der Arabia Petræa*, *M.F.O.B.*, III, pp. 421–3 and Taf. V; Lammens, *La Bâdia et la Ḥîra*, in the *M.F.O.B.*, IV, p. 108, n. 11, and pl. II; van Berchem, *Journal des Savants*, 1909, pp. 301 and 406–8; Musil, *W.Z.K.M.*, XXIV, p. 59; Dieulafoy, *Art in Spain and Portugal*, pp. 15–16, 18, 26, 34, 41, 71, 89, and figs. 1 and 25; G. L. Bell, *Ukhaiḍir*, pp. 114–17, fig. 29, and pls. 79–80; Diez (E.), *Die Kunst der islamischen Völker*, p. 28 and Abb. 36; Moritz (B.), *Bilder aus Palästina*, p. 5 and Abb. 33–4; Creswell, *Vaulting System of the Hindola Maḥal at Māndū*, *J.R.I.B.A.*, XXV, Third Series, pp. 241–2 and fig. 9; reprinted in the *Indian Antiquary*, XLVII, pp. 172–3 and pl. II c; Jaussen and Savignac, *Les Châteaux arabes*, pp. 8, 27, 51–77, 100–108, 114–21, figs. 8–15 and 19, and pls. XIX–XXXIV (the best account of all); King (G. G.), *Mudéjar*, pp. 87, 88, 89, and pl. XXXVII; Kammerer (A.), *Pétra et la Nabatène*, p. 338 n. and pl. 1221; Hassan el-Hawary, in the *J.R.A.S.*, 1930, pp. 328 and 330 and pl. IV (D); Wiet, *Répertoire d'épigraphie arabe*, I, pp. 18–19; Sauvaget, *Remarques sur les Monuments omeyyades*, *Journal Asiatique*, CCXXXI, pp. 16–18; Stern, *Notes sur l'Architecture des Châteaux omeyyades*, *Ars Islamica*, XI–XII, p. 74 and fig. 6; Nabia Abbott, *The Ḳaṣr Kharāna Inscription of 92 H. (710 A.D.), a new reading*, *Ars Islamica*, XI–XII, pp. 190–95, with 1 plate; Sauvaget (J.), *La Mosquée omeyyade de Médine*, pp. 126–7 and figs. 15–16; Marçais (G.), *L'Art de l'Islam*, pp. 29–30; Glueck (Nelson), *The other side of the Jordan*, pp. 38–9; and Harding (G. Lankester), *The Antiquities of Jordan*, pp. 157–9 and pl. 22.

3 *Loc. cit.*, pp. 406–8.

wrote it on Monday three days remaining from Muḥarram of the year ninety-two [= 24th Nov. 710]'.[1] Moritz suggests that ʿAbd al-Malik was probably a member of al-Walīd's suite on his return from the visit which he made to Mekka in 91 H. Kharāna in any case was standing in 710, but the inscription is only a *graffito* and does not prove the Muslim origin of the building. Another significant feature may be cited, the indescribably shoddy construction of the arches,[2] unknown in Umayyad work, their elliptical form recalling Sasanian monuments, and the pilasters, like engaged columns without capitals, from which the transverse arches spring just as in the Martyrion of Mār Tahmazgerd at Kerkūk *c.* A.D. 470 and at Sarvistān (see the chapter on the squinch in *E.M.A.*, 1st ed., II, p. 88).

In any case it is earlier than Quṣayr ʿAmra, and it is therefore the earliest building on the Syrian side of the desert in which the transverse arches, instead of being covered by slabs of basalt, are covered by tunnel-vaults, a modification of Mesopotamian origin.

I revisited Kharāna on 23rd April 1962, and again on 14th May 1964, and was more than ever convinced that it is a Sasanian building, on account (1) of its masonry, which resembles that of Damghān, (2) its squinches, for this device is unknown in Umayyad Syria except for the counterfeited example in the Citadel of ʿAmmān (see the chapter on the squinch, *loc. cit.*, pp. 113–14 and Fig. 111), and (3) the triple engaged columns without capitals, already mentioned.

And here is a new argument. The Umayyad *qaṣrs* were not fortified. For example, in al-Walīd's *qaṣr* at Minya the entrance is not fortified, the towers are all solid, except one open to the sky which served as a latrine, and there are no arrow-slits. The same remarks apply to Jabal Says. Neither is Qaṣr al-Ḥayr al-Gharbī fortified, nor Mafjar, for the entrance is not fortified, the towers are solid and there are no arrow-slits. Exactly the same remarks apply to Mshattā and Qaṣr aṭ-Ṭūba, where the only towers that are hollow served as latrines.

The only Umayyad *qaṣr* with a fortified entrance is Qaṣr al-Ḥayr ash-Sharqī, where there is a mâchicoulis now introduced into Islam for the first time, the idea having been derived from the mâchicoulis of the monastic tower of al-Mundhir, which had been incorporated into Qaṣr al-Ḥayr al-Gharbī two years earlier (see p. 541). But here again the towers are all solid, except one of those flanking the entrance, which once contained a spiral staircase lit by a slit. Moreover, there are no arrow-slits, there are no openings in the western curtain-wall, and those in the southern and eastern curtain-walls and in what remains of the northern are square and served to light the wooden-roofed rooms of the upper floor.

Contrast this with Kharāna, where there are no less than twenty-seven[3] arrow-slits. Their sills average 1·27 m. above the floor, and they are of a type unknown in Syria before the twelfth century, at which time they penetrate it along the Euphrates Valley at Raqqa,[4] Abū Huraira,[5] and Bālis.[6] But centuries before that the same peculiar type was employed at Ukhaidir (*c.* 776), and earlier still in a large fort on the Balkh river near Chihilburj, twenty-eight miles from Zārī, mentioned by Maitland.[7] He says that it was built of 'very large' mud bricks, which makes it probable that it dates from Sasanian times (see the Table in *E.M.A.*, 1st ed., Vol. II, p. 22). But it can be traced much farther back than that. At Ashur the Sargonid fortifications have slits in the floor of the rampart-walk which slope outwards and appear on the face of the outer wall as vertical slits with two sloping bricks as a hood.[8]

I am therefore convinced that Qaṣr Kharāna was built during the Persian occupation, which lasted from A.D. 614 to 628. The form of its *bayts* is its only Syrian feature.

CONCLUSIONS. The foregoing shows that the vaulting system of the audience hall of Quṣayr ʿAmra and Ḥammām aṣ-Ṣarakh, and of the mosque at Quṣayr al-Ḥallābāt is of a perfectly normal local type with one modification—the slabs of basalt usually placed above the transverse arches are replaced by tunnel-vaults. This innovation must have been inspired by Qaṣr Kharāna, which is only ten or twelve miles distant from Quṣayr ʿAmra. In my opinion this is the only non-Syrian strain in the building, a strain due not to a contemporary, but to an earlier pre-Muslim influence of short duration.

[1] *Loc. cit.*, p. 422; and a much more complete reading by Nabia Abbott in *Ars Islamica*, XI–XII, pp. 190–95.

[2] See Jaussen and Savignac, *op. cit.*, pls. XXVI, XXXI (reproduced here, Fig. 489, facing p. 454), and XXXIII.

[3] Ignoring the openings high up on the ground floor, which were obviously for light and ventilation only.

[4] In the minaret outside the walls, known as the Manāra al-Munaiṭir; see Sarre and Herzfeld, *Archäologische Reise*, II, pp. 354–5 and Abb. 328.

[5] *Op. cit.*, I, fig. 57.

[6] Dated 607 H. (1210/11); see J. and D. Sourdel, *Notes d'épigraphie sur la Syrie du Nord*, *Ann. Archéologiques de Syrie*, III, pp. 103–5.

[7] *J.R.A.S.*, 1886, p. 22 and figure.

[8] See Andrae, *Die Festungswerke von Assur*, Abb. 165, 189, and 190; and Loud (G.), *Khorsabad*, pl. 8 *c.*

Result of Analysis. Thus Quṣayr ʿAmra and Ḥammām aṣ-Ṣarakh (and the mosque at Quṣayr al-Ḥallābāt) are thoroughly Syrian buildings. The two bath-houses follow a local type already developed in the sixth century, the very sequence of the roofing systems—tunnel-vault, cross-vault, and dome—being that already adopted in the sixth century at ʿAbda and Ruḥayba. The roofing system of the audience halls and mosque is Syrian, except for the tunnel-vaults above the transverse arches, which replace the slabs of basalt usual hitherto. The low springing of the transverse arches and the famous paintings of Quṣayr ʿAmra are also thoroughly Syrian, likewise the spherical-triangle pendentives used for the dome setting, as we shall see in the next chapter.

The only non-Syrian features are: (1) the modification of the roofing system described above, a modification of Mesopotamian origin, for which the connecting link is Qaṣr Kharāna, and (2) the subject of the painting showing the Enemies of Islam, the composition of which is derived from a Sasanian prototype.

XIV

THE EVOLUTION OF THE PENDENTIVE[1]

High antiquity of the dome—The pendentive a discovery of comparatively recent date: its fundamental importance—Early attempts in Egypt: Dirā' Abu'n-Nagā—Early attempt at Kerch—Early attempts in Italy: Vetulonia—Early attempts in Syria: Phaena, 'Ammān, Umm az-Zaytūn, Shaqqā, Latakia, Ruwayḥā, Ḥāss. and 'Abda—Early attempts in Asia Minor: Mahaletch and Maden Shahr—Early attempts in Roman Africa: Tripoli—Further attempts in Rome under the Empire: the Domus Augustana, Tombs on the Via Nomentana, the Baths of Caracalla, the Temple of Minerva Medica—A satisfactory pendentive unknown to the Romans—Two solutions possible, (*a*) the spherical triangle, and (*b*) the squinch—Earliest examples of a spherical triangle: Quṣayr an-Nūwayjīs, The Baths at Jerash, Samaria, Brād, The Golden Gate and the Double Gate at Jerusalem—First examples outside Syria: The Mausoleum of St. Minas (Abū Mīnā) at Maryūṭ, the Mausoleum of Galla Placidia at Ravenna, Sancta Sophia at Constantinople—Terminology—Sancta Sophia at Salonika.

WE HAVE NOW MET WITH TWO EXAMPLES of a dome on pendentives; we must therefore consider the history and evolution of this structural feature.

It is a curious fact that, whereas domes appear to have been known almost from the dawn of the historical period, the discovery of a satisfactory pendentive was only made at a comparatively recent date.

HIGH ANTIQUITY OF THE DOME. In ancient Egypt the dome was undoubtedly known from very early times. One is accustomed to think of Egyptian architecture as a style of columns, architraves, and massive walls of stone, yet, side by side with this monumental form of construction, there existed vaults and domes in small and unimportant buildings. In the excavations at Rīfa a large number of models of houses dating from the Tenth Dynasty were found. One had a terrace roof with two little rounded domes just emerging through it,[2] exactly like a style of house to be found to-day in many parts of the East, Persia for example. The use of small brick domes for granaries was quite general. According to Perrot and Chipiez, the granaries, barns, and storehouses were almost always dome-shaped. Those which had flat roofs seem to have been very few indeed.[3] Lutz[4] has called attention to a somewhat

[1] The evolution of the pendentive has been discussed by the following: 1855, Isabelle (C. E.), *Les Édifices circulaires et les dômes*, pp. 70–71; — 1866, Rahn (J. R.), *Über den Ursprung und die Entwicklung des christlichen Central- und Kuppelbaus*, pp. 69–81; — 1867, Fergusson (J.), *History of Architecture*, II, pp. 308–10; 3rd ed., I, pp. 433–5; — 1875, Viollet-le-Duc, *Dictionnaire*, IV, pp. 347–67, and VII, pp. 110–14; — 1883, Choisy (A.), *L'Art de bâtir chez les Byzantins*, pp. 79–80, 88–9, 152, and 158–62; — 1885, Dieulafoy, *L'Art antique de la Perse*, IV, pp. 72–5; — 1889, Gosset (A.), *Les Coupoles d'Orient et d'Occident*, pp. 245 and 249–52; — 1894, Lethaby and Swainson, *Sancta Sophia*, pp. 201–3; — 1899, Choisy, *Histoire de l'architecture*, I, pp. 527–8, and II, pp. 11–13; — 1901, Rivoira (G. T.), *Le origini della architettura lombarda*, I, pp. 31–3; 2nd ed., I, pp. 31–6 and 71–2; English transl., I, pp. 29–35 and 63; — 1905, Millet, *Revue Archéologique*, 4me sér., V, p. 102; and his *L'Art byzantin*, in G. Michel's, *Histoire de l'Art*, I, pp. 142–3; — 1906, Anon., *The Builder*, LXXXVIII, p. 530; — Sturgis (R.), *History of Architecture*, I, pp. 92–3; — 1909, Bell (G. L.), in Ramsay and Bell, *Thousand and One Churches*, pp. 438–46; and Porter (A. Kingsley), *Medieval Architecture*, pp. 105–8; — 1910, Bell (Gertrude L.), in the *Journal of Hellenic Studies*, XXX, pp. 78–9; and Diehl, *Manuel d'art byzantin*, pp. 33–7; — 1912, Lasteyrie (C. R. de), *L'Architecture religieuse en France à l'époque romane*, pp. 268–70 and 272–5; Lethaby (W. R.), *Architecture*, pp. 57–8 and 112–13, and Rosintal (J.), *Pendentifs, Trompen und Stalaktiten*, pp. 8–18; French transl., pp. 18–29; — 1913, Jackson (T. G.), *Byzantine and Romanesque Architecture*, I, pp. 39–40; — 1914, Rivoira, *Architettura musulmana*, pp. 239–40; English transl., pp. 234–5; — 1916, Leclerq (H.), art. *Dôme*, in Cabrol and Leclerq, *Dict. d'Archéologie chrétienne*, cols. 1350–74; — 1918, Strzygowski, *Die Baukunst der Armenier*, pp. 359–61, 484–5, and 775–6; — 1919, Strzygowski (J.), *Die Entstehung der Kreuzkuppelkirche*, *Zeitschr. fuer Gesch. der Architektur*, VII, pp. 51–77; — 1920, Strzygowski, *Ursprung der christlichen Kirchenkunst*, p. 52; transl. by Dalton and Braunholtz, p. 59; — 1921, Rivoira, *Architettura romana*, pp. 135–7, 192–8, 210, 213–16, 319, and 328–31; English transl., pp. 108, 152–9, 171, 172–4, 263–4, and 273–5; and Dalton (O. M.), *East Christian Art*, pp. 84–5; — 1923, Giovannoni (G.), in *The Legacy of Rome*, pp. 446–7 (an appalling translation of the author's Italian); expanded in his *La tecnica della costruzione presso i romani*, pp. 34–6; — 1927, Anderson (W. J.) and R. B. Spiers, *Architecture of Ancient Rome*, Ashby's ed., pp. 82 and 138; King (G. G.), *Mudéjar*, pp. 82–4; and Pijoán (J.), *History of Art*, II, pp. 56–7; — 1928, Traquair (R.), *The Origin of the Pendentive*, *J.R.I.B.A.*, XXXV, Third Series, pp. 185–7; — 1929, Camps y Cazorla (E.), *Arquitectura christiana primitiva visigoda y asturiana*, pp. 4–5 and lám. II_1; — 1933, Hamilton (J. A.), *Byzantine Architecture*, pp. 14–20; — 1934, Ebersolt (J.), *Monuments d'Architecture byzantine*, p. 31, n. 1; — 1936, Zaloziecky (W. R.), *Die Sophienkirche in Konstantinopel*, pp. 218–30; — 1940, Swift (Emerson H.), *Hagia Sophia*, p. 163; — 1947, Ward-Perkins, *The Italian Element in Late Roman and Early Medieval Architecture* (*Annual Italian Lecture, British Academy*), pp. 17–18; — 1950, Smith (E. Baldwin), *The Dome*, Chap. III, *passim*; — 1951, Swift (E. H.), *Roman Sources of Christian Art*, pp. 111–25, figs. 60–63 and pls. XX–XXIII; — 1956, Rumpler (Marguerite), *La Coupole dans l'architecture byzantine et musulmane*, p. 75.

[2] See Lethaby, *Architecture*, p. 57 and fig. 13; and W. M. F. Petrie, *Gizeh and Rifeh*, pp. 17 and 19 and pl. XVIII (42).

[3] *History of Art in Ancient Egypt*, II, pp. 36–7 and figs. 24 and 26, where paintings showing dome-shaped granaries are reproduced.

[4] *The oldest monumental evidence of a dome-structure*, *Journ. American Oriental Society*, XXXIX (1910), p. 122.

enigmatic little structure, shown in a hunting scene, carved on a slab of schist, which has since been reproduced by Capart.[1] If he is correct in his interpretation, the existence of little domes in Egypt must be admitted at the beginning of the Dynastic period.

In Chaldaea, and Assyria also, the dome was known from very early times. Fig. 499 shows a bas-relief, now in the British Museum, which was found by Layard in the palace of Sennacherib (705–681 B.C.) at Kuyunjik (Nineveh). Here we see buildings, some with hemispherical cupolas, and some with tall domes approximating to cones in shape. In most cases an eye has been left in the centre to admit light.[2] They undoubtedly represent peasants' huts, which are so constructed at the present day in many villages in the plains of Northern Syria, North-Western Mesopotamia, and Persia.[3]

FIG. 490. Slab found by Layard at Kuyunjik (Nineveh). (From Layard, *Discoveries*.)

In Rome the dome appears to have been known some centuries before our era. It seems to have been introduced as a feature in bath-building, and the only domes known to Vitruvius, who wrote about the beginning of the first century A.D., were those required for the hot chamber of the bath.[4] The ruined dome of the bath at Pompeii (Fig. 491) is a concreted shell of rubble, very conical, just like those shown on Layard's bas-relief.[5]

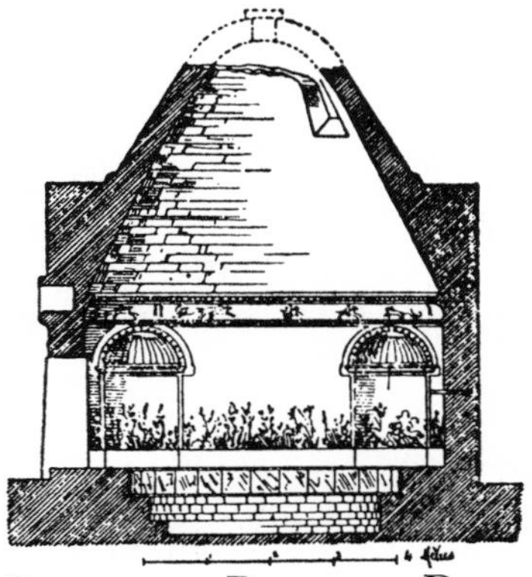

FIG. 491. POMPEII: Dome of Bath. (From. A. Gosset, *Les Coupoles d'Orient et d'Occident*.)

All these domes, however, have one feature in common, they are all small and they are found only in buildings of secondary importance. In Egypt this is invariably the case. In Chaldaea and Assyria the great palaces of Sargon and Sennacherib appear to have been built without domes. Strabo (*d.* A.D. 25), although he did not visit Mesopotamia, describes Asia from the Taurus to India by the aid of contemporary writings, and mentions the narrow vaulted rooms. He says that 'all the houses were vaulted in consequence of the absence of wood'.[6] His statements were confirmed by Place who found curved segments of vaulting, some 4×6 ft., amongst the débris in the rooms of the palace of Khorsābād (721–705 B.C.).[7] He even found rollers of limestone, weighing from 2 to 3 cwt., pierced at each end with a square hole for the insertion of wooden spindles. Similar rollers are used in the East at the present day, to roll the flat terraces on top of the vaulted roofs of sun-burnt clay. These rollers close the cracks, kill the weeds, and make the surface firm. Place also found that the length of nearly every chamber was at least twice the breadth, and in many cases four, five, or even seven times as much. This, of course, precludes the idea of a dome. In the

1 *Les Débuts de l'art en Égypte*, pl. I to face p. 223.

2 Layard, *A Second Series of the Monuments of Nineveh*, p. 3 and pl. 17; and his *Discoveries*, p. 112; Perrot and Chipiez, *History of Art in Chaldaea and Assyria*, I, pp. 144–6 and fig. 43; Dieulafoy, *L'Art antique de la Perse*, IV, p. 47 and fig. 28; Gosset, *Les Coupoles d'Orient et d'Occident*, pp. 2–4 and fig. 1; Sarre, in the *Zeitschr. der Gesellschaft für Erdkunde*, p. 7 and Abb. 48; and Herzfeld, in Sarre and Herzfeld, *Archäologische Reise im Euphrat- und Tigris-Gebiet*, I, p. 118. Rivoira (*Moslem Architecture*, p. 123) suggests that these domes, at least the conical ones, were constructed of bricks set in rings, each projecting beyond the one below, a method which, as he points out, was known at an early date in Italy, e.g. the 'Diavolino' from Vetulonia (see below, pp. 453–4). Although conical domes can certainly be constructed in this manner, the suggestion lacks probability in view of the hemispherical domes shown on the same slab, which, in their upper part at least, could only be constructed with properly radiating beds for each ring.

3 For a study of the present distribution of these bee-hive huts, see Banse, *Die Gubâb-Hütten Nordsyriens und Nordwest-Mesopotamiens*, *Orientalisches Archiv*, II, pp. 173–9 and map on Taf. XXXI; and *Durch den Norden Mesopotamiens*, *Petermanns Mitteilungen*, LVIII, pp. 119–22; see also Brice (W. C.) and Dönmez (Ahmet), *Construction of a house roofed with corbelled domes in Southern Turkey*, *Man*, XLVIII, pp. 135–6, with 5 illus.; and Copeland (P. W.), '*Beehive Villages*' *of North Syria*, *Antiquity*, XXIX, pp. 21–4, pls. V–VII and 2 figs.

4 Bk. V, c. xii, sect. 5.

5 Isabelle, *Les Édifices circulaires*, pp. 33–4 and pl. X; and Gosset, *op. cit.*, pp. 9–10.

6 Bk. LXVI, c. i, sect. 5; quoted by Perrot and Chipiez, *op. cit.*, I, p. 169.

7 Victor Place, *Nirive et l'Assyrie*, pp. 254–5.

palace of Sargon, out of 184 rooms scarcely any are square,[1] and there is nothing to show that these were covered with domes—they may quite well have been vaulted. In palace architecture, therefore, the dome appears to have played no part at all.

THE PENDENTIVE A DISCOVERY OF COMPARATIVELY RECENT DATE: ITS FUNDAMENTAL IMPORTANCE. Now what is the explanation of the fact that the dome, admirable as it is for a roof, was never used in antiquity in buildings of the first importance? Why is it always relegated to small and inferior structures? I consider that the reason is this: a knowledge of dome building is not of much use unless it is accompanied by a knowledge of some device whereby a dome can be set over a square chamber. A circular granary or tomb presents no difficulty, but when it comes to a complex building, an aggregation of cells, like a palace for example, it cannot be composed of circular units, and, failing a satisfactory pendentive, domes must be abandoned in favour of vaults. All the domes mentioned hitherto are either set over circular spaces, e.g. the granaries of Egypt and the bath at Pompeii, or else they are set over a small square space, from 2½ to 4 m. each way, by means of a make-shift pendentive, which could only be trusted on a small scale.

FIG. 492. DIRĀʿ ABU'N-NAGĀ: Primitive pendentives. (From Pieron, *loc. cit.*)

The evolution of the pendentive, therefore, has been of fundamental importance in the history of architecture; it played a predominating part in the transmutation of the Roman into the Byzantine style, and we will now endeavour to trace as completely as possible the various unsatisfactory devices which preceded the discovery of the two possible solutions—the spherical triangle and the squinch.

EARLY ATTEMPTS IN EGYPT: *DIRĀʿ ABU'N-NAGĀ.* For Egypt we have the detailed account, published by Pieron,[2] of a tomb discovered by Gauthier in the course of his excavations at Dirāʿ Abu'n-Nagā in 1906. The author, on archaeological grounds, placed this tomb between the Seventeenth and Twentieth Dynasties at the latest, that is to say about the fifteenth century B.C. It consists of two chambers, partly excavated in the rock and partly built of sun-baked bricks measuring 33×15×6 cm.

One chamber about 2·40 m. square had once been covered by a dome which has disappeared, but the pendentives, such as they are, remain. They are composed of about nine oversailing courses of brick, the lowest of which consists of a single brick set lintel-wise across the angle (Fig. 492), whilst those above form a series of quarter-circles each slightly larger than that below it.

A thousand years saw no further progress, judging from Petrie's excavations at Daphne, where he explored the ruins of a fortress-palace built about 660 B.C. All that remained was a square mass of brickwork about 160 feet each way; 'the interior was an irregular "gridiron" of thick walls, forming 'cells about ten to sixteen feet wide. Many were square, others were oblong; the latter formed "deep 'domed chambers or cells, which were opened from the top". They were much ruined, but several cells '"in the best-preserved parts showed signs of the springing of domes in their corners; the corners are 'rounded and gather in towards the vaulting".'[3] In answer to an inquiry from Professor Lethaby, the following additional details were sent by Professor Petrie: 'Egyptian doming of construction chambers 'is irregular, the sides contracting inwards while the corner increasingly rounds. For open chambers, 'I think the angles in each case are truncated by placing bricks across them.'

[1] Place, *Ninive et l'Assyrie*, pls. 2–7.
[2] *Tombeau égyptien à coupole sur pendentifs*, in the *B.I.F.A.O.*, VI, pp. 173–7.
[3] Lethaby, *Architecture*, pp. 57–8

Early attempt at Kerch. Pendentives of similar construction have been found at Kerch, in the Crimea (the ancient Pantikapion), in a domed mausoleum, known as the Royal Tumulus. This mausoleum, first published by Anton Ashik in 1848,[1] is a domed chamber 4½ m. square, the sides of which rise vertically for nine courses (each measuring 41–42 cm.), above which are twelve diminishing rings of masonry forming a cone. The transition between the square substructure and the circular base of the cone is effected by progressively rounding the fifth to ninth courses at the corners as shown (Fig. 493), and setting forward each curved piece step fashion beyond the course below. The transition, beginning in the fifth course from the ground, is almost completed in the ninth, above which is set the first complete ring. The fact that we have here a cone instead of a dome makes no difference to the problem of the zone of transition, for both have a circular base.

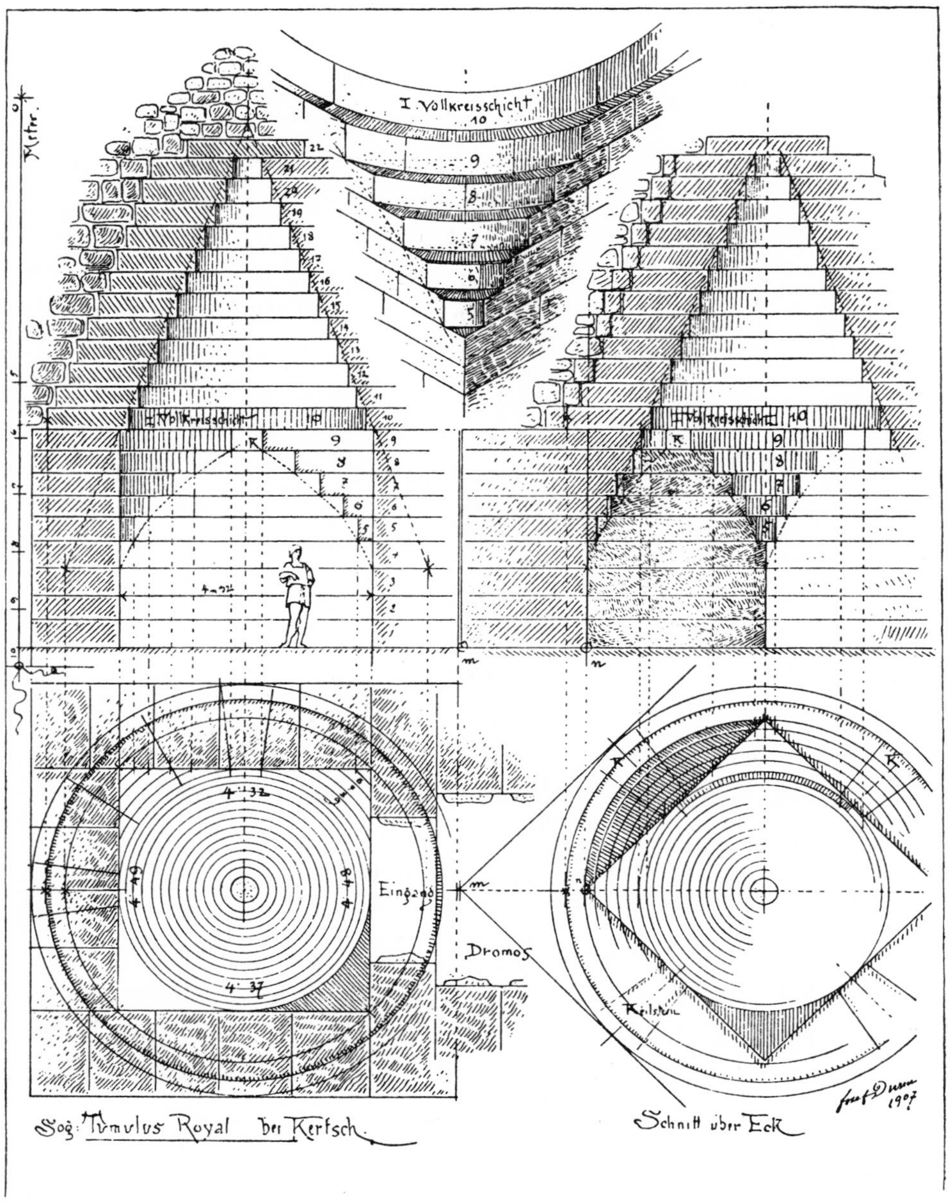

Fig. 493. Kerch: The Royal Tumulus. (From Durm, *Die Kuppelgräber von Pantikapaion*.)

Basing himself on the objects found therein, Ashik attributed the mausoleums of Kerch to the time when the Ionic colony of Pontus was founded (sixth or fifth century B.C.). Dr. von Stern of Odessa, in a letter to Professor Durm, expressed the opinion that these mausoleums could hardly be dated earlier than the fifth century B.C.,[2] an opinion which is shared by Professor Minns.[3] Durm has clearly shown the Mycenaean survivals in the construction of these cones, but the embryonic pendentive is a new development.

Early attempts in Italy: *Vetulonia.* An Etruscan tomb from Vetulonia, attributed to the seventh century B.C., has been set up in recent years in the garden of the Archaeological Museum at Florence. Here again the angles are treated in the same way, five courses of rough blocks, the lowest consisting of one only, are set across each angle, each course projecting beyond that below[4] (Fig. 494, facing p. 454). A base, shaped like a circle with slightly flattened sides, was thus provided on which to set the dome, which unfortunately has not been preserved. It was probably high, conical, and built in horizontal courses

1 *Vosporskoe tsarstvo* (= *The Bosphoran Kingdom*), II, pp. 27–9, with two plates; and *Antiquités du Bosphore cimmérien*, St.-Petersbourg, 1854, pp. cxxvi–cxxxv and pl. A[b] (reduced edition of Reinach, Paris, pp. 32–3); D. McPherson, *Antiquities of Kertch*, pp. 61–2; then by Richardson and Hogg, in *Transactions of the Roy. Society of Literature*, VI, pp. 100 and 115–16 and pl. V; E. S. Poole's Appendix to Lane's *Modern Egyptians*, 1860 ed., p. 587, with figure; Ussher (John), *London to Persepolis*, pp. 52–3; Prisse d'Avennes, *L'Art arabe*, *Texte*, p. 248 and fig. 70; Durm, *Die Kuppelgräber von Pantikapaion*, in the *Jahreshefte des Österreichischen Archäologischen Institutes*, X (1907), pp. 237–41 and figs. 72–5; Minns, *Scythians and Greeks*, pp. 194 and 294 and figs. 86–7; Rosintal, *Pendentifs, Trompen und Stalaktiten*, pp. 14–15 and Abb. 14; and Chapot, in the *Bull. de la Soc. nat. des Antiquaires de France*, 1912, pp. 293–9.

2 Durm, *loc. cit.*, p. 237.

3 *Scythians and Greeks*, p. 294, n. 3.

4 Pinza, *Le origini di alcuni tipi dell'architettura sepolcrale tirrena nell 'età del ferro*, in the *Atti del Congresso Internat. di Scienze Storiche* (Roma, 1903), V, pp. 447 ff., and figs. 100–102; Rivoira, *Lombardic Architecture*, I, pp. 29–30; Milani, *Il R. Museo Archeologico di Firenze*, I, pp. 282–3; and Rivoira, *Moslem Architecture*, p. 123 and fig. 107.

like that of the Treasury of Atreus, at Mycenae. Two other tombs from Vetulonia, known respectively sa 'La Pietrera'[1] and 'Pozzo all'Abate',[2] exhibit the same mode of transition.

For the sake of clearness I propose to study the various unsatisfactory attempts that were made in Syria, Asia Minor, and Imperial Rome before enumerating the earliest examples of the spherical-triangle type of pendentive.

EARLY ATTEMPTS IN SYRIA: *PHAENA*. I must first call attention to the Praetorium at Phaena, the modern Mismīya in the Lejā (Ḥaurān), where the problem of the pendentive is entirely avoided by the employment of a square dome[3] (French, *voûte en arc de cloître*, German, *Klosterkuppel*), a most unsatisfactory device (Figs. 495–6, facing), which possesses none of the advantages of a true dome. It had already fallen when de Vogüé saw this monument, although the substructure does not appear to have given way, but a few courses left at one corner bore witness to its existence. A series of inscriptions,[4] carved on various parts of the building, stated that it was constructed under the Emperors Marcus Aurelius and Lucius Verus (160–69), under the administration of Avidius Cassius, and under the direction of Egnatius Fuscus, centurion of the Third Gallic Legion. This building, unfortunately, no longer exists.[5]

'AMMĀN. Perhaps the earliest solution, certainly the most primitive and least satisfactory, is that adopted in a Roman tomb at 'Ammān, about 300 yards south-west of the mosque. This tomb is a massive structure about 18 ft. square internally, with walls 5 ft. thick. It was once roofed with a dome of cut stone, of which about three-quarters of the two lowest courses remain. The dome is set on the square regardless of the difference at the angles, large voussoirs projecting inwards (Fig. 498 on p. 456), and no special provision is made for its support, except for a very small corbel in each corner. The over-sailing voussoirs are, no doubt, held in place partly by the counterweight of their own centre of gravity, the dome being enormously thick, or by blocks which weight them in the wall.[6]

UMM AZ-ZAYTŪN. At Umm az-Zaytūn in the Ḥaurān we find a great improvement on this arrangement in a little shrine which fortunately bears a Greek inscription with a date corresponding to A.D. 282. The space to be covered by the dome is 5·80 m. square, more than double the measurement of the Egyptian tomb described above. The builders commenced by covering each of the angles of the square by slabs, producing thus an irregular octagon. On this octagon they placed a course of dressed stones, setting one astride each of the eight angles (Fig. 499). Two courses, placed in this fashion, transformed the original square into a polygon of thirty-two unequal sides, which, however, differed so little from a circle that it was possible to use it as the base for the dome which once covered it.[7] De Vogüé on seeing this device was led by it to conclude that it was the prototype from which was ultimately derived the stalactite pendentive so common in the twelfth and thirteenth centuries, as shown in Fig. 500.[8] Now there are two objections against this theory, one serious, the other fatal. In the first place, the most remarkable feature of Syrian stalactite pendentives is that each tier of niches always runs in a straight line across the angle, instead of being curved in plan as in de Vogüé's diagram, that is to say they are conceived as a series of oversailing lintels. In the second place, Rosintal has shown[9] that even if the bricks or blocks of stone were set across the angle in the manner suggested by the very plausible theory of de Vogüé, we do not get, as one would be inclined to think, the circular form desired. On the contrary, there will still be a serious gap between the circular base of the dome and the

[1] Rivoira, *Lombardic Architecture*, I, p. 30; and his *Roman Architecture*, p. 158 and figs. 188–9.

[2] Rivoira, *Roman Architecture*, p. 158 and fig. 190.

[3] Although accepted as an example of a square dome by Strzygowski (*Baukunst der Armenier*, p. 479), I felt bound (in the first edition of this work) to express a certain amount of reserve on this point, firstly because no other example of this method of construction is known in Syria, so far as my knowledge goes, and secondly because Laborde, who travelled in Syria *c.* 1827, or more than thirty years earlier than de Vogüé, illustrates this building on a large scale and shows the central space roofed by an intersecting vault of cut stone (Fig. 496). He shows the same two gaps in the side vault as de Vogüé does, so he was not above drawing defects; see his *Voyage en Syrie*, p. 57 and pl. LI. However, Mr. Spencer Corbett has written to tell me that when he visited Boṣrā in the summer of 1950, he saw an example of this method of construction in a part of the Theatre that had recently been exposed. It covered a crossing place in the *vomitoria* (Fig. 497, facing p. 458).

[4] Waddington, *Inscriptions grecques et latines de la Syrie*, Inscr. Nos. 2524–37; and de Vogüé, *Syrie centrale*, pp. 45–6.

[5] Butler, *Ancient Architecture in Syria, Sect. A: Southern Syria*, p. 440.

[6] C. R. Conder, *Survey of Eastern Palestine*, pp. 43–5.

[7] De Vogüé, *Syrie centrale*, pp. 43–4, pl. 6, and fig. 9.

[8] A. K. Porter (*Medieval Architecture*, I, p. 106) and Diehl (*Manuel d'art byzantin*, p. 34) repeat this suggestion.

[9] *Pendentifs*, pp. 79–81. Phené Spiers had already called attention to de Vogüé's error in his *Stalactite Vaulting*, *Journ. of Proc. of the R.I.B.A.*, Vol. IV, New Series, p. 257; reprinted in his *Architecture: East and West*, p. 47.

Fig. 489. Qaṣr Kharāna: Vaulting system. (From Jaussen and Savignac, *Les Châteaux arabes*)

Fig. 505. Ruwayḥā: Mausoleum of Bizzos, setting of dome

Fig. 494. Etruscan tomb from Vetulonia. (From Rivoira, *Moslem Architecture*)

Fig. 495. Phaena (Mismīya): The Praetorium. (From Laborde, *Voyage de la Syrie*)

Fig. 496. Phaena (Mismīya): The Praetorium. (From de Vogüé, *Syrie centrale*)

top tier of niches, for each tier advances so little in the angle, as shown in Rosintal's diagram (Fig. 501). De Vogüé's elevation is therefore illusory.

Shaqqā. Traces of similar pendentives were found by de Vogüé at Shaqqā, in a little sanctuary, unfortunately without a date.[1] The square covered measured 8·15 m. each way, which is very much larger than anything we have met with hitherto. He also found the same style of pendentives in the palace.[2]

Latakia. Another attempt at a solution of the problem is found at Latakia in a tetrapylon, or four-faced archway, which marks the spot where formerly two colonnaded streets cut each other at right angles.[3] One street having been wider than the other, the arches vary also both in height and width, one pair being 7·80 m. wide, the other pair 4·48 m. only, from which it follows that the base on which the dome is placed is not square but oblong. The pendentives are flat triangles inclined inwards and formed in each case of three horizontal oversailing courses of cut stone, with oblique joints, as shown (Figs. 502–3). The regular octagon thus formed is provided with a very salient cornice, which permits the lower circle of the dome being set on the pendentives without cutting across the angles. In order to adjust the inequality of the two sides of the oblong, the little piece of wall above the narrower arches is inclined forward as shown, a logical and ingenious solution. The low dome is 9·70 m. in diameter, and consists of eleven rings[4] of perfectly cut stone voussoirs with a key-stone at the summit. Domes composed like this one of voussoirs of cut stone are typical of Syria, e.g. Quṣayr an-Nūwayjīs, the Baths at Jerash, the Mausoleum at Samaria, the Mausoleum of Bizzos at Ruwayḥā, the Double Gate and the Golden Gate at Jerusalem, etc., and the occurrence of similar domes in the three Fāṭimid gates of Cairo are one more proof of their Syrian origin. Roman domes at first were always of concrete or brick, which gave way later to concentric rings of earthenware jars laid in an ascending spiral with the tail end of one in the mouth of another, as in San Vitale at Ravenna. De Vogüé places this tetrapylon in the third century, but Choisy speaks of it as fourth–fifth century.[5]

Ruwayḥā. The problem of the pendentive is entirely evaded in two mausoleums, one at Ruwayḥā, and the other at Ḥāss, dating from the early part of the sixth century. The former, first published by de Vogüé, is one of the most important and best-preserved funeral monuments in Northern Syria. According to a Greek inscription,[6] it is the Mausoleum of Bizzos, son of Pardos, whose name is inscribed upon the great west portal of the larger of the two churches at Ruwayḥā, and there seems to be little doubt that both tomb and church belong to the sixth century.[7] De Vogüé,[8] van Berchem,[9] and Butler[10] have all emphasized the special importance of this building for students of Muhammadan architecture, on account of the fact that it is the only ancient structure in Northern Syria that preserves in its completeness an example of a cubical building with a domical roof (Fig. 504, facing p. 458), a prototype of the *welī*, such a characteristic building of the Muhammadan period in Syria, and of the domed mausoleums of the Muslim period in Egypt. In plan it consists of a Greek cross within a square (Fig. 506). Each arm of the cross is covered by a deep arch, three of the recesses thus formed being intended to receive a sarcophagus, whereas the fourth is taken up by the entrance. The haunches of the arches are built up level, so that the top of the cube presents a square platform with a square opening in the centre. The dome was then placed on this platform, but the distance between the outer and inner edge of the latter is such that the dome does not quite touch its outer edge, nor cut across its inner angles. No flat stones were placed across the angles as stated by Butler[11] and Swift,[12] the radius of

1 De Vogüé, *op. cit.*, pp. 41–3 and pl. 6; also Butler, *Architecture and Other Arts*, pp. 396–7 and figs. 140–41. This structure, in Butler's opinion, may probably be assigned to the same epoch as the little shrine at Umm az-Zaytūn.

2 De Vogüé, *op. cit.*, p. 49.

3 Michaud and Poujoulat, *Correspondance d'Orient*, VI, p. 446; de Vogüé, *op. cit.*, pp. 75–6, figs. 29–30, and pl. 29; Coste (Pascal), *Notes et Souvenirs de voyages*, I, p. 425; Dussaud, *Voyage en Syrie*, in the *Revue Archéologique*, 3me sér., XXVIII, p. 326; van Berchem and Fatio, *Voyage en Syrie*, I, pp. 289–90, figs. 166–7, and pl. LVIII; and Hautecœur, *Gazette des Beaux-Arts*, 6me pér., t. VI, p. 32.

4 De Vogüé, *op. cit.*, p. 75; van Berchem, *Voyage*, fig. 167, shows six and a key-stone. I have never visited Latakia.

5 *Histoire de l'architecture*, II, p. 18. Dussaud (*Voyage en Syrie*, *loc. cit.*, p. 326), also expresses the opinion that the date suggested by de Vogüé is 'un peu haute sinon pour l'arc, du moins pour la coupole qui le surmonte'.

6 Waddington, *Inscriptions grecques et latines de la Syrie*, Inscr. No. 2670.

7 Butler, *Architecture and Other Arts*, p. 247.

8 *Syrie centrale*, I, pp. 113–14 and pl. 91.

9 *Voyage en Syrie*, I, p. 204, n. 3, and pl. XLIII.

10 *Op. cit.*, pp. 247–8. Also Mattern, *A travers les villes mortes de Haute Syrie*, *M.U.S.J.*, XVII, pp. 24–5, pl. VII and fig. 5.

11 *Op. cit.*, p. 248; and his *Ancient Architecture in Syria*, *Sect. A: Southern Syria*, Appendix, p. xxv. This error has mislead Diehl, *Manuel d'art byzantin*, p. 36; and Strzygowski, in the *Zeitschrift fuer Geschichte der Architektur*, VII, p. 62.

12 He actually quotes the first edition of this work (p. 310),

Fig. 498. 'Ammān: Western Tomb, showing setting of dome. (From the *Survey of Eastern Palestine.*)

Fig. 499 Umm az-Zaytūn: Dome-setting. (From de Vogüé, *Syrie centrale.*)

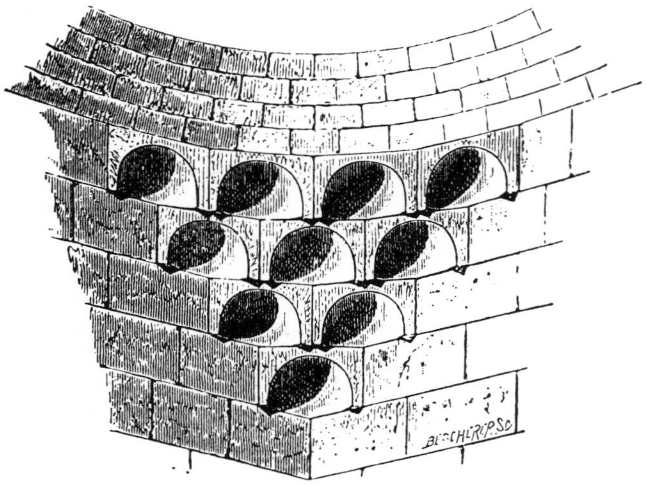

Fig. 500. Suggested origin of stalactite pendentives. (From de Vogüé, *Syrie centrale.*)

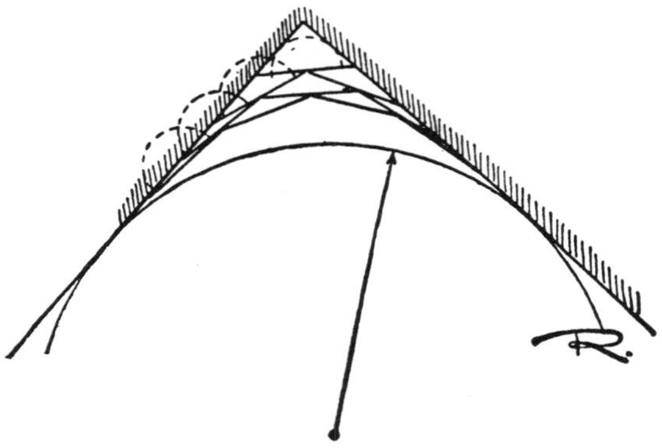

Fig. 501. Plan of stalactite pendentive, constructed after de Vogüé's theory. (From Rosintal, *Pendentifs.*)

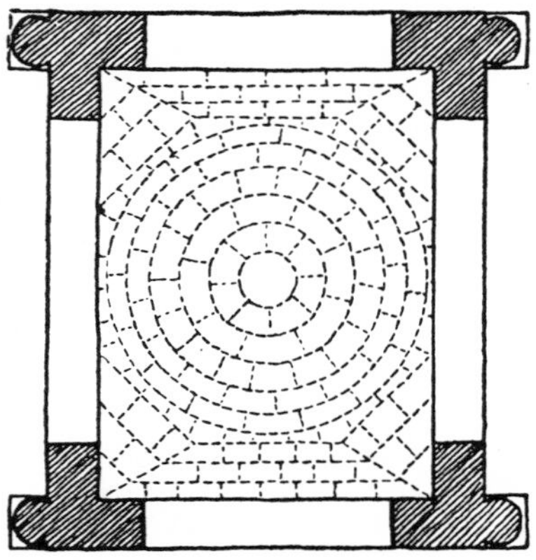

Fig. 502. Latakia: Plan of tetrapylon.

Fig. 503. Latakia: Pendentives of tetrapylon.

(From van Berchem and Fatio, *Voyage en Syrie.*)

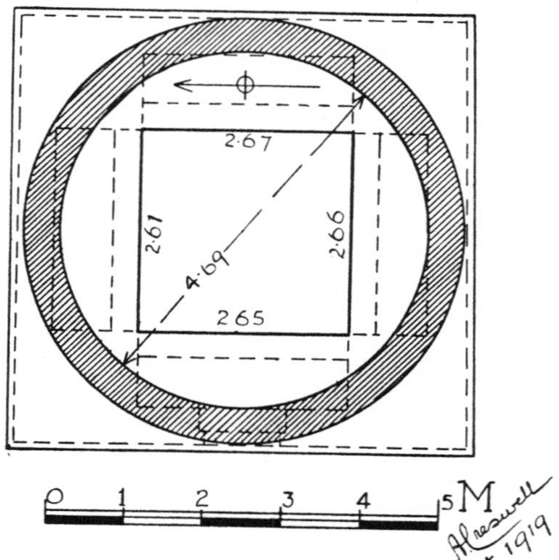

Fig. 506. Ruwayḥā: Plan of Mausoleum of Bizzos, at springing of dome.

the dome being such that there was no need to do this (Fig. 505, facing p. 454). The dome is not built in courses with horizontal beds, but is constructed on true principles with radiating beds, each stone being wedge-shaped, as well as concave internally and convex externally. The whole depends for its stability upon the most perfect stone cutting, for neither mortar nor clamps have been employed.

Ḥass. Here Butler found a somewhat similar mausoleum, which he assigns to the sixth century. It has no dome, but he concludes that it once had a dome of cut stone on account of the number of voussoirs lying about.[1]

'Abda. The dome over the *calidarium* of the Bath described above (p. 440) is set across the corners of the square in the primitive manner shown (Fig. 507), a stone lintel being employed instead of a pendentive. We have seen that this structure probably dates from the second half of the sixth century.

Fig. 507. 'Abda: Dome-setting in Bath. (From Père Vincent's drawing in the *Revue Biblique*.)

Early attempts in Asia Minor: *Mahaletch and Maden Shahr.* If we now turn to Asia Minor we shall find the same lack of a satisfactory pendentive, and the same unsatisfactory attempts to meet the problem.[2] Gertrude Bell, speaking of the interior, says: 'So far as my experience goes the pendentive is not known 'on the plateau till towards the tenth century—No. 12, Tchangli Klisse and 'Irkhala Dere, possibly a little earlier at Miram. Sir W. Ramsay inclines to the ninth century for No. '12 (inscription No. 28). Rott[3] states that he found an example of the continuous sphere [the authoress's 'term for spherical-triangle pendentives, supporting a dome whose curvature is continuous with them] 'at Tomarza. Its existence at so early a date in the centre of Asia Minor was a surprise to me; I visited 'the church myself in 1909 and found that Rott's statement is not correct. The dome has fallen, but 'the four corbel stones, set across the angles of the rectangular substructure, are all in place and the 'construction is therefore the same as that used in the oldest Kara Dagh domes.'[4] The 'oldest Kara Dagh domes' referred to are those of the cruciform church at Mahaletch and church No. 9 at Maden Shahr. Of the former she says: 'Above the four arches, the walls are carried up to the height of 'six narrow courses; in the seventh course a long stone is laid transversely across each corner, changing 'the square into an octagon; in the next course the corners of the octagon are rounded off, and the 'masonry is carried back slightly behind the original lines of the sides of the square so as to produce 'a circle (Fig. 508, facing p. 458).'[5]

In church No. 9 at Maden Shahr[6] the transition is less crude and therefore, I conclude, of somewhat later date. A stone is set across each corner and bevelled off below so as to form a small triangular *glacis*, recalling the treatment at Latakia. The ring of the dome is set back slightly behind the almost regular octagon so formed (Fig. 509, facing p. 458).

Early Attempts in Roman Africa: *Tripoli.* At the spot where formerly two colonnaded streets cut each other at right angles is a Quadrifrons or four-faced archway, still very well preserved. The square is converted into an octagon by four lintels placed across the corners (Fig. 510, facing p. 458), and on the octagon thus formed rests an eight-sided dome. This structure which, according to an inscription, was built by Marcus Aurelius and Lucius Verus, must have been erected between A.D. 163 and 165, for Lucius is called *Armeniacus*, a title which he took in 163, but not *Parthicus*, a title which he added in 165.[7]

where it is expressly stated that 'no flat stones were placed across the angles'.

[1] *Architecture and Other Arts*, pp. 246–7 and fig. 99.

[2] It is true that Choisy, writing over eighty years ago, speaks of pendentives in the Basilica at Philadelphia, in the Church of St. George at Sardis, and in a ruined building at Magnesia on the Meander (*L'Art de bâtir chez les Byzantins*, pp. 90 and 159–62, fig. 175, and pl. XVI), but he does not give any evidence for the dates of these buildings, which do not appear to have been published as yet. Nevertheless his statements have been repeated by the late Gertrude Bell (*Thousand and One Churches*, p. 441), Millet (*L'Art byzantin*, p. 143), and many others. As regards another alleged example, the Triumphal Arch of Salonika, built between 297 (date of the victory over the Perisans which it commemorates) and 311 (death of Galerius), I am equally unconvinced. This arch was a *quadrifrons*, but only the SW. arch now stands. Kinch (*L'Arc de Triomphe de Salonique*, Paris, 1890, p. 7) states that 'les briques de l'arc de décharge placé au-dessus du grand arc, sont façonnées ou posées de manière à servir d'appui à une *voûte sphérique*. Cette voûte, aujourd'hui entièrement détruite, etc.', I cannot distinguish anything of this in his plate showing the SE. (i.e. inner) face of this arch, for there is practically nothing left to go upon.

[3] *Zeitschrift fuer Geschichte der Architektur*, I, p. 160.

[4] *Thousand and One Churches*, p. 442.

[5] *Ibid.*, p. 249.

[6] *Ibid.*, pp. 79–80 and fig. 42.

[7] Trémaux, *Parallèles des édifices*, text to pls. 55–9. He shows it walled-up and converted into a shop, a condition which existed

Further attempts in Rome under the Empire: *The Domus Augustana.* Let us now return to Rome. In the substructure of the 'Domus Augustana' on the Palatine, built by Domitian about the year 85,[1] the square central room, measuring about 7 m. each way, must once have been covered, according to Rivoira, by a dome, which he says was sustained 'by the aid of triangular spherical pendentives formed of lumps of tufa set in irregular courses on a framework of boards and earth, and backed by concrete'.[2]

There is, however, no proof of this. I must emphasize the fact that no spherical-triangle pendentives are to be seen here now, for the remains (Fig. 511, facing) are quite rough and nothing of their original surface is left; they may quite well be the remains of an intersecting vault. Moreover, Mr. M. A. Sisson of the British School at Rome tells me that he has measured this room, and finds that if there had been a dome here it would have come right through the main floor level of the palace above, which is unthinkable. Dr. Ashby likewise believes that the existing remains belong to a cross-vault.[3] To right and left of this room is an octagonal room covered by a dome, but the transition between it and the octagon is slurred over (Fig. 512, facing). On the left at the top of the ramp, before coming to the chapel is a vaulted bay with a headless statue of a small boy. It is roofed by a cross-vault, but the groin in the corners is so worn away that, had the central part of the vault not been preserved, the remains would have been cited by Rivoira as another example of a pendentive.

Tombs on the Via Nomentana. About half a century later we have a tomb in the Via Nomentana, known as 'Sedia del Diavolo', which dates, according to Rivoira, from the time of Hadrian (A.D. 117–38), on account of its peculiar facing: '. . . the ground story, which is 5·20 m. square, was roofed with 'a depressed vault starting from flat pendentives, owing to the very moderate height of the chamber, '. . . The pendentives are formed of lumps of tufa set on a framework of boards; and the vault is made 'of the same material laid by hand. The upper story, or principal room, had a flat cupola, the tri-'angular pendentives of which, set between depressed arches, are formed at the base by rough brick-'work developed from the sides on which they rest, and above this by a surface of lumps of tufa laid 'in rows by hand, just like the cupola itself.'[4]

In another tomb on the Via Nomentana, near the Casale dei Pazzi, the lower chamber, which is 3·70 m. square, has a depressed cross-vault. The upper floor, on the other hand, is covered by a hemispherical dome 'supported by triangular pendentives formed on a framework, and made, like the 'cupola itself, of tufa lumps laid by hand in courses (Fig. 513, facing p. 460). . . . The horizontal 'section of the pendentives which we have been considering is almost flat, a sort of inclined plane from 'the vertical point of view, apparently on account of their small dimensions and the kind of centering 'used for their construction'. Rivoira attributes this tomb also to Hadrian.[5]

The Baths of Caracalla. In the Baths of Caracalla at Rome (A.D. 212–16), where a dome is set on one of the octagonal halls, the transition is not effected by means of eight spherical triangles; on the contrary, 'the spherical character of the pendentives is still not very strongly marked, but only appears 'about half-way up, the lower half forming a re-entrant angle which continues the lines of the walls on 'which the pendentives rest',[6] as may be seen in Fig. 514 (facing p. 460). This effect is of course the result of gradually approximating the octagon to the circle in successive courses, the angle becoming blunter and blunter and finally rounded, a kind of pendentive being thereby formed. As Lethaby

at least as early as Tollot's day (1731), *Nouveau Voyage fait au Levant*, p. 104, and still prevailed in 1877; see Rae (E.), *Country of the Moors*, pp. 68–71. For a recent description see Aurigemma, *L'Arco di Marco Aurelio in Tripoli, Bolletino d'Arte*, 2nd series, V, pp. 554–70 with 12 illus., and his folio monograph with the same title, published by the Reale Accademia d'Italia, fasc. XIII, with 28 plates, Rome, 1937.

[1] Lanciani, *Ruins and Excavations of Ancient Rome*, p. 140; Rivoira, *Lombardic Architecture*, I, p. 30; and his *Roman Architecture*, p. 108 and fig. 122.

[2] *Lombardic Architecture*, I, pp. 30–31.

[3] *Architecture of Ancient Rome*, p. 138; see also Platner and Ashby, *A Topographical Dictionary of Ancient Rome*, p. 162. Yet Swift suggests that the surface has deteriorated between the time when Rivoira's photograph was taken and mine, saying: 'But in view of the fact that Rivoira's observations were made at least two decades before those of the later authorities, etc.' Not so; Rivoira's work, as he tells us in his preface, was written during World War I, and my photographs were taken a few years after.

[4] *Roman Architecture*, p. 152 and figs. 183–4. See also his *Lombardic Architecture*, I, pp. 32–3. For a similar tomb which once existed near San Stefano Rotondo, of which a drawing is preserved in the Topham Collection at Eton, see the *Papers of the Brit. School at Rome*, VII, p. 7 and pl. I; and Ashby, in the *J.R.I.B.A.*, Vol. XXXVII, Third Series, p. 116.

[5] Rivoira, *Roman Architecture*, p. 155 and figs. 185–7. See also his *Lombardic Architecture*, I, pp. 31–2 and fig. 47.

[6] Rivoira, *Lombardic Architecture*, I, p. 33. See also Choisy, *Histoire de l'architecture*, I, p. 527 with diagram; and Rivoira, *Roman Architecture*, p. 169 and figs. 202–3.

FIG. 497. BOṢRĀ: Square dome in Theatre over crossing place in *vomitoria*. (From Mr. Spencer-Corbett)

FIG. 511. ROME: Alleged pendentives in substructure of the Domus Augustana

FIG. 504. RUWAYḤĀ: Mausoleum of Bizzos. (From Butler, *Architecture and Other Arts*)

FIG. 512. ROME: Dome-setting on octagon in substructure of the Domus Augustana

FIG. 509. MADEN SHAHR: Dome-setting in Church No. 9 (From Ramsay and Bell, *Thousand and One Churches*)

FIG. 508. MAHALETCH: Dome-setting over transept of church. (From Ramsay and Bell, *op. cit.*)

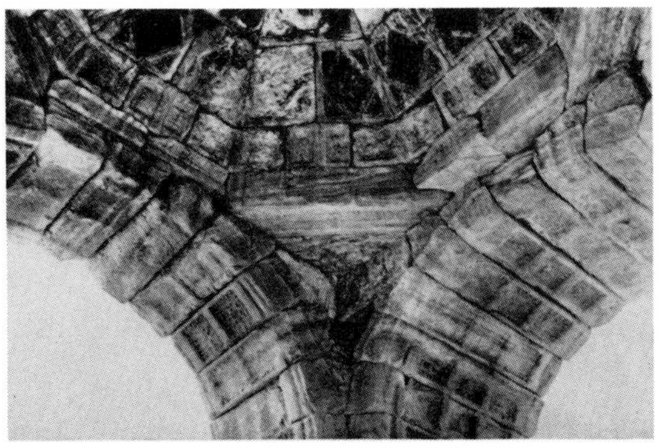

FIG. 510. TRIPOLI (Africa): Quadrifons

remarks when speaking of this building: 'the idea of the dome with its surface running on into the angles forming continuous pendentives was not accepted and the transition was disguised'.[1]

The Temple of Minerva Medica. Of the so-called 'Temple of Minerva Medica', where the dome is set on a ten-sided base (Fig. 515, facing p. 460), Lethaby writes: 'it looks (from below) as if the 'base of the dome proper were set back for some little distance over the sides of the polygon, and thus 'little projection is required at the angles, and the transition is slurred over in the plastering',[2] and Choisy says: 'le pendentif existe, mais réduit à l'état d'un simple encorbellement par assises horizontales, dont la forme est d'ailleurs fort indécise et vague.'[3] In spite of this Lasteyrie[4] and Giovannoni[5] speak of this building and the preceding as though the problem of the pendentive was there solved.

A Satisfactory Pendentive unknown to the Romans. Even Rivoira has to admit that after an 'examination, extending over more than thirty years, of every possible ruin of the Roman period [i.e. down to A.D. 330] in Italy' he has not been able to find any example of a true spherical-triangle pendentive.[6] And in another place, when speaking of the tomb near the Casale dei Pazzi, he says: 'I am 'unable to say whether the process of perfecting them [the pendentives] and their construction in 'courses of brick stands to the credit of the Romans or of the Eastern world. . . . But the proof of this 'is wanting, and, until fresh discoveries take place, the Byzantines must have the credit of the develop- 'ment of pendentives into their perfect form.'[7] Rivoira, therefore, at the last stage in his researches, was no longer prepared to assert that the pendentive was a Roman invention, nor did he have any illusions regarding the rudimentary nature of the device employed in the tombs on the Via Nomentana. This is the best answer to the remarks of Lasteyrie and Giovannoni. Yet well before this we have spherical triangle pendentives in Syria, perfect in theoretical conception and practical execution at Petra, 'Ammān, Jerash, and Samaria.

This, of course, is the explanation of the popularity with the Romans of circular buildings,[8] a popularity which they were never to enjoy again to anything like the same extent, once a satisfactory pendentive had been discovered. In addition to the mighty Pantheon, now known to have been built by Hadrian, a whole series of such structures exists along the Appian Way, e.g. the so-called Mausoleum of the Calatini, the Temple of Romulus (the son of Maxentius), etc.[9] These circular structures were not confined to Rome; the Emperor Trajan, for example, erected one *c.* A. D. 108 in the plain of the Dobrudja near the Danube, to commemorate his victory over the Barbarians,[10] and Diocletian built a circular temple to Jupiter in his famous palace at Spalato. Another example which may be cited is the church of St. George at Salonika, which can scarcely be later than the fourth century. Once a satisfactory pendentive was discovered buildings of this type immediately become scarce.

The Spherical-Triangle Pendentive. There are two possible solutions of the problem which we have been discussing: the spherical-triangle pendentive (German *Hängezwickel*, French *calotte sur pendentifs*) and the squinch. As we have just met with the former in Quṣayr 'Amra and Ḥammām aṣ-Ṣarakh, I propose to discuss its origin here.

But we must first consider the geometrical principle involved before studying its actual realization in brick or stone. It is arrived at in this manner. ABCD is the square space to be covered, and the

1 *Architecture*, p. 113.

2 *Op. cit.*, p. 113. See also Isabelle, *op. cit.*, pp. 58 ff. and pls. XXII–XXIV; Lanciani, *op. cit.*, pp. 402–8; Giovannoni, in the *Annali della Società degli Ingegneri e degli Architetti Italiani*, XIX (1904), pp. 165–201 and tav. iii and iv; *The Builder*, LXXXVIII, pp. 529–31; and Ashby, *op. cit.*, p. 82.

3 *L'Art de bâtir chez les Byzantins*, p. 80.

4 'D'ailleurs les Romains savaient dès cette époque, et même dès le siècle précédent, élever des coupoles sur pendentifs au-dessus de salles carrées. M. Rivoira en a reconnu dans deux monuments funéraires du second siècle qui se sont conservés sur la Voie Nomentaine . . .' *Architecture religieuse en France à l'époque romane*, p. 273.

5 *La tecnica della costruzione presso i Romani*, p. 35.

6 *Lombardic Architecture*, I, p. 33.

7 *Roman Architecture*, pp. 155–7.

8 Fergusson says: 'So far as I know, all the domed buildings erected by the Romans up to the time of Constantine, and indeed long afterwards, were circular in the interior, though, like the temple built by Diocletian at Spalato, they were sometimes octagonal externally'; *Handbook*, p. 346. Swift also notes the Roman fondness for circular buildings; *Roman Sources of Christian Art*, pp. 87, 89, and 99.

9 Montano, *Scielta d. varii tempietti antichi*, tav. 18, 21, 31–3, 41–2, and 53; Canina, *La prima parte della via Appia dalla porta Capena a Boville* (Rome, 1853), II, pls. VI, X, XVI, and XXXVII; Mongeri, *Le rovine di Roma al principio del secolo XVI, Studi del Bramantino*, XLVII, LIII, LIV, LV, and LXIX. Many of the plans of Montano and Bramantino have been reproduced by Rivoira, *Moslem Architecture*, pp. 60–71.

10 Tocilesco (G. G.), *Das Monument von Adamklissi* (Vienna, 1895).

inscribed circle E the dome to be placed over it. Imagine a larger dome FGHI *circumscribed* about the square. Then if the four segments ABG, BCH, etc., are cut off vertically on the lines AB, BC, etc., we get a shallow dome on spherical-triangle pendentives as shown in Fig. 516 (*b*).[1] Yet Jackson, from whose book I have taken these lucid diagrams, says: 'In Syria, however, they never arrived at this method',[2] an extraordinary statement which will not stand for a moment.

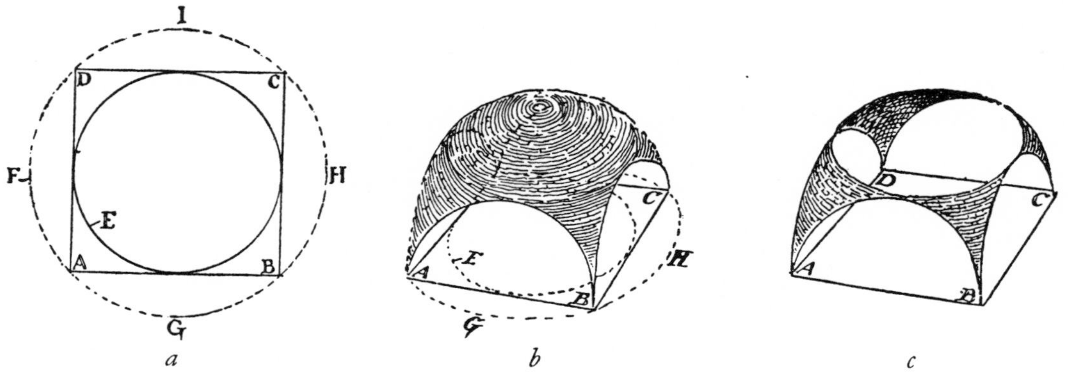

FIG. 516. The spherical-triangle pendentive. (From T. G. Jackson, *op. cit.*)

QUṢAYR AN-NŪWAYJĪS. Probably the earliest practical application of this principle still standing is that found in a mausoleum, known as Quṣayr an-Nūwayjīs, on the outskirts of ʿAmmān (Fig. 504, facing). Here we have a true spherical-triangle pendentive of six courses, the surface of which is a continuation of the curved surface of the dome; the latter is less than a hemisphere, but as the total height of the dome and pendentives is half the diagonal of the square chamber, it follows therefore that the whole—dome and pendentives—would form a complete hemisphere if the sides had not been cut away by the four wall-arches. We therefore have an exact replica in stone of diagram *b*.

Conder, who was the first to publish this building,[3] assigned it to the second century A.D., but without giving his reasons for doing so. Rivoira also, who mentions this building twice in his *Lombardic Architecture* in connexion with San Vitale (I, p. 66) and with the various types of Syrian mausoleums (II, p. 24), accepts it as of the second century, but at that time he presumably did not know its internal construction, for he ignores it in his investigation into the evolution of the pendentive, and cites the Mausoleum of Galla Placidia (*c.* A.D. 440) as the first perfected example. This fact, however, must have been pointed out to him, for in a later work (*Roman Architecture*, p. 173) he writes: 'I must pause 'for a moment to consider the pendentives of the tomb at Qasr al Nuwayjis, the date of which has been 'assigned to the later Roman Empire [amongst others by Rivoira himself, as we have just seen], but 'unsupported by valid arguments or parallels. There is no evidence that this new type of dome-support 'was used in Syria or Palestine at the end of the third century . . .', and he goes on to point out that it is not employed at Umm az-Zaytūn or Latakia (see above, pp. 454–5). His argument, therefore, amounts to this: Enunciation: the spherical triangle pendentive is not known in Syria before the time of Justinian. Proof: no examples of it are to be found. Examples of it, such as Nūwayjīs and Jerash, must therefore be of the time of Justinian or later. A perfect example of argument in a circle! He does not make the slightest attempt to produce the 'valid arguments or parallels' which he reproaches his predecessors for not having provided.

I will therefore attempt to do so. One feature provides a sound basis for argument, viz. the entablature, which on the north, west, and south sides is as shown in Fig. 518 (facing). On these sides of this mausoleum it will be observed that above an architrave with fascia is a curious series of vertical flutes which I propose to call a continuous triglyph motive, surmounted by a regular egg-and-dart border. I have searched for this motive in the works of de Vogüé and Butler and in the elaborately illustrated volumes of the German Baʿalbek expedition, and I have only found one example of it in the whole of Syria—in the so-called temple of Bacchus at Baʿalbek. A frieze of extraordinary richness runs all round the interior, and the lower half of this frieze is composed, not only of a continuous triglyph motive, but of a continuous triglyph motive surmounted by an egg-and-dart border (Fig. 506

[1] See also Hamilton's diagrams, *Byzantine Architecture*, fig. 7.
[2] *Byzantine and Romanesque Architecture*, p. 40.
[3] *Survey of Eastern Palestine*, pp. 172–4. Conder's opinion has received the support of Lethaby and Swainson, *Sancta Sophia*, p. 201.

Fig. 515. Rome: So-called Temple of Minerva Medica, setting of dome on ten-sided base

Fig. 513. Rome: Mausoleum on the Via Nomentana near the 'Casale dei Pazzi', setting of dome

Fig. 514. Rome: Baths of Caracalla, showing transition between octagon and circle

Fig. 517. 'Ammān: Mausoleum known as Quṣayr an-Nūwayjīs, pendentive

Fig. 518. 'Ammān: Mausoleum known as Quṣayr an-Nūwayjīs, cornice with 'continuous triglyph' motive

facing p. 462), exactly as in Quṣayr an-Nūwayjīs. As for the date of the Temple of Bacchus, Krencker says that in style it is not so classical as the Great Temple, but that it corresponds perfectly with the architecture of the great court, which is due to Antoninus Pius (A. D. 138–61).[1] We can therefore safely regard Quṣayr an-Nūwayjīs as dating from the latter part of the second century.

The Baths at Jerash (Gerasa). This example (Fig., 520 facing p. 462) was published by Choisy in 1883.[2] The technique closely resembles that of Quṣayr an-Nūwayjīs; for example, the shallowness of the dome and the curious cutting of the voussoirs, the upper and lower surfaces of the top course of the pendentives not being parallel. That these pendentives are constructed with true radiating beds can be seen from a photograph, published recently,[3] which shows the top course of the pendentive in the south hall, exposed by the fall of the dome.

Rivoira, speaking of these baths, which he had never seen, says:

'Choisy refers to an example, with cupola and pendentives forming part of a single curve, from the ruins of Gerasa. It shows, however, an arrangement exactly like that of the so-called "Double Gate" beneath the mosque of "el-Aksa" at Jerusalem, which in its turn betrays its relationship with that of the vaulting of the "Golden Gate" in the same place: buildings which must be ascribed to the VIth century, or, to be more accurate, to the reign of Justinian (527–65). The period suggested by Choisy, viz. that of the Early Empire, while Dieulafoy puts it later than the IIIrd century of the Christian era, is pure guess-work, and has no support in facts. And also what a singular phenomenon so important a discovery would be . . . making its appearance in Syria, perfect and complete in the days of the Early Empire, . . .!'[4]

What a singular discovery Rivoira would have made if he had ever visited Quṣayr an-Nūwayjīs and looked inside! As for the pendentives of the Double Gate and the Golden Gate, we shall see that the resemblance is not so close as Rivoira maintains.

Feeling sure that the recent excavations at Jerash, carried out by the British School of Archaeology, must have provided definite grounds for a really authoritative dating of this structure, I addressed myself to the excavators. Mr. A. H. M. Jones very kindly sent me the following, which puts the dating of these baths on a really sound basis:

'The baths on the right bank of the stream at Jerash consist of a large block of buildings, roughly T-shaped in plan, all built of fine ashlar and apparently homogeneous in date. The two wings are terminated by square chambers covered by a saucer dome on pendentives; the south dome has collapsed but the north dome is in perfect preservation.

'The building is not dated by any inscription. The periods of building activity at Jerash, however, are clearly defined. The first important period is the second century A. D.; of the principal buildings the North Gate is dated to Trajan, the Propylaea to Antoninus Pius, the South Temple to Marcus Aurelius, and the Nymphaeum to Commodus, by their dedicatory inscriptions. On architectural grounds the two theatres and the North Temple must be of the same period. Inscriptions are abundant during this period and the following half century (the Severan dynasty); they then fail abruptly; except for one inscription of Diocletian and of Constantine (both re-engraved on old inscriptions) there is nothing until the latter half of the fifth century, when a period of renewed building activity begins, lasting well into the sixth century. To this period belong the churches, many repairs to the walls, certain sections of the street colonnades and in all probability the "Forum". The buildings of this period are of a very inferior character, some of them were adaptations of older structure, and for the greater part built of material looted from the older monuments.

'The Baths, then, from the excellent character of their structure, probably belong to the earlier period. A further indication of date is supplied by an inscribed cippus, undated but probably of the end of the second or beginning of the third century, which stands (apparently *in situ*) in one of the colonnaded courts which filled the angles of the T, and which formed an integral part of the design of the baths.'

There is therefore every reason for regarding the pendentives of Jerash as not later than the first half of the third century.

Dieulafoy finds a connexion between the Baths at Jerash and Sarvistān for the following reason. At Sarvistān the courses between the squinches sink as they travel towards the corners; but if we study the lucid diagram of Rosintal,[5] we shall see that they *must do so* from purely geometrical considerations, as is explained when we discuss the squinch (in II, 1st ed., pp. 101–8). Dieulafoy finds traces of this school of craftsmanship in the pendentives of Jerash and the Golden Gate.[6] Now Persian domes in

1 Krencker, von Lüpke, and Winnefeld, *Baalbek: Ergebnisse der Ausgrabungen*, II, p. 86.

2 *L'Art de bâtir chez les Byzantins*, pp. 88–90, pl. XV (1), and figs. 104–5. R. de Scitivaux had already recognized it as a bath in 1860; *Voyage en Orient*, p. 96. Prince Rupprecht of Bavaria has published a plan of this building in the *Zeitschrift des Münchener Alterthums-Vereins, neue Folge*, IX, p. 5. See also Rosintal, *Pendentifs*, pp. 15–17 and Abb. 15–17; and Strzygowski, *Die Baukunst der Armenier*, pp. 361–2 and Abb. 397.

3 Sisson, *Roman Architecture at Jerash*, *J.R.I.B.A.*, XXXV, Third Series, pp. 98–9 and fig. 12.

4 *Lombardic Architecture*, I, pp. 34–5. See also his *Roman Architecture*, pp. 173–4.

5 *Op. cit.*, Abb. 43.

6 *L'Art antique de la Perse*, IV, pp. 71–4.

Sasanian times were tall and elliptical, instead of being very shallow like these; they rested on squinches instead of on spherical-triangles, and Sasanian architecture scarcely knew masonry of cut stone.[1] Not only is the suggestion far-fetched, but the analogy is not even a fair one, for the peculiarity in one case belongs to the tympanums between the squinches, the beds dipping towards the corners, whereas in the other it belongs to the pendentives themselves, the top courses of which thicken towards the corners (Fig. 520 facing).

Samaria. A third example of a really early spherical-triangle pendentive was found nearly sixty years ago by Reisner at Samaria,[2] in a Pagan tomb with a floor level 7·15 m. below the floor of the modern house immediately above it. The tomb is a square chamber preceded by a portico on four columns,

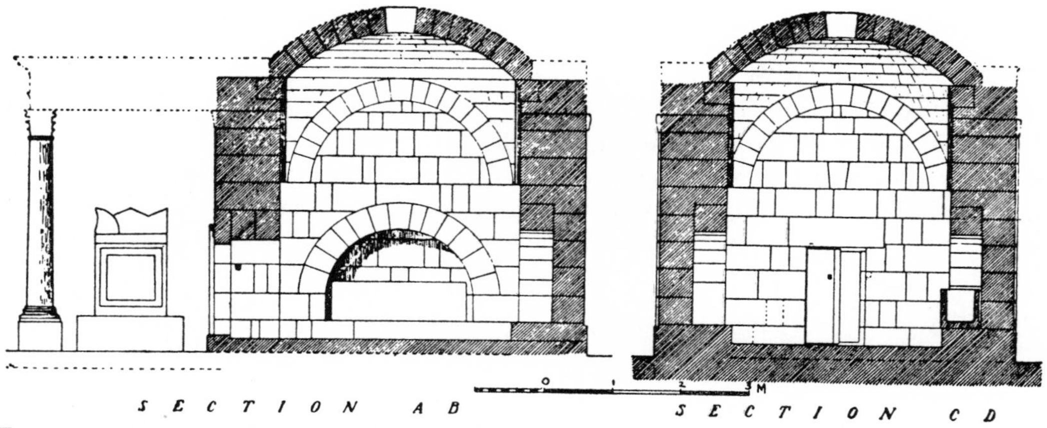

Fig. 521. Samaria: Pagan tomb with dome on pendentives. (From Reisner, *Samaria.*)

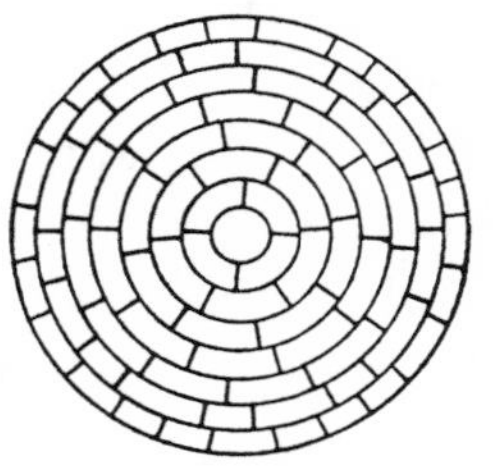

Fig. 522. Samaria: Dome of Pagan tomb. (From Reisner, *Samaria.*)

which extends the whole width of the façade. The interior, to which a stone door, 15 cm. thick, still *in situ* and in perfect working order, gives access, was approximately square, the sides measuring 3·47, 3·50, 3·27, and 3·27 m. respectively. On the north, east, and south sides were arched recesses 2·13 m. wide and 48 cm. deep. On each side of the chamber was a semicircular wall arch, their line of springing being 2·25 m. above the floor. On the tops of these wall arches rested a shallow dome 3·27 m. in diameter and 71 cm. in height. In the four corners between the four arches were spherical-triangle pendentives of five courses of masonry (Fig. 521). The dome itself was formed of seven rings of masonry, an oculus being left in the centre (Fig. 522).

A clue to the date is provided by the best sarcophagus (Fig. 523, facing), which measured 2·50×1·04×1·11 m.

'The long face was divided into two wide panels by short fluted pilasters with Corinthian capitals. These were in high relief and not connected with the base or the top mouldings of the front. From the tops of these pilasters were suspended heavy garlands of laurel leaves with a bunch of fruit(?) hanging from them. In the centre of the spaces were Medusa heads, with a double knot below each. The front was enclosed by a wide flat fascia, 16 cm. in width, with a deeply cut cyma reversa moulding 10 cm. wide inside it. The lid was in the form of a pediment with mouldings similar to those around the lower face. In the centre was a circular medallion portrait of the occupant(?). At the outer corners were two large acroteria.'

Having called the attention of the Department of Antiquities to the importance of this mausoleum for the history of the pendentive, it was further excavated by the Public Works Department in 1937 and a very careful survey of the structure, accompanied by large-scale measured drawings, made by their assistant architect, Mr. Norburn. He was able to confirm that the dome and its pendentives have been struck from a centre on the same level as the centres of the wall arches, and with a radius approxi-

[1] Ṭāq-i-Girrā, a tunnel-vaulted shrine, built with its back against the rocky sides of a pass in the Zagros range, is the only example known, and its Sasanian origin is not certain. This monument, which lies on the borders of Mesopotamia and Persia, in style belongs to the Christian architecture of the former country. The outer end of the vault forms an arch of slightly horse-shoe form, the mouldings of which are bent at right angles and continue horizontally along the façade. It may have been built between the second and the fifth centuries, but it presents several puzzling features. See Ker Porter, *Travels*, II, pp. 207–8; Flandin and Coste, *Voyage en Perse*, *Texte*, p. 465, and *Planches*, IV, pls. 214–15; de Morgan, *Mission scientifique en Perse*, IV: *Recherches archéologiques*, pp. 335–9, pl. XXXIX and fig. 204; and Herzfeld, in Sarre and Herzfeld, *Iranische Felsreliefs*, pp. 232–5, Abb. 112–13, and Taf. XLVII.

[2] G. A. Reisner, *Harvard Excavations at Samaria, 1908–10*, I, pp. 220–23 and figs. 148–52.

FIG. 519. BA'ALBEK: Temple of Bacchus, cornice with 'continuous triglyph' motive. (From Krencker and others, *Baalbek*)

FIG. 523. SAMARIA: Sarcophagus in mausoleum with a dome on pendentives. (From Reisner, *Excavations at Samaria*)

FIG. 520. JERASH: Pendentive in baths

FIG. 524. BRĀD: Pendentive in baths

Fig. 526. Jerusalem: The Golden Gate, pendentive

Fig. 528. Jerusalem: The Double Gate, pendentive

Fig. 529. Abū Mīna: Brick pendentive in Mausoleum of St. Menas

mately equal to half the diagonal of the room, that is to say it conforms to the geometrical construction shown in Fig. 516 *b*.

Hamilton, after a thorough examination of a block from the decorated pediment of the porch, the ornament of three[1] decorated sarcophagi (one is shown in Fig. 523, facing p. 462), and the style and coiffure of the four busts which were also found, comes to the following conclusions, thus fully confirming the date suggested in the first edition of this work.

'The differences in detail observable in the four busts, and the multiplicity of the burials are evidence that the tomb was in use for some generations. The presence of a coin of Constantius II in one of the coffins shows that burials were still taking place towards the middle of the fourth century. It is hardly possible on the evidence available to fix the upper date at all closely, but the coffin containing the coin may from its position be presumed to be one of the latest found, while the style of the others and of the busts (excluding No. 4) points at latest to the first half of the third century. The cornice fragment looks like second- or early third-century work, but might have been re-used.

'It would not be inconsistent with the evidence as a whole to place the building of the tomb in or soon after the reign of Septimius Severus (A.D. 193–211). It would then fall in a period of known architectured activity, of which evidence has been found in all parts of the city of Sebaste.'[2]

Here, therefore, we have a third really early spherical-triangle pendentive.

BRĀD. The baths at Brād,[3] published by Butler,[4] contain a small room, 3 m. square, probably the *calidarium*, which is covered by a dome on spherical-triangle pendentives. These pendentives, in Butler's drawing, are shown as consisting of three courses of masonry, but this is an error; the pendentives are monolithic (Fig. 524, facing p. 462). As for the dome, it is of most curious construction, being composed of a cross in a square as shown (Fig. 525), only seven blocks being employed. This is extended to an octagon by four more blocks, which rest on the four monolithic pendentives and the four walls. The surface of the whole forms a shallow dome. Butler places this building in the third century on architectural grounds, but this is too early. If the cross has been deliberately constructed as a Christian symbol—which seems certain, for it does not arise from structural necessity—then the date cannot be earlier than the fourth century.[5]

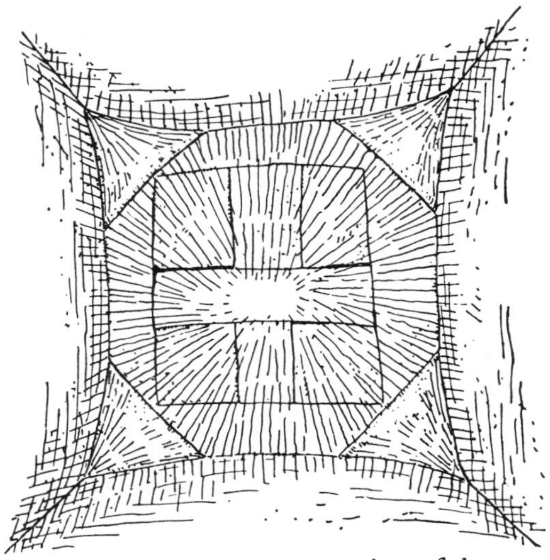

FIG. 525. BRĀD: construction of dome. (Drawn by M. Gaston Rossi, from a photograph.)

JERUSALEM: THE GOLDEN GATE. De Vogüé, who has given us a beautiful architectural study of this fine structure,[6] states his reasons in detail for fixing its date, and comes to the conclusion that it must belong to the sixth century, in which opinion he is followed by Hayter Lewis[7] and Rivoira,[8] both of whom attribute it to Justinian. De Vogüé bases his conclusions partly on the rich carved decoration, e.g. the lower part of the frieze (see my Fig. 68) which resembles a door-lintel at al-Bāra (above, Fig. 66), attributed by him to the sixth century. The resemblance is certainly close, but this lintel, unfortunately, is no more definitely dated than the Golden Gate, so this amounts to arguing in a circle. The same remark applies to nearly all the other parallels, viz. al-Bāra, cornice of pyramidal tomb;[9] Mijlayyā, lintel (above, Fig. 69);[10] Dānā, lintel;[11] and Ruwayḥā, lintel.[12]

There is one, however—the doorway in the atrium of the church at Bābisqā—which is definitely

1 Thirteen stone sarcophagi, whole or fragmentary, were found associated with this mausoleum.

2 Hamilton (R. W.), *The Domed Tomb at Sebastya*, *Quarterly of the Department of Antiquities in Palestine*, VIII, pp. 64–71, pls. XXXVIII–XL, and figs. 1–3.

3 Brād, an almost deserted field of ruins, is in the Jabal Sim'ān, about 25 miles north-west of Aleppo. To reach it, proceed along the old (not the new) Alexandretta road for about 20 miles, and then turn off to the village of Nebbūl on the left. A horse can be obtained here and a two hours' ride along a rocky valley brings one to Brād.

4 *Ancient Architecture in Syria*, *Sect. B: Northern Syria*, pp. 300–303 and Ill. 330–31.

5 Mattern has completely missed both peculiarities, for his drawing shows both pendentive and dome constructed in the ordinary way, and he calls it 'une œuvre entièrement syrienne, du IIe ou IIIe siècle'; *op. cit.*, *M.U.S.J.*, XVII, pp. 110–12 and fig. 25.

6 *Le Temple de Jérusalem*, pp. 12 and 64–8, figs. 10 and 36–8, and pls. VII–XII.

7 *The Holy Places of Jerusalem*, p. 96.

8 *Lombardic Architecture*, I, p. 34, and II, p. 21; and his *Roman Architecture*, p. 174.

9 De Vogüé, *Syrie centrale*, p. 106 and pls. 75–6.

10 *Ibid.*, p. 83 and pl. 32.

11 *Ibid.*, pp. 90–92 and pl. 45.

12 *Ibid.*, p. 102 and pl. 68.

dated 480;[1] it is of the more flowing, and therefore earlier, type closely resembling that at al-Barā, and a similar frieze, but of the stiffer, more conventionalized type, like that of the Golden Gate and Mijlayyā, decorates the main apse[2] of the church of St. Simeon Stylites at Qal'at Sim'ān, which was finished before 560,[3] so on architectural grounds we would be quite justified in attributing the Golden Gate to Justinian, but scarcely to the Empress Eudoxia, as Vincent and Abel do, although she is known to have restored the walls of Jerusalem, for her works were carried out between 438 and 444.[4]

I therefore fully agree with de Vogüé's reasons for placing it at the end of the Byzantine period, and I would be quite prepared to attribute it to Justinian, were it not for other considerations which prevent my doing so. In the first place Procopius, who gives a detailed description of Justinian's works at Jerusalem, and names a number of churches and monasteries restored by him,[5] says nothing about this magnificent and stately gateway. But there is a still more serious objection, to which attention has already been called by Hayter Lewis[6] and Hanauer,[7] viz. a passage in the account of the anonymous pilgrim, usually known as Antoninus of Placentia,[8] who came to Jerusalem *c.* A.D. 570.[9] He ascended from the Garden of Gethsemane and entered by a little postern[10] which, he says, 'adjoins the Gate Beautiful[11] which once belonged to the Temple, and of this gate the sill and doorposts still exist'.[12] It is obvious that it was in ruins, for I cannot believe that any one could refer to the present imposing structure in such terms.

FIG. 527. JERUSALEM: Golden Gate, remains of ancient doorpost. (From de Vogüé, *Temple de Jérusalem*.)

The door-posts referred to by Antoninus still exist, having been incorporated in the present structure, as de Vogüé has shown.[13] They are two great monoliths (A in Fig. 527), one 3·40 m., the other 4·50 m. in height. They are carved with a series of grooves, *c c c*, which do not correspond with the neighbouring courses, but which, as de Vogüé suggests, are no doubt the continuation, into the interior of the gateway, of the joints with drafted edges of the Herodian enclosing walls, long since destroyed at this point.

De Vogüé, however, who cites the passage quoted above, and who remarks that, for Antoninus, there remained of the ancient gate only the great blocks of the entrance, attributes the present structure to the sixth century.[14] Hayter Lewis, who accepts the evidence of this passage as decisive, nevertheless attributes the structure to the last years of Justinian's reign, believing the visit of this pilgrim to have taken place before the Emperor's death (565).[15] Now a *terminus a quo* is provided by the statement in Cap. I that he met the Bishop of Berytus who had known the sufferers in the great earthquake [of 551]. The account must therefore have been written after 551, and his reference to cities destroyed by an earthquake 'in the time of the Emperor Justinian' gives one the impression that that mighty genius was dead. If so, the work must have been written after 565. The Golden Gate, therefore, was still in ruins after Justinian's death.

Let us now turn to the history of the Byzantine Empire about this time. Under Justinian the empire

1 Butler, *Architecture and Other Arts*, pp. 133–5 and illus.; his *Ancient Architecture in Syria, Sect. B: Northern Syria*, pp. 167–9; and Prentice, *Greek and Latin Inscriptions in Syria, Sect. B: Northern Syria*, p. 132.

2 Photograph in my collection.

3 See above, pp. 118–19.

4 *Jérusalem*, II, pp. 834 and 910–11.

5 *De Aedificiis*, Bk. V, c. 6 and 9; Aubrey Stewart's transl., *P.P.T.S.*, II, pp. 138–43 and 147–8.

6 *Op. cit.*, p. 96.

7 *Walks about Jerusalem*, p. 137.

8 Grisar (*Zeitschrift für katholische Theologie*, 1902, pp. 760–70, and 1903, pp. 776–80), has shown that the attribution of this work to a certain Antoninus is incorrect. The pilgrimage was merely made under the protection of Antoninus Martyr, the patron saint of Placentia (Piacenza). See also *Revue Biblique*, XII (1903), p. 159; and Leclercq, in Cabrol and Leclercq, *Dict. d'Archéologie chrétienne*, IV, cols. 1899–2000.

9 Grisar, *loc. cit.*, puts it as late as 580.

10 Probably the little walled-up gateway, a short distance to the south of the Golden Gate, shown by Hanauer, *op. cit.*, fig. 110. This disposes of the suggestion of Vincent and Abel (*op. cit.*, p. 834) that this pilgrim had only seen the Golden Gate from a distance.

11 In Greek *Θύρα ὡραία*; the Greek word *ὡραία*, owing to the similarity in sound, was taken in medieval times as the equivalent of the Latin *aurea*, hence *Porta aurea*, or Golden Gate.

12 'De Gessemani ascendimus ad portam Hierosolima.... Porta civitatis quae cohaerit Portae Speciosae, quae fuit Templi, cujus liminare et tabulatio (Geyer's emendation for the variant readings: trabulacio, trabulatio, tribulatio) stat... ingressi sumus in sanctam civitatem'; Antoninus Martyr, Geyer's ed., pp. 170–71; ed. of Tobler and Molinier, p. 101, quoted by de Vogüé, *Temple*, p. 68, n. 2; see also *P.P.T.S.*, II, pp. 14–15.

13 *Temple de Jérusalem*, p. 12.

14 *Op. cit.*, p. 68.

15 *Op. cit.*, p. 96.

has reached its zenith. In science and art, as in war, his reign will ever be remarkable, his Code and Digest remain monuments of jurisprudence, and the church of Sancta Sophia is universally admitted to be one of the greatest masterpieces in architecture that the world has ever seen. His powerful personality so dominated men's minds that, in the words of Procopius, it seemed as if 'the whole world would not contain him'. But he passed away in 565, and of his successors—Justin, Tiberius, Mauricius, and Phocas—the first was weak and ultimately insane, the second met with an early death, the third, who inherited an empire now bankrupt, was, as it were, foredoomed to failure, and the fourth was an unspeakable ruffian. The revolt of Heraclius gave him the throne in 610, and then followed the disastrous Persian war, the sack of Jerusalem in May 614, and the destruction of the Church of the Holy Sepulchre, with many others.

A monk named Modestus then set forth and travelled throughout Palestine, collecting money for the restoration of the holy places. Contributions were also sent from Egypt by John, Bishop of Alexandria. Modestus, on his return to Jerusalem, was received with favour, and even allowed to commence the rebuilding of the churches,[1] the Persian Government desiring to placate the Christians. This attitude, so free from bigotry, forms a remarkable chapter in history. Sebeos states that Chosroes had sent special orders to treat the captives kindly, resettle them, and restore the public buildings, and quotes a letter, written by Modestus to the Metropolitan of Armenia, saying:

> 'God now has made our adversaries friends, and shown us mercy and pity from our captors. But the Jews . . . who presumed to do battle and to burn those glorious places, are driven out from the Holy City, and must not inhabit it nor see the holy places restored to their magnificence. . . . All the churches of Jerusalem have been set in order . . .'[2]

The conquest of Syria was followed by that of Egypt, and Alexandria fell in 618. A six years' war, waged by Heraclius against the Persians, culminated in the victory of Dastagird in 628, and the recovery of the Holy Rood.[3] In the following year he made a state visit to Jerusalem and celebrated the famous ceremony known as the Exaltation of the Cross, and Modestus appears to have completed the rebuilding of the Church of the Holy Sepulchre in time for this event.[4] Heraclius made his triumphal entry by the Golden Gate, bearing what was believed to be the 'wood of the true cross' on his shoulder. We have been told that Modestus restored the Holy Places; we know that the Golden Gate was one of them, for it was believed by the early Christians to be the Beautiful Gate mentioned in Acts iii, 2 and 10, and I therefore feel justified in attributing it to Modestus, between 616 and 629.

The difference between these pendentives and those already described must now be specified and emphasized. Whereas the others, together with the domes they support, are formed by the penetration of a hemisphere, as shown in Fig. 516 *a* and *b*, in the Golden Gate the dome and pendentives are formed by the penetration of a figure which is *less* than a hemisphere (Fig. 526, facing p. 463).[5] This, of course, is the result of the arches on which they rest being less than a semicircle. The whole system, therefore, of dome and pendentives is much shallower and much more daring, the latter being reduced by about two-fifths in height; nevertheless there is no aesthetic gain—quite the contrary. It was doubtless for this reason that it does not appear to have been repeated, either in Byzantium or in Islam, with the single exception of the Double Gate, which we will now discuss.

JERUSALEM: THE DOUBLE GATE. The structure known as the Double Gate consists of a double doorway, now walled-up, in the south wall of the Ḥaram Area, and a long double passage which rises gradually and ultimately comes out in the Ḥaram Area, in front of the Aqṣā mosque, after having

1 The Churches of the Holy Sepulchre, the Anastasis, Calvary or Golgotha, and Constantine are actually mentioned.

2 Butler, *Arab Conquest of Egypt*, p. 64 (from a MS. transl. by Conybeare); see also Macler's transl., pp. 71–2.

3 Gerland has made a detailed chronological study of this war, which he divides into three campaigns; see *Die persischen Feldzüge des Kaisers Herakleios*, in the *Byzantinische Zeitschrift*, III (1894), pp. 330–73.

4 G. Jeffery, *The Holy Sepulchre*, p. 13.

5 The arches have a span of 4·60 m. and a rise of 1·40 only. They are therefore segments of a circle having a radius of roughly 2·59 m., and the curved surface of dome and pendentives consequently has a radius of

$2{\cdot}59 \times 2$ (= side of ideal square) $\times \sqrt{2} = 7{\cdot}31$ approx
instead of $4{\cdot}60 \times \sqrt{2} = 6{\cdot}30$ approx.

The following figures make the difference clear:

(1)	height pendentives would have been on previous system	2·30	
(2)	height of dome	0·85	
(3)	total (ignoring depth of voussoirs of transverse arches)	3·15	
(1 *a*)	height of present pendentives .	1·40	decrease 39%
(2 *a*)	height of present dome . .	0·78	decrease 8·2%
(3 *a*)	total (ignoring depth of voussoirs of transverse arches) . .	2·18	decrease 30·8%

Four-fifths of the change, therefore, takes place in the pendentives.

passed under the latter a little to the east of the central aisle. Like the Golden Gate it exhibits work of at least two periods, and like it, has been admirably analysed by de Vogüé.[1] The oldest parts date from the Herodian epoch, but the original ceiling has disappeared, as well as the ramps. After a period of ruin, the débris were cleared away, and the remains of the entrance were utilized to form a base for the new one. The walls were refaced,[2] shallow pilasters being left; arches were sprung from these and the present pendentives, domes, and vaults erected. It now consists of two pairs of domes resting on a central column, and two long tunnel-vaults which cover the present ramp (Fig. 528, facing p. 463). These vaults, pendentives, and domes obviously cannot be later than the building which rests partly on them, that is to say the Aqṣā mosque, which almost every writer hitherto has believed to incorporate fragments of Justinian's Church of the Virgin, held by almost universal assent to have been built on this very spot.

But we have seen (above, pp. 31–2) that this cannot have been the case; it is therefore no longer necessary to attribute the domes and pendentives of the Double Gate to Justinian, but what alternative remains? De Vogüé, whose admirable architectural study of these two gateways has frequently been quoted above, points out that there is the closest possible resemblance between them. He says: 'the 'dressing is the same, the ornamentation of the outer archivolt is the same,[3] the interior arrangement 'of depressed arches and domes of cut stone is the same, all is identical, down to the smallest detail, 'such, for example, as the levelling up of the impost blocks of the arches by the aid of little slabs of 'white marble, the remains of an ancient paving.'[4] We may therefore attribute them to Modestus also.

First Examples outside Syria. The Mausoleum of St. Menas (Bu Mīnā) at Maryūṭ. The earliest practical application of this principle known to me outside Syria is in the little mausoleum of Saint Menas at Maryūṭ, in the desert about twenty miles west of Alexandria and about five miles from the coast. The site became a famous place of pilgrimage in the fourth century, and two great basilicas were erected there. One, which was built above the mausoleum of the saint, was consecrated, according to an Ethiopic MS. edited by Budge, under the Emperor Theodosius (379–95) by the Patriarch Theophilus (385–412).[5] The overlapping of these dates gives us A.D. 385–95 for the consecration. To the east of this basilica and in contact with it was built another great basilica which was begun under Arcadius (395–408).[6]

The mausoleum of the saint is a small chamber, only 2·35 m. square, under the altar of the older basilica. It has a shallow dome resting on spherical-triangle pendentives of red brick set in thick layers of mortar (Fig. 463, facing p. 529). Dome and pendentives are of the same curvature. Although Kaufmann, the excavator of these basilicas, has published a photograph of these pendentives,[7] he does not appear to have realized their architectural and archaeological importance and makes no comment on them, nor do they appear to have attracted the attention of any other author.

Ravenna. The next practical application of this principle outside Syria is to be found at Ravenna, in the cruciform building which has only been known as the mausoleum of Galla Placidia since the late Middle Ages. Galla Placidia died at Rome in November 450, and this so-called mausoleum may date from about 440.[8] Here, according to Rivoira, we find the spherical-triangle pendentive in a perfect form. But the shallowness of the dome, the difficulty of examining the construction properly owing to its rich covering of mosaic, and the manner in which the latter is carried round the angles of arches and openings, giving somewhat rounded and uneven forms to the arched lines,[9] prevent the eye

[1] *Temple de Jérusalem*, pp. 8–10 and 68–72, and pls. IV–VI, XIII, and XXXI.

[2] The proof of this work is found at the foot of the wall where the original dressing, covered by the first steps of the staircase, has not been refaced; the later destruction of the staircase has left the wall bare, exposed the drafted blocks, and given the clue to the transformation; de Vogüé, *op. cit.*, p. 9.

[3] See his pl. V, showing the same ornament as that on the frieze of the Golden Gate studied above, p. 120.

[4] *Op. cit.*, p. 69. This identity in design, detail, and date has been reaffirmed by an English architect; see G. Jeffery, *The Holy Sepulchre*, p. 139.

[5] Kaufmann (C. M.), *Die Menasstadt*, pp. 45 and 47.

[6] Severus ibn al-Muqaffa', Evetts' ed., in the *Patrologia Orientalis*, V, p. 122.

[7] *Die Augsgrabung der Menas-Heiligtümer*, fig. 25; *Die Menasstadt*, Taf. 9; and *Die heilige Stadt der Wüste*, Abb. 44.

[8] See C. Ricci, *Il sepolcro di Galla Placidia; Bollettino d'Arte*, 1913, pp. 389–418, 429–44, and 1914, pp. 173–4; and the summary of his researches in van Berchem and Clouzot, *Mosaïques chrétiennes*, pp. 91–2. Rivoira (*Lombardic Architecture*, I, p. 28, and *Roman Architecture*, p. 263) is far too affirmative.

[9] Jackson (*op. cit.*, I, p. 152) says that this treatment in so small a building has a somewhat barbarous effect, and that the interior seems rather as if it had been hewn out of a rock than regularly built.

Fig. 530. Ravenna: Mausoleum of Galla Placidia, pendentive

Fig. 550. Sama: Monastery of St. George. (From Butler, *op. cit.*)

Fig. 552. Qaṣr Ibn Wardān: Church, with pointed arch

Fig. 551. Umm ar-Raṣāṣ: Church tower

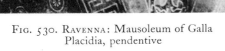

Fig. 584. Villa del Rio: Roman bridge over the Salado; note the joggled voussoirs

from grasping the exact outline of the pendentives, which appear to be somewhat drawn down in the corners (Fig. 530, facing p. 466). The whole effect, in fact, is so confusing that Friedenthal (1908) was led to maintain that the roofing of the central square was effected by an intersecting vault instead of by a dome on pendentives.[1] The late Ugo Monneret, however, informed me that he had had an opportunity of examining the dome from above during the repairs to the roof, which were carried out some years ago, and that he satisfied himself as to the presence of a dome constructed of an ascending spiral of earthenware pipes.

Although the distortion of the pendentives mentioned above may be an optical illusion caused by the mosaic decoration, there is another peculiarity regarding which there can be little doubt. A close examination reveals a sort of re-entrant angle, by which the angle of the walls below is continued upwards, a peculiarity which we have already observed in the Baths of Caracalla (above, pp. 458–9). This effect, as already pointed out, was the result of gradually approximating the octagon to the circle in each succeeding course, the angle becoming gradually rounded, and the cause is probably the same here. If so, it cannot be regarded as a true spherical-triangle pendentive; nevertheless it marks a notable advance from the Roman examples cited above, for it is applied to a square instead of to an octagon as hitherto.

Sancta Sophia at Constantinople. We now come to the supreme example of the spherical-triangle pendentive—the church of Sancta Sophia at Constantinople, the mightiest masterpiece of Byzantine architecture, which was commenced 23rd February 532[2] and solemnly inaugurated 26th December 537.[3]

Here the scale is enormous, for the dome is 107 feet (= 32·61 m.) in diameter from rib to rib.[4] The present dome is not the original one; that fell on 7th May 558 as the result of an earthquake.[5]

Rivoira refers to this disaster in the provocative, arrogant, and disparaging manner so frequently adopted by him when speaking of non-Roman work:

> 'The fact remains, nevertheless, that two eminent architects, Anthemius and the elder Isidorus, were unable to guarantee its stability, for it collapsed in the earthquake of 558. . . . The cause of the catastrophe may also have to be sought in the fact that his dome was the first work of the kind on so vast a scale carried out by Eastern builders (from Isauria), who had not got, like the Romans, a deeply rooted ancient tradition of vault-construction on a grand scale.'[6]

The answer to this is that the Romans *never even attempted* the problem of setting a large dome on a square substructure. When they built a dome of 19 m. (Baths of Caracalla) they put it on an octagonal base; when they built a larger dome of 24 m. (Minerva Medica) they thought it advisable to put it on a ten-sided base; and when they built a still larger dome of 43·20 m. (the Pantheon) they put it on a circular base, thus avoiding the problem of the pendentive altogether. As for Sancta Sophia, its stability is such that, with the exception of the Pantheon, it is 'the only great building in Europe which has endured and been in constant use for nearly 14 centuries'.[7]

The reconstruction of the dome was completed five years later, the church being re-opened on the 24th December 563.[8] Paul the Silentiary, a contemporary of this event, wrote a poem in long Homeric hexameters, which was probably recited at the opening ceremony. He says that 'only the top of the eastern vault (κεραίη) fell, and part of the dome itself, of which part lay on the ground and part, open to the light of day, hung insecurely suspended in the air, a wonder to behold'.[9] The piers of Anthemius, however, remained firm.

That portion of the dome which remained must have been taken down, for it is clear that a structural

1 *Das kreuzförmige Oktogon*, p. 56.

2 Lethaby and Swainson, *Sancta Sophia*, p. 21. I have not been able to find their authority for the day, but Zonaras (XIV, 6) gives the year and month.

3 Marcellinus Comes (contemporary), in Migne, *Patrologia, Series Latina*, LI, p. 943; quoted by Lethaby and Swainson, *op. cit.*, p. 21; Richter, *Quellen der byzantinischen Kunstgeschichte*, p. 51.

4 For the dimensions of Sancta Sophia we are dependent on Salzenberg, who was present during the repairs made by Fossati in 1847, and who made use of the unique opportunity afforded by the scaffolding. He gives the diameter of the dome as 104 ft., but his dimensions being in Prussian feet, 100 of which equal 103 English, the diameter must be just over 107 English feet; *Altchristliche Baudenkmale von Constantinopel*, pp. 54 and 65.

5 Theophanes, Bonn ed., pp. 359–60; and Malalas, Bonn ed., pp. 488–9.

6 *Roman Architecture*, p. 276.

7 Jackson (T. G.), *Byzantine Architecture*, I, p. 101. See also p. 91: 'The original design of the construction is admirable, and the best testimony to its excellence is the fact that it has for so many centuries withstood the violence of nature and of man.'

8 Lethaby, *op. cit.*, p. 29.

9 Verses 187–203; quoted by Lethaby and Swainson, *op. cit.*, pp. 34–6, and by Jackson, *op. cit.*, I, p. 87.

modification, and an important one, was made, all our sources[1] agreeing that the new dome was higher than the old one.

There are no signs, nor can there be any question, of the piers having been raised, as that 'would have involved so much interference with the whole anatomy of the building, which bears no signs of such heroic treatment, that it is hardly credible'.[2] It must, therefore, have been the height of the dome itself which was increased, that is to say, it must have been built with a steeper curvature. Procopius, who watched the building as it rose, speaks of the shallow original dome as appearing 'as though it were suspended from heaven by the fabled golden chain'.[3] Agathias (†582), speaking of the new dome, says that 'it did not frighten the spectators as formerly'.[4]

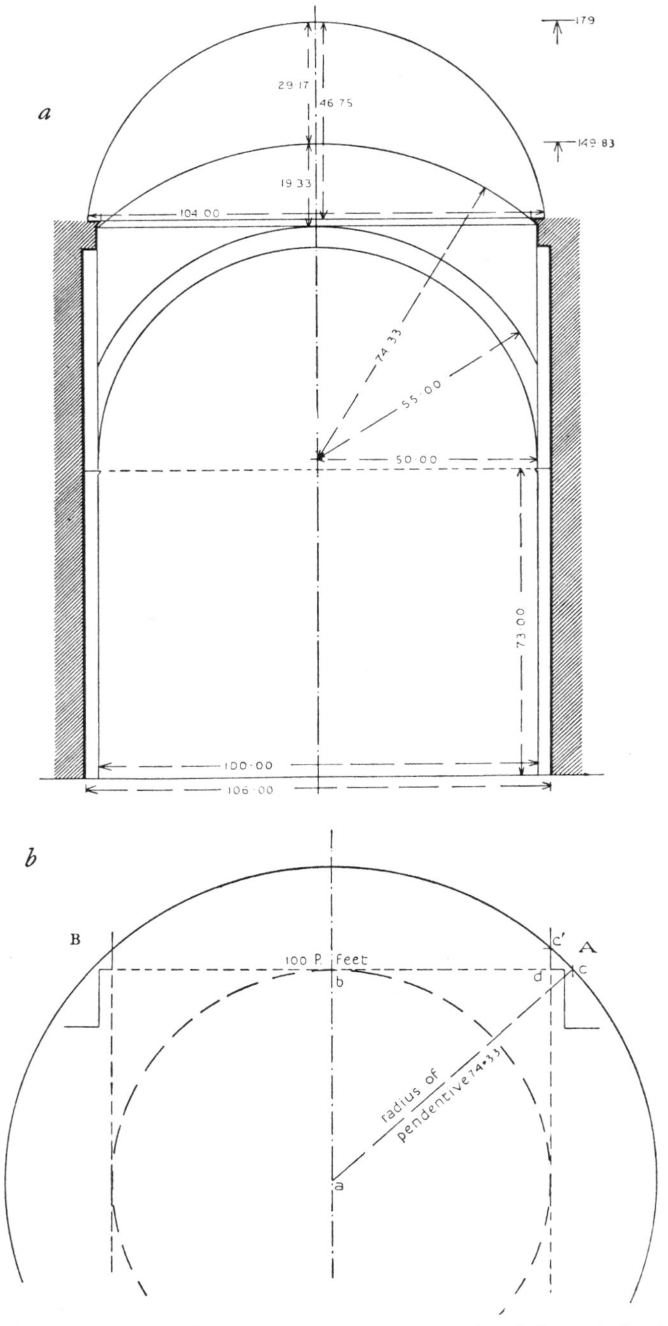

FIG. 531. CONSTANTINOPLE: Sancta Sophia. The original and the present dome.

Rivoira, however, says that 'its want of elevation, 'which goes so badly with its great span, together with 'the dwarfing of the drum, produce in the interior such 'a heavy effect that it seems as if it were about to fall on 'the spectator's head'.[5] Now, in the Pantheon, which Rivoira calls 'this wonderful and superb structure', 'built for all eternity', etc., the dome is nearly, but not quite, a complete hemisphere, that is to say, it is practically the same shape as the dome of Sancta Sophia, and it is *placed much lower*, both actually and relatively, for its diameter is 43·20 m. and the height of its springing *c.* 21·60 m. only above the ground, whereas in Sancta Sophia the corresponding measurements (converted from Salzenberg's Prussian feet) are: diam. 32·65 m.; height of springing 41·52 m.! Comment is superfluous.

Let us now assume that the original dome was struck from the same centre as the pendentives, as in Fig. 531 *b*. What must its radius have been? The arches, according to Salzenberg, have a span of 100 Prussian feet and a depth of 5 ft. (Fig. 531 *a*). The piers are 73 feet in height, but as the arches are stilted $2\frac{1}{2}$ feet, their true springing is $75\frac{1}{2}$ feet above the ground. Now the pendentives are set back on these arches, which complicates the problem, especially as the arches themselves are set with their intrados, instead of their extrados, in contact at the springing. The pendentives consequently do not begin where the arches spring, but at some distance above.

What is the radius of the sphere of which they form part? A in Fig. 531 *b* is the south-east dome pier. It is separated from B by 100 Prussian feet. Now the extrados of the arch AB springs 5 feet beyond *d*, at *c*, and the extrados of the southern arch at *c′*. The radius of the pendentive must therefore be *ac*. But *abc* is a right-angled triangle,

[1] Paul the Silentiary (563), Agathias († 582), Theophanes (†818), Zonaras *c.* 1118, and Malalas (twelfth century). See also Millet's learned study in the *Revue belge de philologie et d'histoire*, II (1923), pp. 599–617. He believes that the original bay covered by the dome was oblong (100 Prussian feet from east to west, and 106 from north to south), and that the original pendentives sprang from the re-entrant angles formed by the four pilasters (see Fig. 531). As a result of this theory he is compelled to maintain that the pendentives were rebuilt as well, which is not stated by any author. In support he cites Agathias, Bonn ed., p. 295, who says that the new dome was of a better shape than the old one, but this may well refer to the elevation.

[2] T. G. Jackson, *op. cit.*, I, p. 88. He thoroughly examined and reported on the building in 1910 at the request of the Turkish Government.

[3] Bk. I, cap. 1; Aubrey Stewart's trans., *P.P.T.S.*, II(γ), p. 9.

[4] Bk. V, cap. 9; Bonn ed., p. 296; quoted by Lethaby and Swainson, *op. cit.*, p. 30; Richter, *op. cit.*, p. 52.

[5] *Op. cit.*, p. 278.

$$\therefore ac \text{ (or radius)} = \sqrt{\{(ab)^2+(bc)^2\}}$$
$$= \sqrt{\{50^2+55^2\}} = \sqrt{5525}$$
$$= 74{\cdot}33 \text{ Prussian feet.}$$

The top of the original dome must therefore have been 73+2·5+74·33 = 149·83 Prussian feet above the ground. The top of the present dome is 179 feet above the ground; difference 29·17 Prussian, or 30·045 English feet. The height of the dome itself must have been 149·83−(73+2·5+55) = 19·33 Prussian, or 19·9 English feet only, which may well have 'frightened the spectators'. The height of the present dome, which rises with a steeper curvature than the pendentives, is 46·75 Prussian feet. The difference in height of the two domes was therefore 46·75−19·33 = 27·42 Prussian, or 28·24 English feet. Thus we have two points of difference: the new dome was 28·24 English feet higher than the old one, but its apex (thanks to the introduction of the cornice) was 30·045 feet higher above the floor-level.

Of the authors quoted above as saying that Justinian raised the dome, only three give the amount, Theophanes[1] saying 20 ft., Zonaras[2] 25, and Malalas 20.[3] Assuming that the unit used was the foot equal to 37 cm. employed under Justinian in Syria,[4] the figure given by Theophanes, the earlier authority, and by Malalas, represents 24 ft. 3 in., and that given by Zonaras 30·31 English feet, which is almost exactly the amount (30·045) given by my calculation.[5]

I am therefore led to the conclusion that the first dome was constructed on the principle shown in Fig. 531 *b*, but that at the rebuilding a fresh start was made from the stage shown in Fig. 531 *a* and the type shown in Fig. 532 produced, which, whether my theory is correct or not, represents the geometrical basis of the present dome.

Rivoira regarded Sancta Sophia as non-Roman. Swift, on the other hand, adopts a somewhat contradictory position. Speaking of Anthemius and Isidorus, he says: '. . . both hailed from Asia 'Minor and were presumably Greeks or of Greek descent; in architecture and building their back-'ground and training must therefore have been Anatolian, that is, entirely Eastern';[6] and on the next page he says: 'They were Greeks of Anatolian origin who practiced their craft and won their reputation in the East.' But how bring in Rome? He then finds the connexion in the fact that Anthemius, according to Agathias, had four brothers, one of whom lived in Rome. Hence the 'certainty' that he had 'often visited him there and had made a thorough study of the great imperial buildings. . . . The 'proof of this conclusion is obvious and unmistakable in the structure of Hagia Sophia itself when the 'latter is compared with the huge vaulted basilicas and magnificent thermae of the later Empire at 'Rome.' Later on he indulges in complete romance and refers to Anthemius as 'the Roman trained architect of Sancta Sophia'.[7]

Now supposing that he did visit his brother in Rome and studied Roman buildings, the only one the influence of which is apparent in Sancta Sophia is the Basilica of Constantine. But he could not have learnt how to construct perfect spherical-triangle pendentives in Rome, for *there were none to be seen there*.

But his partner Isodorus was better placed, for he travelled in the opposite direction, viz. Syria, the country where true spherical-triangle pendentives were to be seen, and he practised there, as is proved by an inscription of A.D. 550 at Chalcis (the modern Qinnasrīn about 18 miles SSW. of Aleppo), which records the rebuilding of the city walls under his direction (see below, p. 543), and in which he is called *μηχανικός*.[8] Massive remains of these walls still exist.[9]

1 Bonn ed., p. 360.

2 Bonn ed., III, p. 171.

3 Bonn ed., p. 490. (ἐπὶ πόδας εἴκοσι); but on p. 495 in figures as λ′ evidently a misprint for κ′ as Millet has pointed out.

4 Butler, *Architecture and Other Arts*, p. 36; and his *Ancient Architecture in Syria, Sect. A: Southern Syria*, p. 73.

5 Difference *c.* 3 inches. Since writing the above I have seen Prost's article in the *Comptes rendus de l'Acad. des Inscr.*, 1909, pp. 252–4, in which he suggests that the original dome was of the same curvature as the pendentives, but he does not enter into exact details or give any calculation. I have also seen Professor Traquair's paper on *The Origin of the Pendentive*, in the *J.R.I.B.A.*, Third Series, XXXV, pp. 185–7, in which he puts forward a similar theory. He realizes that the pendentives are set back on the arches, but adds the set-back to the diagonal, and consequently gets his radius too large. Moreover, he ignores the fact that Salzenberg's measurements are in Prussian feet and those of Theophanes in Greek, both of which differ from the English unit. He thus obtains a difference of level of 27 ft. 9 in., which being really Prussian feet are equal to 28 ft. 5 in. English, between the tops of the two domes.

6 *Roman Sources of Christian Art*, p. 83.

7 *Ibid.*, p. 124, n. 86.

8 Jalabert and Mouterde, *Inscriptions grecques et latines de la Syrie*, II, pp. 202–3. The walls had been ruined by Khusrau I in A.D. 540.

9 See Mouterde and Poidebard, *Le Limes de Chalcis*, pp. 4–7, pl. II–IV and plan I.

Terminology. It should be clear from the foregoing that there is no difference in the pendentives (the radius of which, being half the diagonal of the square, remains unchanged), but only in the dome. I wish to emphasize this point, for a question of terminology is involved. Gertrude Bell, in a short but brilliant summary on pendentives, distinguishes between those whose curvature is continuous with the dome, and those whose curvature is not.[1] The former (my 516 *b*) she calls 'the continuous sphere pendentive', the latter (Fig. 532) she calls the 'true pendentive, i.e. a spherical triangle of which the radius 'is smaller [misprint for *greater*] than the calotte [dome]'. Rivoira falls into exactly the same error: 'It is well known that there are two varieties of the spherical pendentive: 'in the one, the pendentive and the cupola belong to different spherical 'planes and curves; in the other, the dome is continuous with the pendentives';[2] and a few pages farther on: 'the builders of Ravenna boldly 'employed the perfect spherical pendentive continuous with the dome '[he is referring to the Baptistery of Neon (449 or 458–77), where the 'substructure is octagonal and not square!] . . . before the Byzantines 'employed the *other variety* [the italics are mine], in which the dome 'and the pendentives belong to different planes and curves, . . .'[3] Likewise Sisson, speaking of the Baths at Jerash: 'This type of construction appears to be the precursor of the dome on pendentives.'[4] Now it follows from the diagrams that the pendentives are identical in both cases; the dome alone has changed. The pendentives, therefore, should be described in both cases as spherical triangles, and terms found to distinguish the two types of dome; unfortunately 'continuous sphere' and 'non-continuous sphere dome' is scarcely satisfactory.

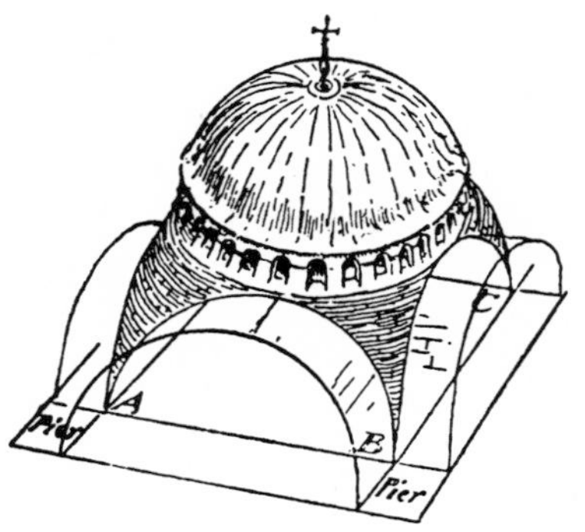

Fig. 532. Diagram of present dome of Sancta Sophia. (From T. G. Jackson, *Byzantine Architecture*.)

Gabriel, in a review of the first edition of this work, suggested that my explanation of the spherical-triangle pendentive (above, pp. 459-60) almost amounted to a waste of time, saying: 'M. C. aurait été bien inspiré en laissant de côté, dans un livre de cette valeur, ces pages de manuel élémentaire, qui n'ont même pas le mérite d'exposer clairement des faits extrêmement simple, bien connus de tous.'[5]

The paragraph above, on terminology, shows that they are far from being well understood by everybody, and misconceptions are still to be found in books written still more recently. Take the following for example: 'La calotte sur pendentifs est distincte de la coupole sur pendentifs. Dans cette dernière, 'le pendentif est un ouvrage indépendant, qui soutient la base circulaire de la coupole. Dans la calotte 'sur pendentifs, la voûte concave et les pendentifs qui la portent sont liés ensemble et *ne peuvent s'établir l'un sans l'autre* [the italics are mine]; ils s'engendrent à la fois et forment une surface 'continue.'[6] This, in a book on architecture published in 1934! It is obvious, as I emphasize once more, that the pendentive is identical in each case; it can be constructed up to the setting of the dome, then left for years if desired, and finally surmounted without undergoing any change by a dome of the same radius as the pendentive, i.e. a calotte, or by a hemispherical dome, according to choice.

And still more recently (1940): '. . . the second dome of Hagia Sophia—that completed in 563—'was the earliest in history to be carried upon true pendentives, that is, pendentives which were independent functional members, distinct, and of different curve from the dome they bore. The curvature 'of the original dome was so flat as to make it practically continuous with its pendentives, dome and 'pendentives forming parts of a single hemisphere whose diameter equaled [*sic*] the diagonal of the 'rectangle covered by the dome. It has been suggested, therefore, that the true pendentives of the second 'dome [the pendentives are the old ones unchanged] were inspired. . . .'[7] Two fine examples of muddled thinking.[8] Later on he writes that the very fact that I am 'compelled to use a separate term, 'continuous sphere pendentive, to distinguish the primitive merging pendentive from the later true pendentive, etc.'[9] This shows careless reading; I never used the term, it was Gertrude Bell who used it

[1] *Thousand and One Churches*, pp. 439 and 443. This distinction is made by Choisy, *L'Art de bâtir chez les Byzantins*, p. 96, but he treats the dome and its pendentives as a *combination*.

[2] *Lombardic Architecture*, I, p. 30.

[3] *Ibid.*, I, p. 34. Same error in his *Roman Architecture*, p. 275.

[4] *J.R.I.B.A.*, vol. XXXV, Third Series, p. 99.

[5] *Syria*, XIV, p. 214.

[6] Ebersolt (J.), *Monuments d'architecture byzantine*, p. 31, n. 1.

[7] Swift (E. H.), *Hagia Sophia* (Columbia University Press, 1940), p. 163.

[8] For a still more recent example see Rumpler, *La Coupole*, p. 75.

[9] *Roman Sources*, p. 117

in *The Thousand and One Churches*, p. 439, and I remarked that the term was 'scarcely satisfactory' in *E.M.A.*, 1st ed., I, p. 322.

And now I would like to make a suggestion. Supposing that the Turkish Government took down the present dome of Sancta Sophia, *without touching the pendentives*, and replaced it by a shallow dome as before, would the present 'true pendentives' cease to be true pendentives? Let Gabriel, Ebersoldt, Swift, Mme Rumpler, and the rest ask themselves this question.

SANCTA SOPHIA AT SALONIKA. I have purposely placed Sancta Sophia of Constantinople third in my list for there is no convincing proof that Sancta Sophia at Salonika was built before it in 495, as Papageorgiu,[1] Lethaby and Swainson,[2] Strzygowski,[3] Rivoira,[4] Diehl,[5] Jackson,[6] Millet,[7] and, quite recently, Tafrali[8] and Ebersoldt (under reserve)[9] have maintained. The sources do not help us, for no mention of the church has been found earlier than A.D. 795,[10] but an inscription with part of a date has been found among the mosaics, which are of two periods. A band of fruit and flowers in the dome is interrupted in two places by a panel with inscriptions belonging to the earlier period, stating that the work was finished in November of the Year of the World 6 . . ., Indiction 4, while Paul was Archbishop. Papageorgiu was convinced that there was only room for one more figure after the 6, and $\overline{\text{ςΔ}}$ or 6004 (= Nov. 495) is the only year that will fit the Fourth Indiction.[11]

This conclusion was brilliantly demolished by Laurent, who showed that the Archbishop of Salonika in A.D. 495 was named Andrew instead of Paul, and that dating from the creation of the world does not occur either in inscriptions or in authors before the seventh century.[12] The month of November of Indiction 4 falls in 6139 (= A.D. 630), 6154 (645), 6169 (660), etc.; an archbishop named Paul is mentioned in the year 649; he therefore decided on A.D. 645 as the date of the work. As this inscription may refer to the mosaics only, it is not absolutely conclusive as to the date of the church, which may therefore be older.

SUMMARY. Thus the dome has been known from very early times, but not the pendentive, although strikingly similar attempts to solve the problem were made in Egypt, the Crimea, and Italy long before the Christian era. Even after, the problem remained unsolved in Italy and Asia Minor, and unsatisfactory substitutes for the pendentive are found in Syria. Nevertheless, it would appear that it was in the latter region that the true solution was found, and a series of examples, perfect in theoretical conception and practical execution, beginning in the second half of the second century A.D., is to be found there. The three earliest examples outside Syria are the Mausoleum of St. Menas at Maryūt, the Mausoleum of Galla Placidia at Ravenna and Sancta Sophia at Constantinople.

1 Ἑστία (Athens), 3rd Oct. (pp. 218–19) and 14th Nov. (p. 317) 1893, quoted by Laurent, *Sur la date des Églises St. Démétrius et Ste. Sophie à Thessalonique*, *Byzantinische Zeitschrift*, IV (1895), pp. 431–2.
2 *Op. cit.*, pp. 202–203; but since withdrawn by Lethaby, *Architecture*, pp. 153–4.
3 *Die Sophienkirche in Salonik*, in *Oriens Christianus*, I, p. 157: 'entweder gleichzeitig oder etwas früher als die Sophienkirche'; also *Kleinasien*, pp. 117–20.
4 *Lombardic Architecture*, I, p. 63.
5 *Manuel d'art byzantin*, pp. 120–21.
6 *Op. cit.*, I, p. 73.
7 *L'Art byzantin*, in André Michel's *Histoire de l'art*, I, p. 145.
8 *Topographie de Thessalonique*, pp. 165–7.
9 *Op. cit.*, p. 161.
10 In a letter of Theodore of Studion, written at Salonika in that year; see Tafrali, *op. cit.*, p. 165.
11 *Loc. cit.*, p. 317.
12 *Op. cit.*, *Byzantinische Zeitschrift*, IV, p. 432; and Dalton, *Byzantine Art*, p. 377.

XV

JABAL SAYS[1]

Position—Description—The entrance tower—The interior—The façades on the court—The unit of measurement employed in setting out the *Qaṣr*—The date—The mosque—The *ḥammām* and audience-hall.

Position. Jabal Says is 105 km. south-east of Damascus. To reach it one must pass through Dumayr to Khān Abū Shāmāt, the last control post on the route to Baghdād, which must be followed for another 20 km. before turning south-east and then south. The volcanic craters known as the Tulūl aṣ-Ṣafā then become visible to the west, and must be kept in sight, otherwise it means that we are too far to the east. Finally a flat-topped mountain comes into sight, and at its foot are the ruins we are seeking, whose existence was first made known by de Vogüé in 1865. In 1893 they were visited by von Oppenheim, in December 1913 by Gertrude Bell, and in 1938 by Sauvaget. I visited it on 5th June 1932 and again, accompanied by Écochard, on 9th June 1933 and made a plan of the mosque and *ḥammām*.

Jabal Says has recently been excavated by Dr. Klaus Brisch with the support of the Deutsche Forschungsgemeinschaft. I am deeply indebted to him for permission to publish the plan of the *qaṣr*, as revealed by his excavations, and also for taking me out and showing me his discoveries on the 9th and 10th of May 1964.

Description. The *qaṣr* at Jabal Says consists of a rectangular enclosure averaging 67·11 m.[2] a side externally, ignoring the projection of the towers, of which there are eight (Fig. 533). Four of these are hollow corner towers and four are placed in the centre of each side. The four corner towers average 8·40 m. in diameter, and three of them appear to rest on socles. In this connexion Sauvaget writes: 'Ces tours d'angles sont établies sur un socle en sallie que A. Poidebard considère comme un 'renforcement postérieur. Cette interprétation est contredite par l'examen de la technique, qui montre 'que ce socle, effectivement contemporain du reste de la construction, est simplement destiné a procurer 'une assiette plus stable aux angles de l'édifice.'[3] But Dr. Brisch has pointed out to me that this is a deception, for the masonry has been added as a reinforcement, so that the three towers are each enclosed in a sort of chemise, 95 cm. thick, which has been added against the *finished face* of each tower. We have seen something very similar in the corner towers of the Dār al-Imāra of Kūfa.

The intermediate towers average 6·50 m. in diameter, with a projection of 3·20 m.,[4] except that on the north side which is larger than the rest (9·17 m.), for the entrance passage passes through it.

The walls vary slightly in thickness, the average being 2·01 m. They are built of dressed basalt blocks on their inner and outer faces, with a filling of lumps of basalt and mortar. There are practically no foundations, for the walls are built directly on the rock and follow its natural inclination towards the north; if we take the south-west tower as zero, the south-east is 36 cm., the north-west 76 cm., and north-east 96 cm. lower.[5] Two courses of basalt, totalling about 70 cm. in height, form the foundations properly speaking, which usually project about 30 cm. beyond the face of the wall. Above this the basalt walls rise 2·20 m., after which the wall was built of mud bricks measuring 40×40×10 cm. Remains of these bricks were found *in situ* alongside the niche of the central tower, on the south and east sides and also to the west of the entrance tower, which shows that the basalt lower part of the walls has practically been preserved to its original height down to the present day.

[1] Bibliography:—1865–77, de Vogüé (Melchior), *Syrie centrale*, p. 71, figs. 26–8 and pl. 25; —1899, Oppenheim (Max von), *Vom Mittelmeer zum Persischen Golf*, I, pp. 243–8, with 1 plate and 4 figs.; — 1901, Dussaud (R.) and F. Macler, *Voyage archéologique au Ṣafâ et dans le Djebel ed-Drûz*, p. 30, and fig. 3; — 1927 Hogarth (D. G.), *Gertrude Bell's Journey to Hayil*, *Geographical Journal*, LXX, p. 4, with 2 illus.; — 1928, Poidebard (A.), *Reconnaissance aérienne au Ledja et au Ṣafa*, *Syria*, IX, p. 123, pls. XLV–XLVI and fig. 3; — 1934, Poidebard (A.), *Le Trace de Rome dans le desert de la Syrie*, pp. 63–5 and pls. LIV–LVII; — 1939, Sauvaget (J.), *Les Ruines omeyyades du Djebel Seis*, *Syria*, XX, pp. 239–56, pls. XL–XLI and 13 figs.; — 1956, Stern (Henri), *Notes sur l'architecture des châteaux omeyyades*, *Ars Islamica*, XI–XII, pp. 76–7 and fig. 9; — 1963, Brisch (Klaus), *Le Château omeyyade de Djebel Seis*, *Les Annales Archéologiques de Syrie*, XIII, pp. 135–58, with 12 illus.; and *Das omayyadische Schloß in Usais*, *Mitteilungen des Deutschen Archäologischen Instituts*, *Abt. Kairo*, XIX, pp. 141–87, Taf. XXXI–XLIII, and 29 figs.; — 1965, Brisch (Klaus), *Das omayyadische Schloß in Usais (II)*, *ibid.*, XX, pp. 138–77, Taf. XLVII–LI, and 52 figs.

[2] The measurements are 67·62 (north), 67·53 (east), 66·83 (south), and 66·48 (west).

[3] *Loc. cit.*, p. 242, n. 2.

[4] They therefore form almost exact semicircles in plan.

[5] Brisch, *loc. cit.*, p. 142.

Brisch is convinced that the exterior of the *qaṣr* had a coating of stucco, for he found traces of it in the east corner of the middle tower on the south side, and quite large surfaces of it to the east and still more to the west of the entrance tower.[1]

THE ENTRANCE TOWER, which is 9·17 m. in width and projects about 4·60, is built entirely of basalt, courses of well-cut blocks frequently alternating with courses of undressed stones; the entrance passage,

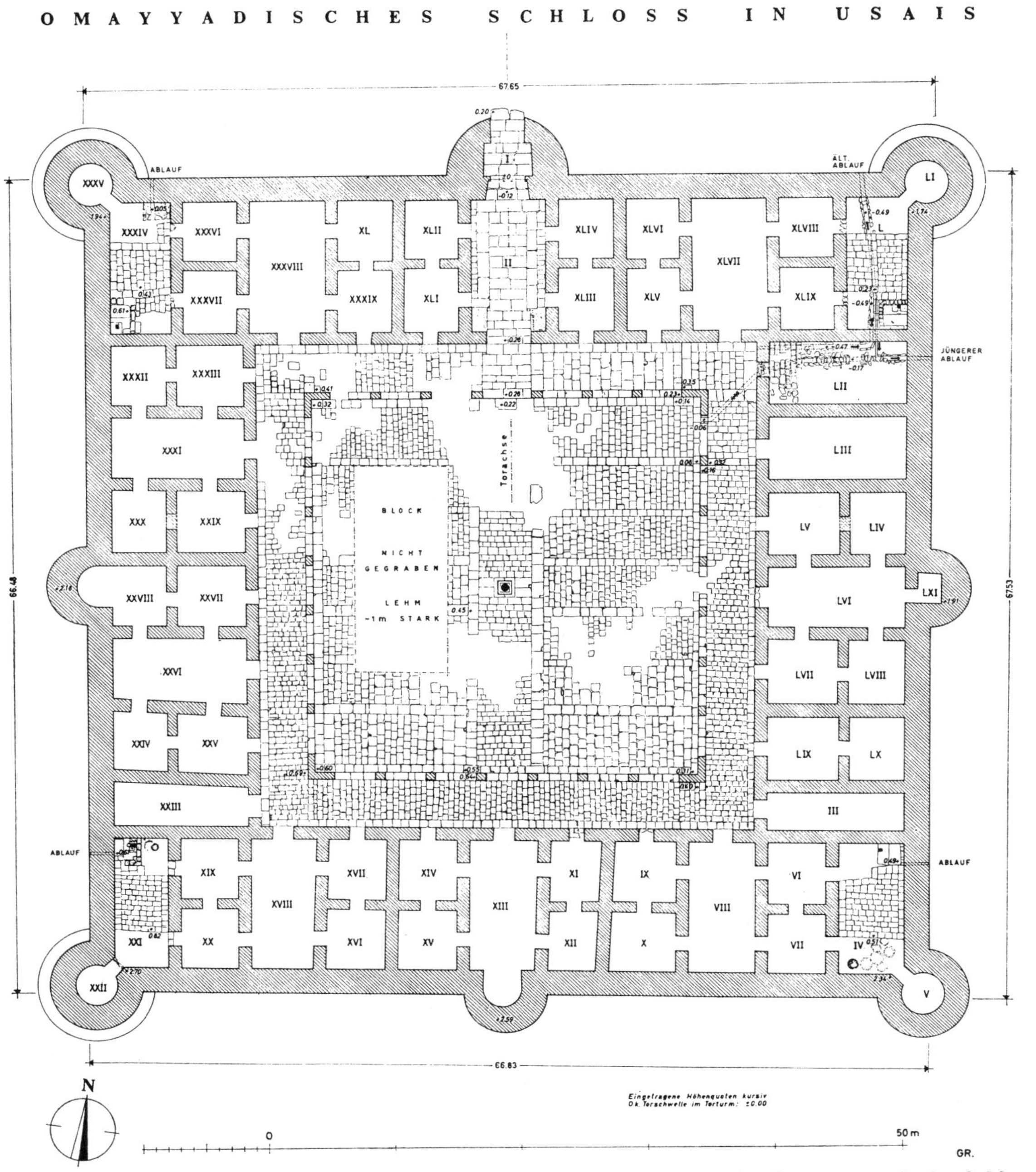

FIG. 533. JABAL SAYS: Plan of the *Qaṣr*. (From Brisch, *Das omayyadische Schloss in Usais.*)

however, is entirely lined with dressed blocks. It is pierced in the centre by an arched opening, 2·72 m. in width and very slightly pointed (Plate 77*c*), which leads into a tunnel-vaulted vestibule, 3·83 m. wide and 2·70 deep, at the back of which is a doorway 2·72 m. wide, opening into a great entrance hall, 5·95 m. wide and 10·90 long. The vault, immediately in front of this doorway, is pierced by an opening, 30 cm. in diameter, which may have been used as a speaking-tube, for interrogating visitors before opening the door.[2] The doorway had a wooden frame and holes to take the door pivots can be seen in the lintel. Corresponding sockets of iron are still in position below.

The masonry of the upper storey, which has the form of a horse-shoe in plan, is exactly the same as that of the lower, both externally and internally. The jambs of two lateral windows remained *in situ*.

[1] *Loc. cit.*, p. 145.

[2] In this connexion compare the east, south, and west gateways of Ukhai ir; *E.M.A.*, II, pp. 57–8 and fig. 38.

The excavators carefully examined the blocks piled up at the foot of the tower and made an inventory of them. Amongst them were blocks belonging to the sills, jambs, and lintels, which showed traces of the holes needed by iron grilles. They were forced to the conclusion that this upper room must have had two more windows and perhaps three. As regards the roof nothing remains, but Brisch[1] points out that de Vogüé speaks of a ' solide construction à deux étages voûtés en brique '.[2]

The Interior. At the inner end of the great entrance hall is an opening 3·56 m. in width, which gives access to an inner court, about 31 m. square surrounded by porticoes 3·80 m. in depth, with seven arches, as at Minya, on each side resting on piers. At the back of this portico were seven doors belonging to the zone of habitation, about 11·80 m. in depth, which consisted of self-contained *bayts*, or groups of rooms, as under:

On the north side there was a five-roomed *bayt* belonging to the entrance of the *qaṣr*, and two six-roomed *bayts* to right and left.

On the east side a five-roomed *bayt* in the centre, flanked to the north by two deep rooms, and to the south by a pair of rooms and one deep room.

On the west side there are two five-roomed *bayts*, and one deep room (XXIII) corresponding with III.

On the south a five-roomed *bayt* in the centre, and two six-roomed *bayts* to right and left. The outer rooms of the latter communicate with the hollow corner tower by a door only 1·80 m. high, with a lintel which rests on the top of the basalt part of the outer wall. Thus the east half of this side corresponds to the west half, except that it is reversed, and the south side as a whole corresponds to the north, except that, in the latter, the pair of outer rooms are not in communication, as we have just seen. There is, however, no such correspondence between the east and west sides.

There is a recess 3 m. wide and 3 m. deep at the back of the central room in the five-roomed *bayt*. Its great size and its position on the north–south axis exactly opposite the entrance of the *qaṣr*[3] make it probable that it was a throne recess, in which case XIII must have been a hall of audience.

This makes five five-roomed and four six-roomed *bayts*, or nine *bayts* in all. The former all have three doors opening on to the portico, but the six-roomed *bayts*, owing to their position (see plan), only have two.

It should be noted that all the lateral rooms of these *bayts*, except the end pair on the north side, are in communication with each other as well as with the central room, which is not the case at Qaṣr aṭ-Ṭūba, and in only two of the four *bayts* at Mshattā.

As regards the two long rooms at either end of the southern portico Brisch, on the analogy of Qaṣr al-Ḥayr al-Gharbī and Kharāna, suggests that they were occupied by staircases to the upper floor.[4]

The entrance, the central court, the passage leading to it, and the porticoes still have their original stone pavement, but hall IV was only partly paved.[5]

The foundations of the interior walls are similar to those of the outer wall, but narrower. As for the walls themselves those next the court have an average thickness of 1·05 m., whereas the partition walls are thinner, being about 85 cm. only.

The Façades of the Court. The excavators, from what they found in the interior, came to the conclusion provisionally that the porticoes consisted of two storeys, the lower of semicircular arches resting on piers, the upper of arches resting on marble columns, some monolithic, from pre-Muslim times, others composite, without capitals or bases and perhaps made especially for the *qaṣr* (Fig. 524). The arches are formed of two concentric rings of brick.

Between the columns of the upper storey were transennae, or balustrades of brick and stucco, just over a metre in height, designed like little arcades (Fig. 522). Some large pieces of the stucco ornament of these little arches were found and put together (Plate 78 *c*). The reconstructed arches bear a close resemblance to similar arches found by the German excavators at Maʿāriḍ, near Ctesiphon (Fig. 536). We shall meet with the same sort of thing in a very elaborate form at Mafjar (below, p. 555 and Plate 100 *b*). The façade was crowned with crenellations, probably with six steps.

[1] *Loc. cit.*, p. 144.
[2] *Syrie centrale*, p. 143.
[3] Compare the position of the Throne-Room at Kūfa and Ukhaiḍir.
[4] *Loc. cit.*, p. 147.
[5] *Ibid.*, p. 142.

THE UNIT OF MEASUREMENT EMPLOYED IN SETTING OUT THE QAṢR. The following table shows that the unit employed must have been the Nilometric cubit of 54·04 cm., which we shall see was also employed at Mafjar (below, pp. 561 and 574), and also in the Mosque of Ibn Ṭūlūn in 263–5 H. (876–9); see *E.M.A.*, 1st. ed., II, pp. 342-3.

East side of enclosure	67·53 m.	=	125 N.C.	=	67·55	Diff.	2 cm.
Entrance tower, width	9·17 m.	=	17 ,,	=	9·18	,,	1 cm.
Length of entrance passage	10·85 m.	=	20 ,,	=	10·80	,,	5 cm.
Width of entrance passage	5·95 m.	=	11 ,,	=	5·94	,,	1 cm.
Depth of porticoes	3·80 m.	=	7 ,,	=	3·78	,,	2 cm.
Width of main entrance	2·72 m.	=	5 ,,	=	2·70	,,	2 cm.

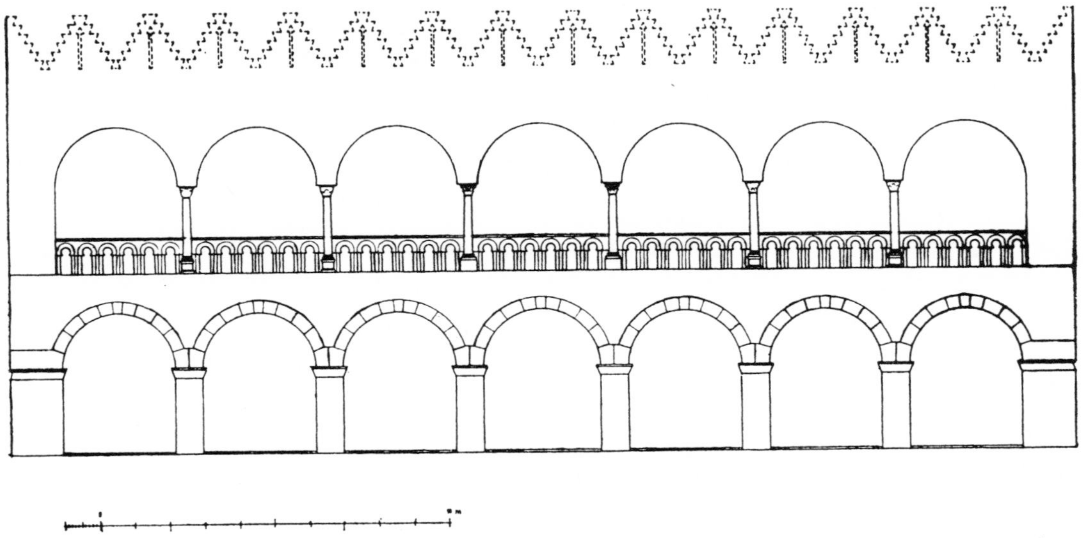

FIG. 534: JABAL SAYS: Arcade round courtyard. .(From Brisch, *loc. cit.*)

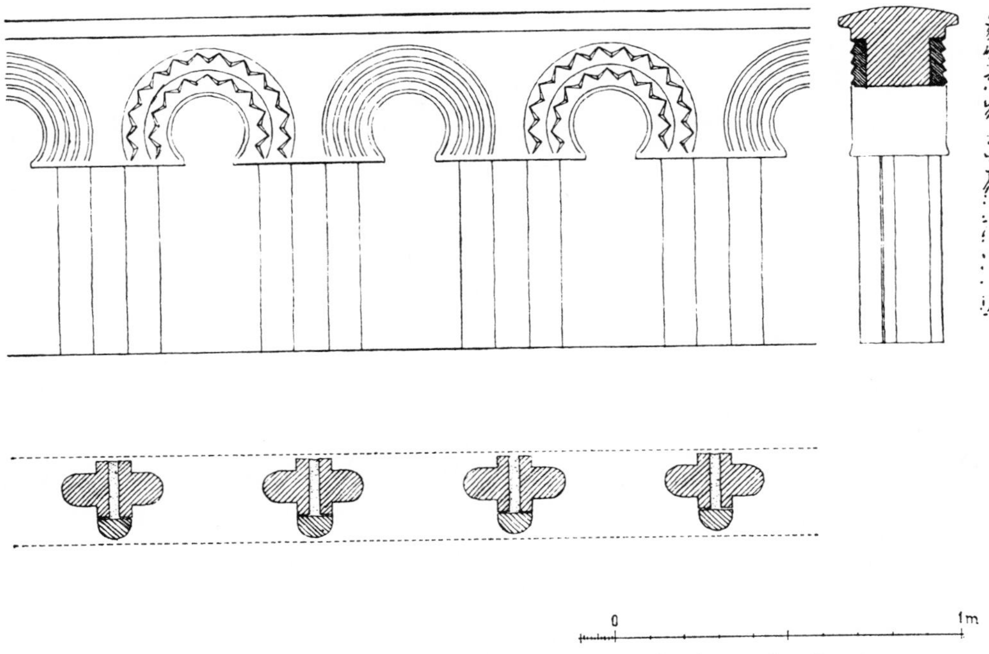

FIG. 535. JABAL SAYS: Arcade round courtyard, detail of balustrade of upper storey. (From Brisch, *loc. cit.*)

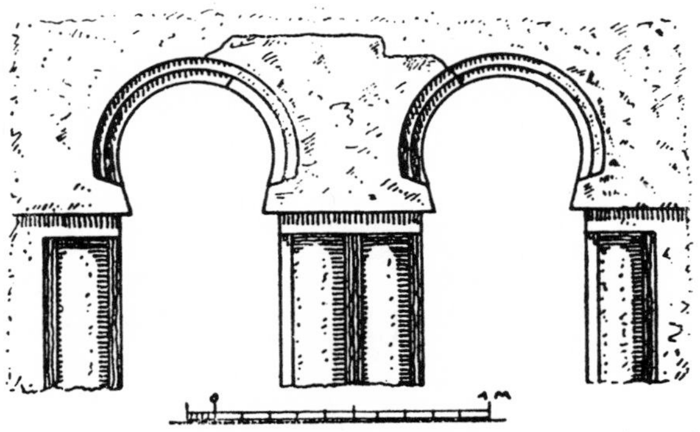

Fig. 536 MA'ĀRIḌ: Little arcades in stucco found near Ctesiphon, by the German excavators

THE DATE. de Vogüé, von Oppenheim, Dussaud, and even Poidebard, all believed that the *qaṣr* was a Roman frontier post, but Musil was able to show that it was Umayyad.[1] He quotes al-Bakrī to the effect that Walīd I had a residence at 'Usays,[2] and Yāqūt who says that 'Usays was a watering-place to the east of Damascus.[3] He adds that the correct name has been corrupted into Seis.

Did al-Walīd build it early or late in his reign? Its monastic simplicity, compared with the luxury of Minya, might lead one to put it earlier, but I believe this is to be explained by its distant and isolated position.

1 *Palmyrena*, p. 282.
2 *Mu'jam*, Wüstenfeld's ed., p. 122.
3 *Mu'jam*, I, p. 272.

Abu'l-Faraj al-'Ush has published quite a number of Arabic graffiti scratched on the rocks in the neighbourhood,[1] some of which are dated. The dates run as follows: 93 H. (712), 100 (718/19), 108 (726/7), 113 (732), and 119 (737). Thus it would seem that the occupation of Jabal Says by the Umayyads began towards the end of the reign of al-Walīd, and continued towards, if not actually until the fall of the dynasty and the systematic destruction of the Umayyad residences by the 'Abbāsids. And if the mosque nearby, which has a concave miḥrāb, is contemporary with the *qaṣr*, then we must put them both after the introduction of this feature at Madīna in 88 or 90 H. (707 or 709) and before the death of al-Walīd I in 100 H. (715).

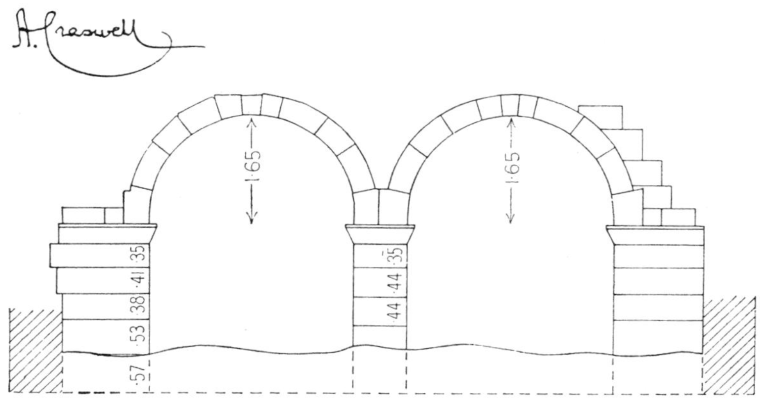

FIG. 537. JABAL SAYS: The Mosque, detail of arches.

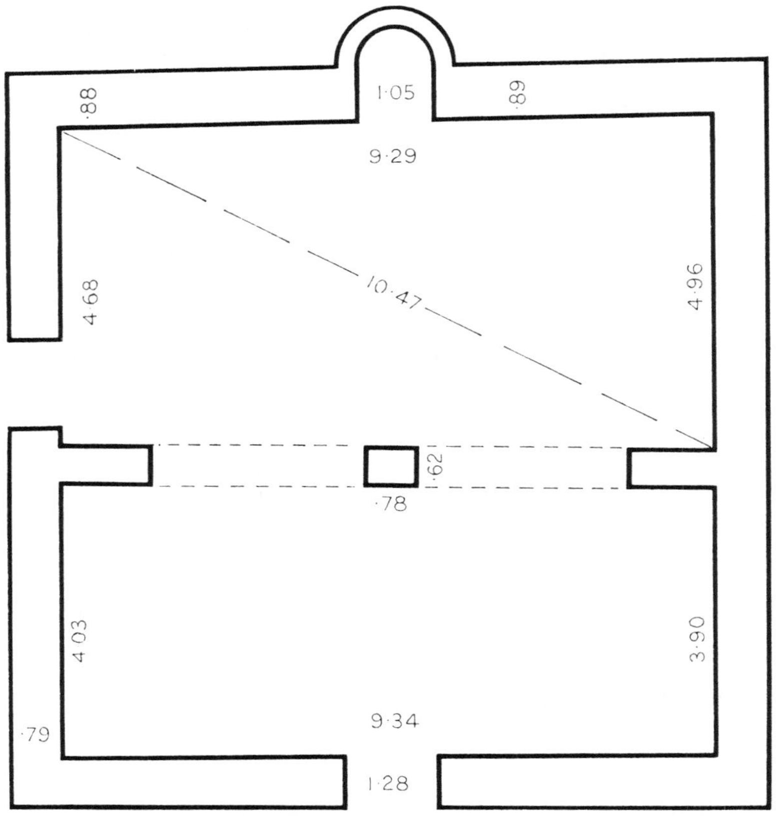

Fig. 538 JABAL SAYS: The Mosque.

THE MOSQUE. At a distance of about 70 m. to the west of the *qaṣr* is a small nearly square mosque (Plate 77 *d-f* and Fig. 537-8), measuring 9·34×9·48 m. internally, with walls of basalt from 80 to 90 cm. thick. It has two doors of which one, in the centre of the north side, is 1·28 m. wide, the other, in the east side, is 1·25 m. only.

The interior is divided into two nearly equal parts by an arcade of two slightly stilted semicircular arches, 2·93 and 2·98 m. in span, which rest on a central pier measuring 60×78 cm. and two wall piers, each 1·28 m. deep. These two arches were still standing when I visited Jabal Says on 9th June 1933, but one has since fallen. The central pier which, like the wall-piers, is crowned by a splay-face moulding, rises 2·52 m. above the sills of the doorways.

The arches rise approximately 1·65 which, added to the height of the piers and allowing, say, 30 cm. for the depth of the voussoirs, gives 9 m. as the height of the roof. The walls, except for the wall piers, are only three courses high, from which Sauvaget concludes, on the analogy of the *qaṣr*, that the part above was of mud brick. He also concludes that the roof was of wood, as such walls would not support a flat stone roof of the Ḥaurān type.[2]

The miḥrāb, partly destroyed, in the centre of the south wall, measures 1·07 m. in width and 1·35 in depth. Its semi-dome, as well as part of its back wall, has fallen, but its frontal arch was still standing in 1893 when it was visited by von Oppenheim.[3] Curiously enough the wall of the semicircular part is only 35 cm. thick (Plate 77*f*).

[1] *Inscriptions arabes inédites à Djabal 'Usays*, in *Annales Archéologiques de Syrie*, XIII, pp. 225–37.
[2] *Syria*, XX, p. 245.
[3] *Op. cit.*, I, illus. on p. 245; Dussaud, *op. cit.*, fig. 3, and Gertrude Bell, *loc. cit.* LXX, p. 4.

THE ḤAMMĀM AND AUDIENCE HALL. About 150 m. east of the *qaṣr* is a building measuring about 16×17 m. (Plate 78 and Fig. 539). Only the lower part is preserved to a height of about a metre above the present ground level. This part is built of basalt, and the rest was doubtless of burnt brick.

It consists of a large tunnel-vaulted hall 4·37 m. wide and about 10 m. long with a semicircular exedra, entered by a slightly narrower arch. Part of the latter has fallen and part of the outer wall of the hall. At the opposite end are two small tunnel-vaulted rooms about 3½ m. deep. The large tunnel-vaulted hall with a semi-domed recess at one end I take to be the audience hall, corresponding to room A at Quṣayr ʿAmra, but the two small rooms which there flank the throne-room recess are here transferred to the far end of the hall. It had three windows, of which two were in the tympanum of the vault above the roof of the two little rooms, and a third in the semicircular exedra shown in de Vogüé's pl. 25, just below the springing of the semi-dome.

The vaulted hall was entered by a door approximately in the centre of the north side. A door on the opposite side leads into a series of rooms, one oblong and tunnel-vaulted as at Quṣayr ʿAmra, the next square, which, on the analogy of Quṣayr ʿAmra and Ḥammām aṣ-Ṣarakh was probably cross-vaulted, and a third room, square with three recesses, which was probably domed.

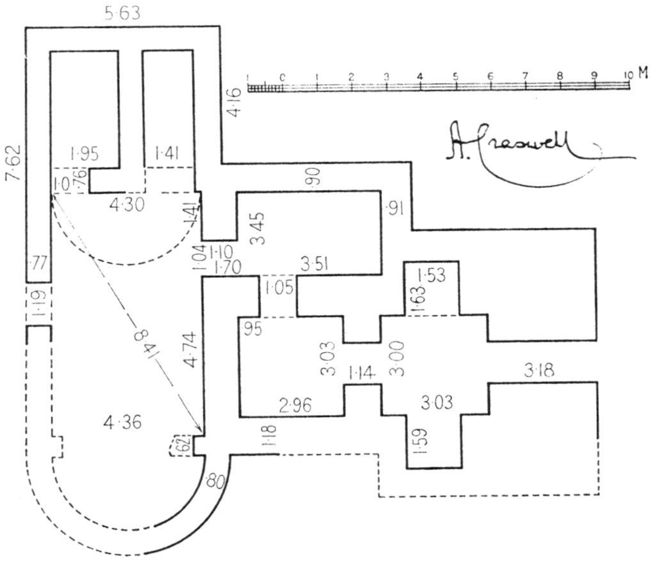

FIG. 539. JABAL SAYS: The Ḥammām.

XVI

‘ANJAR[1]

Description—The interior—The palace—The lesser palace—The mosque—The *ḥammām*—The tetrapylon—The date.

ALTHOUGH SEVERAL SCHOLARS (e.g. Clermont-Ganneau, Mouterde, Sauvaget, etc.) have identified the site, our knowledge of this wonderful layout is due to the extensive excavations of the Emir Maurice Chéhab, the Director-General of Antiquities. Thanks to his kindness I have been able to spend two entire days on the site, and I am especially grateful to him for giving me permission to reproduce Mr. H. Kalayan's great plan (Fig. 540 facing).

Description. ‘Anjar consists of a walled enclosure measuring 370 m. from north to south and 310 from east to west,[2] flanked by solid half-round towers and hollow three-quarter round towers. There is a gateway 3·08 m. wide, flanked by nearly half-round towers, in the centre of each side. There are six intermediate towers on the north and south sides and eight to west and east, making forty in all. Each side is provided with open staircases a metre wide, which run up the inner faces of the walls, behind the four gateways and behind the towers next the corner towers, making twelve in all. The whole enclosure slopes 13 m. from south to north.[3]

The walls are 2 m. thick of dressed stone blocks, in courses 50–60 cm. high externally, but of considerably smaller blocks internally. Between the two is a core of rough blocks and chips embedded in mortar. Some crenellations were found amongst the fallen masonry in front of the gateways and all round the enclosure. This important fact shows that the enclosure must have once reached its full height. Walls and towers are covered with Kufic *graffiti*.

The Interior was divided into four parts by colonnaded streets which ran from each gateway to the one opposite, and crossed in the centre, where there was a tetrapylon of four groups of four columns, each partly re-erected in 1963. About 4·5 m. behind the rows of columns were shops, about 5 m. deep and 3½ wide, with doors corresponding more or less to the intercolumniations. There were thirty-two shops on the west side of the north to south street, southern half, with space for a passage-way between the 10th/11th and 19th/20th counting from the south. At these two points the columns are replaced by T-shaped piers, so the roofing must have intersected here. The road between the columns was about 7½ m. wide, and the distance from shop face to shop face about 19 m. (Plate 78 A).

On the east side there is the same run of ten shops followed by a passage-way, but after that there are seven only. Three shops (=15 m.) are then omitted and replaced by a triple-arched façade on the exact axis of the west entrance of the palace, to which it must have formed a monumental approach. If we continue north we pass seven more shops, after which we come to a building with a triple entrance, apparently related to the mosque immediately behind it.

The Palace measures 71 m. from north to south and 59·5 m. from east to west. Its outer walls are 1·20 m. thick, and it has two entrances only, one (already mentioned) to the west and another exactly opposite; the former is the more richly decorated. Both lead into a room 11 m. deep and 6½ wide from which the central courtyard, 32½ m. square, can be reached.

[1] Bibliography: — d. 813, Theophanes, under the year of the World 6202 = A. D. 711; Bonn ed., p. 577; de Boor's ed., p. 377; — *c.* 846, *Syriac Chronicle*, published by E. W. Brooks, *Z.D.M.G.*, LI, p. 581; — 1900, Clermont-Ganneau, *Chroniques syriaques relatives à la Syrie arabe*, in his *Recueil d'Archéologie orientale*, III, p. 90; — 1912, Bell (H. J.), *Translations of the Greek Aphrodito Papyri in the British Museum*, *Der Islam* III, p. 87; — 1927, Dussaud (René), *Topographie historique de la Syrie antique et médiévale*, pp. 400–402; — 1939, Mouterde (Paul), *Inscriptions en syriaque dialectal à Kamēd*, *Mélanges de l'Université St. Joseph*, XXII, pp. 73–106; — 1940, Sauvaget (J.), *Les ruines Omeyyades de ‘Andjar*, *Bulletin du Musée de Beyrouth*, III, pp. 5–11, and figs. 1–3; — 1944–5, Sauvaget (J.), *Notes de topographie omeyyade*, *Syria*, XXIV, pp. 100–102; — 1947, Sauvaget (J.), *La Mosquée Omeyyade de Médine*, p. 114; — 1958, Sourdel-Thomine (J.), *Ayn al-Djarr*, article in the *Encyclopaedia of Islam*, new ed., I, p. 787; — 1959, Chéhab (Emir Maurice), *Découverte d'un palais omeyyade à ‘Andjar (Liban)*, *Akten des vierundzwanzigsten internat. Orientalisten-Kongresses, München*, 1957, pp. 349–51; — 1963, Chehab (Emir Maurice), *The Umayyad Palace at ‘Anjar*, *Ars Orientalis*, V, pp. 17–25, with 6 pls. and 2 figs.

[2] Area therefore 114·700 sq. m.

[3] Chéhab, in *Ars Orientalis*, V, p. 23; and Dussaud, *op. cit.*, pp. 400–401.

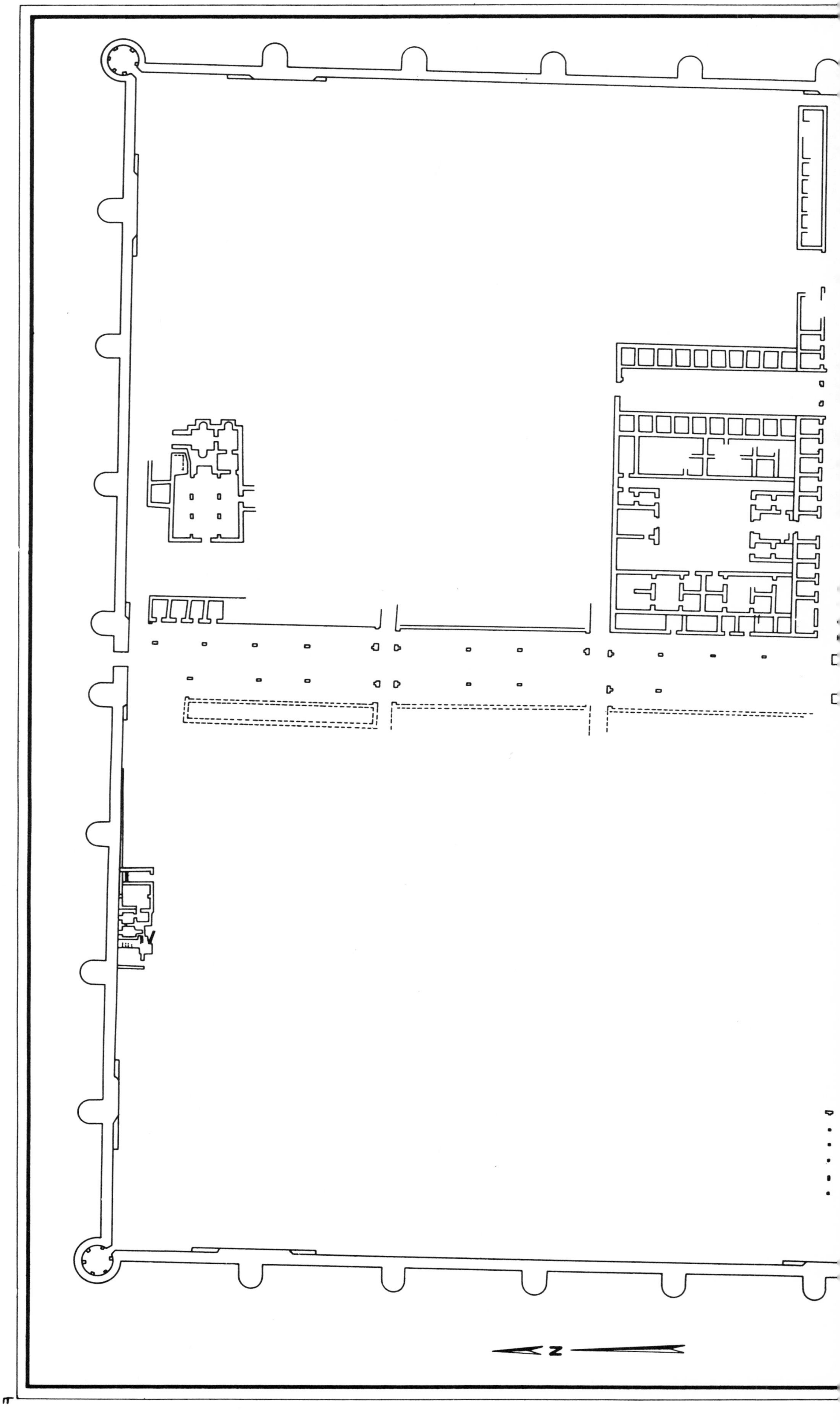
N

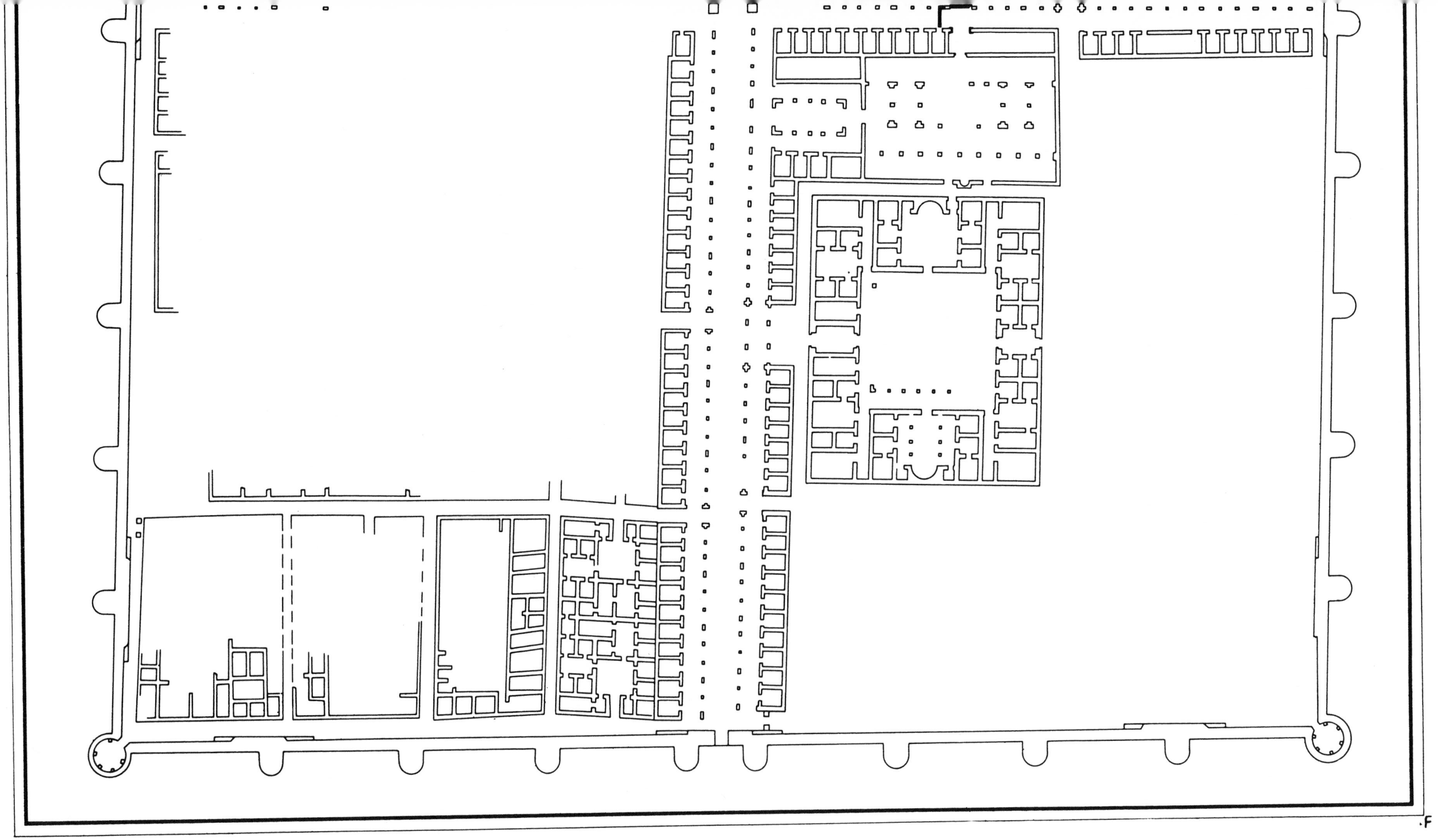

FIG. 540. ‘ANJAR: Plan. (By kind permission of the Emir Chébab.)

Like Mshattā the interior was evidently marked out into one wide and two narrow strips running from north to south. The rooms within are divided into four groups by corridors which run north and south from the four corners of the courtyard. In each outer strip are three five-roomed *bayts*, two of which can only be entered from the corridors. As for the central one, although its plan is the same as the others, it is difficult to accept it as a *bayt* because its central part is a thoroughfare. The courtyard was surrounded by a cloister with six columns a side and L-shaped corner piers, which implies seven arches a side.

Behind it on the south side was a basilical hall, the façade of which had fallen forward during an earthquake, and lay on the ground face downwards just as it had fallen, exactly like the portico at Mafjar, and the façade of the sanctuary of the Great Mosque at Ḥarrān. It has been raised and built up anew by Mr. H. Kalayan, the engineer of the Dept. of Antiquities. It makes an extraordinary impression, for the masonry is composed of courses of stone which alternate with three courses of brick. At first one is astonished, until one recalls a similar treatment of the Bayt al-Māl in the Great Mosque at Damascus and in the hydraulic works at Qaṣr al-Ḥayr ash-Sharqī. However, we must bear in mind that at Damascus this mixed masonry was covered up by a coating of mosaic, and one might have expected that at ʻAnjar the whole façade except the window arches and the continuous mouldings were likewise covered up by a coating of stucco. However, Mr. Kalayan has informed me that no trace of such a coating was found, for the stone surfaces were all well finished and pointed (Plate 78 B).

In the centre is a doorway with lintel and relieving arch, but its jambs do not form one with the brick and stone masonry of the façade. They are built entirely of stone, in courses larger than those of the façade, and are not properly bonded into it. This doorway is flanked to right and left by four arched windows, of which the pair next the entrance are blind. Each window arch is composed of two stone rings, the inner being smooth, whereas the outer is splay-faced and runs along horizontally to the next window, which it runs round, and then continues horizontally as before, in accordance with the practice popular in Syria before Islam, which we have already observed on the south façade of the Great Mosque at Damascus (Plates 42–3), and which we will speak of again when we come to study Mshattā. This is carved in somewhat shallow relief; to left it consists of interlacing semicircles filled with trefoils, to right of a branch with stiff leaves.

The upper part of the façade is treated differently. In the centre corresponding to the upper part of the basilical hall is a tall triple-arched window, flanked to right (and once no doubt to left) by a small arched window like those below. Here again the arches are all linked together by a continuous splay-face moulding.

The raising of the façade has freed the fallen columns of the portico, and the six column-bases and two L-shaped corner-piers thus exposed show that an arcade of seven arches a side must once have run all round the court.

If we pass through the doorway we find ourselves in a basilical hall with four arches a side in two tiers, resting on columns with re-used Roman capitals, surmounted by impost blocks in the shape of a truncated pyramid exactly as in the Great Mosque at Damascus before the great fire of 1893 (Plate 62 *a*). At the south end is an enormous apse 4·83 m. wide. To right and left are three rooms.

From the remains visible it would appear that this basilical hall, together with its flanking rooms and apse, was exactly duplicated on the north side of the courtyard, except for a doorway to the east of the apse, which opened into a street only 3 m. wide, exactly opposite a door of the mosque and immediately to the west of the miḥrāb. This door must presumably be regarded as the door of the *maqṣūra*.

The Mosque is about 47 m. wide and 30 m. deep; three of its supports are missing. It is a somewhat unusual plan, in some respects reminding one of Boṣrā, its *līwān qiblī* being two aisles deep, and likewise the lateral *riwāqs*, but its northern *riwāq* is one aisle deep only. The miḥrāb, which is somewhat out of axis, is 1·93 m. wide.

The Lesser Palace. To the north of the mosque on the other side of the colonnaded street is a palace nearly as large as the one already described. It is entered through what normally would have been a shop, but which presumably became the entrance porch of the palace. At the back of it is a door leading into an oblong room, at the far end of which is another door leading into a square courtyard, flanked to the west by a pair of five-roomed *bayts*. But unlike most Umayyad *bayts*, the entrance to them does not open into the central *līwān* but into an outer room, as shown, the doors of the two *bayts* being close to each other. On the east side we may conclude, in spite of the badly preserved remains, that there were two similar *bayts* there also. On the north side of the courtyard is what looks like another five-roomed *bayt*, of which the western third has disappeared. It should be noted that the western side of this palace is separated from the colonnaded street by a row of shops.

To the east of this palace is what looks like an enclosed bazaar with eleven shops on each side. If we return to the south gate we observe the lower part of two buildings measuring roughly 25×50 and 28×50 m. respectively, the plans of which do not conform to any known type.

Not counting the clear space left free next the city wall, there appear to have been two lesser transverse streets between the north to west street and the north wall and three to the south of it, except that the latter do not run right across because of the palace and mosque complex.

The Tetrapylon consisted of four groups of four columns each, resting on four square plinths 1·74 m. high and roughly 7 m. apart (Fig. 541). They are of very large masonry, some of the blocks measuring as much as 55×194 cm. The north to west and south to east plinths are intact but the south to west has lost its upper moulding. At the north-west corner, the four columns and their entablature have been re-erected; one column measures 4·95 m. not counting its capital and base (Plate 78 C above).

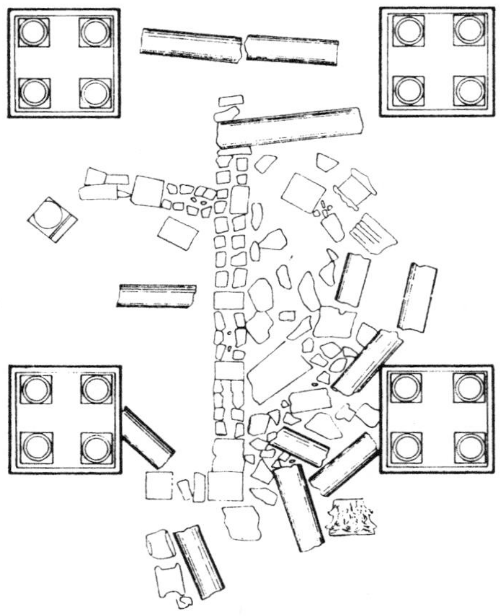

Fig. 541. ‘Anjar: The Tetrapylon. (By kind permission of the Emir Chéhab.)

The Ḥammām. To the left on entering by the north gate was an *ḥammām*, of which the plan has been laid bare. There is a square hall, the roof of which rested on two arcades of three arches each, from which the usual sequence of three rooms can be reached. The third, the *calidarium*, is square and was probably domed, and there is a semicircular recess to right and left, as in Quṣayr ‘Amra and Ḥammām aṣ-Ṣarakh. A fair amount of floor mosaics has been revealed (Plate 78 C below, and Fig. 542).

The Date. In 1897 a fragment of a Syriac manuscript of 846 was published by Brooks.[1] Amongst other things it stated that al-Walīd founded a town called In Gero. Brooks, in a footnote, points out that this fact is also recorded by Theophanes under the year of the World 6202, and also under 6235; he calls the city Garis (Γάρις) and says that it was in the province of Heliopolis (Ba‘albek). Brooks adds the interesting information that Dionysius of Tell Maḥrē calls this place ‘In Gero,[2] and Ibn Wadhi (II, p. 413) ‘Ain Gar. Clermont-Ganneau, shortly after, called attention to Brooks's article and identified the city with a village called ‘Anjar, a contraction of ‘Ain Jar.[3]

But in addition to Theophanes and the Syriac Chronicle we have other evidence for al-Walīd's work here, for Mouterde, in 1939, published a remarkable series of inscriptions, discovered by him in quarries near the village of Kāmed in the Beq‘a, about 20 km. south of the Beyrūt–Damascus road, in which the quarrymen have recorded their names.[4] But some are longer; his no. 10[5] reads: ‘In the year 96 of the Hijra (714/15) in the time therefore of the reign of Walīd son of ‘Abd al-Malik Emīr of the Saracens, this quarry has been opened by (men from) Jezīrat Kurdu (= Jezīrat ibn ‘Umar).’

Nos. 20 and 21 both read: ‘In the year ninety-six under the power of the Arabs. . . .’[6]

No. 28 reads: ‘In the year ninety-six in the days of Walīd Emir of the Higreans [i.e. Muslims] work has begun. . . .’[7]

1 *A Syriac Chronicle of the year* 846; *Z.D.M.G.*, LI, p. 581.
2 Chabot's text, p. 45; transl., p. 40.
3 *Recueil d'Archéologie orientale*, III, p. 90.
4 *Inscriptions en Syriaque dialectal à Kâmed (Beq‘a)*, *Mélanges de l'Université Saint Joseph*, XXII, pp. 71–106.
5 *Ibid.*, pp. 81–2.
6 *Ibid.*, pp. 92–3.
7 *Ibid.*, pp. 96–7.
8 Bell's transl., in *Der Islam*, III, p. 87.

Men also came from Egypt for no. 1434 of the Aphrodito papyri reads: 'Phamenoth 20, by letter of the Governor, by 'Ubayd ibn Shu'aib the courier concerning a labourer [or labourers] at Ainu 'l-Jar who returned to Babylon.'[8]

Sauvaget immediately connected the quarry inscriptions with our monument, which is only about ten miles away, but Mouterde denied the possibility of these quarries having been used for 'Anjar, saying that in February 1947 he visited the ruins of 'Anjar in company with the Professor of Geology of the Engineering School of Beyrouth, according to whom 'la presque totalité des pierres conservées

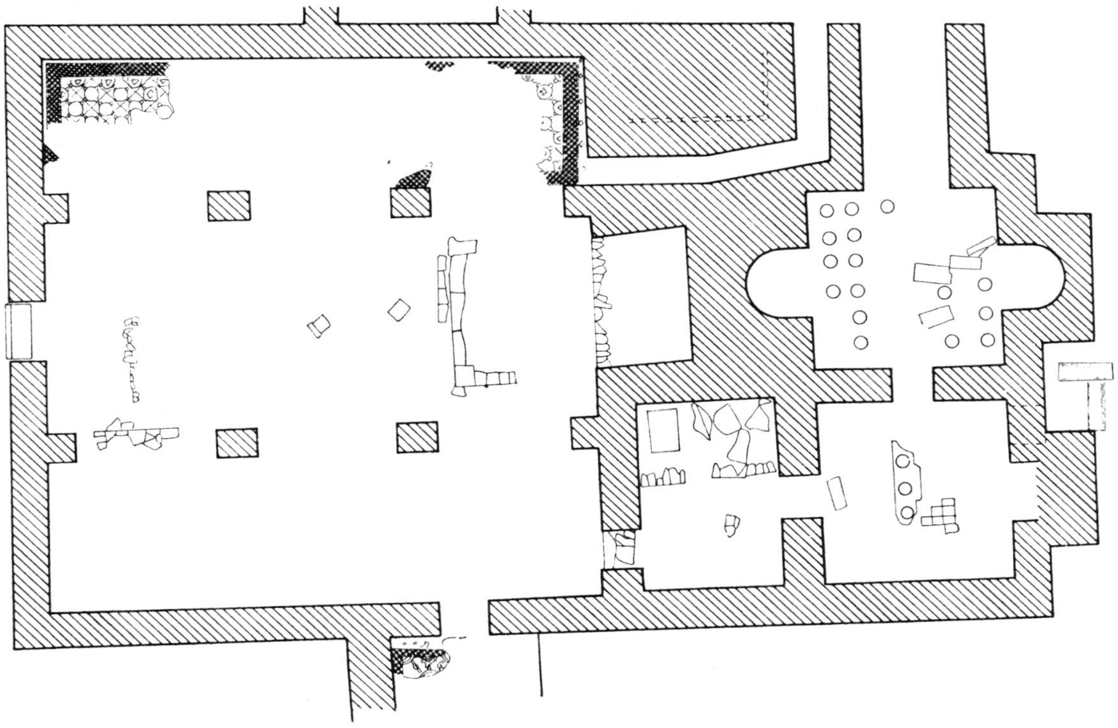

Fig. 542 'ANJAR: The Ḥammān next the North Gate.
(By kind permission of Emir Chéhab.)

étaient non du calcaire nummulitique comme celui de Kâmed, mais du calcaire d'epoque crétacée, plus compact et plus sombre'. And he adds that at a distance of less than 500 m. 'les toutes premières assises de l'Anti-Liban fournissaient en surabondance ce matériau; une carrière ancienne montre qu'on y a recouru'.[1]

I therefore wrote to the Emir Maurice Chéhab, the Director-General of Antiquities, whose very kind reply clears up the whole matter: 'Our engineer, who is in charge of the restoration works at 'Anjar, 'has examined the quarries at Kamed. He has found that the stones with a dressed surface for construc-'tion at 'Anjar definitely come from Kamed. He has noticed that these stones reveal the same technique 'of quarrying as in Kamed.

'The statement of Father Mouterde is due, as you have suggested in your letter, to the fact that when 'he visited 'Anjar, only the interior of the walls were visible and these were built out of the very hard 'limestone that was probably picked from the mountains of the Anti-Lebanon near by. All the stones of 'the outer parts of the walls came from the quarries at Kamed.'

We can now regard 'Anjar as definitely dated 96 H. (714/15) the last year of al-Walīd's reign; he died on 23 February 715.

[1] *M.U.S.J.*, XXVII, pp. 421–2.

XVII

THE WORKS OF THE KHALIFS SULAYMĀN AND YAZĪD II

THE LATER UMAYYAD PERIOD—Sulaymān founds Ramla and builds the Great Mosque—The first Great Mosque at Aleppo—The treasury (*Bayt al-Māl*) in the Mosque of ʿAmr.

THE WORKS OF YAZĪD II—THE SO-CALLED ʿUMAR MOSQUE' AT BOṢRĀ: Description—The interior—The roofing system—The east *riwāq*—The north *riwāq*—The windows—Sauvaget's theories—The miḥrāb—The minaret—The date—Architectural origins—The architectural evolution of the minaret.

AL-MUWAQQAR—The description of Brünnow and von Domaszewski—Musil's account—The condition of the ruins in 1962—The capitals—The water-gauge.

THE LATER UMAYYAD PERIOD. When al-Walīd died in Jumādā II, 96 (Feb. 715) the Umayyad Empire had reached its zenith. Its decline was as rapid as its rise, and it only endured for another thirty-five years.

al-Walīd was succeeded by his brother Sulaymān, a worthless creature who died in Ṣafar 99 (Sept. 717). His cousin ʿUmar II, the son of ʿAbd al-ʿAzīz (brother of ʿAbd al-Malik), succeeded him. ʿUmar who, unlike most of the Umayyads, was an extremely religious man, died after a short and uneventful reign in Rajab 101 (Feb. 720). The respective characters of these three Khalifs have been summed up tersely in the well-known saying that 'under al-Walīd people talked of fine buildings, under Sulaymān of cookery and the fair sex, while in the reign of ʿUmar ibn ʿAbd al-ʿAzīz the Qurān and religion formed favourite topics of conversation'.[1]

ʿUmar was followed by his cousin Yazīd II, the third son of ʿAbd al-Malik. Weakness characterized his reign, which only lasted four years, during which the decadence of the Umayyad dynasty became pronounced. He died in Shaʿbān 105 (Jan. 724) and was succeeded by his brother Hishām.

SULAYMĀN FOUNDS RAMLA AND BUILDS THE GREAT MOSQUE.[2] It is a remarkable fact, as Sauvaget has pointed out,[3] that in contrast to other countries conquered by the Arabs, no town that has acquired importance has ever been founded in Syrian territory since the appearance of Islam. Ramla, the only settlement that has been founded as a new creation, has never risen above the rank of a small market town of the second order. Ramla, according to Balādhurī, was founded by Sulaymān, after he had been appointed Governor of Palestine by the Khalif al-Walīd. Balādhurī says: 'Before Sulaymān there was 'no such city as Ramla, and its site was sand (*raml*), hence its name. The first thing he built was a palace '(*qaṣr*) for himself and the Dār aṣ-Ṣabbāghīn (House of Dyers). He then planned the mosque and began 'its construction, but became Khalif before its completion.'[4] It must therefore have been begun before A.D. 715. A Christian of Ludd, named al-Baṭrīq (the Patriarch) ibn an-Nakā,[5] was appointed to supervise the expenses both of residence and mosque. The works were continued by Sulaymān after he became Khalif, but the mosque was only finished under the reign of his successor ʿUmar II (A.D. 717–20), who, however, diminished the original plan saying: 'The people of ar-Ramla should be content with the size thereof to which I have diminished it.'[6]

Muqaddasī, who saw this mosque in A.D. 985, says that it surpassed 'in elegance and beauty even

[1] Ibn al-Athīr, V, p. 5; Ibn aṭ-Ṭiqṭaqā, *al-Fakhrī*, Derenbourg's ed., p. 173; Amar's transl., p. 203; quoted by Nicholson (R. A.), *Literary History of the Arabs*, p. 203.

[2] BIBLIOGRAPHY: —868, Balādhurī, p. 143; transl. by Le Strange, *Palestine*, pp. 303–4; Hitti's transl., pp. 220–21; —903, Ibn al-Faqīh, p. 102; —923, Ṭabarī, I, p. 2397, l. 9; —956, Masʿūdī, *Tanbīh*, pp. 359–60; Carra de Vaux's transl., pp. 460–61; —985, Muqaddasī, p. 165; transl. by Gildemeister, *Z.D.P.V.*, VII, p. 158; and by Le Strange, *P.P.T.S.*, III (γ), pp. 33–4, and in his *Palestine*, p. 305; Ranking's transl., pp. 271–2; —1047, Nāṣir-i-Khusrau, Schefer's text, p. 21; transl., pp. 63–4; transl. by Le Strange, *op. cit.*, 306–7; —1225, Yāqūt, II, p. 817; —*c.* 1300, Dimashqī, Mehren's transl., p. 272; —1321, Abu'l-Fidā', *Taqwīm*, p. 241; Guyard's transl., II₂, p. 18; —1496, Mujīr ad-Dīn, p. 417; Sauvaire's transl., pp. 206–7; —1822, Rampoldi, *Annali musulmani*, III, p. 206; —1890, Le Strange, *Palestine under the Moslems*, pp. 303–8; and Gildemeister, *Z.D.P.V.*, XIII, p. 15; —1912, Caetani, *Chronographia*, p. 1210; and Reitemeyer (E.), *Städtegründungen der Araber im Islām*, pp. 73–4; —1914, Rivoira, *Architettura musulmana*, pp. 46–7; English transl., p. 44; —1919, Creswell, *Evolution of the Minaret*, *Burlington Magazine*, XLVIII, p. 138; —1936, Honigmann, article *al-Ramla*, in the *Encyclopaedia of Islām*, III, pp. 1115–17.

[3] *Esquisse d'une histoire de la ville de Damas*, in the *Revue des Études islamiques*, 1934, p. 422.

[4] P. 143; Hitti's transl., pp. 220–21; repeated by Ibn al-Faqīh, p. 102; and Yāqūt, II, p. 817.

[5] Ibn al-Faqīh (*Buldān*, p. 102) calls him Ibn Bakā.

[6] Balādhurī, p. 143; Hitti's transl., p. 220; and Masʿūdī, *Tanbīh*, p. 360; Carra de Vaux's transl., p. 461 (erroneously, as 'reduit la ville'). Muqaddasī (p. 165; Gildemeister's transl., *Z.D.P.V.*, VII, p. 158; Ranking's transl., p. 271) attributes it to Hishām, but as Balādhurī wrote a century earlier we must accept his version as more authoritative.

'that of Damascus. It is called the Jāmi' al-Abyaḍ (White Mosque). In all Islam there is not a larger 'miḥrāb than that of this mosque . . . ; it also possesses a beautiful minaret. It (i.e. the mosque)[1] was 'built by Hishām ibn 'Abd al-Malik. (Manuscript C reads instead: "It is a construction of Hishām 'ibn 'Abd al-Malik, erected on beautiful columns of white marble, and panelled likewise with marble.") 'I have heard my uncle relate that when the Khalif was about to build the mosque it was reported to 'him that the Christians possessed columns of marble, which they had prepared for the Church of 'Bāli'ah, lying buried beneath the sand; thereupon Hishām informed the Christians that they must 'either show him where the columns lay, or that he would demolish their church at Lydda (Ludd), in 'order to employ its columns for the building of his mosque. The Christians accordingly unearthed 'their columns, which were very thick and tall and beautiful. The floor of the covered portion of the 'mosque is paved with marble, and the court with cut stone. The doors of the covered part are made 'of cypress wood and cedar, inlaid with carved patterns and very beautiful in appearance'.[2]

As regards the minaret admired by Muqaddasī, we may confidently say that it was a square tower, for in another part of his book he expressly remarks, as one of the customs peculiar to Syria, that all the minarets were square.[3]

A White Mosque is mentioned by Nāṣir-i-Khusrau, who passed through Ramla in 1047, but it must have been a reconstruction, for as-Suyūṭī says that Egypt and Syria were visited by a terrible earthquake in 425 (1033), which destroyed a third of the town of Ramla and reduced the Great Mosque to a heap of ruins.[4]

The First Great Mosque at Aleppo. Sulaymān also built the first Great Mosque at Aleppo, according to Ibn Shaddād (d. 1285) who says: 'The Muslims, at the time of the conquest, acquired 'a piece of ground for the Great Mosque by treaty with the inhabitants. The site during the Byzantine 'period had been a garden belonging to the Cathedral, the foundation of which was attributed to 'Helena, the mother of Constantine . . . the north part of the Great Mosque had been the cemetery of 'the Cathedral.'[5]

Ibn ash-Shiḥna, quoting Ibn al-Adīm, says: 'The Qāḍī Shams ad-Dīn Abū 'Abd Allāh ibn al-'Khiḍr told me: "The Mosque of Aleppo rivalled that of Damascus in its decoration, its marble panel-'ling and its mosaics (*fusaifisā'*)". It is said that it was Sulaymān ibn 'Abd al-Malik who built it, and 'that he wished to make it as beautiful as the work of his brother al-Walīd at Damascus.'[6] He goes on to say that when the 'Abbāsids destroyed the Umayyad monuments of Syria they took away its marble and furniture and transferred it all to the Great Mosque of Anbār, and that it remained in this state until it was burnt by Nicephorus Phocas when he took Aleppo in 351 H. (962).[7] Sayf ad-Dawla (d. 967) rebuilt it, but the oldest part of the present mosque, according to Sobernheim and Herzfeld, only goes back to Malik Shāh[8] (*c.* 1090).

The Treasury (Bayt al-Māl) in the Mosque of 'Amr. 99 H. (717/18). Ibn Duqmāq, quoting Ibn Yūnus, says that it was built by Qurra ibn Sharīk (who died in 96 H.).[9] According to another tradition he says that it was constructed by 'Usāma ibn Zayd at-Tanūkhī in 99 H., when he was Director of Taxation in Egypt under the Khalif Sulaymān.[10] Maqrīzī speaks of it as being above the *Fauwāra* of the mosque, and gives the date, probably by a slip, as 97 H.[11]

We fortunately possess an admirable description of this structure, for Ibn Rusta writing in 903 says: 'The *Bayt al-Māl* of Miṣr is in the congregational mosque in front of (*quddām*) the minbar; it is 'separated from its roofs (*suṭūḥ*) and is not in contact with any part of them. It stands on stone pillars

[1] Le Strange (*op. cit.*, p. 305) interprets the text of Muqaddasī to mean that Hishām built the minaret, but M. Wiet has pointed out to me that *banāhu* being masculine, it must be the mosque (masculine) to which he is referring and not the minaret (feminine). Mujīr ad-Dīn (p. 417; Sauvaire's transl., pp. 206–7) attributes the mosque to Sulaymān.

[2] P. 165; the above is Ranking's rendering, pp. 271–2. This passage has also been translated by Le Strange, *P.P.T.S.*, III (γ), pp. 33–4; and his *Palestine*, p. 305.

[3] P. 182; Gildemeister's transl., *Z.D.P.V.*, VII, p. 218; Ranking's transl., p. 299; Le Strange, *op. cit.*, p. 21.

[4] See above, p. 182, n. 6.

[5] Ibn Shaddād, *ad-Durr*, fol. 61, translated into French by Herzfeld from the MS. at Leningrad; *C.I.A.–Syrie du Nord, Inscriptions et Monuments d'Alep*, p. 143; repeated, with variations, by Ibn ash-Shiḥna, *ad-Durr*, ed. of Sarkis, p. 61; Sauvaget's transl., *Les Perles choisis*, pp. 56–7, also translated by Herzfeld, *Ars Islamica*, XIII–XIV, p. 119 (he attributes it to Ibn al-'Adīm).

[6] *Op. cit.*, pp. 61–2; transl., pp. 56–7.

[7] *Ibid.*

[8] *Encyclopaedia of Islām*, II, p. 235.

[9] IV, p. 64, ll. 26–7.

[10] IV, p. 64, l. 27–8.

[11] *Khiṭaṭ*, II, p. 249, ll. 13–15; and Abu'l-Maḥāsin, I, p. 80, ll. 1–9; see also as-Suyūṭī, *Ḥusn*, II., p. 178, ll. 7–8 (under 99 H.).

'(*asāṭīn*) and is a kind of raised dome, beneath which people sit and pass to and fro. There is 'a bridge (*qanṭara*) of wood there and when it is desired to enter that *bayt* they draw this bridge by 'means of cords (*ḥibāl*) until its end rests on the roof (*saṭḥ*) of the mosque. When they leave the 'chamber, they restore the bridge to its (former) position. It has an iron door with locks (*aqfāl*). 'When the last prayer is finished they make everybody leave the mosque permitting none to remain. 'The doors of the mosque are locked (*tughlaq*). This is how the *Bayt al-Māl* is kept.'[1]

As for the number of columns on which it rested, this is not certain, for Ibn Rusta omits to say, and although Ibn Duqmāq, when enumerating the number of columns in the mosque, states that it rested on ten[2] (exactly as at Ḥarrān, below, p. 645), his description naturally refers to the new Bayt al-Māl of 379 H. (989).

It was therefore a structure similar to that in the Great Mosque of Damascus (above, pp. 179 and 202), except that it did not have a fountain under it until one was added in 379 H. (see first ed., II, p. 172).

THE SO-CALLED 'OMAR MOSQUE' AT BOṢRĀ[3]

The so-called 'Umar Mosque' of Boṣrā stands with its east wall almost directly on the line of the west colonnade of the Via Principalis, or north–south street of Roman Boṣrā. Apart from its many fine marble columns it is built of that hideous material—black basalt—and the depressing effect caused thereby was added to by the ruined condition of the interior when I first saw it in 1919. This state certainly goes back to 1859 when Rey made a poor plan of it,[4] and probably to 1806 when it was visited by Seetzen, the earliest traveller to have left a description of it. He speaks of '18 herrliche Säulen von weissem und buntem Marmor aus einem Stücke, nebst mehrern Basaltsäulen'.[5] Burckhardt, in 1812, speaks of 'sixteen fine variegated marble columns (two less than Seetzen),[6] distinguished both by the 'beauty of the material, and of the execution: fourteen are Corinthian, and two Ionic; they are each 'about sixteen or eighteen feet in height, of a single block, and well polished'.[7] Rey says: 'Les 'colonnes sont de cipolin vert d'eau, avec des chapiteaux d'ordres divers en marbre blanc. J'ai 'surtout remarqué deux chapiteaux ioniques, du plus beau style, portant des guirlandes de chêne 'suspendues à l'entour. . . .'[8]

Buckingham in 1816 mentions a 'pavement of large flat stones laid in diagonal squares'.[9] To-day this is only true of the eastern half of the sanctuary.

The Syrian Department of Antiquities in 1938/9 cleared a great part of the interior.

Description. The walls, which are about 9½ m. high, have been patched in many places; the north wall, for example, is of three periods: the first part next the minaret is of fine masonry with courses about 50 cm. high; it forms one with the socle of the minaret. But this fine masonry only extends westward for about 5 m., after which the masonry is very bad and irregular right up to the summit, with a course of many large drums of columns set in transversely; moreover this bad masonry extends eastwards, above the good masonry, right up to the minaret (Plate 79 *b*). But it does not extend to the

[1] P. 116, ll. 6–13.

[2] IV, p. 61, l. 2.

[3] Bibliography:—1822, Burckhardt (J. L.), *Travels in Syria and the Holy Land*, pp. 228–9; —1825, Buckingham (J. S.), *Travels among the Arab Tribes*, pp. 198–200; —1838, Lindsay, Lord, *Letters on Egypt, Edom, and the Holy Land*, II, p. 137; —1854, Seetzen (U. J.), *Reisen durch Syrien und Palästina*, I, p. 69; —1855, Porter (J. L.), *Five Years in Damascus*, II, p. 151; 2nd ed., p. 235; —1860 (?), Rey (E. G.), *Voyage dans le Haouran*, pp. 181–2, and Atlas, pls. XVI and XVII; —1860, Wetzstein (J. G.), *Reisebericht über Hauran und die Trachonen*, p. 71; —1891, Porter (J. L.), *The Giant Cities of Bashan and Syria's Holy Places*, p. 71 and plate (taken from Rey); —1897, Schumacher (G.), *Das südliche Basan*, *Z.D.P.V.*, XX, pp. 148–9; —1899, Oppenheim (Max von), *Vom Mittelmeer zum Persischen Golf*, I, pp. 198–9 and plate; —1904, Germer-Durand, in *Bull. archéologique du Comité de Travaux hist. et scient.*, 1904, pl. IV; and Kondakov (N. P.), *Arkheologicheskoe puteshestvie po Sirii i Palestinie*, p. 107, pl. 17 and fig. 16; —1909, Brünnow (R. E.) and Domaszewski (Alfred von), *Die Provincia Arabia*, III, pp. 25–9 and 210 and figs. 903–5; —1914, Butler (H. C.), *Ancient Architecture in Syria, Sect. A—Southern Syria*, pp. 289–92, pl. XVIII and illus. 254–8; —1939, Wiet (G.), *Répertoire chronologique d'Épigraphie arabe*, X, p. 183; —1941, Sauvaget (J.), *Les Inscriptions arabes de la Mosquée de Bosra*, *Syria*, XXII, pp. 53–65, pls. VII and VIII and five figs.; —1947, Sauvaget (J.), *La Mosquée omeyyade de Médine*, pp. 101–3 and figs. 7 and 7*bis*; —1949, Littman (Enno), *Arabic Inscriptions* (*Princeton University Archaeological Expeditions to Syria in* 1904–5 *and* 1909, Division IV, Section D, pp. 23–7; —1954, Ouéchek (É. E.) and S. A. Mougdad, *Bosra, Guide historique et archéologique*, pp. 9–13 with 1 plate.

[4] *Voyage*, Atlas, pl. XVII.

[5] *Reisen* (not published until 1854), I, p. 69.

[6] This may be a slip, for Porter in 1855 speaks of seventeen; II, p. 151.

[7] *Travels in Syria*, p. 228. He adds that two columns bore Greek Christian inscriptions.

[8] *Op. cit.*, p. 182.

[9] *Travels*, p. 199.

north-west corner, for there is a complete vertical break, and the last 7–8 m. is of another variety of poor masonry.[1]

The masonry of the left third of the west wall is even worse, and its thickness increases nearly 30 cm. as it goes north from the middle doorway. That of the remainder, however, is better, for the courses are at least horizontal. An open staircase of two flights divided by a landing runs up in the middle of this façade (Plate 79 *b*); it must have been restored by the Department of Antiquities, for there were many gaps in it in Butler's day. Schacht, in a recent article,[2] mentions a number of primitive mosques in North and East Africa, where a sort of sentry box is provided on the roof for the *muʾadhdhin*, the box being reached by a staircase running up the outer wall of the mosque; and he cites the Great Mosque of

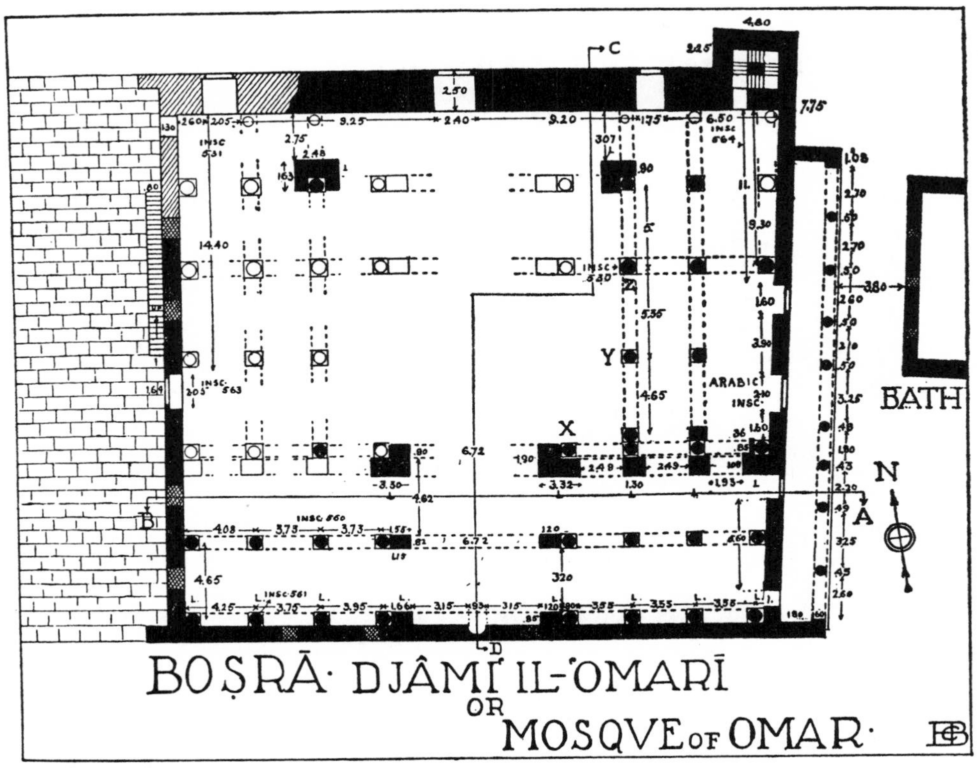

FIG. 543. BOṢRĀ: The so-called ʿUmar Mosque', plan. Scale 1 : 200. From Butler, *op. cit.*

FIG. 544. BOṢRĀ: Great Mosque, miḥrāb (now plastered over.)

Boṣrā as a really early example of the same arrangement. This it certainly is not, for our minaret has its own internal staircase (below, p. 489) and it cannot be entered from the roof, so the outer staircase on the west side of the mosque does not serve it in any way. But he might have mentioned the Mosque of ʿAmr of 53 H. (673) in this connexion, for the arrangement he is describing actually did exist there (above, p. 59).

Houses conceal the lower part of the back wall. The masonry of the east wall is at least fairly regular. The north wall is about 2·50 m. thick, but the other walls are only a little over a metre. The internal measurements are: 33·86 m. (north), 32·53 m. (south), 31·08 m. (east), and 28·96 m. (west). The interior tapers to the extent of 1·33 m. from north to south and 2·12 m. from east to west; the south-western corner is almost a true right angle.

There are three doors in the north wall, four in the eastern and two only in the western. Some of the doors on the east and west sides have Roman door-frames. All these doors have a lintel and some of them a very tall lunette as well (Plate 79 *b*), recalling the lunette of the mosque at Quṣayr al-Ḥallābāt (Plate 84 *d*).

THE INTERIOR when first I saw it in 1919 was intact on the east side and nearly so on the south, but almost all between the northern and western sides of the ṣaḥn and the outer walls had collapsed, leaving piles of débris on the ground, in some places 2 m. deep.

The arrangement of the interior is most unusual. There are three arcades on the south side, but as one

1 For this reason I have not attempted the impossible task of marking the outer wall to show various periods.

2 *Further Notes on the Staircase Minaret*, *Ars Orientalis*, IV, pp. 137–41.

is in contact with the south wall (but not forming one with it), there are only two aisles. The scheme of these three arcades forms one of the most attractive features of the mosque; each consists of a pointed central arch, about 6·70 m. in span, with three semicircular arches about 3 m. wide to right and left. The central arch of the second arcade has been struck from two centres about one-tenth of the span apart.[1] On account of its width it had to be sprung from a level nearly 1½ m. lower than the others (Fig. 545). Butler remarks that 'the combination of the low pier and the high column, where the narrow arches join the broad arch on either side, is a beautiful piece of design'.[2] It would look better still if the voussoirs of the great arch were not so miserably shallow.

Of these three arcades the right half of the outer one has fallen and the left half has been reinforced, at some later date, by an arcade of pointed arches, carried on piers set behind it on its south side but not in close contact with it, for there is a small space between them. Butler remarks that 'this reinforcing arcade served, like the wall arcade, to narrow the space to be spanned by the stone slabs of the roof'.[3] This arcade was removed, I believe rightly, during the works of 1938/9.

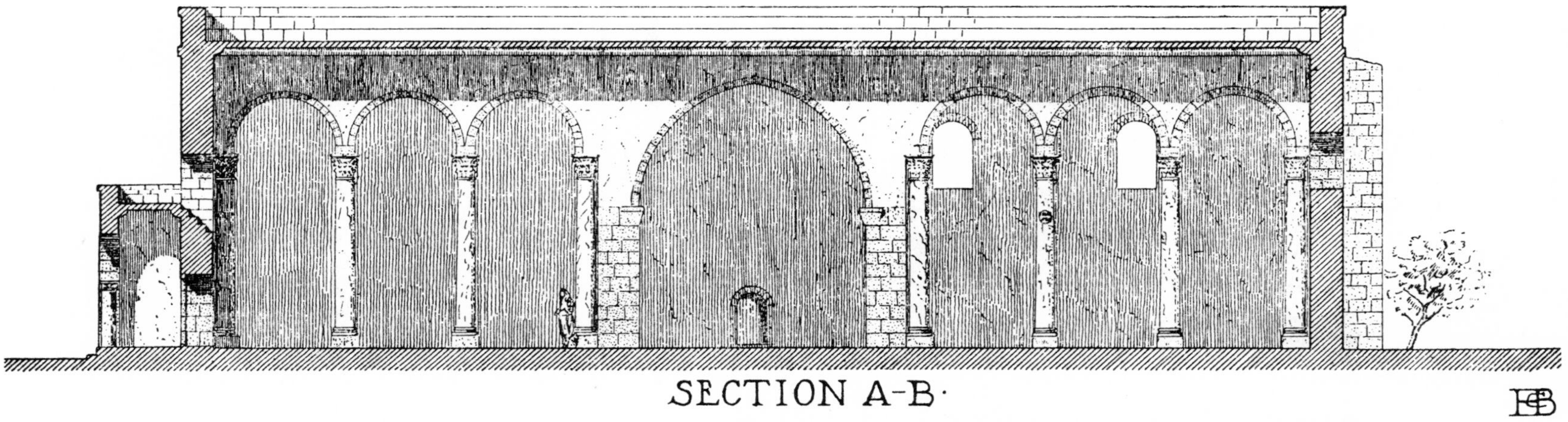

Fig. 545. Boṣrā: The so-called 'Umar Mosque'; section of sanctuary. (From Butler, *op. cit.*)

As regards the third, or wall arcade, he says that 'it has slightly pointed arches resting on Ionic columns of basalt, and it is not one with the south wall, nor anywhere bonded into its masonry'. Moreover, it partly cuts across two of the four windows in the south wall, and behind it can still be seen the remains of fine stucco ornament,[4] probably of the early twelfth century. If so, it may well be the work of Abū Manṣūr Gumushtegīn in 506 H. (1112/13).[5] This proves that the arcade must be an insertion of still later date, perhaps that of 618 H. (1221), recorded by an inscription on the north wall.[6] This explains why its central arch is more pointed than the other, having been struck from two centres one-fourth of the span apart. Butler believes it to have been 'one of the earlier restorations, having been inserted to decrease the width of the aisle and to reduce the required length of the roofing slabs'.[7] This arcade also has been removed.

The Roofing System. The arcades carry a roof of stone slabs resting on a double corbel course, in perfect keeping with the style of roofing typical of the Ḥaurān shown in Fig. 482. The ceiling is 8·55 m. above the floor and 8·60 above the pavement of the ṣaḥn.[8] Butler shows a parapet 1 m. high above the arcades on the ṣaḥn, but in 1919 the only sign of such a parapet was at the top of the wall on the west side. Kondakov, in 1904, shows the east *riwāq* with the whole of its roof intact.[9] Butler, speaking for the whole mosque, says that of the part standing in his day about one-third of the roof

[1] Found by trial and error on an enlarged photograph of Plate 79 *e*.
[2] *Op. cit.*, p. 291.
[3] *Ibid.*, p. 291.
[4] Illustrated by Rey, *Voyage*, Atlas, pl. XVII; and in Sauvaget's article, *loc. cit.*, pl. VIII.
[5] For this inscription see Sauvaget, *loc. cit.*, pp. 59–61 and pl. VIII; Wiet, *Répertoire*, VIII, pp. 93–4; and Littmann, *Arabic Inscriptions*, pp. 23–4.
[6] Sauvaget, *loc. cit.*, pp. 62–3; and Wiet, *Répertoire*, X, p. 183. This inscription is first mentioned by Wetzstein in 1860, *Reisebericht*, p. 71; and then by Schumacher (1897), who gives the Arabic text; *Die südliche Basan*, *Z.D.P.V.*, XX, pp. 148–9.
[7] *Op. cit.*, p. 291.
[8] Its height, as scaled off Butler's fig. is 9·20 m.; difference 65 cm. I have not verified my measurement, as I only noticed this difference after my return to Cairo.
[9] *Op. cit.*, pl. 17; reproduced here, Plate 80 *b*.

was intact.[1] Écochard photographed a *tabula ansata* on one of the basalt roofing slabs with an inscription: 'Work of Ḥaidara in the year 460 (1067/8).'[2]

THE EAST *RIWĀQ*. On the east side two parallel arcades, each of four arches, take off from the façade of the sanctuary and go right through to the north wall[3] instead of stopping against the outer arcade on the north side, as is the almost universal rule. This part had been preserved intact,[4] its roof of stone slabs resting on a double corbel course (Plate 80 *b*) exactly as in Fig. 482, which shows the typical roofing system of the Ḥaurān. The arches of the first two bays were of unequal span, both are semicircular but the narrower one is stilted. The outer springs from an extremely slender column of white marble (Y). The next two columns in each arcade carry two pairs of arches at right angles to each other, one going south–north and the other east–west, and a column is set against the wall to take the return of the latter. This arcade must have continued to the west to form the outer arcade of the north *riwāq*, for the springer block of the first arch of such an arcade can be seen above column Z on the east side (Plate 79 *d*) and the place where this arcade struck the west wall is clearly visible in the masonry, near the top of the wall (Plate 80 *a*). Thus we have established the existence of the outer arcade of the north *riwāq*, which probably had a wide central arch like the arcade opposite, but this has not yet been proved.

As for the inner arcade of the north *riwāq* nothing remains of it, although we might have expected to see its last two arches crossing the eastern *riwāq*, like those of the outer arcade, and ending at a wall column. Butler even suggests that the present system in the north-east corner is the result of a later reconstruction.[5]

THE NORTH *RIWĀQ*. What are we to think of the bases of the three piers (A, B, and C) now about 70 cm. high? At A we have a short drum, about 70 cm. high, set in the south-eastern corner of what remains of a masonry pier about 2 m. square. Fortunately we have Kondakov's photograph (Plate 80 *b*) which shows twelve courses of masonry embracing the column, which has a simple capital, a moulded impost block, and an arch springing from it towards the south. Butler, in his plan (Fig. 543), shows another column D in the north-west corner of the present court, with masonry built round it.[6] This column exists to-day, but the masonry round it has been removed. In between these two are the lower parts of two piers (B and C) measuring 1·90×0·97 m. and 1·95×0·92 m.; they are not shown on Butler's plan. Did these piers replace columns? If so, the spacing here must have been very different from what it is in the sanctuary.

We would naturally expect the west *riwāq*, of which nothing visible is left, to have been similar to the one opposite, but it is impossible to say definitely until some 2 m. of débris have been cleared away so as to expose any existing column bases.[7] But if it actually was like the one opposite, we would then be able to say that the ṣaḥn had two arches to east and west and three to north and south.

THE WINDOWS are simple arched openings and any grilles they may have had have gone. There are four in the back wall of the sanctuary and two at each end. There are three more under the eastern *riwāq* and three under the western, but none in the north wall; total 14.

SAUVAGET'S THEORIES

Sauvaget has some ridiculous remarks to make on this mosque: 'Les monuments omeyyades étant 'habituellement couverts en charpente, et la légèreté des supports montrant que c'est ce mode de 'couverture qui avait été adopté ici, il est clair que si les colonnes se sont déjetées, c'est sous la surcharge

[1] *Op. cit.*, p. 290. To-day, alas, the whole sanctuary is roofed with concrete.

[2] In Sauvaget, *loc. cit.*, p. 58 and pl. VII, no. 3. Now preserved in the Citadel.

[3] Plate 80 *c*, taken since the demolition, shows the springer blocks to take them at their northern end.

[4] I regret to say that the whole of this *riwāq* and its important archaeological evidence (see below) has been swept away since 1919. I have not yet discovered exactly when or by whom. Kondakov's Plate 17 and my Plate 79 *c* and *d* now become historical documents. A new *riwāq* is now (April 1963) in course of construction. My plan (Fig. 546) represents the present state of the mosque, including the newly constructed west *riwāq*, except that I have drawn the demolished east *riwāq* from Butler's plan of over sixty years ago.

[5] *Op. cit.*, p.290.

[6] He says that the north-west corner was 'a mass of ruins preserving one broken column in situ encased by piers on three sides', *op. cit.*, p. 292.

[7] It has since been cleared away. Monsieur Émilie E. Ouéchek, who has been the architect in charge for many years, and who rebuilt this *riwāq*, assured me during my visit on 17th and 18th April 1962 that no column bases were found. On the other hand, Monsieur Mougdad informed me during a later visit (23rd April 1963) that all the bases were found *in situ*, under the débris (as one would expect), and that the present *riwāq* was reconstructed on them.

'que leur imposaient les nouveaux plafonds de pierre, obligeant à bâtir les piliers de soutènement qui les 'épaulaient ici et là.'[1]

To which one may reply that the Umayyads did not adopt uniform rules for the construction of mosques, but varied them according to local conditions. In Syria, where timber was still plentiful, they constructed gable roofs of considerable span at Damascus (12–17 m.), at Qaṣr al-Ḥayr ash-Sharqī

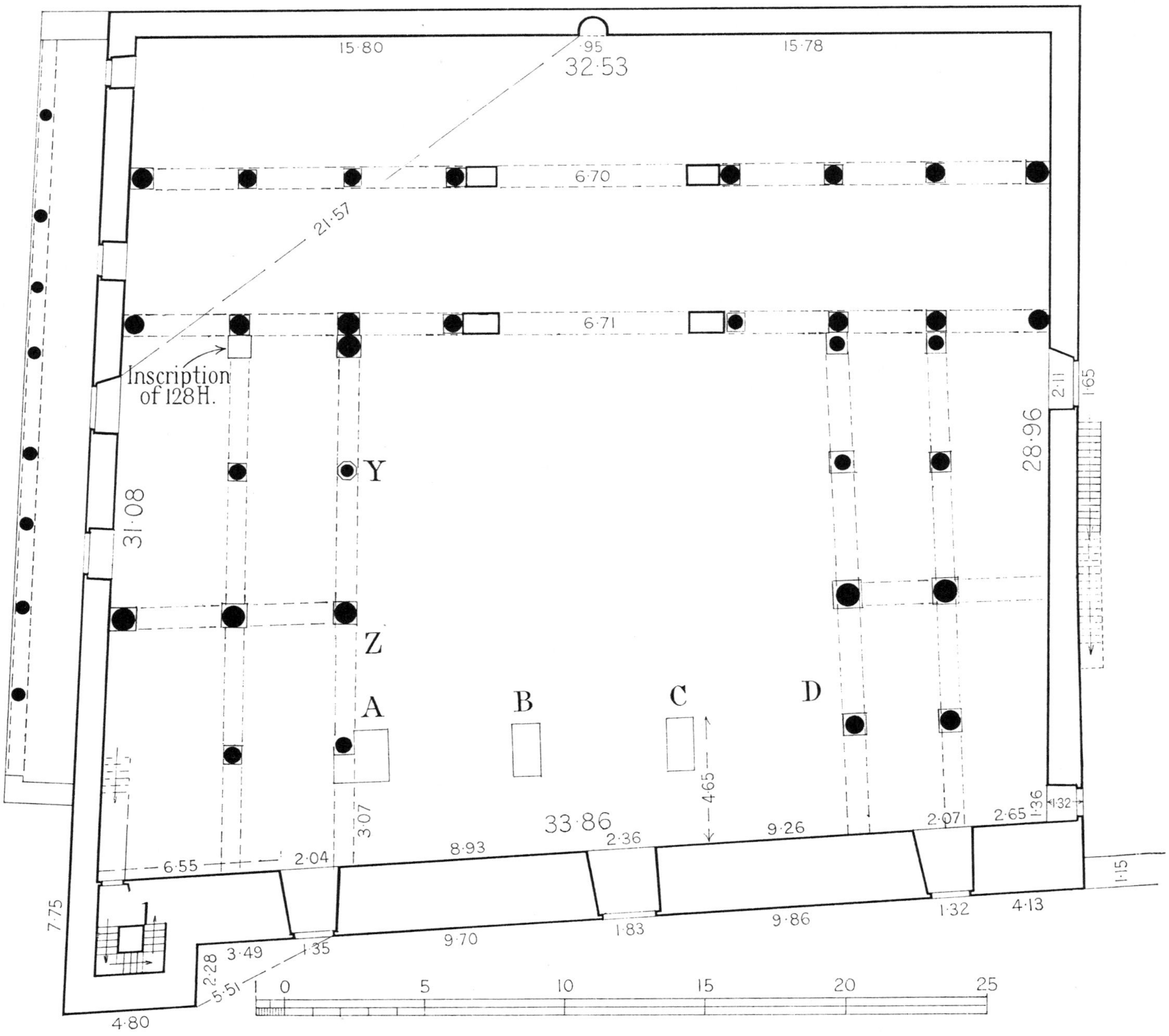

FIG. 546. BOṢRĀ: The so-called 'Umar Mosque'. Author's plan.

(7·30 m.), and Ḥarrān (9·18 m.). In ʿIrāq they built mosques in which the flat timber roof rested directly on the columns without the intermediary of arches, e.g. Kūfa and Wāsiṭ.

But in the treeless Ḥaurān the architecture of all periods, as de Vogüé[2] and Butler[3] have emphasized, 'was the most truly lithic that the world had seen; it was entirely of stone, sometimes even to the doors and window shutters'. This is precisely the case with the door of the minaret of our mosque, yet Sauvaget actually suggests that a gable roof of timber was employed here at the beginning, and blames 'les nouveaux plafonds de pierre' for the state of the mosque, instead of the earthquakes which have been the curse of Syria.

He says: 'A ce plan il ne manque que le détail de l'agencement de la nef axiale, complètement 'oblitéré par une réfection, mais l'existence de cette nef est certaine, les cotes relevées montrant que la 'colonnade ne pouvait se développer d'un côté à l'autre de la salle de prière en conservant partout le

[1] *La Mosquée Omeyyade de Médine*, p. 102. [2] *Syrie centrale*, pp. 6–7. [3] *Op. cit.*, p. 68.

‘même écartement entre ses fûts.[1] On peut admettre que le toit de cette nef reposait, par l'intermédiaire ‘d'arcs longitudinaux, sur des piliers [his plan shows columns only] qu'ont remplacés plus tard les ‘piliers actuels.’[2]

He then gives a plan (reproduced here, Fig. 547) showing how the mosque must have been originally. In it he eliminates the piers in the middle of the arcades of the sanctuary and increases the width of the central part, which he believes had a gable roof of timber, from 6·70 m. to 8·60 m., but he forgets to dot in the lateral arches on which it rested, nor does he make any provision for meeting the thrusts of the arcades which stop against it on either side, by duplicating the columns next the nave, as in the Mosque of al-Azhar, for example. Such a mosque would have quickly collapsed without the aid of an earthquake.

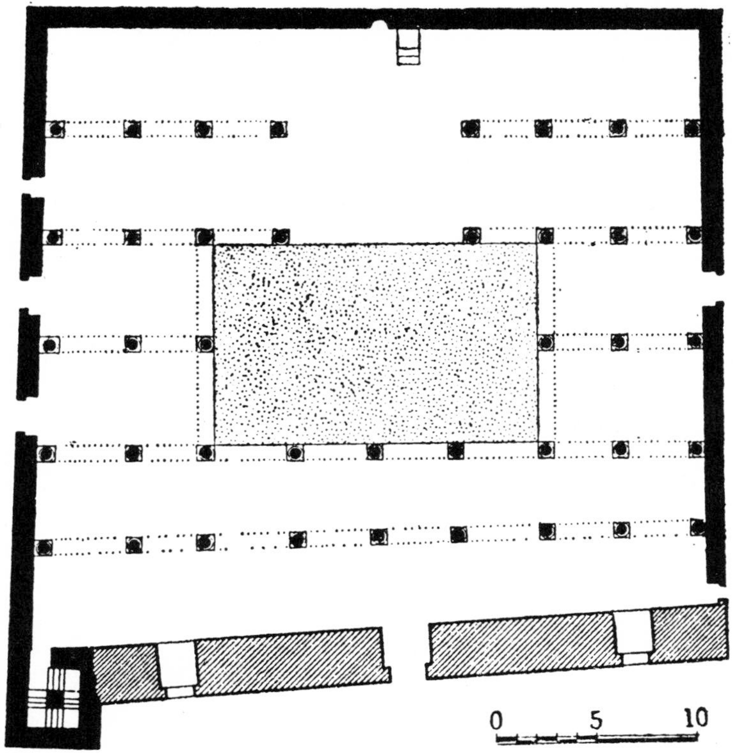

Fig. 547. Mosque of Boṣrā: Sauvaget's, plan. (From Sauvaget, *La Msquée Omeyyade de Médine.*)

The Miḥrāb. The perfectly plain miḥrāb consists of a semicircular niche, 95 cm. wide, 62 cm. deep, and 2·57 m. high to the apex; the semi-dome is cut out of a single block of stone 1·60 m. wide and 70 cm. high (Fig. 544 and Plate 80 *a*, just visible above the débris). It is the earliest concave miḥrāb that has survived intact, for the miḥrāb of al-Walīd at Minya is only preserved to a height of two courses, likewise his miḥrāb at Jabal Says (Plate 77 *f*), and the miḥrāb of the little mosque at Quṣayr al-Ḥallābāt, which was apparently seen intact by Butler, and which may be of about the same date as that of Boṣrā, is now covered by the fallen masonry of the south wall.

The Minaret is placed at the north-east corner so as to make a salient of 2·28 m. on the north façade. It is a square tower of basalt resting on a slightly larger socle about 5 m. high, of large blocks,[3] the courses of which form one with the first 5 m. of the north wall and the first 7·80 m. of the east wall. The sides of this socle are bevelled off above, so as to effect the transition to the slightly smaller shaft which is set somewhat askew. A flight of broken steps in the north-eastern corner of the mosque leads up to a landing in front of the doorway, which is only 1 m. high and 74 cm. wide. The door is a solid piece of stone, so typical of the lithic architecture of the Ḥaurān, which turned[4] on pivots fixed in sockets above and below. We find ourselves in a little vestibule 1·76 m. wide and 77 cm. deep and then ascend in an anti-clockwise fashion round a 98 cm. (east) by 92 cm. (north) newel by sixteen flights of four steps each, making sixty-four in all. On the way we pass a number of windows, 20–30 cm. square. Buckingham says that ‘similar but smaller doors of stone served to close the apertures for light in different stages of the building, as we ascended it, all of them being hung by pivots traversing in sockets above and below’.[5] No such shutters are to be seen to-day. We finally reach a room 3·73 m. high, with a double-arched window divided by a column in the centre of each side. The column on the south side is spirally fluted, the rest are plain. Above was a roof entirely of stone slabs, but only two remain to-day.[6] This room measures 2·19 m. (north)×2·44 (east)×2·14 (south)×2·40 (west).

The Date. In spite of the ruin which has overtaken part of the northern and western *riwāqs*, it is obvious that an important part of the original mosque has survived on the southern and eastern sides,

1 He evidently did not realize that transverse arcades with a very wide central arch are quite normal in the Ḥaurān before Islam; see below, p. 490.

2 *La Mosquée Omeyyade*, p. 102.

3 The first nine courses measure 4·27 m.

4 This stone door unfortunately is no longer in position, but may be seen on the ground leaning against the flight of broken steps which leads up to the door of the minaret.

5 *Travels among the Arab Tribes*, p. 199.

6 In Buckingham's day this ceiling ‘was of solid stone, and every part of the tower strong and perfect’; *op. cit.*, p. 199.

viz. the two arcades which form the sanctuary, which are intact (except for the western half of the one next the ṣaḥn) and the two arcades which take off from it to form the east *riwāq*.

Now one of the columns of this mosque—the column from which the inner arcade of the eastern *riwāq* took off—has been *replaced* by a masonry pier, and on the east face of this pier is an inscription of eight lines, recording the fact and dated 128 H. (745/6).[1] This can only mean that the mosque which has come down to us existed already (apart from patching of the outer walls, building the back arcade of the sanctuary, replacing of roofing slabs, etc.) in 128 H. (745/6). For how long before that? A block of basalt, discovered in the course of the restoration and clearance which were carried out under the direction of Écochard in 1938–40, bears a building inscription of three lines of which the first line has practically been destroyed. It is dated 102 H. (720/21),[2] which falls in the first year of the reign of Yazīd II.

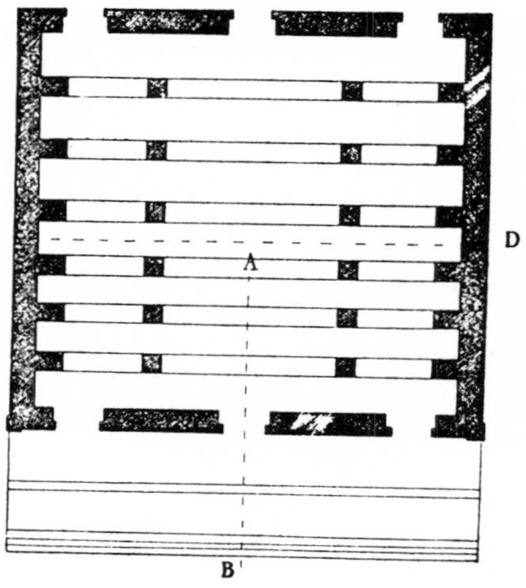

Fig. 548. Shaqqā: Basilica, plan and section. (From Butler, *Early Churches in Syria*.)

The second line begins with the last three letters of a word with a feminine termination which Sauvaget reads as *mi'dhanat*. This is confirmed by the fact that 'its construction' is also in the feminine, for almost all the other parts of a mosque—ṣaḥn, *riwāq*, miḥrāb, etc., are masculine. Our minaret therefore was built in 102 H. (721/21), and it is consequently the earliest in Islam.[3] It is tempting to take this as the foundation inscription of the mosque also.

Now the Khalif 'Umar II died 19 Rajab 101 (4th Feb. 720) and the year 102 ran from 12th July 720 to 30th June 721. If Yazīd II began our mosque he cannot have done so before 5th February 720, which would give him 16–17 months at the most to complete it before the end of 102 H., i.e. 30th June 721. This is not long, and I believe that it may have taken longer, which means that it *may* have been begun by 'Umar before his death. If so, this would explain its popular name 'Mosque of 'Umar'.

Architectural Origins. The Great Mosque of Boṣrā closely follows the building traditions of the Ḥaurān in every respect, viz. its arcades, its roofing system, its outside staircase and its minaret. Let us begin with the arcades. The transverse arcades of the sanctuary, with an arch in the centre of more than double the span of the arches on either side of it, is a feature which occurs in the second to third century basilica at Shaqqā[4] (Fig. 548); also in the Christian convent in the same place, which de Vogüé places in the fifth century.[5] The same feature may be observed in the church at Ṭafḥā,[6] where the central arch measures 6·90 m. against 3·08 m. for the lateral arches, and also in a church at Nimreh,[7] where the central arch has a span of 7·25 m. against 1·53 only.

The roofing system of our mosque is that described above (pp. 444–5 and Fig. 482); it is employed in all the buildings just mentioned, and is used all over the treeless Ḥaurān.

[1] Sauvaget, *loc. cit.*, pp. 56–8, pl. VII and fig.; and Littmann (E.), *Arabic Inscriptions*, pp. 24–5.

[2] Sauvaget, *loc. cit.*, pp. 54–6, pl. VII and fig. Now preserved in the Citadel.

[3] The first minaret *built as such*. At Damascus we have seen that the first minarets were the pre-existing towers at the four corners of the *temenos*.

[4] de Vogüé, *Syrie centrale*, pp. 55–6 and pls. 15 and 16; Butler, *Early Churches in Syria*, pp. 16–17 and illus. 9 and 10.

[5] *Op. cit.*, p. 58 and pl. 18.

[6] de Vogüé, *op. cit.*, p. 57 and pl. 17; Butler, *Architecture and Other Arts*, pp. 408–11, fig. 147 and 5 illus.; and his *Early Churches in Syria*, p. 22 and illus. 17 and 18.

[7] Butler, *Early Churches*, pp. 22–4 and illus. 19 and 20.

Another feature, the outside staircase in which each step is formed of a block of stone with one end embedded in the wall, is also common in the Ḥaurān and may be seen at Shaqqā,[1] and Duma,[1] in House No. III[2] and House XVIII,[3] at Umm al-Jimāl, and also in a house at Jemarrīn.[4]

The Architectural Evolution of the Minaret.[5] The square tower was apparently the only form of tower known in Syria from the first to the beginning of the thirteenth century, when an octagonal minaret appears at Salkhad in 630 H. (1232/3).[6]

Let us confine ourselves to dated examples to begin with.

(1) *Damascus.* At the four corners of the great *temenos* (now the Great Mosque) which we have seen (above, pp. 162–3) dates from the first century A.D., was a tower about 11 m. square and 21 m. high divided into four storeys by wooden floors, and we have seen (above, p. 156) that these towers served as minarets when Damascus was conquered by the Arabs.

(2) *Umm al-Jimāl.* In the fifth century we have a fine square tower in the barracks, *c.* A.D. 412. It is 4·40 m. square and about 15 m. high, marked off into four storeys.[7]

(3) *Qaṣr al-Banāt.* Convent with square tower about 23 m. high with six storeys; built by Kyrios, probably the same as the architect whose name is found on four other churches, the dates of their inscriptions varying from A.D. 390 to 418.[8]

Fig. 549. Umm as-Surab: Church of SS. Sergius and Bacchus. (From Butler, *op. cit.*)

(4) *Umm as-Surab* (in the Southern Ḥaurān). Church of SS. Sergius and Bacchus, with tall, square tower, completely preserved except the roof (Fig. 536). Built A.D. 489.[9]

(5) *Ḥalbān* (in Northern Syria). Tower dated A.D. 543.[10]

(6) *Qaṣr al-Milḥ.* Tower of Monastery built by the Ghassānid al-Mundhir in A.D. 559. Incorporated by Hishām in his palace Qaṣr al-Ḥayr al-Gharbī (below, p. 541, and Fig. 596 facing p. 542).

In addition to this many private houses in the Ḥaurān were provided with a square tower presumably for defence, e.g. at Ṣabḥah, with a tower of three storeys 16 m. high;[11] aṣ-Ṣāfiya,[12] Sammā,[13] Jren (two towers),[14] Umm al-Quṭṭen[15] where there are no less than seven towers (one belonging to a monastery) averaging 5m. square and three to five storeys high, say 15–22 m.; and Burāq[16] where there are two fine square towers.

Thus it was perfectly natural, inevitable even, that the architect of our mosque should build a square tower for his minaret, for no other form of tower was known in the whole of Syria. So far, however, I have not found any forerunner of its charming double windows—two arches resting on a central column—which became so popular in Spain, and also in Boṣrā itself, where it is to be seen in the minaret of the Jāmiʿ al-Khiḍr, 528 H. (1134),[17] of the Jāmiʿ ad-Dabbāgha, 622 H. (1225),[18] and of the Jāmiʿ Dayr al-Muslim,[19] 705 H. (1305/6).

1 de Vogüé, *op. cit.*, pl. 12.
2 Butler, *Ancient Architecture in Syria, Sect. A: Southern Syria*, pp. 197–9 and illus. 176 and 177.
3 *Ibid.*, pp. 200–202 and illus. 181.
4 *Ibid.*, illus. 268.
5 For the origin of the minaret, see above, pp. 59–60.
6 Wetzstein, *Reisebericht über Hauran und die Trachonen*, p. 70; von Oppenheim, *Vom Mittelmeer zum Persischen Golf*, I, pp. 206–7 and illus.; Dussaud and Macler, *Mission dans les régions désertiques de la Syrie Moyenne*, in the *Nouvelles Archives des Missions scientifiques*, X, p. 732; and Wiet, *Répertoire*, XI, pp. 32–3.
7 Butler (H. C.), *Ancient Architecture in Syria, Sect. A: Southern Syria*, p. 170 and illus. 145.
8 Butler (H. C.), *Ancient Architecture in Syria, Sect. B: Northern Syria*, pp. 214–23, illus. 219, and pl. XX; and his *Architecture and Other Arts*, pp. 156–7.
9 Butler (H. C.), *Ancient Architecture in Syria, Sect. A: Southern Syria*, pp. 95–9, and illus. 78; and his *Early Churches in Syria*, pp. 85–7 and illus. 90.
10 Butler, *Ancient Architecture in Syria, Section B: Northern Syria*, p. 18 and illus. 16.
11 Butler, *Ancient Architecture in Syria, Sect A: Southern Syria*, p. 115 and illus. 93.
12 *Ibid.*, p. 126 and illus. 100.
13 *Ibid.*, p. 135 and illus. 113.
14 *Ibid.*, pp. 422–3 and illus. 364.
15 *Ibid.*, pp. 139–42 and illus. 116 and 121–3.
16 *Ibid.*, p. 127 and illus. 101 and 102.
17 van Berchem, in the *Z.D.P.V.*, XIX, p. 107; Brünnow and von Domaszewski, *Die Provincia Arabia*, III, pp. 13 and 210, and figs. 886 and 887; Butler, *op. cit.*, p. 292 and illus. 205; Littmann, *Arabic Inscriptions*, pp. 30–31; *op. cit.*, VIII, p. 188, Wiet.
18 Butler, *op. cit.*, pp. 293–4 and illus. 263; and Wiet, *Répertoire*, X, pp. 222–3. In April 1962 I was sorry to find that the E. and W. columns had gone and that the S. column was leaning.
19 Buckingham expressly mentions the double-arched window near the top, divided by a spirally fluted column; *Travels among the Arab Tribes*, p. 197. For the date see Ouéchek and Mougdad, *Bosra*, p. 15, n. 2.

(7) *Sama* (in the Southern Ḥaurān). Monastery of St. George, with square tower about 12 m. high, completely preserved (Fig. 550, facing p. 466). Built A.D. 624–5.[1]

(8) *Jerāda.* To these examples may be added the well-preserved tower of five storeys adjoining the narthex of the church at Jerāda. Its floors were composed of slabs of stone extending from wall to wall.[2]

(9) *Umm ar-Raṣāṣ.* Square tower, 2·50 m. a side and about 12 m. high (Fig. 551, facing p. 466). Alongside are the ruins of a building which Tristram (1872) believed to be a church, as he was able to distinguish an apse,[3] although Vincent maintains that it was a fort.[4] Brünnow and von Domaszewski say that the destroyed building was 'gewiss die Kirche'.[5] As a matter of fact there are two buildings quite close to each other. One is obviously a fortified tower (perhaps all that remains of the town wall), the other, much ruined, but almost in contact with our tower, I take to have been the church. A Greek cross is carved on the east and west faces of the tower.

It should now be clear that the square minaret at Ramla, the minaret of Boṣrā and the minaret of Qaizawān to which we are coming, (p. 518), are merely a continuation of the traditions of pre-Muslim Syria. It is difficult to imagine how Thiersch can say of the latter that 'die Ähnlichkeit des Minarets mit dem alten dreigeschossigen Pharos ist in die Augen springend'.[6] The octagonal and circular storeys are wanting, and the top storey, as we shall see, is not original. One cannot claim, as Thiersch does, that every minaret with storeys which are successively square, octagonal, and circular is a direct descendant of the Pharos, and then claim the same thing for another minaret, all the storeys of which are square in plan! Even the proportions observed for the lower storeys in each case are not similar, as Thiersch maintains: in the Pharos the base of the lower storey was to its height as 5 : 12, whereas at Qairawān the proportion is roughly 5 : 9. On the other hand, the resemblance of the minaret at Qairawān to Syrian church towers (some of which taper, e.g. Sama, Fig. 550, facing p. 466) and tower houses needs no emphasizing.

We can now say with confidence that the idea of the minaret arose in Syria under the Umayyad dynasty, the first minarets being the four ancient corner towers of the *Temenos* at Damascus, and that the first minarets built by the Muslims were derived architecturally from Syrian towers.[7] In addition to this the Syrian minaret was destined to remain true to its traditions for many centuries as may be seen from the following sequence:

QAṢR AL-ḤAYR ASH-SHARQĪ. Minaret between the two enclosures, 110 H. (728/9). See below, p. 532.

DAMASCUS. The northern minaret of the Great Mosque, seen by Muqaddasī, which occupied the site of the present Ma'dhanat al-'Arūs (Minaret of the Bride). It is not possible to determine the date of this minaret, which Muqaddasī (985) refers to as *muḥdatha* (above, p. 177). I therefore suggest *c.* A.D. 900. Whether it was built by al-Walīd or shortly before Muqaddasī's visit does not concern us here. If Rivoira is right in believing that the first few courses of the present minaret, which are larger than the rest, belong to the previous one, then it must have been square also.

ḤOMṢ. Square minaret, known as *al-ma'dhanat al-maktūma*. Built, according to an inscription, by Abu'l-Fawāris Bakjūr as-Sayfī, in 381 H. (980).[8]

ALEPPO. The beautiful minaret of the Great Mosque, dated 483 H. (1090/91).[9]

BOṢRĀ. Mosque of al-Khiḍr, dated 528 H. (1134),[10] with square minaret.

ḤAMĀ. Great Mosque, south-eastern minaret dated 529 H. (1135).[11]

MA'ARRAT AN-NU'MĀN. Great Mosque with square minaret dated 575 H. (1179).[12]

DAMASCUS. Great Mosque; present northern minaret (*Ma'dhanat al-'Arūs*), built between 570 H. (1174/5) and 580 H. (1184). See above, p. 177.

[1] Butler, *op. cit.*, pp. 83–6 and illus. 64 and 65; and his *Early Churches in Syria*, pp. 89–90 and illus. 92.

[2] Butler, *Architecture and Other Arts*, p. 153. and illus.

[3] *Land of Moab*, pp. 145–6, with plate. Described also in Buckingham, *Travels among the Arab Tribes*, pp. 99–100.

[4] *Revue Biblique*, 1898, p. 434.

[5] *Die Provincia Arabia*, II, pp. 70–72 and fig. 653.

[6] *Pharos, Antike, Islām und Occident*, p. 124.

[7] Gottheil (*Journ. Amer. Oriental Socy.*, XXX, p. 138); Thiersch (*op. cit.*, pp. 99–110) and Diez (*Encyc. of Islām*, III, p. 228) are in agreement on this point.

[8] Van Berchem and Fatio, *Voyage en Syrie*, I, p. 166; Sarre and Herzfeld, *Archäologische Reise*, II, p. 355; and Wiet, *Répertoire*, V, pp. 139–40. In 1919 I sought for this minaret and was shown the place where it had stood. I was told that it had been pulled down during the war, according to some on account of its being in a dangerous condition, according to others, for the sake of its stone.

[9] Abu'l-Fidā', III, p. 268; and Herzfeld, in Djemal Pascha, *Alte Denkmäler aus Syrien*, text to Taf. 39 and 40; and Herzfeld, *C.I.A. Inscriptions et Monuments d'Alep*, pp. 150–64, pls. LVI–LXIII and figs. 60–61.

[10] See above, p. 491.

[11] Wiet, *Répertoire d'Épigraphie arabe*, VIII, pp. 195–6.

[12] Sarre and Herzfeld, *Archäologische Reise*, II, p. 355.

Aleppo. Minaret of the Jāmiʿ ad-Dabbāgha al-ʿAtīqa, built *c.* 1200 according to Herzfeld.[1]

Aleppo. Great Mosque in the Citadel, with square minaret, mosque is dated 610 H. (1213/14).[2]

This type even penetrated into the northern part of Mesopotamia. Two examples of this intrusion may be cited:

Raqqa. Square minaret in mosque outside the walls.[3]

Ḥarrān. Great Mosque, with minaret—a tall square shaft—near the centre of the north side (recalling the arrangement at Damascus); below, p. 644 and Plate 140 *a*.

The first departure in Syria from the square type is (1) the octagonal minaret of Bālis, of which the date 607 H. (1210/11) was first read by Janine and Dominique Sourdel,[4] and (2) the octagonal minaret of Salkhad, dated 630 H. (1232/3).[5]

Before leaving the question, however, one must admit that although the square type, judging by existing monuments, appears to have been the invariable rule in Syria for many centuries, yet three anomalies existed in North Africa, if we can accept the evidence of early travellers: (1) al-Bakrī (1068) says that the mosque at Al-Qaṣr al-Qadīm, a town founded in 184 H. (800), had a tower of cylindrical form, constructed of bricks and ornamented with columns arranged in seven storeys.[6] (2) The same author says that at Ajedābīya in Barqa, the Great Mosque, which had been founded by Abu'l-Qāsim (934–945), had an octagonal minaret (*saumaʿa muthammana*).[7] (3) The Shaykh at-Tijānī, who travelled in Tunisia between 706 and 708 H. (1306–9), says that the minaret of the Mosque of Tripoli had been built in 300 (912), and that its lower half was round, the upper half octagonal.[8] This type cannot be matched by any existing example, and Thiersch is not justified in calling it 'ein . . . Minaret mit echt ägyptischem Formenwechsel',[9] as the circular part in Egyptian minarets always comes above the octagonal, which in its turn rests on a square lower storey.[10]

AL-MUWAQQAR[11]

Owing to the almost complete destruction of this monument I have felt it advisable to adopt an unusual procedure, viz.: first to give the accounts of the famous archaeologists, Brünnow and von Domaszewski, who saw it in April 1898, and Musil who saw it in June of the same year, and again in 1901. I shall then add a very brief account of the state of the site when I visited it on the 23rd April 1962.

The Description of Brünnow and von Domaszewski. Here is what Brünnow and von Domaszewski saw in April 1898:

'The ruin rests partly on the summit and is partly built out on the eastern slope, where the level sur-'face was to have been extended on this side by means of a terrace resting on tunnel-vaults, of which 'only the western half is preserved.

'Of the north and south walls only fragments are preserved; at the western end of the north wall a 'door jamb is still to be seen with a reveal and an arch above (*a*) whilst in the upper part of the wall is

1 *Mshattâ, Ḥîra und Bâdiya*, in the *Jahrb. der Preuszischen Kunstsammlungen*, XLII, p. 143 and Taf. 10(1).

2 Bischoff, *Tuḥaf al-Anbāʾ fī Taʾrīkh Ḥalab*, p. 135; van Berchem, *Inschriften aus Syrien*, p. 40; and Herzfeld, *C.I.A., Inscriptions et Monuments d'Alep*, pp. 132–3.

3 See Gertrude Bell, *Amurath to Amurath*, pp. 55–6, and fig. 35; and Herzfeld, in Sarre and Herzfeld, *Archäologische Reise*, II, pp. 354–5 and Abb. 327–9.

4 *Notes d'Épigraphie et de Topographie sur la Syrie du Nord*, in *Les Annales archéol. de Syrie*, III, pp. 103–5.

5 Dussaud and Macler, *Mission*, p. 732, n. 10bis; and Wiet, *Répertoire*, XI, p. 33.

6 P. 28; de Slane's transl., p. 71 [64].

7 *Op. cit.*, p. 5; transl., p. 15 [16–17]; also the *Kitāb al-Istibṣār*, p. 30; Fagnan's transl., p. 58. See also Marçais, *Manuel*, I, pp. 37–9.

8 *Riḥla*, Rousseau's transl., *Journal Asiatique*, 5me sér., t. I (1852), p. 154.

9 *Op. cit.*, p. 126.

10 See 'Sequence of Minarets' in my *Muslim Architecture of Egypt*, I and II.

11 Bibliography:—1902, Musil (Alois), *Kuṣejr ʿAmra und andere Schlösser östlich von Moab, Sitzungsberichte der Kais. Akad. der Wissenschaften in Wien, phil.-hist. Classe*, CXLIV, pp. 12–14 and Abb. 5; — 1905, Brünnow (R. E.) and von Domaszewski (A.), *Die Provincia Arabia*, II, pp. 182–9, Taf. XLIX, and figs. 757–71; — 1907, Musil (Alois), *Kuṣejr ʿAmra*, pp. 27–9 and figs. 20–30 and 87–9; — 1910, Herzfeld (E.), *Die Genesis der islamischen Kunst, Der Islam*, I, pp. 128–31; — 1922, Jaussen (J. A.) and Savignac, *Les Châteaux arabes de Qeṣeir ʿAmra, Ḥarâneh et Ṭûba*, p. 8 and pls. I–II; — 1939, Sauvaget (J.), *Remarques sur les monuments omeyyades, Journal Asiatique*, CCXXXI, pp. 35–6; — 1946, Hamilton (R. W.), *Some Eighth-century Capitals from al Muwaqqar, Quarterly of the Dept. of Antiquities in Palestine*, XII, pp. 63–9, pls. XXI–XXII and figs. 1–12; and *An Eighth-century Water-Gauge at al Muwaqqar, ibid.*, XII, pp. 70–72 and pl. XXIII; and Mayer (L. A.), *Note on the Inscription from al Muwaqqar, ibid.*, XII, pp. 73–4; — 1947, Sauvaget (J.), *La Mosquée omeyyade de Médine*, pp. 125–6 and fig. 14.

'a partly preserved arched window (Figs. 758–9). At 20·20 m. to the west of this door jamb is a wall 'running from north to south, which may be original in its lower part, for at its two ends parts are still 'preserved of the two pieces of the transverse wall lying in exactly the same alignment as the two main 'parts. In its present state however it is of later origin for it is not built of limestone blocks like the 'others, but of rough flint blocks. If we assume that the door *a* stood in the middle of the north wall, 'we then obtain 38 m. for the inner width of the whole building; the length between the north and 'south walls amounts to 35 m. only. The outer walls are 1·12 m. thick.

'The north and south walls do not stand on the terrace but on the ground itself, they thus slope 'towards the east. The terrace is built up between them, and is carried by eight tunnel-vaults of varying 'width; the two measured by us were 3·65 and 3·95 m. respectively, whereas Musil, I think gives '3·72 m. as the average. Its depth, so far as it is preserved, up to the hill, amounts to *c.* 6 m.; its height 'about 2 m. From the apex of the vault to the surface of the terrace I measured 45 cms. A similar 'vault has been built with a breadth of 3·65 m. on the outer side of the north wall; however it does not 'spring, like the two outer vaults at the end of the inner terrace, from the wall itself, but rests on a 'supporting wall 55 cm. thick built against it. A vault has likewise been built against the south wall, 'but it is separated from it not only by a supporting wall 2 m. thick, but also by a piece of wall project-'ing in front of it. The surface of the terrace is still partly paved with stone slabs.

'Of the inner structure only a small amount has been preserved. On the inner side of the north wall, 'about 75 cm. above the ground, the remains of steps about 3 m. wide can still be recognized, they 'followed the wall and must have led to an upper storey; the staircase was obviously lit by the window 'mentioned above. At a distance of 8·30 m. from the north wall are two socles, 1·25 m. long and 90 cm. 'wide, placed 2·75 m. apart, of which the inner is 45 cm. beyond the alignment of the door jamb '(Fig. 766). There is a similar pair 13 m. south of it, but I have only seen the outer socle. Between the 'two outer, and at a distance of 3·95 m. from the northern socle, is a column base, 53 cm. square; 'from these measurements it follows that its centre lies at a distance from the southern socle equal to 'twice the distance from the northern one, so that between it and the former [i.e. the southern socle] 'a similar base must be restored (3·95+0·53+3·95+0·53+3·95 = 12·91). To the west of it a similar 'pair of bases must be assumed between the two inner socles. The peculiarly decorated capitals of 'these columns and pilasters partly lay about on the ground (Figs. 760–65).

• 'This inner building appears to have had the form of a basilica; however it does not stand sym-'metrically between the outer walls, so that these can scarcely be regarded as the actual limit of the 'building. A piece of masonry 1·07 m. thick, attached to the southern socle, appears to have limited 'the inner room on this side; a similar wall was probably attached to the northern socle. A more exact 'knowledge of the structure could only be obtained by excavation.

'About 50° S. of E. from the main building and at a distance of about 8 minutes is a smaller building 'of which the purpose is not clear (Fig. 771, plan and sections Figs. 767–9). It consists of three 'tunnel-vaulted rooms lying side by side, of which only the middle one is to some extent preserved. 'Its outer breadth amounts to 13·38 m., the length along the best preserved west wall is 13·86 m. The 'two inner walls, each carrying two vaults are 88 cm. thick in their upper part, where they are pierced 'by open arches; in the middle vault I noticed that on both sides, directly below the arched opening, 'is a projection of 6 cm. and if this is also the case with the two outer—which unfortunately I did not 'verify—the proper thickness of the wall would be 1 m. This lower thicker part of the wall rises about '90 cm. above the present ground-level, raised by the accumulation of débris; from the ledge to the 'springing of the tunnel-vault I have measured *c.* 1·64 m., to the apex 3·20. The openings of the row of 'arches are 1·07 m. wide and the height to the apex 1·10 m.; the voussoirs are 31 cm. deep. The piers 'between the arches are 62 cm. wide and the height from the ledge to the springing of the arches is '58 cm.

'One of the outer walls is nearly all destroyed, the other, on the contrary is fairly well preserved, and 'in it are two rectangular windows, 70 cm. high and 28 cm. wide, which are 5·80 m. apart and set 'immediately below the springing of the vault. The centre of the space between the windows may be 'the centre of the building, and if we assume that the windows are likewise at the same distance from 'the end walls as they are from each other, we thereby obtain *c.* 18 m. as the original inner length of the 'building, or with the end walls, *c.* 19·60. At the northern end of the east wall I thought I could dis-'tinguish a corner, the position of which would agree well with this supposition.'[1]

Musil's Account. Here is Musil's description of the ruins[2] which he saw in June 1898:

'[The palace-ruin] crowns a 910 m. high summit of a range of the same name which goes from 'west to east....

'The whole construction consists of three parts: the palace, some ruined dwelling places as well as 'some caves and a tower to the west of the palace, and finally a tank with a larger building at the 'south-east foot of the summit.

'The almost completely ruined palace forms—as far as one is still able to perceive—a rectangle of '65 m. in length (E.–W.) and 39 m. in width. Its 1·15 m. thick enclosing walls are flanked by two 'round and two rectangular towers. As one finds foundation walls everywhere next the N.E., E. and 'S. enclosing walls, one is compelled to conclude that the building originally covered a wider extent.

'The interior of the palace is divided into two unequal halves by a transverse wall, 1 m. thick, which 'is reinforced by a tower-like pier. The eastern half has in the north and south enclosing wall 2 doors, '1·50 m. wide. It ends in the E., where the ground is sloping, with a substructure built up of a row of 'tunnel vaults on low abutment walls. Within the enclosing wall are 8 tunnel-vaults of 3·72 m. average 'width, whilst a similar one is constructed outside of it. On top of the substructure are remains of piers, 'columns and pieces of walls in situ.

'Numerous cut stones from piers and drums of columns, especially bases and capitals richly orna-'mented with vine, palm leaves, lillies and other motifs, lie about in the débris nearby. The vaulted 'substructure with its colonnaded construction above doubtless once extended beyond the present 'breaking-off, since the enclosing walls in their ruinous state still extend beyond it and as the above-'mentioned remains of piers and columns do not show an organic ending. This lay-out, with its 'columned hall open towards the east, reminded me vividly of Khirbet ad-Dayr at al-Faṭūma in Wādī 'Mūsā (Petra). The walls of the vaults were covered with mortar, and pitted here and there in order to 'give the fine lime plaster a better grip. I found the same plaster and the same pitting in Qaṣr aṭ-Ṭūba 'and Quṣayr 'Amra. The decoration of a stone slab which I found in the débris, by a circle about '30 cm. in diameter, in which a cross is incised, and smaller circles between the arms of the cross, 'makes it probable that Christians have lived here. To-day, the palace serves, like those in its imme-'diate neighbourhood, as a burial-place for the Ṣḫūr. The southern and south-eastern slope of the hill 'in addition to ruined walls contains very many bulb-shaped cisterns which serve as a resting place for 'numberless pigeons. To the SSE., at the foot of the hill, is a tank, 34 m. long (E.–W.) and 31·50 wide. 'Its enclosing wall is 1·90 m. thick, with a core of rubble and earth. Staircases at its inner north-west 'and south-west corners lead down to the bottom. A few metres SSE. of the tank are the remains of 'a building from 13·50 m. to 17 m. long from N. to S. and 13·26 wide, with three rooms each 3·42 m. 'in width. These rooms were covered with tunnel-vaults of which only the central one remains. They 'communicate with each other by ten round vaulted openings in the 90 cm. thick separation-walls, 'which are built on a continuous socle. Here the construction of ordinary dwelling rooms is applied 'for a special purpose which, however, excludes its being used for dwelling or religious purposes. The 'exterior walls are only 60 cm. thick and have narrow window openings.

'Apparently the southern end of the central room formed a half round apse; however I was not 'able to verify this point on account of the burials of Bedawīn, which were scattered all over the place. 'About 3·5 m. from the outer walls, and 5 m. from the existing piers, one observes the remains of a wall '80 cm. thick, which surrounds the whole enclosure.

The Condition of the Ruins in 1962. I visited Muwaqqar on 23rd April 1962, and found that terrible damage had been done to what remained when Brünnow and von Domaszewski and Musil visited it in 1898.

To begin with, the eight parallel tunnel-vaults, by which the platform of the palace was extended towards the east, still exist, but a wall with eight doorways has been built a couple of metres or so in

[1] *Op. cit.*, II, pp. 182–7.

[2] *Ḳuṣeir 'Amra*, pp. 27–9.

front of their broken ends, and the vault continued by a miserable ceiling of branches, matting, etc. The partition walls between the rooms have been continued in poor masonry.

As for the surface of the platform, I was only able to discover a piece of its pavement about 2 m. square near the south-east corner. The rest was covered with rubble débris from a foot to over 2 feet deep, and I could not distinguish any traces of the remains so carefully described by Brünnow and von Domaszewski, except for about 3 m. of what appeared to be the south wall near the piece of pavement just mentioned. The tank is still in use but the remains of the vaulted ruin, 100 yards to the south-east of it, are no longer to be seen.

THE CAPITALS EMPLOYED AT AL-MUWAQQAR. Fortunately eighteen beautiful capitals (Plates 81-2) have been saved from this wreck, and they have been admirably published by Hamilton,[1] who has kindly allowed me to give a short account of them here. A full list of them is given in the table. They are very interesting for a number of them are decorated with motifs employed some twenty years later at Mshattā, for which it had not been possible to find antecedents before the publication of these capitals. All, as far as is known, belonged to the palace, except No. 18, which belonged to the water-gauge of the tank.

LIST OF CAPITALS

No.	*Type*	*Illustrated*	*Brünnow*	*Musil*	*Savignac*	*Whereabouts in 1943*
1	Column	Pl. XXI	Fig. 760, Pl. XLIX	..	Pl. II	Unknown.
2	”	”	Fig. 761, Pl. XLIX	..	Pl. II	Palestine Archaeological Museum.
3	Engaged half-column	Not illustrated, cf. No. 16	Fig. 762	..	Pl. II	Unknown.
4	Column	Pl. XXI	Fig. 763, Pl. XLIX	..	Pl. II	Unknown.
5	Engaged half-column	”	Fig. 764, Pl. XLIX	..	Pl. II	Palestine Archaeological Museum.
6	”	Fig. 5 *a*, *b*, *c*, p. 65	..	..	Pl. I (3)	Unknown.
7	Column	Fig. 2, p. 65	..	..	Pls. I, II	Unknown.
8	”	Fig. 4, p. 65	..	..	Pl. I (2)	Unkown.
9	Pilaster	Fig. 6, p. 66	..	Fig. 87, p. 102	..	Unknown.
10	Column	Pl. XXI	..	..	..	Muwaqqar, damaged.
11	? Fragment	”	..	..	..	Muwaqqar.
12	Column	”	..	..	..	Muwaqqar.
13	”	Fig. 3, p. 65	..	..	..	Unknown. Seen at Muwaqqar before 1943.
14	”	Pl. XXII	..	..	..	Muwaqqar.
15	”	”	..	..	..	Muwaqqar.
16	”	”	..	..	..	Muwaqqar.
17	”	”	..	..	..	Muwaqqar.
18	”	”	..	..	..	Muwaqqar (now in ‘Ammān).

THE WATER-GAUGE. Amongst the most interesting discoveries at al-Muwaqqar has been the capital and part of the shaft of the water-gauge of the reservoir, found in a house in 1943. Hamilton was informed that it had been recently found in the mud, when the reservoir[2] in the small valley south-east of the palace was cleaned out. This curious capital is shown on Plate 82 *g-i*. ‘Three of the sides are ‘decorated by a row of acanthus leaves separated by paired volutes. . . . The junction of the three ‘sides with the shaft is marked by a double collar composed of a rope ornament and a row of folded ‘half-palmettes.’[3] The fourth side is occupied by an inscription of ten lines: ‘Bismillāh . . . Hath ‘ordered the building of this pool (*birka*) the Servant of God, Yazīd, the Commander of the ‘Faithful. . . . It hath been built by the care of ‘Abd Allāh ibn Sulaym.’[4] In small characters between the 8th and 9th lines are the words ‘fifteenth cubit’. Hamilton has convincingly shown that the inscription and the leaf and the rope ornament must have been carved at the same time.[5]

[1] *Some Eighth-century Capitals from al Muwaqqar*, *Quarterly of the Department of Antiquities in Palestine*, XII, pp. 63–9.

[2] *Loc. cit.*, p. 70.

[3] *Ibid.*

[4] *Ibid.*; and Mayer, *Note on the Inscription from al Muwaqqar*, *Quarterly of the Department of Antiquities in Palestine*, XII, p. 73.

[5] *Loc. cit.*, p. 71.

The foot of the column and part of the top drum were found shortly after. On the former was the word *dhirā‘* (cubit), on the latter ‘fourteenth cubit’. At the top of the latter is the date ‘year 104‘ = A. D. 722/3.[1] In other words we can now say that the reservoir was constructed by the Khalif Yazīd II in 104 H., in spite of Mayer's doubts, due to the fact that, although al-Muwaqqar is mentioned several times by Umayyad poets, no author earlier than Yāqūt mentions his name in connexion with it.

Hamilton points out that if we take the top lines of the inscription at each cubit as the level intended, we get 45 cm. for the 11th cubit and 44·5 cm. for the 12th. The average of these two measurements, 44·75 cm., falls within half of a centimetre of a cubit based on one and a half standard Roman feet of 29·6 cm., viz. 44·4 cm. This multiplied by fifteen gives 6·71 m. as the approximate height of the column and the maximum depth of water anticipated.[2]

[1] *Loc. cit.*, p. 72.

[2] *Loc. cit.*, pp. 71–2.

XVIII

THE WORKS OF THE KHALIF HISHĀM

Ḥammām aṣ-Ṣarakh—Detailed description—Material—The decoration—The date—The Mosque at Quṣayr al-Ḥallābāt—Description—The date—The Mosques at Khān az-Zebīb and Umm al-Walīd.

Qaṣr al-Ḥayr al-Gharbī—The site—The Khān—The date—The Palace—The entrance—The entrance passage—The courtyard—The rooms of the interior—The upper floor—The lighting arrangements—The decoration—The bas-relief of a Khalif—The decoration of the portico and *bayts*—The staircase rooms—The first fresco—The second fresco—Identification and date—Architectural Origins—The general design.

The Minaret of the Great Mosque at Qairawān—History—Description of the present minaret—Is the present minaret that built by Hishām?—Architectural origins.

HISHĀM SUCCEEDED YAZĪD II in Sha'bān 105 (Jan. 724). His reign—a comparatively long one of nineteen years—was mild and generally conscientious, in fact Muir regards it, 'if we except occasional outbreaks of cruel tyranny', as 'one of the most exemplary of the Caliphate either before or after'.[1] His reign witnessed the rise of a new claimant to the Khalifate—Muḥammad, great-grandson of 'Abbās, the Prophet's uncle. The unsuccessful revolt of Zayd, grandson of Ḥusayn, in 124 H. (740) and the resulting collapse of the 'Alīds, left the way clear for the former, whose party was destined to succeed in founding the 'Abbāsid Khalifate ten years later.

ḤAMMĀM AṢ-ṢARAKH[2]

Ḥammām aṣ-Ṣarakh was discovered by the late H. C. Butler of the Princeton Expedition in 1905. He sighted it from Quṣayr al-Ḥallābāt, standing out alone on the plain about three miles to the south-east.[3] He visited it during a driving snowstorm and was only able to devote half an hour to it, yet in spite of these unfavourable conditions he managed to plan it with considerable accuracy. He visited it again in March 1909, photographed and examined it at leisure, and corrected some of his earlier observations.

I visited it on the 23rd of November 1926,[4] in company with Père Vincent, to whom I am indebted for the beautiful drawings reproduced here (Figs. 553-4).

Ḥammām aṣ-Ṣarakh is strikingly like Quṣayr 'Amra in plan and arrangement but, thanks to its well-finished masonry which has taken a beautiful amber tint, it makes a very much better impression (Plates 83 and 84 *a* and *b*), especially the semi-domed recesses of the bath, which are a pleasure to look upon. Like Quṣayr 'Amra it is composed of two principal elements: (1) a rectangular audience hall measuring 8·95×7·90 m. (against 8·75×7·58), with an alcove, corresponding to the throne-recess of Quṣayr 'Amra, opening on the south-east side, flanked by two rooms H and H₁, each lit by three small splayed windows, and (2) a bath, consisting of three little rooms L, M, and N, the first tunnel-vaulted, the second cross-vaulted, and the third covered by a dome—the same sequence of roofing systems as at Quṣayr 'Amra, the only difference being that to pass out of L one must turn to the right instead of to the left. On the north-east side of N is a tunnel-vaulted passage O, leading into an enclosure P of which the walls, although partly standing at the time of Butler's visit,[5] have now almost completely disappeared.

Detailed Description. On the analogy of Quṣayr 'Amra, one would have expected to find the entrance of the audience hall in the centre of the side opposite the alcove, but this is not the case;

[1] *Caliphate* (Weir's ed.), pp. 399–400.

[2] Bibliography: —1907, Musil (A.), *Kuṣejr 'Amra*, p. 148; Strzygowski, *Amra als Bauwerk*, in the *Zeitschr. für Geschichte der Architektur*, I, p. 64; —1909, Butler (H. C.), *Ancient Architecture in Syria, Section A: Southern Syria*, pp. 77–80, and Illus. 59–60, and Appendix, pp. xix–xxv and Illus. *59a–60c*; —1914, Bell (G. L.), *Ukhaiḍir*, pp. 111–12 and 165; —1922, Jaussen and Savignac, *Mission archéologique en Arabie, III: Les châteaux arabes*, pp. 112–14; —1927, Pijoán (J.), *History of Art*, II, p. 209 and fig. 313; and Musil (A.), *Arabia Deserta: a Topographical Itinerary*, p. 351 and figs. 84–91; —1933, Pauty (Edmond), *Les Hammams du Caire*, pp. 17–21 and fig. 3; —1943, Écochard (Michel) and Claude le Cœur, *Les Bains de Damas*, pp. 126–8 and fig. cxxxviii (5); —1949, Pijoán (José), *Summa Artis, XII—Arte islámico*, p. 35 and fig. 45; —1959, Harding (G. L.), *The Antiquities of Jordan*, p. 152; —1960, Field (Henry), *North Arabian Desert Archaeological Survey*, p. 67 and figs. 65–6 and 70 *a*.

[3] He says (*op. cit.*, p. 77) 'scarcely a mile east', but this is a mistake.

[4] We went by car from 'Ammān to Ḥammām az-Zerqā, and there found an Arab of the Dajar tribe, who accompanied us as guide. We travelled east for about twenty miles, until we saw Ḥammām aṣ-Ṣarakh lying in the plain at the end of a valley running from west to east. (See map on p. 404.)

[5] *Op. cit.*, p. 78 and Illus. 59, 60, and 60 *a*. He calls it 'a sort of vestibule, now much ruined'.

although two-thirds of the wall on this side have been preserved[1] there is no door to be seen. One must therefore conclude that it was at B₁ in the centre of the south-western side, but it is not possible to verify this conclusion, for the whole of this wall has fallen and any trace of a door-sill, if such exists, is buried under the débris. The audience hall is roofed, as at Quṣayr ʿAmra, by three parallel tunnel-vaults[2] resting on two transverse arches which spring from very low responds, only a little over a metre high. Both these transverse arches have fallen but, according to Père Vincent's reconstruction, they measured 5 m. to the apex (against 4·70 at Quṣayr ʿAmra).

At the back of the central nave is an alcove covered by a tunnel-vault of cut stone, part of which still stands, the crown being only 5 m. above the ground level, instead of just over 7 m. like the crowns of the tunnel-vaults. The sides of this recess, as at Quṣayr ʿAmra, are flush with the wall piers of the central nave. A quarter-round moulding runs all round the main hall at a height of 5½ m. Below this moulding, at the west end of each tunnel-vault, is an arched window, but it is not possible to say whether there were corresponding windows at the opposite end, for the wall has not been preserved to its full height on this side; if there were, they must have been above the moulding in order to clear the tunnel-vaults of the alcove and lateral rooms, the crowns of which reach nearly to the moulding. The south-western wall having fallen, it is not possible to say whether there were windows in it, but it is probable that there were none, as at Quṣayr ʿAmra, for the winter rains would beat against this side. The opposite side, unlike Quṣayr ʿAmra, is without windows.

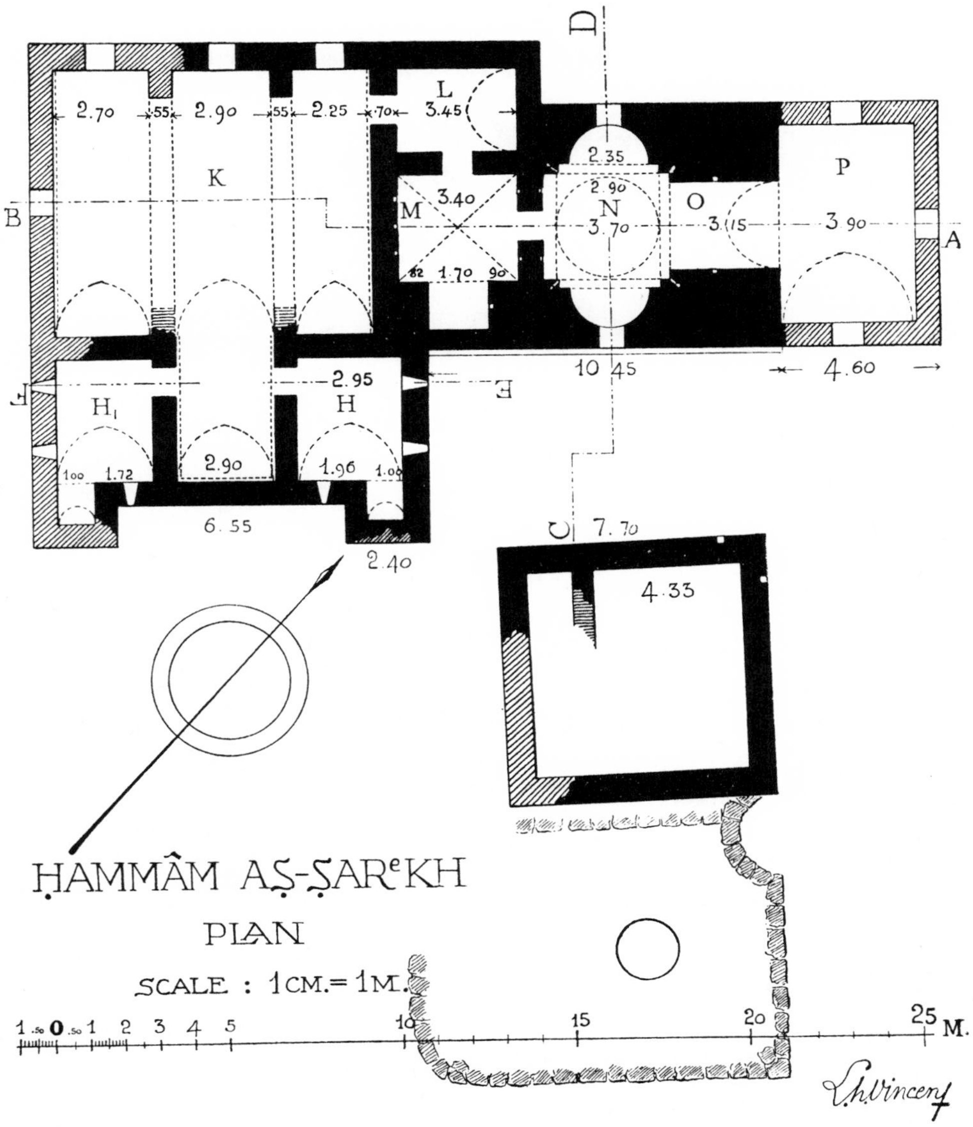

FIG. 553. ḤAMMĀM AṢ-ṢARAKH: Plan.

A small doorway with lintel and relieving arch opens on the left side of the alcove into the lateral room H, of the same depth as the alcove and roofed with a stone tunnel-vault of the same height. There was a similar room to the right of the alcove, but it is now completely ruined, only the foundations and the first three courses of one side of the vault remaining. The moulding, however, which runs round the alcove at the springing of the vault, is lacking in the side rooms. At the back of the latter in the outer corners are two small arched recesses, a metre wide and 1·20 deep, which form salients on the south-east wall. These little rooms, unlike the corresponding ones at Quṣayr ʿAmra, are each provided with three splayed windows, as shown on the plan (Fig. 553).

A door in the north corner of the main hall leads into the little tunnel-vaulted *apodyterium* (L), which measures 2·50×3·45 m. and which is without windows. There are no remains of benches. In the centre of the south-east side is a door, 90 cm. in width, which leads into the *tepidarium* (M), a cross-vaulted room measuring 3·40×3·20 m., on the far side of which, exactly as at Quṣayr ʿAmra, is a little tunnel-

[1] I revisited Ḥammām aṣ-Ṣarakh on 20th May 1928 for the purpose of reading over this description on the spot, and was grieved to find that another third of this wall had fallen, doubtless during the earthquake of July 1927. Plate 83 *d* shows its present state.

[2] It is a curious fact that the north-east tunnel-vault is narrower than the rest, being only 2·25 m. against 2·90 for the central vault and 2·70 for the other.

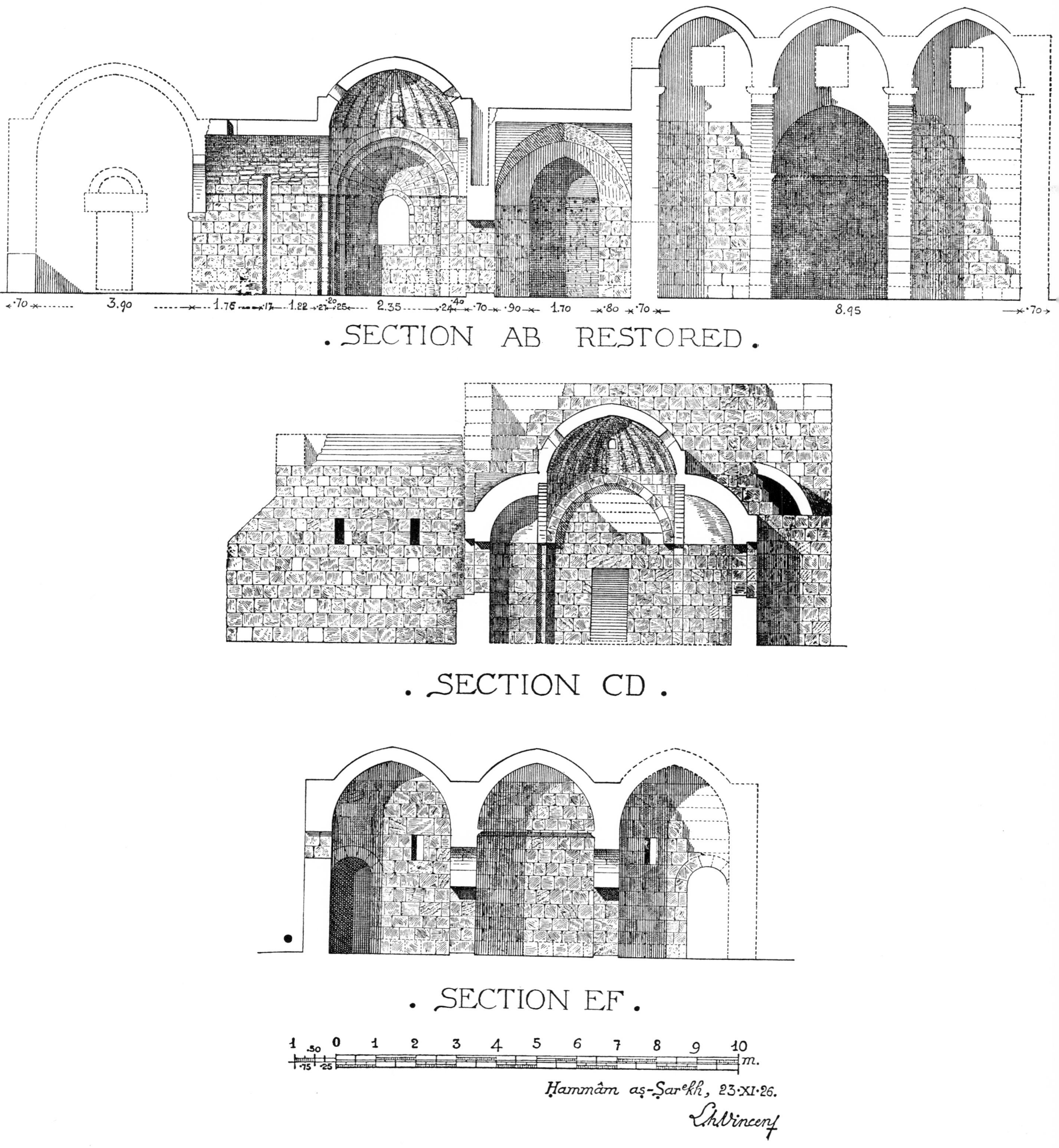

FIG. 554. ḤAMMĀM AṢ-ṢARAKH: Sections.

vaulted recess, 1·70 m. wide and 1·20 deep. In the upper part of the walls are six vertical grooves, no doubt intended to receive earthenware water-pipes.

Almost in the centre of the north-east wall is a door, similar to the last, leading into the *calidarium* (N), a rectangular chamber, 3·70 m. long and 3·20 wide, with a semicircular recess to right and left, less deep than those of Quṣayr ʿAmra. At the back of each semi-dome is a small arched window 75 cm. wide. The semi-domes are beautifully constructed with voussoirs which radiate from a saddle-like block placed above the summit of the window arch, which is distinctly pointed (Plate 83 *e*). The central part of the chamber is covered by a dome, slightly less than a hemisphere, resting on spherical-triangle pendentives of four courses of stone (Plates 83 *a–c* and 84 *b*). There appear to have been eight small circular windows in the dome, but some have now become large holes. The dome is built with nineteen projecting ribs[1] composed of long, thin wedge-shaped pieces of shale entirely unhewn, and the filling between the ribs is of shale also. Butler believes that it was originally completely covered with plaster.[2] The crown has fallen in, so that the original shape cannot be exactly determined, but, as Butler remarks, the curve of the ribs shows almost conclusively that it was slightly pointed. It has an outer covering of fine waterproof cement, which, from its pinkish colour, probably contains crushed pottery.

On the east side of N is a tunnel-vaulted passage, 2·60 m. wide and 3·15 long, opening into P, of which hardly anything remains. The walls forming the sides of O are of enormous thickness (2·15 m.), much thicker in fact than they need have been to take the thrust of the vault. On looking at the plan it would appear that this thickness is due to a desire that the outer walls should present a straight façade.

MATERIAL. The walls, which vary in thickness from 70 to 80 cm., are constructed of blocks of limestone averaging 32 cm. in height. The courses run along regularly, except on the north-western face, where there is a curious irregularity—not a clean vertical break—at the junction of the audience hall and room L. This irregularity, however, only begins at the third course.[3] Some at least of the material must have been taken from an older building, for Butler noticed that ‘the outer end of one of the vaulting stones of the niche on the [south-] east side, which was originally embedded in mortar and covered with waterproof cement, is moulded with the profile of an archivolt’ which he assigned to the fourth or fifth century.[4]

The tunnel-vault of L and the cross-vault of M are constructed of longitudinal courses[5] of narrow, flat voussoirs of undressed shale; both were covered on the outside with waterproof cement like that on the dome. The three tunnel-vaults of the main hall, which no longer exist, were composed, according to Butler, ‘of a light concrete composed largely of volcanic scoriae, or cinders, like those of the mosque on the hill’.[6]

THE DECORATION. The whole building appears to have been devoid of carved ornament, but rooms L and M were coated with stucco, apparently decorated with paintings, for Butler, on the springing of the vault of the little recess in M, saw the remains of a painted medallion which had contained the bust of a life-sized human figure.[7] Only the shoulder, part of the neck, an ear with an ear-ring, and part of a head-dress could be seen; these were executed in good colours that were still bright. The background was yellow, the drapery of the shoulder dark red, and the head-dress was painted to represent a filmy white material, the transparency of which was well indicated.[8] But there appears to have been more than this, for Musil, who visited it in 1909, says: ‘On all the unimpaired walls are remains of paintings and it is evident that all the rooms were once painted; . . .’[9] Unfortunately every trace of painting has disappeared.

THE DATE. Ḥammām aṣ-Ṣarakh, bath and audience hall like Quṣayr ʿAmra, to which it bears the closest resemblance, must have been built for an Umayyad prince for his own personal use. But although the resemblance is so close throughout in plan, in dimensions, and in the very sequence of

1 Not twenty, as stated by Butler, *op. cit.*, p. xxi.

2 *Op. cit.*, p. xxi.

3 Jaussen and Savignac (*op. cit.*, p. 112, n. 3) compare this to the arrangement of the masonry at the north-west corner of Quṣayr ʿAmra, for which see above, pp. 394–5.

4 *Op. cit.*, p. xxii.

5 They must therefore have been built on a centering.

6 *Ibid.*, p. xxii. For this mosque, see below, pp. 502–5.

7 On the analogy of Quṣayr ʿAmra (above, p. 397) I conclude that this medallion was held above the head of a female figure painted on the side of the recess.

8 *Ibid.*, p. xxiii.

9 *Arabia Deserta*, p. 351.

the vaulting systems—tunnel-vault, cross-vault, and dome—it is better built, and its arches are perceptibly more pointed than those of Quṣayr ʿAmra (separation of centres one-seventh to one-sixth of the span) though not yet so pointed as the vaults of Mshattā (one-fifth). I therefore place it midway between these two buildings, say A. D. 725–30.

THE MOSQUE AT QUṢAYR AL-ḤALLĀBĀT[1]

Description. About three miles north of Ḥammām aṣ-Ṣarakh is the Roman fortress known as Quṣayr al-Ḥallābāt (see map on p. 404), the nucleus of which was built under Caracalla in A.D. 213–17 and the rest under Justinian in A. D. 529. It was discovered by Butler and Littmann in the winter of 1904–5, together with the little mosque which stands about 15 m. from its south-east corner.[2]

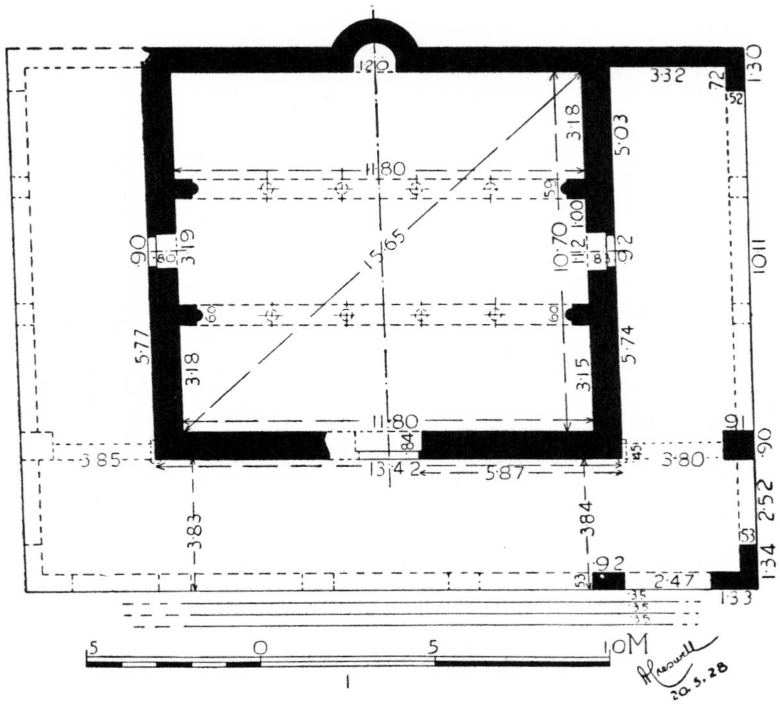

Fig. 555. Mosque at Quṣayr al-Ḥallābāt: Plan.

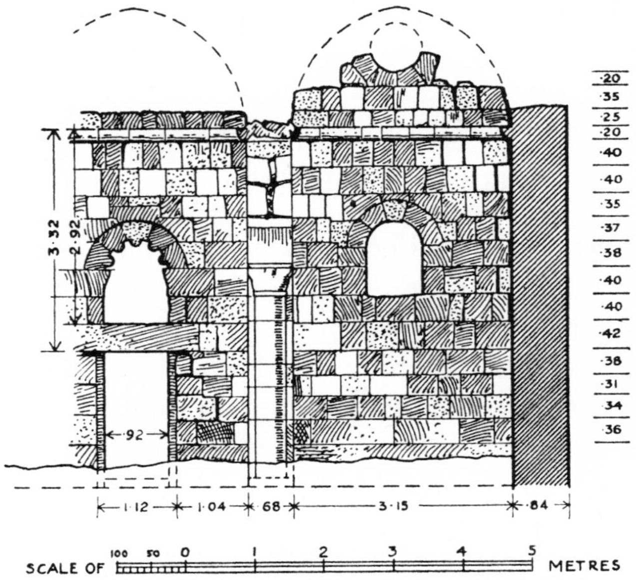

Fig. 556. Mosque at Quṣayr al-Ḥallābāt: Interior, west side. Measured by K. A. C. Creswell and drawn by M. Lyon.

This little mosque is a rectangular building of stone, measuring internally 10·70 m. from north to south and 11·80 m. from east to west (Fig. 555). Two wall piers, with the springing of arches above them (Plate 84 *d* and Fig. 556), suffice to indicate that the interior was divided into three aisles by two rows of arches, and Butler's measurement of the curve of one showed that the radius was such that there must have been five arches in each arcade. These arches rested on columns, but their bases are completely hidden by the accumulation of débris.[3]

The main entrance was in the centre of the north side, and there was a lateral entrance approximately in the centre of the east and west sides. These entrances are not splayed as shown by Butler. The exterior was surrounded on three sides by a portico, consisting of arches on piers supporting a timber roof, and ten of the holes which received the beams can be seen near the top of the west façade (Plate 84 *c*). This portico averaged 3·30 m. in depth excluding the piers. Of the latter, only the bases of three now remain, together with the wall which closed the south end of the western portico. The existing piers are 53 cm. deep. A splay-faced capital at the north ends of the west and east sides of the main building shows that it must have been connected with the portico by two arches, as shown (Fig. 555,

[1] Bibliography: —1909, Butler (H. C.), *Ancient Architecture in Syria, Sect. A: Southern Syria*, pp. 74–7 and illus. 57–8, and Appendix, pp. xvii–xix and illus. 57 *a*–58 *a*; —1918, Creswell, *Vaulting System of the Hindola Maḥal at Māndū, J.R.I.B.A.*, XXV, Third Series, pp. 243–4 and fig. 11; reprinted in the *Indian Antiquary*, XLVII, p. 175 and fig. 5; —1922, Jaussen and Savignac, *Mission archéologique en Arabie, III: Les Châteaux arabes*, pp. 113–14; —1927, Pijoán (J.), *History of Art*, II, p. 209 and figs. 311–12; and Musil, *Arabia Deserta: a Topographical Itinerary*, Fig. 93; —1940, Glueck (Nelson), *The other side of the Jordan*, p. 37 and fig. 12; —1960, Field (Henry), *North Arabian Desert Archaeological Survey*, fig. 69 (3 illus.).

[2] Butler, *op. cit.*, pp. 70–74, illus. 55, and pl. VI, and Appendix, p. xvii.

[3] Butler (*op. cit.*, p. xviii), speaking of his second visit, says: 'I was able to prove that the arrangement of two rows of four columns each in the interior is correct.'

see also Plate 84 *c* for the springing of the arch), the two piers concerned being of nearly double depth to take the thrust. There were no such arches on the north side. Three steps, each 35 cm. wide, run along the greater part of the northern front, but it is not now possible to say exactly where they stopped.[1]

The walls are 82 cm. thick, and are built of squared blocks of limestone averaging 40 cm. in height, laid dry, like the best pre-Muslim work in the Ḥaurān. The west side is almost intact, and so was the south side when Butler saw it; the east side is only half its full height, and part of the eastern half of the north wall has gone, the other half being almost intact. The east door jamb of the northern entrance no longer exists, but Butler found the lintel on the ground, also a pilaster cap which probably supported an end of it (Fig. 557, C and D).

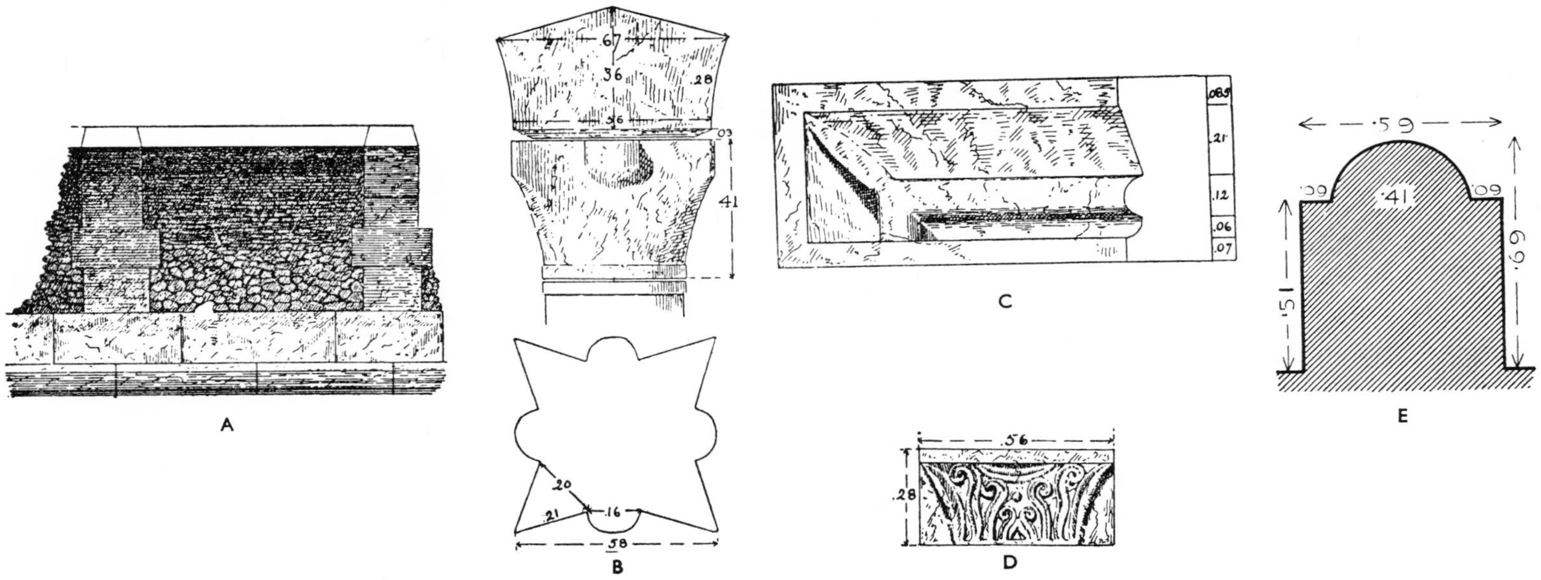

FIG. 557. MOSQUE AT QUṢAYR AL-ḤALLĀBĀT: Details. A—Remains of vault. B—Capital of column and springer block. C—Lintel of northern entrance. D—Pilaster cap from northern entrance. E—Plan of wall piers. (From Butler, *op. cit.*, except E.)

The western entrance is only 92 cm. wide and is spanned by a lintel 35 cm. deep, above which is a very attractively treated relieving arch, cusped by a series of billets, one to each voussoir. At a slightly higher level are two round arched windows 83 cm. wide which light the north and south aisles of the interior.[2]

In the south wall, before two-thirds of it collapsed, was a miḥrāb 1·20 m. wide 'built like the apses of baptisteries in Northern Syria',[3] except that 'it was very low [as at Boṣrā], unlike the apses of Christian buildings'.[4] Butler examined the miḥrāb with particular care, and was able to establish the fact that it 'was built with the walls'.[5] He says that there was a circular window over this miḥrāb, but no other opening in the south wall.

A quarter-round moulding runs round the interior at a level of 2·10 m. above the springing of the arches, and what remains above this moulding, at the summit of the south wall, gives us a decisive clue to the method by which the mosque was roofed (Fig. 557 A). There were evidently three parallel tunnel-vaults, running from east to west, and resting on the north and south walls and the two intermediate arcades, the spandrels of which must have been filled up level, and crowned with the same quarter-round moulding. The existing remains show that the ends of these vaults must have been lit by a bull's-eye window. Butler has called special attention to the construction of the vaults which, he says, 'were 'certainly built upon a centering. A complete system of transverse arches was constructed correspond-'ing to the columnar supports. These arches were bevelled upwards on both faces. A filling of concrete 'composed largely of light volcanic scoriae or cinders (a material found in great quantities in the craters 'of the extinct volcanoes of the Ḥaurân), was then laid between the arches. When this had hardened, 'each cell of vaulting was a solid mass held firmly in place owing to the wedge form of the arches. 'A remnant of this vaulting is still well preserved at the top of the south wall of the mosque'[6] (Fig. 557 A).

1 Butler (*op. cit.*, illus. 58) shows them as extending farther west than east, which seems scarcely probable.

2 There must have been corresponding windows in the east wall (the side of one still exists), but there are none in the north wall.

3 Butler, *op. cit.*, p. 76.

4 *Ibid.*, p. xviii.

5 *Ibid.*, pp. 76 and xviii.

6 *Op. cit.*, p. 76.

Fig. 558 shows Butler's restoration of the west façade. There are obviously several errors in it. In the first place his plan shows that the piers (excepting the corner piers) are of equal width, whereas in his elevation the second pier is shown as wider than the third and fourth.[1] Secondly, the arches were not all of equal span, the outer ones being narrower than the rest, as was also the case in the north portico (see plan). As for Butler's fifth arch, I could not find any trace of the wall on which it rests in his drawing, so I omit it, although traces of it may exist. But in any case the fifth pier does not project behind the rear façade of the mosque, as shown by Butler, although there is a splay-faced moulding on its south side (Plate 84 *c* and Fig. 555), which may indicate that there was another arch here.

Fig. 558. Mosque at Quṣayr al-Ḥallābāt: Butler's restoration of west façade.

Finally, I cannot believe that the vaults were covered by a gable roof of timber. At Quṣayr 'Amra in the same region a similar roofing system is adopted, as we have seen (above, p. 391), yet the vaults are left exposed and merely covered with a waterproof cement. I feel sure that it must have been the same here. In the whole of Syria I do not believe that there is a single example of a vault covered with a timber roof. I therefore restore the west façade as shown (Fig. 559).

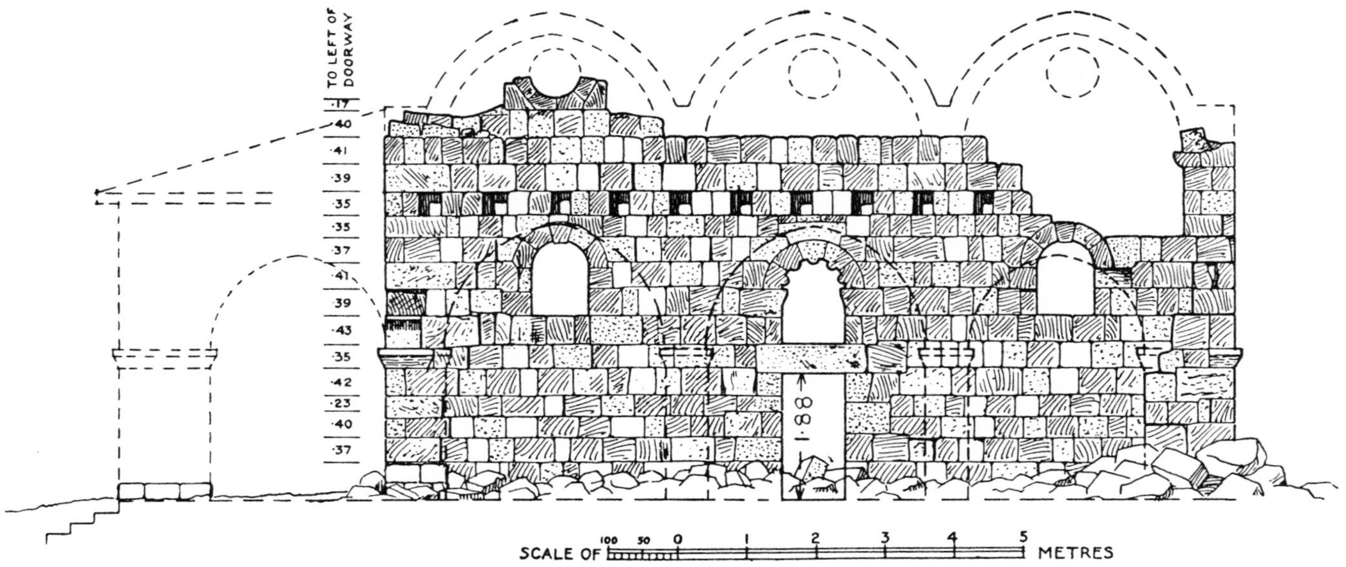

Fig. 559. Mosque at Quṣayr al-Ḥallābāt: Author's restoration of west façade. Measured by K. A. C. Creswell and drawn by M. Lyon.

The Date. Butler has already emphasized the fact that this mosque, well built of new material without the use of mortar, differs completely from the mosques of the twelfth and thirteenth centuries existing in the Ḥaurān, all of which are of very poor workmanship and built of re-used materials set in mortar, often with a filling of rubble and concrete.[2] On the other hand, the close resemblance that its masonry bears to that of Ḥammām aṣ-Ṣarakh, and the use of the same vaulting system as in the audience halls of Quṣayr 'Amra and Ḥammām aṣ-Ṣarakh, justify us in grouping all three together. Moreover, we have seen that the concave miḥrāb was first introduced in 707–9 at Madīna (above, pp. 147–8), so we must place it after that date, and in view of the known historical conditions (see

[1] Even his plan (*op. cit.*, illus. 58) does not agree with the dimensions marked on it. For example, he shows the depth of the north portico (including the piers) as 4·18 m., whereas the dimensions given by him for the corner pier (1·32) and the first arch (2·50) show that its real depth must be 1·32+2·50 = 3·82 m., which agrees closely with my measurement, 3·87. Or, to check it in another way, if we take his depth 3·28 for the portico, minus the piers, and add 50 cm., the depth given by him for the piers, we get 3·78 as the depth *with the piers*, yet this dimension is marked on his plan as 4·18, a difference of 40 cm.! Moreover, the piers are flush with the edge of the plinth and not slightly set back as shown by Butler.

[2] *Op. cit.*, pp. 76 and xix.

above, pp. 403–6) it is scarcely conceivable that it can have been built after the fall of the Umayyad dynasty, in A.D. 750.[1]

We have seen that the half-Bedawīn Umayyad Khalifs occupied some of the forts of the Roman *limes* in Transjordan, and Butler's suggestion that this little mosque was built by an Umayyad Prince who had taken up his residence in the fort alongside seems highly probable.

THE MOSQUES AT KHĀN AZ-ZEBĪB AND UMM AL-WALĪD. I must now refer to two little buildings farther south in Transjordan, at Khān az-Zebīb (about five miles west of Quṭrānī) and Umm al-Walīd (about six miles west of Zīza, see map on p. 404), published by Tristram many years ago[2] and more recently by Brünnow and von Domaszewski.[3]

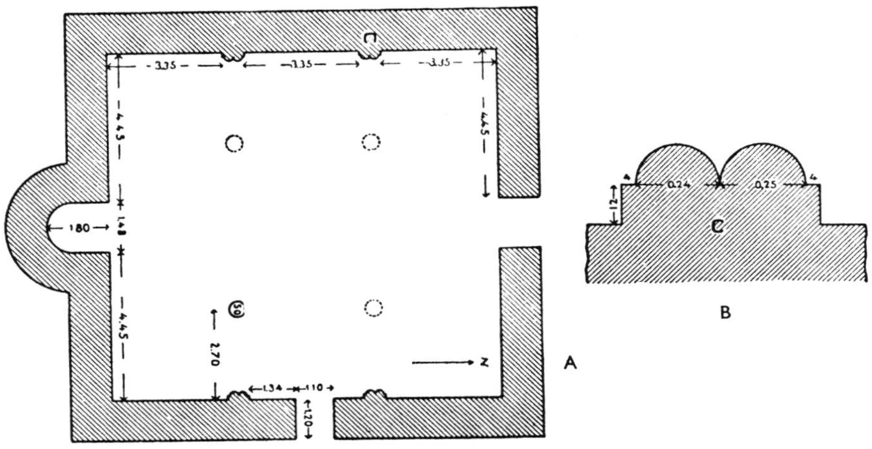

FIG. 560. KHĀN AZ-ZEBĪB: Mosque. A—Plan, scale 1 : 200. B—Wall piers, scale 1 : 20. (From Brünnow and von Domaszewski, *op. cit.*)

I have visited Khān az-Zebīb only to find that the Khān has suffered very much since Brünnow and von Domaszewski visited it in 1898, and that the mosque and the other building mentioned by them have practically disappeared. The mosque in fact now consists of four ridges of débris which form a rectangle about 11 m. square. A Bedawī of the Banū Ṣakhr, who accompanied me from Qalʿat aḍ-Ḍabaʿa, told me that when he first saw it the walls were standing to the height of a man, but that it was wrecked during the construction of the Ḥijāz Railway, its stones being employed for the culverts which are very numerous.[4]

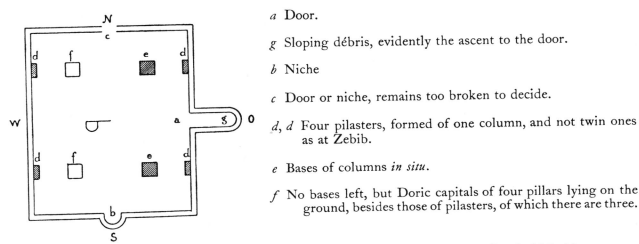

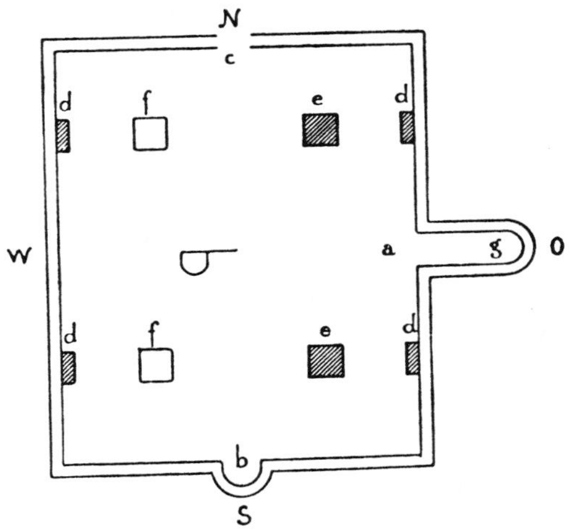

a Door.

g Sloping débris, evidently the ascent to the door.

b Niche

c Door or niche, remains too broken to decide.

d, *d* Four pilasters, formed of one column, and not twin ones as at Zebib.

e Bases of columns *in situ*.

f No bases left, but Doric capitals of four pillars lying on the ground, besides those of pilasters, of which there are three.

FIG. 561. UMM AL-WALĪD: Mosque. (From Tristram, *Land of Moab*.)

According to Brünnow, it consisted of a rectangle measuring 11·21 by 10·38 m. internally (almost the same as that of the mosque just described), with a door in the centre of its north and east sides, a recess 1·48 m. wide and 1·80 deep in the centre of its south side, a pair of pilasters, each composed of two coupled semi-columns, to right and left (Fig. 547), and the remains of a column *in situ*. Brünnow and von Domaszewski call this recess an apse, in spite of the fact that it points south (the direction of Mekka to an observer in Transjordan), and insist that it was a church. Herzfeld, however, has recognized it as a mosque,[5] a verdict which no one acquainted with the mosque at Quṣayr al-Ḥallābāt will dispute.

1 Jaussen and Savignac share this view, *op. cit.*, p. 113.
2 *Land of Moab*, pp. 173 and 180–81, and fig. 15.
3 *Die Provincia Arabia*, II, p. 81 and Abb. 665–6, p. 90 and Abb. 671.
4 The shameful acts of vandalism committed at this time have yet to be reckoned up, for no one, as yet, has been over the ground so thoroughly covered by Brünnow and von Domaszewski a few years earlier. We know, however, that Mshattā suffered badly, likewise Qasṭal.
5 *Mshattâ, Ḥîra and Bâdiya*, in the *Jahrbuch der Preuszischen Kunstsammlungen*, XLII, p. 130.

The second building, which stands just[1] outside the east gate of Umm al-Walīd, is a similar structure to the last; it measures twelve yards from north to south and ten from east to west, according to Tristram, whose sketch-plan is reproduced here (Fig. 561). 'Inside the doorway the bases of two columns remain *in situ*; and four plain Doric capitals, and portions of shafts are lying about.'[2]

Thus we have three little mosques in Transjordan strikingly similar in size and plan, which are undoubtedly Umayyad, but which must have been built after A.D. 708 on account of their concave miḥrābs (see above, pp. 147–8).

QAṢR AL-ḤAYR AL-GHARBĪ, 105–9 H. (724–7)

THE SITE. On the track from Damascus to Palmyra at about twenty-six miles east of Qaryatayn and about thirty-seven miles before reaching Palmyra is a ruin known as Qaṣr al-Ḥayr, also called Qaṣr al-Ḥayr al-Gharbī to distinguish it from another site of the same name about forty miles to the east of Palmyra. Wood and Dawkins, who passed it in 1751, say: 'In nine hours from Carietein we came to 'a ruined tower, on which we observed, in two or three places, the Maltese cross. Near it are the ruins 'of a very rich building, as appeared by a white marble door-case, which is the only part standing and 'not covered with sand; its proportions and ornaments are exactly the same as those on plate XLVIII.'[3] Since then many travellers en route for Palmyra have passed it.[4] Langenegger in 1905 gives a photograph of the gateway (plate to face p. 380), the lintel of which is still about a metre above the ground, but when I first saw it in 1927 on my way to Qaṣr al-Ḥayr ash-Sharqī the earth was right up to it.

THE KHĀN[5]

Only the gateway, composed of two monolithic door posts and a lintel, both antique, were visible before the excavations, for the walls had been of mud brick resting on a base of well-cut stone. The mud brick, however, had melted away leaving the stone, which was just visible at ground level. The Khān forms a great rectangle measuring 55·75 m. (east), 54·10 m. (north), 55·90 m. (west), and 55·10 m. (south); average 55·21 m.; none of its angles is a right angle (Fig. 562). Within was a central court, measuring about 22·50 × 23 m., surrounded by a portico about 2½ m. deep, with four L-shaped corner piers and the stone bases of the other supports, which Schlumberger believes to have been of wood.[6] Behind this portico, on the north, west, and south sides are three narrow rooms nearly 48 m. long and about 4·80 m. wide which, so to speak, overlap at the corners in an extraordinary fashion. Each could be entered from the court by two doors. On the side of the entrance (east) are six rooms of varying dimensions, and a vestibule as shown (Fig. 562). Immediately to the right on entering the yard is a block of masonry which served the staircase to the roof, the first two steps of which were extant.

Two wings advance 18 m. from each end of the façade. That on the left was a mosque, as is proved by the remains of a miḥrāb; the other had a portico on three columns, probably of wood, with a drinking trough at the back.

THE DATE of the khān is given by an inscription on the lintel, the most extraordinary inscription in Islam. It was sometimes the Roman practice not to carve an inscription on stone, but to cast the letters separately in bronze with pegs at the back and to fix them thereby to a stone block. Our inscription must have been executed in this fashion, but the metal letters have disappeared, leaving the holes in-

[1] Perhaps I should say 'stood', for I was unable to identify it during a short visit which I paid to this enormous field of ruins, and I am rather doubtful whether Brünnow himself actually saw it in 1897, for he contents himself with reproducing Tristram's rather crude plan.

[2] *Land of Moab*, pp. 180–81.

[3] Wood (Robert) and Dawkins, *The Ruins of Palmyra*, p. 35. Schlumberger identifies it with Heliaramia of the Peutinger Table; *Syria*, XX, p. 363, n. 1.

[4] Porter (J. L.), *Five Years in Damascus*, I, 250; 2nd ed., p. 94; Mordtmann, *Neue Beiträge zur Kunde Palmyra's* in the *Sitzungberichte der Bayerischen Acad. der Wiss., philos.-philog. und hist. Classe*, 1875, II, Supp. III, pp. 87–8; Sachau (E.), *Reise in Syrien und Mesopotamien*, p. 49; Moritz (B.), *Zur antiken Topographie der Palmyrene*, *Abh. der Kgl. Akad.*, *Berlin*, *phil.-hist. Abh.*, 1889, pp. 12–13; Peters (J. P.), *Nippur*, II, pp. 25–7, with 3 figs.; von Oppenheim, *Vom Mittelmeer zum Persischen Golf*, I, p. 273; Hoffmeister (E. von), *Kairo–Bagdad–Konstantinopel*, pp. 64–5, with illus.; Langenegger (F.), *Durch verlorne Lande*, pp. 380–82, with 4 illus. (one shows the tower and another the lintel of the gateway); Savignac (R.), *Mission épigraphique à Palmyre*, *Revue Biblique*, XXXIX, pp. 366–7 and figs. 2–5.

[5] BIBLIOGRAPHY:— 1932, Wiegand (Theodore), *Palmyra*, pp. 8–9 and Abb. 11; — 1934, Poidebard (A.), *La Trace de Rome dans le désert de Syrie*, p. 190; — 1939, Schlumberger (Daniel), *Les Fouilles de Qasr el-Heir el-Gharbi*, *Syrie*, XX, pp. 209–13 and figs. 6–8: — 1931, Wiet (G.), *Répertoire chronologique d'Épigraphie arabe*, I, p. 23.

[6] *Loc. cit.*, XX, p. 211.

tended to take the pegs, and shallow grooves for the letters (Plate 85 *c*). It runs: 'The execution of this work has been ordered by the slave of God, Hishām, Amīr al-Mu'minīn . . . in Rajab 109 (Nov. 727).'[1] It is an extraordinary example, unique of its kind, of the survival of antique methods in early Islam. This lintel has since been brought in to the Museum at Damascus; unfortunately it was broken in two places in the process.

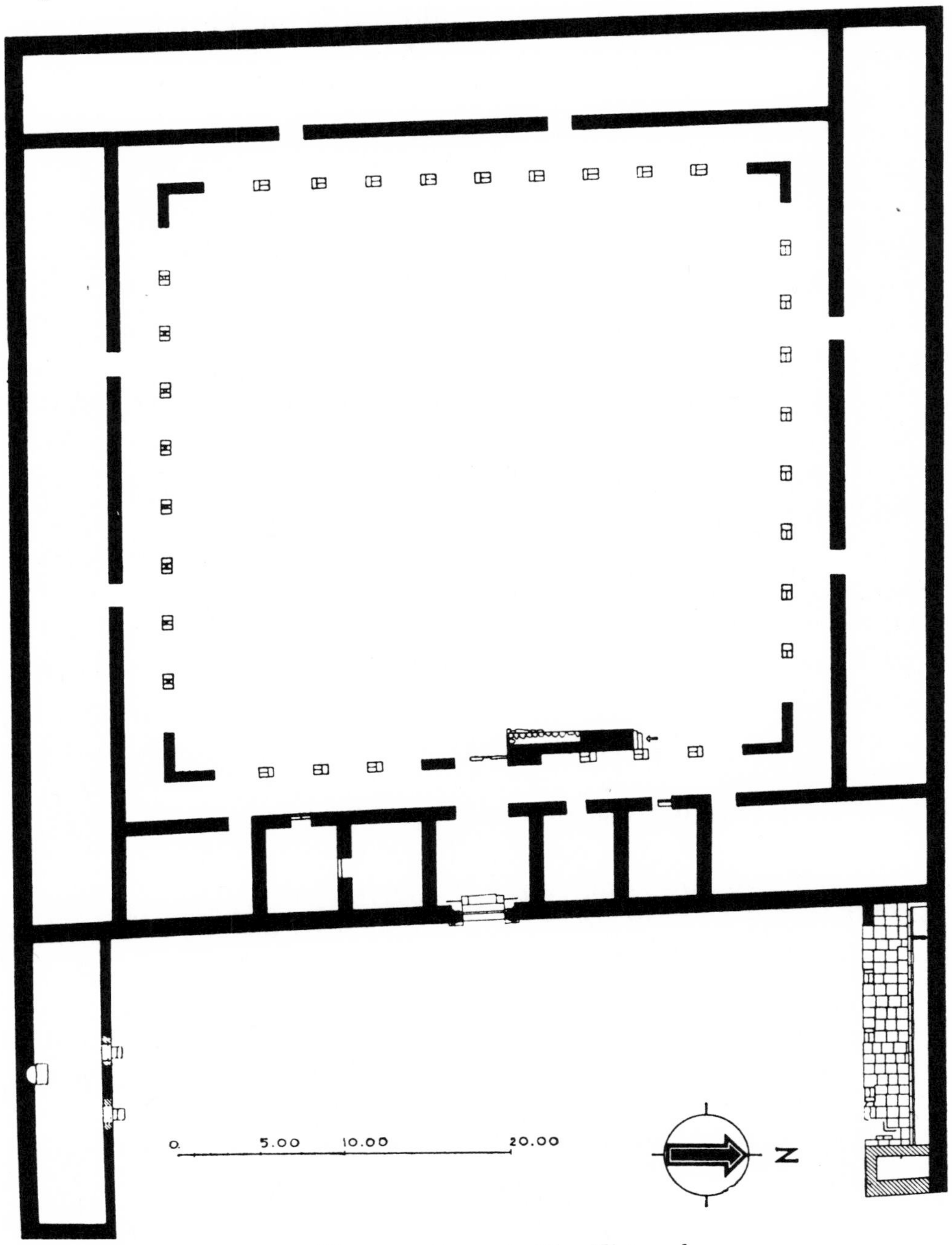

FIG. 562. QAṢR AL-ḤAYR AL-GHARBĪ: The Khān, plan.

This technique was widely spread in Roman times, e.g. the Maison carrée at Nîmes and the Arch of Triumph at Orange. In both cases the inscription can be reconstructed from the holes left.[2] Detached bronze letters with a tenon at the back have been found at Attaleia.

Schlumberger has pointed out to me an example in Norther Syria—Ḥiṣn Sulaymān, near Tortosa.[3]

THE PALACE[4]

The palace is a rectangle which, excluding the towers, measures 71·45 m. (east), 70·45 m. (north), 73·03 m. (west), and 71·05 m. (south), average 71·50 m., with an entrance flanked by two half-round

1 Wiet, *Répertoire*, I, p. 23.

2 See Cagnat's article, *Inscriptions*, in Daremberg and Saglio, III$_{(1)}$, pp. 533–4 and figs. 4069–70.

3 Krencker (Daniel) and W. Zschietzschmann, *Römische Tempel in Syrien*, p. 98, Abb. 131 and Taf. 51.

4 BIBLIOGRAPHY: — 1932, Wiegand (Th.), *Palmyra*, p. 6–9, Abb. 7–14 and Taf. III; — 1934, Poidebard (A.), *La Trace de Rome dans le désert de Syrie*, pp. 187–9 and pls. XXXIII–XXXVII; — 1936–7, Schlumberger (D.), *Comptes des fouilles*, *Comptes rendus de l'Acad. des Inscriptions*, 1936, p. 216, and 1937, pp. 134–9, with 6 illus.; — 1939, Schlumberger (D.), *Les Fouilles de Qasr el-Heir el-Gharbi (1936–1938)*, *Syria*, XX, pp. 195–238,

towers in the centre of the east face. There are three round corner towers, the place of the fourth being taken by the tower of the monastery which the builders decided to incorporate in the enclosure, as shown (Fig. 563, facing p. 510), though why they did not set the palace a few metres more to the east, in order that the tower should make a salient on both flanks, is puzzling. There are also three intermediate towers.

The outer wall of the enclosure, which is about 2 m. thick, is of dressed stone with a rubble core for the first 2 m., above this is a zone of burnt brick and above this mud brick. It is no wonder that centuries of winter rains have caused this upper part to melt away.

The Entrance is preceded by a pavement 10 m. wide, which is raised half a metre, and thus masks part of the base moulding of the two flanking towers. Schlumberger is convinced that this was a later addition to prevent flood water entering the building after heavy rain, as nearly happened in 1938.[1] The gateway itself, the lintel of which had been seen peeping out of the ground by many travellers before the excavations (above, p. 506), is 3 m. wide. It is formed by two jambs 4 m. high and a monolithic lintel, all richly decorated and presumably taken from some building at Palmyra.[2] The proportion 3:4 gives it a very squat appearance, as Schlumberger remarks 'plus trapues que celles d'aucune porte romaine que je connaisse en Syrie',[3] and he suggests that the door-posts have been shortened before being re-employed. A remarkable fact: part of the carved vine ornament, which had been eaten away near the ground by the well-known combination of salt and moisture (see below, p. 530), had been restored in stucco.[4]

These door-posts were placed at the two ends of a block which formed the sill. When the whole gateway was transported to Damascus this sill was turned over and a Greek inscription painted in red was revealed, recording the construction of the doorway of a monastery by Arethas, i.e. the famous Ghassānid Phylarch[5] al-Ḥārith ibn Jabala in 870 Sel. = A.D. 559,[6] the monastery in question being undoubtedly that to which the great tower at the north-west corner belonged.

The Entrance Passage. The roof of the entrance passage, which is about 11 m. long, was supported by two transverse arches resting on pilasters, their thrust being taken by buttresses on the other side of the wall in the adjacent rooms II, III, IV, and V. The entrance passage of Mshattā (Fig. 636) was designed on similar lines, but with four transverse arches instead of two. Between these pilasters are three stone ledges, the central one on each side being provided with stone pillows, exactly as at Khirbet al-Mafjar (below, p. 551 and Plates 101-2).

The Courtyard. The entrance passage leads into a courtyard measuring about 45 m. square which is reduced to 37 m. by a portico about 4 m. deep running all round. Of this portico nothing remained except the four corner piers, preserved to various heights, and the column bases, all *in situ* except one. They are nearly all antique, mostly with Attic bases, in every way similar to those of the colonnades of the second and third centuries at Palmyra; some in the east portico are capitals placed upside down. No columns were found, and it is not possible to say whether the missing columns carried an entablature or an arcade.[7] The pavement of the portico is separated from that of the court by a step as at Mafjar; a gutter runs all round and in the centre was a small basin.

pls. XXVII–XXXIX and 11 illus.; pp. 324–73, pls. XLIV–XLVII and 18 illus.; — 1940, Schlumberger (D.), *Les Fouilles de Qasr el-Heir el-Gharbi*, *Sixième Congrès Internat. d'Études byzantines, Alger, 2–7 Octobre 1939*, *Résumes*, pp. 185–7; and *Les Origines antiques de l'art islamique à la lumière des fouilles de Qasr el-Heir*, *Bericht über den VI. Internationalen Kongress für Archäologie, Berlin, 21–26., August 1939*, pp. 241–9; — 1946–8, Schlumberger (D.), *Deux fresques omeyyades*, *Syria*, XXV, pp. 86–102, with 2 plates and 7 illus.; — 1946, Stern (Henri), *Notes sur l'architecture des châteaux omeyyades*, *Ars Islamica*, pp. 73–74 and figs. 1 and 23; — 1951, 'Abd al-Ḥaqq (Sélīm), *I'āda Tashyīd Janāḥ Qaṣr al-Ḥair al-Gharbī fī Mathaf Dimishq*, *Les Annales Archéologiques de Syrie*, I, pp. ٥ — ٥٨, with 32 illus. on 16 plates and 2 figs., synopsis in French, pp. 129–33; — 1953, Dunand (M.), *De l'Amanus au Sinai: sites et monuments*, pp. 142–5, with 1 illus.; — 1954, Huxley (Julian), *From an Antique Land*, p. 138 and pl. 35; — 1956, Franz (H. G.), *Die Stuckfenster im Qasr al-Hair al-Gharbi*, *Wissenschaftliche Annalen*, V, pp. 465–83, with 22 illus.; — 1962, Ettinghausen (Richard), *Arab Painting*, pp. 33–6 and coloured illus. on pp. 35 and 37.

[1] *Loc. cit.*, XX, p. 225.

[2] Wiegand compares its decoration to that of a building usually regarded as the *castrum* of Diocletian at Palmyra, *Palmyra*, p. 6. But see Schlumberger's, *Le Prétendu Camp de Dioclétien à Palmyre*, in the *Mél. de l'Université Saint Joseph*, XXXVIII, pp. 79–97.

[3] *Loc. cit.*, XX, p. 225.

[4] *Ibid.*, pp. 225–6 and pl. XXXIII_2.

[5] The Ghassānids were Jacobite Christians, see below, pp. 630–1.

[6] This inscription has been very fully studied by Schlumberger, *ibid.*, pp. 366–72; and more recently (1959) by Jalabert and Mouterde, *Inscriptions grecques et latines de la Syrie, V: Emésène*, pp. 239–45, with 2 figs.

[7] *Ibid.*, p. 226, n. 1.

The Rooms of the Interior. Behind the portico is a series of rooms 11 m. deep on every side. Of the fifty-nine rooms into which the interior is divided, six are entirely independent and open directly into the porticoes. Two of these, XXXVIII and XLI, in the north-west and south-west corners respectively, are single rooms; two others, XIV and XIX, are occupied by staircases, the last two are merely passages of which one (XL) leads to the tower of the monastery, the other (LIV), paved like the courtyard and almost completely open to it, gave access to the cistern.

If we leave these six pieces aside, the chambers left over consist of six halls (VI, VII, XXIV, XXIX, LII, and LV), similar in plan and proportions, to each of which a number of smaller rooms are attached. The main halls run right through from the portico to the outer wall, a distance of about 11 m. The rooms linked with them are either next to the outer wall, or next to the portico. Each of these halls, together with the rooms depending on them, form a self-contained set of rooms without any connexion with the other sets, and each of these six groups is provided with a latrine which emphasizes their self-sufficiency. The main hall of each group, or *bayt*, is divided into two bays by a transverse arch resting on pilasters, both being of cut stone. Abutment is provided by the wall which divides the smaller rooms and which runs on the same alignment throughout. In each bay are two doorways, opposite to each other, which give access to the rooms of the group. They are all placed in exact alignment, so that it is possible to see from one end of the group to the other, in some cases through six consecutive rooms.

The Upper Floor. We have seen that there are two staircases; did they merely lead to the roof or to an upper storey? Schlumberger points out (i) that the existence, in each of the latrines of the ground floor, of a central pillar of masonry containing a vertical pipe (Plate 88 *d*), can only be the drain belonging to a latrine on the upper floor, and (ii) that fragments of stucco panels found all round the court, and of which the putting together is now (1939) well advanced, were certainly *transennae*, or closure-slabs which, being fixed between the columns of the upper portico, formed a continuous balustrade, as at Mafjar.[1]

He also concludes that the plan of this upper storey was practically the same as that of the ground floor. For example, above the main hall of each of the ground floor groups there must have been a similar hall, because every time fragments of the stucco decoration of the lateral doorways have been found on the ground floor, other pieces belonging to a second arch have been found, which can only belong to the arch of the corresponding doorway above. If there were slight differences, it may have been in the arrangement of the rooms above the cistern room LIV and above the passage leading to the tower of the monastery, supposing it was not open to the sky.[2]

The Lighting Arrangements. As the walls have not been preserved up to the level at which there might have been windows, we are reduced to conjecture. It is tempting to assume, as does Schlumberger,[3] that the rooms next the outer wall were lit by narrow openings placed high in the wall, but this is by no means certain for the rooms on the ground floor next the outer wall at Qaṣr al-Ḥayr ash-Sharqī have no such windows, and can only have been lit by the doorway, or by a lunette above it when the door was closed.[4] As for the rooms next the court, they were probably lit by windows under the portico. The central hall would be lit by a grille in the lunette above the entrance, as well as by a diffused light from the lunettes above the doors of the side rooms.

The Decoration. We must now study the decoration, beginning with the monumental entrance. When the excavations began the ground near the entrance was found to be full of fragments of stucco ornament. Schlumberger, by a stroke of genius, marked off the ground in squares, put the fragments found in each square in a separate box, numbered and well packed with straw, and sent them to Damascus.[5] He then made several squares of four planks of wood, about 3 m. long and 25 cm. wide, laid them out on the ground and filled them with sand.[6] They thus formed tables on which the fragments could

1 *Ibid.*, p. 229.

2 *Ibid.*, p. 229.

3 *Ibid.*, pp. 229–30.

4 It is possible that many of the rooms there were not subdivided but ran right through from the courtyard to the outer wall.

5 Thousands of fragments of window-grilles and other pieces of ornament found in the rooms of the palace were carefully packed in boxes, numbered according to the room in which they had been found. In all some 50,000 fragments were dealt with.

6 Because the fragments were of varying sizes and thickness, and it was easy to push them into the sand until their upper surfaces were uniform and level.

be laid out and assembled in a gigantic jig-saw puzzle. The result was a brilliant success, for it has enabled the decoration of the gateway and its flanking towers to be reconstructed with a very small margin of error. Once this was done, two brick towers were erected, of the same width and depth as the originals, and the reconstructed stucco ornament (set in concave chassis, 1·10 × 1·05 m.), was fixed to them. This work was finished in 1944.[1] A tentative reconstruction[2] was made by Écochard, and Plate 87 *d* gives the final result after the fragments had been affixed to the tower. It will be noted that the elliptical arch has been replaced by a slightly stilted semicircular one. Cubes of mosaic were found adhering to fragments of this arch.

The only points on which doubts exist are the following:

(i) The exact level of frieze 1. Schlumberger says that a bare surface at the extremity of this frieze must indicate the part masked by the consoles of the doorway.[3] But what has happened to the consoles? They do not appear either in Écochard's proposed reconstruction, or in the re-erected gateway, although one is shown laying on the ground in Langenneger's photograph taken over fifty years ago.[4] Schlumberger adds that this contact can be obtained at a level lower than that which has been chosen. The maximum downward displacement is 50 cm.[5] This downward displacement was evidently decided on during the final setting in position (see Plate 87 *d*), the total height being reduced to 14·45 m.[6] He also adds that this displacement can be effected without modifying the position of the arch because, although the extremity of this arch is joined to a piece of the frame of panel *2*, the exact position of this piece in the whole panel has not been fixed.

(ii) The liaison between motif *10* and motif *11*.

(iii) The reconstruction of the zone in the central part corresponding with panels *4* and *5* on the towers. He remarks 'it is probable that we must place there semidomes supported on consoles, a motif of which we possess fragments'. The final decision is shown on Plate 87 *d*.

(iv) The arrangement of the panels (or niches) under gables, and the windows under arches in the central part.

(v) The reconstruction of the top of the central part both above and below the band *14/15*.

With these reserves we can now describe the result. The stucco decoration begins with a frieze of wind-blown acanthus, its upper edge being on a level with the underside of the lintel, i.e. 4 m. from the ground (Plate 87 *f*). Above this, on each tower, were three great oblong panels, about 3¼ m. high, set vertically, each with different designs, those on the right tower corresponding to those on the left, but in reverse order. The pattern on the panels next the doorway (2 b and 2 c) consist of hexagon coffers in contact by their points, a lozenge-shaped space being left between; the central panels (2 a and 2 d) are covered with a network of bands drawn from right and left at an angle of 45°, which form squares set diagonally and filled with various acanthus and other motifs.

Separated from these panels by a band of little medallions and a splay-face moulding is a series of seven panels, alternately square and oblong (*4* and *5*) surmounted by a narrow frieze of palmettes (*6*). Above this is a row of colonnettes (*7*) supporting an alternation of gables (*8*) and shell-hoods (*9*), between which, apparently, a number of female busts were inserted. Above this was a band (*10*) formed by a meander filled by palmettes and rosettes alternately. Each tower was crowned by five stepped and undercut crenellations, unusually tall and narrow, with an arrow-slit in the centre.

Of all the above the liaison between part *1* and part *10* is certain, also the liaison of the crenellations with *11* and the level of band *15* with respect to band *11*, on which the crenellations rest, is likewise certain because the vertical part which joins them has been preserved. The only uncertainties are (1) the liaison of band *10* with band *11*, and (2) the exact level of *1* with respect to the entrance.

The Bas-relief of a Khalif. Fragments were also found of the bas-relief of a sovereign, approximately life-size, seated, with feet close together and knees wide apart (Plate 86 *d*) just like a figure of a Sasanian king. The latter, however, generally has his hands resting on the pommel of a sword but here there is no sword. The tunic, very open at the neck, has wide sleeves and is bordered with a row of pearls.

[1] Selīm 'Abd al-Ḥaqq, *Les Annales Archéologiques de Syrie*, I, p. 130.
[2] See *Syria*, XX, p. 326 and fig. 13.
[3] *Syria*, XX, p. 326.
[4] *Durch verlorne Lande*, plate facing p. 380.
[5] *Syria*, XX, p. 326.
[6] *Les Annales Archéologiques*, I, p. 131.

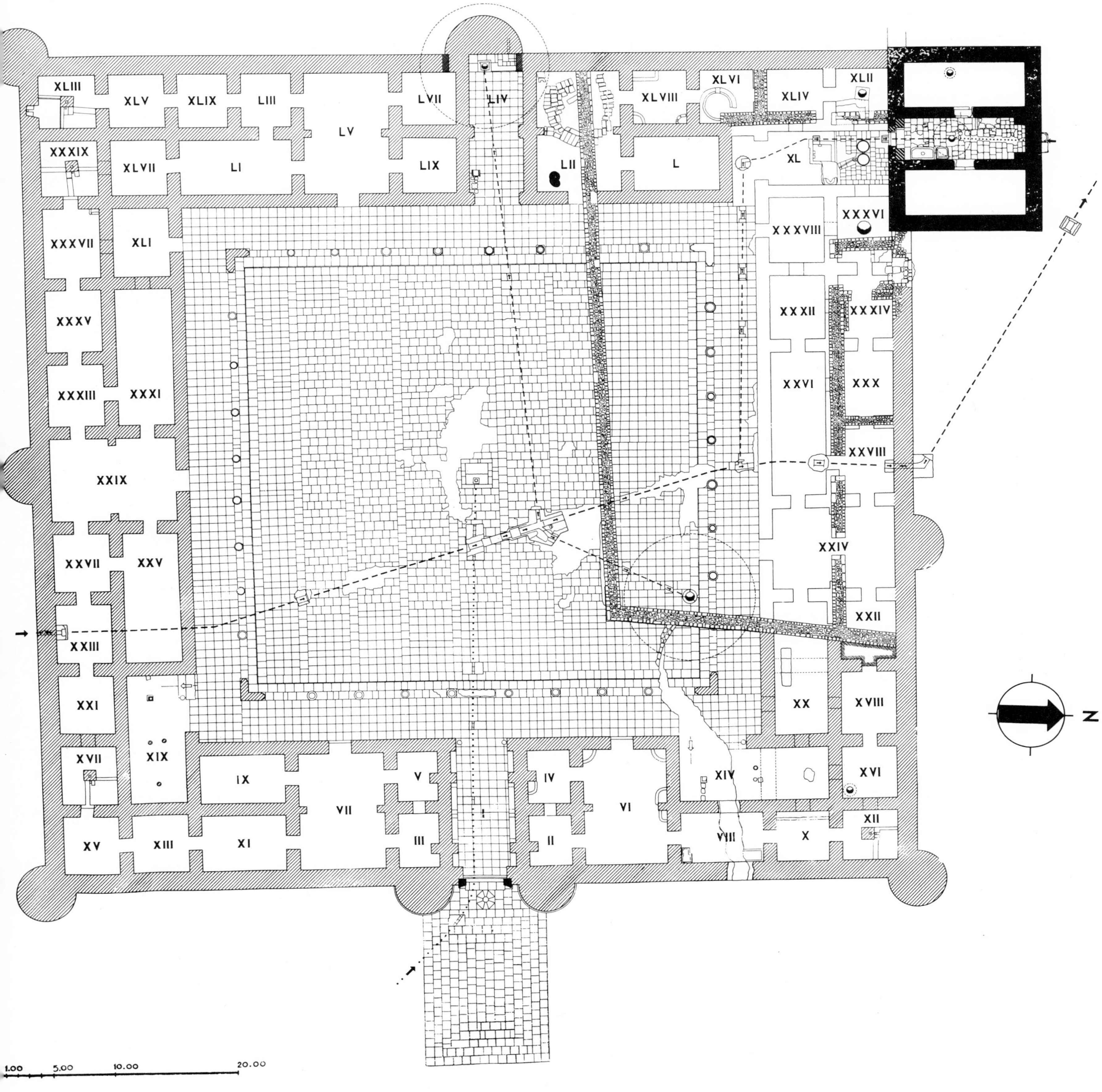

FIG. 563. QAṢR AL-ḤAYR AL-GHARBĪ: Plan.

By kind permission of M. Daniel Schlumberger.

It forms a sort of apron in front, which covers the top of the loose and baggy trousers, the outer seams of which are hidden by a row of pearls. Schlumberger considers it highly probable that this royal figure occupied the tympanum of the arch over the entrance.[1]

Another remarkable piece of sculpture was found, a person standing next to a seated figure, both without heads but with skilfully executed classical drapery.

THE DECORATION OF THE PORTICO AND *BAYTS*. The decoration of the portico consisted of panels of stucco, of which three were inserted as a parapet in each intercolumniation of the gallery on the first floor (Plate 89).

As for the rooms, the ornament was apparently confined to the doorways, all of which had a wooden lintel (which has disappeared in every case) and a lunette formed by a semicircular relieving arch. The arches were of brick decorated with beautiful stucco ornament, and a stucco grille occupied the tympanum. Schlumberger remarks that a great diversity reigned in the decoration of the arches, thanks to which diversity the sorting out of the fragments and the reconstitution of the arched bands could be effected without hesitation (see Plates 88–9). 'The number of arches reconstructed in each hall is ten. 'As each hall has five doors, and as the débris of two arches was found at the foot of each door, we may 'be sure that five belonged to the ground floor and five to the doors of the hall above.'[2] Similarly at the entrance of the isolated room XLI fragments of two arches only were found, of which one must belong to the ground floor and the other to the room above.

This is *the first introduction of stucco ornament into Muslim architecture*, in which connexion I would like to quote Hamilton's remarks on its result (although he is speaking of the stucco ornament of Mafjar: 'The ease with which plaster could be carved was itself an invitation and encouragement to add to and 'enrich the traditional stock of ornament. It is clear that the artists who designed these balustrades 'commanded a wider range of motifs, and handled them with greater freedom and boldness, than did 'their predecessors who had carved the lintels, chancel-screens, window-grilles, pulpits, or sarcophagi 'of pre-Islamic Syria.'[3]

As for the walls, the decoration painted on those of the ground floor, as a rule, has no human figures. Three types may be distinguished. The first simply consists of wide horizontal bands, the colours employed being white, yellow ochre, and wine dregs. The second is distinguished from the former by a high dado, coarsely imitating a marble panelling. The third is composed of great, brightly coloured rosettes with geometrical or plant ornament except one respresenting a hippogriff (Plate 86 *e*),[4] earlier, therefore, than the one carved on the façade of Mshattā.

THE STAIRCASE ROOMS. A curious problem presented itself during the excavations. In the oblong rooms XIX and XIV which measured 12·12×4·45 and 10·87×4·45 m. respectively, the floor in each case was occupied by a fresco in a remarkable state of preservation, and four supports of unequal height.[5] In room XIX three of these supports (columns) and the part of a fourth (a pier) were still standing. In XIV there were two column bases and a square slab; a circular gap in the fresco indicated the place of a fourth support. How explain why the frescoes, although on the floor, were not worn by people walking over them, and what could be the *raison d'être* of four supports all of different heights?

However, a solution of the problem was found: the four supports of unequal height were intended to carry the frame of a wooden staircase to the state-rooms on the east side of the upper floor, and the paintings could have been admired by looking over the banisters on the way up.

THE FIRST FRESCO, which has a floral border, is divided horizontally into three unequal parts. In the upper one two musicians are shown standing under two horse-shoe arches resting on badly drawn columns and crude impost blocks. The place of the middle impost block is nearly all occupied by a column of the staircase. Under the left arch is a woman playing a lute. Under the other is a man playing a flute and wearing a long robe, beneath which very baggy pantaloons appear (Plate 91).

The second picture represents a young unbearded man on horseback hunting gazelles. He is riding

1 *Syria*, XX, pp. 328–9.

2 *Ibid.*, p. 331.

3 *Plaster Balustrades from Khirbat al Mafjar*, *Quarterly of the Department of Antiquities in Palestine*, XIII, p. 56.

4 *Syria*, XX, pp. 324–5 and fig. 26.

5 This discovery was made in Nov. 1936; *Syria*, XXV, p. 86. In 1937 they were transferred to the Museum in Damascus.

a black horse with a tail dyed with henna and tied in a fantastic knot; the horse's hoofs are also stained with henna. The rider, who is seated on a white saddle-cloth, has black curly hair tied with a floating ribbon, and floating ribbons, Sasanian style, are attached to his belt. His brown shoes and green pantaloons appear beneath his long dress, and, most remarkable of all, he is using stirrups. This must be one of the earliest known representations of them. He has just shot a gazelle with a typical Turkish bow of double curvature.

In connexion with this type of bow, Dr. Schumberger has called my attention to a very interesting article[1] according to which its superiority over the long bow of the West was due to the fact that it exerted a steady driving force on the arrow, whereas the other sort exerted a great driving force at the moment of release, but which diminished rapidly. As a result, a bow of double curvature could shoot an arrow almost twice as far as the long bow.

The problem of the stirrup, which was quite unknown to the Greeks, Romans, and Sasanians, has given rise to a considerable literature, the latest author to discuss the subject, and more or less summarize our information, being Lynn White, Jr.[2] He cites a decisive passage from al-Jāḥiẓ (d. A.D. 868), in which he describes the contempt of the Persian Shu'ūbīya for the Arabs, as saying: 'You were 'accustomed to ride your horses in battle bareback, and whenever a horse did have a saddle on its 'back it was made of leather but had no stirrups. But stirrups are among the best trappings of war for 'both the lancer who wields his spear and the swordsman who brandishes his sword, since they may 'stand in them or use them as support.' To which al-Jāḥiẓ replies: 'As to stirrups, it is agreed that 'they are very old, but iron stirrups were not used by the Arabs before the days of the Azraqites.'[3]

White continues: 'The reference to the sect of the Azraqites is clarified by a passage from the 'writings of another ninth-century author al-Mubarrad (d. A.D. 898) who tells us that "stirrups were 'first made of wood and therefore broke very easily, with the result that whenever (the warrior) wished 'to brandish his sword, or the lancer to strike with his spear, he had no support. Consequently al-'Muhallab ordered that they be made of iron. He thus became the first to have stirrups made of iron."' This was presumably in A.D. 694 when al-Muhallab was campaigning against the Azraqites in Central Persia.[4] White concludes that stirrups had recently reached Persia from Turkistan.

The upper part of the third picture has suffered badly, but one can still see a hunting dog chasing a hare. In the lower part a man with a large key attached to a ribbon leads a horned animal with divided hoofs. Schlumberger has made the very good suggestion[5] that this man is a slave leading a captured animal towards the *Ḥayr*, or Game Preserve.

THE SECOND FRESCO is surrounded by a border composed of an undulating vine scroll which forms loops, in each of which are two bunches of grapes. In the centre is a great medallion, 1·80 m. in diameter, occupied by the bust of a woman with a background of foliage. Round her neck is a collar of pearls and below that a reddish snake, the head of which appears above her right shoulder and the tail above the left. Her hands are holding up a napkin full of fruit (Plate 90). Schlumberger compares this allegoric figure to Gē (Γη) in the mosaics of Antioch, the Earth being feminine in Greek.[6] The frame being oblong the medallion divides it into two parts of which the upper is well preserved. It is occupied by two marine monsters, rather like Lapiths, because each consists of the head and body of a very muscular man with the hind legs of a horse and a tail like an enormous black snake coiled into three. Each monster holds a javelin in his right hand. Of the lower part nothing has survived except the faint outline of several foxes, a heron, etc.

IDENTIFICATION AND DATE. In 1939 Sauvaget devoted 12 pages of special pleading to an attempt to prove that Zaytūna and Qaṣr al-Ḥayr ash-Sharqī were one and the same place.[7]

I give here the relative texts in chronological order and my conclusions from them.

[1] Medinger, *L'Arc turquois et les archers parthes à la bataille de Carrhes*, *Revue Archéologique*, 6me série, II (1932), pp. 226–34, with 2 figs.

[2] *Medieval Technology and Social Change*, Oxford, 1962.

[3] *al-Bayān wa'l-Tabyīn* (Cairo, 1926–7), III, 8, 12, extracted in White, *op. cit.*, p. 18.

[4] Pp. 18–19.

[5] *Syria*, XXV, p. 93.

[6] *Ibid.*, p. 99.

[7] *Remarques sur les Monuments omeyyades*, *Journal Asiatique*, CCXXXI, pp. 1–12.

Theophanes (d. 818) says:

'And he (Hishām) began to found palaces in open country and town, and to create sown fields and gardens and to make water channels (καὶ ὕδατα ἐκβαλλειν, lit. to bring up water).'

Bonn ed., p. 620; de Boor's ed., p. 403.

Balādhurī (868) says:

'As for Ruṣāfat-Hishām, it was built by Hishām ibn 'Abd al-Malik, who previous to its foundation lived at az-Zaytūna.'

Futūḥ, p. 179; Hitti's transl., p. 280.

Ṭabarī (915) says:

'Hishām used to live at Ruṣāfa . . . Aḥmad ibn Zuhayr has related to me from 'Alī ibn Muḥammad, 'saying: The Khalifs and their sons used to flee from the plague. They would therefore go to live in 'the desert away from the people. When Hishām wanted to live at Ruṣāfa someone said to him: Do 'not go, for Khalifs do not catch the plague, no Khalif was ever seen with the plague. But Hishām 'replied: Do you wish to make an experiment with me? So he went to live at Ruṣāfa which is [in the] 'desert, and built two *qaṣrs* there. Ruṣāfa was a Rūmī town which had been built by the Rūm.'

Secunda Series, p. 1737, l. 16–p. 1738, l. 5.

In another place (pp. 1466–7) he says: 'Muḥammad ibn 'Umar relates from someone who told him 'that the Khalifate came to Hishām whilst he was in Zaytūna in a little house of his there. Muḥammad 'ibn 'Umar said: I have seen it and it was small. The postal courier brought him the sceptre (*'aṣā*) and 'the seal and addressed him as Khalif. Then Hishām rode from Ruṣāfa to Damascus.'[1]

The last sentence has been the cause of all the trouble. It is obviously a slip of the pen because our Ruṣāfa, i.e. Ruṣāfat-Hishām, or Qaṣr al-Ḥayr ash-Sharqī, had not been founded at that time. Sauvaget's explanation is fantastic, viz. that it refers to two successive states of the same place, and that the narrator has first described how the insignia of the Khalifate reached Hishām at Zaytūna, and that in continuing his account he has mechanically dropped the first name and used the name it took later. This, if you please, in the same sentence(!). Moreover, it begs the question by assuming that the name Zaytūna was actually changed to Ruṣāfa, although he cannot quote any Arabic author to that effect, and nothing can be clearer than Balādhurī's statement that Zaytūna was the place where Hishām lived before he built Ruṣāfat-Hishām.

'Hishām went to live at Ruṣāfa. It was [in the] desert. There had been a Rūmī city there, built 'formerly by the Rūm, where they had made cisterns and *qanāt* coming from a long way off in the 'desert.[2] It had subsequently fallen into ruin: Hishām restored it and built two castles there.'

Anon. *Kitāb al-'Uyūn*, Vth–VIth (XIth–XIIth) century in de Goeje and de Jong, *Fragmenta historicorum arabicorum*, I, p. 101, ll. 12–15.

Yāqūt (1225):

'Zaytūna . . . this is a place in the Syrian desert where the Khalif Hishām lived before he built Ruṣāfa.'

Mu'jam, II, p. 965.

Thus we have the statement of Ṭabarī and the *Kitāb al-'Uyūn* that he lived at Ruṣāfa and built two *qaṣr* there, which identifies Qaṣr al-Ḥayr ash-Sharqī with Ruṣāfa; and Balādhurī's statement (repeated by Yāqūt) that before Hishām built Ruṣāfat-Hishām[3] he lived at az-Zaytūna, which identifies the latter with Qaṣr al-Ḥayr al-Gharbī.

The whole sequence of events is now clear. It was in a small house at az-Zaytūna, then a small settlement with a Ghassānid monastery depending on the water provided by the barrage of Harbaqa, that Hishām received news of his accession to the Khalifate,[4] which followed the death of Yazīd II on 26th Sha'bān 105 (28th Jan. 724). It was after this, presumably, that he began the *qaṣr*, garden, and *khān*, the latter being dated Rajab 109 H. (Nov. 727), i.e. not quite four years after his accession.

But fear of the plague made him move some 100 miles ENE. and build a new residence, Qaṣr al-Ḥayr ash-Sharqī, finished two years later in 110 H. (728/9), where he lived for fifteen years, until his

1 *Remarques sur les monuments omeyyades*, *Journal Asiatique*, CCXXXI, pp. 2–13.

2 For this *qanāt*, seen by Sir Eyre Coote in 1771, Eyles Irwin in 1781, and Rousseau in 1808; see below, p. 535.

3 So called to distinguish it from the famous Ruṣāfa-Sergiopolis, the pilgrimage city of St. Sergius, forty miles to the north.

4 Ṭabarī, Secunda series, pp. 1466–7.

death on 6 Rabīʿ II 125 (6th Feb. 743).[1] And whereas his previous residence had been on the main road from Damascus to Palmyra, his new residence is a long way off the main road from Palmyra to Dayr az-Zor on the Euphrates; as Ṭabarī puts it 'in the desert away from the people', which seems to confirm his fear of the plague.

I must add that Sauvaget, five years after his attempt to prove that Zaytūna was the same as Qaṣr al-Ḥayr ash-Sharqī, abandoned his theory and insisted that it must be sought for in the region of Raqqa.[2]

ARCHITECTURAL ORIGINS

THE GENERAL DESIGN. How explain the fortified appearance of Umayyad palaces and answer van Berchem's query—'Why should the masters of Asia to beyond the borders of Persia have perpetuated the type so close to their capital? Their *limes* were not in Moab, but in Transoxiana and beyond the Indus.'[3]

Let us consider for a moment the route taken by the armies of the conquest. They followed approximately the line of the modern Ḥijāz railway, until one detachment turned left at the level of Jerusalem, a second at the level of Damascus, whilst a third turned 45° to the right to the conquest of ʿIrāq. Now these armies passed a long series of Roman frontier forts, the *castra* of the Roman *limes*, which ran from the Gulf of ʿAqaba to Damascus, and from Damascus to Palmyra.[4] The most important of these, going from south to north, are:

Odhroḥ	built by Trajan (98–117).
Daʿjanīya	probably Trajanic.
Lajjūn	,, ,,
Bshayr	inscription of Diocletian (284–305).
Dumayr	A.D. 162.

Some of these frontier forts were lived in by Umayyad princes. For example, al-Walīd II sometimes lived at Azraq,[5] which was rebuilt in 634 H. (1236/7), but which in the time of al-Walīd II, i.e. in A.D. 744, was a Roman fort of Diocletian and Maximian.[6] When he was attacked by conspirators he fled north to the Qaṣr al-Bakhrāʾ, which is the Arabic name of a Roman fort about fifteen miles south-west of Palmyra.[7]

In Transjordan, about twenty miles east of Zerka, is a Roman fort of which the modern name is Quṣayr al-Ḥallābāt. The nucleus of it was built by Caracalla in A.D. 213–17, the rest by Justinian in A.D. 529. About 15 m. from its south-east corner is a little mosque of the first half of the eighth century (see above, pp. 502–5), built doubtless by an Umayyad prince who had taken up his residence in the Roman fort alongside.

Now the result of this was twofold. It not only gave the Umayyads the necessary knowledge when they wanted to build fortresses on the Byzantine frontier to cover Antioch (see below, p. 656 under 105 H), but it affected the design of the palaces of the Umayyad Khalifs. Here is a list of them:

1. al-Walīd's palace at Minya on Lake Tiberias } 708–15.
2. ,, *qaṣr* at Jabal Says }
3. Hishām's palace of Qaṣr al-Ḥayr al-Gharbī, *c.* 727.
4. ,, ,, ,, Qaṣr al-Ḥayr ash-Sharqī, 110 H. (729).
5. ,, ,, at Khirbat al-Mafjar.
6. al-Walīd II's palace of Mshattā } *c.* A.D. 744.
7. ,, ,, ,, Qaṣr aṭ-Ṭūba }

[1] Masʿūdī, *Tanbīh*, p. 322; transl. p. 416.

[2] *Notes de topographie omeyyade*, *Syria*, XXIV, p. 103.

[3] *Au Pays de Moab et d'Edom*, *Journal des Savants*, 1909, p. 406.

[4] Many have been described in Brünnow and von Domaszewski's great work *Die Provincia Arabia*; supplemented and extended by Poidebard's remarkable aerial survey, *La Trace de Rome dans le Désert de Syrie. Le Limes de Trajan à la conquête arabe* (Paris, 1934).

[5] Ṭabarī, Secunda Series, p. 1743, quoted by Musil, *Ḳuṣejr ʿAmra*, p. 156, and n. 233 with other sources.

[6] Azraq is a Roman fort of the time of Diocletian and Maximian (dedication on stone in court), reconstructed by Malik Muʿaẓẓam ʿĪsā in 634 H. (1236/7); see above, p. 405, n. 1; see Dussaud and Macler, *Mission dans les régions désertiques de la Syrie moyenne*, pp. 30–31, 268–9, and 337, and pls. V–VI; Musil in the *Kaiserl. Akad., der Wiss., Sitzungsberichte*, CXLIV, pp. 2–4; Jaussen and Savignac, *Mission archéologique en Arabie*, III, pp. 12–13 and pl. IV.

[7] Masʿūdī, *Prairies*, VI, p. 1; and his *Tanbīh*, transl., p. 419; also Musil, *op. cit.*, p. 162, and sources cited.

All these palaces, although built in the midst of Muslim territory, look externally like forts, for they are stone enclosures with round flanking towers. Nos. 1–5 are approximately 70 m. square and No. 6 is four times as large, i.e. 145 m. square. No. 7 is twice as large—70×140 m. Why this fortified appearance when it was not necessary? My conclusion is that having been in the habit of occupying forts belonging to the Roman *limes*, they came to look upon a rectangular enclosure flanked by towers as a necessary part of a princely residence, a *sine qua non*, the 'correct thing', so to speak.

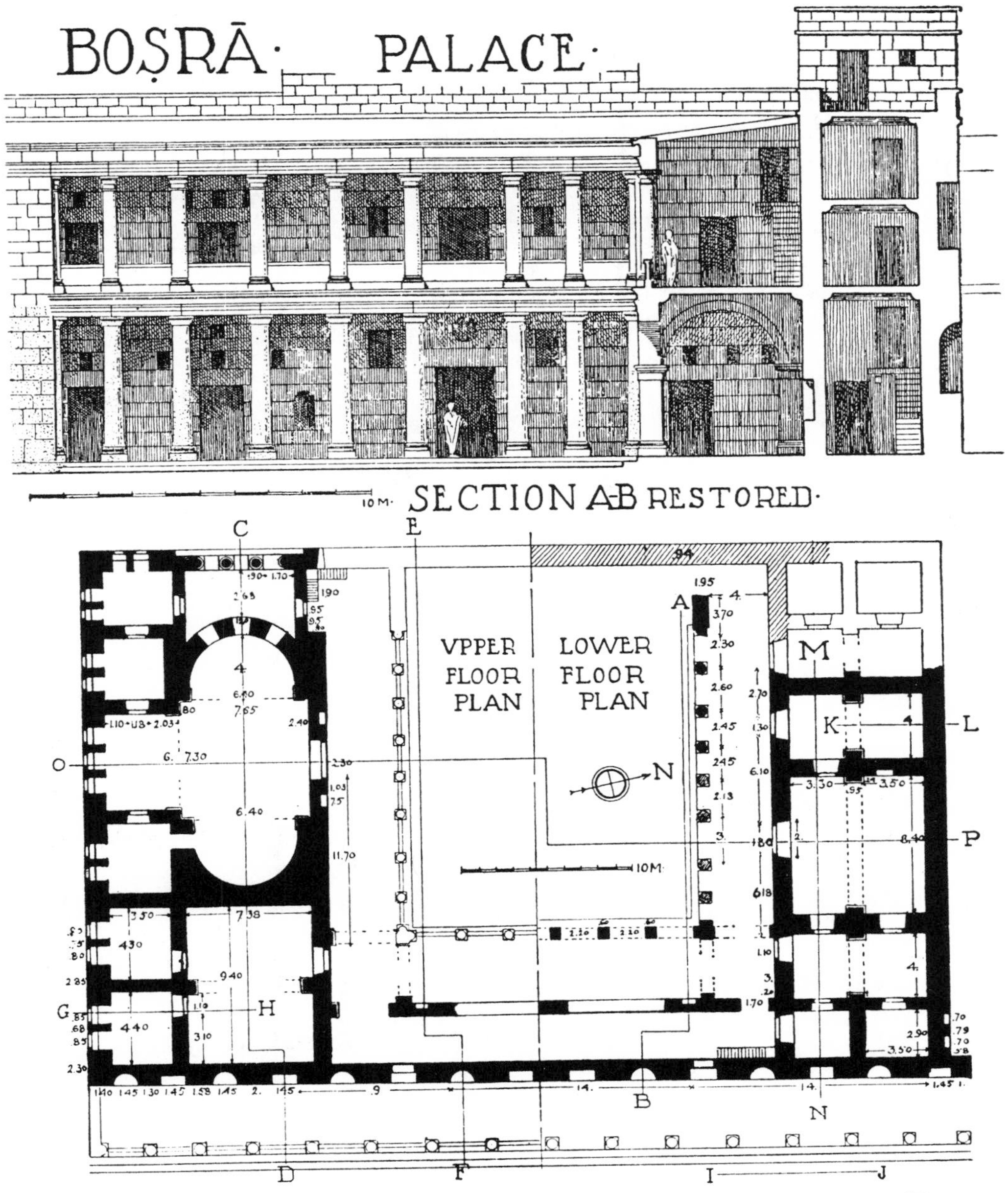

FIG. 564. Plan and section of the Palace of the Roman Governor, BOṢRĀ. (From Butler, *op. cit.*)

THE *BAYTS*. But where can we find a central open court with two storeys of rooms next the walls and a colonnaded portico, also in two storeys, in front of them, such as we have at Minya, 'Usays, Qaṣr al-Ḥayr al-Gharbī, Qaṣr al-Ḥayr ash-Sharqī, and Mafjar.

We have precisely this type at Boṣrā in the palace of the Roman Governor (Fig. 564), a monument which has been *completely ignored* in all discussions on the origin of the Umayyad palace and its *bayts*. Regarding the date Butler says: 'All the details, like the pier-cap and the corbel course . . . resemble the 'earliest work of the Roman period in the Ḥaurân, and is not unlike late examples of Nabataean work; for 'the ornaments shown in the meander pattern of the pier-cap include the crescent moon and the wine-jar 'which may be taken as symbols of Allāt and Dushara. The fragments of the minor order of the 'colonnade are almost exactly similar to the details of the order of the colonnade at the top of the *cavea* 'of the Theatre which is certainly a building of the best Roman period in Syria.'[1] And he comes to the

[1] *Ancient Architecture in Syria, A: Southern Syria*, p. 260.

conclusion that there is nothing to prevent us from attributing it to the first Roman Governor, after the creation of the Provincia Arabia in A.D. 106.

Here is Butler's plan and elevation (Fig. 564), a clear forerunner of the scheme we find at Minya, Jabal Says, 'Anjar, Qaṣr al-Ḥayr al-Gharbī, and Mafjar. And there is even a *bayt*, i.e. a central hall flanked by a pair of rooms on either side. But these side rooms, instead of being separated by a wall without a door, as in Mshattā and Qaṣr aṭ-Ṭūba, are merely divided by an open arch, exactly what Grabar has found during his excavations on the west side of al-Walīd's palace at Minya,[1] the earliest Umayyad palace that has come down to us. Although almost completely hidden by modern buildings, Butler

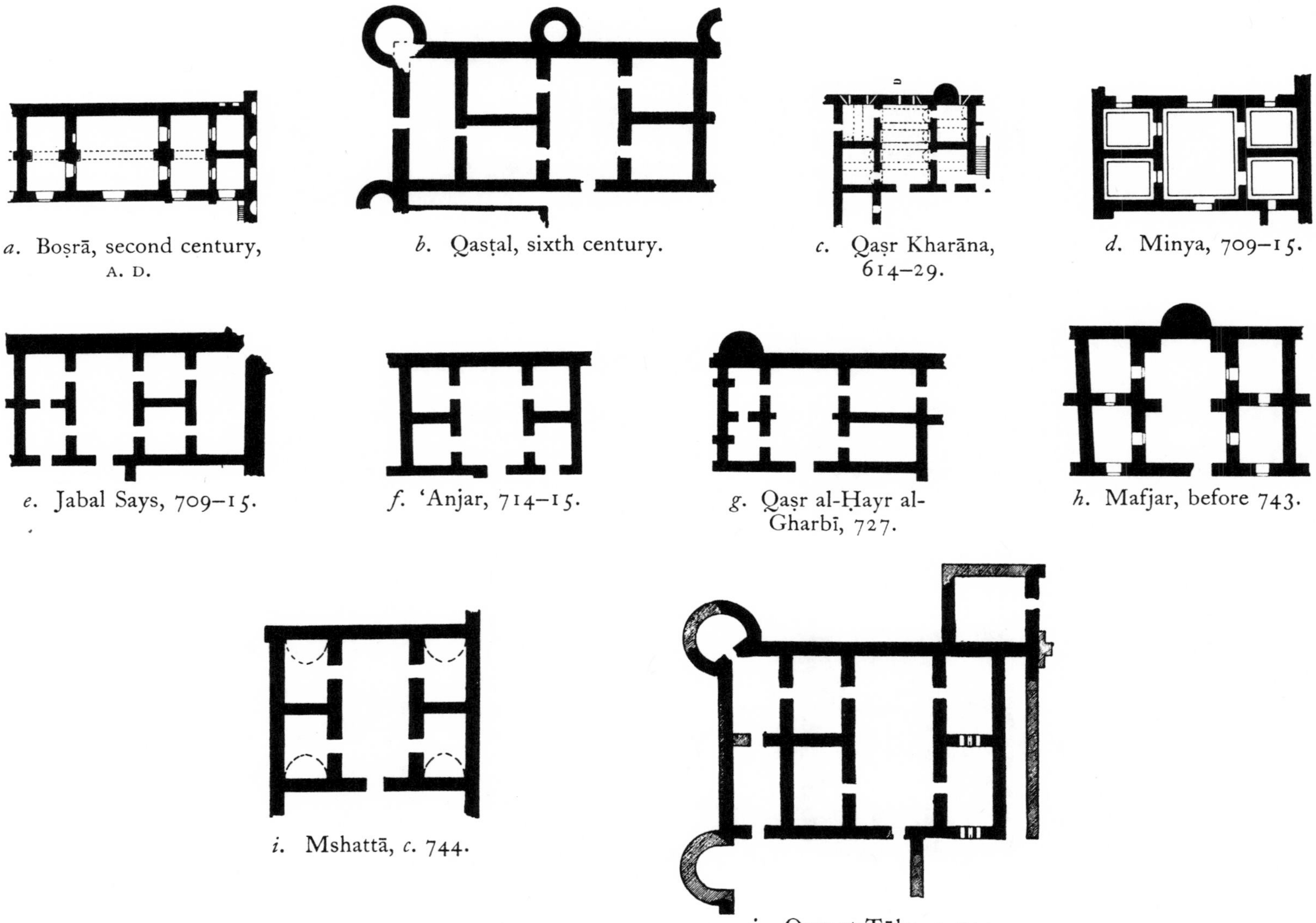

a. Boṣrā, second century, A.D. *b.* Qasṭal, sixth century. *c.* Qaṣr Kharāna, 614–29. *d.* Minya, 709–15. *e.* Jabal Says, 709–15. *f.* 'Anjar, 714–15. *g.* Qaṣr al-Ḥayr al-Gharbī, 727. *h.* Mafjar, before 743. *i.* Mshattā, *c.* 744. *j.* Qaṣr aṭ-Ṭūba, *c.* 744.

FIG. 565. Sequence of Syrian *Bayts*.

emphasizes that 'almost all the apartments on the ground floor are in a perfect state of conservation'.[2] Here we have the central courtyard, and on one side of it are two perfect *bayts*, one above the other, with a colonnaded portico, also in two storeys, in front of them. This incidentaly disposes of Sauvaget's argument that Qasṭal and Kharāna must necessarily be Umayyad because both had a portico in front of the rooms, an argument to which the Ghassānid house at al-Ḥayyāt (see below, pp. 636–7) deals yet another blow. And the *bayt* likewise disposes of the argument that Qasṭal and Kharāna must be Umayyad because of their *bayts*.

Thanks to the kindness of Mr. Mougdad, the Inspector of Monuments, I was able to visit the remains of this palace, although occupied by families, on 23rd April 1963.

The great court has almost completely disappeared, as well as the colonnade, except part of the west end-pier. But the *bayt* behind it, or rather the ground-floor part (the upper floor has almost gone), was more or less intact, especially the great central hall, measuring some 8 m. in depth. It now has three

[1] *Sondages à Khirbet el-Minyah, Israel Exploration Journal*, X, p. 233 and fig. 5.

[2] *Op. cit.*, p. 256.

transverse arches, all quite modern, but the western pilaster of the original single transverse arch is still partly visible behind the new one. Of the two western flanking rooms, a door opens from each into the main hall, but one has been blocked up. The third door of Butler's façade, like the first, is on the axis of the two lateral rooms and not displaced towards the north-west corner, as he shows it. The doors leading from these two rooms into the central hall are partly blocked by the pilasters of the two modern transverse arches. The two small rooms still farther east are now used as stables.

Our next example is Qasṭal, about five miles west of Mshattā (see map on p. 404). Externally it resembles the fortresses of the Roman *limes* in Transjordan, but internally it is quite different, for the rooms are grouped into six *bayts* and arranged round the interior of the walls so as to leave a central court over (Fig. 565 *b*).[1]

This remarkable arrangement of the interior is not found in any other fort of the *limes*, so it can scarcely belong to the second or third century, in which it might have been placed on account of its excellent ashlar masonry. In view of what is said below (pp. 626 and 627–8) regarding masonry in Transjordan there only remains one possible alternative—the sixth century.

But how explain the arrangement of the interior? I think it can only be explained by the assumption that Qasṭal was built for an Oriental. In the sixth century the care of the frontier was handed over to the Ghassānid Phylarchs, and this leads me to believe that it was built for one of them. And this is confirmed by Ḥamza al-Iṣfahānī (tenth century) who says that it was built by Jabala ibn al-Ḥārith.[2]

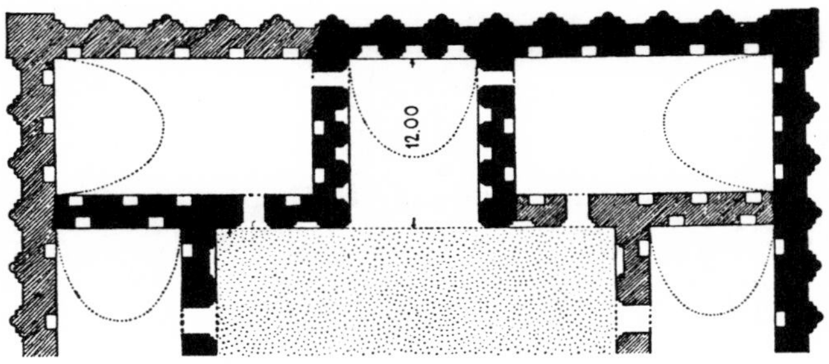

a. Fīrūzābād (*c*. 226).

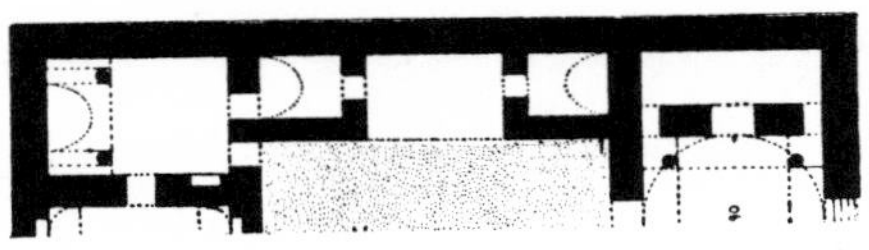

b. Sarvistān (early fifth century).

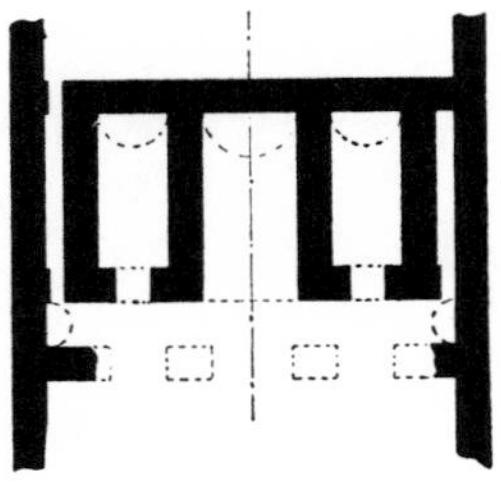

c. Qaṣr-i-Shīrīn (590–628).

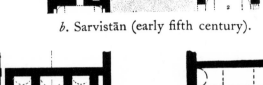

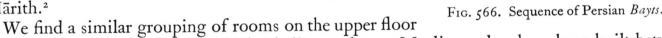

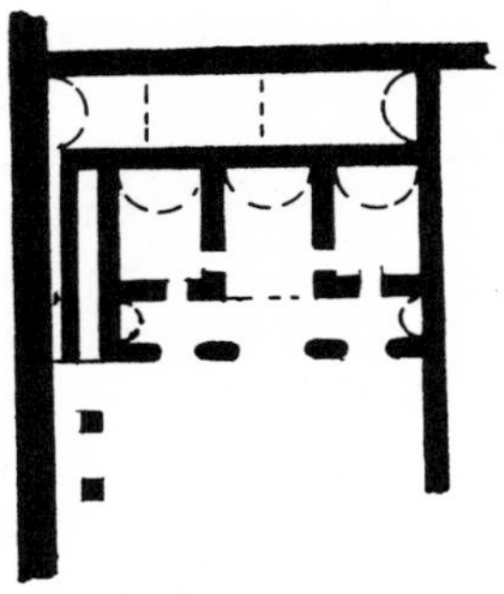

d. Ukhaiḍir (last quarter of eighth century).

FIG. 566. Sequence of Persian *Bayts*.

We find a similar grouping of rooms on the upper floor of Qaṣr Kharāna (Fig. 565 *c*), which I believe to be pre-Muslim and to have been built between 614 and 628 (see above, pp. 447–8). The *bayts* here are identical to those of Mshattā; those of Qasṭal, in which two small rooms giving access to the corner tower (? a latrine) are added at one side, bear the closest possible resemblance to those of Qaṣr aṭ-Ṭūba.

The earliest Syrian *bayts* under Islam (see table in Fig. 565) are to be found in al-Walīd's palace at Minya on Lake Tiberias. Here we have a five-roomed *bayt* on the south side, next to the basilical audience hall (above, pp. 386–7 and Fig. 448). Moreover, from the spacing of the remains of walls, taking off from the inner side of the west wall (*ibid.*), there must have been two more here. Grabar's excavations had as their object a final conclusive proof of this, but unfortunately they ceased after a couple of weeks' work. However, they were carried on long enough to establish the fact that the northern lateral rooms of the southern *bayt* were connected with each other by a widely open arch instead of by a door, exactly as at Boṣrā.

At Jabal Says there is what might be regarded as a new development—the addition of a large room (or court) on one side, in connexion with the hollow corner tower which may have served as a latrine, as at Mshattā. Thus we get a six-roomed *bayt*.[3] But it is not really an innovation, for the *bayt* in the palace of the Roman Governor at Boṣrā is likewise extended on one side.

At 'Anjar we have the simple five-roomed *bayt* once more, but at Qaṣr al-Ḥayr al-Gharbī we have, as Brisch has pointed out, 'a very advanced variant of the five-room group, in which the lateral rooms lying along the façade are extended by a further series of oblong rooms, set parallel to the outer walls'.[3]

1 For a detailed description of Qasṭal, see Brünnow and von Domaszewski, *Die Provincia Arabia*, II, pp. 95–103, figs. 676–85, and Taf. XLIV.

2 Gottwaldt's ed., p. 117; quoted by Brünnow and von Domaszewski, *op. cit.*, p. 100.

3 *Usais*, *Mitteilungen des Deutschen Archaölogischen Instituts, Abteilung Kairo*, XIX, p. 176.

Now, for the sake of comparison, let us consider early Persian *bayts* (Fig. 566).

At Fīrūzābād (*c.* A.D. 226) we have two *bayts* on either side of the great court. Each consists of an *īwān* with a pair of flanking chambers, which can be entered from it or from the court (Fig. 566 *a*). At Sarvistān (early fifth century) we have the same arrangement, except that the flanking rooms are square and entered from the *īwān* only (Fig. 566 *b*).

At Qaṣr-i-Shīrīn, in the palace of Khusrau Parvēz (A.D. 590–628), a distinct advance is shown. The *īwān* and its flanking chambers have become much deeper, and in front of them is a portico (*ṭarma*) of three arches. A passage at the side leads into a court at the back (Fig. 566*c*).[1]

At Ukhaiḍir (second half of eighth century) the arrangement is almost identical (Fig. 566 *d*), that is to say the ʿAbbāsids followed the Sasanian tradition.

THE MINARET OF THE GREAT MOSQUE AT QAIRAWĀN[2]

HISTORY. Al-Bakrī, our oldest authority (A.D. 1068) for this building, says that

'the miḥrāb of this mosque was constructed for the first time by ʿUqba ibn Nāfiʿ. All the edifice, with the exception of the miḥrāb, was pulled down and reconstructed by Ḥassān.[3] It was he who transported hither from an ancient church the two red columns spotted with yellow, which are of matchless beauty. . . . Hishām, the son of ʿAbd al-Malik, having ascended the throne of the Khalifate [Shaʿbān 105 H. = Jan. 724] received a despatch from the Governor of Qairawān [at that time Bishr ibn Ṣafwān] in which he stated that the mosque was not large enough to hold the assembly of the Faithful, and that immediately to the north of the edifice was a vast garden belonging to the Banū Fihr. In his reply the Khalif ordered the purchase of this land and its inclusion in the area of the mosque. The Governor obeyed; then he constructed in the ṣaḥn of the mosque a cistern(*mājil*)[4] which is designated to-day by the name *al-Mājil al-Qadīm* (the old cistern) which is situated to the west of the porticoes (*balāṭ*). Above the well which was in this garden, he built a minaret (*ṣaumaʿa*), the foundations of which were established in the water and, by a curious chance, he observed that this structure occupied the exact centre of the northern wall. Devout men carefully avoid praying in the part added to the mosque, and, to justify their conduct, say that the Governor had used compulsion to force the owners of the garden to sell it. To-day the minaret is just as Ḥassān had constructed it; it is 60 cubits high and 25 wide. One enters it by two doorways, one of which faces the east and the other the west. The jambs and lintels of these doorways are of marble ornamented with sculpture.'[5]

The phrase—'to-day the minaret is just as Ḥassān had constructed it'—contradicts, as Rivoira has pointed out,[6] the details already given by al-Bakrī, viz. that the minaret of his day was that built by the Governor of Qairawān (Bishr ibn Ṣafwān) by order of the Khalif Hishām. In fact it is clearly stated that the very site of the northern part of the mosque and the minaret was only purchased at that time. The name of Ḥassān, therefore, must be a slip on the part of al-Bakrī, or more probably a copyist's error. Bishr was Governor from 103 (721/2) to 109[7] (727/8), but the fact that he received his orders from Hishām narrows down the possible date for our minaret from Shaʿbān 105 (Jan. 724) to 109 (727/8).

DESCRIPTION OF THE PRESENT MINARET. The existing structure is a tower of three storeys, all square in plan, the lowest of which measures 18·87 m. in height without its crenellations, the second 5 m., and the third about 7·5 m., the total height without the finial being 31·5 m. (Fig. 568). The base of the lowest storey, according to Marçais, averages 10·50 m. a side.[8] I found the south-east side to measure 10·67 m. at the base and 10·20 m. at the summit, so the extent to which the first storey tapers has been much exaggerated, photographers having tilted their cameras when taking it. The photograph here published (Plate 85 *a*) was taken after the camera had been carefully levelled, and it consequently gives a more exact idea of the true form of the minaret. The two upper storeys do not taper; they average 7·59[9] and 5·46 m. a side respectively; both unfortunately have been whitewashed.

[1] The German-American excavations at Ctesiphon have revealed examples of the same grouping; see Wachtsmuth, in *Die Ausgrabungen der zweiten Ktesiphon-Expedition*, pp. 9–11.

[2] For previous history of the mosque, see above, pp. 61 and 138–41.

[3] 69–78 H. (688/9–697/8).

[4] For this word see Dozy and de Goeje, *Edrisi*, Glossary, pp. 268–9.

[5] Pp. 22–3; de Slane's transl., pp. 57–9 [52–4]; reprinted in Saladin's *Mosquée de Sidi Okba*, pp. 18–20.

[6] *Moslem Architecture*, pp. 37–8.

[7] An-Nuwayrī, de Slane's transl., *Journal Asiatique*, 3me sér., t. XI, p. 581.

[8] *Manuel d'art musulman*, I, p. 27.

[9] SE. 7·63; NE. 7·55; NW. 7·58 m. The south-west side of the terrace is obstructed by a little hut for the *mu'adhdhin*.

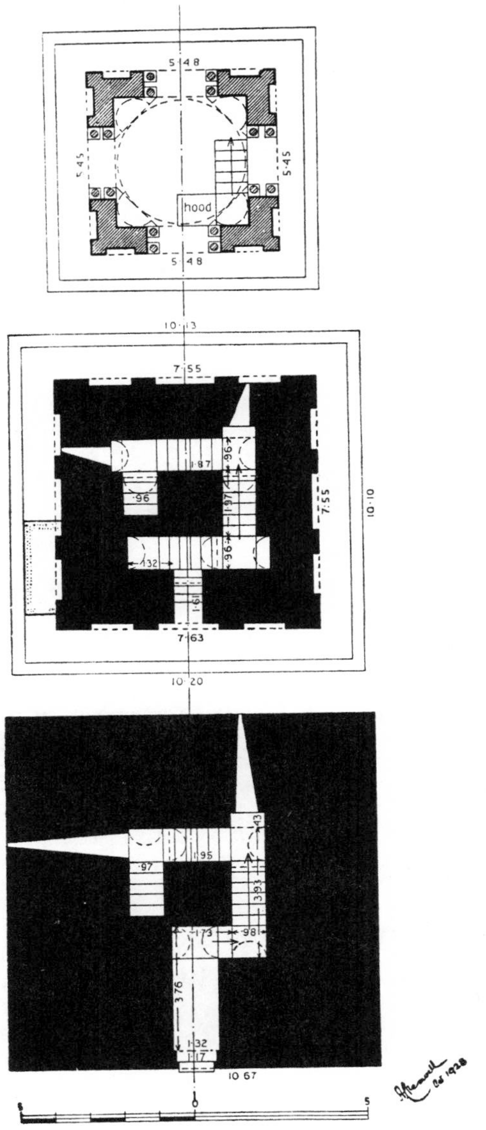

FIG. 567. QAIRAWĀN: Minaret of Great Mosque, plan. Scale 1 : 200.

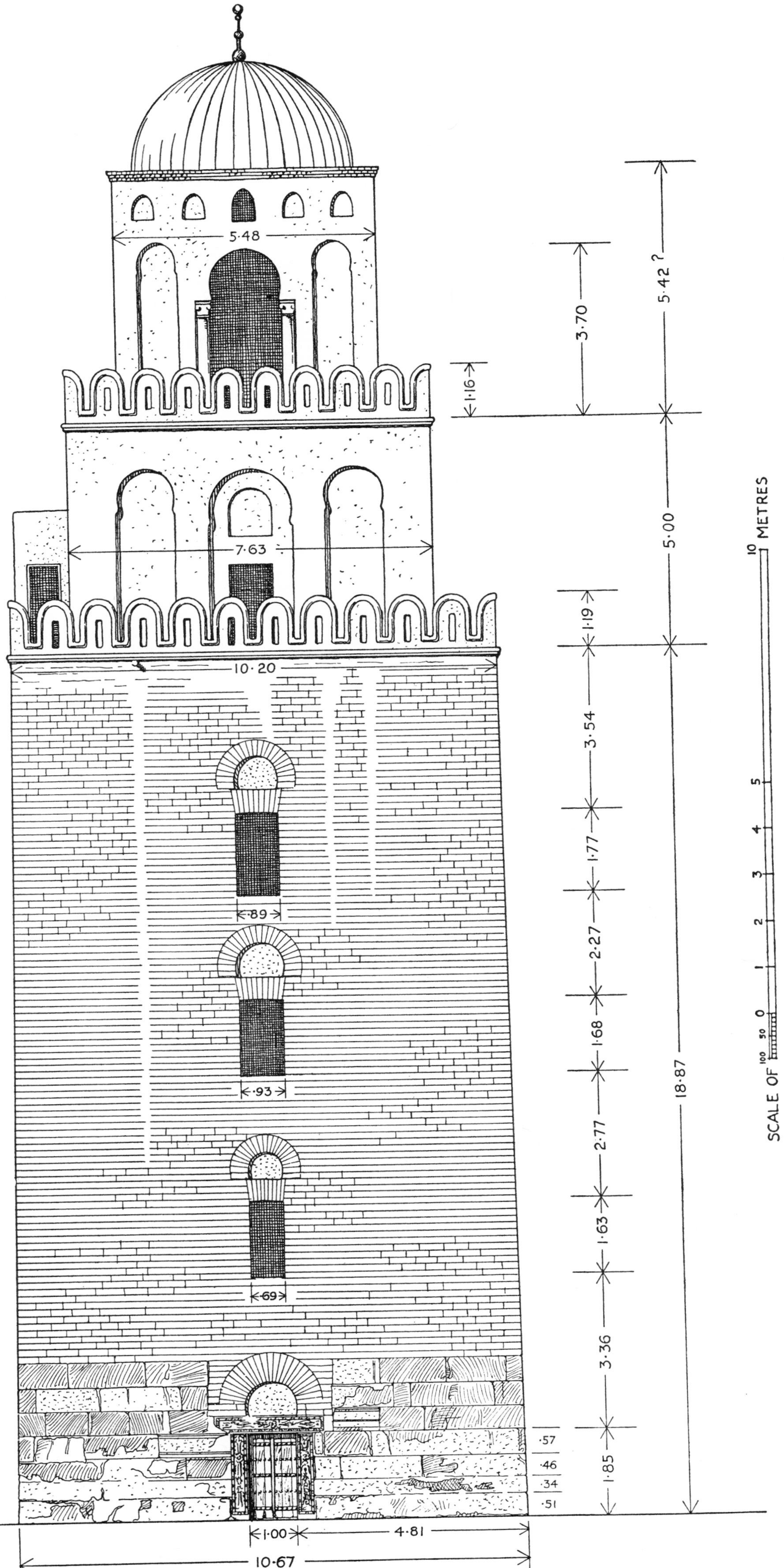

FIG. 568. QAIRAWĀN: Minaret of the Great Mosque.

Measured by K. A. C. Creswell and drawn by M. Lyon.

The entrance (Plate 85 *b*), which is a metre wide and 1·85 high, is formed by two jambs and a lintel, all of marble, carved Roman fragments perhaps taken from Carthage. The lintel is surmounted by a small horse-shoe relieving arch. The first seven courses are formed of large blocks of stone taken from Roman monuments, of which the first four average 47 cm. in height. Several of them bear Latin inscriptions of the time of Marcus Aurelius and Septimius Severus[1] (A.D. 179–208) embedded upside-down. The rest of the tower is built of small stone blocks 13·5 cm. thick (average of nine courses), which at a distance look like bricks.[2] A number of small cannon balls are embedded in the east side of the lowest storey.[3] The entrance is paved with borrowed fragments, which include a ceiling slab resembling a classical fragment in the Museum of St. Louis at Carthage.[4]

The staircase, which, curiously enough, is not quite in the centre of the tower, is 97 cm. wide and, the square core round which it is carried only averaging 1·92 m. a side, it follows that a space of no less than 3·30–3·50 m. is left for the side walls of the main storey—an enormous thickness. This staircase is lit by three windows on the south-east side of the lower storey directly over the entrance. Each window is covered by a horizontal arch, with a horse-shoe relieving arch above, after the pattern of the entrance below. In addition there are three windows like arrow-slits in the north-western, and two in the south-western face. Each flight of the staircase is covered by a short nearly horizontal tunnel-vault, semicircular or nearly so. The leading end of each rests on a little arch, placed just before the turn, after which another tunnel-vault takes off at right angles at a higher level. The vaults thus rise in steps corresponding to the flights of the staircase, and the problem of intersection is avoided.

A door, with lintel and relieving arch treated exactly like the windows on the south-east side, gives access to the roof of the arcades on either side (one can be seen in Plate 85 *a*). The second storey opens on to the terrace of the first by a rectangular doorway set in a shallow horse-shoe arched recess, flanked by a similar but slightly narrower recess on either side. The other sides of this storey are each decorated by three similar blind recesses The staircase continues through the second storey and, after 123 steps,[5] comes out under the little domed pavilion. The latter opens on to the terrace on all four sides by horse-shoe arches 3·70 m. in height, each springing from two pairs of columns.

The summits of the first and second storeys are crowned by peculiar rounded crenellations, each pierced by an arrow-slit. They measure 1·19 and 1·16 m. respectively in height. The top storey measures about 5·40 m. to the cornice, and the dome above about two metres. Four squinches, resting on a string course which runs round the interior at a height of 4·25 m., support a little hemispherical dome fluted externally. Between the squinches on the side of the ṣaḥn is a little window. This zone of transition is about a metre in height, and it is marked externally on each face by a row of five little arched recesses, placed about 65 cm. above the four archways. They are all blind except the central one on the side of the ṣaḥn, which is formed by the little window just mentioned.

Is the Present Minaret that Built by Hishām? Rivoira says: 'At the point where the tower is set back a second storey begins. . . . The materials, so far as can be judged from the very little which is visible inside, are different from those of the lower stage of the tower.'[6] This is not the case to-day; the masonry of the sides and newel of the staircase is visible all the way up; it is absolutely uniform and unbroken, and there can be no shadow of doubt that the first and second storeys are all one piece of work. As regards the top storey, there appears to be reason for believing that it dates from the first half of the nineteenth century.[7] As Marçais has pointed out,[8] the present tower corresponds closely with the particulars given by al-Bakrī. The latter, as we have seen, says that the minaret of his day measured 25 cubits a side. Now the average measurement of the sides of the present minaret is 10·63 m., which

[1] Pellisier, *Lettre à M. Hase*, in the *Revue Archéologique*, IVe année, p. 263; *Corpus Inscriptionum Latinarum*, VIII, pars I, No. 80, and *Supplement*, No. 11218; Broadley (A. M.), *Tunis, Past and Present*, II, pp. 164–5; Houdas and Basset, *Épigraphie tunisienne*, in the *Bulletin de correspondance africaine*, I, p. 176; Boddy (A. A.), *To Kairwân the Holy*, pp. 169–71; and Saladin, *Mosquée de Sidi Okba*, p. 49, n. 1.

[2] Hence Rae's remark that 'it seemed to be of brownish brick for a great part of its height, and of a creamy white above'; *The Country of the Moors*, p. 216.

[3] According to Penet (*Kairawan*, pp. 6–7), they are due to Yūnus, grandnephew of the Bey Ḥassān, who besieged Qairawān in 1740. Rae, however, says: 'The brick and plaster of this massive tower are defaced by marks of gunshot, fired by the Government troops during the insurrection [began 1864], when they retook the city from the insurgents'; *op. cit.*, p. 287.

[4] Saladin, *op. cit.*, p. 50 and figs. 13–14.

[5] Three in the entrance and twenty flights of six steps each.

[6] *Op. cit.*, p. 37. Diez also suggests that the two upper storeys are of later date; *Encyc. of Islām*, III, p. 229.

[7] Rivoira, *op. cit.*, p. 37.

[8] *Op. cit.*, p. 27.

gives 42·5 cm. for al-Bakrī's cubits. Al-Bakrī gives the height as 60 cubits; this at 42·5 cm. a cubit = 25·51 m. against my measurement of 25·03 m. to the top of the crenellations of the second storey—a remarkably close agreement. It would therefore appear that the two lower storeys are those described by al-Bakrī in A.D. 1068, and that the top storey is a later addition. In view of the early date of al-Bakrī and his circumstantial account of the construction of the minaret, we would be fairly well justified in dating it *c.* A.D. 724, the year of the Khalif Hishām's accession.

Nevertheless, although I am convinced that the present minaret is that described by al-Bakrī, I would like to make a reservation here. The masonry of the minaret is so exactly like the exposed masonry of the buttresses on the south-east side of the mosque, which cannot be earlier than 221 H. (836), that I cannot help feeling that this minaret, which I have placed here in homage to the text of al-Bakrī, may really form part of the new mosque built by Ziyadāt Allāh in that year. In this connexion we must remember that al-Bakrī did not visit North Africa himself, but compiled his book from other writers, mostly of the first half of the eleventh century, and from contemporary official reports made by agents of the Umayyad government of Spain[1] and in one case, he attributed to Ziyadāt Allāh in 221 H. work which appears to have been due to his successor Abū Ibrāhīm Aḥmad in 248 (862). But even if we attribute the minaret to Ziyadāt Allāh it still remains the oldest existing in Islam with the exception of that of the Great Mosque at Boṣrā, and the possible exception of that at Qaṣr al-Ḥayr ash-Sharqī (below, p. 532).

One more point remains to be considered. Al-Bakrī says that the minaret had two doors, one to the east and one to the west, and that the jambs and lintels of these doors were of marble decorated with carving. Now the present entrance corresponds to the above description, but it opens to the south-east (= the south, or *qiblī* of al-Bakrī), and he cannot be referring to the doors opening on to the roof, for they are quite plain. Assuming that he has got his directions wrong, there still remains the problem of the second entrance, of which I could find no traces in the present minaret, within or without.[2]

ARCHITECTURAL ORIGINS. The most striking architectural detail of this minaret is the treatment of the doorway, which at once recalls the little entrance to the tower of Shaykh ʻAlī Kāsūn, ten miles north of Ḥamā (Fig. 106, facing p. 200). A similar treatment may be seen in the Great Mosque at Ḥamā, where the entrance to the very early lower part of the south-east minaret is treated in the same way. As the minaret of Qairawān was constructed by order of an Umayyad Khalif, Syrian influence is just what we should expect.

1 See de Slane's introduction to his edition of al-Bakrī, *Description de l'Afrique septentrionale*, 2me éd., pp. 13–15; and Marçais, *Les Faïences de la Grande Mosquée de Kairouan*, pp. 8–9.

2 The ground at the back of the minaret has risen considerably, but it can scarcely hide a second entrance, for such an entrance would have to be at a higher level than the other on account of the staircase.

XIX

QAṢR AL-ḤAYR ASH-SHARQĪ.[1] 110 H. (728/9)

Description—The Lesser Enclosure—The Interior—The Greater Enclosure—Cause of the present condition of the two enclosures—The Mosque—Form of the Arches—The date—The Hydraulic Works—The meaning of the word al-Ḥayr.

ARCHITECTURAL ORIGINS: Joggled voussoirs—The mâchicoulis—The combination of brick and stone—The construction of the vaults.

QAṢR AL-ḤAYR ASH-SHARQĪ LIES IN THE DESERT nearly sixty miles north-east of Palmyra and about forty miles south of Ruṣāfa.[2] The nearest village is Ṭaiyiba, which is about twelve miles north-north-west. The latter was a station on the old overland route from Aleppo to Baghdād and Baṣra,[3] and Qaṣr al-Ḥayr was consequently seen by several seventeenth-, eighteenth-, and early nineteenth-century travellers, e.g. Pietro della Valle in 1616 and 1625, Godinho in 1663,[4] Beawes in 1745,[5] Charmichael in 1751,[6] Sir Eyre Coote in 1771,[7] Parsons in 1774, Capper in 1778, Evers

[1] BIBLIOGRAPHY: — 1616, Pietro della Valle, *Viaggi* (Rome, 1662), I, p. 372 and IV, pp. 410–11; French transl. (Paris, 1661–4), I_2, p. 13, and IV, p. 480; — 1663, Godinho (Manoel), *Relação do novo caminho . . . vindo da India para Portugal* (Lisboa, 1665), p. 147; — 1745, Beawes (W.), *Remarks and occurrences in a Journey from Aleppo to Bassora, by way of the Desert, in 1745*, in the *Asiatic Journal*, VI (1818), p. 269; — 1751, Charmichael (John), *A Journal from Aleppo over the Desart to Busserah*, published as an Appendix to Vol. I of the New (3rd) ed. of J. H. Grose's *Voyage to the East Indies* (London, 1772), pp. 9–10; reprinted by Douglas Carruthers in *The Desert Route to India*, pp. 143–5; — 1764, Niebuhr (C.), *Reisebeschreibung*, II, p. 236; French transl. (1780 ed.), II, p. 193; — 1771, *Diary of a Journey with Sir Eyre Coote from Bussora to Aleppo in 1780 (?) from the original MS. communicated by Sir Woodbine Parish*, in the *Journal of the Roy. Geographical Socy.*, XXX (1860), p. 207; — 1774, Parsons (Abraham), *Travels in Asia and Africa; including a Journey from Scanderoon to Aleppo, and over the Desert to Bagdad and Bussora*, pp. 86 and 89; — 1778, Capper (James), *Observations on the Passage to India through Egypt, and across the Great Desert*, pp. 65–6; — 1779, Anon. (Evers, Samuel), *A Journal, kept on a Journey from Bassora to Bagdad; over the Little Desert, to Aleppo . . . in the year 1779. By a Gentleman, late an Officer in the service of the Hon. East India Company* (Lee, Horsham, 1784), pp. 78–82; — 1781, Irwin (Eyles), *A Series of Adventures in the course of a Voyage up the Red Sea . . .*, 3rd ed., II, pp. 300–302; — 1789, Taylor (John), *Travels from England to India, in the year 1789*, I, p. 232; — 1797, Olivier (G. A.), *Voyage dans l'Empire othoman* (Paris, 1807), VI, pp. 349–50; — 1808, Rousseau (J. B. L. J.), *Voyage de Bagdad à Alep, publié, d'après le manuscrit inédit de l'auteur par L. Poinssot*, pp. 146–54 and plate; — 1895, Østrup (J.), *Historisk-topografiske bidrag til kendskabet til den syriske Ørken; Det Kongelige Danske Videnskabernes Selskabs Skrifter, Historisk og filosofisk Afdeling*, Række VI, bind IV, pp. 66–9 and fig. 3; — 1900, Clermont-Ganneau, *Une inscription du calife Hichâm; Recueil d'archéologie orientale*, III, pp. 285–93, pls. VII A and VIII, and p. 358; — 1927, Dussaud (René), *Topographie historique de la Syrie antique et médiévale*, pp. 258–60 and 514; Gabriel (A.), *Kaṣr el-Ḥeir*, in *Syria* VIII, pp. 302–29, pls. LXXXV–XCIV and figs. 4–15; — 1928, Musil (A.), *Palmyrena: A Topographical Itinerary* (*American Geographical Society, Oriental Explorations and Studies*, No. 4), pp. 77–9 and figs. 15–24; — 1929, Carruthers (D.), *The Desert Route to India*, pp. xxi, 15, 133, 140, 143–5, and plate facing p. 144; — 1931, Dussaud (R.), P. Deschamps and H. Seyrig, *La Syrie antique et médiévale illustrée*, pls. 84–6 and relative text; Seyrig (H.), *Antiquités syriennes, I.—Les Jardins de Kaṣr el-Heir*, *Syria*, XII, pp. 316–18 and pl. LXII; and Wiet (G.), *Répertoire chronologique d'épigraphie arabe*, I, pp. 23–4; — 1932, Gabriel, *A propos de Kasr el-Heir, à l'est de Palmyre*, *Syria*, XIII, pp. 317–20; — 1934, Poidebard (A.), *La Trace de Rome dans le Désert de la Syrie*, p. 91 and pl. XCI_1; and Seyrig, *Antiquités syriennes. 16—Retour aux jardins de Kasr el-Heir*, *Syria*, XV, pp. 24–32, pls. VII–VIII and figs. 1–3; — 1935, Sauvaget (J.), in the *Bulletin d'Études orientales*, V, pp. 136–7; — 1937, Creswell (K. A. C.), *Another word on Qaṣr Al-Hair*, *Syria*, XVIII, pp. 232–3; and Grant (C. P.), *The Syrian Desert*, pp. 196–7 and plate facing p. 197; — 1939, Sauvaget (J.), *Remarques sur les monuments omeyyades*, *Journal Asiatique*, CXXXI, pp. 1–13; — [1947], Marçais (Georges), *L'Art de l'Islam*, p. 17; and Stern (Henri), *Notes sur l'architecture des châteaux omeyyades*, *Ars Islamica*, XI–XII, pp. 75–6 and figs. 8, 21, and 22; — Pijoán (José), *Summa Artis, XII—Arte Islámico*, pp. 41–4 and 51–6; — 1953, Dunand (M.), *De l'Amanus au Sinai: Sites et Monuments*, pp. 145–6, with 3 illus.; — 1965, Grabar (Oleg), Qaṣr al-Hayr al-Sharqī. Preliminary Report on the First Season of Excavations, Part I, *Les Annales archéologiques de Syrie*, XV (2), pp. 107–20, with 23 illus.

[2] It must not be confused with the fortified tower of the same name between Qaryatain and Palmyra, which was incorporated in Qaṣr al-Ḥayr al-Gharbī, and for which see below, p. 541,

[3] Parsons says: 'The caravans from Aleppo to Bussora [= Baṣra] keep the same track as those from Aleppo to Bagdad, as far as Taiba; afterwards the track of the Bussora caravans is about one point of the compass more to the southward. This is called going over the great desart, wheras the route to Bagdad is over the little desart'; *op. cit.*, p. 86. This explains why Ukhaiḍir was more rarely seen by European travellers of those days than Qaṣr al-Ḥayr.

[4] *Relação*, p. 147. There can be little doubt that the 'magnificent building of cut stone, much ruined', which Godinho, coming from 'Āna, saw just before reaching Ṭaiyiba, was Qaṣr al-Ḥayr, although he speaks of it as built of marble.

[5] After leaving 'Ain ul Kom' on the 11th of August, he writes: 'We passed this morning by the ruins of a castle called Gussorah Seveyge; the building has been large and of a square figure; at present most of the southward is standing, built of stone, with turrets at equal distances, but within there are no remains'; *loc. cit.*, p. 269.

[6] In J. H. Grose, *op. cit.*, I, Appendix, pp. 9–10; and Carruthers, *The Desert Route to India*, pp. 143–4. Carruthers (p. 135) points out that the date, 1771, given by Grose is incorrect, for Charmichael mentions his meeting with Brabazon Ellis, the English Resident at Baṣra. The latter was appointed in 1751, and there had been at least four others by 1771. Moreover, Ives's map, published in his *Voyage from England to India in the year 1754*, shows a route described as that of 'Mr. Carmichael in the year M.D.CCLI'.

[7] The date 1780, suggested in the *J.R.G.S.*, for Sir Eyre Coote's journey must be corrected, for Irwin says: 'The consul being at a loss himself, was not too proud to apply to Mr. Smith, who prevailed on Abdul Azah—the shaik who conducted the late Sir Eyre Coote over the desart, in the year 1771, . . . to accept the trust'; *op. cit.*, II, p. 281. See also Parsons, *op. cit.*, p. 10: '. . . General Sir Eyre Coote (who was here [Scanderoon] in March 1771, on his return from India by way of Bussora). . . .'

in 1779,[1] Irwin in 1781, Major John Taylor in 1789,[2] Olivier in 1797,[3] and Rousseau in 1808. Tenrreyro, who passed through Ṭaiyiba in 1523 and 1528,[4] and Plaisted, who arrived there on the 17th of July 1750, on his twenty-first day's march from Baṣra, must have passed within a very short distance of it,[5] likewise the Chevalier de St.-Lubin in 1756, Rousseau's own father in 1782, Latouche in 1785, and Sir Harford Jones, for Rousseau, in 1807, found the names of all four written on the monolithic gate of Ṭaiyiba.[6] To these may be added the anonymous Englishman whose journey, made in 1780, has been published

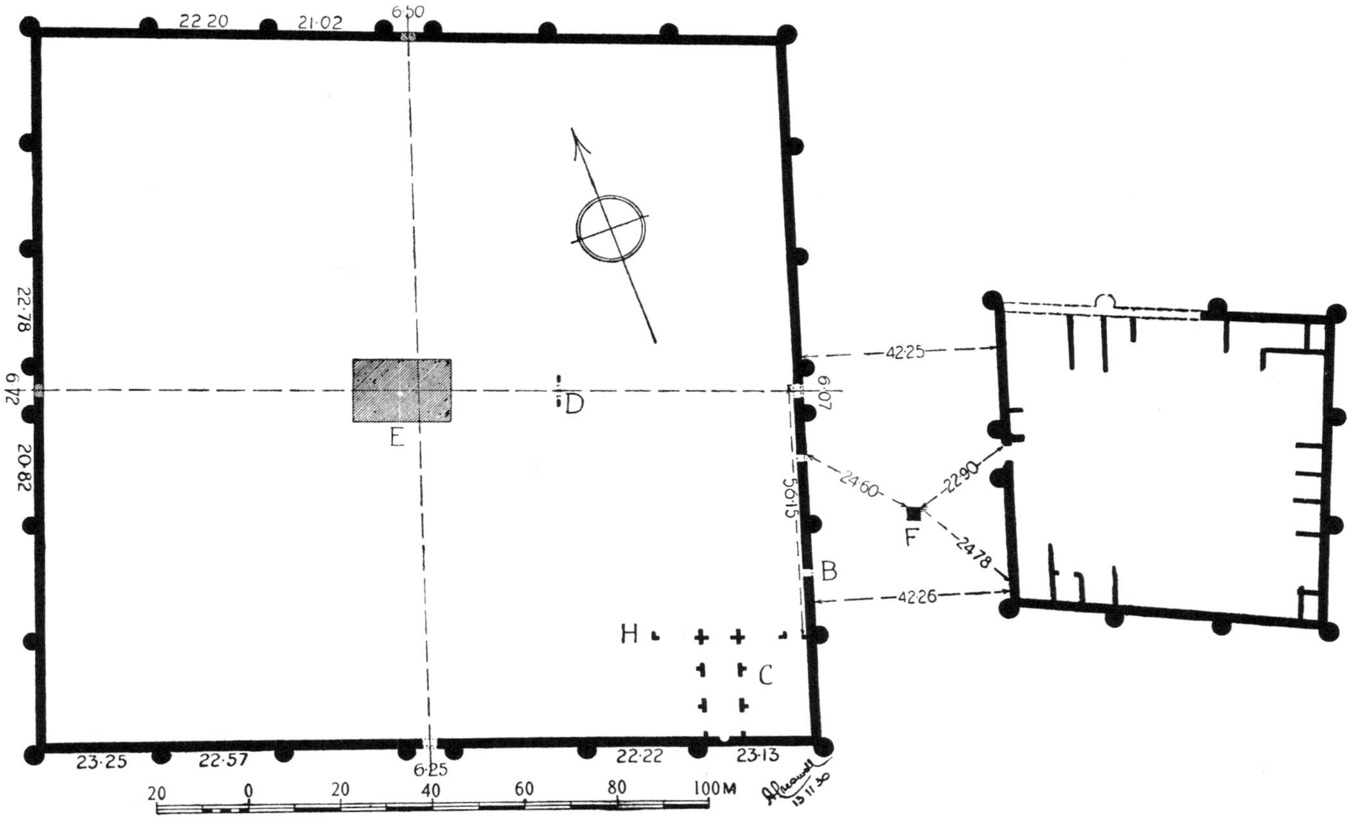

FIG. 569. QAṢR AL-ḤAYR ASH-SHARQĪ: Plan.

by Lusignan,[7] and Julius Griffiths who passed through 'Ain al-Kōm, on his way from Aleppo to Kerbelā' and Baṣra, in June 1786.[8] It must also have been known to Niebuhr for, in his list of places on the road from Baṣra to Aleppo, he mentions it as '*Kussur el choên*, sont deux vieux châteaux dans cette contrée'.[9] And when the Bedawīn who had their tents south of the Khābūr told Sachau in 1880 that there was a ruin in the desert 'behind Ruṣāfa' which they called the *gaṣr čebīr* (= *qaṣr kabīr*) and named Ga'āra,[10] they can only have referred to Qaṣr al-Ḥayr.

But its rediscovery after nearly 120 years of oblivion and its adequate publication are due to M. Albert Gabriel who visited it in April 1925 and to whom I am indebted for permission to use many of the drawings reproduced here.[11]

1 'May 16 . . . about noon came in sight of the ruins of Kassar Luckween or the two brothers. . . . They appeared to have been surrounded by a canal of water for about five miles. . . . The cornices in the front are ornamented in a very elegant manner, one entire pillar of black marble is still standing, as also one of oriental granite, the capital of which seems to be of the Corinthian order. In front of the ruins is a large square tower, which I suppose was used as a watch-house; we ascended to the top of it by a flight of steps . . . an Arabic inscription on one of the arches, containing a pious exhortation . . .'; *op. cit.*, pp. 78 and 80.

2 'This day we passed near the remains of a small castle in the Gothic style. The name of this place, we were informed, signified in Arabic, the Brother's Buildings'; *op. cit.*, I, p. 232.

3 'Nous campâmes entre deux gros bourgs abandonnés depuis un grand nombre d'années, et distans l'un de l'autre de deux ou trois milles. Nous n'eûmes pas la force d'aller voir quelle avait été leur étendue et leur importance. Nous avions rencontré, un peu avant de mettre pied à terre, trois aqueducs fort anciens et solidement bâtis; ils ne recevaient plus d'eau: le premier, que nous pûmes suivre des yeux à plus de demi-lieue de distance, était à quelques pieds seulement au dessus du sol.' 'Le 27 [de juin], nous marchâmes deux heures et demie, et nous campâmes au dessous de *Taïb* ou Taïbéh'; *op. cit.*, II, pp. 349–50.

4 *Itinerario*, Coimbra, 1560, fols. 85 *a* and 98 *a*. Pedro Teixeira would probably have seen it in 1605 on his way from 'Āna to Ṭaiyiba, if his camel men had not insisted on turning south at 'Ketef el Hel' to go to Sukhna, instead of following the direct route: *Travels*, Sinclair's transl. (Hakluyt Society), pp. 98–9.

5 *A Journal . . . to Busserah: from thence across the Great Desart to Aleppo*, London, 1757, p. 62.

6 *Op. cit.*, p. 155.

7 L. (S.) [Saviour Lusignan], *A History of the Revolt of Ali Bey, against the Ottoman Porte . . . To which are added . . . and the Journal of a Gentleman who travelled from Aleppo to Bassora*, 2nd ed., London, 1784, pp. 228–9. For some reason he passed through 'Ain al-Kōm instead of Ṭaiyiba.

8 *Travels in Europe, Asia Minor, and Arabia*, London, 1805, p. 360.

9 *Op. cit.*, French transl. (1780 ed.), II, p. 193.

10 *Reise*, p. 249.

11 Musil had already seen it in 1908, but he did not publish his description and drawings of it until twenty years later.

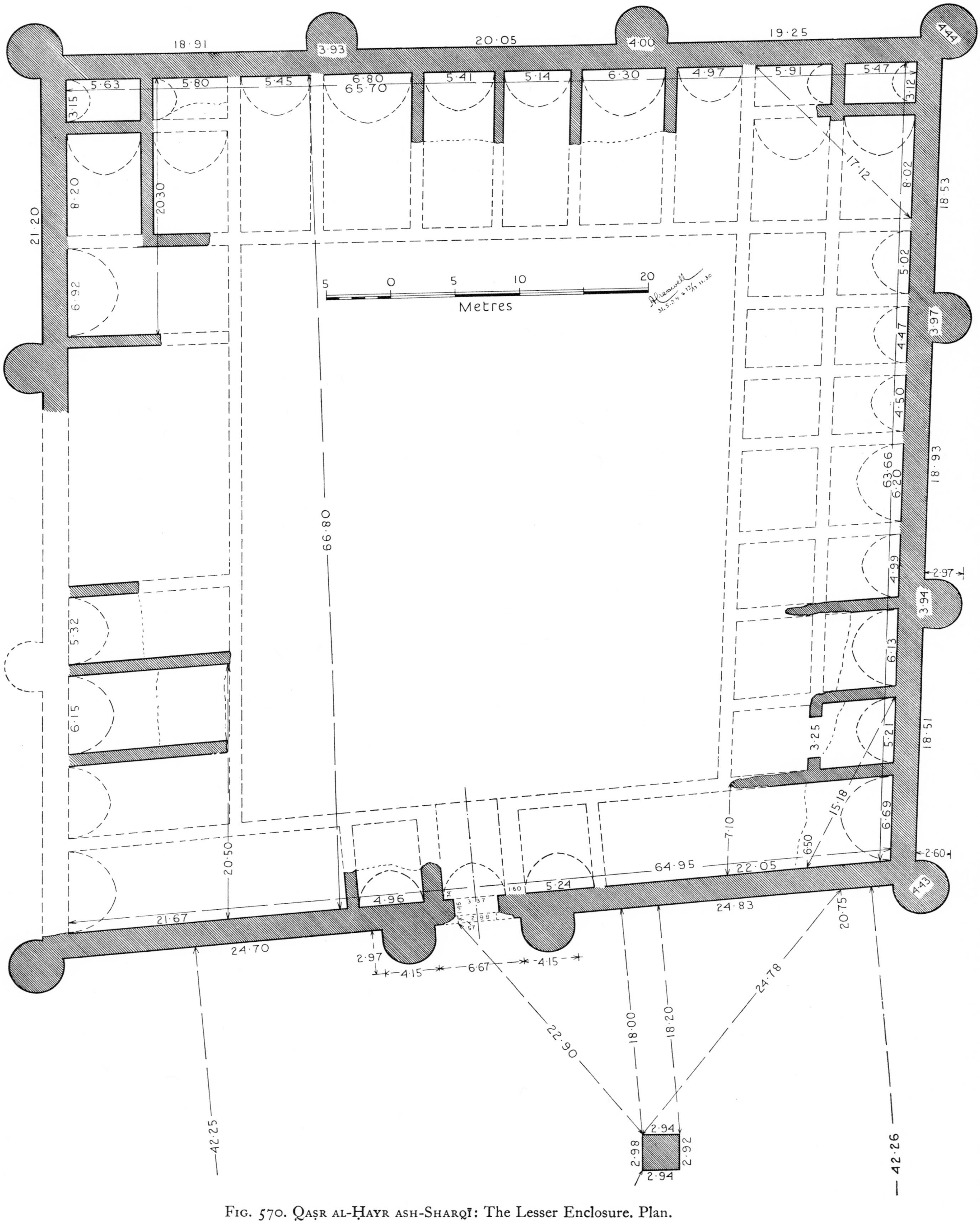

Fig. 570. Qaṣr al-Ḥayr ash-Sharqī: The Lesser Enclosure. Plan.

It may well be asked—Why this gap between 1808 and 1925? I think the following must be the explanation: In 1840 a company known as 'The Transit Co.' was formed for the conveyance of passengers from Alexandria to Suez and vice versa in connexion with the P. and O. service. They were sent along the Maḥmūdīya Canal in native sailing boats from Alexandria to Aṭfīḥ on the Nile, from Aṭfīḥ to Būlāq (the port of Cairo) in the company's steamers, accommodated in the Hôtel d'Orient founded in that year, and sent next day by omnibus to Suez. The fare, with a free allowance of 400 lb. of luggage, was £8. 12*s*.[1] This route became so popular that by 1844 some 100 passengers or more passed each way twice a month.[2] From this moment the Aleppo–Baṣra route to India was dead so far as European travellers were concerned.

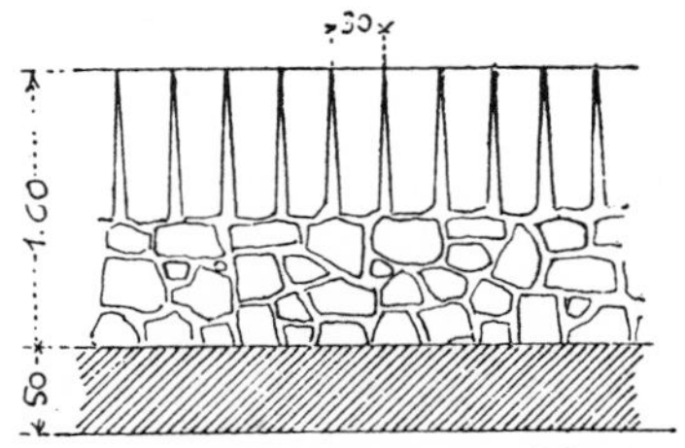

FIG. 571. QAṢR AL-ḤAYR: Nature of masonry. (From Gabriel, *op. cit.*)

I visited Qaṣr al-Ḥayr on the 31st of May and the 1st of June 1928, and again on the 12th and 13th of November 1930. I went by car from Palmyra to Sukhna[3] (68 km.) and the Shaykh of that village showed me the way to Qaṣr al-Ḥayr. I returned in the evening and passed the night in his house, leaving again next morning for the Qaṣr. On this occasion I took a villager who agreed to act, after my work was finished, as a guide to Ṭaiyiba, 19 km., Ruṣāfa (via 'Ain al-Kōm,), 61 km., and Raqqa, 51 km.[4]

DESCRIPTION. The ruins consist of two fortified enclosures (Plates 92–8 and Fig. 569), roughly square, both flanked with half-round towers; one averages nearly 66 m. and the other about 160 m. a side internally. They are placed with their sides approximately facing the four cardinal points, the larger to the west, the smaller to the east, with a space of 42·25 m. between them. As Gabriel points out, they are not on the same axis, the east–west axis of the Greater Enclosure being about 10 m. (I make it about 10·50 m.) farther north than the other.[5] They are of great importance, for they are the *oldest Muslim fortified enclosures in existence*.[6]

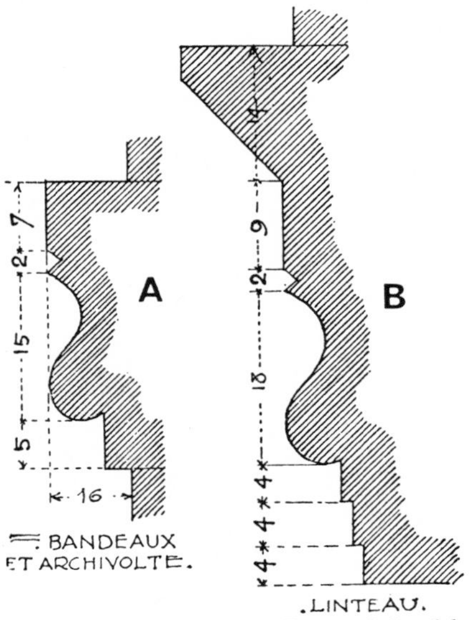

FIG. 572. QAṢR AL-ḤAYR: Mouldings. (From Gabriel, *op. cit.*)

THE LESSER ENCLOSURE (Plates 92–4 and Figs. 570–4) is formed by a curtain wall 2·03 m.[7] thick, flanked by half-round towers, one at each corner and two intermediate ones on each face, making twelve in all. The corner towers average 4·43 m. in diameter, the intermediate ones 3·96 m.,[8] except the pair which flank the entrance, which are roughly 4·15 m. in width with a projection of 2·97 m. On the east and south faces the distance between the towers varies from 18·51 to 20·05 m., but on the west face the intermediate towers, which flank the only entrance, are only 6·67 m. apart. This enclosure is in a much better condition than the other, the walls being preserved to the level of the ramparts, except on the north side where nearly two-thirds of the wall have fallen.[9] Of the towers only the four corner ones and the pair flanking the entrance have been preserved above the rampart level. Each has a small domed chamber, except that flanking the entrance to the north, which appears to have

1 See Olin (S.), *Travels in Egypt*, I, pp. 334–5; Tillotson (John), *The Overland Route to India* (Lloyd, London, n.d.); Yates (W. H.), *The Modern History and Condition of Egypt*, I, pp. 500–504; Wilkinson (Sir Gardner), *Modern Egypt and Thebes*, I, pp. 473–6; Anon, *The Route of the Overland Mail to India* (Atchley & Co., London, n.d.); Richardson (D. L.), *The Anglo-Indian Passage*, pp. 30–31, 57–64, and 183; A. F. C. de Cosson, *The Old Overland Route across Egypt to India*, in *Bengal, Past and Present*, X (1915), pp. 211–21; and Sidebottom (John K.), *The Overland Mail*, 1948, pp. 15–81.

2 M. A. Titmarsh [= W. M. Thackeray], *Notes of a Journey from Cornhill to Grand Cairo*, 2nd ed., p. 187.

3 For a vivid description of Sukhna, see Langenegger, *Durch verlorne Lande*, pp. 306–10. See also T. J. Ellis, *On a Raft and through the Desert*, II, pp. 77–8.

4 The surface is quite good except for the first 6 km. or so after 'Ain al-Kōm.

5 *Syria*, VIII, p. 311.

6 The only records of earlier Muslim works of fortification known to me are the following: (1) a fortress known as al-Manṣūr, built in Ziyād in 38 H. (658/9), between Iṣṭakhr and Baidha; (2) the restoration of the walls of Maṣṣīṣa by 'Abd al-Malik in 83–4 H. (702/3); (3) a little castle of black stone (? basalt) constructed by Maslama at Aleppo in 90 H. (708/9); (4) the restoration of the fortifications of Latakia in 100 H. (718/19); (5) the fortress of al-Muthaqqab constructed by Ḥassān ibn Māhawayh al-Anṭākī (near Maṣṣīṣa) in 105 H. (724); (6) the castle of Qaṭarghāsh constructed by 'Abd al-'Azīz ibn Ḥayyān al-Anṭākī; (7–9) the castles of Mūra, Būqā, and Baghrās constructed by order of Hishām, like the three preceding, in the same year; see the *Chronology* at the end of volume.

7 Measured at the entrance.

8 Direct measurements across the top of the four intermediate towers on the south and east sides gave 3·94, 3·97, 4·00, and 3·93 m. (going from left to right). The towers do not taper.

9 This condition dates from Rousseau's day; see his sketch published by Clermont-Ganneau, *loc. cit.*, pl. VIII.

contained a spiral staircase, but all the steps have disappeared and nothing but a hollow shaft is to be seen. From the rampart walk down to the under side of the joggled lintel of the doorway measures 7·47 m., and the doorway itself must have been at least 4·20 m. high. The height of the curtain walls must therefore have been 4·20+7·47+2·60 (parapet, see below) = 14·27 m.

The stone, which has taken a beautiful amber tint, is a fine-grained limestone, which Gabriel believes to have come from Ṭaiyiba.[1] It is well dressed with very fine joints, and the courses are about 35 cm. in height. This fine jointing has not been obtained by a perfect dressing of the surfaces of the blocks, but by cutting them so that they taper slightly inwards, as may be observed on walking along the ramparts (Fig. 571). I brought away some pieces of cement from some joints which had opened in the masonry of the rooms in the south-east corner. Mr. A. Lucas, who has rendered such valuable services in the chemical treatment of objects found in the Tomb of Tut-ankhamen, has kindly analysed them for me. He writes as follows: 'The cement is a good quality of gypsum plaster (plaster of Paris) containing small proportions of fine quartz sand and of carbonate of lime, both probably natural impurities and not artificial additions.'

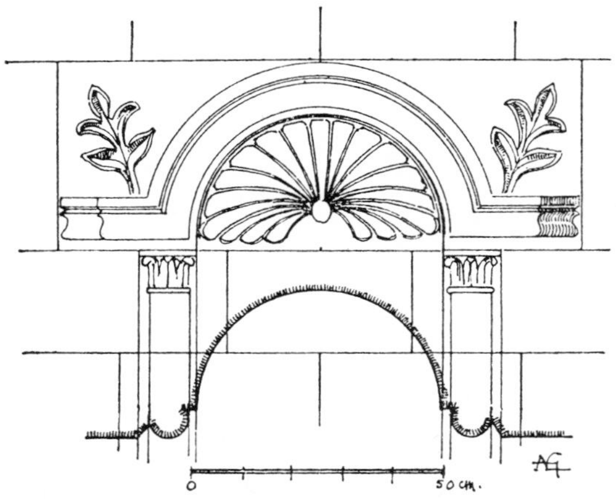

Fig. 573. Qaṣr al-Ḥayr: Niche flanking entrance of Lesser Enclosure. (From Gabriel, *op. cit.*)

The entrance is a well-designed piece of work. The opening is 2·98 m. in width, but its height cannot be measured, for sand and débris reach to within 1·50 m. of the lintel; Gabriel suggests 4·20 m. The door-jambs have crumbled away, but the flat arch in the form of a lintel still remains in position (Plate 93 *c*). It is carved with a moulding which must have returned round the jambs, and is surmounted by a splay-faced moulding (Fig. 572, B). Above it is a semicircular relieving arch, with a similar moulding on a slightly smaller scale (Fig. 572, A), which is prolonged to right and left at the springing until it strikes the flanking towers; the towers themselves are encircled with a similar moulding at a slightly lower level. The tympanum is filled in with plain masonry, but the spandrels are occupied by two little semicircular niches with fluted shell-like hoods resting on engaged columns (Fig. 573). Beneath each niche are the remains of a bracket.

The towers at their summits exhibit a most original and charming decorative scheme, carried out in brick and stucco (Plates 92 *c*, 93 *a* and *b*, 94 *c*, and Fig. 574). This decoration commences below with a cyma recta moulding, similar to that which runs round the towers almost on a level with the door-lintel; then there are two courses of brickwork, then a row of small bricks about 10 cm. square set lozenge-wise, and then another course of brickwork. Immediately above this is the last course of stone-work and on this rests the attractive blind arcading. The latter is executed in stucco and consists of a series of rectangular panels divided by pairs of little columns, the shafts of which are composed of a series of chevrons. The face of the arch above is decorated with acanthus foliage, but the design in the panels is more difficult to make out, for the stucco, which is of a dark greyish colour,[2] has lost its original sharpness; there appear to be leaves and grapes[3] attached to an undulating stem. This decoration, as Gabriel has pointed out, is not carved but moulded, and four moulds appear to have been used: one for the colonnettes, a second for the pairs of capitals, a third for the sunken panel, and a fourth for the tympanums, arch-faces, and spandrels. The whole is surmounted by a course of bricks placed so as to produce a dog-tooth motif, then six (or perhaps more—Gabriel says nine) courses of vertical brickwork, and then several projecting bricks, capping the whole and forming a cornice, of which traces remain here and there. Above this, set back from the face of the wall, rises the brick dome crowning the tower. This is the *earliest stucco decoration in Islam*.

The decorative frieze just described runs across the summit of the curtain wall between the towers with a small modification: the ornamental band of brickwork is placed above the last course of stone instead of below it. In the centre is a mâchicoulis of two openings resting on three stone brackets. The

[1] *Loc. cit.*, p. 312.

[2] Gabriel (p. 315) says that it is composed of lime, plaster, and ashes.

[3] Gabriel speaks of flowers, but I could not with certainty distinguish any.

upper part of this mâchicoulis, which is no longer complete, is of brickwork decoratively treated, of which a dog-tooth course is still preserved and three rows of small, square bricks placed lozenge-wise (Plate 92 *c*).

The curtain walls, with the exception of that in which the entrance is set, are treated as follows: the smooth, beautifully finished masonry rises to just above the level of the moulding crowning the masonry of the two towers just described; then come five courses of brickwork, all stretchers as elsewhere, then three more courses of stone, then a band of small, square bricks set lozenge-wise, above which is ordinary brickwork, but how many courses there were when it was complete cannot be determined; to the right of the towers flanking the entrance there is a short length of eighteen courses, to the left is another short length of twenty-three courses. The latter must be almost if not quite complete, for it rises to the base of the dome. The summit of the latter piece of wall is about 2·60 m. above the level of the rampart walk, of which it forms the parapet, so it cannot have run unbroken from tower to tower, but, as it has disappeared down to the level of the rampart, the form taken by the embrasures cannot be determined. Gabriel gives a conjectural restoration of it on his pl. XCIV. The rampart walk is a little over 1·50 m. in width and the parapet has a thickness of 50 cm.

The remaining towers are treated as follows: the first band of brickwork, of five courses, which runs along the curtain walls, is carried round each tower, then come three courses of masonry, then a band of small square bricks set lozenge-wise, then three more courses of stone, and then a final band of four or five courses of brickwork, surmounted by a brick dome (Fig. 574, facing p. 532). The bricks are 24 to 25 cm. square and 4·5 cm. thick (I could not find any larger than this), and the joints 2·5 cm.

FIG. 574. QAṢR AL-ḤAYR: Decorative scheme at summit of towers flanking entrance to Lesser Enclosure. (From Gabriel, *op. cit.*)

THE INTERIOR is in an advanced state of ruin; nevertheless it is still possible to see that the lower storey consisted of a number of tunnel-vaulted chambers about 12 m. in depth but of varying width, arranged round a central court (Plates 93 *d* and 94), now full of débris which must be more than 3 m. in depth, for it reaches in almost every chamber up to the springing of the vault, and in some cases even higher. It is obvious from my plan that this central court must have measured about 37 m. from north to south and 47 narrowing to 37 m. from east to west. The vaults are constructed as follows: the vault begins with from ten to thirteen courses of brick, laid horizontally in slightly oversailing courses adjusted to the curve of the vault; above this are two rings (in one case three) of flat, square bricks set vertically with their flat sides at right angles to the axis of the vault; these rings are covered by an outer ring of bricks set edgeways (Plate 94 *d*). We shall discuss this system later (p. 544). It is possible to see that the two best-preserved chambers on the south side were divided into an inner and outer length by a partition wall, so I conclude that the rest were similarly treated.

Above these vaulted chambers was a second storey, the rooms of which corresponded to the vaulted chambers below, for the bonding stones which project from the enclosure walls correspond in every case with the partition walls below. This upper storey, part of which still remains in the north-eastern corner and on the south side, must have had a flat wooden roof, for a series of beam holes are to be seen all along in the enclosure walls, about a metre and a half below the ramparts (Plate 94 *d*).

The ramparts were reached by a spiral staircase in the tower to the north of the entrance, but all the steps have disappeared and the ramparts can only be reached by clambering up in the south-west corner (Plate 93 *d*).

Grabar and his assistants carried out excavations here from 10th September to 30th October 1964.[1] They started work within the entrance and found that there was a vestibule 5·30 m. wide and 7 m. deep, with a stone pavement. It was flanked by two rooms of approximately the same size, each of which communicated with it by a door. The vestibule and these two rooms opened on to a portico, 5 m. deep, formed by an arcade on columns, of which five bases were recovered. The space between them varied from 4 m. in the axial one to 3·50 for the southernmost one. Parts of ten columns were found in the entrance bay, lying in a south-easterly direction, just as they had fallen. They were about 55 cm. in diameter and 3·70 m. in length and clearly belonged to the bases. Three capitals were discovered, two of which were remarkable. One was a beautiful composition carved in stucco, which formed as it were a sheath to a stone capital, apparently Corinthian.[2] Four columns were slenderer and shorter than the rest and Grabar suggests that they come from a second storey.

The second point excavated was in the south-east corner; here Grabar found the L-shaped corner pier of the arcade which clearly ran all round the enclosure in front of the rooms, and the cruciform piece of masonry belonging to the corner rooms. It looks as though the long room flanked by two doors on the east side and one (possibly two) on the west side may turn out to be part of a five-roomed *bayt*.

We now have the arcaded courtyard with rooms behind at Minya, Jabal Says, Qaṣr al-Ḥayr al-Gharbī, and Mafjar, yet Grabar actually has the nerve to say (p. 109): 'The problems of the purposes, dates, and identifications of the spectacular ruins of Qaṣr al-Ḥayr al-Sharqi still remain as major puzzles in the archaeological history of Syria.'

The Greater Enclosure is formed by a curtain wall 2·12 m. in thickness,[3] flanked by half-round towers about 4 m. in diameter, with an entrance in the centre of each side. There is a tower at each corner and six intermediate towers on each face, making twenty-eight in all. Their pitch averages 26·25 m. from axis to axis,[4] except the middle pair on each face; as these flank the four entrances their pitch is reduced to 10½ m. In addition to these four main entrances there is a small postern gate B, 1·47 m. wide (Fig. 576), to the south of the east entrance,[5] which escaped the notice of Gabriel; it was probably covered by débris, for there are signs of a clearance having been effected here. Still farther south in the same side is a third entrance B, which Gabriel calls a postern, but which we shall see served quite another purpose. This enclosure is built of larger masonry than the other, the courses varying from 50 to 70 cm. in height. Unfortunately it is in a very bad state, whole curtain walls having fallen down, and many towers are badly ruined; in fact, the south-eastern one has collapsed and been roughly rebuilt with blocks of stone laid dry. Two curtain walls on the south side have been almost entirely rebuilt in the same fashion.

As all the towers appear to have been solid, the ramparts must have been reached by staircases running up the inner face of the curtain walls, but none is visible to-day, so one must conclude with Gabriel[6] that they belonged to some of the curtain walls that have fallen. It is possible, however, in one or two places to reach the ramparts by climbing up. The parapet, unlike that of the Lesser Enclosure, is of stone; in many places it remains to a height of two courses; I measured the latter on the north side and found them to be 60 and 53 cm. respectively, total 1·13 m. with a thickness of 41 cm. As in the Lesser Enclosure, there is nothing to show what the form of the battlements was.[7] The parapet appears to have been strengthened by a series of buttresses 41 cm. square placed about 1·75 m. apart (Fig. 575).

The curtain walls and towers are not decorated with bands of brickwork, but the upper part of the

[1] *Les Annales Archéologiques de Syrie*, XV (2), pp. 107–20.

[2] *Ibid.*, p. 111 and fig. 9.

[3] Gabriel (p. 317) says 2·05; but this is what I found the thickness to be, measured at the east and south entrances. The other two have been walled up.

[4] It is only possible to measure a few (see my plan) on account of the piles of stones from the fallen curtain walls. With a couple of ladders, however, this difficulty could be overcome, for many of the towers are intact, or nearly so.

[5] Axis to axis = 11·95 m.

[6] *Loc. cit.*, p. 319.

[7] If we may trust Rousseau's sketch (*op. cit.*, figure facing p. 146) there were no battlements at all, but merely a continuous parapet joining the discharging chambers at the summits of the towers.

latter is entirely constructed of this material from a point one course below the level of the ramparts. This may still be observed in spite of the ruined state of the enclosure, on the west side—2nd, 3rd, and 6th intermediate towers—and on the north side in the 1st, 2nd, and 3rd intermediate towers from the north-west corner. In the brick upper part of these towers is a small discharging chamber with an arrow-slit to right and left, giving a flanking fire, and one pointing outwards (Fig. 575). The arrow-slits are covered by slabs of stone. Rousseau's sketch[1] shows that these towers, like those of the Lesser Enclosure, were each crowned by a brick dome.

The best-preserved curtain wall is that to the west of the northern entrance. From the rampart level to the top of the entrance measures 5·75 m. From the latter point to the present ground level is only 2·45 m., but as this entrance must have been at least 4 m. high we get a total height of about 9·75 m.

The four main entrances are almost identical (Plate 95 *a-c*); each consists of a rectangular doorway not quite 3 m. wide, with a joggled lintel surmounted by a stilted and slightly pointed relieving arch, the tympanum being filled up with masonry, the face of which is set back about 4 cm. from the face of the arch. Behind the lintel, on each side, is a hole for the beam in which the upper ends of the door spindles were set. Above each entrance is a mâchicoulis of two openings resting on three brackets, each composed of three tiers of mouldings. For some reason or other the mâchicoulis over the northern entrance is wider and rests on five elaborate brackets, the central one being decorated with a sun-flower.[2] In addition to this a small bracket, in line with the front of the mâchicoulis, projects from the side of each tower, so that the mâchicoulis balcony must have run right across from tower to tower (Plate 96 *a* and *b*). This northern entrance, following the custom of the East, was doubtless called the Ruṣāfa Gate, from the name of the city towards which it faces. Now Ruṣāfa was the chosen residence of the Khalif Hishām who built the enclosure we are discussing (see below, p. 537). I suggest that this is why the mâchicoulis over the Ruṣāfa Gate is more elaborately decorated than the others.

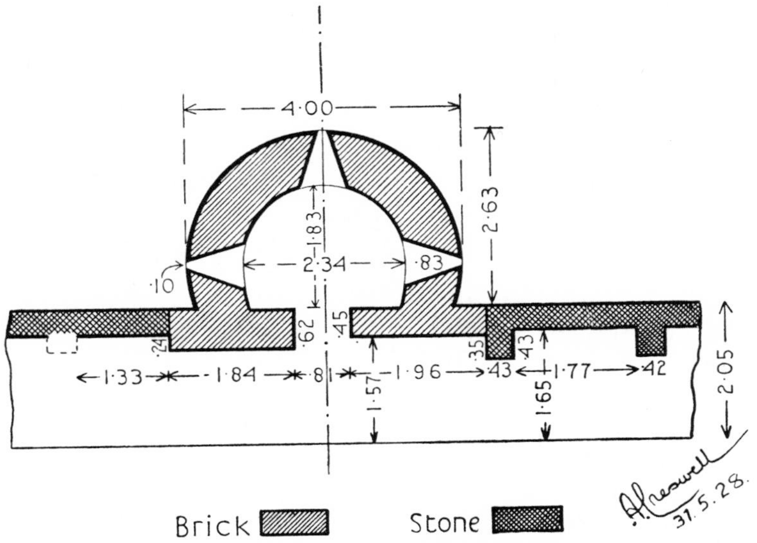

FIG. 575. QAṢR AL-ḤAYR: Greater Enclosure, plan at summit of a tower.

To return to the sunk tympanums, which are pitted with holes about 2 cm. in diameter regularly spaced 25 cm. apart; Gabriel suggests that these tympanums were embellished with a ceramic decoration and that these holes were intended to give a grip to the cement with which it was fixed.[3] Although numerous fragments of pottery, similar to Raqqa pottery, have, according to him, been found in this enclosure, I cannot bring myself to believe that ceramic decoration was used in Muslim architecture at this early date. It seems more probable that there was a panel of stucco ornament here, for stucco ornament is used, as we have seen, on the towers flanking the entrance of the Lesser Enclosure.

The interior is almost devoid of structures except for the remains of a building in the south-east corner which we shall discuss presently. The surface of the ground presents a series of mounds and craters, like ground that has been heavily shelled, caused in this case by treasure-hunters.[4] At the intersection of the two axes of the enclosure is a great rectangular excavation, E, partly filled up; it is still partly covered by a brick tunnel-vault and, as Rousseau and Gabriel have suggested, was probably a cistern. At D is a curious pointed arch springing from two piers and decorated with a coarsely executed chevron pattern.[5] It was above this arch that Rousseau saw a half-effaced Arabic inscription, of which

1 Published by Clermont-Ganneau, *loc. cit.*, pl. VIII.

2 Illustrated by Musil, *op. cit.*, fig. 24, but erroneously marked 'Western entrance'.

3 *Loc. cit.*, p. 320.

4 The same thing may be observed at Bālis, Raqqa, and no doubt many other places. Nothing can be more unfortunate, for once a site is riddled and turned upside-down in this fashion, for the sake of pottery, etc., it is spoilt for ever so far as scientific archaeological excavation is concerned. At Raqqa, for example, in addition to searching for the now famous pottery, the very foundations of buildings have been dug up to obtain the fine 'Abbāsid bricks with which the present Circassian settlement has been constructed at the south-west corner of al-Manṣūr's enclosure.

5 Illustrated by Musil, *Palmyrena*, fig. 17.

he translated part;[1] it has been re-read by Musil as: 'Al-Malik Saʿīd ibn Jamāl ad-Dīn . . . tishrīn the second, eight hundred and ten [Nov. 1407]. Manṣūr wrote this.'[2]

Cause of the Present Condition of the Two Enclosures. Parsons gives the following explanation of the sad state of these two enclosures: 'A Turkish gentleman in our caravan says, that he has been 'informed that both these towns were destroyed by the order of the emperor Amurath the fourth, on his 'return from the taking of Bagdad from the Persians [1638], as he thought them formidable places 'which some rebel pasha might occasionally possess, and bid defiance to his authority.'[3]

This, however, does not explain the peculiar nature of the damage. Any one unaccustomed to conditions in Egypt is certain to be puzzled by the way in which the walls of the two enclosures are eaten away for a distance of a metre or a metre and a half above ground level. This disintegration is accompanied by a white incrustation or efflorescence. Similar damage may be observed at Qaṣr aṭ-Ṭūba.

This disintegration is entirely a physical and not a chemical phenomenon, and is caused by the crystallization of various salts, chiefly sodium chloride (or common salt), underneath the surface of the stone. For such crystallization to take place three conditions are necessary: first the presence of salts soluble in water, second the presence of water to dissolve the salts, and thirdly opportunity for the salts to be brought to the surface of the stone and there to crystallize out by the evaporation of the water holding them in solution. Thin layers of the stone are then partly forced off by the growth of the crystals underneath.[4]

At Qaṣr al-Ḥayr the winter showers soak the ground which, like so much desert land, contains salt; the salty water is drawn up from the ground into the limestone by capillary attraction, the water evaporates at the surface of the stone, the salts crystallize out (this forms the white efflorescence), and, by the sheer force of their growth, the crystals rupture the surface of the stone and cause a thin layer to scale off. This process, repeated every winter, has even led to the collapse of several curtain walls. The same thing may be observed at Palmyra where the whole southern side of the *temenos* is in danger from the same cause; the base of the wall has been eaten away and the whole south wall is leaning inwards in an alarming fashion.[5]

The Mosque (Plates 96 *c*, 97, and 98 *a*, and Figs. 576 and 578, facing p. 532). In the south-east corner are the remains of a building, c, which must have been constructed after the enclosure was finished, for there is a complete vertical break between its masonry and the three piers which are in contact with it. Rousseau calls this building 'un corps de logis'[6] and Gabriel 'portique ou mosquée'. There can be no doubt that it is the latter,[7] the arcade running parallel to the south (i.e. qibla) wall being the façade on the ṣaḥn, and a moment's examination suffices to show that the two arcades of three arches each, which run from north to south, are nothing else but a transept, the piers being T-shaped, and the two arcades which divided the sanctuary into three aisles must have stopped against their outer faces (Plate 96 *c* and 97 *a*). The brick walls, over 4 m. high,[8] which rise above these two arcades, and which Gabriel regards as evidence of another storey, must surely be the walls of the clerestory, as in the Great Mosque at Damascus.

As for the 'isolated' pier H (Plate 96 *c* and Figs. 576 and 578, facing p. 532) which stands in a line with the northern arcade, it is of course a continuation of it; it corresponds in shape and dimensions with pier J and it is separated from the transept pier by almost exactly the same distance (7·61 against 7·57 m.). But as the one existing arch of the façade is 3·28 m. in span and the transept arch 4·80, one cannot imagine that the other arches, which spring from exactly the same level, were 7·57 m. in span, for that would involve an impossible rise, impossible because it would completely derange the façade. No, there must be a support missing on each side of the transept. And there, lying on the ground at the very spot required,

1 *Op. cit.*, p. 150.

2 *Op. cit.*, p. 77.

3 *Op. cit.*, p. 86; see also p. 89.

4 See Lucas (A.), *Disintegration and Preservation of Building Stones in Egypt* (National Printing Dept., Cairo, 1902), pp. 1–12; 2nd ed. (1915), pp. 2–5. For exactly the same phenomenon in Sind, see Cousens, in the *Archaeological Survey of India: Annual Report, 1909–10*, p. 82; and his *Antiquities of Sind* (*Archaeological Survey of India, New Imperial Series*, Vol. XLVI), pp. 111 and 122.

5 The Service of Antiquities in 1930 built a number of buttresses to prevent its collapse.

6 *Op. cit.*, p. 151.

7 Musil had already recognized it as a mosque, *Palmyrena*, p. 77.

8 Timber was let into this brickwork between every eleven courses; the timber has perished, but the grooves which it occupied remain (see Plates 96 *c* and 97 *a*).

is a column composed of four drums of black granite about 54 cm. in diameter (c in Fig. 576). On the other side of the transept is a similar column (at c[1]) more than half-buried in earth, and upside-down on the ground in front of the transept arch is a Corinthian capital, D. Restoring our façade accordingly we get a central arch 4·80 m. in span flanked by three of 3·25 (Fig. 576). But why are piers J and H

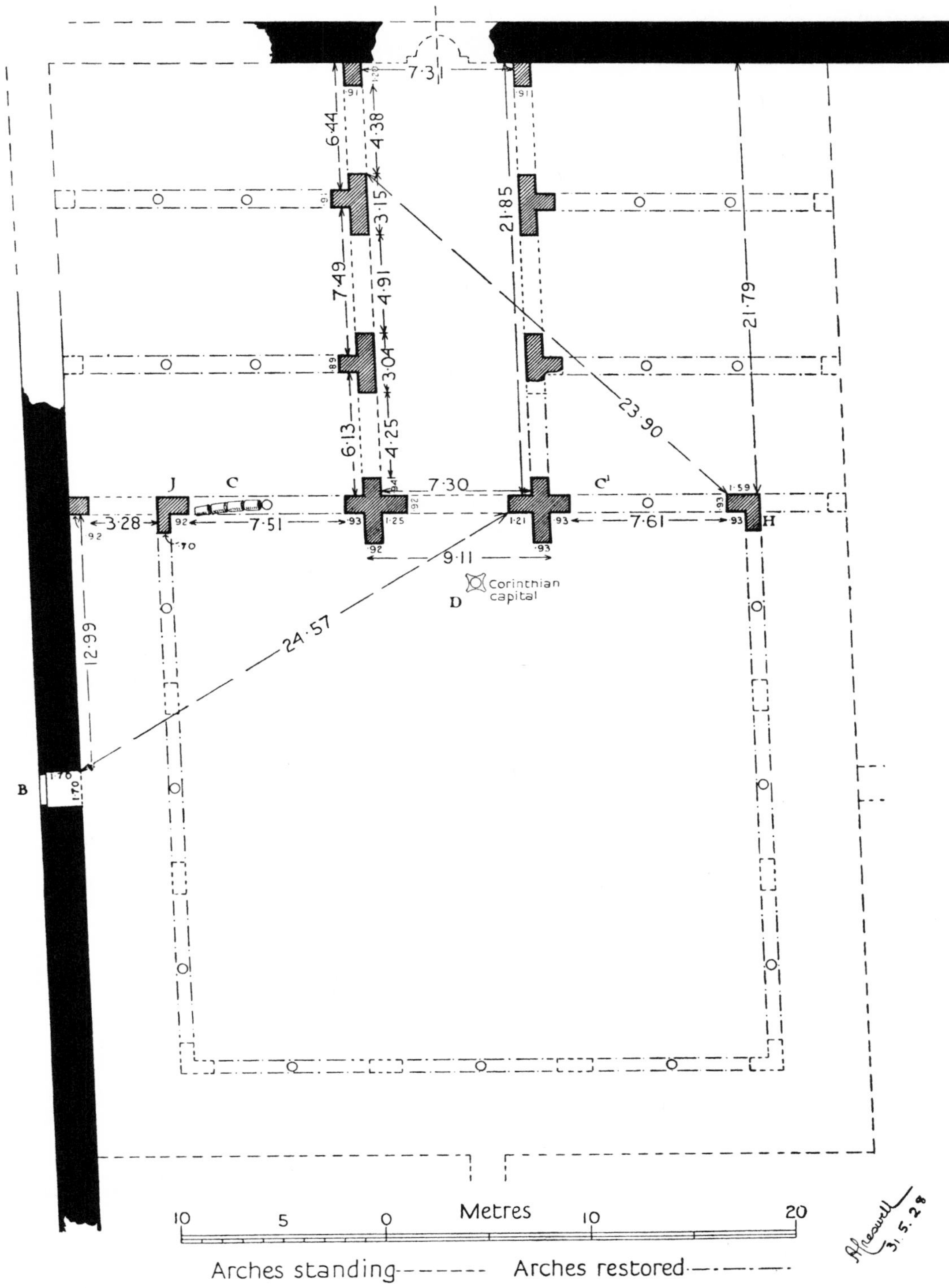

FIG. 576. QAṢR AL-ḤAYR: Greater Enclosure. Plan of mosque.

L-shaped? Surely because they were the corner piers of the ṣaḥn from which the side *riwāqs* took off. Let us therefore repeat the spacing of the façade along the sides. This gives us a ṣaḥn 28 m. square. The level of the ceilings of these *riwāqs* is given by the beam-holes A (Fig. 578, facing p. 532).

As for the so-called postern gate B, which is placed, not close against the side of a tower like the true postern, but almost in the centre of a curtain wall, a glance at the plan shows that it must have been intended to give direct access from the exterior into the ṣaḥn of the mosque, exactly as in the palace mosque at Khirbet al-Minya (above, p. 383 and Fig. 448). Another glance at the plan brings additional confirmation to this view, for the axis of B corresponds almost exactly with the centre of the west side of the ṣaḥn in my proposed restoration, the difference being less than 30 cm.

If we assume the north wall of the ṣaḥn to have abutted against a tower, as the façade of the sanctuary actually does, then we have just room for a ṣaḥn bounded by side *riwāqs* of six arches each.

The arches of the sanctuary must have corresponded to those of the façade, but from what did they spring, piers or columns? On the analogy of the Great Mosque at Damascus, one would expect them to have sprung from columns, and evidence to that effect is fortunately provided by Sir Eyre Coote, who says: 'We saw a number of arches supported by pillars of white marble finely polished; as the rubbish 'had covered up one half, we could only see the upper part; the capitals had double flowers, exceedingly 'well finished; several broken pillars of marble were scattered about the area, . . .'[1] This was in 1771; an anonymous Englishman (Evers) in 1779 says: '. . . one entire pillar of black marble is still standing, as also one of oriental granite, the capital of which seems to be of the Corinthian order.'[2] When Rousseau passed in 1807 only the existing arcades were left.[3]

It is not possible to say how high the transept originally was; I have merely shown its minimum height as fixed by the present height of the brick walls which rise above its arches. It may well have been one or two metres higher. But whether my reconstruction of this, the third oldest of existing congregational mosques, is correct or not, there is not very much margin for error, and the actual remains suffice to confirm the dominating influence of the Great Mosque of Damascus on the early mosques of Syria.

The east wall of the sanctuary and half the south wall, including the part which must have contained the miḥrāb, have fallen, but, in spite of its loss, it is surprising that any doubt has ever existed as to the function of this building which, fortunately, is dated.

FORM OF THE ARCHES. The five existing arches of the transept are stilted and very slightly pointed, and the central arch of the transept is very slightly pointed but not stilted (Plate 97 *a–b*). The left-hand arch of the façade is more pointed and has a distinct return (Plate 98 *a*); it is the earliest example of a pointed horse-shoe arch known to me.

THE DATE. Rousseau found an inscription high up on pier H, and had it transported to Aleppo, where he made a careful sketch of it.[4] The inscription reads: 'Bismillāh . . . This city (*madīna*) has 'been built by order of 'Abd Allāh Hishām, Prince of Believers. This is one of the monuments which 'the inhabitants of Ḥomṣ have erected by the hands of Sulaymān the son of 'Ubayd in the year '[1]10'[5] [= A.D. 728/9].

THE MINARET. Between the two enclosures is a square tower, F, averaging 2·94 m. a side, with an entrance to its spiral staircase in the south face, which some writers have regarded as a watch-tower.[6] Any watching required could have been done from the ramparts on either side, which command the same field, and it is difficult to imagine what additional advantage this isolated tower could have had, to say nothing of the difficulty of provisioning its garrison during a siege. But the identification of Rousseau's 'corps de logis' as a mosque throws a new light on the function of this tower, which I believe was a minaret intended to serve the inhabitants of both enclosures.[7] It is about 10 m. in height, but its upper part is missing. Its present summit, therefore, is just on a level with what must have been the level of the parapet of the Lesser Enclosure. It may well have been two or three metres higher, and so have commanded both enclosures. If it really is a minaret and contemporary with the two enclosures, then it is the third oldest existing minaret in Islam.[8] Its form, a perfectly plain square shaft, is quite in keeping with what has been said above (pp. 491–3) regarding the architectural origin of the minaret.

THE HYDRAULIC WORKS. When one goes to Qaṣr al-Ḥayr from Sukhna, that is to say, when one approaches from the south-west, one sees another structure at some little distance on the right which,

[1] *Loc. cit.*, p. 207. Capper in 1777 also mentions columns; *op. cit.*, 2nd ed., p. 66.

[2] *Journey from Bassora to Baghdad*, p. 78.

[3] *Op. cit.*, pp. 150–51 and plate facing, p. 146.

[4] This sketch, although in his diary, was not published by Poinssot, but may be found reproduced with a commentary by Clermont-Ganneau, in his *R.A.O.*, III, pp. 285–90 and pl. VIII.

[5] Rousseau, *op. cit.*, p. 151; Clermont-Ganneau, *loc. cit.*; Dussaud, *op. cit.*, p. 259; Gabriel, *loc. cit.*, p. 321; and Wiet, *Répertoire*, I, pp. 23–4.

[6] E.g. Gabriel, *loc. cit.*, p. 322.

[7] Clermont-Ganneau thought that it might be a minaret; *Recueil d'archéologie orientale*, III, p. 289.

[8] Gabriel (*loc. cit.*, p. 321, n. 3) thinks that it is 'bien de date plus récente que le grand ḳaṣr', but he does not specify his reasons.

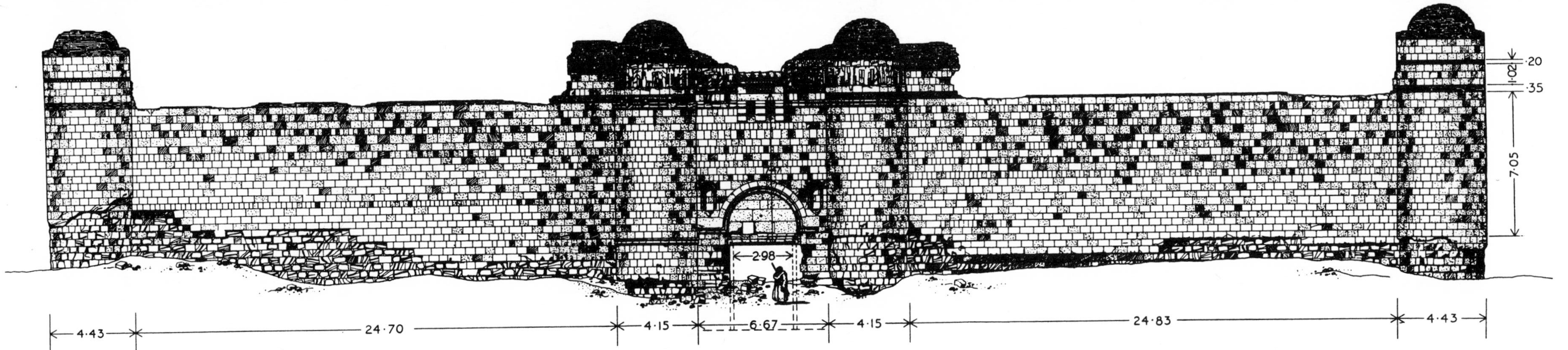

FIG. 577. QASR AL-HAYR ASH-SHARQI: Lesser enclosure, west façade. Measured by K. A. C. Creswell and drawn by M. Lyon

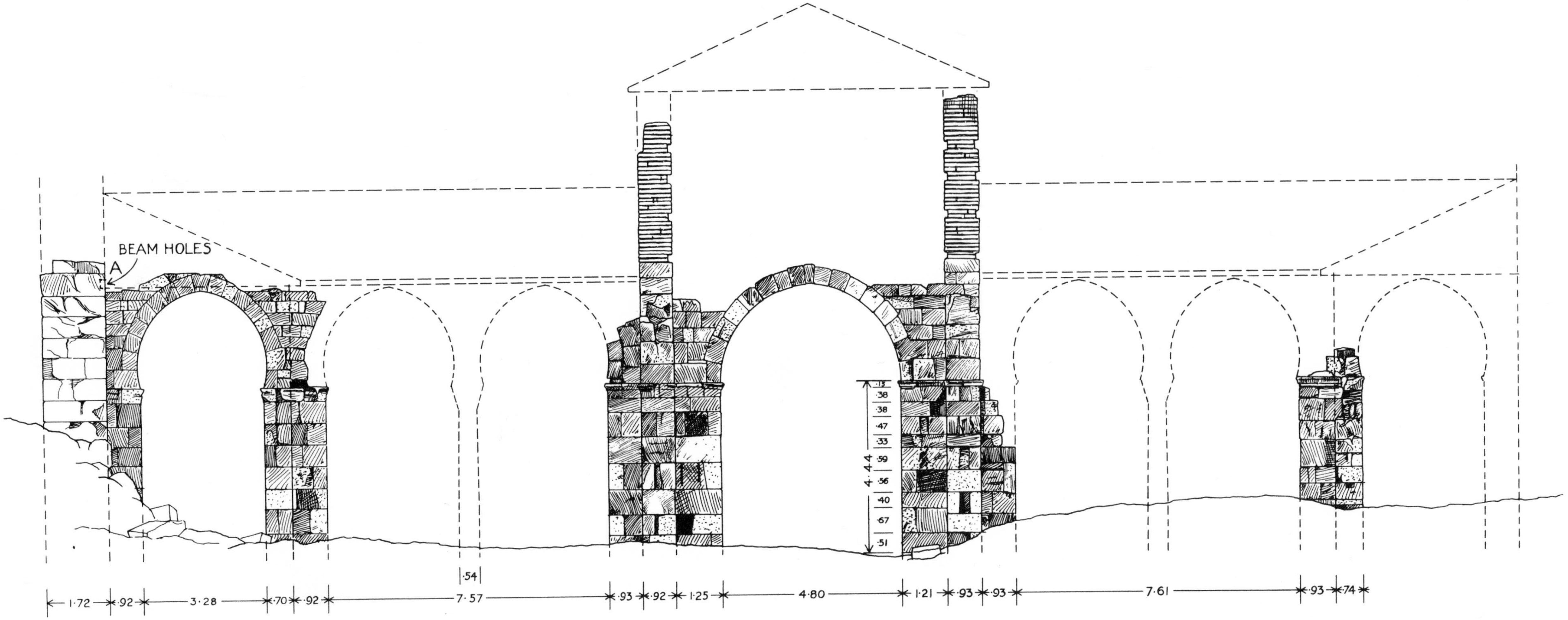

FIG. 578. QASR AL-HAYR ASH-SHARQI: Façade of Sanctuary of Mosque. Measured by K. A. C. Creswell and drawn by M. Lyon

when approached, resolves itself into two lengths of wall, a little over 4 m. in height, running approximately north-west and north-east (Plate 98 *c* and Figs. 579–81). These two lengths, which measure 63 m. and 162 m. respectively, meet at an angle of about 80°. These walls, on their outer faces, are strengthened by semicircular buttresses placed about 12 m. from axis to axis. On the other side are rough projections of masonry which are probably the remains of corresponding buttresses; the triangular form given to them in Gabriel's drawing (Fig. 581) is, as he points out, conjectural.[1]

In each bay at ground level are arched openings 1·10 m. wide and 2·05 m. high; the sills are formed of stone slabs which appear to have been polished by the flow of water. The arches, which are semi-

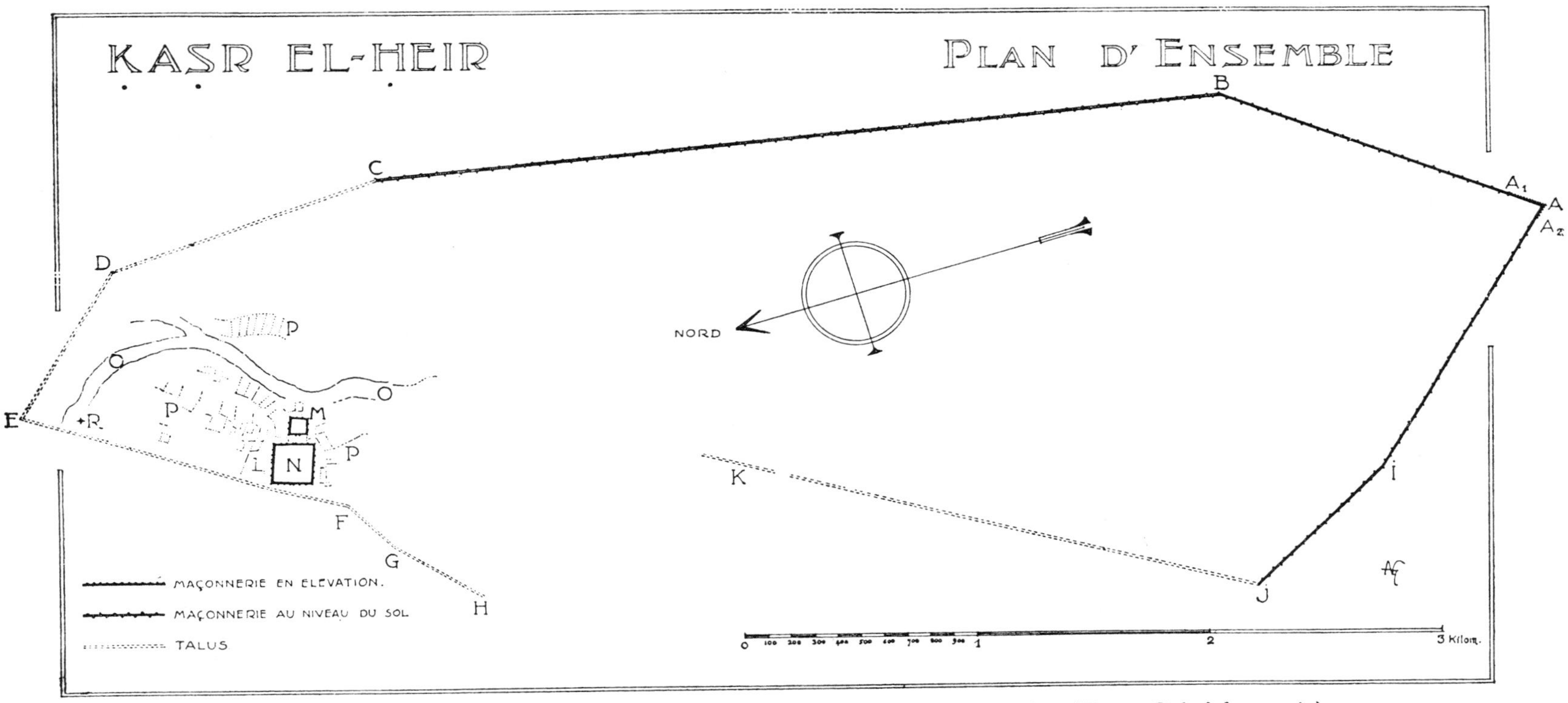

FIG. 579. QAṢR AL-ḤAYR: The two enclosures and the hydraulic works. (From Gabriel, *op. cit.*)

circular in form, are of stone on their inner and brick on their outer faces. The thickness of the wall (1·55 m.) is reduced to 1·10 m. by a glacis of two courses of masonry which slopes back at an angle of 45° immediately above the extrados of the arches. Above the glacis is a string course of five courses of brick,[2] then a course of stone, and a covering course of flat slabs, fragments of which are still preserved here and there.

The two bays next the point of junction are shorter than the rest and have only one opening each on account of a little vaulted chamber which occupies the angle; the remainder, four to the north-west and twelve to the north-east, are approximately uniform in length and have four openings each, except in two cases—the third bay to the north-east where there are five openings, and the fourth which has three only.

The length running north-west (A—A_2) is prolonged without change of direction for 1,360 m. (A_2—I) by another wall, now destroyed almost to ground level. It is 1·12 m. thick with a rubble core and has rounded buttresses 32 m. apart, placed so that those on the inner face come midway between those on the outer. After this the wall changes its bearing and runs in a direction slightly more to the north for 750 m. (I—J). From J a low ridge runs north-east in a straight line for about 2 km. before losing itself in the ground.

Let us now return to our starting-point. The north-east length of wall is prolonged by another wall (A_1—B) similar to A_2—I and 1,300 m. in length. This wall changes its direction at B and runs almost due north for 3,600 m. (B—C). Up to this point the wall retains its constructive features, but after C only a ridge can be distinguished, running due north for 1,200 m. (C—D). From D it runs north-west for 750 m. to E. After E its traces become almost unrecognizable, but possibly the course marked by Gabriel may be justified.

[1] *Op. cit.*, p. 307.

[2] The bricks measure 30×30×4 cm., and the joints 2·5 cm.

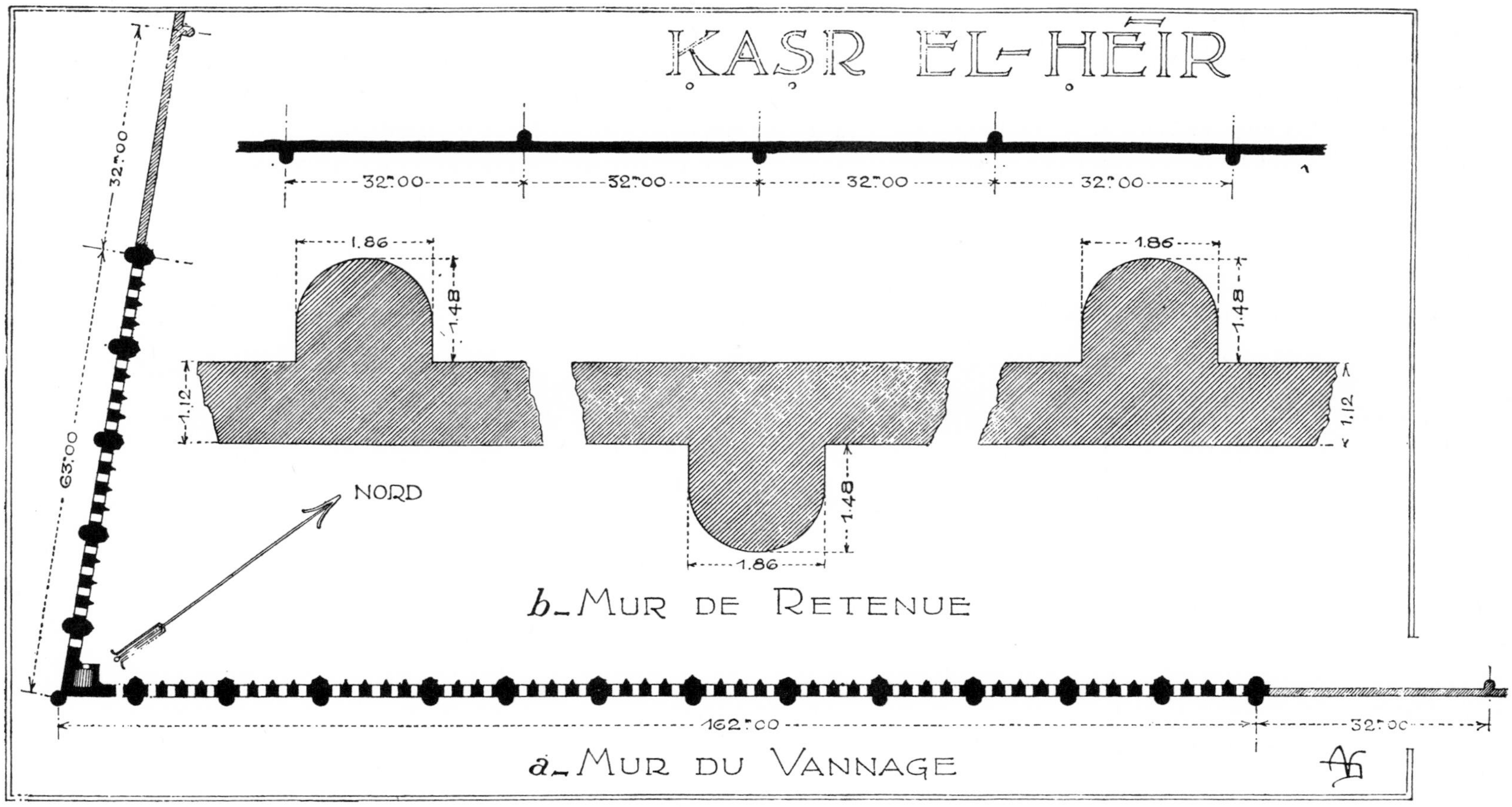

Fig. 580. Qaṣr al-Ḥayr: The Dam, plan.
(From Gabriel, *op. cit.*)

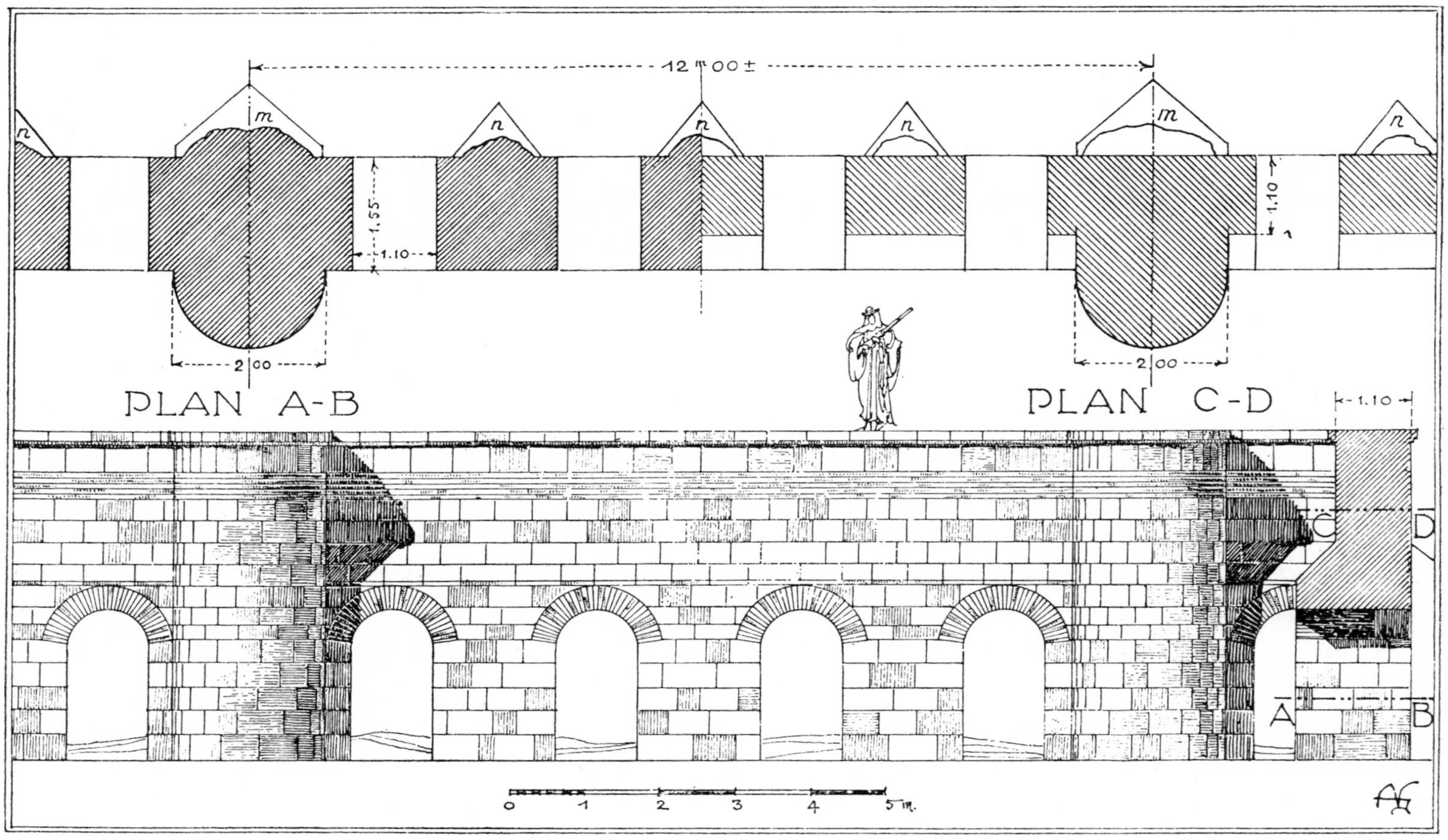

Fig. 581. Qaṣr al-Ḥayr: The Dam, elevation.
(From Gabriel, *op. cit.*)

Gabriel points out that these walls cannot belong to a fortified enclosure; the towers, for example, which only project a metre, are merely buttresses, and their alternation on the two faces of the wall is contrary to the principles of fortification.[1] Finally the sluice gates show that the whole was designed for the retention of water, which the sluice gates were intended to control; and he draws a very interesting comparison with the type of reservoir met with in Tunisia (e.g. the Aghlabid cisterns, outside the Bāb Tūnis at Qairawān, for which see Vol. II, 1st. ed.), the walls of which exhibit the same alternation of rounded buttresses on either face.

According to his theory there must therefore have been, at certain seasons of the year, a shallow artificial lake extending southwards from Qaṣr al-Ḥayr, with a maximum width of 2 km. and a length of over 5 km.

Whence came the water supply? Gabriel, in the limited time at his disposal, did not locate any aqueduct, nor did I, but Rousseau speaks of an aqueduct coming from Kowan (? ʿAin al-Kōm, as Eyles Irwin says, quoted below) which he places four leagues to the north.[2] Musil on his map[3] marks two aqueducts coming from Ṭaiyiba (to the north-west); one, marked 'Ḳenāt an-Nedwijje', passes to the north of Ṭaiyiba, the other, marked 'Ḳenāt as-Shejm', passes to the south of the same place. Sir Eyre Coote refers vaguely to an aqueduct, as follows: 'There was the ruin of an aqueduct that came from the mountains on the right to this palace, and from thence across the pain into the other building.'[4]

Now the name *qanāt* indicates that these aqueducts did not consist of a file of arches carrying a water channel, but rather a subterranean channel cut well below the surface and connected with it by vertical shafts at intervals of 30 or 40 yards, a type of work in universal use in Persia and Central Asia; in the latter region it is designated under the name *kārīz*.[5] It is found as far west as Morocco.[6]

And, in confirmation, here is what Irwin saw in 1781: 'We quitted our ground about seven this 'morning, and leaving Teibe to our right, kept an E.S.E. course. . . . At nine o'clock the advanced 'party on horseback hit, by accident, on a broken aqueduct. This raising our curiosity, we alighted, 'and descended into the broken place, where we found the building to be of hewn stone and neat work-'manship. Our Arabs tell us, that this aqueduct runs from the wells of Il Coom, to Kaser Il Aukhein, 'a ruined structure, which we are to visit this forenoon. One of our company discharged a musket into 'the aqueduct, in order to start any game that might be concealed in it. This effect was not produced; 'but the report of the musket served to disclose the direction, in which the channel run [*sic*]. As we advanced 'we traced the aqueduct on the road, by the wells which opened into it at different places, for the con-'viency of drawing water. A very little expence might restore this antient work to its original use.'[7]

Seyrig, guided by a villager, was able to follow one of these *qanāts* which starts at ʿAin al-Kōm and follows the bottom of a *wādī* for more than 30 km. to within about 1 km. from the small set of sluice gates at R. The *qanāt* is only visible in the last part of its course, where the carefully dressed extrados of its vault emerges above the ground in several places. In the earlier part of its course, however, it can be traced by its numerous peep-holes and the mounds near them, composed of earth taken out when the aqueduct has been cleaned. Another *qanāt*, which he did not follow, flows into the former at a point about 10 km. from ʿAin al-Kōm.[8]

I accepted this theory in the first edition of this work, but Seyrig in 1931 suggested that instead of a lake there was, on the contrary, 'a vast garden enclosure protected by a defensive work that would certainly not have resisted a sufficiently organized enemy, but which would suffice to repulse a razzia such as might be feared from nomad tribes'.[9] Gabriel contested this suggestion[10] but Seyrig, being still convinced that he was right, decided to make further researches on the spot.

He found that the long walls of stone, especially on the west side of the enclosure, were still surmounted in places by remains of a wall of mud bricks, 42 cm. square and 9 cm. thick. It was two and a half bricks thick, i.e. 1·06 m.; allowing for the mud bond it must have been 1·10 m. thick like the stone part below it. In some places the wall had fallen *en bloc* and some of the fallen pieces consisted

1 *Loc. cit.*, p. 309.
2 *Op. cit.*, p. 153.
3 *Map of Northern Arabia*, New York, 1927.
4 *Loc. cit.*, p. 207.
5 See Streck's article, *Ḳanāt*, in the *Encyclopaedia of Islām*, II, pp. 708–9; and Bogdanov, in *Islamic Culture*, V, pp. 410–11. For an excellent article on the construction of *qanāts* in Persia, see E. Noel, *Qanats*, in the *Journal of the Royal Central Asian Socy.*, XXXI, pp. 191–202.
6 Harris (W. B.), *Tafilet*, pp. 215–16.
7 *Op. cit.*, 3rd ed., II, p. 300.
8 *Syria*, XV, p. 28.
9 *Syria*, XII, pp. 317–18.
10 *Ibid.*, XIII, pp. 317–18.

of twenty courses, equal to fully 2 m. which, added to 1·50 m. for the stone wall, gives 3·50 m. for the minimum total height, and it may well have been even more. Amongst the débris were a number of well-cut blocks of stone which may have been cap-stones.

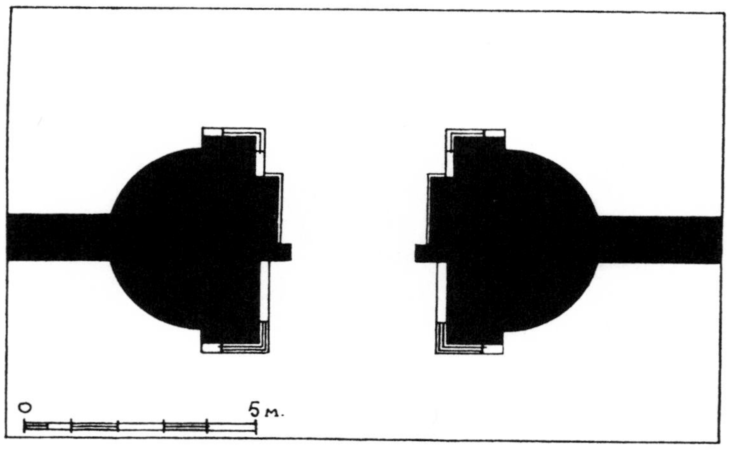

FIG. 582. QAṢR AL-ḤAYR ASH-SHARQĪ: One of the gates of the *ḥayr*. (From Seyrig, *loc. cit.*)

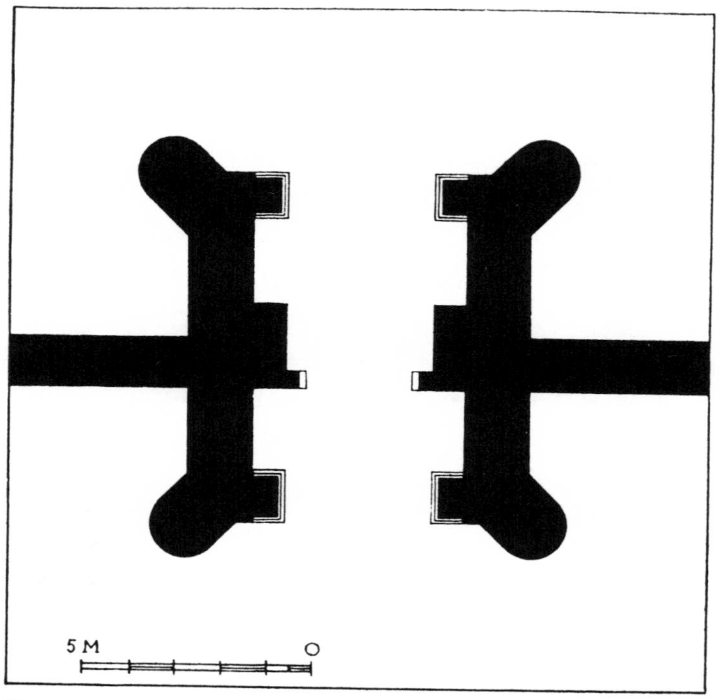

FIG. 583. QAṢR AL-ḤAYR ASH-SHARQĪ: Another gate. (From Seyrig, *loc. cit.*)

He also found that the semicircular buttresses were continued upwards by courses of mud bricks which were not square but trapezoidal in form, so as to facilitate their setting in a semicircle. Seyrig remarks: 'It is evidently the presence of the wall of bricks that 'has compelled the builder to place his buttresses, the 'utility of which would appear doubtful if the height 'had been 1·50 m. only, on both faces of the wall.'

Seyrig was able to follow JK to a point, north of O where it stops almost in a line with the south side of the Greater Enclosure. In addition to this he actually discovered the bases of two monumental entrances. The first (Fig. 582) about 100 m. to the south of B, is provided with a projecting sill. The second about one kilometre north of J, is of the remarkable form shown in Fig. 583, which might be described as a miniature double *propugnaculum* with corner buttresses. Both clearly form one with the long walls being, like them, of stone below and brick above.

He also found a second set of sluice gates at R, the highest point of the enclosure, standing at least 2 m. above the ground level, and of the same type as that described above. At least four bays were visible, and there may have been a few more but scarcely more than a dozen.

He concludes that we have to do with a great enclosed garden or *paradeisos*, 850 hectares in area, protected by a wall strong enough to keep out Bedawīn pillaging parties. This explains the modern name Bustān (garden) given to this area by the villagers of Sukhna and Ṭaiyiba.

THE MEANING OF THE WORD AL-ḤAYR. But what does the word *ḥayr* mean? I submit quotations from two early Arabic historians which I maintain throw light on this question.[1]

(1) Ya'qūbī, describing the foundation of Sāmarrā by the Khalif al-Mu'taṣim in A.D. 836, says: 'And wherever these streets of al-Ḥayr touched land granted to other people, he would order the wall '[of al-Ḥayr] to be built farther back. Behind the wall were wild animals, gazelles, wild asses, deer, 'hares and ostriches, kept in by an enclosing wall, in a fine broad open tract.'[2]

(2) Miskawaih, under the year 315 H. (925/6) says: 'This year there was a rising of the disbanded 'cavalry, who went out to the Oratory, plundered the Palace called ath-Thurayyā (the Palace of the 'Pleiades at Baghdād), *and slaughtered the game in the Ḥayr*.'[3]

I maintain, therefore, that the enclosure 5 km. long and 1,500 m. wide at Qaṣr al-Ḥayr was neither an artificial lake nor a garden, but a game preserve for the Khalif Hishām, and that the walls were meant, not to keep the Bedawīn out but to keep the animals in.

In other words it was a *Paradeisos*, the very word used by Theophanes, when speaking of the works of

[1] The following first appeared in 1937 in *Syria*, XVIII, pp. 232–3.
[2] *Buldān*, p. 263.
[3] Text of Amedroz and Margoliouth, I, p. 159; transl., I, p. 179.

the Khalif Hishām in the desert; 'And he began to found palaces in open country and town, and to create sown fields and *Paradeisous*, and to make water channels.'[1]

The name Qaṣr al-Ḥayr should therefore be translated as 'Palace of the Game Preserve'.

The Date. We have a fixed point for the dating in the inscription of 110 H. (728/9) seen by Rousseau on a pier of the mosque. This inscription dates the Greater Enclosure, for it refers to the *madīna* (city) built for the Khalif Hishām. The mosque cannot be earlier, for its east and south sides are formed by the city walls, and I believe it to have been the city mosque, expressly built immediately after the enclosure was completed.

As for the Lesser Enclosure, Gabriel points out[2] that it is of mixed construction, stone and brick being employed together as at Qaṣr Ibn Wardān and Mshattā, with this difference, that at Qaṣr Ibn Wardān the courses of brickwork alternate regularly with courses of stone after the Byzantine fashion, whereas at Mshattā the outer walls are *entirely* of stone and the inner *entirely* of brick. The Lesser Enclosure at Qaṣr al-Ḥayr therefore occupies an intermediate position; a band of five courses of brickwork exists near the summit of the wall, where it serves to separate the curtain wall proper from the parapet, and at the same time marks the level of the rampart walk. It therefore plays a purely aesthetic role. In all three buildings the vaults are entirely of brick. Gabriel goes on to point out that, in the Lesser Enclosure, we have Mesopotamian elements, such as the stucco panels at the top of the entrance towers, and the technique of the brickwork (joints thinner than the bricks, instead of equal to them in thickness, as in Byzantine work at Qaṣr Ibn Wardān and Bālis), mixed with Syrian elements such as the finely jointed masonry, semicircular entrance arch,[3] mouldings, etc. Finally, he comes to the conclusion that it may be considered on the one hand as one of the stages that marked the diffusion eastward of structural and decorative forms belonging to Syria, and on the other hand as an instructive example of the way in which Syrian architecture enriched itself by ingenious, economic, and rapid processes borrowed from the East.[4] Yet instead of taking this, as might have been expected, as an argument for an Umayyad date, when the two regions involved formed part of one empire for the first time, and when contemporary documents show that workmen were sent from one part of the empire to another to be employed on public works, e.g. from Persia to Mekka (above, p. 63), from Egypt and Syria to Madīna (above, pp. 142–3, and from Egypt to Damascus (above, p. 151) and Jerusalem (p. 373),[5] facts which would lead us to expect the very blending of technical processes observed at Qaṣr al-Ḥayr, he decides to place it and the irrigation works in the fifth to sixth centuries, or a little later at the end of the sixth century.

However, my argument that this blending of technical processes indicates an Umayyad date is strongly reinforced by two documents which, in my opinion, cast a decisive light upon the matter: (1) Ibn ash-Shiḥna, speaking of Hishām, says: 'And he went out to Ruṣāfa because it was in the desert, and for that reason he had two castles (*qaṣrayn*) built there';[6] and (2) Theophanes (d. 818) says: 'And he (Hishām) began to found palaces in country and town, and to create sown fields and gardens and to make water channels (?).'[7]

Thus we have: (1) Hishām built two castles in the desert of Ruṣāfa; we have seen that the Greater Enclosure is one, therefore it is difficult to avoid the conclusion that the Lesser Enclosure is the other; (2) he carried out irrigation works and created gardens and fields in open country. The open country referred to must be the desert of Ruṣāfa, which was his known place of residence,[8] so we are brought to the region mentioned by Ṭabarī and Ibn ash-Shiḥna, and there can be little room for doubt that the irrigation works referred to are those described above.

1 Bonn ed., p. 620; de Boor's ed., p. 403.

2 *Op. cit.*, pp. 324–5.

3 Gabriel over-emphasizes this, saying (p. 327): 'les constructeurs du petit château avaient systématiquement proscrit' the pointed form! This is the *only* arch in the enclosure, whereas in the other enclosure there are eleven (four for the gates and seven in the mosque). But many of the vaults in the Lesser Enclosure have a pointed form (see Plate 93 *d*).

4 *Loc. cit.*, p. 327.

5 Bell, *Translations of the Greek Aphrodito Papyri in the British Museum*, in *Der Islam*, II, p. 383.

6 *Rauḍa*, Leyden MS., fol. 82. The late Maḥmūd 'Aqqūsh pointed out to me that this passage must have been taken from Ṭabarī, II, p. 1738, ll. 4–5, where the same fact is related in almost the same words.

7 Under year 6216 = A. D. 725; Bonn ed., p. 620; de Boor's ed., p. 403: *Καὶ ἤρξατο κτίζειν κατὰ χώραν καὶ πόλιν παλάτια, καὶ κατασπορὰς ποιεῖν καὶ παραδείσους, καὶ ὕδατα ἐκβάλλειν.*

8 See above, p. 513.

Finally we have: (1) The Greater Enclosure (*madīna*) linked with Hishām by Rousseau's inscription of 110 H. (728/9); (2) The Lesser, or Royal Enclosure linked with it by Ṭabarī's reference to *qaṣrayn* (the dual of *qaṣr*); (3) The Lesser Enclosure linked with the irrigation works by the close similarity of its masonry decorated with a string course of brick;[1] and (4) the irrigation works linked with Hishām by the text of Theophanes.

These three structures being thus indissolubly interlocked, and one being due to Hishām in 110 H., I attribute all three to him *c.* 110 H. (= A. D. 728/9).

ARCHITECTURAL ORIGINS

JOGGLED VOUSSOIRS, although rare before the rise of Islam, are found scattered over a very wide area extending from Spain to the Euphrates. They are employed in a Roman bridge, over the Salado, near Villa del Rio (Fig. 584, facing p. 466), near Km. 53 on the road from Cadiz to Madrid, and also in another Roman bridge, over the Pedroches, 3 km. from Cordova, of which the joggled springer blocks of the arches still remain.[2] They also occur in the Roman theatre at Orange (Fig. 585), which was probably begun shortly after the foundation of the town in 46 B.C., and finished under Augustus (30 B.C.–A.D. 15).[3] They also occur at Spalato in the Porta Aurea (Fig. 586), facing p. 542)[4] and the Porta Ferrea[5] of Diocletian's palace, built *c.* A.D. 303–5,[6] and at Ravenna, where eight semicircular arches with joggled voussoirs (Fig. 587, facing p. 542) occur in the lower storey of Theodoric's mausoleum, which was built *c.* A.D. 519.[7]

In Egypt this feature first appears in Ptolemaic times, 'when it is found, among other places, in the tombs of Kōm Abū Billo in the Delta (Fig. 588). In these tombs, which are of limestone, the arch is rather ovoid than semicircular, with a span of some seven feet'.[8]

This feature is also found in the pre-Muslim architecture of Syria: (1) at Jerusalem where a doorway, in a piece of wall belonging to the edifices which surrounded the Roman Forum of Aelia Capitolina, is spanned by a lintel with a relieving arch above, the voussoirs of which are joggled in a slightly more elaborate manner:[9] according to Vincent it cannot be later than Constantine; (2) in two transverse arches of 10 m. span (Fig. 589) belonging to a ruined church at Ṣamma in the Ḥaurān, which Butler attributes to the early part of the fourth century;[10] (3) at Bethlehem, in the Church of the Nativity, where the central doorway of the façade of the narthex (Fig. 590) is covered by a horizontal arch with joggled voussoirs of the simplest type;[11] (4) at Ruṣāfa, in the Basilica of Sergios, *c.* A.D. 600, where the nave arches are built in two rings, the inner having joggled voussoirs (Fig. 591, facing p. 542);[12] and (5) at Jerusalem over the lateral entrance on the south side of the Golden Gate, which I have attributed to Modestus between A.D. 616 and 629 (above, pp. 463–5).

The joggled voussoirs of Qaṣr al-Ḥayr were no doubt directly derived from Ruṣāfa, which is only a little over forty miles away, and the seat of the Khalif who built these two enclosures.

[1] Admitted by Gabriel: '. . . ils offrent avec le petit château de telles similitudes de construction, qu'on peut sans aucun doute les dater de la même époque'; *loc. cit.*, p. 327; and again, 'on retrouve dans ces murs, les matériaux, calcaire et briques, employés dans le petit ḳaṣr. Ils offrent les mêmes échantillons, sont mis en œuvre suivant les mêmes procédés et témoignent des mêmes qualités techniques'; p. 309.

[2] I owe this information to Don Félix Hernández, who very kindly took me to see the first-named bridge.

[3] Formigé (Jules), *Remarques diverses sur les théâtres romains à propos de ceux d'Arles et d'Orange*, *Mém. de l'Acad. des Inscr. et Belles-Lettres*, XIII, pp. 26–8.

[4] For a beautifully executed detail drawing, see Monneret de Villard, *Les Couvents près de Sohâg*, fig. 108.

[5] For an illustration of the Porta Ferrea, see Hébrard and Zeiller, *Le Palais de Dioclétien*, figs. on pp. 45 and 48; and Jackson (T. G.), *Byzantine and Romanesque Architecture*, I, fig. 5.

[6] Hébrard and Zeiller, *op. cit.*, pp. 155 ff. and 172; and Jackson, *op. cit.*, I, p. 21.

[7] Rivoira, *Lombardic Architecture*, I, pp. 53–5, and his *Roman Architecture*, pp. 197–9.

[8] Somers Clarke and Engelbach, *Ancient Egyptian Masonry*, p. 187 and fig. 224. Mr. Engelbach, at my request, very kindly looked up the Egyptian Museum Register containing an inventory of the jewellery and other objects found in this tomb, and informed me that all were undoubtedly of the Ptolemaic period.

[9] Vincent and Abel, *Jérusalem*, II, p. 82 and fig. 51.

[10] *Ancient Architecture in Syria, Sect. A: Southern Syria*, pp. 134–5 and Ill. 111–12; also H. Glück, *Der Breit- und Langhausbau in Syrien; Zeitschr. für Geschichte der Architektur*, Beiheft 14, p. 12 and Abb. 2; and Beyer, *Der syrische Kirchenbau*, p. 115 and Abb. 72.

[11] See Harvey, Lethaby, etc., *The Church of the Nativity*, fig. 17 and pl. VI; and Vincent and Abel, *Bethléem*, fig. 35 and pl. IV, partly reproduced here. The researches of Harvey and Richmond in 1934 have shown that the whole of this wall and its doors must date from the alterations of Justinian; *Q.D.A.P.*, V, pp. 75 ff. and Plate XXXVI.

[12] Spanner and Guyer, *Rusafa*, pp. 52–5 and Taf. 14; see also Sarre and Herzfeld, *Archäologische Reise*, Taf. LIX, right-hand top corner.

A curious counterfeited example occurs at Qaṣr al-Mudakhkhin, near the point where the old Roman road from Antioch enters the plain of Sermedā. On the north side of a little chapel, a long stone, placed above the lintel, is cut to form a segmental arch. The face of the stone is carved with deep lines that simulate the joints of voussoirs, each joint being provided with a mortice and tenon (Fig. 592).[1]

The next example after Qaṣr al-Ḥayr is found in the Kharpūt Gate at Diyārbakr. In the left salient, above a niche, is a lintel hollowed out underneath; above this is a shallow relieving arch of three

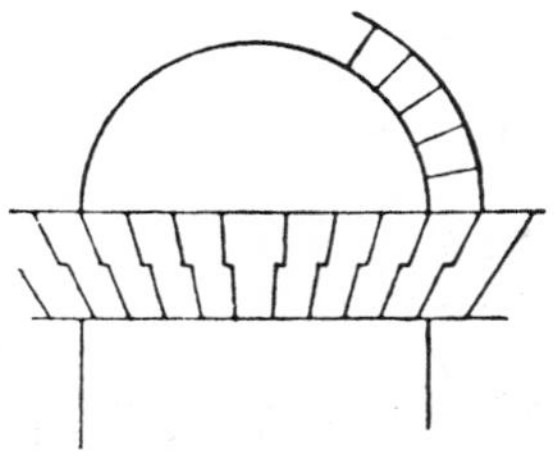

FIG. 585. ORANGE: Joggled voussoirs in Roman theatre. (From Sturgis, *History of Architecture.*)

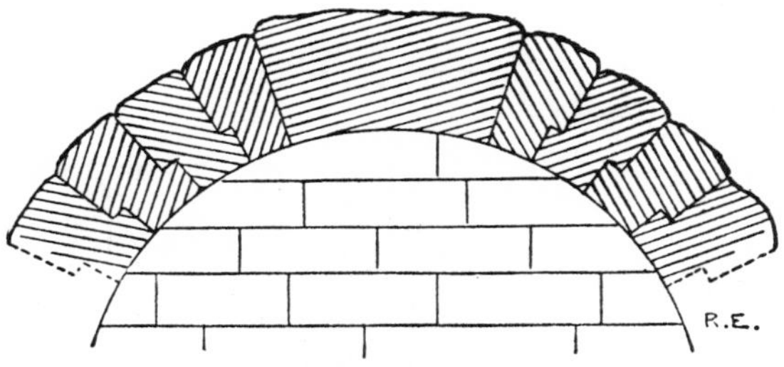

FIG. 588. KŌM ABŪ BILLO: Joggled arch in Ptolemaic tomb. (From Somers Clarke and Engelbach, *op. cit.*)

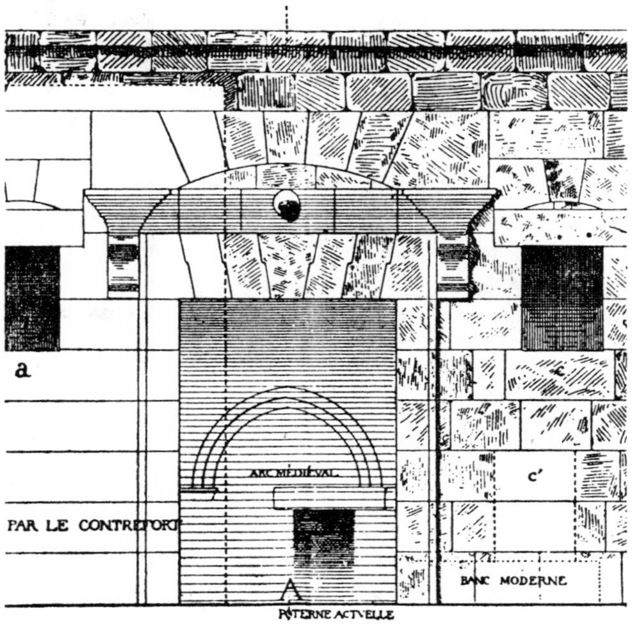

FIG. 590. BETHLEHEM: Church of the Nativity, joggled voussoirs. (From Vincent and Abel, *op. cit.*)

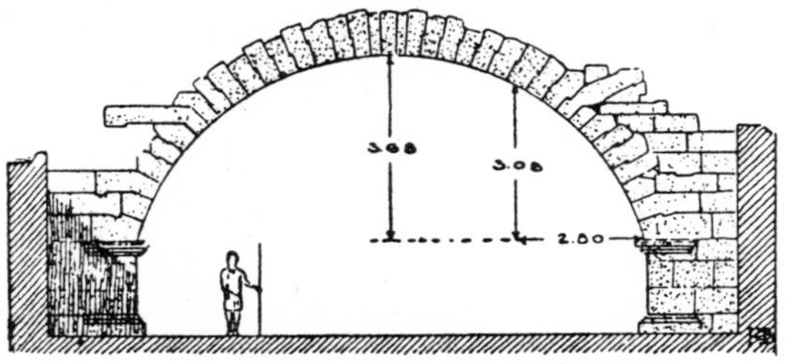

FIG. 589. ṢAMMA: Transverse arch of church. (From Butler, *op. cit.*)

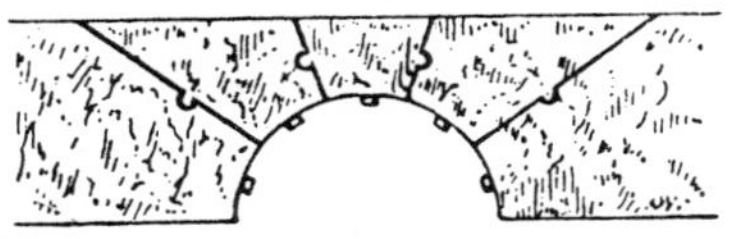

FIG. 592. QAṢR AL-MUDAKHKHIN: Arch with joggled joints counterfeited. (From Butler, *Ancient Architecture in Syria, Sect. B: Northern Syria.*)

joggled voussoirs. This gate is dated 297 H. (909/10), and one of the dating inscriptions is cut on the course immediately above this relieving arch.[2]

Another example (unpublished) is found over the entrance to the tall octagonal minaret of the Great Mosque at Urfa, where there is a deep joggled voussoir above the lintel of the doorway. The date of this minaret is not known, but it is certainly early,[3] although I do not feel convinced that Sachau[4] is right in assigning it to the Byzantine period, for all the surviving examples of Syrian church towers are square.

It first appears in Muslim Egypt in the Fāṭimid gates of Cairo and after that is widely used, and attains considerable elaboration even before the end of the Fāṭimid period, e.g. in the Mosque of al-Aqmar (519 H. = 1125), over the entrance.[5] Only the simplest form, however, is found in the Citadel (Saladin, 579 H. = 1183/4).

[1] Butler, *Ancient Architecture in Syria, Sect. B: Northern Syria*, p. 209 and fig. 216.

[2] See van Berchem, in van Berchem and Strzygowski, *Amida*, p. 18 and pl. III_2.

[3] Rivoira (*Moslem Architecture*, p. 134) says that it must be ascribed to the twelfth century, though without supplying the necessary evidence, 'a practice which', as *he himself remarks* in another place (p. 121), 'is more convenient than convincing'.

[4] *Reise in Syrien und Mesopotamien*, p. 194.

[5] See my *Muslim Architecture of Egypt*, I, Plate 83 *c*.

MÂCHICOULIS. The earliest examples of stone[1] mâchicoulis occur in the pre-Muhammadan architecture of Northern Syria, and three of these are dated: (1) at Kfellūsīn (Fig. 593), in a tower built A.D. 492, according to an inscription on the lintel over the entrance;[2] (2) at Refāda, in a two-storey house, dated A.D. 516;[3] and (3) at Dār Qītā, in a watch-tower dated A.D. 551.[4] Other examples, undated however, may be seen at Jerāda (Fig. 595 *b*, facing p. 542), in a tower-house assigned by Butler to the fourth century,[5] at Sarjibla, in a house of five storeys (Fig. 594) assigned by Butler to the sixth century,[6] at Kafr Ḥauwār, in four towers standing in a row on the edge of the town,[7] at Refāda, in a tower,[8] at Khirbet Ḥāss,[9] and at Dayr Qula, a monastery in Palestine, assigned by Conder to the sixth century.[10]

FIG. 593. KFELLŪSĪN: Tower. (From Butler, *Ancient Architecture in Syria, Sect. B: Northern Syria.*)

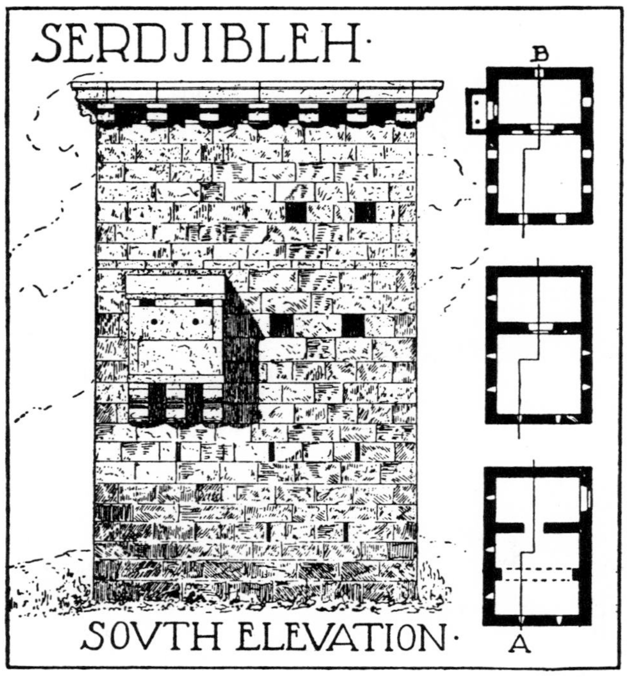

FIG. 594. SARJIBLA: Tower. (From Butler, *op. cit.*)

In the Ḥaurān an example in the barracks at Umm al-Jimāl (? Θαυτια), probably built *c.* A.D. 412, has been published by Butler.[11]

Of these ten examples only three can possibly have been for the purpose usually assigned to mâchicoulis, viz.: to enable the besieged to drop molten lead, boiling oil, or projectiles on a storming party attacking a doorway below. All the others are latrines and cannot have served any other purpose. The oldest example, that at Jerāda, is found in a tower six storeys high completely preserved to its uppermost cornice. It is within the town and is an integral part of the town wall, which is formed for the greater part by the rear walls of houses. It measures 5½ m. square and 28 m. high, and it is set in a re-entrant angle. It was divided into six storeys, and on one side, at the top storey but one, is a small compartment, built out from the wall upon two large corbels. This overhanging chamber, which is entered by a narrow doorway, is about 2·25 m. high, 2·30 m. wide, and 80 cm. deep on the inside. In the middle of the stone floor is a circular aperture 25 cm. in diameter. Butler says that there can be no

[1] Similar structures of brick resting on a pair of stone corbels occur on the walls of Rome in work of the second period due to Maxentius in A.D. 354. They were known in early medieval Latin as *necessaria*, and had a sanitary and not a defensive function; see Richmond (I. A.), *The City Wall of Imperial Rome*, pp. 84–6.

[2] Butler (H. C.), *Ancient Architecture in Syria, Sect. B: Northern Syria*, p. 225 and illus. 227–8. One figure being uncertain, the date may be read as equivalent to A.D. 492 or 522, but the profile of the cornice according to Butler is more in keeping with the earlier date.

[3] *Ibid.*, pp. 256–7 and illus. 269.

[4] *Ibid.*, pp. 189–90.

[5] Butler, *Architecture and Other Arts*, pp. 128–9 with illus.

[6] *Ibid.*, pp. 253–5 with two illus.; and *Ancient Architecture in Syria, Sect. B: Northern Syria*, pp. 230–31 and illus. 232.

[7] *Ibid.*, pp. 232–5 and illus. 234.

[8] *Ibid.*, p. 258 and illus. 275.

[9] De Vogüé, *Syrie centrale*, I, p. 95 and pl. 58. Also Mattern, *A travers les villes mortes de Haute Syrie*, *M.U.S.J.*, XVII, p. 50 and fig. 11.

[10] *Survey of Western Palestine*, II, pp. 315–19.

[11] *Ancient Architecture in Syria, Sect. A: Southern Syria*, pp. 170–71 and illus. 144–5.

doubt that this closet was the *latrina* of the watch, and could have had no other purpose, for it is on the town side of the tower and not above any point of attack. Moreover, he adds that a mass of broken cylinders of clay was found in the ruins beside the wall, suggesting that an earthen conduit may have led from the closet to a sewer of some sort.

The tower at Kfellūsīn, dated A.D. 492 (or 522), is 15 m. high and is divided into four storeys. The top floor was provided with a large latrine corbelled out from the west wall, whereas the entrance to the tower is on the opposite side. Double corbels carry a large flat stone, which constituted the floor, pierced with two holes. Upon this floor were built the walls, consisting of three high courses of stone only 12 cm. thick. The whole was covered by a slightly slanting roof of stone slabs, which were carried under the main cornice of the building.

The two-storey house at Refāda, dated A.D. 516, has an overhanging latrine on the upper floor in the east wall.

The tower-house at Sarjibla, assigned by Butler to the sixth century, is oblong in plan (9 m. × 6·20 m.), over 17 m. high, and divided into five storeys (Fig. 594). On the third storey is a rectangular structure built out from the walls and supported on three brackets. Its walls are of thin slabs of stone, pierced with small round windows, and there is a slanting roof of stone slabs. From inside a small doorway opens into the overhanging structure, which, having two round apertures in its stone floor, can only have been a latrine. Butler thinks it must once have been connected with a main sewer of some sort, as many broken pieces of tile-pipe were found in the débris below it. Here again the entrance to the tower is on the opposite side to this projecting structure, which therefore does not command it.

At Kafr Ḥauwār the four little towers mentioned above are each provided with a latrine, placed on the south side, the side away from the entrance. The construction, however, is somewhat different from those already described, there being no real corbels, as the floor is composed of a single slab, projecting on both sides of the wall. This treatment is rendered possible by the extremely small scale of the structure, which is only about 60 cm. wide internally and about 1·66 m. high. There is one small circular hole in the floor. Butler does not suggest a date.

The watch-tower at Refāda appears to have been four storeys high, and in the second storey, at the angle, is an overhanging latrine like that just described. The entrance to the tower is not on this side.

We thus have six examples which can only have been latrines, and which cannot possibly have served to protect an entrance. We will now discuss those examples which were for defensive purposes. The earliest of these is found at Dār Qītā in what appears to have been an isolated watch-tower (dated A.D. 551) standing a little to the north-west of the centre of the town. It is about 5½ m. square, with an entrance on the west side, and three storeys of it are still preserved. In the third storey, and directly over the entrance, are two brackets carrying a slab with a hole pierced in it; round the edges of the slab are the remains of thin walls which once surrounded it, just as at Kafr Ḥauwār. Butler is convinced that this little overhanging chamber was undoubtedly built for the delivery of missiles upon an enemy attempting to force an entrance, and that similar ones placed over entrances are probably the prototype of the continuous machicolations which frequently surmount the walls of later medieval fortifications. These remarks would of course apply to the little tower of the guard at Khirbet Ḥāss, published by de Vogüé,[1] which has a similar overhanging chamber above the entrance, and also to the tower set astride the only approach to the Monastery of Dayr Qula in Palestine.[2] To these examples must be added the fortified tower[3] between Qaryatain and Palmyra, incorporated in Qaṣr al-Ḥayr al-Gharbī, already mentioned. On the south side, high up and directly over the entrance, which is buried in the ground but visible from within, are the remains of a fine mâchicoulis (Fig. 596, facing p. 542). This tower is built of fine ashlar masonry which appears to have been dry set.

Of the eleven examples of mâchicoulis cited we may therefore say that their function is clear in every case, but there is another, the tower at the south-east corner of the barracks at Umm al-Jimāl, which offers difficulties. This tower, which is exceedingly well preserved, is six storeys high and in the top storey in the centre of each side is a little bottomless overhanging chamber resting on corbels. Two sides of this tower coincide with the outer walls of the barracks, but none of these mâchicoulis

1 *Syrie centrale*, I, p. 95, and pl. 58.
2 *Survey of Western Palestine*, II, illus. on p. 315.
3 For this tower see above, pp. 448, 506 and 508.

commands a doorway, nor can they have been used as latrines, for there is no floor. Butler suggests that the tower may have been a belfry, in which some sort of resounding instrument, the *semanterium* perhaps, was placed, in which case the ropes or chains for ringing it would have passed through these bracketed chambers; but why is this tower provided with four? Butler in another place, when discussing these curious chambers, admits that he can find no satisfactory explanation for this last example.[1]

The mâchicoulis at Qaṣr al-Ḥayr ash-Sharqī, which is of great importance as the earliest in Islam, may therefore be regarded as Syrian in origin.

I have already remarked (above, pp. 25–6) that the architecture of Northern Mesopotamia at this time formed one with that of Northern Syria. Hence it is not surprising to find that the mâchicoulis was apparently employed at Amida (Diyārbakr) in A.D. 504 according to a passage in Joshua Stylites (*c.* A.D. 515) which runs: 'It was difficult [for the Byzantine army] to fight with them [the Persians] 'because being on the crest of the wall, and having built little houses all along the rampart in which they 'hid themselves, they could fight without . . . being seen by those who were outside.'[2] A very good non-technical description of a mâchicoulis.

The Arabic word for this feature, as Sauvaget has pointed out,[3] is shown by a passage in Abū Darr who, speaking of the Ẓāhirīya Madrassa at Aleppo, says that the people in it defended it against the Mongols by making a *saqqāṭa* above the entrance and repelling the assailants by throwing stones upon them.[4] This madrasa, which still exists,[5] has a recessed entrance porch with the usual stalactite vault; there is a large roughly made hole in this vault, by means of which people above could drop heavy stones on anyone attempting to force the door. It thus served exactly the same purpose as the holes in the floor of a mâchicoulis, for which the word *saqqāṭa* (falling) is obviously the Arabic equivalent.

The later history of the mâchicoulis is discussed in my *Muslim Architecture of Egypt*, II, pp. 60-61.

THE COMBINATION OF BRICK AND STONE. The use of brick at Qaṣr al-Ḥayr constitutes an anomaly, for Syria before Islam was a country of stone architecture, with two notable exceptions: Qaṣr Ibn Wardān and the great *castrum* at Andarīn.

Qaṣr Ibn Wardān consists of a group of buildings (palace, church, and barracks) similar in plan, style, and, for the greater part, in materials to the imperial edifices of Constantinople under Justinian. The three buildings comprising this group have been carefully measured, drawn, and described by Butler.[6]

The materials are brick and basalt; the bricks which are large, flat, and nearly square are of two sizes—$30 \times 34 \times 3{\cdot}5$ and $34 \times 37 \times 4$ cm.—and are of the quality and colour of those used in the Church of Sancta Sophia, and in the so-called Palace of Justinian at Constantinople. They are used in conjunction with basalt in the walls, and *exclusively* in the vaults and domes. The walls are composed of bricks and basalt in alternate bands about 1 m. high, a fine-grained white limestone is used for many door and window frames, and a polychrome effect is produced not found in any other building in Syria except Andarīn. Vaults of brick also appear in the greatest variety of forms, tunnel-vaults, ordinary cross-vaults, domed cross-vaults, and elliptical vaults with complicated twisted surfaces. All these, as Butler remarks,[7] 'seem strangely out of place in a region where vaults of any kind were rare, especially in 'ecclesiastical architecture, where vaults of brick in any form are never found, and where cross-vaults 'are unknown, except in one or two later buildings in the immediate vicinity, which may very well 'have been copied from these excellent examples. The carved ornament, too, is exotic in this locality. '. . . The entire group of structures, in materials, in construction, and in details, presents an architec-'tural ensemble that is closely related to the buildings erected by Justinian's great architects beside the 'Bosphorus: the dates on two of the buildings (A.D. 561 and 564), fall within the reign of Justinian [he 'died in November 565], and there is no doubt that the entire group was erected within a few years. 'It seems probable that we have here a suite of imperial edifices, erected under direct influence from 'Constantinople, designed by the imperial architects, and, to all appearances, built, in part at least, of

[1] *Ancient Architecture in Syria, Sect. B: Northern Syria*, p. 234.

[2] Joshua Stylites, *Chronicle*, Martin's text, p. 62; transl., p. lxii; Wright's text, p. 69; transl., pp. 59–60.

[3] '*Les Perles choises' d'Ibn ash-Chihna*, pp. 116 and 212.

[4] Text, ed. of Sarkis (Beyrut, 1909), p. 113.

[5] See Bell, *Amurath to Amurath*, p. 12 and fig. 5; Creswell, *Origin of the Cruciform Plan of Cairene Madrasas, B.I.F.A.O.*, XXI, p. 15, fig. 4, and pls. III–IV; Kamīl al-Ghazzī, *Kitāb Nahr adh-Dhahab fī Ta'rīkh Ḥalab*, II, pp. 299–300; Sauvaget, *Inventaire des monuments historiques de la ville d'Alep, Revue des Études islamiques*, 1931, pp. 81–2.

[6] *Ibid.*, pp. 26–45. For a bibliography of this building, see above, p. 442.

[7] *Op. cit.*, p. 27.

Fig. 586. Spalato: Porta Aurea. (From Rivoira, *Moslem Architecture*)

Fig. 587. Ravenna: Mausoleum of Theodoric

(*a*) (*b*)

Fig. 595. Tower Houses with Mâchicoulis: (*a*) Kfellūsīn, (*b*) Jerāda. (From Butler, *op. cit.*)

Fig. 591. Ruṣāfa: Basilica of Sergios, joggled voussoirs

Fig. 596. Qaṣr al-Ḥayr al-Gharbī: Mâchicoulis

'materials imported from the capital. The only other structure that I have seen in all Central Syria, that 'bears the least resemblance to these buildings, is the great *castrum* of il-Anderîn, the nearest large 'city.[1] This building was constructed of alternate bands of basalt and brick-work, in about the same 'proportions as at Ḳaṣr Ibn Wardân; it was completed in the year 558 A.D.'[2]

Butler continues by pointing out that according to Procopius (*De Aedificiis*, II, 8), an architect named Isidoros, a nephew of the Isidoros of Miletus, who collaborated in the design of Sancta Sophia, was engaged in extensive government building operations in Euphratesia, and that it is probable that he actually built the walls of Chalcis (Qinnasrīn), on the north-west edge of this very district, for an inscription dated A.D. 550 and giving the name of Isidoros as a state official, has been found in the ruins of that city.[3]

As a further proof of the Byzantine origin of this building, Butler calls attention to the existence of domed cross-vaults[4] separated by arches with broad soffits, like those common in the churches of Constantinople. As for the use of brick, he says: 'I have looked in vain for ancient bricks in the 'mediaeval and modern architecture of Syria; the only ancient material of this sort that I have found 'has been roof tiling, which is now used, not for roofs, but in ordinary wall building, mixed with other 'materials . . . if other material than the native basalt was desired for building purposes, it had to be 'imported in any circumstances. Brick was the lightest material to transport, and the easiest to handle. '. . . If the architect was trained in Byzantine construction, and if Byzantine vaults and domes were 'planned for, it was necessary to have the special material that had made the development of these things 'possible. It remains only to be known whether brick makers or the bricks themselves were imported, 'and I believe it was the latter. I have not compared the bricks of Kaṣr Ibn Wardân with those used in 'Constantinople, side by side; but from a careful examination of the colour and texture of both separ-'ately, and at times only a few weeks apart, the similarity between the two indicates to my mind that 'they were burnt in the same kilns, or, at least, in exactly similar kilns, where brickmaking was a great 'industry, which it was not at Antioch.'[5]

Referring to Strzygowski's suggestion that Antioch was a brick-building centre,[6] he remarks: 'This 'learned writer, however, seems to prefer to trace the origin of these buildings, the source of the material 'used in them, and the habitat of the masons employed upon them, to Antioch rather than to the capital. 'Nothing whatever remains of the great churches of Antioch, and practically the only remnants of the 'architecture of that great city to be seen to-day are the walls on the mountain and the aqueduct bridges 'in a neighbouring valley; neither of these is built of brick. Even the vaults and cisterns, connected 'with the fortifications on the mountain top, are made of rough stone laid in mortar. Had brick been 'used on an extensive scale in a city so large as Antioch, such imperishable material as brick of the 'quality found at Ḳaṣr Ibn Wardân would have been used again and again, and would still be seen in 'the buildings of the present occupants of the site; but this is not the case. . . . Antioch was situated 'in the midst of good quarries, and I am of the opinion that it was a city of stone, and that the archi-'tecture of the city, during the sixth century, is exemplified in that of the towns in the suburbs, i.e. the 'Djebel il-A'lā, the Djebel Bārîshā, and the Djebel Sim'ân; for I cannot believe that such a style as that 'illustrated by the churches of St. Simeon Stylites at Ḳal'at Sim'ân was developed in the suburban towns 'in the neighbourhood and independently of the style of the metropolis.'[7]

At Andarīn (*Androna*), twelve miles north-east of Qaṣr Ibn Wardān, is a great *castrum*, built, according to an inscription on the lintel, in November, 1st day, Indiction 8 (= Nov. 559).[8] 'The greater 'part of the lower story was built up in courses of basalt; above this bands of brickwork alternated with 'bands of basalt coursing. . . . The vaulting, of course, was of brick, and of the same character as the 'vaulting at Ḳaṣr Ibn Wardân; the bricks are of the same sizes, and the mortar is of the same quality.'[9]

But the bricks of Qaṣr al-Ḥayr are smaller than Byzantine bricks, and in size and texture resemble those in use in 'Irāq, about this time, for the Baghdād Gate of Raqqa (A.D. 772); moreover the

1 About twelve miles to the north-east.

2 Butler, *op. cit.*, pp. 27–8.

3 *Ibid.*, p. 28.

4 For this kind of vault and its construction, see the beautiful isometric projections of Choisy, *L'Art de bâtir chez les Byzantins*, pls. 11 and 13.

5 *Op. cit.*, p. 43.

6 *Kleinasien*, p. 131.

7 *Op. cit.*, p. 43. Herzfeld is in complete agreement with Butler's view; see his *Mschattâ, Ḥîra und Bâdiya, Jahrbuch der Preuszischen Kunstsammlungen*, XLII, p. 122.

8 Prentice (W. K.), *Greek and Latin Inscriptions, Sect. B: Northern Syria*, pp. 45–7.

9 Butler, *op. cit.*, p. 51.

layers of mortar are less in thickness than the bricks, another Mesopotamian feature. The brickwork of Qaṣr al-Ḥayr, therefore, shows a mixture of two influences; the decorative use of brickwork to give a striped effect to masonry, is Byzantine, but the bricks themselves and the technique are Mesopotamian.

THE CONSTRUCTION OF THE VAULTS. There are two methods of vault construction in brick. In one, that employed in the West, the bricks are laid in horizontal rows on either side of a centering, one above the other, until they meet at the top. A centering is absolutely essential when this method is adopted, for it is obvious that without it the two halves would not stand until completed and joined at the crown.

FIG. 597. THEBES: The Ramesseum—method of vault construction. (From Clarke and Engelbach, *Ancient Egyptian Masonry*.)

But there is another system, in which centering may be avoided, and this system is found in very early times in Egypt and Assyria, i.e. in those countries where the scarcity of wood rendered it imperative that the prohibitive cost of centering should be avoided. In this system the flat, square bricks employed are set vertically instead of horizontally, so that the vault is composed of a series of rings, or slices as Choisy calls them,[1] in which the joints and not the beds radiate from the centre. Each brick was bedded against the previous one by means of a very viscous clay mortar, adhesive enough to keep it in place until the ring was finished and thereby locked.[2] When this is done it forms a solid support, on which the bricklayer stands and against which he applies the next ring. In order to lessen the span, three or four courses of brick are usually laid horizontally at the springing, each one overhanging that beneath. In some of the vaults at Qaṣr al-Ḥayr there are as many as thirteen such courses. Such vaults, however, must be begun against an end-wall, against which the rings lean slightly, and if the ends are to be left open an end-wall must be constructed and removed afterwards, or an arch must be built on a centering and the vault begun against it. Vaults constructed on this system occur in the Ramesseum at Thebes[3] (Fig. 597) built by Ramesses II (1292–1225 B. C.), and similar ones were found by Place at Khorsābād (Sargon, 722–705 B. C.).

The great vault at Ctesiphon is constructed in this fashion, and this system, which was unknown at Rome, appears in Byzantine architecture, which must therefore have derived it from the East. Choisy gives an example from Sancta Sophia[4] (A. D. 535), it occurs in the Palace at Qaṣr Ibn Wardān (A. D. 564),[5] and Jackson records an example at Constantinople dating from A. D. 587.[6]

[1] *L'Art de bâtir*, p. 32 ff.

[2] This method of construction has been described and discussed by Place (V.), *Ninive*, p. 265; Choisy (A.), *Note sur la construction des voûtes sans cintrage pendant la période byzantine*, in the *Annales des Ponts et Chaussées*, 5me pér., t. XII (1876), pp. 439–49; and in *L'Art de bâtir chez les Byzantins*, pp. 31–41; Perrot (G.), and C. Chipiez, *History of Art in Chaldæa and Assyria*, I, pp. 167–8; Dieulafoy (M.), *L'Art antique de la Perse*, IV, pp. 13–18; Schulz, *Mschatta*, in the *Jahrb. der Kgl. Preusz. Kunstsammlungen*, XXV, pp. 214–15; Choisy (A.), *Histoire de l'architecture*, I, pp. 20–22; Spiers (R. P.), *Architecture: East and West*, pp. 62–3 and 76–7; Herzfeld (E.), *Samarra: Aufnahmen und Untersuchungen*, pp. 16–18; Clarke (S.), *Christian Antiquities in the Nile Valley*, pp. 26–7; Reuther (O.), *Ocheïdir*, pp. 4–5; Jackson (T. G.), *Byzantine and Romanesque Architecture*, I, pp. 35–7; Benoit (F.), *L'Architecture: L'Orient, médiéval et moderne*, pp. 14–15; Dalton (O. M.), *East Christian Art*, pp. 77–8; and Clarke (S.) and R. Engelbach, *Ancient Egyptian Masonry*, pp. 181–2.

[3] Clarke and Engelbach, *op. cit.*, p. 182 and figs. 214–15.

[4] *L'Art de bâtir chez les Byzantins*, pl. II.

[5] Butler (H. C.), *Ancient Architecture in Syria, Sect. B: Northern Syria*, Illus. 37.

[6] In a building believed to be the Carian Portico (*Καριανὸν Ἔμβολον*) erected by the Emperor Maurice; *op. cit.*, I, p. 37. See also Mordtmann, *Esquisse topographique de Constantinople*, p. 39; and van Milligan, *Byzantine Constantinople: The Walls*, p. 196.

XX

KHIRBAT AL-MAFJAR[1]

General description—The water supply—Apparently never finished.

THE PALACE: The panel-and-post balustrades—The central archway and porch—The entrance hall—The four lunettes—The decoration of the vault—The palace proper—The staircases—The courtyard—The panel-and-post balustrades—The *sirdāb*—The upper floor—The windows—A tracery window.

THE MOSQUE.

THE FORECOURT, POOL, AND PAVILION. The cubit employed.

THE BATH. The porch—The great hall—The exedrae—The main hall, or *frigidarium*—The clerestorey—The bathing pool—The floor mosaics—The *Dīwān*—The dome cap—The cold rooms—The hot rooms and furnace—The latrine—The unit of measurement employed—The date.

BIBLIOGRAPHY.

THE SITE OF KHIRBAT AL-MAFJAR[2] was first visited by Warren and Conder in 1873[3] and again by Bliss and Hunter in 1894.[4] Bliss found three distinct mounds aligned roughly north and south, the northern one of which had recently been pillaged for stone. Bliss reproduced some lumps of carved plaster which can now be identified as fragments of the balustrades belonging to the southern building.

After the First World War the mounds were again pillaged, and the small Franciscan monastery in Jericho was largely constructed with material brought from the site; police proceedings revealed that some 2,500 blocks of stone had been removed, as well as columns, capitals, frescoes, polished marble slabs, etc.[5] This led the Department of Antiquities in 1934/5 to begin excavations, which lasted for twelve seasons, ending in March 1948, when the Palestine Mandate was given up.

Since then work has been continued in the Palestine Museum, where a mass of broken stucco ornament like a gigantic jig-saw puzzle has been re-assembled with remarkable success by Mubarak Saad, the Formatore of the Museum.

GENERAL DESCRIPTION. The remains consist of five principal buildings, as follows:

(1) A two-storeyed *Qaṣr*, roughly 65 m. square internally.

(2) Next to the north side of the *Qaṣr* and continuing the alignment of its east side is a mosque with a concave miḥrāb but with only one *riwāq* of two aisles. A staircase descends to it from the upper floor of the *Qaṣr*.

(3) On the same alignment as the western side of the *Qaṣr* is a wall about 20 m. long, which ends in a three-quarter round tower, and then turns east to form (with the west side of the mosque) a courtyard measuring about 20×25 m. Its north side is formed by the *Ḥammām*.

(4) The *Ḥammām* was reached by a covered arcade which crossed this courtyard from a door in the north wall of the palace; it was a most elaborate affair, measuring about 30 m. square, with a monumental entrance on the east side opening into a courtyard formed by prolonging the east wall of the mosque. On the south side of this courtyard are three doors leading into the mosque.

(5) *The Forecourt.* In front of all these buildings extended a great forecourt, measuring 54 m. from east to west and 135 m. from north to south. Its southern wall took off from the south-eastern corner tower of the palace, and in its centre was a projecting porch, originally rectangular, but which was subsequently modified on reaching the third course by giving it quarter-round corners. It had been paved with flagstones, the impression of which is still visible in the mortar bedding. The entrance passage was provided with *masṭabas*, or stone benches, on either side like the gateway of the Garden at Qaṣr al-Ḥayr ash-Sharqī (above, p. 536).

The west side of this forecourt was formed by the monumental entrance of the palace, with its two-storeyed portico. Then came the remains of five massive towers or buttresses (Fig. 629),

[1] In writing this abbreviated account of Khirbat al-Mafjar I am deeply indebted to Mr. R. W. Hamilton for putting all his knowledge and material at my disposal, and likewise his advice on many occasions.

[2] For Bibliography, see end of chapter.

[3] *Survey of Western Palestine*, III, pp. 211–12.

[4] *P.E.F., Q.St.*, 1894, pp. 177–81.

[5] Hamilton, *Khirbat al Mafjar*, p. 1, n. 4.

which must have carried some heavy superstructure of which nothing remains and, finally, a portico of four arches, the back wall of which is a prolongation of the east wall of palace and mosque. A door leading into the forecourt of the *Ḥammām* comes opposite the second intercolumniation.

(6) The Fountain. Near the exact centre of this court was a square pool with an octagonal pavilion of very massive construction. The centre of the pool was aligned exactly on the north wall of the palace, and within a metre of the centre line of the court.

This forecourt and its central pavilion, as Hamilton points out, 'was the one feature which 'gave a semblance of architectural unity to the whole complex, the palace, mosque, and baths 'being themselves strung together at haphazard without any attempt at integration in a uniform 'scheme'.[1]

(7) The Ḥayr. Eastward of the main enclosure is a long meandering wall now flush with the ground. It is re-inforced by half-round buttresses, placed first on one side and then on the other alternately, exactly as at Qaṣr al-Ḥayr ash-Sharqī. This justifies us in calling it the Ḥayr—game enclosure or park—with an area of about 150 acres.

The Water Supply. Hamilton writes: 'For the palace and the baths it is certain that the water re-'quired was brought from 'Ain ad Duyūk and 'Ain an Nuway'imah by an aqueduct, of which the line 'can still be followed over the greater part of its length. This is the structure described on pp. 722–5 of 'the Memoir accompanying Sheet XVIII of the Survey [of Western Palestine]. At two points the 'channel was carried by bridges across the *wadi* . . . (Plate 99 *b*). About 700 m. north-west of the palace 'the waters were gathered in a reservoir or *birkah*, between which and the palace the fall of some 80 feet 'in the land was used to turn three or more water-mills; . . . On reaching a point about 30 m. from the 'west wall of the baths the channel turned at right angles to the north and supplied, first, a square open 'cistern near the west wall of the baths . . . and secondly, the baths themselves.'[2]

Apparently never finished. Baramki points out that Mafjar 'does not appear to have been com-'pletely finished. It was seen that the carving of the stucco over the north wall of the Entrance Hall had 'not been completed; one of the plaster screens in Room II (*a*) had only just been started; the marble 'screens in the North Hall were complete only in parts; the walls in Rooms II′ (*a′*) and (*b′*), III′ (*a′*) 'and (*b′*) and Hall III′ were either half done or not even started, and the tiles stacked in Hall III′ were 'prepared and never used. . . . Not only does this show an abandonment of work, but a sudden and 'simultaneous interruption all over the site'

THE PALACE

The Palace is built throughout of a light porous sandstone from Khirbat as-Samrā', a large quarry five kilometres to the north.[3] Its outer walls (Fig. 605) face the four cardinal points; their measurements are:

East	61·26 m.	internally and	63·86 m.	externally.
South	64·68 m.	,, ,,	67·28 m.	,,
West	64·68 m.	,, ,,	67·28 m.	,,
North	64·61 m.	,, ,,	67·21 m.	,,

Hamilton has pointed out that the cubit of 44·75 cm. employed for the water gauge of Muwaqqar (above, pp. 496-7) must have been used in marking out the palace at Mafjar for the external measurements of the south and west sides equal 150 such cubits plus 16 cm.; on the north side the difference is 9 cm. only.[4] There were three-quarter round towers at the four corners, and a semicircular one in the middle of the north and west sides. All these towers were solid up to the point preserved.

In the centre of the east side was the entrance tower, 14 m. wide with a projection of 6·10 m., flanked on either side by a two-storeyed portico. The façade was not symmetrical, for there were five arches to the left of the gateway and only four to the right. The lower arcade was supported by masonry piers,

[1] *Op. cit.*, p. 5.
[2] *Ibid.*, pp. 5–6.
[3] Baramki, in the *Q.D.A.P.*, V, p. 134.
[4] *Op. cit.*, pp. 39–40.

each consisting of four closely set cylindrical shafts with moulded bases[1] and acanthus capitals standing on moulded cubical bases (Fig. C_1). The arches of the upper and lower galleries and the columns on which they rested lay on the ground face downwards, just as they had fallen during an earthquake, perhaps that of A.D. 747 (see above, p. 374, n. 3). Two other arcades at right angles abutted on the northern and southernmost pier. The southern arcade formed a portico (some of the bases were found *in situ*), which turned and continued along the eastern side of the forecourt; the northern one appears to have formed some sort of link with the pool of the fountain, by which I am completely mystified.

The excavators found that all the arches at Mafjar must have been very slightly pointed, with two centres separated by distances varying from one-twelfth to perhaps one-fifth of the span. The commonest ratio in arches it was possible to measure was between one-eighth and one-sixth.[2]

Of the columns found on the northern side four were monoliths of granite and a fifth of hard pink limestone; on the southern side five were of white marble.[3] With their capitals and bases, of which six were recovered, the supports of the upper galleries could be measured as standing 3·10 m. high. Curiously enough it appears certain that there was one more arch in the upper storey than below,[4] so there was no vertical correspondence. A similar peculiarity is shown in the mosaic at Ravenna, intended to represent the Palace of Theodoric (Fig. 102, facing p. 200), and also in the façade of Ṭāq-i-Kisrā at Ctesiphon.

Above one of the arches of the southern gallery as it lay spread on the ground were four courses of superimposed masonry, 1·05 m. high. This enables us to estimate the height of the porticoes as follows:

Datum to floor level of first storey . .	8·20 m. (see below, p. 550)
First-storey columns, with capitals and bases	3·10 m.
Arches	2·50 m.
Superimposed masonry	1·05 m.
	14·85 m.[5]

THE PANEL-AND-POST BALUSTRADES. Between each column of the upper storey was a pair of pierced ornamental panels, exactly as in Qaṣr al-Ḥayr al-Gharbī. The remarkably beautiful balustrade panels, according to Hamilton, must have been made in a workshop and brought to Mafjar all finished and ready for installation, whereas the posts that held them in position were not pre-fabricated but made on the spot.[6]

In the forecourt were found the shattered remains of thirteen different panels, of which the central fields were all alike, the borders alone differing.[7] The central part in every case consisted of two superimposed arcades of five arches above and six below, carried by clusters of four little columns, with alternately straight and spiral flutings and acanthus capitals. Plate 100 *b* shows one assembled from fragments and now in the Palestine Museum.[8] Hamilton has reached the conclusion that an error has been made in the reconstruction, saying that 'the border scroll at the bottom should emerge from a single 'basket placed at the centre, not from two baskets as presupposed by the reconstruction. There should, 'consequently, be six arches in the bottom row, not nine. Plate, LXV [my Plate 100 *b*], showing a long continuous strip 'of lower border in the same panel, confirms this; for the half-palmette just visible beside the plaster 'lacuna at the left end of that strip belongs to a corner motif, and the border really turned upwards at 'that point, thus revealing the full length of the central panel in the six arches it subtends.'[9]

But there is a more decisive argument than this: the panel as reconstructed is 2 m. long, whereas the space between the posts in the gallery of the forecourt is only just over a metre and a half (see his Plate CI [my Fig. 599*c*]), so the panel as reconstructed is much too long to fit.

The borders of these panels consisted either of stalks, in some cases rising out of a vase in the centre and forming loops to right and left, or fantastic flower motifs linked together below. Some (Fig. 598) closely resemble the decoration of the bronze coverings of the tie-beams in the Dome of the Rock.

1 Baramki has pointed out that whereas in the north portico there is a common square base for the cluster of four columns, in the south portico the base is divided into four parts, each part corresponding to one of the columns; *Q.D.A.P.*, X, p. 154.

2 On this question, see Hamilton, *op. cit.*, pp. 18–22.

3 *Ibid.*, p. 21.

4 *Ibid.*, pp. 21–2.

5 *Ibid.*, p. 22.

6 *Ibid.*, p. 241.

7 *Ibid.*, p. 245.

8 Hamilton's plate LXVI_1 shows another.

9 *Ibid.*, p. 260, n.

It was noticed that the same scroll pattern was repeated on one side of every panel, whereas, on the reverse, the borders all differed from each other. Hamilton suggests that the panels were set so that the former all faced one way and the latter another. I suggest that all the varying patterns were set to face the courtyard, whence all could be seen at a glance, and that the repeated ones faced inwards.

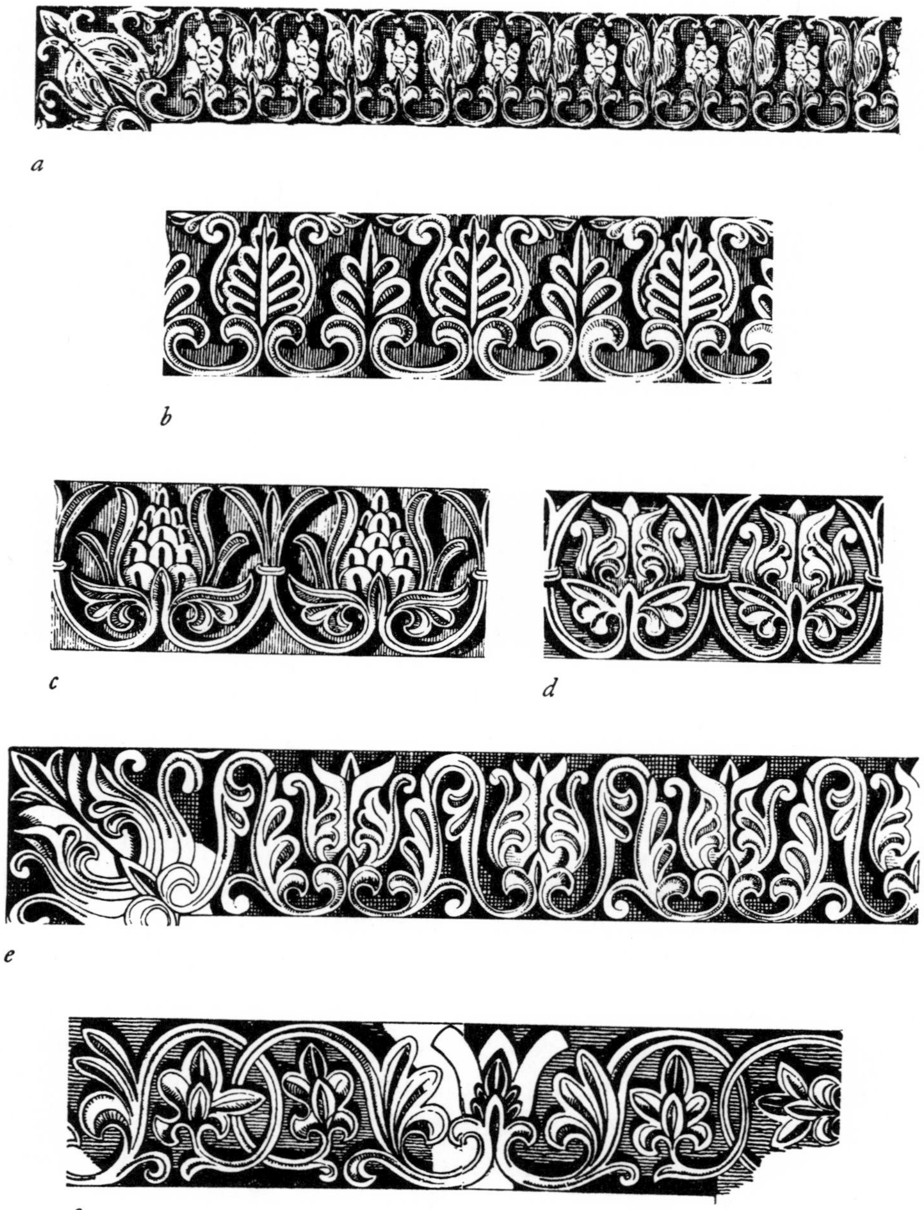

Fig. 598. Mafjar: Linked-flower borders from the balustrade panels of the forecourt. (From Hamilton, *op. cit.*)

Hamilton says: 'Unlike the panels, the posts appear to have been built up by hand and carved in the 'positions where they had to stand; for where they stood next to a column they were rounded to the 'curvature of the shaft and to the base mouldings, while the intermediate ones were securely stuck to 'the edges of the panels they held.'[1] Each post was about 1·05 m. high, but their widths varied from 15 to 23 cm.; each had an onion-shaped knob on top, resting on a moulded collar (Plate 100 *a*).

The Central Archway and Porch. The great archway in the centre was about 4·70 m. wide, and the slightly stilted arch sprang at a height of about 4·50 m. from the floor. It formed one end of an open porch of the same depth as the portico. Its outer face consisted of a series of voussoirs treated as radiating niches between decorated colonnettes, some fluted. These colonnettes turned inwards under the arch and continued horizontally along the surface of the vault (Plate 99 *c*) as shown (Fig. 600).[2] This vault was penetrated by the vaults of the side recesses, a cross-vault being thereby formed over the passage-way.

[1] *Op. cit.*, p. 267.

[2] Corbett's reconstruction of this vaulting is based on the measurements of a dozen of the front voussoirs and about six stones from the groins, *ibid.*, pp. 12–13.

At a level of 1·84 above the sill was a cyma recta moulding 27 cm. high (Fig. 586) with floral motifs on looped stalks, which ran across the north, east, and south faces of the tower and passed in under the arch to traverse the north and south walls of the porch, until it terminated on either side against the jambs of the gate itself (Plate 101, *b* and *d*).

FIG. 599. MAFJAR: Palace front, restored elevation. (From Hamilton, *op. cit.*)

On either side of the porch is a bench, each with three head- or arm-rests, one in section a quarter circle, at each end, and a semicircular one in the middle. Four courses above these benches, or at a level of 1·84 m. above the sill, was the continuation of the cyma recta moulding just mentioned. Resting on it (i.e. at a level of 2·09 m. above the sill) were four niches with flanking colonnettes, of which there were three on each wall and a fourth on the jamb of the archway. A number of niche heads

FIG. 600. MAFJAR: Palace gateway and entrance hall, restored long-section. (From Hamilton, *op. cit.*)

decorated with various designs in relief, such as vines growing out of cornucopias, anthemions, etc., were found in the porch or just outside it.[1] Vestiges of a carved capital showed that the niches themselves were 1·30 m. high; if we add 63 cm. for the hood we obtain 1·93 m., or 4·02 m. above the sill. This is the highest point that can be directly measured.[2]

Fragments of a second string course, 27 cm. high, decorated with acanthus whorls (Fig. 602) with the background painted red, found in the porch, suggest that there was a second string-course, as shown

1 Baramki, in the *Q.D.A.P.*, VI, p. 157; and Hamilton, *op. cit.*, pp. 12–13.
2 Hamilton, *op. cit.*, p. 13.

in Fig. 600. Assuming that the vault was semicircular and sprang at a level of 30 cm. above this cornice, we get 7·42 for the height of the crown above the front step of the porch. Adding 67 cm. for the depth of the voussoirs and, say, 11 cm. for the bedding and surfacing, we get 8·20 m. for the general level of the first floor of the palace.

FIG. 601. Palace porch, string course and niche. (From Hamilton, *op. cit.*)

Let us return for a moment to the front of the tower. A number of decorated blocks of stone were found on the ground in front of the gateway. They could be assembled into two groups, one running horizontally, the other vertically. The ornament consisted of ribbons, projecting 7 cm., carved with a simple design, and interlaced so as to form quatrefoils in the horizontal (Plate 99 *d*), and circles

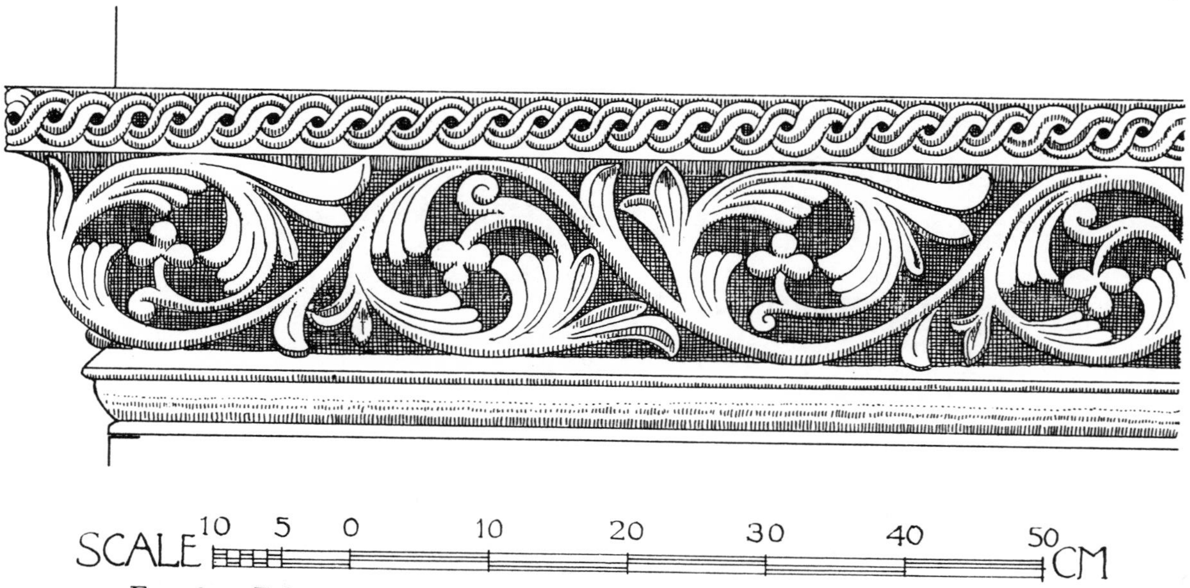

FIG. 602. Palace porch, scroll cornice. (From Hamilton, *op. cit.*)

in the vertical group, both being linked by circular loops.[1] Hamilton noticed that one of the stones belonging to the horizontal band was cut to fit the extrados of an arch of a curvature agreeing with the curvature of the entrance arch. The slope of the junction showed that the lower edge of the ornament must have butted on the curve of the extrados 1·20 m. above the springing, and he also found that at this

[1] See Hamilton, *op. cit.*, pl. XV, 2 and 3.

level there would be just enough room for two complete quatrefoils plus the one cut short by the curve of the arch. As for the vertical bands, Hamiton suggests that they may have framed the window of a room on the upper floor above the porch and entrance hall.[1]

A double row of acanthus leaves (Plate 100 *e*), carved on a number of stones totalling nearly 3 m. in length, were found lying in front of the gateway. They had a shallow channel sunk in their top surface 21 cm. behind the front edge. A number of crenellations were also found, 99 cm. high, with four undercut steps and decorated with grooves filled with red (Plate 100 *c*). Hamilton believes that they surmounted the acanthus cornice just mentioned, and he calculates that fourteen whole and two half crenellations would have been needed to crown the 13·98 m. wide tower.[2]

A place must be found somewhere in the façade of the tower for three or more hexagonal medallions, each composed of six triangular stones, of which one is shown in Plate 99 *d*, and a whole medallion, 1·08 m. in diameter, has been reconstructed by Hamilton.[3] The stones varied from 66 to 82 cm. in depth, and the decorated part projected 12 cm. from the surface. In order to bring out the decoration the background is painted red. Hamilton thinks it unlikely that all have survived, so he adds one for symmetry, and places them at the summit of the façade (Fig. 599).[4]

THE ENTRANCE HALL. At the back of the porch was a double-leafed door of which the left jamb has been preserved to a height of 3·10 m. The jambs are carved with a panel decoration; ten panels exist on the left jamb and the lintel apparently had twelve. The latter, which had fallen, was made in three pieces, two long ones and an hexagonal piece in the centre (Plate 101 *a*). The weakness of this eccentric arrangement was probably reduced by having a relieving arch above it. Beyond this doorway was a long vaulted hall (Plate 103 *a*), open at the far end and leading into the cloister round the central courtyard.

On either side are three massive wall piers and stone benches, each with three arm-rests (or head-rests) between them exactly like those in the porch (Plates 101 *d* and 102 *b*). The stucco behind them was found to be carved (Plate 102 *e*), showing that the head-rests were an afterthought. The piers are built to look like clusters of columns; their rough moulded bases are made up with a layer of plaster 4 cm. thick, as also are the columns (Plate 102 *b*).[5] The roof consisted of a brick tunnel-vault, penetrated by the vaults of the side recesses. All this hall was decorated with stucco ornament. By combining the fragments *in situ* with those that have fallen, it was clear that the space between the wall piers was divided by an acanthus cornice, which presumably ran across the recesses immediately below the springing of the vault. Each recess was divided by a broad vertical strip; and each panel was then divided horizontally, making sixteen nearly square panels, or 'carpets' as Hamilton calls them.

A small piece of ornament, preserved at the top edge of the right-hand lower panel of the south wall (Plate 102 *f*), could be recognized as identical with the panel *in situ* at the left side of the same wall.[6] This suggests that each group of four panels was filled by two different compositions arranged so that the top left was the same as the bottom right and vice versa. Of the different compositions of the sixteen panels, only three can be reconstructed to-day, plus a small fragment of one of the four vertical strips. The latter consists of a vine stem with bunches of grapes, which rises from the corner and leans against a scalloped semicircle filled by radiating pointed leaves. The whole of this strip was framed by a border of heart-shaped petals and beads (Plate 102 *e*).

The panel on the south wall, west bay, west half consists of a diagonal pattern of swastikas alternating with rosettes, and framed by a chain design between borders of beads (Plate 102 *f*).[7] Hamilton points out that the vertical borders do not cut the outer rosettes through their exact centre, but are drawn so as to leave their blobs intact.[8] As the panel is an exact square, this had to be compensated for by leaving a small space between the bottom row of rosettes and the border.

Panel 3, south wall, west bay, east half (Plate 101 *e*). The border is the same as in panel 2, but the main part consists of cruciform compartments, each containing a fleur-de-lis.

Panel 4, north wall, west bay (Plate 102 *f*).[9] On the north wall, as far as we can tell, the standard

[1] *Op. cit.*, pp. 15–16.
[2] *Ibid.*, p. 17.
[3] *Op. cit.*, fig. 86.
[4] *Op. cit.*, p. 17.
[5] Baramki, *Q.D.A.P.*, VI, pp. 158–9.
[6] Hamilton, *op. cit.*, p. 159.
[7] The diagonal square in the centre of the panel does not appear in the composition, but is here inserted in the centre to show the geometrical basis of the design.
[8] *Ibid.*, p. 162.
[9] See also Hamilton, *op. cit.*, pl. XXXIV_4, for detail.

border consisted of a guilloche between borders of beads. Within, swastikas rotating to left and right formed **T**-shaped compartments, filled with three whirling palmettes joined by short stems.

Hamilton[1] says that there are joining fragments to prove that the acanthus cornice mentioned above immediately surmounted the 'carpets', and above this cornice were the four lunettes formed by the vaulting.

Fig. 603. Mafjar: Panel 2 in entrance hall. South wall, west bay, west half. (From Hamilton, *op. cit.*)

The Four Lunettes (Plate 102 *a* and *c*). Three pieces of stucco were found belonging to the lunettes, viz. the panel with heads, the plaster statue, which are shown here, and a niche hood. The statue must have rested on the acanthus cornice, for two human feet were found attached to fragments of it.[2] The composition, shown in Plate 102 *a*, apparently filled the lunette; it has been set out on a network of equilateral triangles, as shown in Fig. 604, on which has been drawn beaded bands so as to form circles linked together by small loops. Human busts peer out from each circle. As regards the niche with its statue, Hamilton is convinced that these niches were inserted afterwards, and another niche was found with the impression of two human busts and the interlacing bands belonging to them.[3]

Fig. 604. Mafjar: Geometrical scheme of panel 5. (From Hamilton, *op. cit.*)

The Decoration of the Vault. Although it has not been possible to reconstruct it from the many thousands of fragments, it is nevertheless clear that the design consisted of a series of vines peopled with

[1] *Ibid.*, p. 165.

[2] One is shown in Hamilton, *op. cit.*, pl. XXXV_8.

[3] *Ibid.*, pl. XXXV_{10}.

figures of men and animals.[1] The vine leaves have three or five lobes with eyelets drilled between them and surrounded by concentric ridges, and the bunches of grapes were pear-shaped, with a drill hole in each grape. It was, however, possible to put together a considerable part of the ornament on one of the groins.[2]

THE PALACE PROPER. Within the four walls of the palace were rows of single rooms running along the east and south sides. All these rooms, which opened on to the cloisters, were isolated from each

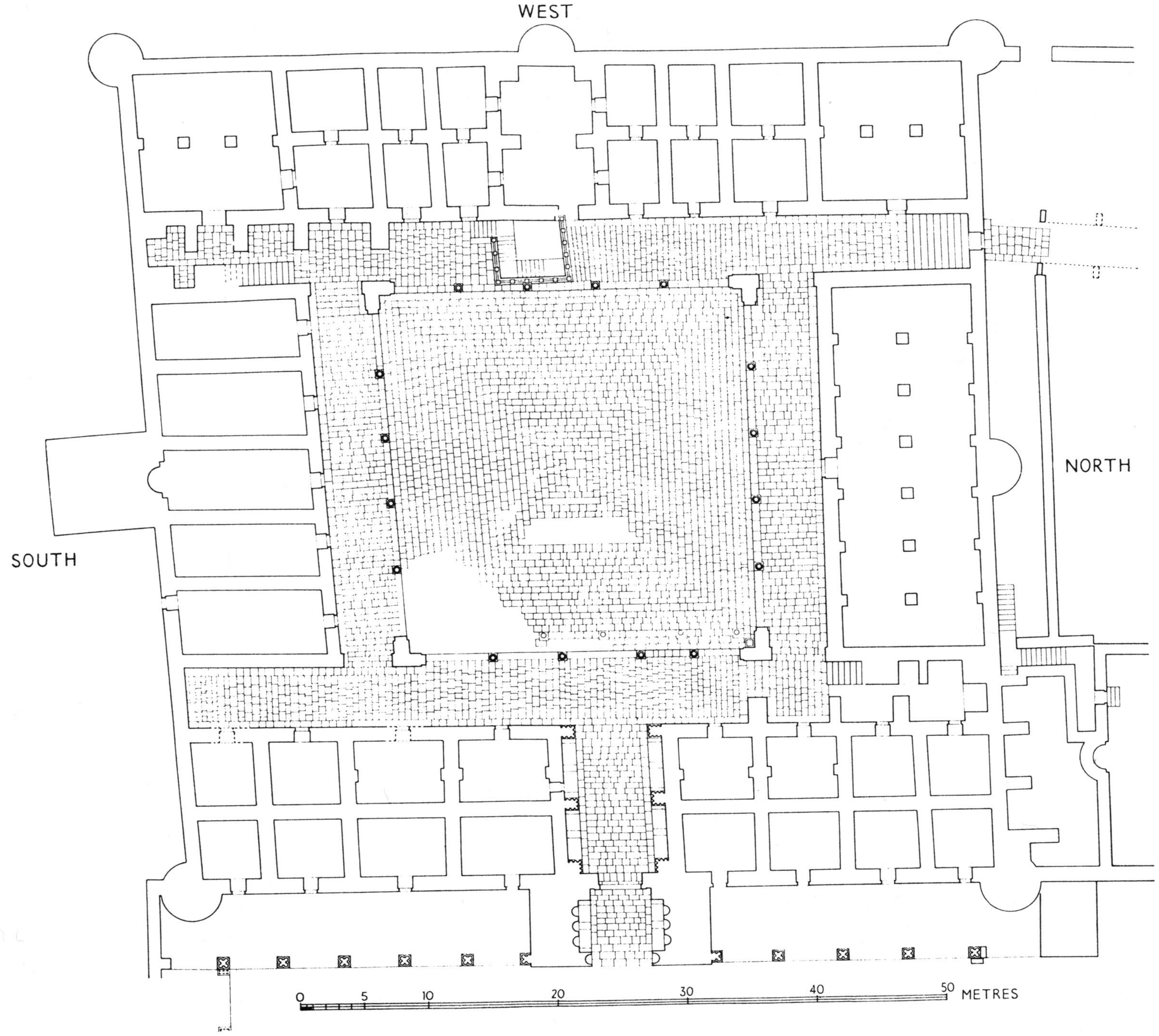

FIG. 605. MAFJAR: Plan of Palace. (From Hamilton, *op. cit.*)

other. On the west side the rooms were arranged in pairs, one behind the other, except the group of five rooms in the centre, the lateral rooms of which communicate with the central room and with each other;[3] the central room opens into the cloister and likewise the outer lateral rooms. The central room appears to have had a barrel vault of brick supported, but not penetrated, by three masonry arches springing from three pairs of piers, as shown (Fig. 605); these piers were not bonded into the walls. The bricks were of two sizes, 33 × 33 × 4 and 25 × 25 × 4 cm.[4] The floor of the hall, which was paved

1 *Ibid.*, pls. XXXVI–XXXVIII. 2 *Ibid.*, pl. XXXV, 7.
3 The lateral rooms communicate with each other at Minya, but not in Mshattā and Qaṣr aṭ-Ṭūba.
4 Baramki, in the *Q.D.A.P.*, V, p. 132.

with concrete (*madda*) about 2 cm. thick, sloped towards the court. As for the two outer rooms which only measure about $5\times3\frac{1}{2}$ m., no bricks were found in them, so Baramki concludes that they had a wooden roof.[1]

There remain two rooms roughly 11 m. square to be mentioned, in the north-west and south-west corners respectively. There are two square piers[2] and corresponding wall-piers in each, from which we may conclude that they were vaulted in the same way as the long room on the north side. Baramki points out that the floors of all the rooms on this side were either not finished or not even started.[3]

The room in the centre of the south side, provided with a niche with flanking colonnettes (Plate 102 *d*), was certainly a mosque resembling that of Mshattā (below, pp. 583–4). Square holes to take clamps have been cut in the masonry at the bottom edge of the fourth course in each wall, presumably to take a marble panelling, and the tower behind, nearly 5 m. square, which occupies the place of the usual half-round tower, was doubtless the base of a square minaret, the only type known in Umayyad architecture.[4]

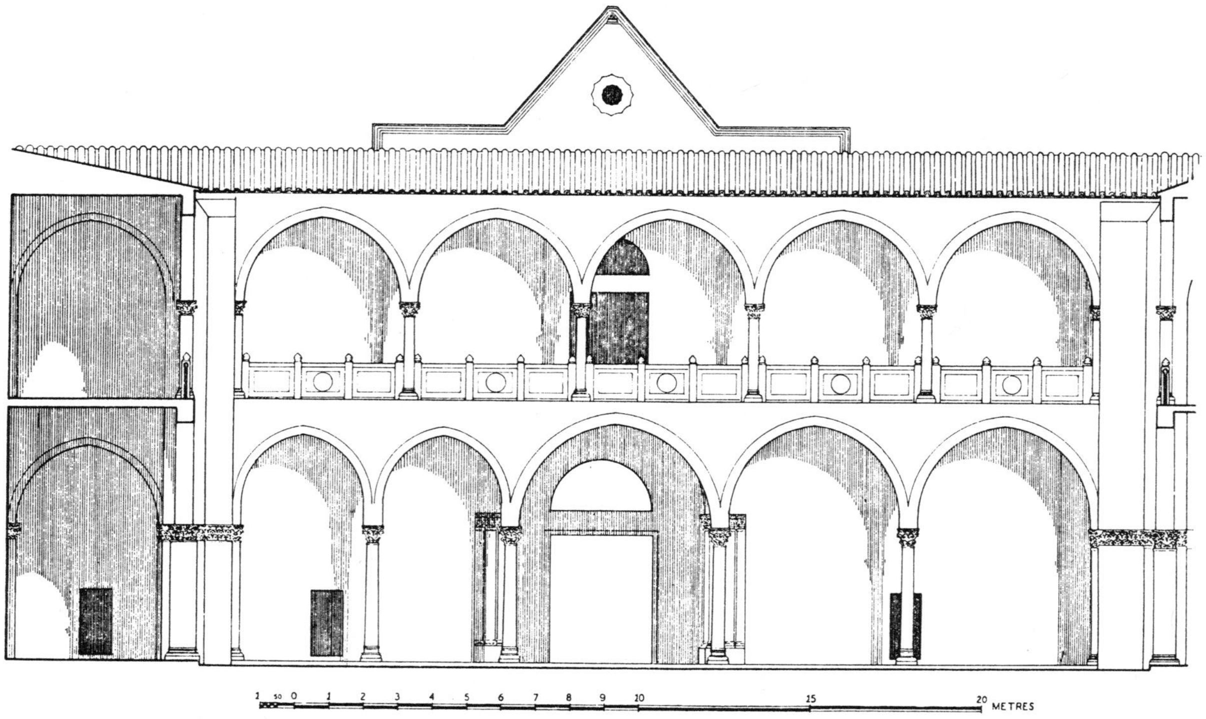

FIG. 606. MAFJAR: Palace courtyard, east side; restored elevation. (From Hamilton, *op. cit.*)

The north side was occupied by a very large room, 28·59 m. wide and 10·90 m. deep, with a row of six square piers down the centre; the corresponding wall piers to north and south show that there must have been six arcades of two arches each, which must have carried seven tunnel-vaults of sun-dried bricks which were found lying disintegrated on the floor.[5]

The Staircases. The arrangement of the ground floor rooms left a passage in each of the four corners of the building, which continued the east and west walks of the portico as far as the outer walls. Of these the one in the south-east corner provided access to rooms 13 and 15, another in the north-west corner led, by a flight of shallow steps, to a door in the outer wall which served the loggia leading to the baths. The two in the north-east and south-west corners contained double-flights of steps which mounted on arches to the first floor. These staircases can almost be described as monumental, whereas in medieval Muslim palaces the staircases are generally steep, and tucked away in a corner.

THE COURTYARD was paved throughout with a bituminous limestone, of a sort known locally as 'Nabī Mūsā' stone. The pavement of the four cloisters was raised 15 cm. above the central part, which measured 27·73 m. wide and 28·95 deep, and the column-bases were aligned along its edge. There were four columns on each side, and at each corner an L-shaped pier with two pilasters. In the court, at a distance of 1·08 m. from the east side and parallel to it, is a gutter 17 cm. wide and 2 cm. deep, which

[1] *Ibid.*, p. 134.

[2] In the south-west room some of the voussoirs of the central arcade were found in the débris, *ibid.*, VI, p. 163.

[3] *Ibid.*, VI, p. 163.

[4] *Ibid.*, VIII, p. 51; and Hamilton, *op. cit.*, p. 34.

[5] *Q.D.A.P.*, VI, pp. 165–6.

slopes towards the centre and then turns east to run out below the entrance hall. In it are small sumps which communicated with an underground drain by trefoil holes.[1]

The columns and bases varied in height, but their combined average height was 3·48 m. If we add 52 cm. for the capitals we get 4 m. for the level at which the arcades sprang. We have seen that the level of the first floor must have been 8·20 m., so the lower arcades and the masonry above them must have been 3·70 m., as shown in Fig. 606. The columns were not evenly spaced; for example, in the east portico, the central arch corresponding to the entrance hall was wider than the rest and placed slightly north of the centre, so that the two arches on its north side were narrower than the two on the south. And if we assume that the columns above were evenly spaced they cannot have come vertically above those below. Charred remains of beams lying across the portico here and there make it certain that these porticoes had timber ceilings,[2] and one may add that the upper had a tiled roof, for a quantity of unused roofing tiles were found stacked in the large room W_1.

THE PANEL-AND-POST BALUSTRADES. The upper floor galleries had panel-and-post balustrades of stucco between the columns. There were three panels between each pair of columns, instead of two only as in the forecourt. All the panels described below belonged to the first floor galleries of the palace.[3] They were composed of rectangular slabs of plaster, 10–11 cm. thick, carved on both sides and firmly held in position by posts, two placed against the columns and two in between, as shown (Fig. 606).

The designs all consisted of a rectangular central part within a border. It appears that every panel made for the central court had a different design on either side, and also that each design was repeated once, but once only. Thirty different designs have been identified, representing thirty panels. As sixty panels would have been needed for the twenty intercolumniations of the upper gallery, it would appear that the excavators have recovered half of them.[4]

From the unfinished panel and others, it is clear that they had been made by pouring liquid plaster into forms of the required size and shape and laid, whilst still damp, on a piece of woven material spread on the ground. There the designs were drawn and carved. 'The drawing equipment included a ruler, a scoring tool, a blunt point, a pair of dividers, and a taut string. Excavation of the background and modelling required a narrow triangular chisel, knife or broader chisel, and a drill. . . .'[5] It is obvious that the actual ornament was executed by hand and not cast in moulds, so that even duplicates were separately drawn and carved.[6]

When I first published the marble window grilles of the Great Mosque at Damascus, I pointed out that one must have been set out on a network of equilateral triangles, and the other on a network of squares set on their points.[7] I also pointed out that the same principle underlay the setting out of the three original windows of the Mosque of Ibn Ṭūlūn,[8] and the geometrical decoration on the soffits of the arches, where SW. 8, SW. 9, and SW. 10 have obviously been set out on a mesh of equilateral triangles, and SW. 4 and SW. 5 on the other principle—a network of squares,[9] and I proposed to classify these two types as 60° designs and 45° designs.[10]

This has now been confirmed by the discovery of an unfinished balustrade slab at Khirbat al-Mafjar, in a workshop which had been established in a room on the west side of the court. The border has been carved and finished whilst work on the central part has only advanced as far as the marking out of the network of equilateral triangles (Plate 104 *d*).[11] Of the panels belonging to the court ten[12] belong to the 60° group and nineteen to the 45° group.[13] Here is Hamilton's analysis :

'In the panels of the central court there were two sorts of field designs: repeating patterns that 'covered the whole field, and self-contained circular designs, which touched the top and bottom

[1] Baramki, *Q.D.A.P.*, VI, p. 160 and Pl. LIII_{2-3}.
[2] Hamilton, *op. cit.*, pp. 28–9.
[3] Hamilton, *op. cit.*, p. 242.
[4] Hamilton, *op. cit.*, pp. 244–5.
[5] *Ibid.*, p. 273.
[6] *Ibid.*, p. 242.
[7] *Early Muslim Architecture*, I, pp. 140–41, Plates 46 *b* and *c*, and Figs. 85 and 89.
[8] *Op. cit.*, II, p. 347, Pls. 111 *e* and 112 and figs. 253–5.
[9] *Op. cit.*, II, pp. 344–5, Pls. 103–5 and figs. 248–9.
[10] *A Short Account of Early Muslim Architecture* (Penguin Book), pp. 311–14.
[11] Baramki, in the *Q.D.A.P.*, VI, pp. 162–3; and Hamilton, *op. cit.*, p. 242 and pl. LXI.
[12] Nos. 1, 2, 4, 5, 6a, 9, 10a, 13, 14, and 15.
[13] Nos. 1a, 2a, 3, 3a, 5a, 6, 7, 7a, 8, 8a, 9a, 10, 11, 12, 12a, 13a, 14a, 15, and 18.

'borders but left a space at each end to be filled by independent motifs. On one panel two circular 'medallions were contained in the field side by side.

'The repeating patterns were all geometrical. . . . We can distinguish six types of geometrical 'framework:

'(i) Round, square or lobed compartments linked at their points of contact by loops (his Figs. 181–5).

'(ii) A lattice-work of straps tracing swastikas at alternate intersections, and so forming six-sided compartments (his Figs. 186 and 187).

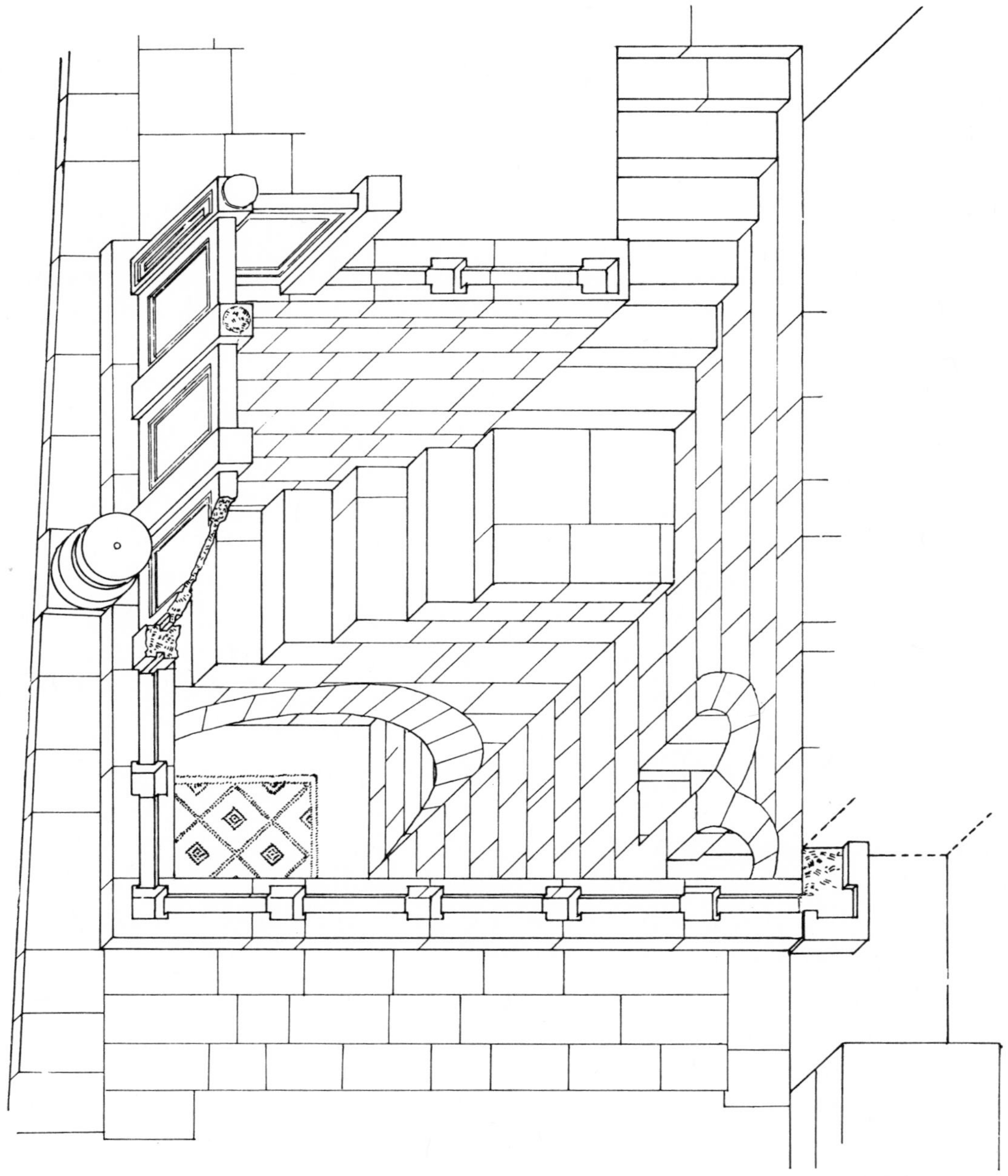

FIG. 607. MAFJAR: Stair-well of *sirdāb* under west portico. (From Hamilton, *op. cit.*)

'(iii) An all-over fretwork of swastikas (square or skewed) alternating with floral compartments (my Plate 104*c* and his Figs. 188–93, 203).

'(iv) The field partitioned by diagonal bands of three or four interwoven straps (his Figs. 194–6).

'(v) Over-all patterns based on interlacing or overlapping circles (his Figs. 198–202).

'(vi) A close fretwork of meandering straps leaving T-shaped or cross-shaped voids (Figs. 204–5).[1]

'(vii) Circular designs depending on interlacings . . . but rounded off in a closed and logically complete system (Figs. 206–10 and my Plate 104*a*)'.[2]

[1] Hamilton, *op. cit.*, pp. 245–53.

[2] *Op. cit.*, p. 257.

THE *SIRDĀB*. In the centre of the west cloister, and in front of the central room of the five-room group, is a staircase which descends in three short flights, first towards the north, then towards the east and then north again, to a small open court not quite 5 m. below the cloister. It is paved with mosaics, in style resembling the 'rainbow matting patterns' of exedrae VI, VIII, and X in the great *frigidarium* (below, pp. 564–6), and its west side is formed by the façade of the *sirdāb*. The latter has a tall narrow doorway spanned by a lintel with lunette above, and a small arched window high up to the right and left. Inside is a rectangular room, with two arched recesses to right and left, a fine mosaic floor and a tunnel vault of brick above. At 7½ m. from the entrance is a partition rendered with waterproof cement and provided with two steps as shown in Plate 103 *d*. Behind is a tank or bath, supplied with cold water from a hole above; this section is paved with concrete. Owing to the porous nature of the masonry the whole of the west wall and part of the north and south walls are faced with bricks and plastered.[1]

THE UPPER FLOOR. That the two staircases did not merely lead up to the roof but to an upper storey is proved by a number of white marble columns, 26 cm. in diameter and 2·30 m. long, which were

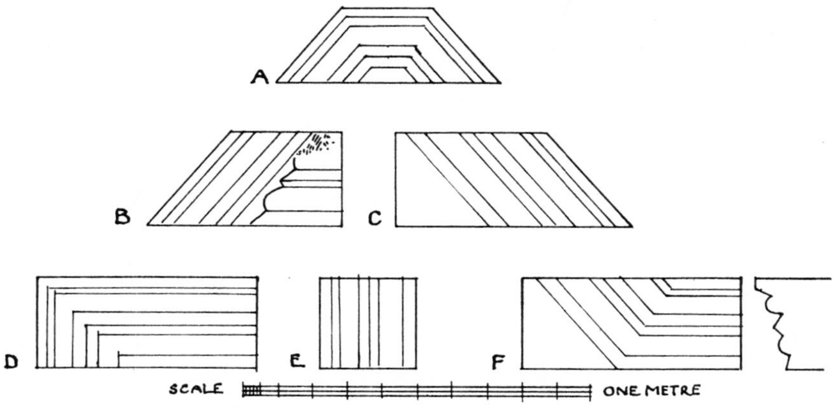

FIG. 608. Palace: elements of a moulded feature in the east range. (From Hamilton, *op. cit.*, Fig 15.)

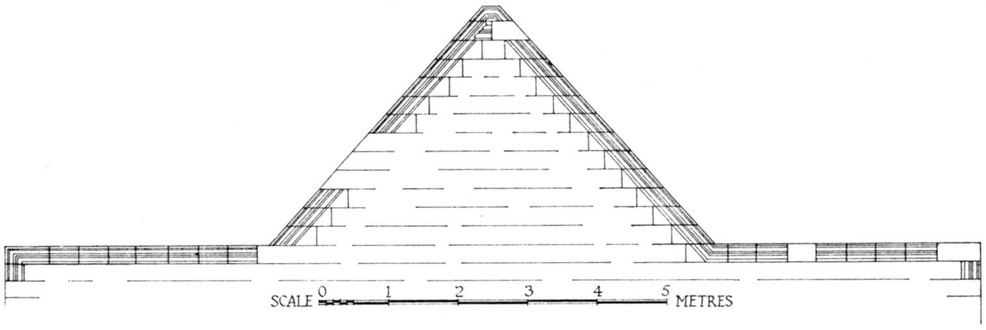

FIG. 609. Palace: conjectural reassembly of moulded stones from the east range of the palace. (From Hamilton, *op. cit.*, Fig. 16.)

found lying in the court in front of the larger columns. Bases and capitals belonging to these columns were found in the east and west cloisters; the bases had grooves on two of their opposite sides to take the closure-slabs.[2] Hamilton's Fig. 15 gives 'the essential elements of a moulded feature of which the 'fragments were found scattered in the ruins of the palace gateway and entrance hall. Of thirty-eight 'stones fifteen, including D and F, composed 6·59 m. run of horizontal moulding; eleven like Fig. 15 *c* 'showed the same moulding rising toward the left, a total rise of about 3 m.; nine others, including B, 'rose 2·47 m. toward the right; and in A we may see the junction of these two raking lines. On two 'stones, E, both 27 cm. long, the moulding was probably vertical. It is clear that the moulding formed a 'cornice crowning a wall which rose in the centre to a gable-end.'[3] By combining the pieces as in his Fig. 16, which shows every stone that exists and the minimum number of gaps, Hamilton obtained a width for the whole equal within 5 cm. of the width of the gate tower. As all these pieces were found

[1] Baramki, in the *Q.D.A.P.*, V, pp. 136–7, and pls. LXXXIII–LXXXIV; VI, pp. 164–5 and pls. LXI–LXIII; and Hamilton, *op. cit.*, pp. 31–4.

[2] Baramki, in the *Q.D.A.P.*, VI, pp. 166–7.

[3] Hamilton, *op. cit.*, p. 35.

in the region of the entrance tower 'it is hard to resist the conclusion that the first-floor apartments over the gate had a ridge-roof of which the gable formed the end' (see Fig. 606). The gable itself only measures 6·40 m. at its base, so Hamilton suggests that there was here a basilical hall with a central nave about 6 m. wide covered by a gable roof, and side aisles of 4 m. each with flat or nearly flat roofs. And he suggests[1] that we may have had here, what is not to be found on the ground floor, an audience hall of basilical form, like Mshattā.

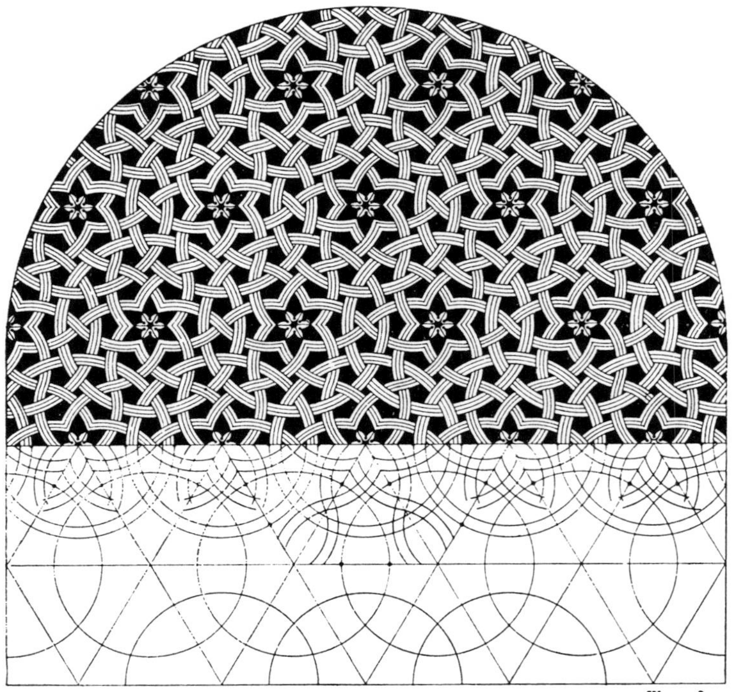

W = 1·18 m.

Fig. 610. Mafjar: Window-grille belonging to Palace, reconstructed from fragments. (From Hamilton, *op. cit.*)

The Windows. Fragments of window-grilles were found in the eastern rooms of the palace, from which it was possible to recover the designs of eight. All belonged to round-headed openings; some no doubt filled the lunettes above the lintels of the doorways, as at Qaṣr al-Ḥayr al-Gharbī. Those found in the palace can be distinguished from those of the bath, in that all of them appear to have been painted red or brownish-gold on one side, the colour penetrating about 2 cm. into the openings.

B_1, P_1, P_6, and P_7 were all drawn on a network of equilateral triangles, and P_2, P_3, and P_5 on a network of squares,[2] in other words the first four may be classed as 60° and the rest as 45° designs.

A Tracery Window. A group of curiously shaped stones was found in the well of the staircase in the centre of the western cloister which gave access to the *sirdāb*. The only decoration on them was a raised band, 16 cm. wide, decorated with two poor bead and reel mouldings set in parallel V-shaped grooves. There were ninety-two stones in all, differing slightly in size and shape, but all had one or more curved surfaces. They were successfully put together as a round window filled with a six-pointed star in interlacing strapwork, as shown in Plate 103 *c*, where they have been set up for convenience on a low wall. Of the 106 stones required for the original window, 92 have been saved and used in the reconstruction. Both sides of the window are the same, except that the knots loop in opposite directions. The diameter is about 2·04 m., and there are four different shapes of stone employed. The outer sides of the stones composing the circular frame were roughly dressed and showed traces of mortar, proving that the whole structure had been a window built into a wall, of which the thickness must have been between 85 and 90 cm. The two faces are bonded together by varying the depth of adjacent stones, as shown.[3]

Though cut in the light and porous limestone, Hamilton[4] estimates its weight as not less than 3½ tons. This was carried, naturally, by the two lowest points and, to avoid the inevitable crushing, the keel-like edges were re-inforced by a cushion running through from a point 21 cm. from either face.

The geometrical basis is as follows: 'The radius of the arcs forming the outline of the star equals 'the radius of the enclosing circle. The design results, in other words, from the overlapping of seven 'equal circles. The centres of the knots in the star lie on the circumference of a circle of half the same 'radius. The width of the interlacing bands equals the radius of the knots and is given by the distance 'from their centre to the middle points of the arcs.'[5]

As most of the stones had fallen into the well of the staircase mentioned above, Hamilton suggests that the window probably belonged to the east wall of the central room of the upper floor on the west side, and looked on to the court across the roof of the cloister.[6]

1 Hamilton, *op. cit.*, pp. 36–7.

2 Hamilton, *op. cit.*, pp. 281–90, figs. 238–50, and pl. LXIX.

3 Hamilton, in the *Q.D.A.P.*, XII, p. 12; and *Khirbat al Mafjar*, pp. 37–8 and pl. XII$_5$.

4 *Q.D.A.P.*, XII, p. 12.

5 *Loc. cit.*, pp. 12–13.

6 *Khirbat al Mafjar*, p. 38.

THE MOSQUE

At a distance of 7 m. from the north-east corner of the palace are the remains of a mosque, which measures 17·10 m. in width internally and 23·60 m. in depth. Its east side continues the east side of the palace. It could have been entered in two ways, one by a door to the right of the miḥrāb, served by the staircase already mentioned, which descended from the first floor of the palace, and by three doors on the north side which faced a courtyard in front of the *Ḥammām*; these doors opened into a sort of narthex, on the opposite side of which were three more doors opening into the mosque (Fig. 629).

The courtyard was not surrounded by arcades on all four sides, but on the qibla side only, in which respect it resembled the Great Mosque of Cordova in A. D. 787,[1] the Great Mosque of Qairawān in 836,[2] and the Great Mosque of Tunis in 864.[3] This south *riwāq* was 10·35 m. deep, and Hamilton concludes, from the total absence of fallen brickwork, that it had a wooden roof. The greater part of the southern arcade lay fanned out on the ground, just as it had fallen, and Hamilton found it an easy matter to recover the form of a complete arch. It turned out to be slightly pointed with its two centres one-seventh of the span apart.[4] The arches were $6\frac{1}{2}$ m. high, but no remains of a cornice or parapet were found.

The qibla wall was only preserved to a height of three courses; in the centre was a semicircular miḥrāb with flanking columns composed of short drums. It had a coating of white plaster on which was no trace of decoration.

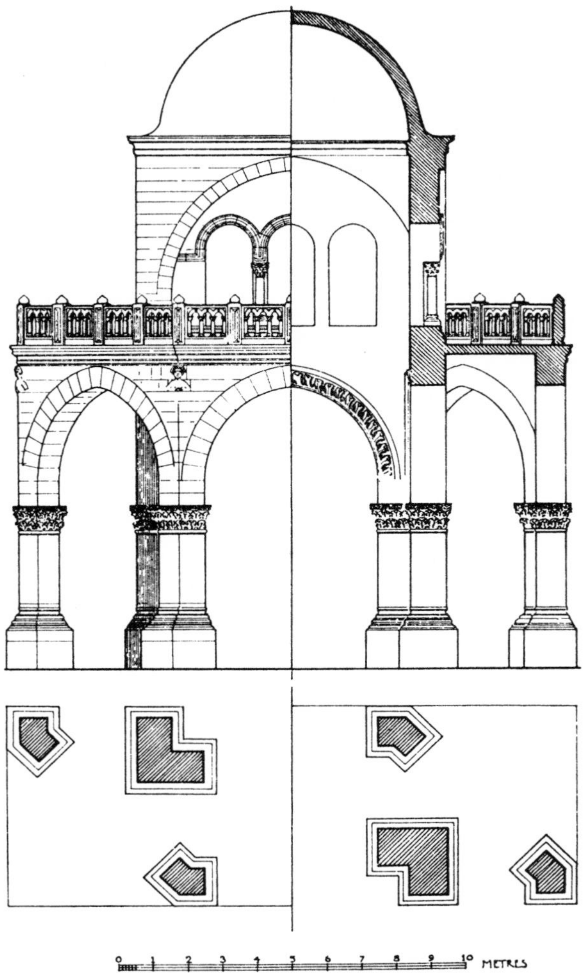

FIG. 611. MAFJAR: Forecourt pavilion, restored elevation and cross-section. (From Hamilton, *op. cit.*)

THE FORECOURT, POOL, and PAVILION. Of the forecourt so little remains, except at the south end, that it seems to have been hardly begun. Nothing remains of its east side except two parallel foundation trenches connected by cross trenches and filled with rubble concrete. Baramki takes them to be the remains of a portico,[5] but Hamilton suggests that they may have been meant for a series of rooms for stabling.[6]

The fountain already mentioned (p. 546) stood in a masonry pool just over 16 m. square with a cement floor and walls 1 m. thick and 25 cm. high. The pool and the inner surface of its four walls were covered with waterproof cement, and outside it was a walk 3 m. broad, paved with Nabī Mūsā stone and enclosed by a stone border 20 cm. high and 40 cm. broad, immediately within which was a shallow gutter provided with three drains.

The fountain was a very massive octagonal building, resting on four L-shaped piers arranged to form a square, and set within an octagon resting on eight piers and just big enough to stand within the pool (Plate 105 *a*). None of these twelve piers stood more than 80 cm. high, but it was possible from a number of fallen blocks to reconstitute the plinth moulding between the heavy pedestal and the slighter shaft. On the analogy of the Bath, Hamilton concludes that these piers were 4·86 m. in height, of which 75 cm. belonged to the capitals. There must have been twelve arches with a span of 4·56 m. Two different kinds of voussoirs were found, one consisting of blocks 66 cm. deep and measuring 1·06 m. from front to back, and decorated with an acanthus moulding on one face only. This latter dimension is exactly equal to the thickness of the L-shaped piers, which shows that they must have belonged to the arches of the central square.[7] The second group of voussoirs were perfectly plain and one of them—a keystone—shows that the radius must have been about 2·80 m. As the span was 4·86 m., the two centres must have been 74 cm. or about one-sixth of the span apart.[8]

[1] *E.M.A.*, II, p. 154.
[2] *Ibid.*, p. 219.
[3] *Ibid.*, p. 324.
[4] *Khirbat al Mafjar*, p. 106.
[5] *Q.D.A.P.*, X, p. 155.
[6] *Op. cit.*, p. 110.
[7] Hamilton, *op. cit.*, pp. 114–15.
[8] Baramki, in the *Q.D.A.P.*, XI, pl. XVI A; and Hamilton, *op. cit.*, p. 115 and fig. 60.

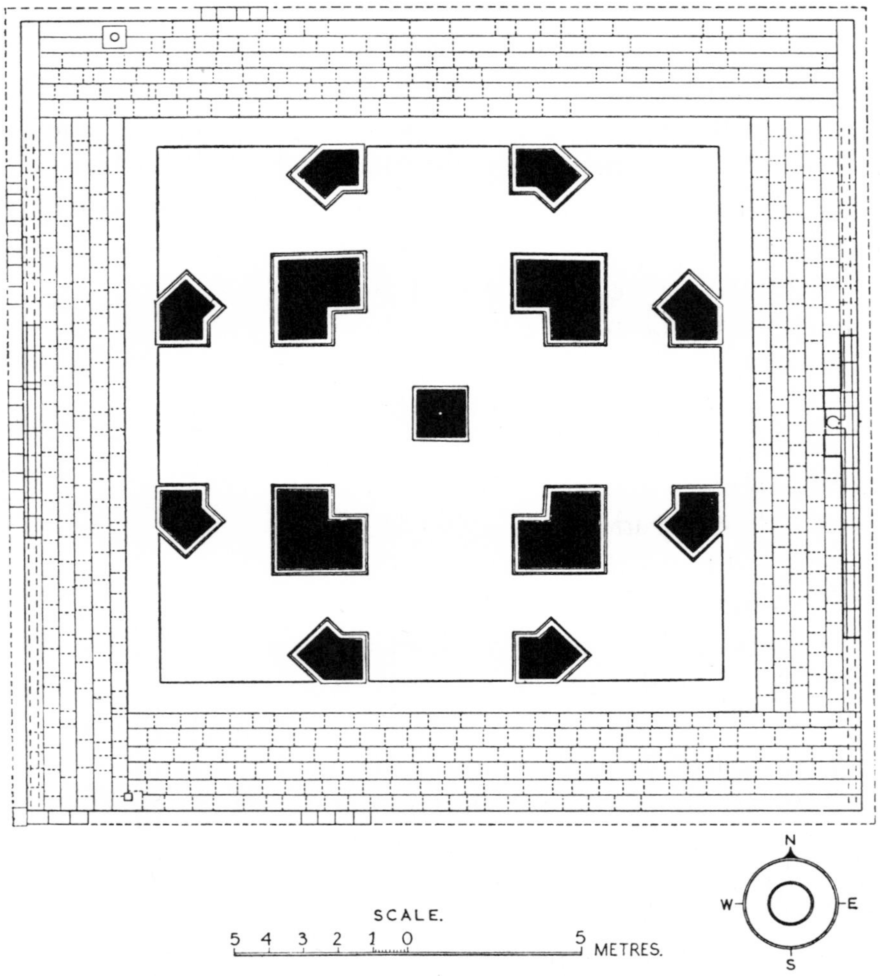

FIG. 612. MAFJAR: The Pool. (From Hamilton, *op. cit.*)

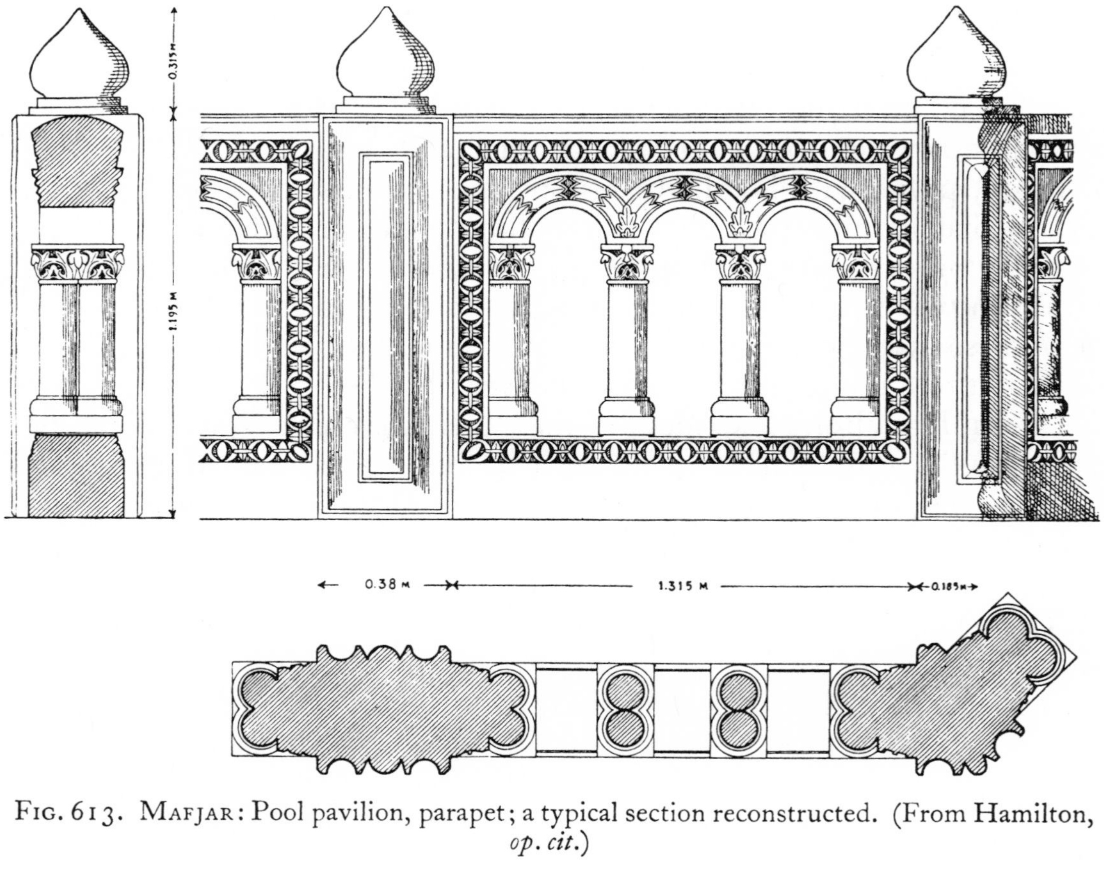

FIG. 613. MAFJAR: Pool pavilion, parapet; a typical section reconstructed. (From Hamilton, *op. cit.*)

A cornice 62 cm. high crowned the octagonal part of the pavilion. A corner stone belonging to it was found, on the top surface of which mason's guide lines had been scored for the posts and panels of a stone parapet, of which part may be seen reassembled in Plate 105 *b*; see also Fig. 613. It was 1·195 m. high, plus 31 cm. for the bulbous tops of the posts. Four of these panels and the five posts belonging to them exactly filled one side of the octagon.[1] The space between the arches of the octagonal and square systems measured about 2·35 m. across on the axes of the square and barely 50 cm. on the line of the diagonals. This area must have been covered over because it was provided with a parapet, and on account of its small size and awkward angles it seems probable that it was given a flat wooden roof.

Four moulded voussoirs, two impost blocks, and two capitals were found in the pool, apparently belonging to windows in the upper part of the central square above the terrace. Hamilton estimates that there was space for three on each side.[2] As for the covering of the central square, the fallen bricks mentioned by Baramki[3] make it more than probable that there was a brick dome, which must have rested on spherical-triangle pendentives, *for the squinch was unknown in Syria in Umayyad times*, except for the counterfeited example in the Citadel of ʿAmmān.[4]

The plan will be recognized immediately as having been set out on two crossed squares, like the Dome of the Rock (above, pp. 73–4 and Figs. 22–3) and the Qubbat aṣ-Ṣulaybīya at Sāmarrā.[5]

THE CUBIT EMPLOYED. We have seen above (p. 546) that the palace was set out with the cubit of 44·75 cm. which had been used for the water-gauge of Yazīd II at Muwaqqar. But not so our pool and pavilion, for which the Nilometric cubit of 54·04 cm. was certainly employed. For example:

Span of arches 4·86 m. = 9 N.C. = 4·863 m. Diff. 3 m/m.
Inner sides of pool, average 16·212 = 32 N.C. = 16·212. Diff. nil.

We shall see that it was also employed for the *Ḥammām* (below, p. 574).

THE BATH

Just over 40 m. to the north of the palace, and exactly parallel to it, are the remains of the largest and finest *ḥammām* so far discovered in Islam. It is the best preserved part of the whole complex, for it has suffered least from stone-robbers, its ground plan is perfectly preserved and its elevation can be constructed with certainty up to the springing of the principal arches.

THE PORCH. From the remains still standing and from fragments picked out from a mass of fallen material Hamilton, by a complicated but convincing reasoning, has made a remarkable reconstruction.

The façade, which faced east, was 8·45 m. wide; it was entered by an arched opening 3·91 m. wide[6] above which was a semi-domed niche with a statue of the Khalif, nearly life-size (Plate 105 *d*), wearing a small sword. He is standing on a pedestal, with two squatting lions back to back, but looking forward. This niche was flanked by two smaller niches at a level about a metre lower. At the top edge of the porch were stepped and undercut crenellations of brick, 70 cm. high, of which three were recovered.[7] Total height 10·63 m.

FIG. 614. MAFJAR: The Bath Porch, reconstruction. (From Hamilton, *op. cit.*)

1 Hamilton, *op. cit.*, p. 115.
2 *Ibid.*, p. 118–20.
3 *Q.D.A.P.*, XI, p. 156.
4 *E.M.A.*, II, pp. 113–14 and fig. 111 facing p. 114.
5 *Ibid.*, p. 285 and fig. 226.
6 Hamilton found that this arch had been sprung from two centres about one-seventh of the span apart; *op. cit.*, p. 93.
7 *Op. cit.*, pp. 102–3 and fig. 53.

In the jambs of the arch were two facing niches, one of which with its finely carved hood was recovered nearly complete. Within the porch was another pair of arched recesses, each 2·55 m. wide, and at the back was a doorway with moulded jambs and a decorated lintel (Plate 105*c*), surmounted by an arch treated rather like that leading into the vestibule of the palace.[1] It was 2·50 m. wide and opened into the *frigidarium*.

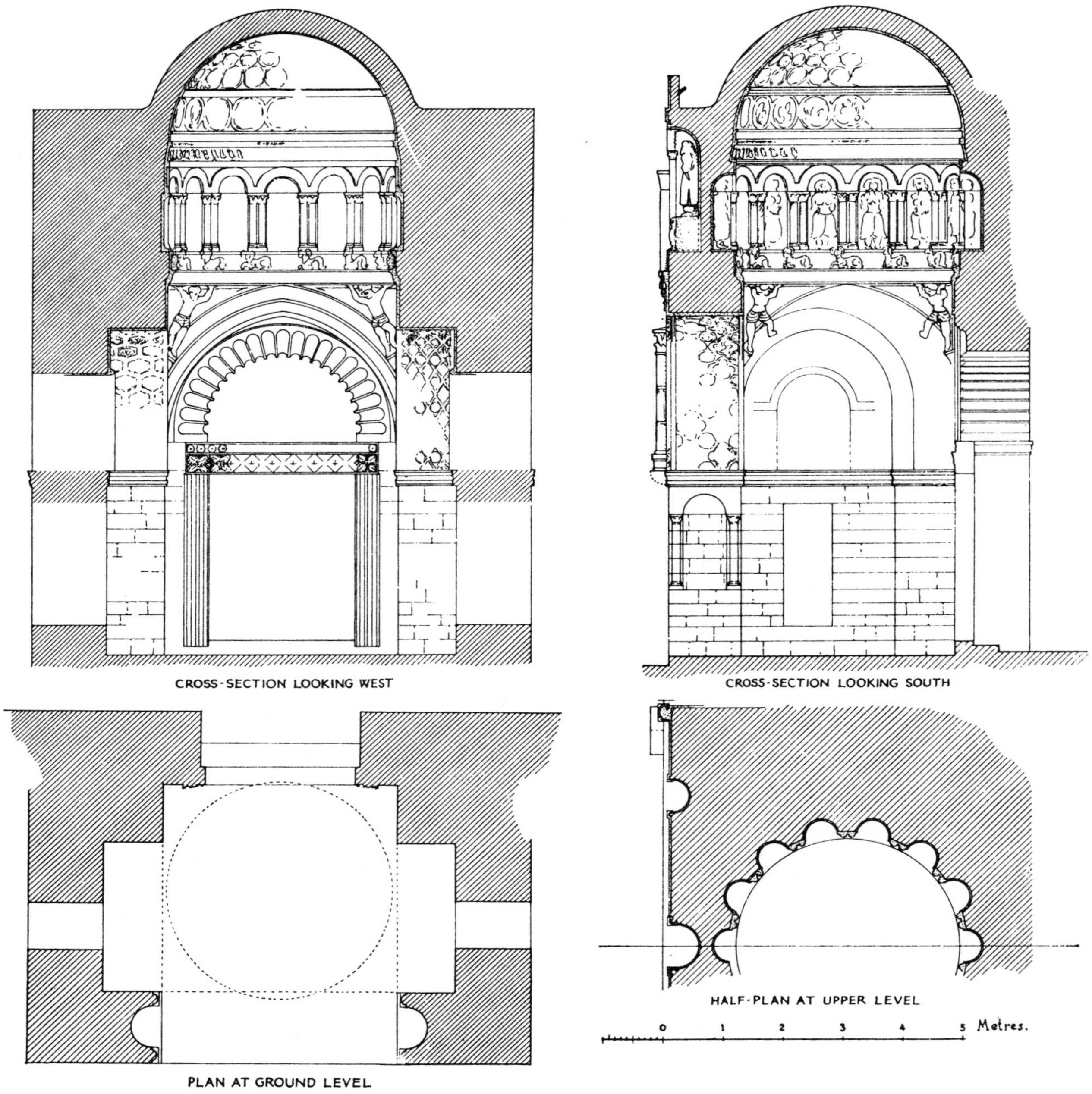

FIG. 615. MAFJAR: The Bath Porch, reconstruction. (From Hamilton, *op. cit.*)

From the fragments recovered it is clear that the porch was covered by a brick dome which rested on spherical-triangle pendentives. 'The most prominent feature in the decoration of each pendentive was a human figure, which projected in high relief from a background of vine and acanthus foliage.'[2] Their arms appear to sustain the cornice, 24 cm. high, of wind-blown acanthus (Plate 106 *a*), the top of which formed a narrow shelf on which rested a row of gazelles and fat-tailed sheep in stucco.[3] Above this came the masonry drum in which were fourteen niches (Fig. 615), each with a plaster statue.[4] Its height, calculated from parts reassembled on the spot by Baramki, was 2·12 m. Hamilton calculates that the top of the drum was 8·16 m. above the datum.[5]

The base of the dome was decorated with an elaborate border, about 63 cm. broad, of flowers sprouting from split vine leaves, above which 'the whole surface seems to have been covered by concentric

[1] *Ibid.*, p. 48 and pl. XVIII_1.
[2] *Ibid.*, pp. 190–91 and 237.
[3] *Ibid.*, p. 96 and pl. XLIV_4 and fig. 50.
[4] *Ibid.*, p. 48.
[5] *Ibid.*, p. 97 and pl. XIV_8.

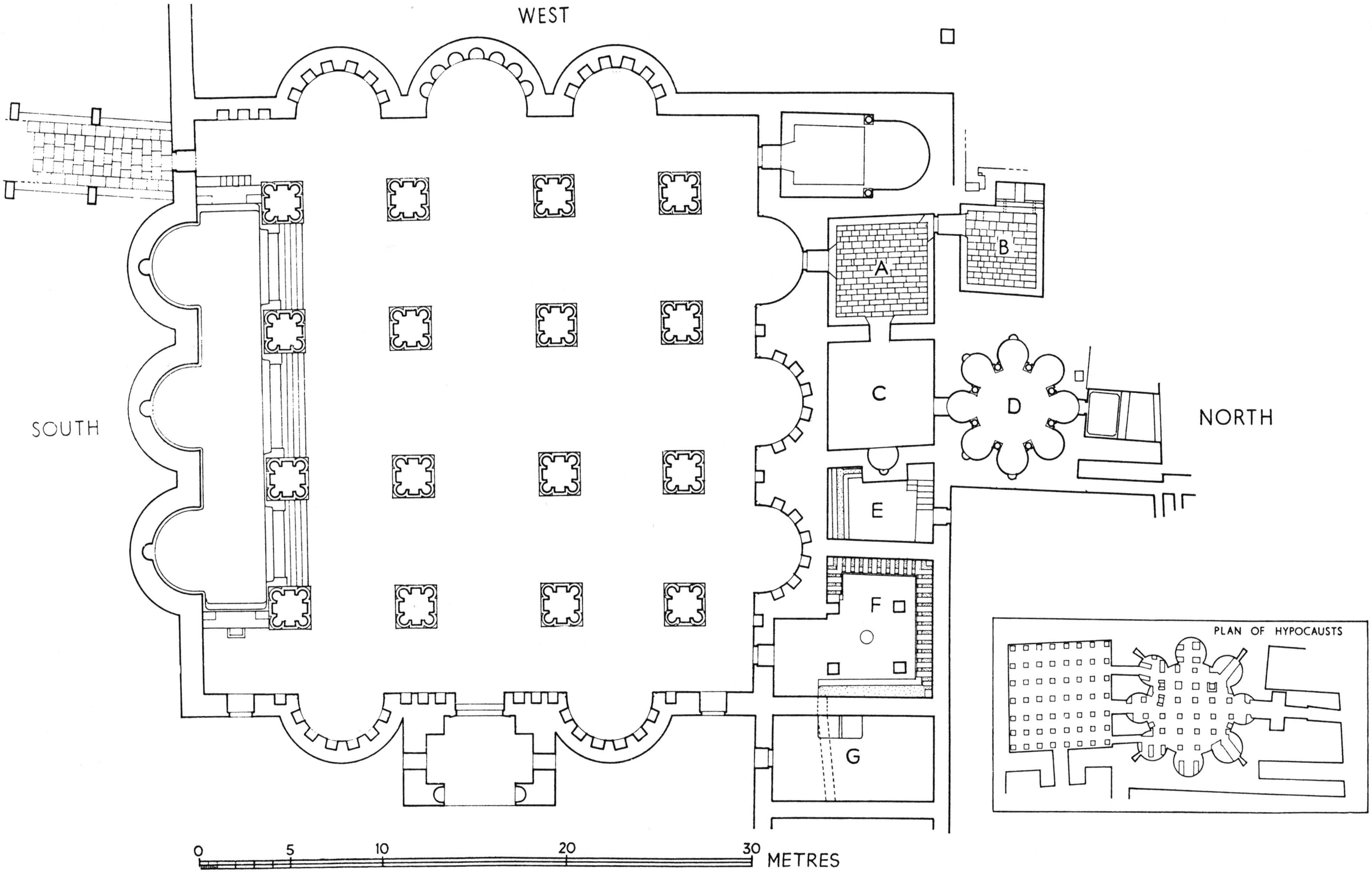

Fig. 616. Mafjar: Bath plan. Scale 1 : 200. (From Hamilton, *op. cit.*)

rings of tangent circles, diminishing in size towards the centre, like the design on the famous bowl of Chosroes in the Bibliothèque Nationale'.[1] Each circle was filled with a flower composition.

THE *FRIGIDARIUM* was approximately 30 m. square,[2] with three semicircular exedrae on each side except the east, where there are two only because of the entrance porch. The exedrae all formed external salients except those on the north side (Fig. 616). There was a secondary entrance also at each end of the east side, and another at the west end of the south side, which was evidently a private entrance for the Khalif, for it gave admission from the long paved loggia, already mentioned (p. 554) which led from the western cloister of the palace.

FIG. 617. MAFJAR: Bath hall, south-west corner, sketch showing disposition of vaulting, string course, and niches. (From Hamilton, *op. cit.*)

THE EXEDRAE. Each of the eleven exedrae was flanked by a pair of engaged columns, the bases of which were a little less than a metre above the floor; several of their acanthus capitals were recovered. All round the walls, in the exedrae and between them, excepting only in the south wall, was a series of small niches 55 cm. square and just over a metre high, with arched heads. In the northern ambulatory (apse VIII), parts of the walls could be rebuilt up to one course above the niches (Plate 106 *c*), their sills being four courses above the floor. It was also possible to reconstruct eight courses, 2·07 m. in height, of the west jamb of the south-west door.

Let us now turn to Fig. 617. 'It so happened that just outside the middle apse (apse II) on the south 'side of the hall a chunk of masonry from the semi-dome was found lying almost as one piece on the

[1] *Ibid.*, p. 192.

[2] The execution of the plan is inaccurate for the sides vary as follows: north 30·28 m., south 30·33 m., west 30·42 m., and east 29·79 m., average 30·21 m.

'ground as the earthquake had thrown it. At the base of the fragment, part of a cornice moulding 'remained in contact with the springing of the semi-dome. We knew already that that moulding en-'circled the exedrae; this fragment proved, what might in any case have been surmised, that it did so 'directly below the semi-dome at the top of the apse wall. In immediate contact with the lower edge of 'the same moulding there lay a niche-head, clearly undisturbed since its fall. This proved that the 'cornice supporting the semi-dome directly surmounted an upper order of niches.'[1] Justification for making the decorated moulding surrounding the apse arches descend vertically alongside a niche and

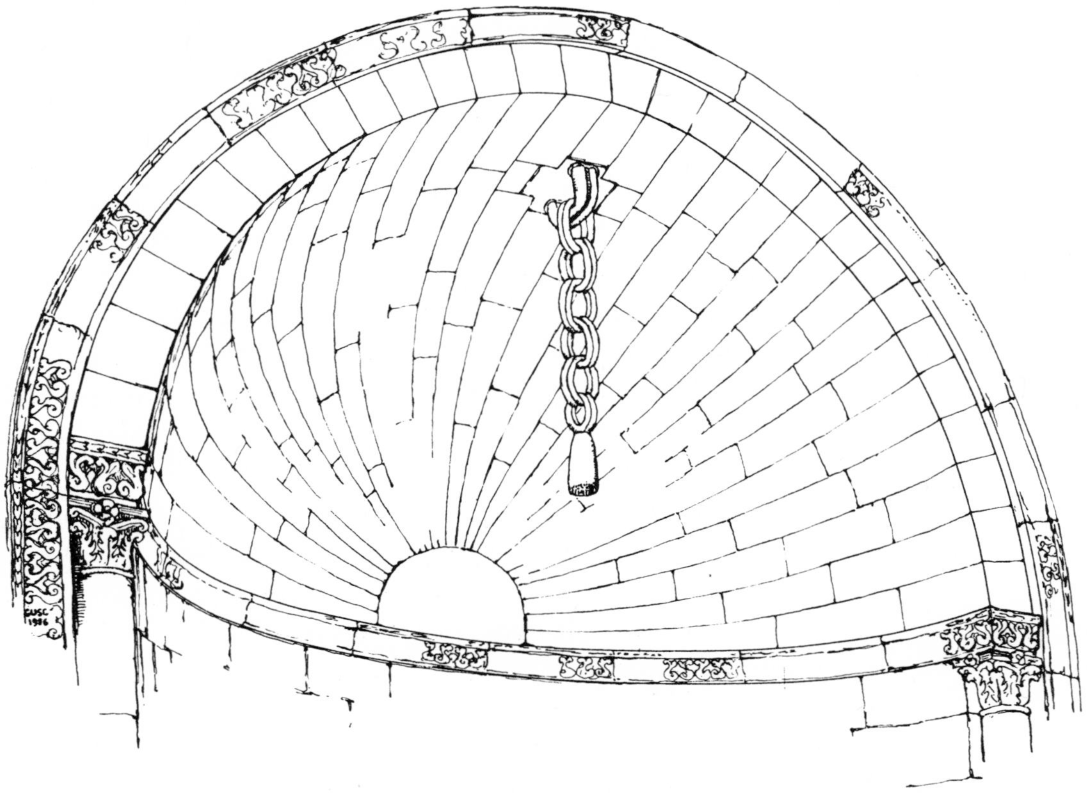

FIG. 618. MAFJAR: Bath hall, apse V, semi-dome as reassembled. (From Hamilton, *op. cit.*)

then run horizontally below the upper tier was provided by a stone[2] on which part of the moulding rises vertically beside a niche. The moulding which ran round the great semi-domes of the apses was not cut on the front voussoirs but on an outer ring of covering stones, as shown (Figs. 617 and 618).

As for the construction of the great semi-domes, several rings of voussoirs were found lying comparatively undisturbed as they had fallen in apse IV. From these Corbett was enabled to restore the complete semi-dome as shown in Hamilton's Fig. 48, according to which it was slightly more than a quarter-sphere, the centre being 38 cm. behind the chord of the apse. The front arch was slightly pointed.

Exedra V (Fig. 618) formed an exception, for its semi-dome was built in courses radiating from a saddle-block at the back, exactly as in the *calidarium* of Ḥammām aṣ-Ṣarakh (above, p. 501, and Plate 83 *e*). Nine measurable voussoirs survived from its frontal arch. Directly behind the keystone on the diameter of the apse was a cross-shaped voussoir with a ring below it cut in the same stone. The ring was oval in section and its attachment to the voussoir was reinforced by an iron band sunk into the body of the stone. As found the stone ring was broken into several pieces and with it, among the fallen blocks of the semi-dome, were fragments of six other rings of oval form and figure-of-eight section together with a drop-shaped stone pendant. All these fragments could be reassembled to form a chain and pendant about a metre and a half long, as shown in Plate 103 *f*; all carved out of a single block of stone, a stone-mason's *tour-de-force*, which would have caught the eye of all who entered by the main door.[3]

The roof of this great hall was supported by sixteen massive stone piers, each 2·26 m. square and about 4·80 m. in height, with acanthus capitals and moulded bases on plain square plinths. They had three-quarter-round shafts at the corners and square pilasters between, and were set in four rows of four

[1] Hamilton, *op. cit.*, p. 86.
[2] *Ibid.*, pl. XIV$_6$.
[3] *Ibid.*, p. 91.

each. 'Their spacing was such that on each main axis the central aisle was from 5·50 to 5·60 wide; the 'intermediate aisles from 4·40 to 4·60 m.; and the four aisles on the outside from 2·50 to 3·36 m. 'wide.'[1]

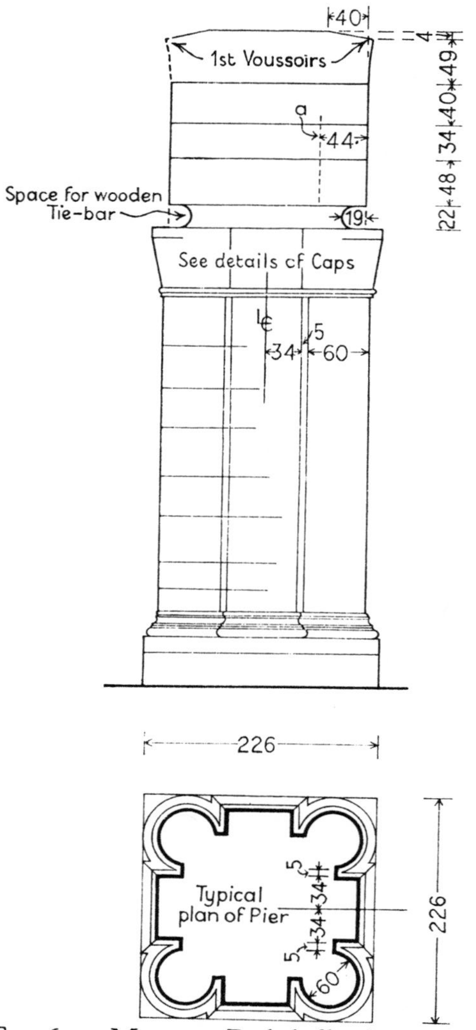

FIG. 619. MAFJAR: Bath hall, plan and elevation of a typical pier with the impost, measured from pier 9. From Hamilton, *op. cit.*)

'From fallen voussoirs, many of which lay in recognizable series, 'it was clear that the sixteen piers had been interconnected by stone-'built arches, which carried walls intersecting to form nine square or 'rectangular compartments. It was further apparent that each of these 'walls was pierced by a number of windows, some of which could be 'judged, by details in the plaster rendering of their jambs and by traces 'of glazing, to have been outside windows, while others had merely 'served to connect adjoining compartments of the interior.'[2]

At a level which was probably a few feet below the windows, the walls were traversed by a cornice moulding, of which the profile is shown in Fig. 621 'The wall spaces between the windows were decorated 'on their inside faces with small recessed niches arranged in groups of 'three [one above two].[3] Like the rest of the interior these niches were 'plastered over and painted with imitation marble revetments, flanking 'colonnettes, and crude shell niches. . . . Vast quantities of fallen brick-'work showed that the greater part, if not the whole, of the structure 'had been vaulted in brick.'[4]

The highest feature of the nine central bays, of which the level could be calculated by direct measurements, was the crown of the main arches of the axial aisles which were roughly 9 m. above the sill of the south-western door. It was possible to fix this level because the semi-cylindrical corner shaft of one of the fallen piers was found so little disturbed that every course could be measured. Its total height from the top of its plinth to the top of its capital was 4·22 m. As the plinth was 5 cm. below the datum, the top of the capital must have been 4·17 m. above it. The capital of another pier was found with a lump of masonry still attached to the top of it, from which it was clear that the main arches of the hall were stilted, having three courses of stonework plus a timber tie-bar, 1·44 m. high in all, intervening between the top of the capital and the springing (Fig. 619). This added to the height of the measured pier gives 5·61 m. above the datum as the level of the springing, or about 6·20 m. above the floor.[5]

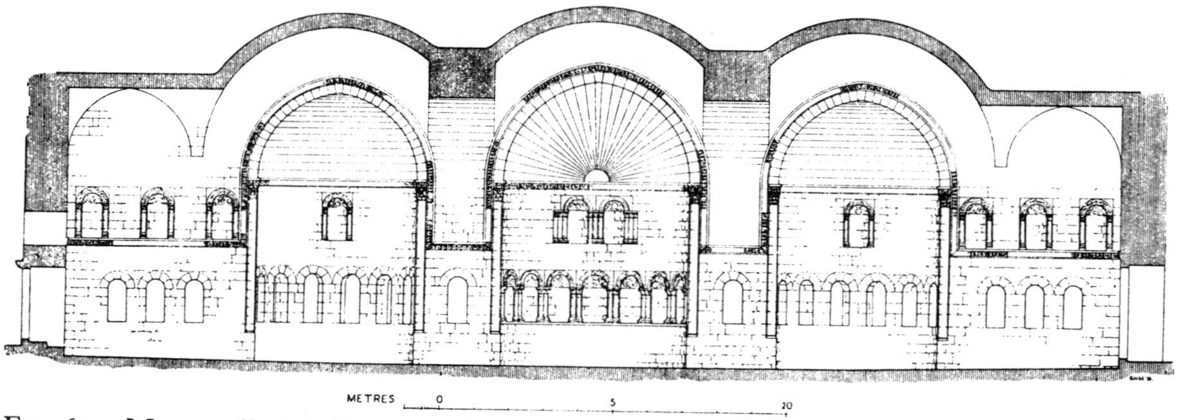

FIG. 620. MAFJAR: Bath hall, west ambulatory, inferred long section and elevation. (From Hamilton, *op. cit.*)

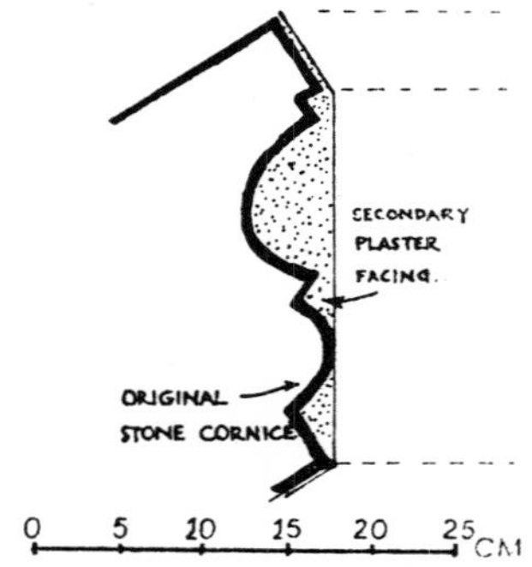

FIG. 621 MAFJAR: Bath-hall, cornice moulding from above the main arches. (From Hamilton, *op. cit.*)

We have seen that the width of the central aisle was 5·62 m., but as the arches were set back 18½ cm. at the springing besides being stilted, their span must have been 5·99 m. It was fortunately possible to measure ten voussoirs belonging to one particular arch, from which the radius was deduced as 3·39 m. From

[1] Hamilton, *op. cit.*, p. 49.
[2] *Ibid.*, pp. 51–2.
[3] *Ibid.*, pl. XIII₆.
[4] *Ibid.*, p. 52.
[5] *Ibid.*, pp. 68–9.

this it follows that its centres must have been 79 cm. apart,[1] or between one-seventh and one-eighth of the span. Fifteen voussoirs 41 cm. deep, belonging to an arch of one of the intermediate aisle arches was also measured; its radius worked out as 2·90 m. and its height to the soffit 2·88 m. or to the extrados 3·29 m. giving a total height of 8·90 m. above the datum, or about 9·5 m. above the ground. It will thus have stood about half a metre lower than the arches of the axial naves.[2]

The Clerestory. The walls above all these arches rose high enough to provide room for windows, some of which overlooked the roofs of the outer aisles, whereas others merely opened into the neighbouring bays as shown in Fig. 622. The masonry between these windows has fallen in such large pieces, some almost intact and measuring 1·32 m. square, that it was obvious that the walls at this level were 1·32 m. thick and that the windows were placed 1·32 m. apart.

In certain places the walls above the arches must have been traversed by a plastered and painted moulding, of which fragments were found widely scattered. In a few cases the stones composing the moulding had been cut to follow gently rising curves, which Hamilton takes to represent the back of arches which impinged on the line of the moulding, and as these curved pieces were comparatively rare he suggests that not all the arches so interfered with the horizontal continuity. In other words it was the arches of the axial naves which impinged on the line of the moulding, and not the others which were 50 cm. lower. By measuring the stones assembled in his Plate XIII$_8$, it was found that the level at which the moulding impinged on the outer curve of the arch was about 25 cm. below the apex, and that the moulding itself, 25 cm. high, had been laid at 9·18 m. above the datum. By a wonderful piece of luck the stones shown in his Fig. 31 were found cohering, and they show that there were not less than three courses of masonry, 80 cm. high, above the moulded course and below any window. Hamilton points out that the least possible height of the window-sills must therefore have been 9·18 + 0·26 + 0·80 = 10·24 m. above the datum[3] (or about 10·86 above the ground) but as there is no indication of a window-sill on its top surface, he assumes one more course in his reconstruction (his Fig. 31). As the spacing of the windows was constant, it follows that the windows on the short sides of the oblong bays must have been narrower than the others. Thanks to numerous cohering blocks of masonry it was possible to see that the window-jambs had been 1·49 m. high and that the window openings had been arched. Assuming that they were round-headed their full height must have been 1·49 + 0·66 = 2·15 m.

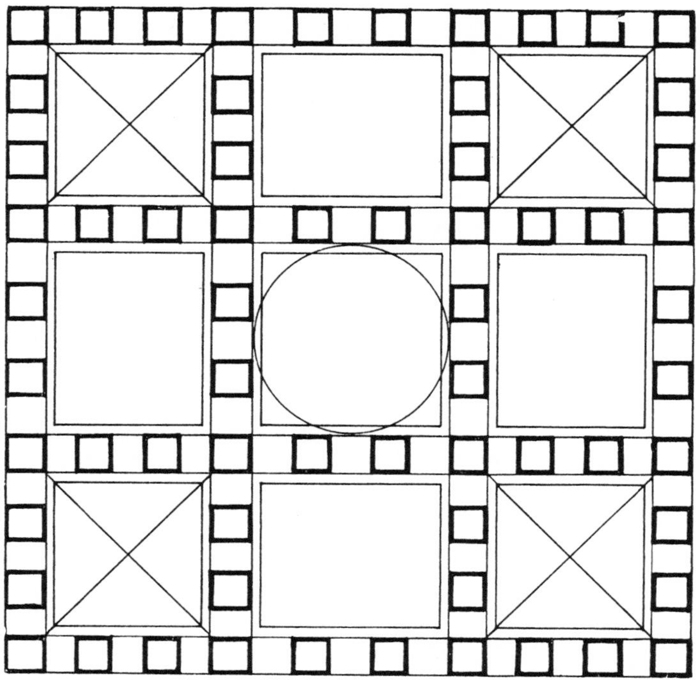

Fig. 622. Mafjar: Bath hall, central bays: schematic plan at clerestory level. (From Hamilton, *op. cit.*)

From the above-mentioned moulding upwards, the internal walls of the nine central bays were decorated with painted designs now half effaced, but this decoration was varied between each pair of windows, by groups of three little niches recessed in the wall face already mentioned and shown in Hamilton's Fig. 33. Certain fragments of adhering plaster grilles showed that only the external windows were glazed.[4] Of the nine bays at this level, four were squares averaging 5·52 m., four rectangles averaging 6·57×5·52 m., and the central compartment a square of 6·57 m. Hamilton in his restoration proposes to put cross-vaults over the four corner bays, and tunnel-vaults over the oblong axial bays.

As for the central one he believes that there was a dome on a drum with windows, a conclusion with which one can readily agree without accepting either of the two reconstructions published by him.

The Bathing Pool. A barrier to enclose a bathing pool had been built between the four piers that stood nearest to the south wall; this barrier, which was 1·25 m. high, turned at right angles at each end

[1] The distance apart = 2 R–S = 6·78–5·99 = 79 cm.
[2] *Ibid.*, pp. 69–70.
[3] *Ibid.*, pp. 70–71.
[4] *Ibid.*, p. 71.

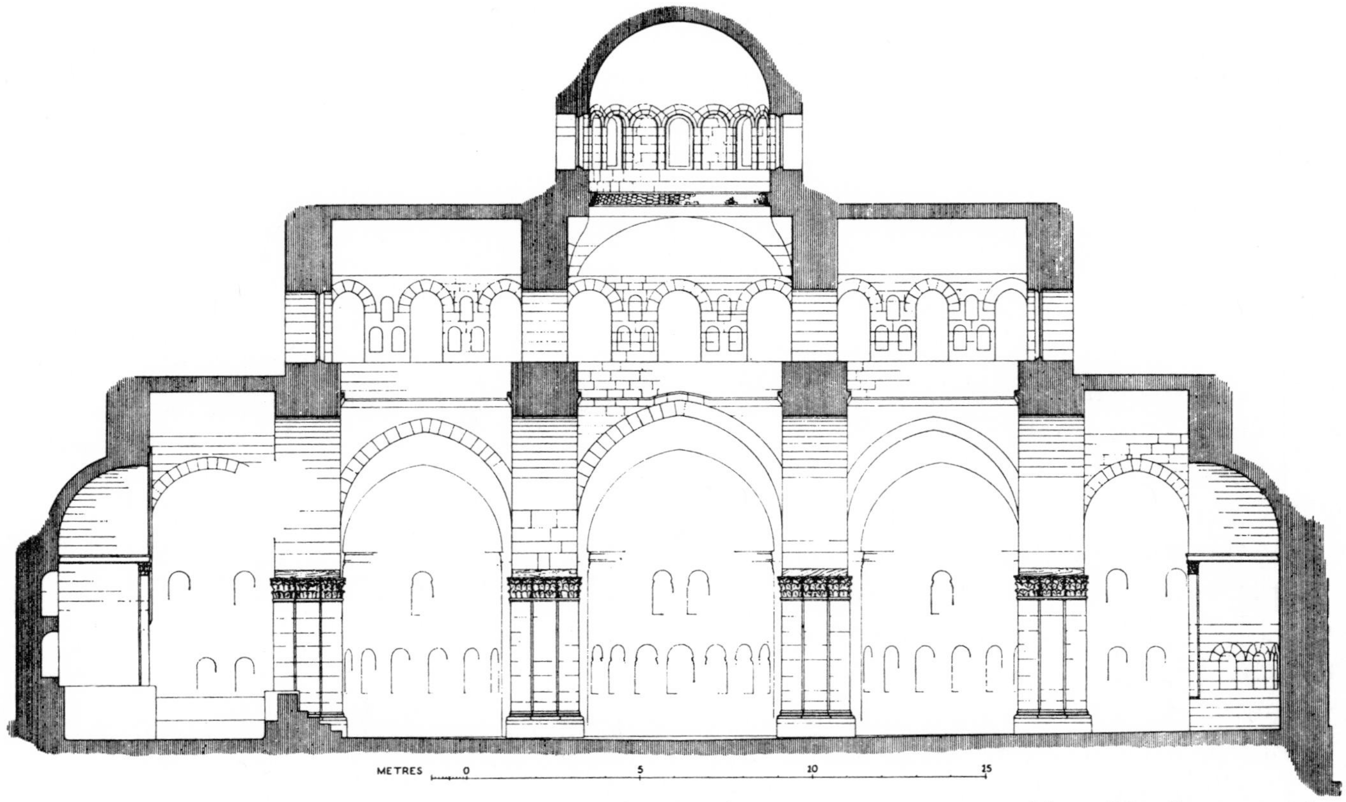

FIG. 623. MAFJAR: Bath hall, inferred cross-section, looking west. (From Hamilton, *op. cit.*)

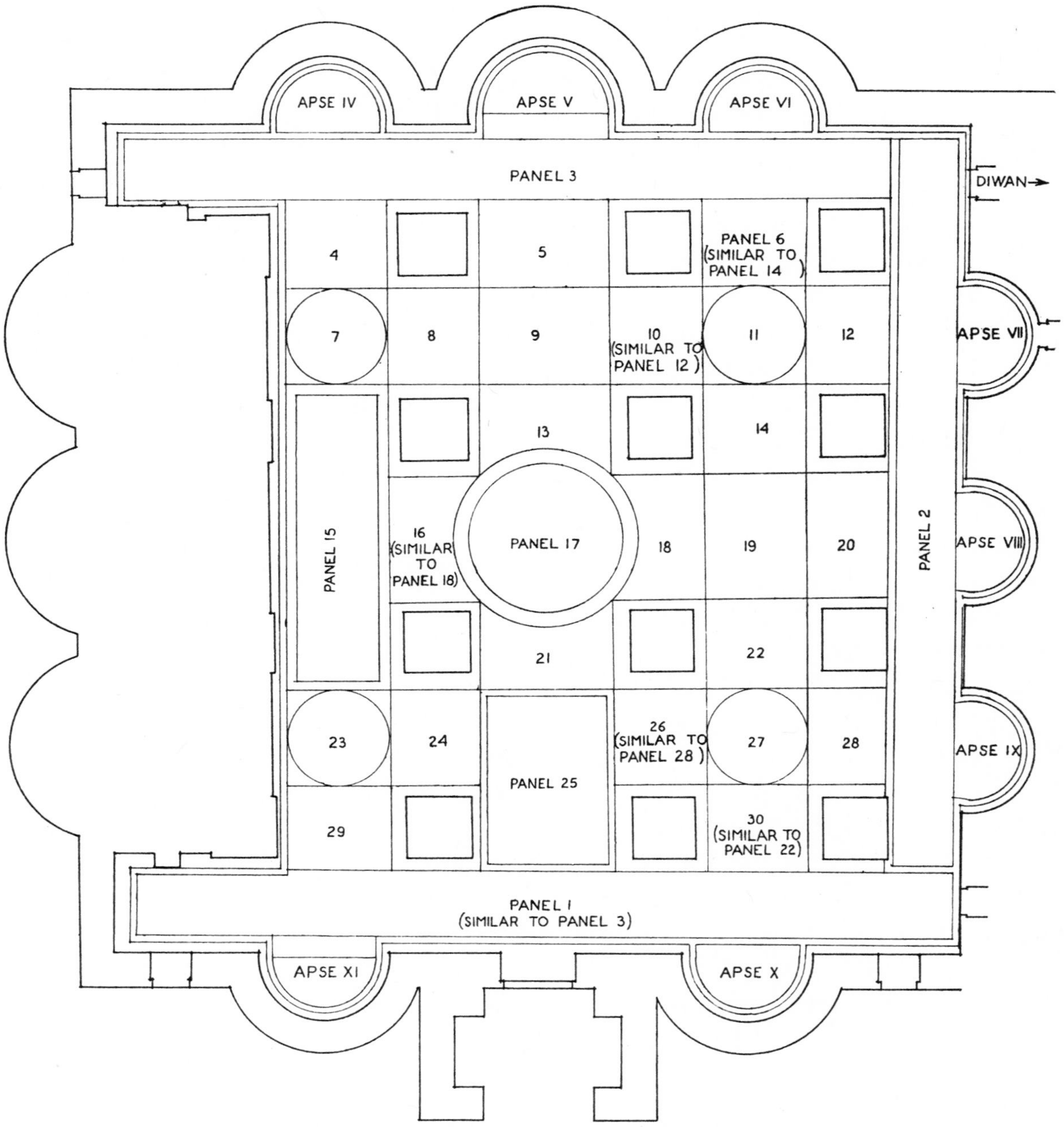

FIG. 624. Bath hall, index plan of mosaic floor.

to meet the wall. This pool was 19·50 m. long and 3·40 m. wide to which must be added the area of the three exedrae. It was accessible on the side facing the hall by three broad flights of steps between the four piers, leaving a parapet at the top 50 cm. high and 50 cm. thick. All was revetted with slabs of bituminous Nabī Mūsā stone. Another flight of six steps was built against the short west wall alongside the doorway leading to the palace (Plate 106 *b*). The inner surfaces of the pool were lined with a waterproof cement of lime and crushed pottery on a backing of brickwork.

There was no trace of an inlet for water which, presumably, was higher up than the surviving masonry. The floor sloped towards the east end, where there was a pipe for emptying the pool. Near the top of the barrier at the same point was an overflow pipe. 'Four other pipes traversed the barrier, one at the 'west end of the pool and the others between the piers on the north side at an intermediate level flush 'with the lowest of the outside steps. When the pool was filled these could be opened to let water flow 'out through grooves cut in the top surface of the step on to the mosaic floor of the hall. This arrange- 'ment could have been used for washing the floor, which itself was drained by four pierced marble 'slabs let into the surface along the east–west axis of the hall.'[1]

THE FLOOR MOSAICS. The great glory of the *frigidarium* was its polychrome mosaic floor found almost intact, except where it had been dented by falling masonry, under some three or four metres of débris. It formed a continuous surface of mosaic, as may be seen in Plates 107–9 and Fig. 624, divided by the pier bases into 38 different 'carpets', as Hamilton calls them.[2]

On entering by the porch we cross a long transverse panel (No. 1) running from end to end of the eastern ambulatory, and have a vista in front of us in which an oblong panel (No. 25) leads the eye towards the great circular composition (No. 17) immediately under the dome (Plate 107 *c*), and beyond that to the central exedra on the west side with its magnificent semicircular carpet (Plate 107 *d*). In front of it is the long transverse panel of the western ambulatory, the design of which is similar to No. 1. In the case of three out of the five circular compositions (Nos. 11, 17, and 27), the adjoining carpets are made to match. Thus of the four panels flanking No. 11, 10 matches 12 and 6 matches 14; of the panels flanking No 17, 13 matches 21 and 16 matches 18; and of the panels flanking No. 27, 22 matches 30 and 26 matches 28. Each of the eight exedrae has its own semicircular carpet; that of the largest, facing the main entrance, being particularly magnificent, as already stated. All the designs are geometrical compositions.

There are thirty-eight panels in all; but as seven designs are duplicated (1 = 3, 6 = 14, 10 = 12, 13 = 21, 16 = 18, 22 = 30, and 26 = 28) it follows that there are thirty-one different designs instead of thirty-eight. These are classified by Hamilton[3] into seven types, as follows:

1. *Rectilinear diapers or reticulations*: panels 6, 8, 10, 12, 14, 16, 18, 22, 24, 26, 28, 29, 30.
2. *Interlacings on rectangular grid*: panels 1, 2, 3, 4, 5, 9, 15, 25, and the front of apse XI.
3. *Concentric interlacings*: panels 7, 11, 23, 27, and apse XI.
4. *Sprig patterns*: panels 13, 20, 21, apses IV and IX.
5. *Rainbow matting patterns*: apses VI, VII, VIII, and X and *Dīwān* ante-room.
6. *Basketry patterns*: panels 17 and apse V.
7. *Overlapping circles*: panel 19.

Two remarks are called for. All these patterns are 45° patterns with a single exception, for the only example of a 60° pattern occurs under the dome of the *Dīwān*. Hamilton has already expressed surprise that the semi-domed recess there contains the only realistic pictorial mosaic in the whole complex.[4] It seems probable that the *Dīwān* mosaics were executed by a craftsman with ideas of his own, and that the rest of the mosaics were executed by a group of craftsman belonging to the same school.

Another feature calls for remark. It will be noticed that whenever octagons are used in the designs they nearly always have four long sides alternating with four short ones, e.g. panels 8, 22, 24, 28, and 30. This feature occurs in the mosaics of the Church of St. George at Jerash and is due to the setting-out of the octagons on squared paper, as was first pointed out by Crowfoot (see above, p. 202). I would class these designs as last in the order of merit, and Hamilton seems to be of the same opinion.[5]

[1] *Ibid.*, p. 49.
[2] *Ibid.*, p. 327.
[3] *Ibid.*, pp. 329–37.
[4] *Ibid.*, pp. 337–9.
[5] *Ibid.*, pp. 329–31.

In apse IV the pattern is composed of imbrications, each occupied by a sprig. A grid of imbrications is used for the grille above the lintel of the western door of the Dome of the Rock (Plate 4). In the rainbow matting patterns in apses VI, VII, VIII, and X, the rainbow effect is 'produced by bands of two or three different colour-groups following each other in recurrent sequence and each graded in tone from light to dark'.[1]

The basketry group consists of two panels only, No. 17 and apse V, which occupy the most important positions in the *frigidarium*, one under the dome and the other in the apse opposite the entrance, that is to say they form part of the vista seen on entering by the porch, and so were presumably regarded by the craftsmen as their best work, in any case they certainly deserved to be. As Hamilton puts it: 'None of the pre-Islamic floors on record can be compared in variety of colouring, fineness of articulation, or over-all size with panel 17'.[2] It consists of a network of concentric circles increasing in diameter as they advance, and intersected by two sets of curved lines rotating in opposite directions. These three sets of lines form isosceles triangles, their bases lying on the concentric circles and their sides on the two rotating curved lines. Hamilton estimates that there must be nearly 8,000 coloured triangles in the main pattern.[3] For some reason or other a pair of black and white triangles, in the fifteenth ring from the exterior,[4] has been turned round, perhaps a deliberate imperfection to avert the evil eye.

The *Dīwān*. The western door on the north side opened into what must have been the most richly decorated part of the whole great complex, the audience hall, or *Dīwān* of the Khalif or Prince who was the owner of the palace. Significantly it is exactly opposite the door at the southern end of the same aisle which gave access to the covered loggia leading to the western cloister of the palace. It was a domed room about 4·80 m. square with a deep semi-domed recess on the north side. On three sides, about 60 cm. above the floor were deep ledges which could have served as benches, and the floor of the apsidal part was on the same level (Fig. 625).

Both parts of the room as well as the tops of the benches were paved with coloured stone mosaics and the fronts of the latter were plastered and painted in imitation of a marble dado. Both floors and benches were found in perfect preservation (Plate 108), which is most fortunate for the mosaic of the apsidal recess (Plate 108 *c* (colour)) is certainly the most beautiful floor mosaic ever discovered in Palestine. It represents an orange tree, full of fruit, with leaves in three shades of green, beneath which to the left are two antelopes, one of which nibbles at its leaves, and to the right a lion pounces on the back of another antelope, an old-as-the-hills motif of Scythian art. It is the only pictorial mosaic in the whole complex which Hamilton well describes as 'drawn as a succession of superimposed silhouettes, each plane 'of colour forming the background to one lighter in tone than itself, thus passing by gradations from 'the deepest gray or black through shades of gray, blue-green, and green to pale lemon-yellow'.[5]

The walls, on the contrary, had been destroyed down to the level of the benches, except round the apse, where up to five courses (1·5 m.) survived in places. The remains of a carved stucco revetment, which Hamilton rightly describes as 'of quite outstanding quality', adhered to the wall (Plate 109 *b–c*).

The whole room was filled with débris consisting of masses of fallen material—carved stucco fragments, broken bricks, and masonry. From a careful examination and sorting out of this material it was clear that the square part had been covered by a brick dome resting, by the intermediary of spherical-triangle pendentives, on a stone drum with eight windows, fitted with pierced stucco grilles, which apparently were not glazed. There was also a lunette over the door. The whole of the apse and its semi-dome were of ashlar.

Two columns, encrusted with stucco ornament in the form of imbrications, carried the frontal arch of the apse. An acanthus cornice ran round the walls of the square part, and probably of the apse also. Its level was estimated as 2·96 m. above the floor.[6] If we assume that the pendentives were true spherical-triangle pendentives, then their top edge must have been 2·35 m. above the cornice. The height of the drum, computed from measurements of its fallen ornament, must have been about 1·75 m.; the springing of the dome was therefore 7·06 m. above the floor. 'An interesting point revealed by remains of the

[1] *Ibid.*, p. 334.

[2] *Ibid.*, p. 336.

[3] *Ibid.*, p. 335.

[4] To the left, on a vertical line dropped from the centre in Plate 107 *c*.

[5] *Q.D.A.P.*, XIV, p. 120.

[6] Most of the vertical measurements were deduced from measured fragments of the ornament and the theoretical height of the panels as they would be if their ornament were completed.

'internal decoration . . . was that the springing level of the dome was the same as that of the window 'arches; so that the heads of the drum windows penetrated the hemispherical shell of the dome.'[1] Fallen fragments of the dome showed that its outer surface had been plastered over and painted yellow. Hamilton believes that the little stone edicule,[2] which was found in the débris of the room, must originally have formed a miniature lantern at the summit of the dome.[3]

FIG. 625. MAFJAR: *Dīwān*, restored perspective view of the interior. (From Hamilton, *op. cit.*)

Except for the semicircular lunettes between the pendentives, the entire inner surface was encrusted with stucco ornament, superior in design and execution to any other in the whole great complex. The decoration was divided into three zones by two acanthus cornices, one, already mentioned, directly below the springing of the pendentives, and a second round the base of the drum. Below the first cornice the walls were divided into nine panels, two to right, two to left, one on each side of the door,

[1] *Khirbat al Mafjar*, p. 66. [2] Shown in his pl. XII_3. [3] *Op. cit.*, p. 66.

and three in the apse. Each panel was surrounded by a triple border, consisting of a curious motif in effect rather like an inverted egg and dart, then by a series of acanthus whorls, recalling those on the dome piers of the Dome of the Rock (Plate 36 *a*) and then by a series of overlapping heart-shaped motifs. Fragments of the lower acanthus cornice were found joined to the upper border of one of the panels, from which it follows that if we can reconstruct a panel we know what was the level of this cornice.

FIG. 6.26 MAFJAR: window grille B1, from *dīwān* of bath. (From Hamilton, *op. cit.*)

It was possible to reconstruct the two most beautiful panels (Nos. 18 and 19) of which a considerable part still adhered to the wall of the apse (Plate 109 *b*, and Hamilton's Figs. 140 and 144) and one other (No. 17) from which it appeared that their heights worked out as 1·42 m.[1] Substantial remains were found of panel 20, in which rows of pomegranate flowers, which Hamilton[2] compares to those of Qalʿa-i-Kuhna, play the principal part.

The columns of the apse arch were decorated with beaded imbrications, filled with sprigs of acanthus (Plate 109 *b*) which recall the decorations of the great brick columns of the Sassanian palace at Dāmghān.[3] The face of the arch itself was decorated with swastikas and trefoils, and an outer bead-and-reel border.

Fairly large fragments of the pendentives show that they were each decorated with a wreath of minute acanthus leaves enclosing a winged horse in relief.[4] The three triangular spaces, left over between the wreath and the edges of the pendentives, were filled with vine scrolls.[5]

Directly above the pendentives the base of the drum wall was encircled by a row of some eighty or a hundred partridges, above which was a second acanthus cornice on which rested eight round-headed windows, flanked by little colonnettes and filled with stucco grilles. Only one (Plate 109 *a* and Fig. 626) was recovered complete. It is a 60° design and is practically identical to the marble grille on the south side of the western vestibule of the Great Mosque at Damascus (above, Plate 59 *b*). Three others were reconstructed from fragments; all were 45° designs, two of them composed entirely of straight lines, whereas the fourth was based on compass work.[6]

A very elaborate border ran round the arched part of each window, continued along horizontally across the space between, and then rose again to run round the next. It consisted of a central band of interlacing ribbons forming circles and enclosing six-lobed motifs set between an inner and outer bead-and-reel border and a hollow moulding. The whole effect is very rich (Plate 109 *a*).

The transition between this border and the dome cap proper was effected by eight five-sided panels. They all had egg-and-leaf borders, but no single panel was recovered at all complete.

THE DOME CAP. Incredible as it may seem, this fragile ornament has been almost perfectly preserved although it had fallen from the summit of the dome. In the centre is a six-lobed rosette, composed of six very large acanthus leaves with curved-over tips, standing boldly away from their background, with two smaller rosettes in the centre. Six human heads, alternately male and female, rise up in high relief between the acanthus leaves. 'They were all identical in form and only distinguished by 'black-painted moustaches and trim beards in the men and globular pendent ear-rings in the women. 'The hair and eyebrows of all were painted black and the lips tinted red. The drilled pupils of the eyes 'and the eyelids were black. The women's ear-rings were yellow'[7] (Plate 110 *a–b*). This part was enclosed

[1] Hamilton, *op. cit.*, pp. 197–8.
[2] *Ibid.*, p. 202.
[3] *Ibid.*, pp. 220–21.
[4] See Hamilton, pl. LIV 1 and 2.
[5] *Ibid.*, pp. 205–7.
[6] *Ibid.*, pp. 207 and 281–5.
[7] *Ibid.*, p. 211.

by a six-lobed bead-and-reel border, and then by a free-standing vine scroll, each loop containing a five-lobed vine leaf. This in turn was enclosed by another bead-and-reel border, beyond which came a remarkable border composed of two undulating stalks forming eighteen loops, each occupied by a fantastic flower (Hamilton calls it a 'winged strawberry flower') on a split-palmette calyx.[1] Then comes a third bead-and-reel border, and a hollow moulding which must have been in contact with the eight five-sided panels.

THE COLD ROOMS. A door in the western exedra on the north side opens in room A. This had a door on the far side leading into B, and one on the right leading into the hot rooms. It had benches round all four walls, but was not heated. The walls and floor including the benches had once been encased with marble slabs which had been systematically removed. The same thing had happened to room B, which is a little smaller than A, and which also had benches all round. Above the benches the walls were coated with waterproof cement, and incorporated in the west wall were two tanks, the use of which is not clear.[2]

THE HOT ROOMS AND FURNACES. To reach the *calidarium* one first had to enter A and then pass into C, a room about 5½ metres square, with a niche on the east side (Plate 110 *d*). The floor has collapsed, exposing the hypocausts. The brick piers ran in rows from east to west, spaced 42 to 49 cm. apart, and covered by basalt slabs or large bricks. The hypocaust was heated by a furnace in the stoke-hole E, placed just under the niche. This stoke-hole was not accessible from the bath proper but only from the exterior by a door on the north. The hot air from the hypocaust was carried up the walls by short pottery pipes fitted into each other and hidden by marble panelling, the existence of which is proved by a few small fragments still adhering and a few bronze clamps.[3]

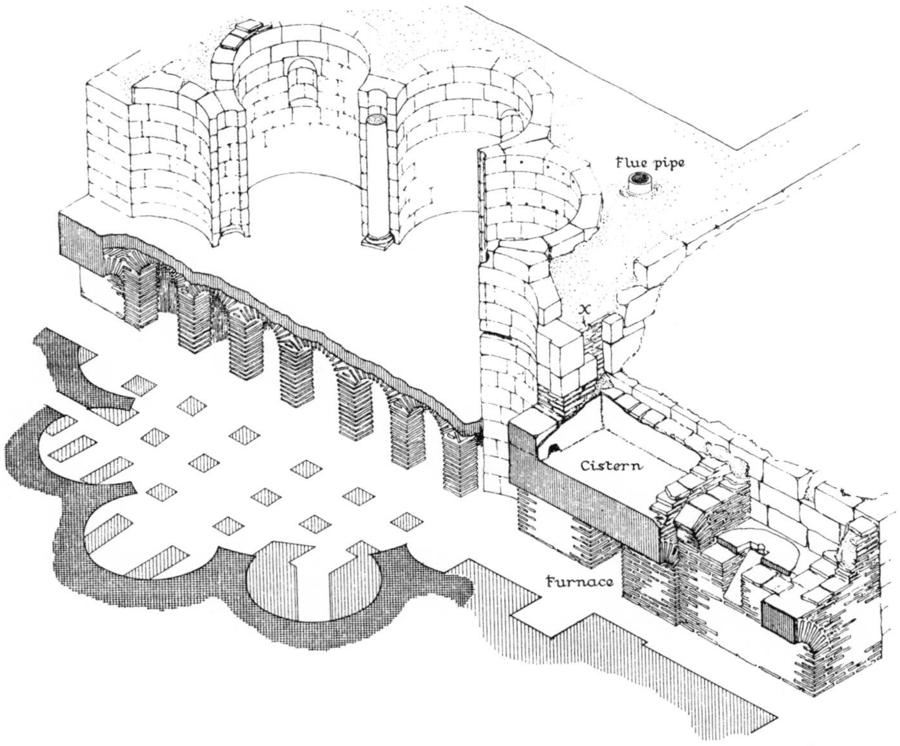

FIG. 627. Room D, with furnace, as seen from the north-east. (From Hamilton, *op. cit.*)

From this room people would have passed into a second hot room D, a circular chamber with eight horse-shoe shaped niches, one containing the door (Plate 110 *c*). In each of the four niches nearest the door from room C is a small round-headed recess, and in one of them on the west side was the springing of a semi-dome in brick, about 2 m. above the floor level (Fig. 627). Here again the floor has collapsed, exposing the hypocaust. Eight small columns stood against the narrow segments of wall between the niches, but only the base of one remains. The diameter between opposite columns was about 4·25 m. Hamilton suggests a central dome and eight little domes.[4] I believe that there was a central dome resting on eight arches, springing from the engaged columns and surrounded by eight semi-domes, for the recesses are only 90 cm. wide and about 50 cm. deep if we omit the engaged columns for the reason just given.

THE LATRINE (F) was an L-shaped room entered by the easternmost door on the north side. Three piers and a wall pier, which together form a square, were doubtless joined by four arches which served as supports for four brick tunnel-vaults, parallel to the four walls, the square in all probability being left open to the sky. Large pieces of these vaults were found lying here and there. In the centre was an ornamental fountain, consisting of a scalloped stone basin, with a copper jet in the middle. It was plastered and painted yellow.

[1] *Ibid.*, p. 210 and fig. 154. [2] *Op. cit.*, pp. 52–5. [3] *Ibid.*, pp. 55–9. [4] *Op. cit.*, p. 59.

Under these vaults on three sides were plastered masonry seats, separated by slots 19 cm. wide, opening into a deep drain which ran all round and passed out eastwards under G in Fig. 629. Seats and drain were all coated with a strong waterproof cement. The seats, at some unknown date, had been altered so that they were composed of rows of projecting stones corbelled out at intervals of 30 cm. from the back wall, and 'met by corresponding stones projecting slightly inwards from a continuous screen wall in front '(Fig. 628). . . . What proves that the present form of the seats is secondary . . . is the existence under 'each of the corbelled stones of a quarter-round moulding, now filled up with plaster and invisible. It is 'clear that in the original scheme this moulding was meant to be seen, and that the screen wall, which now 'hides it, must have been absent. The only original elements 'are the corbels and the narrow ledge that now skirts the seat 'but was then a relatively broad step or foot-rest.'[1] Hamilton remarks that 'it seems clear, from both stages of the installa-'tion, that the Roman habit of sitting on a seat had tem-'porarily displaced, in Umayyad aristocratic circles, the 'more hygienic and ancient oriental practice of squatting on 'foot-rests established at floor level'.[2]

FIG. 628. The Latrine. (From Hamilton, *op. cit.*)

It is not generally known that similar latrines, with water carriage, are still to be seen in the Madrasa of Sultan Ḥasan at Cairo and the Mosque of Barsbāy at Khānqā (841 H. = 1437). In the former there are four massive L-shaped piers joined by four arches, supporting four tunnel-vaults parallel to the sides. Each unit is enclosed in a cell with a pointed-arched doorway, the seat is on the right on entering, and there is a washing basin opposite the entrance.

THE UNIT OF MEASUREMENT EMPLOYED. Here again, as in the Pavilion, the Nilometric cubit appears to have been employed in setting out the Ḥammām.

North wall	30·28 m. =	56 N.c. =	30·26 m.	Diff. 2 cm.
South ,,	30·33 m.	,,	,,	,, 7 cm.
Height of porch	5·43 m. =	10 N.c. =	5·404	,, 2½ cm.
,, ,, façade	9·72 m. =	18 N.c. =	9·727	,, 7 mm.
Internal diameter of drum of dome	3·74 m. =	7 N.c. =	3·78	,, 4 cm.
Dīwān sides (average)	4·69 m. =	8½ N.c. =	4·59	,, 10 cm.

From this it would appear to be a fair deduction that Copts played an important part at Mafjar, as they must have at Mshattā (below, pp. 620-22).

THE DATE. During the excavations of 1936/7, Baramki discovered fragments of marble slabs and mosaic chippings in front of the south-eastern corner tower, and among them was a small broken slab of white marble on which a man named 'Ubayd Allāh had written in ink a message of goodwill to the Khalif Hishām.[3] As it is unthinkable that such a message would ever have been dedicated to anybody but the reigning Khalif, it may be taken as definite proof that the complex was built during his reign, i.e. between A.D. 724 and 743. Hamilton, however, is not willing to admit that this graffito means that Hishām was the builder or the owner of the palace; he says: 'certain aspects of the establishment suggest 'a warning that that conclusion might be wrong. A certain extravagance in the architecture and orna-'ment of the bath, even a suggestion of profligacy, may be felt to be out of character with the parsimony 'and gravity of demeanour attributed by Arabic historians to Hishām.' But Hishām's palace of Qaṣr al-Ḥayr al-Gharbī had highly decorated closure-slabs, great paintings, and an elaborate decorated entrance. On the other hand 'we cannot exclude the possibility that some other person of exceptional wealth and 'princely standing, perhaps a close relative of the Caliph or an official wielding high authority in the 'province, might have built for himself . . . a winter lodge or *mashta*, with a mosque for public prayer 'and other amenities attached to it'.[4] Finally he attributes Mafjar to Walīd II.

[1] Hamilton, *op. cit.*, pp. 60–61 and fig. 23. [2] *Ibid.*, p. 62. [3] *Q.D.A.P.*, VIII, p. 53 and pl. XXXIV$_2$. [4] *Op. cit.*, p. 7.

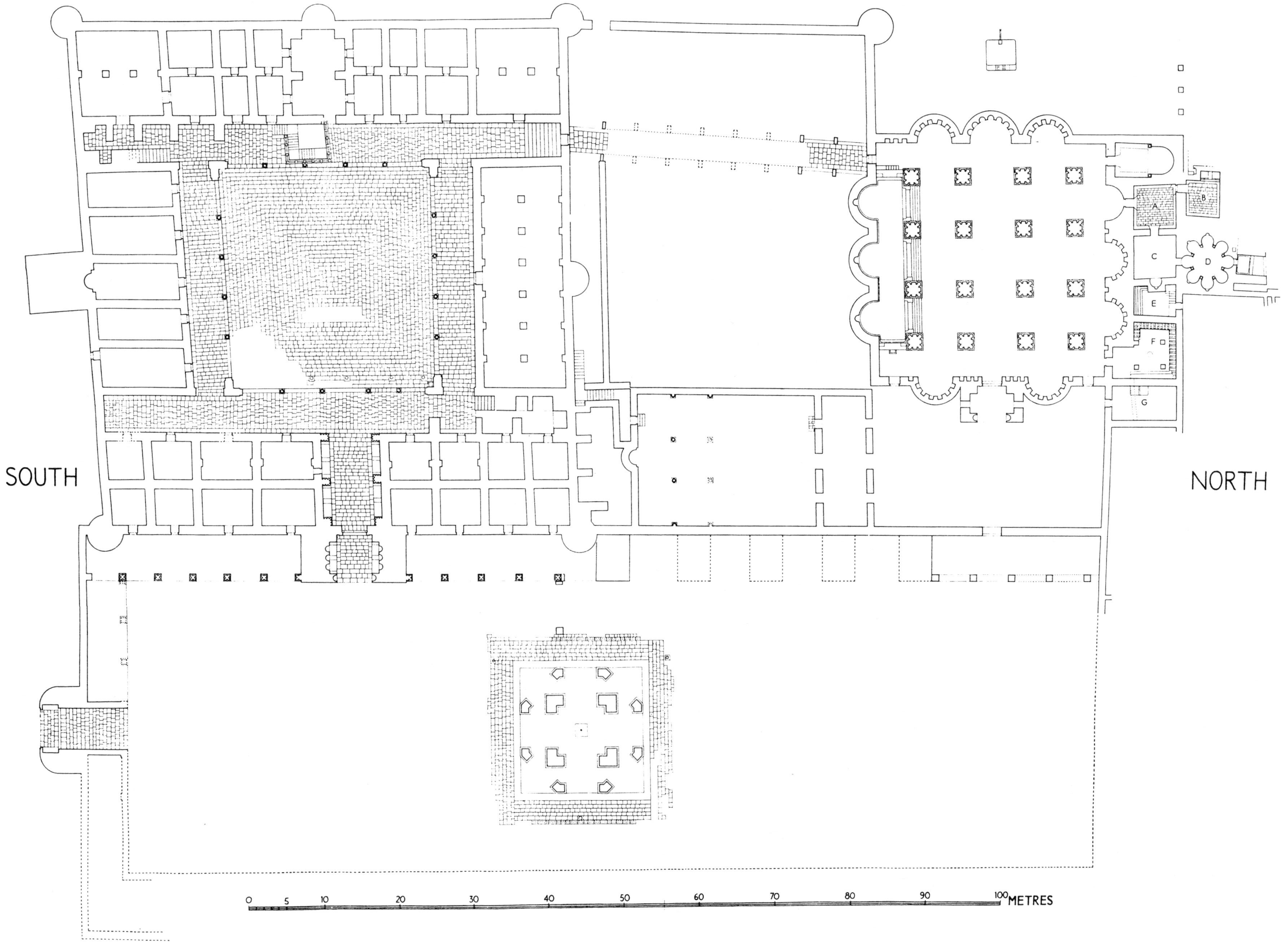

FIG. 629. MAFJAR: General Plan of the Palace, Mosque, Bath, and Forecourt. (From Hamilton, *op. cit.*)

As regards the statue, belonging to the porch of the bath, of a man standing on a pedestal, on the front of which are two squatting lions, back to back but looking forward, he admits that it can only depict a ruler, for lions were an attribute of sovereignty. Who else can it be intended for but Hishām? Yet he actually suggests that 'the recorded distaste of the Khalif Hishām for frivolous relaxation and unprofitable expenditure must rule out any suggestion that he was the builder of the bath and, consequently, of the palace',[1] and he attributes it to Walīd II, interpreting the statue 'as a self-portrait of al Walīd himself, depicted by anticipation in the sovereign estate he hoped and intended one day to assume'.[2]

This suggestion seems to me to be untenable for several reasons. The first is that Walīd II was on the worst possible terms with his uncle Hishām who, by various humiliations, made things unendurable for him at his court. *The Kitāb al-Aghānī* says: 'Hishām was displeased with al-Walīd [II] and his 'associates, so al-Walīd went away [from Ruṣāfa] having with him a party of his associates and clients, 'and stayed at Abraq between the territory of [the tribes of] Balqain and Fazāra and a water called Aghdaf.'[3] This makes it improbable that Hishām would have left him with the wealth needed to build and decorate Mafjar. And in another place the *Kitāb al-Aghānī*[4] again speaks of al-Walīd's departure for Abraq and adds the important information 'and stayed there until Hishām died', so he could not have been busy building a great palace complex near Jericho. To this may be added the statement of Ibn 'Abd Rabbihi (*c.* 913) that al-Walīd had lived in the desert for twenty years before he became Khalif, and that even when he was Khalif he never set foot in a town.[5]

We have seen above that Mafjar was unfinished when it was destroyed by an earthquake, presumably that of 747/8.[6] If we accept the Khalif Hishām as the builder then we may assume that all work stopped on his death in 743. Moreover, the insecurity of life caused Khalifs and Sultans, as the case may be, to press on with their building operations at the maximum possible speed, e.g. the well-known example in Cairo, where the immense complex of Qalā'ūn—Hospital, Mausoleum, and Madrasa—was completed in thirteen months after the preparation of the site.[7] So we may say that as Mafjar was unfinished in 743 it was unlikely that its building had been going on for more than a few years, say three, or four at the outside, which would put it in the period 739–43.

BIBLIOGRAPHY

1883 CONDER and KITCHENER, Survey of Western Palestine, Memoirs, III, pp. 211–12.

1894 BLISS (F. J.), Notes on the Plain of Jericho. *Palestine Exploration Fund, Q.St.*, 1894, pp. 177–81, with 3 figs.

1931 SCHNEIDER (A. M.), Das byzantinische Gilgal (*chirbet mefdschir*). *Zeitschr. des Deutschen Palästina Vereins*, LI, pp. 50–59, with 3 figs.

1936–40 BARAMKI (D. C.), Excavations at Khirbet el Mefjer. *Quarterly of the Department of Antiquities in Palestine*, V, pp. 132–8, pls. LXXIV–LXXXVIII and 3 figs.; VI, pp. 157–68, pls. XLIII–LXVI; VIII, pp. 51–3, pls. XXXIV–XXXV and 1 fig.; X, pp. 153–9, pls. XXX–XXXIV and 1 fig.

1938 BARAMKI (D. C.), Where an 8th-century Caliph hoped to spend congenial winters. The excavation of Hisham's elaborately equipped and gorgeously decorated palace in the Jordan Valley. *The Illustrated London News*, CXCIII, 3rd Sept., pp. 407–9, with 15 illus.

1945 BARAMKI (D. C.), One of the finest and best preserved mosaic pavements found. *The Illustrated London News*, CCVII, 14th July, pp. 52–3, with 3 illus.

1944–5 HAMILTON (R. W.), Stone Sculpture. *Quarterly of the Department of Antiquities in Palestine*, XI, pp. 47–66 and pls. XIII–XVI, with 21 figs.; XII, pp. 1–19 and pls. I–X, with 14 figs.

1945 SCHWABE (M.), Khirbat Mafjar. Greek inscribed fragments. *Quarterly of the Department of Antiquities in Palestine*, XII, pp. 20–30 and pl. XI.

1947 HAMILTON (R. W.), Plaster Balustrades from Khirbat al Mafjar. *Quarterly of the Department of Antiquities in Palestine*, XIII, pp. 1–58 and pls. I–XXIII, with 68 figs.

1947 BARAMKI (D. C.), Guide to the Umayyad Palace at Khirbat al Mafjar, 12mo., Jerusalem, 1947.

1949 BARAMKI (D. C.), 'The Stately Pleasure Dome' of the Caliph Hisham: revealed in recent excavations near Jericho. *The Illustrated London News*, CCIV, 28th May, pp. 726–8, with 16 illus.

— ANON. The Winter Palace of the Great Khalif: discoveries near Jericho. *The Illustrated London News*, CCIV, 28th May, p. 728.

1949 HAMILTON (R. W.), The Baths at Khirbat Mafjar. *Palestine Exploration Quarterly*, LXXXI, pp. 40–51, pls. IV–V and 1 fig.

1950 HAMILTON (R. W.), The Sculpture of living forms at Khirbat al Mafjar. *Quarterly of the Department of Antiquities*

[1] *Op. cit.*, p. 346.

[2] *Op. cit.*, p. 232.

[3] VI, p. 104, ll. 27–8. See also Ya'qūbī, *Ta'rīkh*, II, p. 394; Ṭabarī, Secunda Series, p. 1743, ll. 11–14, quoted by Musil, *Palmyrena*, p. 277. Musil seems to suggest that this event took place in the first half of A.D. 735, *Kuṣejr 'Amra*, p. 160; and his *Palmyrena*, p. 277. Musil identifies Aghdaf with the Wādī Ghadaf, eighty miles south-east of 'Ammān, on which Qaṣr aṭ-Ṭūba stands, and Nöldeke agrees; *Z.D.M.G.* IXI, p. 226.

[4] II, p. 79, ll. 1–4.

[5] *al-'Iqd al-Farīd* (ed. of 1302 H.), II, p. 351, ll. 28–9, quoted by Nöldeke, *Z.D.M.G.*, LXI, p. 226.

[6] See above, p. 374.

[7] See my *Muslim Architecture in Egypt*, II, p. 210.

in Palestine, XIV, pp. 100–119 and pls. XXXV–XLV, with 2 figs.

1950 HAMILTON (R. W.), A Mosaic Carpet of Umayyad date at Khirbat al Mafjar. *Quarterly of the Department of Antiquities in Palestine*, XIV, p. 120, pl. XLVI (coloured) and folding plan of whole complex.

1953 HAMILTON (R. W.), Carved Plaster in Umayyad Architecture. *Iraq*, XV, pp. 43–55 and pls. VI–VII.

1955 GRABAR (Oleg), The Umayyad Palace of Khirbat al-Mafjar. *Archaeology*, VIII, pp. 228–35, with 10 illus.

1956 FRANZ (Heinrich Gerhard), Das Omayyadenschloss von Khirbat al Mafjar. Eine Übersicht über die Ergebnisse der Ausgrabungen. *Forschungen und Fortschritte*, XXX, pp. 298–305, with 12 illus.

1956 STERN (Henri), Notes sur l'architecture des châteaux omeyyades. *Ars Islamica*, XI–XII, pp. 72–3 and fig. 2.

1958 BARĀMKĪ (Dimītrī) Taṭawwur al-Handasa al-Mi'mārīya, wa'l-Fann fī 'Ahd al-Umawīyīn. [Development of Architectural Technique and Art in the Umayyad Period.] *al-Mu'tamar ath-Thānī li'l-Āthār fi'l-Bilād al-'Arabīya*, Baghdād, 18th–28th Nov. 1958, pp. 135–7, and pls. 1–3.

— DAJJĀNĪ ('Aunī Khalīl), Ḥafā'ir fī Madīna Arīḥā, al-Urdun. [Excavations in the town of Jericho, Jordan.] *Ibid.*, pp. 197–9 and pls. 1–2.

1959 HAMILTON (R. W.), Khirbat al Mafjar: an Arabian Mansion in the Jordan Valley. With a contribution by Oleg Grabar. Large 4to, Oxford, 1959.

1962 ETTINGHAUSEN (Richard), Arab Painting, pp. 36–40, and coloured illus. on p. 39.

XXI

MSHATTĀ

MSHATTĀ:—Discovered by Tristram—General description—Detailed description—The enclosure wall—The masonry—Masons' marks, etc.—The gateway—Successive symmetrical subdivision of the interior—The Gateway Block—A latrine—The mosque—The Great Court—The Main Building—The triple-apsed hall—The latrines—The bricks—The side divisions of the Main Building—The vaults—The doorways—The decoration of the Main Building—The side tracts—Proposed reconstructions of Brünnow and Schulz—Author's proposed reconstruction—The channels in the enclosure walls—The decoration of the south façade—BIBLIOGRAPHY OF MSHATTĀ.

MSHATTĀ[1]

THE NOW FAMOUS PALACE OF MSHATTĀ was discovered by Layard in 1840[2] and, independently, by Tristram in February 1872,[3] but Seetzen had already heard its name mentioned in 1806 amongst a list of places in the Belqā.[4] It lies about twenty miles south of 'Ammān and about four miles north-east of the station of Zīza on the Ḥijāz Railway (see map, p. 404). The first thorough investigation of this monument was made by Brünnow,[5] who visited it in 1895, 1897, and 1898. His researches were supplemented in many important respects by the excavations of Schulz.[6] I have been greatly helped by their admirable descriptions.

GENERAL DESCRIPTION. Mshattā consists of a great walled enclosure of fine masonry, nearly 144 m. square internally, flanked by half-round towers, and with an entrance in the centre of the south side. Internally it is divided into three tracts running from north to south, the central one being 57 m. in width and the lateral ones about 42 m. (Fig. 630). The buildings intended to occupy the lateral tracts have never been begun, and even those projected for the central tract have never been finished. Of the latter, however, the group at the north end must have been very nearly finished, and the plan of the group at the south end can be clearly seen, for a great stone grid is visible, formed by the foundation courses of beautiful, smooth stone blocks, which just projects above the ground.

Immediately behind the gateway is an entrance hall 17·40 m. long, leading into a court, 27·14 m. broad and 23 m. deep; these two elements were flanked by other rooms and courts. I shall call this group the Gateway Block. Beyond the court just mentioned is an enormous central court, just over 57 m. square, on the north side of which is a triple-arched entrance (the arches have fallen) leading into a great basilical hall, 22·91 m. deep, ending in a 'triconchos'. This basilical hall is flanked by two symmetrical complexes composed as follows: on either side of an oblong court, placed perpendicular to the basilical hall, is another court at right angles to it, flanked on each side by a pair of vaulted chambers. I shall call this northern group the Main Building.

DETAILED DESCRIPTION. THE ENCLOSURE WALL is 1·70 m. in thickness, so that the external measurement of the enclosure is about 147 m. each way.[7] Its main axis runs about 12° east of north

The round towers at the corners are about 7 m. in diameter, and as they have been struck from centres which lie somewhat outside the ideal corners of the enclosure, it follows that the curve of the towers springs with a slight bulge from the face of the wall. There are five round intermediate towers about 19 m. apart[8] on the west, north, and east sides. These towers are about 5·25 m. in diameter, and they also have been struck from centres placed a little beyond the outer face of the wall, so that the

[1] For Bibliography, see pp. 604–6.

[2] His account, however, was not published until 1887, in his *Early Adventures*, I, p. 395.

[3] *Land of Moab*, pp. 195 ff.

[4] *Reisen durch Syrien*, I, p. 395.

[5] Brünnow and von Domaszewski, *Die Provincia Arabia*, II, pp. 105–76 and 308–11.

[6] Schulz and Strzygowski, *Mschattā*, in the *Jahrbuch der Kgl. Preuszischen Kunstsammlungen*, XXV, pp. 205–373.

[7] Brünnow and von Domaszewski (*op. cit.*, II, p. 105) give the internal measurements from north to south as 143·60 m. measured on the main axis, and 143·47 m. measured along the west wall. From east to west on the transverse axis they obtained 143·80 m., and for the west half of the south wall 71·82 m., which gives 143·64 m. for the whole side, if the entrance is in the exact centre. I should add that all the measurements in this account, except those of the main building which are mine, taken after Dr. Dajani's clearance, are taken from their careful description, for some parts, the Gateway Block, for example, have suffered so much that only a part of their measurements could be checked to-day.

[8] Those measured by Brünnow varied from 18·60 to 19·75 m.' *op. cit.*, II, p. 105.

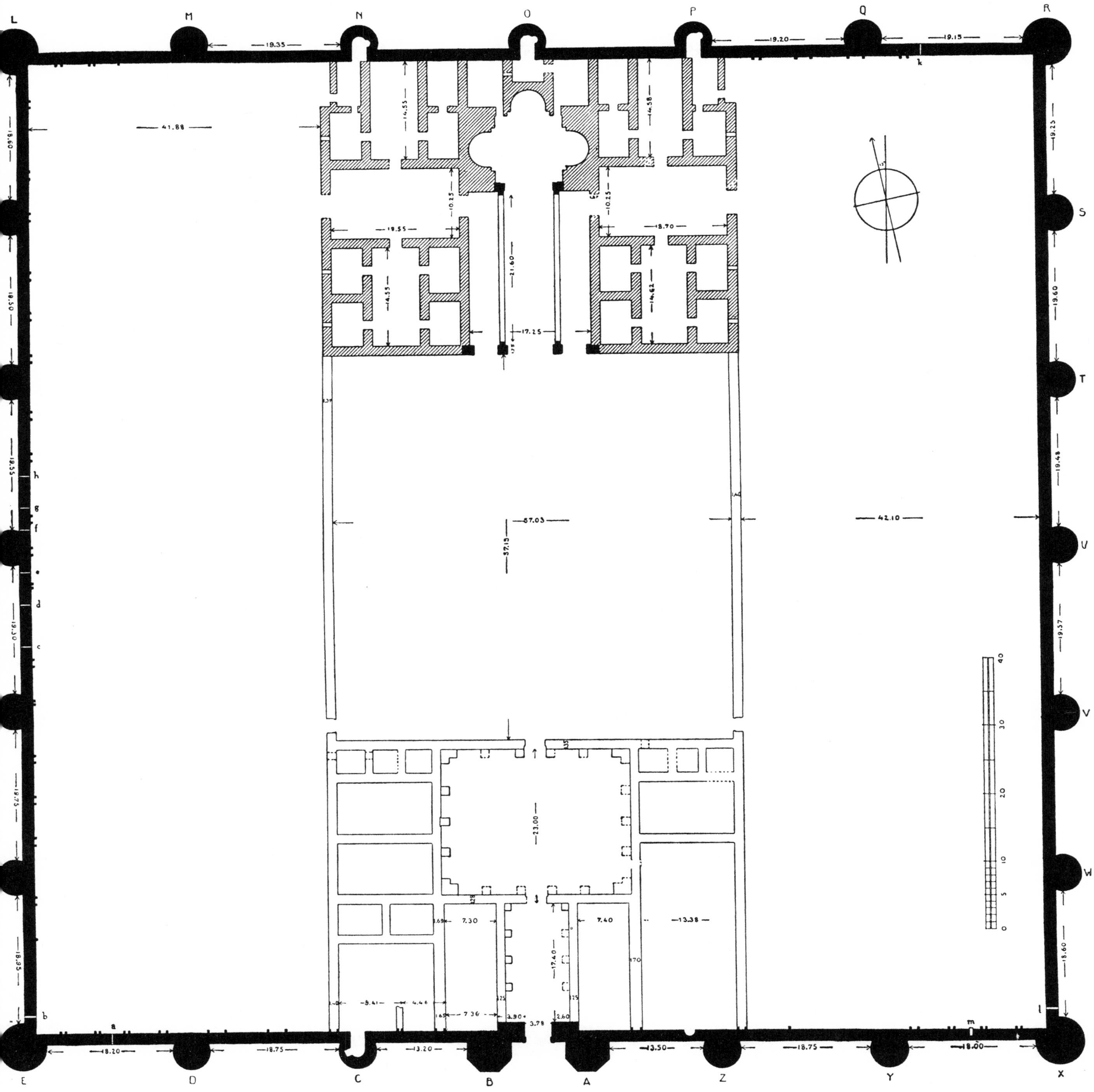

FIG. 630. MSHATTĀ: Plan. (From Brünnow and von Domaszewski, *op. cit.*)

curve of the tower, if continued, would just touch the inner face of the wall, or nearly so[1] (Figs. 630). All the towers with the exception of four (C, N, O, and P) are solid.

On the south side the arrangement is different, for here in place of the central tower is the entrance, flanked by two towers which exhibit the five sides of an octagon (Fig. 636). Their diameter at the socle is 6·30 m., but their depth to the inner face of the wall is only 5·90 m., so that the octagon, if completed, would project internally. The three outer faces of the octagon, measured at the socle, vary from 2·50 to 2·52 m., but the sides perpendicular to the wall only measure from 2·34 to 2·43 m. These two towers are 7·84 m. apart and the entrance which they flank is 3·46 m. in width. The curtain walls between

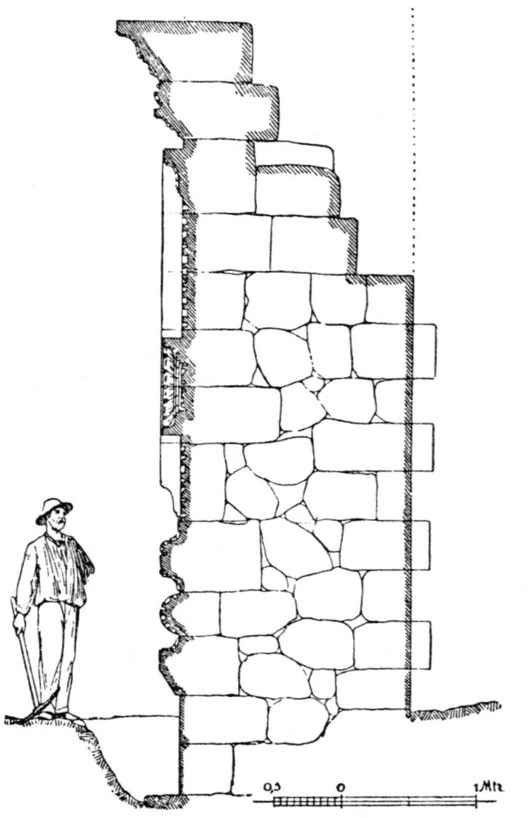

FIG. 631. MSHATTĀ: Section of façade showing nature of masonry. (From Schulz and Strzygowski, *loc. cit.*)

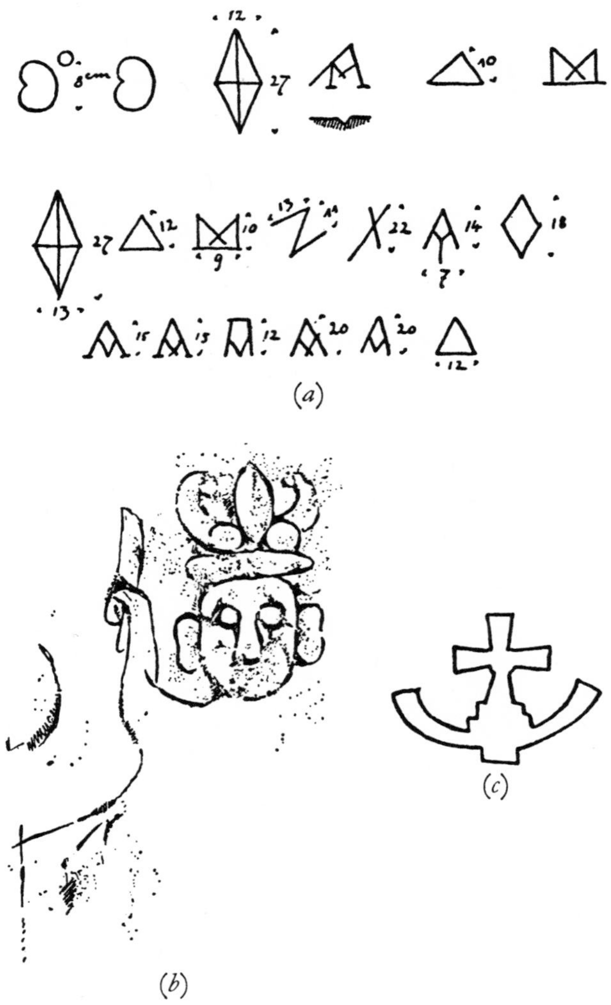

FIG. 632. MSHATTĀ: Masons' marks. (From Schulz and Strzygowski, *loc. cit.*)

them and towers C and Z measure 13·20 and 13·50 m. respectively. These two curtain walls, as well as the ten faces of the half-octagonal towers and the short strip of wall between the latter and the door-posts, are decorated with the famous carving of unrivalled richness, the greater part of which is now in the Staatliche Museen at Berlin (Plates 120–34 and 136).[2] The four remaining intermediate towers are placed at distances varying from 18 to 18·75 m.

THE MASONRY. The enclosure wall and towers are built of beautiful, slightly porous limestone, which when freshly cut was dead white, but which has taken an amber-brown tint, no doubt due to the presence of iron. It has been erected, without a real foundation, on a filling of broken blocks and lime mortar. The masonry is smoothly dressed with very fine joints, and the courses vary from 37 to 43 cm. in height.[3] The wall itself consists of an outer and inner facing with rubble between, and the courses of the inner and outer faces do not correspond (Fig. 631). The bond is very defective in places, for one

[1] In tower N the distance from the inner face of the wall to the outer periphery of the tower measures 5·23 m., whilst its diameter is 5·16 m. In tower C the corresponding measurements are 5·33 and 5·25 m. The slight differences may be due to errors of measurement; Brünnow, *op. cit.*, II, p. 105, n. 2.

[2] Thanks to the friendly intervention of the late Ernst Kühnel on my behalf, it was arranged that the photographs reproduced on Plates 120–31 should be especially taken for this new edition by the Staatliche Museen, to whom I offer my sincere thanks.

[3] In towers on east side, 32–8 cm.; in curtain wall on east side of Gateway Block, 43 cm.

or more stretchers only 20 to 40 cm. deep and averaging 90 cm. in length alternate with headers up to a metre in length. Moreover, the fine joints are deceptive, for the blocks taper slightly inwards, as we have seen at Qaṣr al-Ḥayr (p. 571), and the joints consequently only close properly at the surface. The filling consists of lumps, of various sizes, of the same limestone mixed with small pieces of flint, and bonded with a mortar composed of lime, ashes, and powdered limestone, with an occasional admixture of pounded bricks and potsherds. In 1897 the east side was still in good condition,[1] whereas on the other sides most of the outer blocks had already been pulled out, exposing the rubble interior.[2]

Masons' Marks, etc. Schulz found a number of masons' marks on the blocks of the main façade when dismantled for transport to Berlin (Fig. 632 *a*). He also found, on the inner faces of these blocks, roughly scratched sketches made by the workmen in their idle moments, such as a horse, the head of a man (Fig. 632 *b*) surmounted by an ornament recalling the insignia of Chosroes as it occurs on coins and bas-reliefs. He also noticed a cross (Fig. 632 *c*), which shows that there must have been Christians among the workmen.

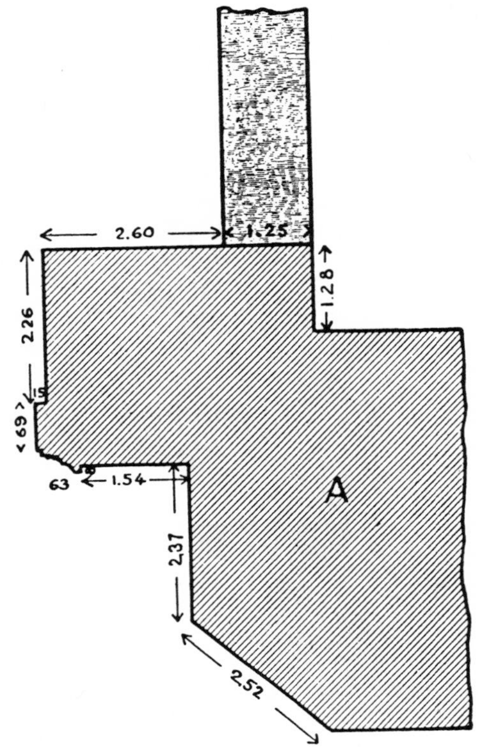

Fig. 633. Mshattā: Entrance, plan of eastern door-post with tower A.

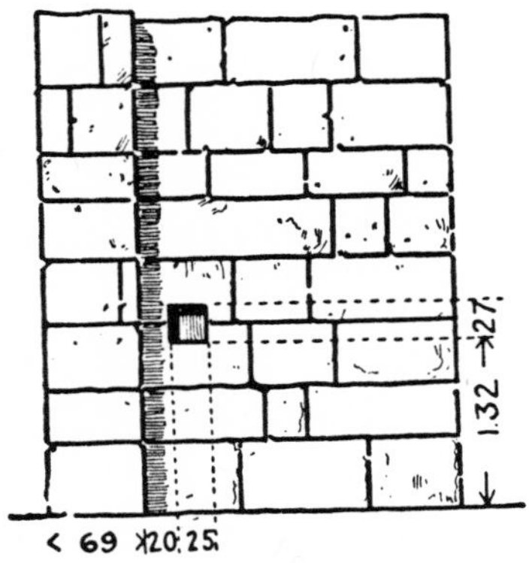

Fig. 634 Mshattā: Entrance, elevation of west side.

(From Brünnow and von Domaszewski, *op. cit.*)

The Gateway. The massive door-jambs are built in courses most of which correspond to those of the flanking towers and curtain wall. The width of the opening is 3·46 m. and behind the jambs 3·78; the height preserved is about 3·80 m. The outer faces of the jambs are bevelled off for a distance of 63 cm., and this oblique face is decorated with ornament (Plates 130–31) similar to that on the entablature of the façade. The masonry of the entrance is a very massive piece of construction, for it projects 1·28 m. beyond the inner face of the wall, as shown (Fig. 633), and returns against it for 3·85 m. On each side, at a distance of 20 cm. behind the jamb of the door and 1·32 m. above the present ground level, is a hole 27 × 25 cm. intended for the reception of the beam which bolted the door (Fig. 634). The hole in the west jamb is only 26 cm. deep, so the opposite one must have a depth of at least 4·30 m. to permit the pushing back of the beam.[3]

Successive Symmetrical Subdivision of the Interior. Thanks to the nearly finished Main Building and the stone grid elsewhere, it is easy to see that the interior is divided into three sections by two walls, 1·40 m. thick, running from north to south. The two outer sections have a width of about 42 m. and are at present great open areas, but on the inner face of the enclosure wall project bonding stones to which we shall refer later on. The middle tract, which is 57 m. wide, is divided into three main divisions of which the northern and southern are both approximately 42 m. deep (the same as the width of the side courts). The central division is therefore a regular square, 57 m. a side, placed at the same distance from all four walls.[4] This rectangle must have been a great open court, whereas the smaller rectangles contained the principal buildings, and a glance at the plan shows that the successive (generally

1 Brünnow, *op. cit.*, II, p. 109 and fig. 689. The east side has since suffered badly; compare Brünnow's fig. 689, with my Plate 112 *a*.

2 Brünnow, *op. cit.*, figs. 687–8.

3 Brünnow (II, p. 109) was able to measure it to a depth of 3·30 m., but the end was choked up with rubbish.

4 The sum of the measurements give for the southern rectangle a depth varying from 41·68 to 41·85 m., and for the northern 42·15 m. The central court is 57·15 m. from north to south and 57·03 from east to west; Brünnow, *op. cit.*, II, p. 111.

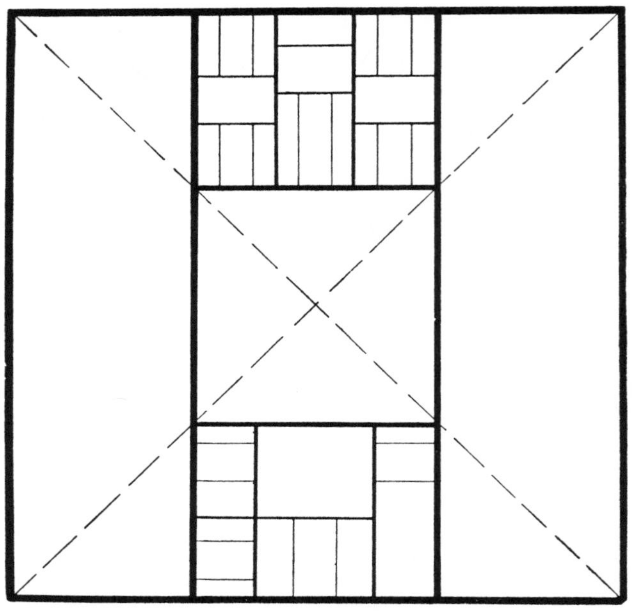

Fig. 635. Mshattā: Diagram showing successive symmetrical subdivision of the interior into three.

symmetrical) subdivision into three is to be found here also, especially in the northern rectangle (Fig. 635).[1]

The Gateway Block. Immediately within the entrance is a hall *r*, 17·40 m. deep and 9·23 m. wide, of which the side walls, about 1·25 m. thick, are directly attached at their outer ends to the two door-piers (Fig. 636). On each side is a row of four rectangular plinths, 1·10 m. deep and 95 cm. wide, placed 2·78 m. apart.[2] It seems probable that these plinths were intended to support columns carrying transverse arches. I suggest that these carried transverse vaults, in which case the vaulting system would resemble that of the audience hall at Quṣayr ʿAmra and Ḥammām aṣ-Ṣarakh, the Mosque at Quṣayr al-Ḥallabāt, Qaṣr al-Ḥayr al-Gharbī, the Ṭāqāt at Baghdād, etc. There must also have been plinths in the two southern corners, and one in fact was laid bare by Schulz, but, as the spacing is slightly wider here, Brünnow[3] suggests

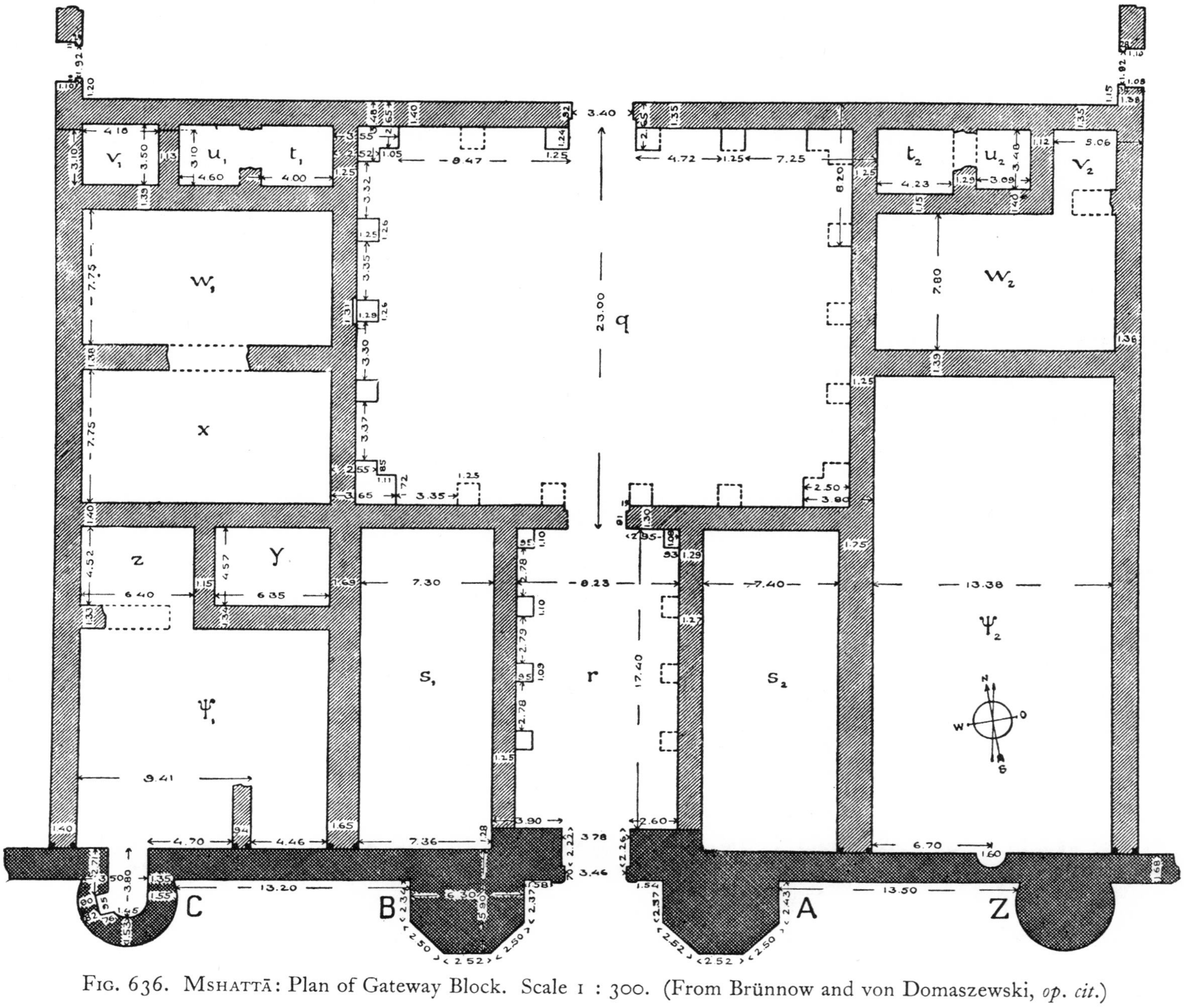

Fig. 636. Mshattā: Plan of Gateway Block. Scale 1 : 300. (From Brünnow and von Domaszewski, *op. cit.*)

[1] In this drawing the divisions do not show the actual thicknesses of the walls; they are graduated in thickness so as to distinguish the grouping into threes as clearly as possible.

[2] Three of those on the east side were first laid bare by Schulz.

[3] *Op. cit.*, II, p. 111.

that there were intended to have been doors here leading into the two outer halls s_1 and s_2, which are 7·30 and 7·40 m. wide respectively. These two lateral halls are slightly longer than the entrance hall because they are not curtailed by the masonry of the entrance. The outer walls of s_1 and s_2 are 1·70 m. thick, i.e. 30 cm. thicker than any other wall of this block. Schulz has suggested[1] that the walls here were intended to be carried up higher than elsewhere, but it is possible that these rooms were intended to be vaulted, and that the extra thickness of the outer lateral walls was intended to meet the thrust. Abutment would be provided on the inner lateral sides by the transverse arches of the entrance hall. It should be noted that these two walls, and their thinner continuations which form the sides of the court, divide the Gateway Block into three rectangles of which the western is 13·90m. broad, the eastern 13·38, and the central 26·45. The latter is divided into two nearly equal parts, of which the southern is formed by the entrance hall and the two lateral rooms, and the northern half by a court *q*, 21·70 m. deep and 27·40 wide, which is reached from *r* by a door 3·40 m. in width. On the main axis, opposite this door, is another of similar width leading into the great central court. These are the only two doors in this block of which the position can be fixed with certainty, for the masonry alongside them is two courses high : the first course serves as the sill and the second forms the sides of the doorway. The jambs of both are on the outside, so the doors must have been intended to open inwards into *q*.

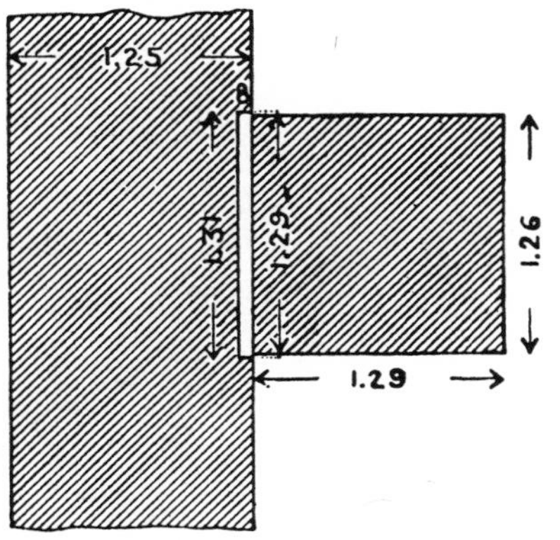

FIG. 637. Middle plinth on west side. (From Brünnow and von Domaszewski, *op. cit.*)

Against the four walls of the court (*q*) are placed plinths similar to those in *r*, except that they are larger, averaging 1·25 m. square, and are placed from 3·30 to 3·40 m. apart. They, also, may have been intended to support columns, more especially as they are square. The plinths in the corners are L-shaped as shown, presumably for coupled columns; if so, there must have been twenty-two columns in all.

Brünnow is very positive that all the plinths in this court and the entrance hall were meant for columns, but the possibility of brick piers is not excluded. However, in this court, he noticed the following feature which adds to the probability that columns were intended here, viz. that the wall behind the middle plinth on the west side has been cut away to a depth of 8 cm. on a width of 1·31 m. (Fig. 637) apparently to leave more room behind a column which it was intended to place here.

The wall between *q* and *r* continues through the western rectangle, dividing it also into two nearly equal parts of which the northern is subdivided into three. Of these the northern is again subdivided into three little rooms t_1, u_1, and v_1. Brünnow thought that he could recognize signs of a door in the west wall of v_1. If this is correct one could have passed from v_1 into the great western side tract. The southern half of the western rectangle is also subdivided, as shown; on its north side are two rooms *y* and *z*, and Schulz's excavations have shown that there were three little rooms on the south side.[2]

A LATRINE. In tower C, which lies just behind one of these little rooms, is a peculiar arrangement which occurs again in three towers, N, O, and P, behind the Main Building. A small room, 2·15 m. wide, has been hollowed out, which extends 3·80 into the interior of the tower and terminates in a semicircle at a distance of 1·53 m. from the outer periphery of the tower. On the western side of this recess, approximately at the beginning of the curve, was a rectangular niche,[3] about 95 cm. wide and 75 cm. deep. In this niche, which was cleared by Schulz, is set a block of stone as shown in Plate 117 *c*; in the centre of it is a slit 25 cm. wide which slopes steeply and ends in a drain running downwards and outwards (as in tower N; see Fig. 645). There can be no doubt as to its function, for it closely resembles the type of latrine used all over Syria at the present day.

The eastern rectangle of the Gateway Block is much more simply divided up than the western, only the four rooms at the northern end being represented by the corresponding rooms t_2, u_2, v_2, and w_2.

THE MOSQUE. The place of the remaining rooms is occupied by an area 13·40 m. broad and 27·30 m. deep, the south wall of which is formed by the enclosure wall. Exactly in the middle of the latter is a semicircular niche, 1·62 m. across, flanked by recesses intended to take nook-shafts (Fig. 638). This

[1] *Loc. cit.*, p. 212.
[2] *Loc. cit.*, Taf. II and VII.
[3] It will be seen that when my photograph was taken (1929) the course forming the niche had already disappeared.

deep court with bare walls and a niche in the centre of its south side repeats the form of the Palace mosque at Mafjar (above, p. 554). The whole of this court as well as the miḥrāb was cleared down to the pavement by Dr. ʿAunī Dajānī in 1963. A number of curved blocks belonging to the miḥrāb were put back into position, so that there are now four complete courses, totalling 1·69 m. in height (Plate 115 *b*).[1] The miḥrāb was found to have a raised sill 35 cm. in height, an unusual feature which, however, we have already met with at Minya (above p. 384, n. 1). I must emphasize that all five courses correspond exactly with the courses of the wall to right and left.

FIG. 638. MSHATTĀ: Remains of miḥrāb in ψ_2. Measured by K. A. C. Creswell and drawn by M. Lyon.

THE GREAT COURT. One passes through the northern door of *q* into the central court measuring roughly 57 m. square,[2] which is limited to north and south by the Main Building and the Gateway Block, and separated by walls from the two great lateral courts. In these two side walls, at a distance of 1·15 and 1·20 m. from the south end, are two doors, 1·92 m. wide, with jambs on the inner side, so that the doors opened towards the side courts. There is a similar door in the north-western corner[3] and one opposite (damaged).

Schulz, in the south-west part of this court, found a basin of brickwork measuring roughly 8 × 6 m., its sides carefully cemented 'in Roman fashion',[4] by which I conclude that he means with reddish waterproof cement. He was right in assuming that there were three others in keeping with the rule of symmetry which dominates here, for they have all been laid bare in recent times.

THE MAIN BUILDING[5] (see Figs. 639–50 and Plates 114–19), which is the only completely built structure in the enclosure, forms the central point of the whole and must be considered as the royal part of the palace. As stated above, the foundations of the burnt-brick walls consist of four courses of limestone blocks, of which three and a half courses rise 1·51 m. above the floor level.[6]

This rectangle, like the southern, is divided into three main divisions by two walls 1·35 m. thick; the two outer are 18·60 and 18·76 m. wide respectively, and the middle one has a breadth of 17·30 m. (Fig. 644). The two former are closed towards the south, but the latter was entered from the Great Court by a triple-arched entrance resting on two free-standing and two engaged piers (Fig. 639).

The free-standing and engaged piers (Figs. 639–43) are of ashlar,[7] and the blocks of the latter are carried back well into the brickwork so as to form a thorough bond with it (Plate 114). All the piers have a depth of 1·07 m., and the two free-standing ones are 1·40 m. wide. The lower part of each engaged pier forms one with the limestone courses below the brickwork and the socles of all four piers are flush with it, but the faces of the piers are set back about 13 cm. (Fig. 644). The bases of the pilasters, which rest on a smooth socle, are 45 cm. high and bear a general resemblance to bases of the Corinthian order (Fig. 640). The smooth part from the bases to the capitals measures about 3·11 m. The capitals are all

[1] The courses from below upwards measure 38, 37, 38, and 56 cm.
[2] See above, p. 581, 4.
[3] Clearly shown in Brünnow and von Domaszewski, *op. cit.*, II, fig. 698.
[4] *Loc. cit.*, pp. 220–21.
[5] The appearance of this part has been transformed, thanks to Dr. Dajani, who in 1963 completely cleared the basilical hall and the triconchos down to the pavement, as well as the courts and vaulted chambers flanking them.
[6] The plinths forming the sides of the Great Court are now only one course high; this course appears to correspond with the bottom course of the Main Building.
[7] The two southern corners of the Main Building were of ashlar also (as may be seen in Brünnow and von Domaszewski, *op. cit.*, II, figs. 698–9), but most of it has fallen.

FIG. 639. MSHATTĀ: Main Building, triple entrance to basilical hall. (From Schulz and Strzysgowski, *loc. cit.*)

FIG. 641. MSHATTĀ: Main Building. Capital of coupled middle pier of outer entrance from the south-west. (From Brünnow and von Domaszewski, *op. cit.*)

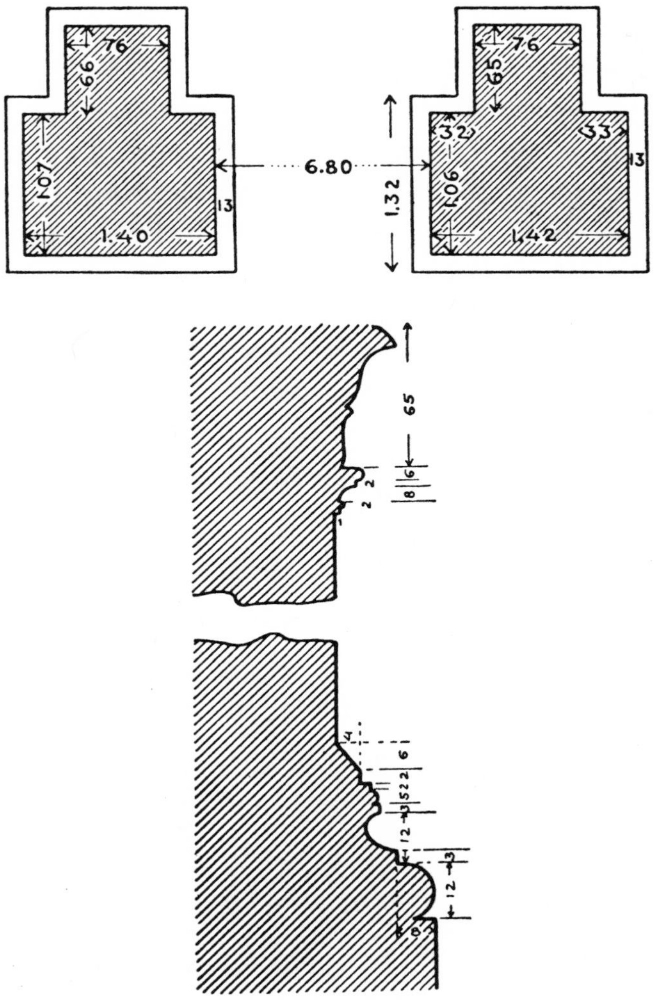

FIG. 640. MSHATTĀ: Main Building. Base and capital of pilaster of outer entrance. (From Brünnow and von Domaszewski, *op. cit.*)

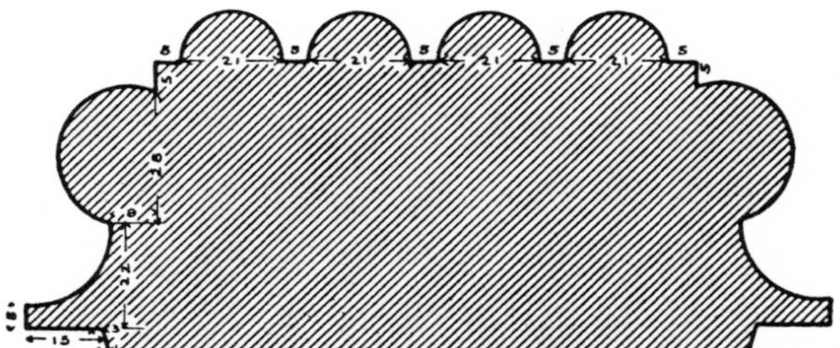

FIG. 642. MSHATTĀ: Main Building. Section of fallen arch of outer entrance. Scale 1 : 20. (From Brünnow and von Domaszewski, *op. cit.*)

alike and consist of a cornice-like base 12 cm. high, above which rises the calyx, formed of two tiers of acanthus leaves totalling 65 cm. in height (Plate 114 *c* and *d*). The capitals of the two middle piers are coupled with those of the pilasters attached to them.

The lateral arches had a span of about 3 m. and the central one about 6·54 m.; all three arches have been thrown down, apparently by an earthquake, and their moulded voussoirs lie in disorder on the ground. The late A. H. Cristie gave me some very old photographs, taken by a member of the Norfolk family of Buxton in 1872; one shows the voussoirs laying almost exactly as they had fallen (Plate 114 *e*). When Schulz saw them they were still lying in contact with each other, exactly as they had fallen.[1] He was able to turn over the blocks, measure them, fix their original position from the place they occupied on the ground, and establish the reconstruction shown with certainty (Fig. 639).[2]

Schulz points out that although there is now nothing above the capitals of these piers, they must once have been surmounted by a perfectly plain impost block, for one still exists above the east pier of the corresponding arch at the other end of the hall. It was 31 cm. high and between it and the capital was a single course of brickwork 9 cm. high. Embedded in this brickwork was a piece of wood 9 × 9 cm. in cross-section, the remains of a tie-beam, of which each arch had a pair. He consequently inserted this feature in his restoration of the main façade. He found that the arches of the latter must have been stilted semicircles. Their intrados was formed of four torus mouldings, and there was a moulding on each face, as shown (Fig. 642). This outer moulding ran round each arch, then horizontally above the impost block, then round the next arch and so on, finally running up vertically at each side and turning at right angles to run horizontally across the top, so as to form a rectangular frame. The whole of this frame and of the spandrels is constructed of limestone blocks, and the surface above each side arch was decorated with three six-lobed rosettes, resembling those in the upright triangles of the outer façade; they even project the same amount (14 cm.). Schulz noticed that the background of these rosettes bore traces of red paint.[3] Above the top of the moulded frame was one more course of smooth masonry.

A similar moulding ran round the inner edge of the arches, but instead of running up vertically on each side it stopped dead on meeting the walls.

On the inner face of the free-standing piers are two pilasters, 76 cm. wide and 65 deep, to which similar pilasters, 74 cm. wide and 53 deep, correspond at the northern end of the hall. Between these two pairs of pilasters is a foundation wall 20 cm. high and 1 m. wide of large well-cut blocks, whereby the hall is divided into three aisles (Plate 115 *c* and 116 *b*). The eastern wall shows no sign of columns having been erected upon it, but Schulz, who laid bare the western, found the grey marble base of the first column from the north still in position and a place cut for the second.[4] To-day, thanks to Dr. Dajani's clearance, four sockets can be seen, 77 cm. square, 3 cm. deep, and 3 m. apart which, together with the column-base still in position, show that there must have been five columns, i.e. six arches. He also found a monolithic shaft of cipollino in the middle of the room, as well as two other shafts which had been broken, apparently by the arch of the triconchos falling upon them.[5] A Corinthian capital of the same grey marble as the base was found in the triple-apsed room beyond. It was 55 cm. high and bore traces of painting; blue for the background and gold (over red) for the stems and leaves.[6]

The central aisle of hall *a* opened into *b* by an archway, all the voussoirs of which have fallen. This arch was of almost the same width[7] as the central arch of the outer portal. The piers on which it stood are of cut stone bonded into the brick wall behind (Plates 116 *a–b* and 117 *a–b*).

A pilaster is attached to two of their free faces; one, on their south faces, is that already mentioned as belonging to the row of arches, the other, 1·13 cm. wide, on their inner faces, forms the side of the archway. Although their bases, uncovered by Schulz, and their neck moulding have the same form as those of the triple archway, their capitals are quite different; they have a convex form decorated with a fine network of vine tendrils (Plate 116 *d* and *e*, and Fig. 643).

The arch was decorated with the same mouldings as those of the façade, except that the torus moulding

[1] A similar state of affairs exists at Ḥarrān where the two wings of the façade of the sanctuary of the Great Mosque have fallen and the blocks lie in order on the ground. The blocks are large, but with the necessary personnel it would be possible to turn them over, effect a few small adjustments, and reconstruct the whole façade, which appears to have been richly carved.

[2] *Loc. cit.*, pp. 216–17.

[3] *Ibid.*, p. 217. This suggests that they were gilt, for surfaces to be gilt are generally given a preliminary coating of red paint.

[4] See his Taf. I.

[5] *Ibid.*, pp. 217–18.

[6] This capital is now in the Staatliche Museen, Berlin.

[7] Brünnow says 6·87 m.; my measurement was 6·75 m.

on its two faces, instead of being left smooth, has been carved with a pair of beautiful vine tendrils which repeatedly cross each other, forming loops with little rosettes at their crossings (Plate 116 *c*). Each loop is occupied by a bunch of grapes,[1] or a three-lobed or five-lobed vine leaf, the latter having three grapes superimposed at the point of junction with the stalk. The hollow moulding next this torus moulding is carved with rows of acanthus leaves.

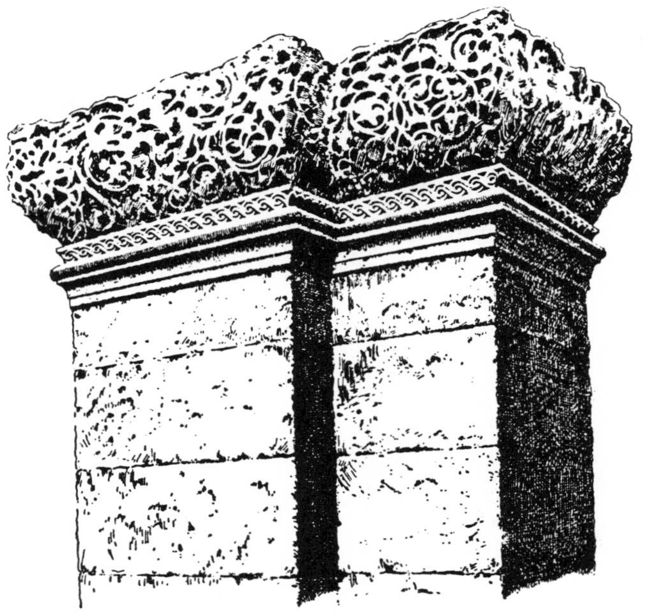

Fig. 643. Mshattā: Capital of eastern pier of inner arch, from the south-west. (From Brünnow and von Domaszewski, *op. cit.*)

The Triple-apsed Hall (Plates 116 *a* and 117 *a–b*). The room which we now enter is exactly 9·78 m. square. In each of its three side walls is a great apsidal recess 5·25 m. wide and about 3·90 m. deep, their plan being a stilted semicircle. On looking at the plan it will be seen that the thickness of wall left at the back of these niches is the same as the thickness of the side walls of d_1 and d_2. The corners of these apsidal recesses are cut away rectangularly to a depth of from 50 to 60 cm., obviously for the reception of engaged columns, of which, however, Schulz found no

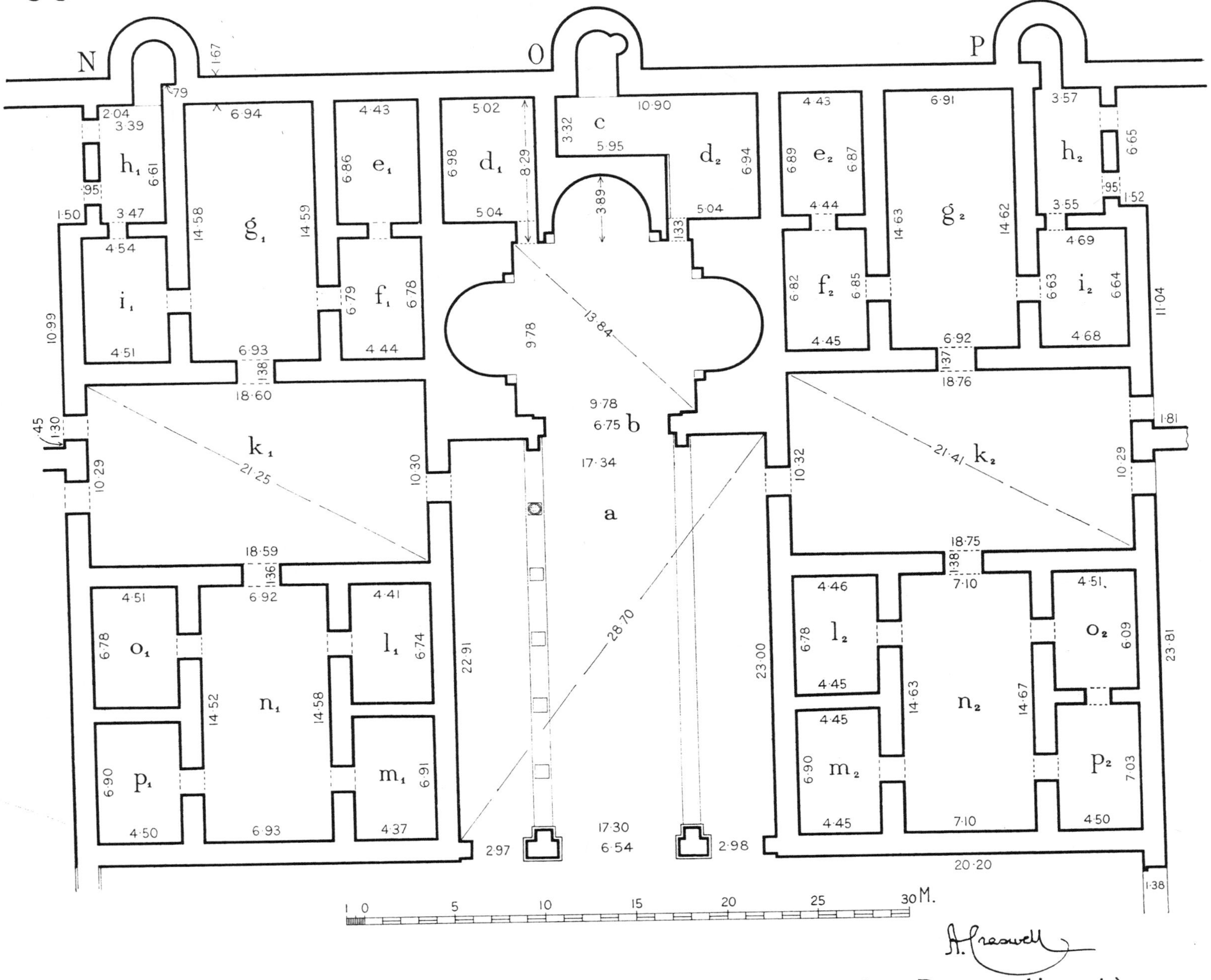

Fig. 644. Mshattā: Main Building, plan. (From Brünnow and von Domaszewski, *op. cit.*)

[1] Strzygowski, *loc. cit.*, Abb. 73. Three of the voussoirs of the eastern half of this arch, together with the impost block, are now in the Staatliche Museen, Berlin (Plate 116 *c*).

fragments.[1] These excisions begin in the top course of the masonry and terminate at a height of 5·05 m. above the floor level, at which point a course of stone, 48 cm. high, which runs right back to the corners, is let into the brickwork, as shown (Plate 117*b*). There can be no doubt that these niches ended in semi-domes, although no gradual curving over is visible, for they have only been preserved for 12 to 15 courses above the inserted blocks of stone.[2] The frontal arches of these recesses, together with the fallen arch, may have carried a dome, which, according to Brünnow[3] and Schulz,[4] was intended here. The débris here is about 2 m. deep, from which Schulz concludes that this dome was actually built. If we assume that it was hemispherical its apex must have been just over 13 m. above the floor. But see below, p. 616.

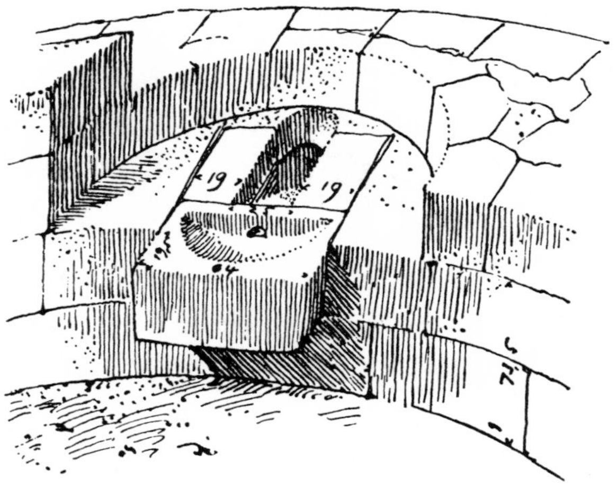

Fig. 645. Mshattā: Latrine in tower n. (From Schulz and Strzygowski, *loc. cit.*)

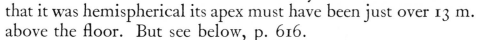

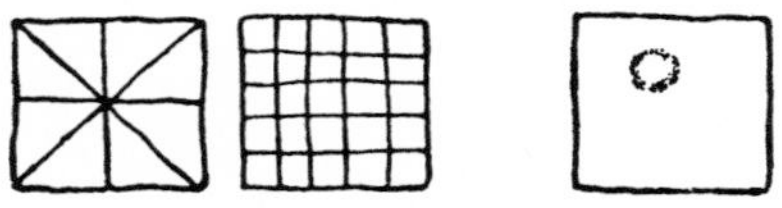

(*a*) (*b*)

Fig. 646. Mshattā: Markings on bricks: (*a*) lines made with a pointed instrument; (*b*) circle made with the finger. (From Schulz and Strzygowski, *loc. cit.*)

On either side of the northern recess are doors, 1·05 m. wide and 4·00 m. high, spanned by pointed arches, leading into the rooms, d_1 and d_2, which measure 6·98 × 5·04 m. and 69·4 × 5·04 m. A door leads from d_2 into a smaller chamber *e*, measuring 3·30 × 4·58 m., which is placed immediately behind the apsidal recess. This completes the central third of the Main Building.

The Latrines. I must, however, mention that a small room leads out of d_2. It has been hollowed out in the middle tower (o) of the north side; it measures 2·15 m. wide and 3·76 deep, and ends in a semicircular termination. It has a small window looking into d_1. Towers n and p each contain a similar chamber. Schulz cleared out all these rooms, and found that each had a small semicircular recess in their curved end wall, containing a latrine stone (Fig. 645) exactly like that already mentioned in tower c.[5]

The Bricks are of two sizes, 21 × 21 and 28 × 28 cm. square and 6½ cm. thick. Some have marks as shown (Fig. 646) to help the bond. The joints are about 2½ cm. thick (height of eight courses, 72 cm.).

The Side Divisions of the Main Building. These two divisions are built to the same pattern, except that they are reversed in relation to each other; the description of one therefore holds good for both.[6]

Here again we observe that successive subdivision into three which is the keynote of the plan. Each rectangle is divided by two cross walls, 1·40 m. thick, into three rectangles of which the middle ones, k_1 and k_2, are 18·60 to 18·76 m. wide and 10·30 m. deep, and in communication with the basilical hall by doors about 3 m. wide (Fig. 649). In the middle of their two long sides is a door leading into the northern and southern rectangles; these are again subdivided into three parts, of which the central ones g_1 and g_2 measure 14·60 × 6·93 m. The flanking sections are each subdivided into two rooms varying from 6·75 to 7 m. in length and with a width of about 4·50 m., with the exception of h_1 and h_2, which are reduced in width because the outer wall is here set back for some reason which I am unable to explain. All these vaulted rooms are in direct communication with g_1, g_2, n_1, or n_2 as the case may be, except h_1, h_2, e_1, and e_2.

The Vaults. These rooms, all of which run parallel to the main axis, were roofed with pointed tunnel-vaults, but only two of these are standing and these are not intact. They spring with an offset of 5 cm. at a height of 5·25 m. from the ground level, and at their apex attain a height of 7·75 m. (Fig. 647). They therefore have a rise of 2·50 m. on a span of 4·40 m. The best-preserved vault is shown in Plate

[1] *Loc. cit.*, p. 218.

[2] Brünnow (II, p. 126) explicitly mentions their gradual curving over, but I think this must be a slip, for their condition to-day appears to be exactly the same as that shown in his photograph (*op. cit.*, II, fig. 718).

[3] II, p. 126.

[4] *Loc. cit.*, p. 218.

[5] *Loc. cit.*, pp. 218–19. No latrine stone is now visible in o or p, and in the case of n it has been overturned and is lying on its side.

[6] The only difference to be observed is that o_2 and p_2 are in communication, whereas there is no doorway between o_1 and p_1. I have specially confirmed this point, which was noted by Brünnow, *op. cit.*, II, p. 128.

117*e*, which photograph was taken from the ruined enclosure wall (Plate 118*a*, to right), with the camera almost on a level with the springing of the vault. It shows clearly that the section of the vault is a pointed arch struck from two centres one-fifth of the span apart, the earliest example of this ratio.

The vaults are constructed as shown in Plate 118*b* and *c* and Fig. 648 : there are two horizontal courses above the offset, above which is the vault proper, a brick and a half (= 40 cm.) thick, composed of rings of flat, square bricks set edgeways, i.e. with their faces parallel to the end-wall, just as in the Lesser Enclosure at Qaṣr al-Ḥayr ash-Sharqī (above, p. 527 and Plate 93 *d*), but there is no covering ring of bricks laid flat.

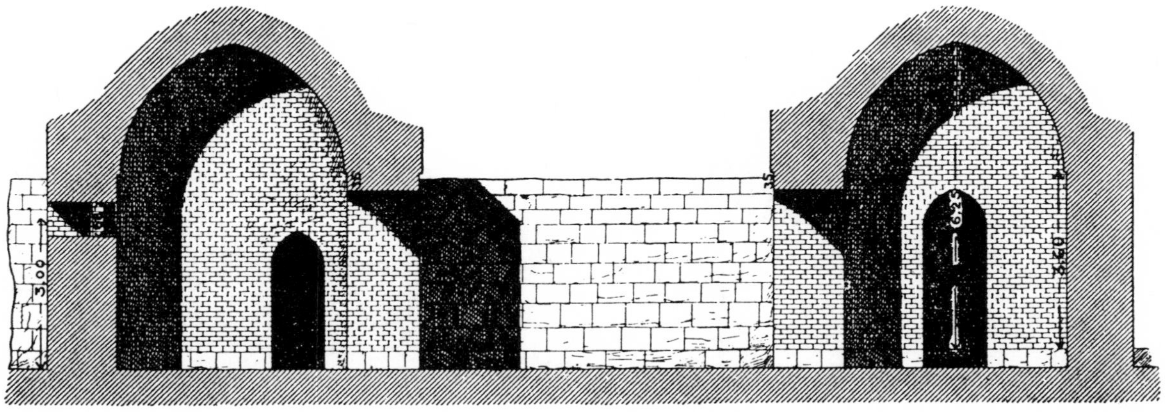

FIG. 647. MSHATTĀ: Main Building. Section through rooms i_1, g_1, and f_1.
(From Brünnow and Domaszewski, *op. cit.*)

THE DOORWAYS, which are almost invariably in the centre of the wall in question,[1] have a width varying from 1·30 to 1·35 m.[2] Their construction should be specially noted, for we shall meet with it again in Qaṣr aṭ-Ṭūba. The openings are spanned by a stilted pointed arch of slightly greater width than the opening (Plate 117 *d* and Fig. 649) the apex of which is 4·75 m. above the floor level. This arch is of similar construction to the vaults, being composed of an inner ring of square bricks set with their flat face outwards, and an outer ring of bricks set edgewise. In the brickwork at the sides of the doorway, three courses below the springing, is a gap which extends right through the wall, from which one might conclude that a stone lintel or wooden beam had been pulled out.[3] Schulz, however, who examined all the doorways very carefully over sixty years ago, was then able to find traces which convinced him that there was first of all a solid wooden ceiling, 12½ cm. thick, the whole depth of the doorway, its underside being about 66 cm. below the springing and, on top of it, a layer of bricks set vertically.[4] The object, of course, was to give a rectangular top to the doorway, and in the wooden ceiling it was easy to make a socket for the door spindle. The tympanum would serve to admit light when the door was shut, supposing g_1, g_2, n_1, and n_2 were open courts.

And this brings us to the problem of these rectangles. Were they vaulted? The outer rooms i_1, o_1, and p_1, and i_2, o_2, and p_2 all have bull's-eye windows, placed high up (Fig. 650), but f_1, f_2, l_1, l_2, m_1, and m_2 have not. The latter, therefore, must have been practically without light if the rectangles referred to were vaulted, for these rectangles, instead of being open at one end (like a *līwān*) into k_1 and k_2 respectively, were separated from it by a wall with a door in it. Yet the side walls of these rectangles are set forward in the same way, and at almost the same height[5] as the side walls of the vaulted rooms already described. In the latter, however, there are only two horizontal courses above the offset, from the upper of which spring the rings of the vault. Here, however, at least sixteen courses have been preserved without any really perceptible signs of a forward curve.[6] Brünnow confines himself to the observation that if there was a vault, it must have been considerably higher than the others,[7] but Schulz,

[1] The only exceptions are in rooms h_1, h_2, d_1, and d_2.

[2] Except the doors between i_1 and h_1, i_2 and h_2, which are only 99 cm. wide.

[3] A similar peculiarity occurs in the doorways of Qaṣr Kharāna, but there it may be seen, from several intact doorways, that the horizontal part was formed by two lintels, one at the back and one at the front, with a wooden beam between, in which was set the socket of the door spindle; see Jaussen and Savignac, *Les Châteaux arabes* pp. 55–6, fig. 8, and pl. XXII.

[4] *Loc. cit.*, p. 215.

[5] About four bricks higher.

[6] I have looked at the brickwork from below on several occasions; sometimes I have thought that it curved forward slightly, sometimes I have come to the conclusion that it did not.

[7] *Op. cit.*, II, p. 127.

who points out that the fallen débris here is a metre deep, is convinced that there was a vault and shows one in his restoration[1] and, to get over the lighting difficulty, assumes that there were openings for light along the sides of the vault.

The vault, if there was one, must have risen well above the tops of the side vaults, in order that such openings could have been made, but I cannot believe that such openings ever did exist, for such construction is unthinkable in Syria, ʿIrāq, or Egypt at this time, nor can I recall any examples, even centuries later. However, although far from certain, it is possible, partly on account of the offset and partly on account of the metre depth of débris, that there was a vault over these rectangles, and that the windowless rooms were actually very dark and intended for repose in the heat of the day like those flanking the throne recess at Quṣayr ʿAmra, which are very dark yet not completely so.

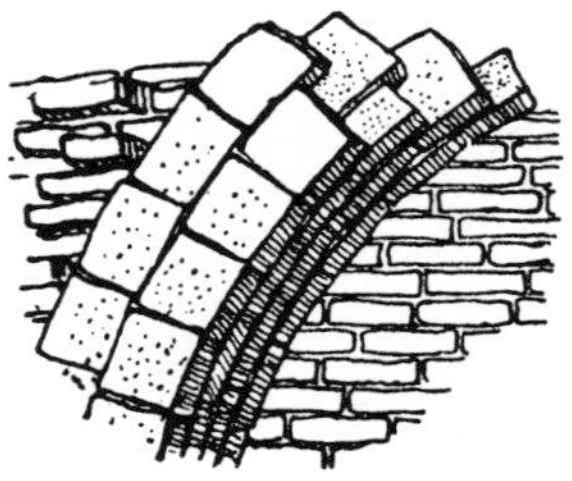

Fig. 648. Mshattā: Construction of vaults with bricks and half bricks. (From Schulz and Strzygowski, *loc. cit.*)

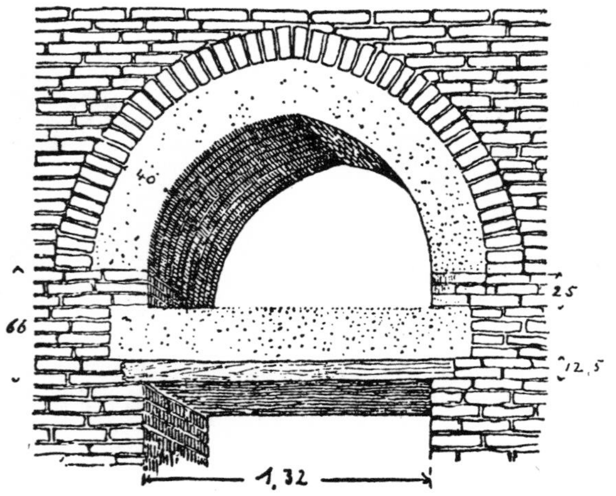

Fig. 649. Mshattā: Construction of the doorways in the Main Building. (From Schulz and Strzygowski, *loc. cit.*)

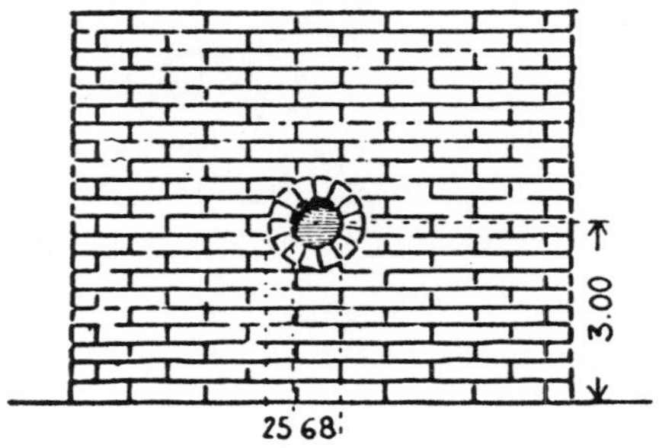

Fig. 650. Mshattā: Main Building, window in outer wall of room p_1, from within. (From Brünnow and von Domaszewski, *op. cit.*)

The Decoration of the Main Building was apparently never even begun, but it was evidently intended to have had a dado of green stone, for Schulz[1] and Jaussen and Savignac[2] found several great blocks of a magnificent green stone (exactly like that which is now brought to Jerusalem from Mār-Sāba, Dayr Dosī, and Teqūʿa), lying in the east side tract, which had evidently been the place where the masons worked. They had already been partly sawn into slabs, two or three centimetres thick, for use as a panelling. The blocks used for Mshattā, however, must have come from a shorter distance, for Jaussen and Savignac found rocks of this material near the ruin called Qaṣr al-Ḥammām, which is only about sixteen miles to the south-east.[4]

The Side Tracts. No foundation walls are to be seen in the side tracts, nor were traces of any found by Schulz on excavation. However, the bonding stones left for the attachment of transverse walls, which are to be seen on the inner walls of the enclosure (Plate 119*a* and Fig. 651), show that such were meant to be constructed. These bonding stones are arranged in pairs, in vertical rows, jutting out from the wall in every alternate course; their outer faces are dressed smooth, the inner face being left rough hewn. The outer breadth of these pairs varies from 97 cm. to 1·41 m., that is to say they indicate the same range of wall thickness that we have already met with except, however, in four places where the breadths vary from 2·50 to 2·95 m. The distances apart of the various pairs must, of course, indicate the width of the rooms built against the wall. The smallest pitch is 3·20, the largest about 12·40 m. These attachments can only be fully recorded on the south and west sides of the western court, for the inner face of the wall elsewhere is too damaged, and was so even in Brünnow's day. Nevertheless, as

[1] *Loc. cit.*, p. 214 and Taf. VI.

[2] *Loc. cit.*, p. 221.

[3] *Les Châteaux arabes*, p. 17.

[4] *Ibid.* Mr. O. H. Little of the Geological Survey of Egypt, to whom I submitted a piece of the green stone from Mshattā, writes to me as follows: 'The rock would be classed as a marble, but it is really a calc-schist in which the green colouring material is not serpentine but most probably chlorite.' He was kind enough to have the piece ground, and found that it took a fair polish.

symmetry was obviously the rule everywhere else, we can safely restore the missing parts from those opposite.

Proposed Reconstructions of Brünnow and Schulz. This is how Brünnow proceeds to reconstruct the architect's intentions:

If we go along the south wall from the south-western corner (tower E) towards the east, we find a room 3·30 m. wide, after that a wall of 1·03 m., then a room of 3·93 m., a wall of 99 cm., a room of 3·20 m.,

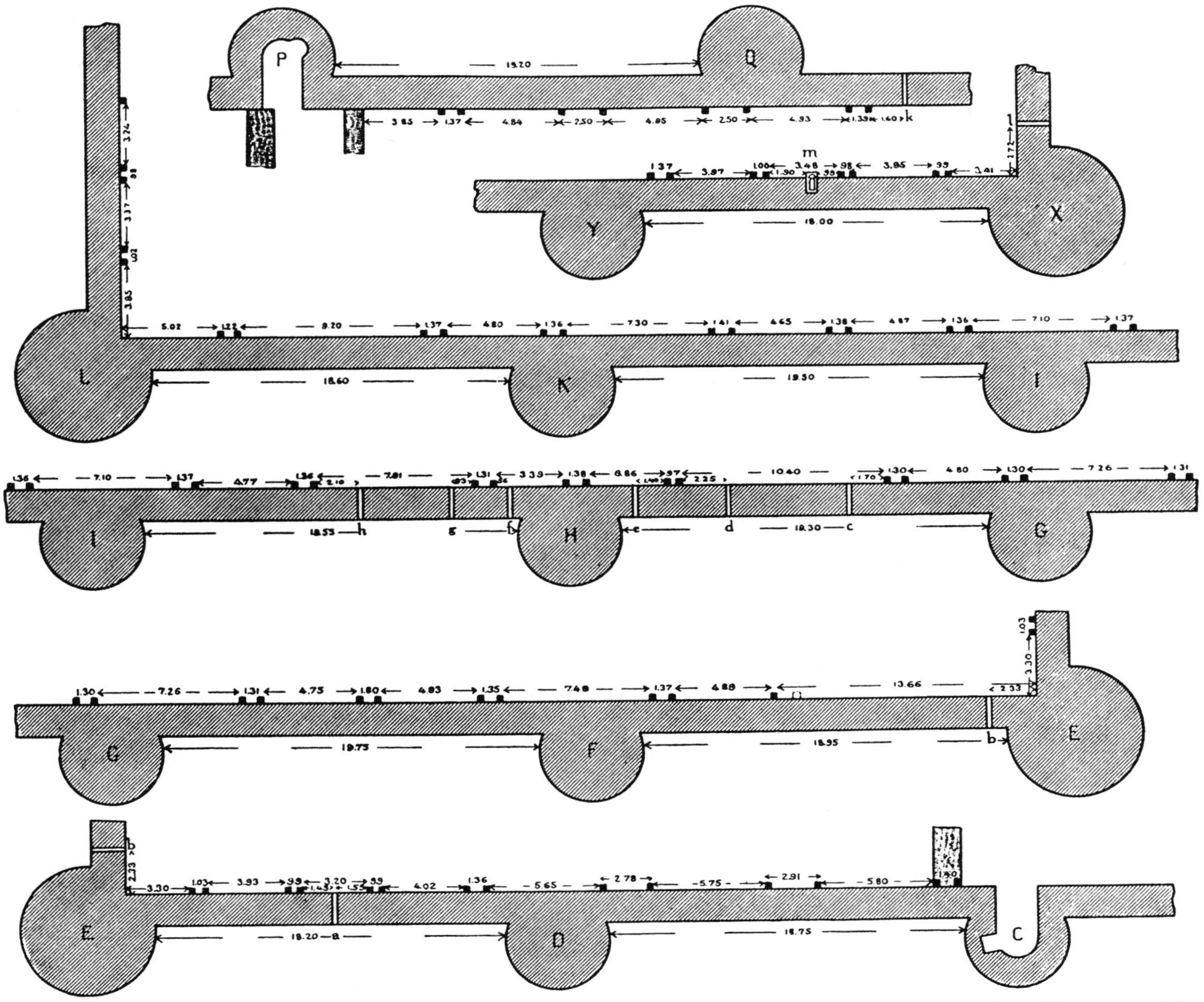

Fig. 651. Mshattā: Details of enclosure walls, showing projecting bonding stones. (From Brünnow and von Domaszewski, *op. cit.*)

a wall of 99 cm., a room of 4·02 m., and, finally, a wall of 1·36 at tower D. Then follow: a room of 5·65, a wall of 2·78, a room of 5·75, a wall of 2·91, and a room of 5·80 m., which abuts against the western wall of the gateway block at tower C. He concludes that there were two distinct groups of rooms here, 17·46 and 22·89 m. wide respectively. At the northern end of this court (tower L) he was only able to find attachments for the first three rooms, the remainder having been destroyed; the measurements were 3·95, 1·02, 3·37, 0·98, and 3·24 m., which, added together, give 12·56 m., almost the same figure as the corresponding measurement (12·45) at the south end.

In the eastern side court, only the first group on the south side (towers X–Y) and the second group on the north side (towers P–Q) are preserved. The measurements of the former taken from the corner are: 3·41, 0·99, 3·95, 0·98, 3·48, 1·00, and 3·97 m., totalling 17·78 m., with which we again arrive at a wall of 1·37 m. These two totals of 17·46 and 17·78 m. are quite in keeping with the fact that the east court is about 21 cm. broader than the western. A space of 17·30 m. remains over for the second group (towers Y–Z), which is quite destroyed, as we have said, with the exception of the attachment of the last room next the main building, the width of which must have been 6·05 m. against 5·80 of the corresponding room in the western court. The corresponding group on the northern side (towers P–Q), however, has fortunately been preserved. It is 17·78 m. in width, or 48 cm. more than its fellow, and its layout is somewhat different, for the two inner walls only measure 2·50 and the three inner rooms vary from 4·84 to 4·95 m. As a result a room, 3·85 m. wide, remains over towards the Main Building, and fits into the space left by the setting back of the outer wall of the latter alongside h_2, to which attention has already been called.

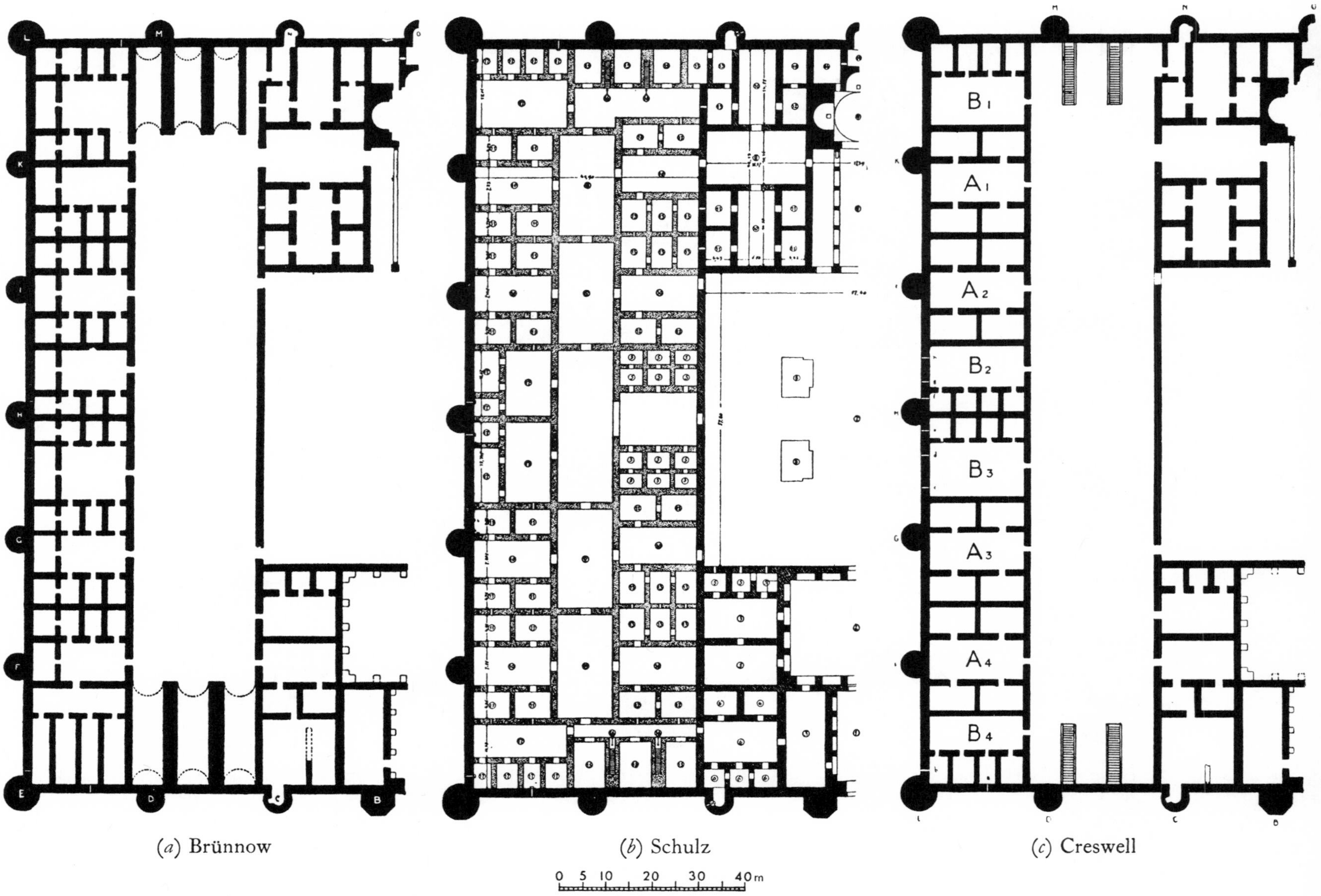

(*a*) Brünnow (*b*) Schulz (*c*) Creswell

FIG. 652. MSHATTĀ: Western side court, attempted reconstructions.

Brünnow then assumes that the approximately equal width of the first group in both lateral courts is the depth of the row of rooms set against the long side walls of these courts, that is to say that the wall about 1·40 m. thick ran the whole length of the court. He then divides up the space, thus cut off, according to the attachments visible along the west wall. He then assumes the wider spaces to have been open courts and subdivides all the rectangles flanking them into four rooms corresponding to the first group of attachments along the north and south walls (Fig. 652 *a*). As for the massive walls, he concludes that these served to support vaults, as shown.

Schulz, independently of Brünnow, also attempted a solution of this problem with very different results. He calls attention to the fact that in the Main Building a group of five rooms combined as shown (Fig. 652) occurs four times and that there are no less than four places where such a group, if turned round, may be placed lengthways against the west wall as shown (Fig. 652 *b*). The north-western corner section divides up obviously into four little rooms and a court, and he treats the south-western corner section in the same way although no attachment for the east-to-west wall was found. As regards the massive walls, 2·50 m. thick or more, he suggests that these must have been intended for staircases leading up to the top of the enclosure wall. He then divides up the east side of the tract in what appears to me to be an unjustifiable fashion.

AUTHOR'S RECONSTRUCTION. I do not believe that there were any rooms on this side, for two reasons: (i) the flanks of the Main Building are absolutely smooth and do not exhibit any preparation for the attachment of walls, and (ii) rooms *i*, *o*, and *p* are each provided with a bull's-eye window in their outer walls. Moreover, in Schulz's restoration, the three doors[1] opening into this side track, viz. two from the great court and one from rectangle k_1, open into what is the central court of one of the 5–6 room units, private family residences or *bayts*, which certainly cannot have been used as thoroughfares.

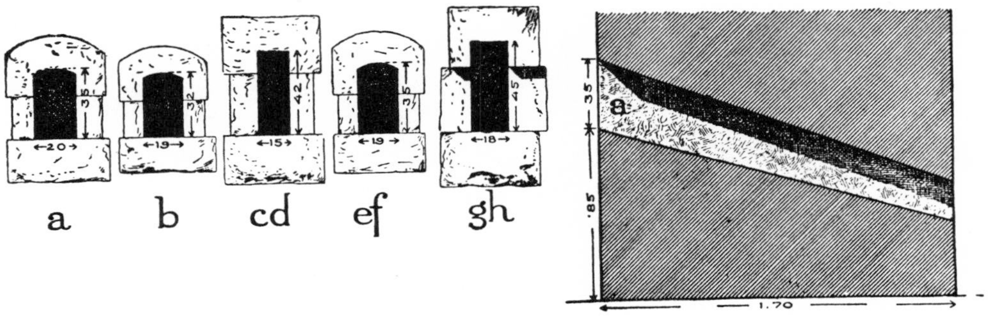

FIG. 653. MSHATTĀ: Sketches of the openings on the inner side of the western side court (see Fig. 651) and section of opening *a*. (From Brünnow and von Domaszewski, *op. cit.*)

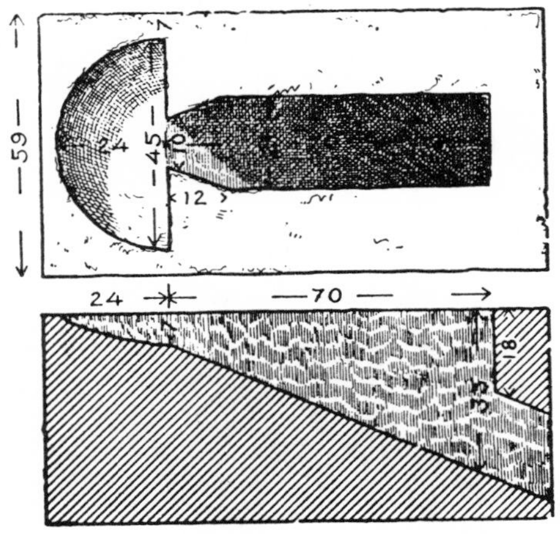

FIG. 654. MSHATTĀ: Plan and section of latrine stone *m* between towers X and Y. (From Brünnow and von Domaszewski, *op. cit.*)

I therefore propose to sweep away all the rooms shown by Schulz on the east side of this tract, to make the alignment of the façade of those on the west side correspond with the fourth and thicker wall attachment to north and south, to modify his division of the two central groups, so as to be in keeping with the north-western corner room, to which their dimensions very closely correspond, and to accept his suggestion regarding the staircases. The result of this is shown in Fig. 652 *c*.

THE CHANNELS IN THE ENCLOSURE WALL. In several of these rooms are curious rectangular openings (Fig. 653) which run right through the wall, the function of which is obscure; the greatest number occur in the four middle rooms of the west wall. The two small middle rooms each contain one of these openings (*e*, *f*). They are straight below and slightly arched above, both measure 19 cm. wide and 35 cm. high and they are placed about 1·35 m. above the present ground level. They run downwards towards the exterior, tapering slightly at the same time, as shown. In each of the two broader rectangles (courts?) alongside are two rectangular openings (*c*, *d*, *g*, *h*), which, on the contrary, are only slightly above the ground level, and run through the wall horizontally without tapering. In the southern room, which is 10·40 m. broad, they measure 15 × 42 cm. (*c* and *d*); in the northern, which is only 7·91 m. wide, they measure 18 × 45 cm. All these openings are placed at irregular distances from the attachments. In the west wall there is only one more opening (*b*); it is 2·35 m. from the south end, and is exactly like the two middle ones except that it is only 32 cm. high instead of 35.

In the south wall of the western tract there is only one opening, *a*, approximately in the middle of the third room from the corner. It is about 85 cm. above the present ground level, and measures 20 × 35 cm.; in other respects it is exactly like the two middle openings *e* and *f* described above. The north wall of this tract is too much damaged for one to say whether openings existed here or not; but there is one resembling *e* and *f* in the corresponding wall of the eastern court, and it is so placed that it would come[2] approximately in the middle of the fourth room from the corner, between towers Q and R.

1 I say three but the position of two only is certain; the door in the centre of the side of the great court shown by Schulz is admitted by him (p. 220) to be conjectural.

2 That is to say, judging from the attachments opposite, for the attachments have been destroyed here, as we have seen above, p. 590.

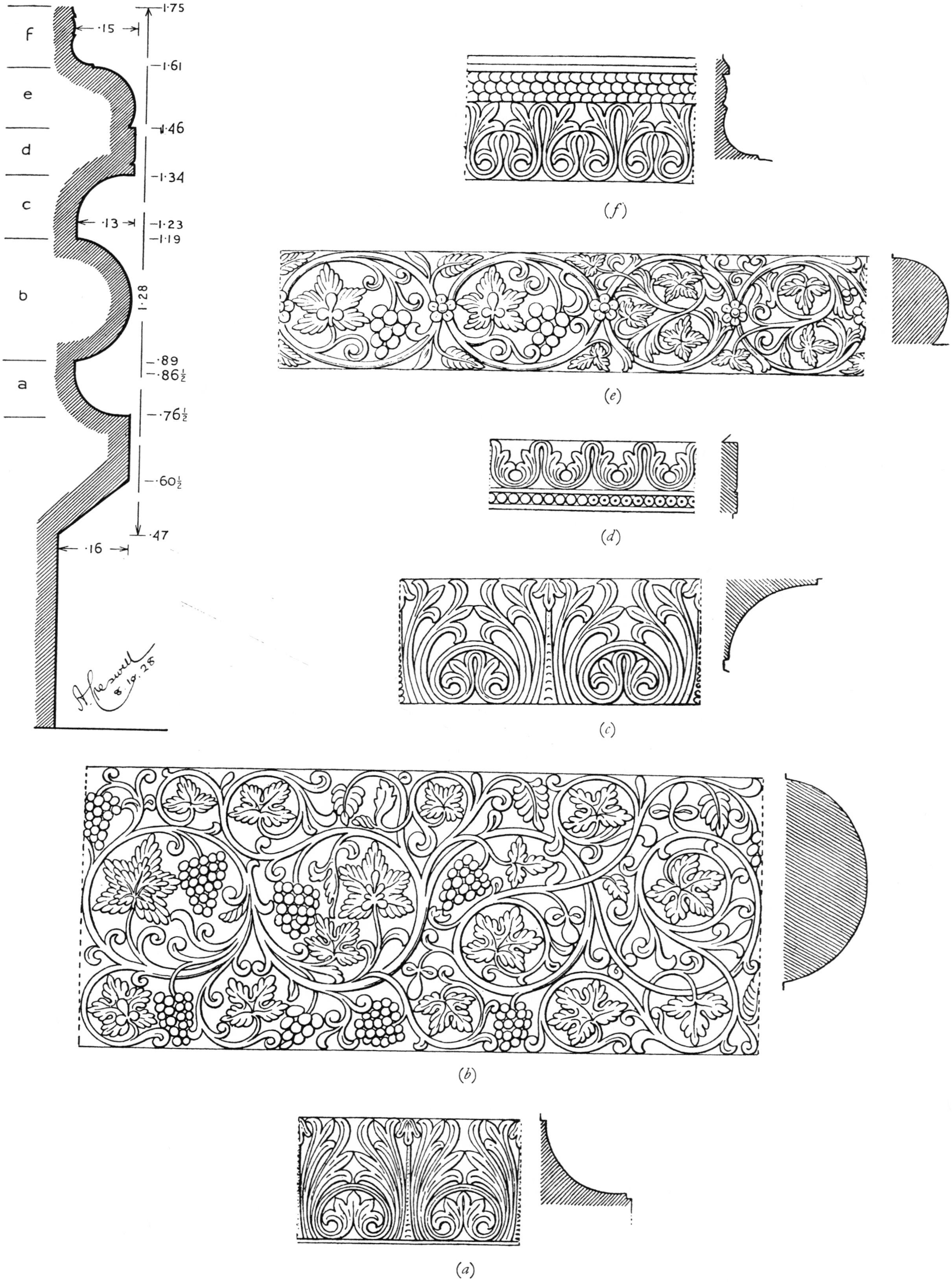

FIG. 655. MSHATTĀ: Façade, analysis of base moulding. (From Schulz and Strzygowski, *loc. cit.*)

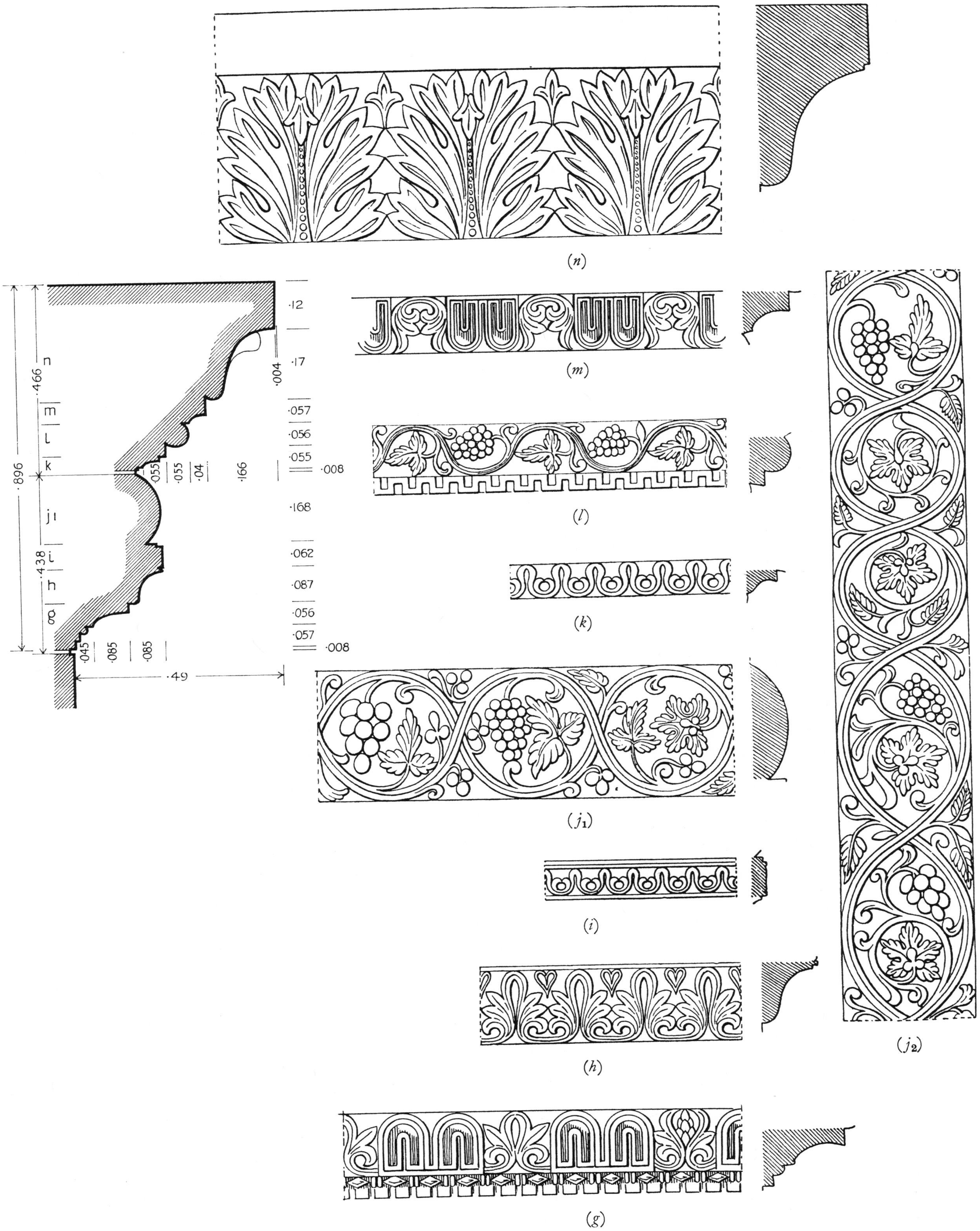

FIG. 656. MSHATTĀ: Façade, analysis of cornice. (From Schulz and Strzygowski, *loc. cit.*, except that *g* and *m* have been slightly modified.)

The east wall of the eastern tract is so damaged that Brünnow was only able to find one opening, 2·72 m. distant from the south-east corner (*l* in Fig. 630); it is rectangular in form, placed high, and slopes downwards towards the exterior.

In the south wall of this tract, in exactly the same place as *a* in the south wall of the western tract, is the remains of what must have been a recess with a latrine stone, like those already mentioned in towers D, N, O, and P. The wall is only preserved here to half the height of a man, and the latrine stone, which is 1·20 m. long by 60 cm. broad, is embedded in the top course at right angles to the wall, from which it projects about 35 cm. Its upper face is hollowed out into a semicircular basin-like depression 45 cm. wide (Fig. 654). Behind this is a cavity 21 cm. broad and 70 long; its front end tapers to 10 cm. and joins the basin, whilst its lower face slopes outwards, ending in a canal 17 cm. square.

The function of this block, as well as those in towers D, N, O, and P, is sufficiently clear; as for the sloping channels described above it is probable that they were for the carrying away of liquids, but what can have been the function of those placed near the ground and running horizontally outwards? I am unable to say.

THE DECORATION OF THE SOUTH FAÇADE. The sumptuously decorated façade,[1] now so famous, between towers C and Z consists of a plain socle 47 cm. high, a richly decorated base 1·28 m. in height, a decorated wall-face 2·95 m. in height and an entablature of 90·4 cm. The latter runs vertically down at the two ends, turns again at right angles somewhat above the base, and stops suddenly against the flanks of the two towers.

The base consists of a torus moulding (Fig. 655 *b*) with a hollow moulding (*a* and *c*) above and below it, the whole being surmounted by a quarter-round moulding (*e*). The torus moulding is decorated with a network of interlacing vine tendrils which form loops. In the left-hand part, which is the best preserved, it is easy to see that in each loop a leaf, rising upwards, is generally paired with a bunch of grapes which hangs downwards, just as on some of the tie-beams in the Dome of the Rock (Plate 27*a*). The grapes stand out in well-rounded relief and the cutting is from 5 to 6 cm. deep. Sometimes three grapes are superimposed at the junction of leaf with stalk. Sometimes, however, there are leaves only without grapes. The two hollow mouldings, which form quarter circles in section, are decorated with rows of anthemions (*a* and *c*), those in the lower moulding being more closely set.[2] Above this is a band 12 cm. high, decorated with a row of pearls and split palmettes (*d*), then a quarter-round moulding decorated with a pair of vine tendrils, which cross each other regularly forming loops, mostly oval, with a little rosette at their points of intersection (*e*). Above this is a hollow moulding decorated with another row of anthemions, surmounted by a triple row of scales (*f*).

The entablature is divided into three parts (Fig. 656). The architrave, only separated from the wall-face by a dentil moulding, springs forward like a cornice. The lower concave half (*g*) bears an ornament resting on a bead and reel, consisting of a pair of double-hoop motifs separated by anthemions; the upper convex half (*h*) is decorated with split palmettes. Separated from it by a narrow border (*i*) is the frieze j_1—a torus of slight projection—decorated with interlacing vine tendrils resembling those of the base torus. The decoration on that part which runs down vertically at the left side of the façade is somewhat different (j_2). The torus is separated from the cornice by a second band *k*, somewhat similar to *i*. The cornice proper, like the architrave, springs boldly forward. The bed moulding (*l*) is decorated

[1] To the late Josef Strzygowski is due the credit of having urged Dr. Bode to bring the façade to Berlin. Thanks to the interest displayed by the German Emperor and his influence with Sultan ʿAbd al-Ḥamīd, the latter consented; see Diez, in the *Encyclopaedia of Islām*, III, p. 613. The removal of the façade was effected under the superintendence of Dr. Schumacher of Haifa and Prof. Schulz of Charlottenburg in the winter of 1903/4; it was sent in 422 cases to Beyrut by land and thence to Hamburg by sea; see *Führer durch die Staatlichen Museen zu Berlin: Das Kaiser-Friedrich-Museum*, 8te Aufl., p. 57; and Kühnel, *Mschatta*, p. 4.

Needless to say this removal was criticized. The answer is provided by the following events. A few years after its removal the Ḥijāz Railway was begun and the Turkish engineers engaged on it, needing stone, looted every building within two or three miles of its course. Before this the east side of Mshattā was intact, as shown in Brünnow and von Domaszewski, *Die Provincia Arabia*, II, Fig. 689. The engineers referred to stripped off all the smooth cut-stone facing blocks and exposed the rubble interior. This sort of thing went on throughout Transjordan but, so far, no one has followed the line of the railway, with Brünnow and von Domaszewski's book in hand, and compared the present state of the forts of the Roman *limes* and many other monuments with the condition shown in Brünnow von Domaszewski's photographs taken in 1895–8.

If the marvellous triangles of the south façade had not been safe in Berlin, their stones would have served to build railway culverts.

[2] As a result of this the upper anthemions only occasionally correspond with those of the lower row.

with a meandering vine tendril resting on peculiar dentils. The corona (*m*) resembles *g*, except that the anthemions are here replaced by split palmettes. The crowning member (*n*) is decorated with a row of great outward-curving acanthus leaves.

The wall-surface between the socle and the entablature is divided into twenty upright and twenty inverted triangles by a cornice-like moulding, which runs up and down zigzag fashion from the socle to the architrave. To these forty triangles must be added four half-triangles, viz. one at each end of the façade and one on either side of the entrance. The outer edge of this moulding projects 13 cm. at right angles to the wall, its inner side being concave (Fig. 657). Its outer edge is decorated with a series of quatrefoils, and the inner with a dentil moulding similar to *g*, the curved space between being filled with bold acanthus leaves (*Acanthus spinosus*) perpendicular to the direction of the moulding, except at the corners of the zigzags where the angle is filled by a larger, upright acanthus.

FIG. 657. MSHATTĀ: Façade, zigzag moulding. (From Schulz and Strzygowski, *loc. cit.*)

The triangles are *c.* 2·85 m. in height and 2·50 in width at the base. Exactly in the centre of each is a great rosette which projects exactly as much as the zigzag moulding; those in the upright triangles are lobed hexagons, those in the inverted triangles are straight-sided octagons. Each rosette is formed, as it were, of a piece of the zigzag moulding bent to shape and enclosing a round kernel which is formed in a great variety of ways (Fig. 658). The four half-triangles each contain half a rosette only.

The remaining wall-surface is decorated with sculpture in relief, but in various stages of execution; in the upright triangles it has been completely, or almost completely, carved, but in the inverted triangles only those of the left half of the façade are filled, sometimes only partly, with carving, whereas those of the right half of the façade only bear isolated traces of decoration. Carved outlines can still be clearly recognized alongside certain finished places.

The rosettes divide the triangles into three parts of roughly equal height, viz. a broad lower strip, two small surfaces flanking the rosette, and the little triangle above it. In the three upright triangles at the west end the lower strips are clearly divided off from the upper part by small horizontal bands, but in the remainder the decoration runs unbroken throughout.

I shall designate the upright triangles and half-triangles going from east to west by the letters of the alphabet, and the inverted ones with the letters of the two adjoining vertical ones.

A (Plate 120). In the lowest section are four circles connected by loops and decorated with beads, above which is a horizontal band, similarly decorated, forming a border. The circles are filled with vine tendrils and bunches of grapes; in each circle are two birds which peck at the fruit. In the second section, to right and left, below the rosette, is a smaller circle with a bird amidst vine tendrils which continue upwards to the topmost section. In the centre of it, just above the rosette, sits a cat-like animal, turned to the right, with a human face[1] turned forwards and surmounted by a conical cap which fills the point of the triangle. The kernel of the rosette is composed of a double flower, surrounded by six objects like pine-cones (Fig. 658).

A–B (Plate 121). Only the upper half of the little triangle below the rosette is finished; one can see two vine tendrils forming a circle, each with a bird within. Below are merely a few slightly indicated outlines. The kernel of the rosette is composed of a little flower, surrounded by eight objects like pine-cones, set radially, between which appear the points of similar objects (Fig. 658).

B (Plate 121). Only partly executed. In the centre of the lowest division is a basket or chalice with three large bunches of grapes (Strzygowski believes them to be pine-apples). Rising up behind the grapes, apparently out of the vase, are two richly articulated stems (unlike vine stems) coiled into circles to right and left and giving birth to vine tendrils and bunches of grapes. The outer circle to the left has not been executed.[2] In each of the three existing circles is a bird, and a fourth fills up

[1] Strzygowski (*Jahrbuch*, XXV, p. 309) calls it a Sphinx or Gorgon.

[2] Brünnow (*op. cit.*, II, p. 138) speaks of several faint outlines being recognizable.

the right corner. A small band forms the upper border. Strzygowski calls attention to the cornucopia-like calices, as in the Dome of the Rock.[1] Only the right half of the middle division has been finished. Between two confronted birds with heads averted rises a strong vine stem which continues up to the lower part of the upper triangle, the decoration of which is only roughly carved in outline, while the upper part has been left bare. Kernel of rosette as in A–B, but surrounded by a circle, outside which are six more objects like pine-cones (Fig. 658).

Fig. 658. Mshattā: Façade, kernels of rosettes. (From Schulz and Stryzgowski, *loc. cit.*)

B–C (Plates 121–2). Only the part below the rosette has been executed. Vine tendrils rise up apparently anyhow and three birds peck at the grapes. Rosette exactly as in A–B (Fig. 658).

C (Plate 122). In the lowest division are nine intersecting double hoops of which the two outer are partly cut off by the zigzag moulding. Eight pointed oval fields are thus formed with small triangular fields between. The former are occupied by a sunflower and a bird alternately, the bird being in the midst of vine tendrils. Here again a band forms the upper border. To the right of the rosette is a circle with a bird in the midst of vine tendrils, which continue upwards to above the rosette. To the left of the rosette are vine stems formed as in B. The lower part only of the upper triangle has been marked

[1] *Loc. cit.*, p. 310.

out; between the tendrils is a bird, standing on the rosette. Kernel of rosette as in A–B, but with twelve instead of eight pine-cones (Fig. 658).

C–D (Plates 122–3). Only the rosette has been executed. It consists as usual of two courses of stone, and the kernel consists of two entirely different patterns put together presumably by mistake. The lower half is exactly as in A, but the upper half is entirely filled by a double (sun- ?) flower the centre part of which matches that of the lower half (Fig. 658).

D (Plate 123). In the middle, below the rosette, is a richly decorated amphora, out of which, to right and left, rise two vine stems which coil themselves into great circles, two large ones below and a smaller one above, from which further tendrils rise up into the upper part of the triangle. The entire field thus forms a single whole for the first time. In each of the two middle circles stands a winged griffin-like animal facing the other; the left is four-footed and has a fox-like head with long pointed ears, whilst that to the right, with its clearly indicated mane, rather resembles a hyena, but it only possesses fore-legs, for its hind-quarters merge into a mass like a cluster of grapes. The outer circles are filled as follows: the lower left-hand circle contains a great bird, perhaps a turkey, and a very large bunch of grapes, the upper a little griffin; on the right side, the lower contains a slightly larger griffin, the upper a little bird. In the vine stems above the rosette is a great bird, like a pheasant, above which the triangle remains bare. The kernel of the rosette is formed by a little flower, surrounded by six tripartite leaves, the panicles of which are bound together on both sides, so that they form a star. Between the leaves are pine-cones as in A–B (Fig. 658).

D–E (Plates 123–4). Only the triangle below the rosette is finished. In the bottom corner is a great three-pointed leaf like chicory, above that, vine tendrils and two birds. The kernel of the rosette is composed of a little flower surrounded by four radiating pine-cones; between each is a fleur-de-lis turned inwards (Fig. 658).

E (Plate 124). In the middle of the lower part is a bowl flanked by a zebu-ox and a lion which drink from it. The two animals are surrounded with the usual tendrils which entirely cover the whole surface up to the unfinished apex. To right and left of the rosette and in the middle of the upper triangle is a bird, and there is a fourth in the lower right-hand corner. The kernel of the rosette is a double sun-flower, surrounded by six pine-cones pointing inwards.

E–F (Plates 124–5). As tower B begins here, the triangle is divided into two halves at right angles to each other. The left half is quite bare and the right half is nearly so, except just below the rosette where there is a vine tendril curled in a circle, with a bird. In order that the rosette may appear symmetrical to the observer, the inner part containing the kernel has been elongated; in the centre is a huge sun-flower reaching above and below to the inner border, but the spaces at the side of it are filled at their widest part with two pine-cones, set horizontally and pointing inwards; clinging to them is a spiral-like convolvulus, and in the corners a little leaf with a serrated edge (Fig. 658).

F (Plate 125). In the centre is a small vase out of which rise two vine stems, which spread over the whole field, each forming one large and two small circles as in D. The decoration of the whole field has been completed here, as it has also on the remaining four upright triangles of this tower. Of the two large circles the left contains a griffin, the right apparently a centaur. In the two outer circles is a bird, but of the two upper ones the left is occupied by a griffin, the right by a pheasant. Above the rosette are two more birds. The kernel of the rosette, as in C–D, is composed of two designs that do not match, as shown in Fig. 658.

F–G (Plates 125–6). Here the whole field up to a point level with the top of the rosette has been almost completely executed, except that to the left at the very top only the hollows have been carved out. The decoration consists of the usual vine tendrils and birds. In the rosette, which is set on the corner, the kernel remains a regular octagon, but the outer border is drawn out sideways. The kernel, for the third time, is composed of two halves which do not match, the lower half resembling A–B and the upper half G–H (Fig. 658).

G (Plate 126). As in D and F, two vine stems rising out of a fluted chalice form six circles, two large ones in the middle and two lying one above the other on either side. In the chalice on each side of the vine stems, which are joined at the bottom, sit two birds looking outwards (see Fig. 268); above, between the diverging stems, is a great bunch of grapes. The chalice is flanked by a pair of confronted lions sitting with a fore-paw raised. The lion on the right is quite within the right central circle, but the one on the left is larger and its hind-quarters are in the small outer circle. In the latter, and also in the one above and in both the lower corners, is a bird. The lower right-hand circle is occupied by a turkey, and the upper by what appears to be a hare. In the upper triangle, which is completely filled by the last runners of the stems coming up from below, are four birds, two large ones in the lower part, and two small ones in the upper. The kernel of the rosette is composed of a double sunflower surrounded by six pine-cones pointing inwards as in A and E.

G–H (Plates 126–7). A strong vine stem rises up out of the point of the triangle and branches out to right and left. Only the right half, however, continues beyond the lower part of the rosette and even then does not quite reach the entablature. The kernel of the rosette follows the same pattern as the upper half of F–G (Fig. 658).

H (Plate 127). Below in the centre a pair of sitting lions drink out of a chalice from which arises a group of leaves. Behind each lion a stout vine stalk shoots up from the ground and rises past the rosette to the apex of the triangle. In each of the two lower corners is a bird; above to the left two, to the right four more birds; in the upper triangle three more. The kernel of the rosette is exactly as in B (Fig. 658).

H–I (Plates 127–8). Tendril work similar to that of G–H. The left half has been nearly finished, but the right half, for the greater part, has only been marked out. The kernel of the rosette is a little flower surrounded by eight pine-cones (Fig. 658).

I (Plate 128). A lion on the left and a griffin on the right drink out of a chalice in the centre. The background is completely covered with tendril treatment resembling that in H. In the left lower corner is an animal difficult to identify; in the right lower corner is a lion sitting erect on its haunches. Below the rosette to the left are three birds, to the right two. Above the rosette are two more birds, above which are three circles formed of tendrils and arranged pyramid fashion; there is a bird in the left lower one. This upper triangle has not been completely finished, and there are only outlines in the upper part. The kernel of the rosette is formed of six five-pointed leaves with a little trilobate leaf inserted between the upper and lower pair, and a sunflower (?) in the centre (Fig. 658).

I–J (Plates 128–9). A tendril rises up towards both sides as in G–H and H–I. To right and left below the rosette is a bird, the former extremely well preserved. In the upper part, to the left, the work has been completely marked out and partly begun; the clearly marked outlines of four circles formed of tendrils can be distinguished, and in the left upper one is a bird. The inner part of the rosette has been entirely destroyed.

J (Plate 129). This is the first triangle without a chalice. Two thick vine stems grow directly out of the ground in the centre, cross each other, and form two large central and four smaller circles as in D, F, and G. Each of the two central circles contains a quadruped looking outwards, but they have weathered badly and it is difficult to say what they are. The filling of the left lower circle has half crumbled away, but the circle above it contains a bird. The right lower circle contains a small, roughly executed human figure, striding outwards and carrying a basket full of grapes, whilst the upper circle is filled with a large five-pointed vine leaf on which are three grapes at the point of junction with the stalk. Nearly half the upper triangle has weathered away, but it appears to have contained a bird. The kernel of the rosette has suffered badly, but Schulz's reconstruction (Fig. 658), which agrees with Brünnow's description,[1] appears to be justified.

J–K (Plates 129–30). Re-entrant angle of tower. The two zigzag mouldings do not meet each other directly, but are joined by a short horizontal piece. In consequence of this, the two halves of the inverted triangle are broader than elsewhere, and the rosette is not in the corner as usual, but in the right half, lying on the enclosure wall, which alone is decorated although unfinished. The kernel of the rosette is composed of a flower, surrounded by eight badly weathered pine-cones similar to H–I (Fig. 658).

K (Plate 130). Tendril work closely resembling that in J, but only worked up to the middle of the rosette. In the right circle next the door-post is an animal looking left, in the left circle is a lion moving to the right, in the upper circle a bird. Kernel of rosette destroyed. Schulz points out[2] that the distance (1·58 and 1·54 m.) between the side of each tower and the outer edge of the door-post has evidently been calculated so as to allow room for the whole entablature of the façade to turn up vertically

[1] *Op. cit.*, II, p. 140. [2] *Loc. cit.*, p. 211 and Taf. III.

at right angles, before forming a relieving arch over the lintel Syrian fashion (e.g. Qal'at Sim'ān (Fig. 663 facing p. 620)), as was almost certainly intended.

Door-posts (Plates 130–31). The mouldings of the door-posts (Fig. 659) resemble the entablature of the façade, except that they are more simply decorated. The inner part, corresponding to the architrave, is decorated with a dentil band and anthemions. The part corresponding to the frieze consists, as in the entablature, of a torus decorated with vine stems, which spring out of a fluted long-necked amphora, except that in the former there is a band decorated with leaf ornaments on the inner side, whereas here the torus moulding is separated from this, as well as from the cornice by an undecorated groove with a right-angled profile. The cornice consists of a dentil band on which rest large anthemions. A broad undecorated strip forms the outer edge, as in the entablature.

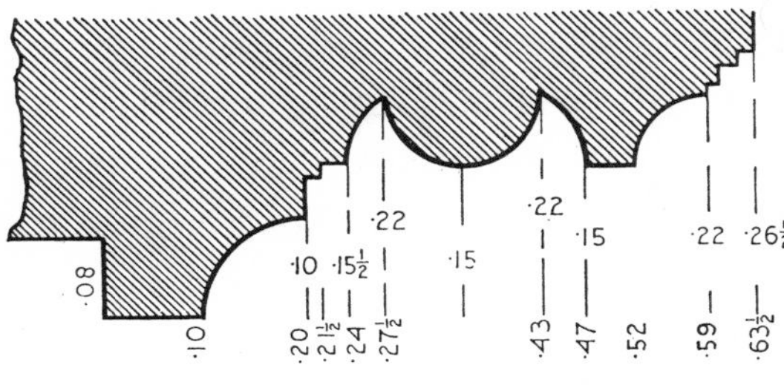

Fig. 659. Mshattā: Moulding of door-posts.

L (Plate 131). Next the door-post is a chalice out of which a sitting lion drinks. Behind the lion a thick vine stem shoots up with three birds amidst the foliage. Only the two lower courses of stone reaching to the middle of the rosette have been finished, the rest is only partly worked. The kernel of the rosette is composed of a central flower surrounded by six enclosed palmettes turned inwards.

The upper half of the rest of the façade had been completely removed, even when Tristram saw it, so that the rosettes of all the inverted triangles are missing.

L–M (Plates 131 and 132 *a*). The two zigzag mouldings are joined by a horizontal piece, as in J–K. The work has been partly marked out on the left half only, and a few tendrils and a bird have been begun below. The rosette is missing.

M (Plate 132 *a*). In the centre a pair of vine tendrils spring out of a little two-handled vase and coil into circles. As Strzygowski points out,[1] this stem does not start thick and gradually taper, but is uniformly thin throughout, the circles are smaller and more numerous, and the leaves are mostly three-lobed, everything in fact being done to give an even effect to the whole field. The kernel of the rosette is formed of a six-petalled object surrounded by six pine-cones (Fig. 658).

M–N (Plate 132). Unworked.

N (Plate 132 *b*). Tendril work similar to M, but the small vase from which the tendrils spring has no handles. The kernel of the rosette consists of a six-lobed flower surrounded by eight pine-cones (two large, four medium, and two small) with little leaves between (Fig. 658).

N–O (Plates 132–3). Unworked.

O (Plate 133 *a*). Tendril work as in M and N, except that the tendrils rise out of the ground instead of a vase. But in the centre is an object like a tree crowned with a winged palmette similar to that in Fig. 289. A smaller example of the same motif can be seen near the left corner. Kernel of rosette as in N.

O–P (Plate 133). Unworked.

P (Plate 133 *b*). The blocks composing this triangle, which were all lying on the ground at the time of Brünnow's visit,[2] were identified and brought to Berlin by Schulz. Two tendrils spring up behind an acanthus root in the centre, cross each other, and form circles as before. On the centre line, set one above the other, are two examples of the curious motif[3] which we have already observed several times in the mosaics of the Dome of the Rock (Plates 7 *a*, 18 *a*, 20 *a*, and Figs. 319–320), and a third, much weathered, can be distinguished a little to the right. Kernel of rosette as in G (Fig. 658).

P–Q (Plate 134). Unworked.

Q (Plate 134 *a*). Completed by Schulz. The design, which consists of irregularly interlacing vine tendrils rising out of a long-necked vase, has been carved out, but the modelling has not been finished. Kernel of rosette as in L.

Q–R (Plate 134). Unworked.

Although the socle still remains intact, the four following triangles, which were not taken to Berlin,

[1] *Jahrbuch*, XXV, p. 314.

[2] And in 1875 also; see Plate 113 *a*. For this photograph, and that reproduced on Plate 113 *b*, see *The American Expedition*, in the *P.E.F.*, *Q.St.*, 1876, pp. 50–51.

[3] Strzygowski calls it a 'Flügelpalmette'.

have either been thrown down or taken away. Some blocks were used for the sake of their stone during the construction of the Ḥijāz Railway. Their disappearance is a complete answer to those who criticized the transport of the rest of the façade to Berlin.

I have tried in vain to get good photographs of this part of the façade. First I tried to get Brünnow's, but I learnt that he was dead and that all his photographs had passed into the possession of an American university. I wrote, and was informed that, although they had photographs and other material of his, they had not got any photographs corresponding to the illustrations of the façade of Mshattā published in his *Provincia Arabia*. I then tried the Palestine Exploration Society without result. Finally, I found some prints of the part I required in Notre-Dame de France at Jerusalem. They had been taken by Père Germer-Durand about 1896. The prints had faded, and I had to spend two afternoons going through over two thousand glass negatives before I found the originals. These unfortunately had spots of mildew on them; they were cleaned as well as possible and are reproduced here (Plates 134 *b* and 135 *a* and *d*.) I shall be extremely grateful to anyone who will let me know of the existence of better ones.

R (Plate 134 *b-c* also *a*, to right). The western third of this triangle was taken to Berlin, the middle third is *in situ* up to the centre of the rosette, and the eastern third, or at least the border moulding, is lying on the ground.[1] Below in the middle is a great beaker, out of which rise two vine tendrils. The latter have become more regular again, and form circles as in previous triangles. Winged palmette to left. Only the first course has been decorated; the left part of the next course has been partly blocked out. Kernel of rosette as in G and P, except that the sunflower is a triple one (Fig. 658).

R–S. Unworked.

S (Plate 135 *a*). All carved out but only partly modelled. The tendril work, resembling M, is formed by two stems which rise directly out of the ground. Kernel of rosette as in A, E, G, P, and R.

S–T. Brünnow says that only a few outlines were to be recognized.

T (Plate 135 *d*). Filled in a remarkable fashion, for the tendrils spread out from a root in the centre, in a manner which Strzygowski has well compared to the tentacles of a cuttle-fish.[2] Kernel of rosette as in R (Fig. 658). This rosette (Plate 135 *c*), which resembles the last, has been taken away and built in over the doorway of a house on the east edge of Zīza village.[3]

T–U (Plate 135 *d*). In the point, several tendrils, some executed, some only marked out.

U (Plate 135 *d*, to right).[4] The surface is divided into circles as in D, F, G, H, only the lines are harder and more rigidly geometrical. There is no suggestion of vine leaves, but there are a number of objects like pine-cones which may be bunches of grapes merely blocked out. In fact they probably are, as Strzygowski has already suggested,[5] for there is an object on the lintel of Qaṣr aṭ-Ṭūba (Plate 138 *a*) which is similar in size and shape, and in which the grapes are quite distinct.

There are also several tulip-like forms resembling some in the mosaics of the Dome of the Rock (Fig. 319) and also those on the same lintel at Qaṣr aṭ-Ṭūba. Three are placed, one over the other, immediately below the rosette. The kernel of this rosette is as in N.

U–V.[6] Only the lower point of the triangle existed in Brünnow's day. A tendril runs spiral fashion within a circle so as to form a second circle concentric with the first, and terminates in a pear-shaped fruit surrounded by six leaves. On the outer side of the tendril are a dozen little leaves which fill the space between it and the outer circle.

V (Plate 136 *b* and *c*).[7] Nearly all that remained of this triangle was fortunately taken to Berlin. Only the part below the rosette had been carved. In the centre is a medallion which reaches from the base to the rosette; in the two corners are two smaller ones. All these circles are superimposed on a background, with which they have no organic connexion, consisting of tendrils and fruit somewhat resembling that of U, except that the tendrils do not coil in circles. Above the left circle, amongst the

[1] It is to be hoped that the Department of Antiquities will restore this and many other fallen pieces to their place in the façade, and transfer hither the missing rosettes from the house in Zīza village (see note 3).

[2] *Mschattā*, *loc. cit.*, p. 317.

[3] Half a rosette, of a type resembling H, has been built in as a hood to a doorway on the east side of this same building, and another rosette is built into the south wall of a courtyard to which this doorway gives access. I omitted to photograph it. As for the half-rosette, I cannot place it, for it does not correspond to Brünnow's photographs of the rosettes which are now missing.

[4] For detail, see Schulz and Strzygowski, *loc. cit.*, Abb. 92. Two blocks, forming part of the course below the rosette, are preserved in the Mshattā Room of the Staatliche Museen, Berlin.

[5] *Ibid.*, p. 318.

[6] Brünnow and von Domaszeski, *op. cit.*, II, fig. 753.

[7] See also Brünnow and von Domaszewski, *op. cit.*, II, fig. 754 (reproduced here, Plate 136 *b*); and Schulz and Strzygowski, *loc. cit.*, Abb. 93.

fruit, is a winged palmette like that of the rosette at Qaṣr aṭ-Ṭūba (Plate 138 *a* and Fig. 289); another can be distinguished to the right of the central circle. The middle circle has a plain outside border, enclosing a circle of anthemion-like objects (rather like Fig. 656 *k*) with an inner border of little beads. In the interior is an anchor-cross, formed of C-shaped motifs rather like enclosed palmettes, with a little flower in the centre. The smaller medallions consist of a circle of quatrefoils, like those that form a border to all the rosettes in the façade, enclosed by an outer and inner border decorated with beads. The interior of the right-hand circle consists of leaf-work, but the left one was apparently more elaborate; less than half of it has been preserved. Kernel of rosette: an eight-petalled flower within a circle of six pine-cones pointing inwards, each being set in a U-shaped frame, the ends of which curl outwards and touch the next one.

When the façade was erected in Berlin a rosette was placed here. Dr. Kühnel was the first to notice that the kernel of this rosette does not correspond with the one shown in position, before the removal, in Brünnow and von Domaszewski, *op. cit.*, II, Fig. 754, and in Schulz and Strzygowski, *loc. cit.*, Taf. VIII (reproduced here, Plate 136 *c*). These illustrations are from different photographs, for the stones in the foreground are not in the same position, but neither is sharp and clear. However, Brünnow and von Domaszewski say that the kernel somewhat resembled A, L, and Q.[1] As regards the substituted rosette (Plate 136 *b*) its kernel consists of an endless undulating stalk of which six loops, turning inwards, form a star-shaped space containing a little flower. The same undulating stalk, on approaching the border of the rosette, again turns inwards to support six five-lobed leaves which lie within heart-shaped spaces. It therefore corresponds to the type marked 'Hallenfassade' in the table of Schulz (Fig. 658), so I conclude that it was found on the ground in front of the triple-arched façade.

Some twenty years ago I photographed a complete rosette, built in over the doorway of a house in Zīza village, which I was told was used by the mounted police. On referring to the table we find that the kernel corresponds to A, E, G, P, R, S, and T. It cannot belong to A, E, G, or P, for these are still intact, nor to R, of which the lower half was still in position at the time of my last visit (Plate 134 *c*). This leaves S and T. The wavy horizontal joint and the ornament which remains below to right and left clearly corresponds to T in Germer-Durand's photograph (Plate 135 *d*). It must therefore have belonged to this triangle, which unfortunately was not taken to Berlin by the Germans, but was looted later on by the local inhabitants, together with the stones of triangles S and U. On the same occasion I photographed half a rosette, built in over a doorway in the courtyard of the same house (Plate 135 *b*). Its kernel corresponds to B and H in the table, but as both these are still intact one must conclude that it must have come, like the substituted rosette, from the only other possible place—the triple-arched façade.

Termination of Façade. At the west end of the façade the descending part of the cornice strikes against the left side of triangle A, low down, immediately turns at right angles, and continues horizontally, without being in contact with its horizontal continuation (Plate 120). At the east end, however, the treatment is somewhat different, for the vertical part of the cornice clears the sloping side of V, turns at right angles, and continues in contact with its horizontal continuation (Plate 136 *c* and *d*). The eastern half-triangle thus becomes blunt-pointed. Only the lower part of it has been preserved, in which leaves and little fruit have been partly carved out in relief.

As Brünnow has pointed out,[2] the various triangles can to a certain extent be grouped according to their varying compositions. Thus the triangles (A–J) to the west of the entrance, as well as the two half-triangles flanking it, all contain figures of animals, but those of the eastern half (M–V) only contain plant compositions. Only three human figures appear, viz. the head in the point of A, the centaur in F, and the little dwarf figure in the right-hand corner of J. The first three triangles, in their lower divisions, exhibit similar compositions, the field being divided into two parts by a horizontal line, whereas elsewhere the field is a whole. The six following (D–I) also form a clearly characterized group; they all contain two confronted animals with a vase between them. Another curious point: the animals which are not drinking (D, F, and G) sit in tendril-work coiled in circles, whereas in the case of those that drink (E, H, and I) the tendrils shoot straight up. But no symmetrical arrangement of the kernels of the rosettes can be established.

1 My description in the first edition of this work (p. 372) refers to the kernel of the substituted rosette.

2 *Op. cit.*, II, pp. 142–3.

BIBLIOGRAPY OF MSHATTĀ

1873 Tristram (H. B.), The Land of Moab, pp. 195–216 and 367–85, figs. 20–23 and 4 plates.

— Anon., Brilliant Architectural Discoveries in Eastern Syria. *The Builder*, XXXI, pp. 397–8 and 2 figs. on p. 403.

1874 Fergusson (James), History of Architecture (2nd ed.), I, pp. 387–92 and figs. 262–6; 3rd ed., I, pp. 401–7 and figs. 265–9.

1876 Rawlinson (G.), The Seventh Great Oriental Monarchy, pp. 594–9, pl. 10, and figs. 62–4.

1878 Fergusson (J.), The Temples of the Jews, pp. 168–70 and fig. 43.

1881 Merrill (S.), East of the Jordan, pp. 256–63, with 4 illus.

1886 Conder (C. R.), Syrian Stone-Lore, pp. 353–5.

— Thomson (W. M.), The Land and the Book, III, pp. 630–34.

1887 Dieulafoy (M.), L'Art antique de la Perse, V, pp. 88–95 and figs. 63–8.

— Layard (Sir Henry), Early Adventures in Persia, Susiana and Babylonia, I, pp. 114–15.

1888 Doughty (C. M.), Travels in Arabia Deserta, I, p. 16.

1890 Hill (Gray), Mashita. *P.E.F.*, *Q.St.*, 1890, pp. 173–4.

— Spiers (R. Phené), Sassanian Architecture. *J.R.I.B.A.*, VII, pp. 56 and 59; reprinted in his *Architecture: East and West*, pp. 83–4 and 86.

1891 Berchem (M. van), Notes d'archéologie arabe. *Journal Asiatique*, 8me sér., t. XVII, p. 428, n. 1.

— Hill (Gray), With the Beduins, pp. 55–6 and 58–9 and 2 illus.

— Merrill (S.), Visits to M'Shita. *P.E.F.*, *Q.St.*, 1891, pp. 75–6.

— Riegl (A.), Altorientalische Teppiche, pp. 134–7 and fig. 23.

1893 Séjourné (P. M.), Voyage au delà du Jordain. *Revue Biblique*, II, pp. 131–4, with plan and 3 illus.

1895 Bliss (F. J.), Narrative of an Expedition to Moab and Gilead. *P.E.F.*, *Q.St.*, 1895, pp. 229–34, with 2 plans and 3 illus.

— Brünnow (R.), Reisebericht. *Mitth. und Nachr. D. P. V.*, I, pp. 81–8 and figs. 21–6.

— Gayet (Al.), L'Art persan, pp. 109–12, with 1 fig.

1896 Berchem (M. van), Corpus Inscriptionum Arabicarum, I: Égypte, pp. 266–7.

— Vailhé (S.), Dans les Montagnes bleues. *Echo de Notre-Dame* (Jerusalem), 1896, pp. 224–9, with 3 illus.

1898 Lammens (H.), Les Ruines d'al-Mochatta. *Al-Machriq*, I, pp. 481–7 and 630–37, with 4 illus. (In Arabic.)

— Peters (J. P.), Nippur, II, p. 357.

1899 Oppenheim (Max von), Vom Mittelmeer zum Persischen Golf, I, pp. 104–6, with plate (from Rawlinson).

1901 Dussaud (R.) and F. Macler, Voyage archéologique au Ṣafâ et dans le Djebel ed-Drûz, p. 44.

— Gautier (L.), Autour de la Mer Morte, pp. 113–18 and figs. 25–31.

— Nies (J. B.), Notes on a Cross Jordan Trip. *P.E.F.*, *Q.St.*, 1901, pp. 366–8.

1902 Gurlitt (C.), Geschichte der Kunst, I, p. 215 and plate.

— Musil (A.), Ḳuṣejr 'Amra und andere Schlösser östlich von Moab. *Sitzungsberichte der Kaiserl. Akad. der Wissenschaften in Wien*, *Phil.-hist. Classe*, CXLIV, Abh. vii, pp. 14–15 and 46–7 and figs. 6–10.

1904 Borrmann (R.), Die Baukunst des Altertums und des Islam im Mittelalter, pp. 314–16 and fig. 249.

— Saladin (H.), Le Palais de Machitta. *Bulletin Archéologique*, pp. 409–14, and pls. XLIV–XLVI.

1904 Sarre (F.), in the *Deutsche Reichsanzeiger*, 19th Jan.

— Schulz (B.) and J. Strzygowski, Mschatta. *Jahrbuch der Kgl. Preuszischen Kunstsammlungen*, XXV, pp. 205–373, Abb. 1–119 and Taf. I–XI.

1905 Brünnow (R. E.) and A. von Domaszewski, Die Provincia Arabia, II, pp. 105–76, figs. 686–754 and Taf. XLV–XLVIII, also pp. 308–11.

— Rhodokanakis (N.), in the *W.Z.K.M.*, XIX, pp. 289–313 (review of Strzygowski's *Mschatta*).

— Ameseder (R.), in the *Byzantinische Zeitschrift*, XIV, pp. 626–30 (a review of Schulz and Strzygowski).

— Berchem (M. van), Mechatta. *Journal des Savants*, 1905, pp. 472–7 (a review of Schulz and Strzygowski).

1906 Clermont-Ganneau, in the *Journal des Savants*, 1906, p. 52 (review of *Die Provincia Arabia*, Bd. II).

— Becker (C. H.), in the *Zeitschrift für Assyriologie*, XIX, pp. 419–32.

— Poppelreuther, Zur Datierungsfrage der Fassade von M'schatta. *Sitzungsbericht der Kunstgeschichtlichen Gesellschaft in Berlin*, II, pp. 12–14.

— Reinach (S.), La Date de la façade de M'schatta. *Revue Archéologique*, 4me sér., t. VII, p. 485.

1907 Dussaud (R.), Les Arabes en Syrie avant l'Islam, pp. 39–56 and fig. 12.

— Herzfeld (Ernst), Samarra: Aufnahmen und Untersuchungen, p. 18.

— Musil (A.), Arabia Petraea, I, pp. 196–203 and Abb. 83–92.

— Musil (A.), Ḳuṣejr 'Amra, pp. 30–32 and figs. 32, 60, 62–70, 90, 91, and 118.

— Brünnow (R.), in the *W.Z.K.M.*, XXI, pp. 283–6, 288–93, and 295 (review of Musil's *Ḳuṣejr 'Amra*).

— Nöldeke (Th.), in the *Z.D.M.G.*, LXI, pp. 228–9 (review of Musil's *Ḳuṣejr 'Amra*).

— Strzygowski (J.), in the *Byzantinische Zeitschrift*, XVI, pp. 721–2 (review of Dussaud's *Les Arabes en Syrie*).

1908 Littmann (E.), in the *Göttingische gelehrte Anzeigen*, 170 Jahrg., pp. 150–51 (a review of Dussaud's *Les Arabes en Syrie*).

— Guthe (Hermann), Palästina, pp. 158–9 and Abb. 140–41; 2te Aufl., p. 163 and Abb. 157–8 (*Monographien zur Erdkunde*, No. 21).

— Moritz (B.), Ausflüge in der Arabia Petræa. *M.F.O.B.*, III, pp. 427–32.

— Rhodokanakis (N.), in the *W.Z.K.M.*, XXII, pp. 211–13 (a review of Dussaud's book).

— Lammens (H.), La Bâdia et la Ḥîra sous les Omaiyades. *Al-Machriq*, XI, pp. 772–3. (In Arabic.)

— Bréhier (L.), L'Art oriental à la fin de l'Antiquité. Le palais de Mschatta. *Revue des Idées*, V₂, pp. 79–84.

1909 Berchem (M. van), Au pays de Moab et d'Edom. *Journal des Savants*, 1909, pp. 300–301 and 402–8.

— Thiersch (H.), Pharos, Antike, Islam und Occident, p. 240 and Abb. 436.

1910 Dalton (O. M.), in Harvey, Lethaby, etc., The Church of the Nativity at Bethlehem, pp. 29–30.

— Diehl (C.), Manuel d'art byzantin, pp. 45–9 and fig. 17; 2me éd., pp. 50–55.

— Lammens (H.), La Bâdia et la Ḥîra sous les Omaiyades. *Mélanges de la Faculté orientale, Beyrout*, IV, pp. 109–11; reprinted and augmented in his *Études sur le siècle des Omayyades*, pp. 345–50.

— Herzfeld (E.), Die Genesis der islamischen Kunst. *Der Islam*, I, pp. 105–44, Abb. 1–3 and Taf. V.

1910 STRZYGOWSKI (J.), in van Berchem and Strzygowski, Amida, pp. 205, 328, and 339–41, and Abb. 124, 275, and 288.

1911 DALTON (O. M.), Byzantine Art and Archaeology, pp. 54, 67, 170–71, 202, 206, 278–9, 692, 694, 697–8, 704, and 705, and fig. 447.

— RHODOKANAKIS (N.), Wort- und Sachforschung im Arabischen, in *Wörter und Sachen*, III, pp. 119–20, and Abb. 1.

— RAHTGENS (H.), Die Kirche S. Maria im Kapitol zu Köln, pp. 134–5 and Abb. 93.

1912 BENOIT (F.), L'Architecture: L'Orient, p. 105 and fig. 65.

— BRÜNNOW (R. E.), Zur neuesten Entwickelung der Meschatta-Frage. *Zeitschr. für Assyriologie*, XXVII, pp. 129–38.

— HERZFELD (E.), Erster vorläufiger Bericht über die Ausgrabungen von Samarra, pp. 39–40.

1913 BELL (G. L.), Churches and Monasteries of the Ṭûr 'Abdîn. *Zeitschrift für Geschichte der Architektur*, Beiheft 9, pp. 107–8.

— DIEULAFOY (M.), Art in Spain and Portugal, pp. 7 and 15 and figs. 4 and 39.

1914 BELL (G. L.), Palace and Mosque at Ukhaiḍir, pp. 111, 113, 117–18, 120, 133, n. 4, 135, 138, n. 5, 141, 142, 162, and 165 and pl. 81.

— MANN (Traugott), Der Islam einst und jetzt (*Monographien zur Weltgeschichte*, Band 32), Abb. 35–6.

— RIVOIRA (G. T.), Architettura musulmana, p. 134; English transl., p. 132.

— STRZYGOWSKI (J.), Erworbene Rechte der österreichischen Kunstforschung in Nahen Orient. *Österr. Monatsschrift für den Orient*, XL, p. 6 and Abb. 3.

1915 DIEZ (E.), Die Kunst der islamischen Völker, pp. 29–33, 37–8, and 204, Taf. I and Abb. 23, 31–3, 86 and 88.

— LAMMENS (H.), L'Attitude de l'Islam primitif en face des arts figurés. *Journal Asiatique*, 11me sér., t. VI, pp. 258–9. Reprinted in his *Études sur la siècle des Omayyades*, pp. 251–90.

1916 MORITZ (B.), Bilder aus Palästina, p. 5 and Abb. 27–8.

— STRZYGOWSKI (J.), Die bildende Kunst des Ostens, pp. 21–3 and Abb. 7.

1917 STRZYGOWSKI (J.), Altai-Iran und Völkerwanderung, pp. 72–3.

— STRZYGOWSKI (J.), Die Baukunst der Armenier und Europa, pp. 637–8 and 645–6, and Abb. 632–4 and 639.

1918 STRZYGOWSKI (J.), Persischer Hellenismus in christlicher Zierkunst, in *Repertorium für Kunstwissenschaft*, XLI, pp. 125–7.

1919 STRZYGOWSKI (J.), Ursprung der christlichen Kirchenkunst, pp. 97, 105, 114, 125 and 129; transl. of Dalton and Braunholtz, pp. 22, 113–14, 123, 134, 147, 151, and 239, and figs. 34 and 51.

1920 VINCENT (H.), in the *Revue Archéologique*, 5me sér., t. XI, pp. 98–100 and fig. 12.

— WOERMANN (Karl), Geschichte der Kunst (2. Aufl.), II, pp. 117–18, 377–8, and Abb. 317.

1921 HERZFELD (E.), Mshattâ, Ḥîra und Bâdiya. *Jahrb. d. Preuszischen Kunstsammlungen*, XLII, pp. 104–6, 133–46, and Taf. I.

— LAMMENS (H.), La Syrie: Précis historique, I, pp. 96–8.

1922 JAUSSEN and SAVIGNAC, Mission archéologique en Arabie, III: Les Châteaux arabes, pp. 17, 28, 121–6, and pls. XIV–XV and XVIII.

— OELMANN (Franz), in the *Bonner Jahrbücher*, Heft 127, p. 174 and Abb. 15.

— OELMANN (Franz), Hilani und Liwanhaus. *Bonner Jahrbücher*, Heft 127, p. 226 and Abb. 34 *c*.

1923 AHLENSTIEL-ENGEL (E.), Arabische Kunst, pp. 9, 13, 16, 17, 55, 57, plan on p. 12, and Taf. 27.

1923/4 OELMANN (F.), Zur Kenntnis der karolingischen und omaijadischen Spätantike. *Mitteilungen des Deutschen Archaeologischen Instituts, Roemische Abteilung*, XXXVIII/XXXIX, pp. 226 ff.

1924 BRØNDSTED (J.), Early English Ornament, pp. 25–6, 312, and 314, and figs. 7–8 and 210.

— WOERMANN (Karl), Geschichte der Kunst aller Zeiten und Völker, II, pp. 377–8 and Abb. 317.

1925 DALTON (O. M.), East Christian Art, pp. 108–9, 118–19, 200, and 368.

— GLÜCK (H.) and E. DIEZ, Die Kunst des Islam, pp. 17, 25–6, 531, Abb. 2, 134, and Taf. I.

— GRÖBER (Karl), Palästina, Arabien und Syrien (*Orbis Terrarum*), p. xii and Abb. 202.

— MONNERET DE VILLARD (U.), Les Couvents près de Sohâg, p. 54 and fig. 51.

1926 BUTLER (A. J.), Islamic Pottery, p. 112.

— ANON., Führer durch die Staatlichen Museen zu Berlin: Das Kaiser-Friedrich-Museum, 8. Aufl., pp. 57–9.

— JERPHANION (G. de), Le Calice d'Antioche, p. 124.

— STRZYGOWSKI (J.), Das Schicksal der Berliner Museen. *Preussische Jahrbücher*, CCIII, pp. 163–4 and 184 (transfer of façade to Berlin).

1927 DUSSAUD (R.), in *Syria*, VIII, pp. 73–4.

— MIGEON (G.), Manuel d'art musulman, 2me éd., I, pp. 229–30.

— PIJOÁN (J.), History of Art, I, pp. 463–5 and fig. 762, and II, p. 207.

1928 MUSIL (A.), Palmyrena, pp. 283–5.

1929 COHN-WIENER (Ernst), Asia, pp. 123–5 and Abb. 93.

— KÜHNEL (Ernst), Kunst des Orients, p. 22 and Abb. 38.

— KÜHNEL (Ernst), in Springer's *Handbuch der Kunstgeschichte*, VI, pp. 377–9, 385, and Abb. 361 and 363–5.

— MUNTHE (Gustaf), Islams konst, pp. 44–7, with 1 illus.

— STRZYGOWSKI (J.), Les Éléments proprement asiatique dans l'art. *Revue des arts asiatiques*, VI, pp. 26–7 and pl. VI *b*.

— WACHTSMUTH (Friedrich), Der Raum, I, pp. 206–10 and Abb. 126–8.

1929/30 KAMMERER (A.), *Pétra et la Nabatène*, pp. 337–8 and pls. 125–8.

1930 STRZYGOWSKI (J.), Asiens bildende Kunst, pp. 100–106, 197–8, 315, 385–7, 445, 448, 455–7, 488, 511 and 713; and Abb. 90–94, 191, 319, 402, 451–2, 482, 501, and 629.

1932 DIEZ (E.), Mshattā, article in the *Encyclopaedia of Islām*, III, pp. 612–14, with plate.

— LAMMENS (H.), al-Walīd ibn Yazīd, article in the *Encyclopaedia of Islām*, IV, p. 1112.

— TERRASSE (H.), L'Art hispano-mauresque, pp. 25–7.

1933 BERENSON (Mary), A Modern Pilgrimage, pp. 100–102 and 333–4.

— KÜHNEL (E.), Mschatta (*Bilderhefte der Islamischen Kunstabteilung*, Heft 2).

— SARRE (Friedrich), Die Islamische Kunstabteilung in Berlin. *Kunst und Künstler*, XXXII, p. 43, with 1 illus.

1936 STRZYGOWSKI (J.), L'Ancien art chrétien de Syrie; see Index.

1937 DIMAND (M. S.), Studies in Islamic Ornament. I. Some Aspects of Omaiyad and Early 'Abbāsid Ornament. *Ars Islamica*, IV, pp. 317 and 324–37, and figs. 36–7, 47–55, and 59–62.

1938 SAUVAGET (J.), Remarques sur l'art sassanide. *Revue d'Études Islamiques*, 1938, pp. 123–4 and fig. 16.

1939 CRESWELL (K. A. C.), Coptic Influences on Early Muslim Architecture. *Bull. de la Société d'Archéologie Copte*, V, pp. 34–42, pls. IV–VII and 6 figs.

1939 SAUVAGET (J.), Remarques sur les monuments omeyyades. *Journal Asiatique*, CCXXXI, pp. 31–5.

1947 MARÇAIS (Georges), L'Art de l'Islam, pp. 27–9 and 32, pl. IV and fig. 4.

1948 BISSING (F. W. von), Äusserer Anhalt zur Datierung der Fassade des Schlosses von Mschatta. *Forschungen und Fortschritte*, XXIV, pp. 124–5.

1948–50 ALTHEIM (Franz), Literatur und Gesellschaft im ausgehenden Altertum, I, pp. 254–63 and Taf. XXIII.

1949 PIJOÁN (José), Summa Artis, XII—Arte islámico, pp. 36–40 and figs. 46–50.

1952 ALTHEIM (Franz), and Ruth STIEHL, Asien und Rom, pp. 41–56 and Abb. 12–29.

1954 ERDMANN (Kurt), Die sasanidische Krone an der Fassade von Mschatta. *Forschungen und Fortschritte*, XXVIII, pp. 242–5, with 16 figs.

1955 BETTINO (Sergio), Il castillo di Mschattà in Transgiordania nell'ambito dell'‘Arte di potenza’ tardoantica. *Anthemon : scritti . . . in onore di Carlo Anti*, pp. 321–66 and tav. XXXIII–XLIX.

— DUSSAUD (René), La Pénétration des Arabes en Syrie avant l'Islam, pp. 65–9 and figs. 15–16.

1956 STERN (Henri), Notes sur l'architecture des châteaux omeyyades. *Ars Islamica*, XI–XII, pp. 75, 82–3 and figs. 7 and 15.

1957 ERDMANN (Kurt), Ein Beitrag zur Datierung der Fassade von Mschatta. *Proc. of the Twenty-Second Congress of Orientalists . . . Istanbul . . . 1951*, II, pp. 614–19, with 13 figs.

1959 HARDING (G. Lankester), The Antiquities of Jordan, pp. 160–62 and pl. 23–4.

1960 FIELD (Henry), North Arabian Desert Archaeological Survey, p. 74 and fig. 57, below (wrongly described as Qaṣr aṭ-Ṭūba).

— GRABAR (Oleg), al-Mushatta, Baghdād and Wāsiṭ, in *The World of Islam* (*Studies in honour of P. K. Hitti*), pp. pp. 99–108 and pls. II–IV.

1962 TRÜMPELMANN (Leo), Mschatta. Ein Beitrag zur Bestimmung des Kunstkreises, zur Datierung und zum Stil der Ornamentik. Tubingen, 1962.

1964 ALTHEIM (Franz), and Ruth STIEHL, Die Araber in den alten Welt, I, Beilage 2: Mšattā und der Beginn der arabischen Kunst, pp. 592–8 and Abb. 6–9 and 12.

XXII

QAṢR AṬ-ṬŪBA[1]

QAṢR AṬ-ṬŪBA:—The outer walls—The interior—The eastern half.

QAṢR AṬ-ṬŪBA IN THE WĀDĪ GHADAF, about sixty miles south-east of ʿAmmān (see map on p. 404), was discovered by Musil in 1898, a few days before his famous discovery of Quṣayr ʿAmra.[2] It is an enormous oblong enclosure, lying roughly east and west and measuring 140·50 m. by 72·85 m.[3]—almost a double square[4] (Fig. 648). The north side is nearly intact (Plate 137 *a*) and several lengths of curtain wall exist on the west side; the two other sides are almost entirely destroyed, although their plan can be followed (Plate 137 *d*).

The enclosure was flanked by five semicircular towers on the south side, and by two on the east and west sides, in addition to which there was a round tower at each corner, the circumference of which was struck from the ideal corners. On the north side the arrangement was different on account of the two gateways C and F, flanked by two square rooms which, as Jaussen and Savignac have pointed out,[5] in no way resemble defensive works. In the curtain wall between is a ruined semicircular tower larger than any of the others (a little over 8 m. across instead of slightly over 7 m.). Each gateway opened on to a passage leading straight to a large court roughly 30 m. square. Jaussen and Savignac checked Musil's plan on the spot, in 1912, and modified it in certain respects, the main correction being the replacement of Musil's central court by the complex V, X, T, T′, V′, X′, etc., of which the foundations can still be seen.[6]

In the plan (Fig. 648) the parts shown in black are still standing in varying states of completeness; in those hatched the walls have disappeared down to the ground level, but their trace can still be followed with certainty, owing to the white lines made by the disintegrated stone showing up clearly against the dark colour of the basalt chips with which this district is covered (Plate 137 *d*).

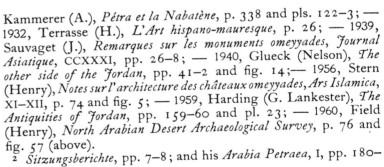

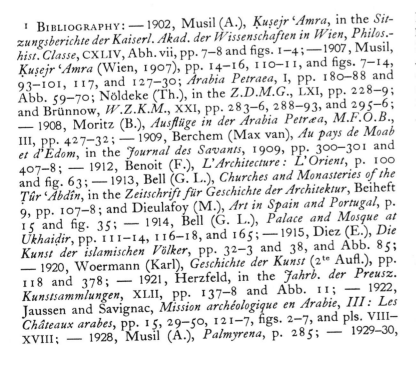

FIG. 660. QAṢR AṬ-ṬŪBA: Inner border of jamb of gateway C. (From Herzfeld, *Jahrbuch der preusz. Kunstsammlungen.*)

THE OUTER WALLS. The great gateway C, 3·54 m. in width, which leads into the western half of the enclosure, is preceded by a passage 6·42 m. in width, flanked by two nearly square rooms B and B′. In 1912, when Jaussen and Savignac visited Ṭūba, the west jamb of this doorway had already disappeared, but two finely decorated blocks still remained of the upper part of the other side (see their pl. XVII$_3$), which permitted them to calculate the width of the opening as having been 3·54 m.[7] The inner border of the door-frame is given here (Fig. 660). The door opening into B is spanned by an elaborately decorated lintel—the finest piece of ornament at Ṭūba (Plates 137 *c* and 138 *a*)[8]—above which was a relieving arch.[9]

1 BIBLIOGRAPHY: — 1902, Musil (A.), *Kuṣejr ʿAmra*, in the *Sitzungsberichte der Kaiserl. Akad. der Wissenschaften in Wien, Philos.-hist. Classe*, CXLIV, Abh. vii, pp. 7–8 and figs. 1–4; — 1907, Musil, *Kuṣejr ʿAmra* (Wien, 1907), pp. 14–16, 110–11, and figs. 7–14, 93–101, 117, and 127–30; *Arabia Petraea*, I, pp. 180–88 and Abb. 59–70; Nöldeke (Th.), in the *Z.D.M.G.*, LXI, pp. 228–9; and Brünnow, *W.Z.K.M.*, XXI, pp. 283–6, 288–93, and 295–6; — 1908, Moritz (B.), *Ausflüge in der Arabia Petræa, M.F.O.B.*, III, pp. 427–32; — 1909, Berchem (Max van), *Au pays de Moab et d'Edom*, in the *Journal des Savants*, 1909, pp. 300–301 and 407–8; — 1912, Benoit (F.), *L'Architecture: L'Orient*, p. 100 and fig. 63; — 1913, Bell (G. L.), *Churches and Monasteries of the Ṭûr ʿAbdîn*, in the *Zeitschrift für Geschichte der Architektur*, Beiheft 9, pp. 107–8; and Dieulafoy (M.), *Art in Spain and Portugal*, p. 15 and fig. 35; — 1914, Bell (G. L.), *Palace and Mosque at Ukhaiḍir*, pp. 111–14, 116–18, and 165; — 1915, Diez (E.), *Die Kunst der islamischen Völker*, pp. 32–3 and 38, and Abb. 85; — 1920, Woermann (Karl), *Geschichte der Kunst* (2te Aufl.), pp. 118 and 378; — 1921, Herzfeld, in the *Jahrb. der Preusz. Kunstsammlungen*, XLII, pp. 137–8 and Abb. 11; — 1922, Jaussen and Savignac, *Mission archéologique en Arabie, III: Les Châteaux arabes*, pp. 15, 29–50, 121–7, figs. 2–7, and pls. VIII–XVIII; — 1928, Musil (A.), *Palmyrena*, p. 285; — 1929–30, Kammerer (A.), *Pétra et la Nabatène*, p. 338 and pls. 122–3; — 1932, Terrasse (H.), *L'Art hispano-mauresque*, p. 26; — 1939, Sauvaget (J.), *Remarques sur les monuments omeyyades, Journal Asiatique*, CCXXXI, pp. 26–8; — 1940, Glueck (Nelson), *The other side of the Jordan*, pp. 41–2 and fig. 14; — 1956, Stern (Henry), *Notes sur l'architecture des châteaux omeyyades, Ars Islamica*, XI–XII, p. 74 and fig. 5; — 1959, Harding (G. Lankester), *The Antiquities of Jordan*, pp. 159–60 and pl. 23; — 1960, Field (Henry), *North Arabian Desert Archaeological Survey*, p. 76 and fig. 57 (above).

2 *Sitzungsberichte*, pp. 7–8; and his *Arabia Petraea*, I, pp. 180–88.

3 Excluding the projection of the towers.

4 We shall see that it actually consists of two square and symmetrical enclosures placed side by side.

5 *Op. cit.*, p. 29.

6 *Ibid.*

7 *Op. cit.*, pp. 31–2.

8 This lintel measures 2·20×0·45 m. and the ornamented surface 1·82×0·39 m.

9 See Jaussen and Savignac, *op. cit.*, pl. X$_1$, which shows that some of the voussoirs had already half crumbled away. They have since disappeared, as may be seen from my plate (127 *c*).

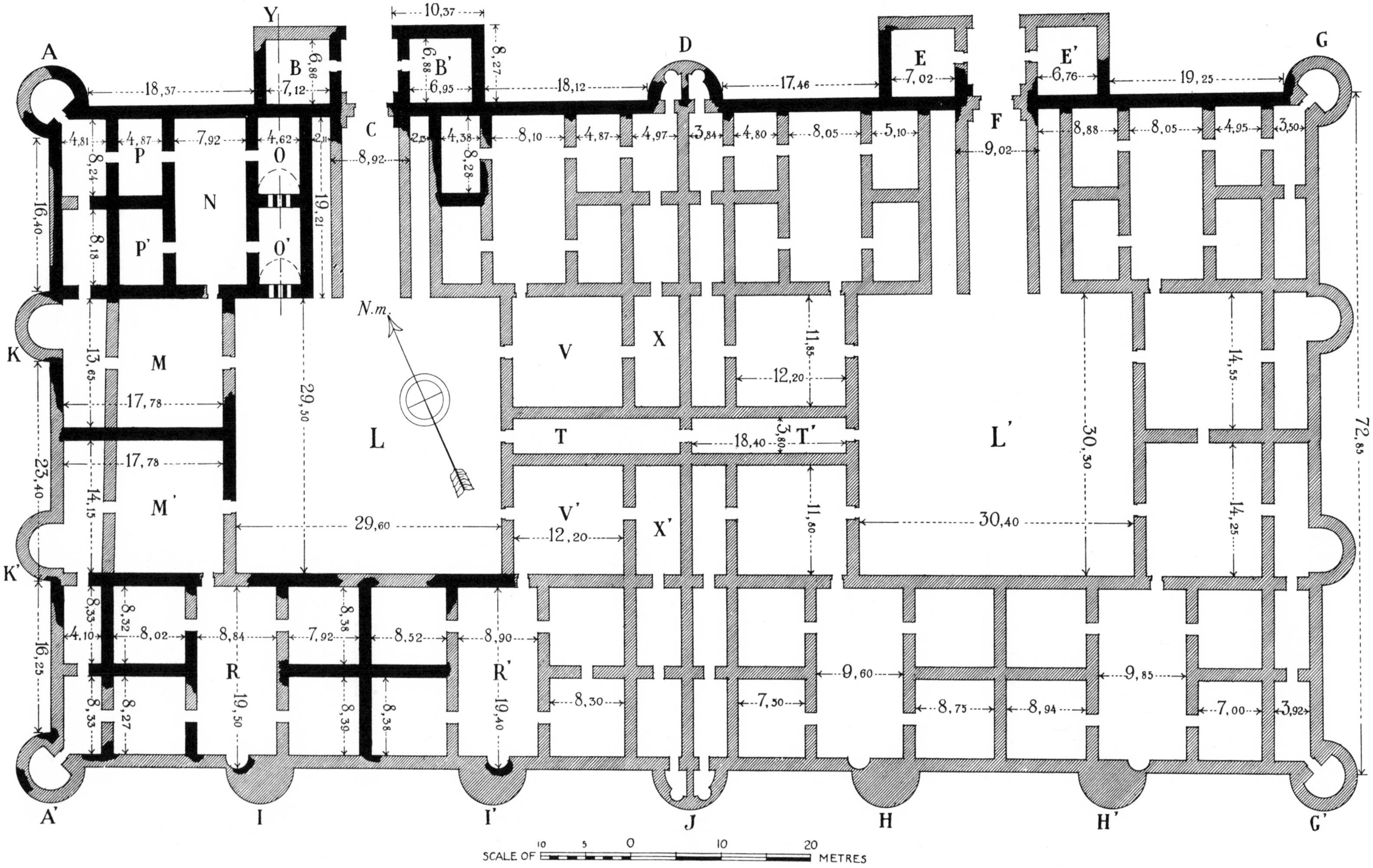

Fig. 661. Qaṣr aṭ-Ṭūba: Plan. (From Jaussen and Savignac, *op. cit.*, with slight modifications.)

Some of the stones framing this doorway have disappeared, and it is a marvel that the lintel still remains in position. Behind the lintel on each side is a deep hole, 19×26 cm., no doubt intended to receive the beam in which the door-spindle was set.[1] The room measures 7·12 m. from east to west and 6·86 from north to south; its northern wall has almost entirely disappeared. The eastern wall of this room is built of stone throughout; as to the other three walls, although their outer faces are of stone, their inner faces are only so for the first six courses, the upper part being of brick.

Room B′ is a few centimetres smaller than B. Its walls are better preserved, likewise its door-posts round which the decoration of the lintel is carried,[2] but parts of this decoration have unfortunately flaked off since Savignac's photographs were taken. The doorway is 1·04 m. wide externally and 1·18 internally. The form of the relieving arch is segmental externally and semicircular internally, the reason being that externally it springs from the top of the lintel, whereas internally it continues down, springing from the door-posts at a point level with the underside of the lintel.[3] Savignac's plate also shows that the inner face of the walls of B′, like those of B, are constructed with a lower part of six courses of cut stone and an upper part of brick, the wall next the entrance passage alone being of stone throughout. At the outer north-eastern corner the wall is 2·90 m. in height; it consists of ten courses of which the two lowest have almost entirely crumbled away; those which remain measure 30, 30, 36, 26, 28, 20, and 31 cm. in height according to my measurements. The stones have been carefully dressed and set with a thin layer of good mortar.

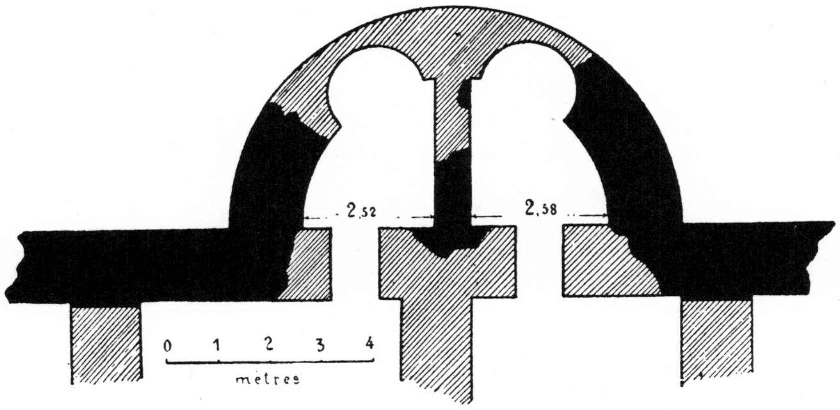

Fig. 662. Qaṣr aṭ-Ṭūba: Plan of tower D. (From Jaussen and Savignac, *op. cit.*)

The wall between B′ and D is of eight courses only and measures 2·35 m. in height above the present ground level. The semicircular tower D, placed almost exactly midway between B′ and E, is the only one of its kind (Figs. 661–2). It is very much ruined, nevertheless enough remains to show that it was divided internally by a thin wall into two quarter-circles and that at the outer corners of each was a little recess. No explanation of these little recesses has been suggested hitherto, even their existence escaped Musil. On the analogy of Mshattā I would suggest that they were latrines, although the pierced blocks, which settle the question at Mshattā, are not now to be seen here. It is quite possible, however, that they still exist under the mass of fallen débris.

The curtain wall beyond D continues of uniform height as far as the north-east corner, although the lowest courses have been almost entirely eaten away in some places.

The great gateway F, leading into the eastern half of the enclosure, is similar to C in every respect except that it is less well preserved; the works in fact appear to have been less advanced. A fragment of carving at the foot of the west jamb[4] shows that the door frame was decorated in the same style as C. Part of the north wall of E and the whole of the north wall of E′ have disappeared.

The curtain wall from E′ to the corner tower measures 19·25 m., whereas the corresponding curtain wall at the opposite end measures 18·37, a difference of 88 cm. Similarly the two lengths of curtain wall to right and left of D measure 18·12 and 17·46 m. respectively, a difference of 66 cm. Thus although a symmetrical façade has certainly been intended, it has not been laid out with great accuracy.

The north-east corner tower G, although very far gone, appears to have been similar to A, of which a fair amount remains. The latter has been struck with an internal radius of nearly 2·50 m. and the wall is 1·20 m. thick. A doorway 1·05 m. in width puts it in communication with the corner room. The tower is not placed exactly on the corner, for the wall to the right and left of the doorway measures 1·92 and 1·20 m. respectively.

The curtain walls on the western face do not appear to have been so high as those on the north for, in the best-preserved parts, there are only seven courses of masonry. The first length of curtain wall

1 The hole on the south side is now plugged with a rough block of stone.

2 Jaussen and Savignac, *op. cit.*, pl. XI.

3 *Ibid.*, pl. XII.

4 This fragment has since disappeared.

measures 16·40 m. and although the greater part of the first tower is ruined, its attachments to the wall remain; they are 7·60 m. apart, so that the tower, being semicircular, must have been struck with a radius of 3·80 m. externally and 2·40 internally if we assume the thickness of its walls, like the curtain walls, to have been 1·40 m. The next tower K′ is still more ruined, but its position can nevertheless be fixed with accuracy for the attachment of its south side to the curtain wall still exists. Allowing 7·60 m. for this tower, the curtain wall between it and K must has been 23·40 – 7·60 = 15·80 m. From it to the corner tower A′ is 16·25 m. The western façade was therefore divided by two towers into three lengths of curtain wall evidently intended to be equal (16·40, 15·80, and 16·25 m.).

Although the curtain walls of the south façade have entirely disappeared,[1] two of the towers I and I′ are still standing to a height of a metre and a half, although they have lost their outer facing. From their pitch it is easy to see that there must have been three more, that is to say five in all, dividing up the south façade into six lengths of curtain wall. The first tower I forms a great rounded mass of masonry 6·75 m. long and 3·90 deep. As this block is solid, although a metre and a half in height, it may have been intended to be so to its full height, like most of the towers of Mshattā. On its inner face, however, is a little niche of well-dressed masonry of which seven and a half courses have been preserved, forming an arc 1·84 across and 35 cm. deep (see II, 1st ed., Plate 120 *c*). Jaussen and Savignac calculate that its depth when complete must have been equal to the depth of the wall, i.e. 1·40 m. This recess must have been very like a miḥrāb, as they suggest, and the possibility of its having been one is increased by the fact that it is in the centre of one of the walls of the court R and that that wall is the one which faces Mekka. Unfortunately neither this niche nor the next one in court R′ are sufficiently well preserved to show whether there were recesses at the outer corners for nook-shafts. Both this tower and the next are placed without regard for these niches, as may be seen from the plan. From I′ onward the towers, as well as the curtain walls, have almost entirely disappeared, and the two little niches shown in H and H′ are conjectural: I would suggest that tower J corresponded to D, and I have restored it accordingly, although Jaussen and Savignac do not do so. Sufficient remains of the corner tower G′ to show that it must have been exactly like the others.

The eastern façade is ruined to the ground level, but its plan is quite clear. Like the opposite side it was divided by two semicircular towers into three lengths of curtain wall, roughly 17, 16, and 16·50 m. in length.

THE INTERIOR. If we enter by the great gateway C, we find ourselves in a broad passage, 6·25 m. in width, which runs between ruined walls to the main court L. To right and left of this passage are two narrower ones, 2·11 wide and 19·21 long, of which the purpose is not clear, for they are both closed at the north end (Plate 138 *b*-*c*). The main court is practically square, for it measures 29·50 × 29·60 m. On its west side are two doorways leading into two smaller courts M and M′, which are almost alike. The walls on the north and south side of M are almost intact, but on the other two sides they are partly destroyed. The lower part of these walls is composed of three courses of well-dressed stone, above which they are of brick exactly as at Mshattā.

There is a small door in the north-east corner of M, of which the east jamb is partly preserved; the three upper blocks, which are the best preserved, are carved with great richness.[2] This door leads into a smaller court N, out of which open four chambers, two on the east side and two on the west. The two former are each 4·62 m. wide, and 8·22 (O′) and 8·26 (O) long (Fig. 661). The walls of O are formed below of three courses of stone totalling 82 cm. in height. In the top course, the stones next the door-opening are 5 or 6 cm. higher than the rest (Plate 137 *e*). The walls of O are identical to those of O′ with the exception of that on the north side which, being part of the enclosure wall, begins with six courses of stone instead of three.

As Jaussen and Savignac point out, the courses of the inner walls and those of the north wall do not correspond, which proves that they were not constructed simultaneously. The enclosure was built first[3] and it had been the builder's intention to construct the lateral walls of this chamber with a lower part

[1] They are indicated, however, by a broad line of débris, conspicuous by its white colour against the black basalt chips which cover the plain; see Plate 137 *d*.

[2] Jaussen and Savignac, pl. XVIII$_1$, Two of these blocks have fallen since their visit. A block from this doorway (illustrated in Musil's *Kuṣejr ʿAmra*, Abb. 130; and reproduced in Diez, *op. cit.*, Abb. 85) may be seen in the Staatliche Museen, Berlin.

[3] *Op. cit.*, p. 40.

of six courses of stone like the enclosure wall, for bonding stones have been provided in the fifth course of the north wall at the points where the side walls strike it. The brickwork is constructed of bricks 25 cm. square and 7 cm. thick, separated by courses of mortar averaging 2 cm. in thickness.

These two rooms are the only ones in the whole enclosure that now possess vaults. They spring at a height of 4·15 m. from the ground level, and begin with two courses of bricks, placed flat and set forward 4 cm. Above this a series of rings are sprung in the ordinary way, each ring being slightly inclined against the end wall. In addition to this the two vaults have a slightly pointed section (Plate 138 *d*), so that they resemble those of Mshattā in every respect. The vaults are 39 cm. thick, i.e. a brick and a half. Part of the outer covering of mortar still exists.

The first ring in hall o must have been stuck against the south wall; then, as the work advanced, the bricklayer tended to incline each ring somewhat backwards instead of making them vertical, so that

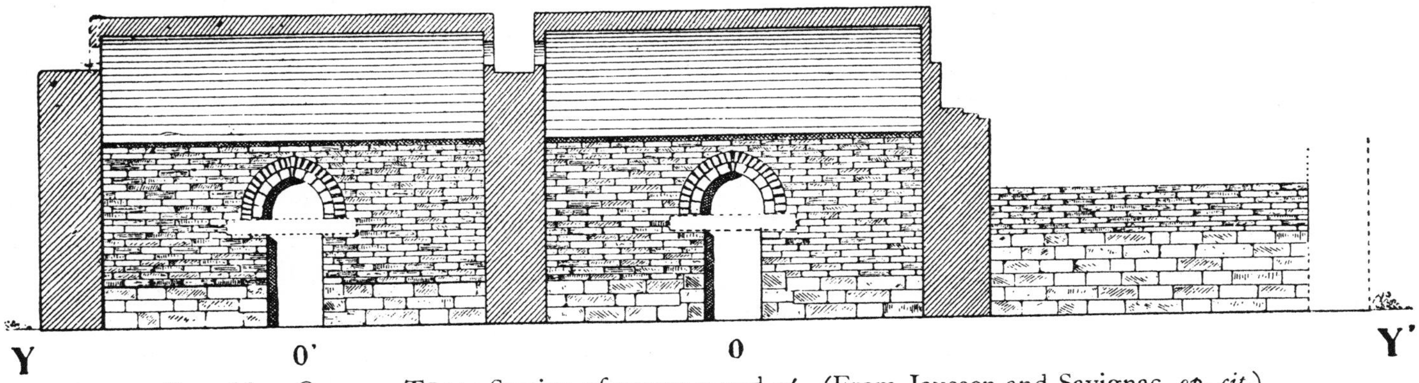

Fig. 663. Qaṣr at Ṭūba: Section of rooms o and o′. (From Jaussen and Savignac, *op. cit.*)

each brick held more readily to the face of the previous ring, centering being entirely dispensed with. When he arrived at the end of the vault he had to add part of an extra ring above to fill the gap between the top of the vault and the other end wall, as may be seen in Plate 138 *b* and *e*. This is the same as the method adopted at Mshattā.

The two rooms o and o′ are separated by a wall 1·32 m. thick, pierced by two pointed-arched windows, 0·52 m. wide and 1·10 high, which put the two rooms in communication; the base line of these windows is at the same level as the springing of the vault (Plate 138 *d*). Immediately above the course of bricks which runs above the tops of these windows is a ring of bricks forming a bull's-eye opening, the top edge of which touches the summit of the vault. The opening has a diameter of 49 cm. and the outer circle of the ring 77½ cm. The thick wall of separation stops just below the bull's-eye and is replaced by two walls, each 25 cm. thick and about 80 cm. apart (Plate 138 *e* and Fig. 663), so that the bull's-eye, unlike the two windows below it, admits light from without. Although everyone is agreed that Mshattā and Qaṣr aṭ-Ṭūba must be of practically the same date, this slight improvement in the lighting arrangements may be taken as evidence that Qaṣr aṭ-Ṭūba is of slightly later date than Mshattā. At the south end of o′ are two pointed-arched windows like the last, pierced in the thick end wall; the wall above them is reduced to 25 cm. and pierced with a bull's-eye, now almost ruined (Plate 138 *c*). The wall closing the south end of o′ has been treated somewhat like a gable, each course of bricks being shorter than the previous one, a sort of staircase being thereby formed on each side. At the northern end of o the filling is even rougher and the brickwork thinner. In this room, on the top course of the masonry just below the brickwork, are a number of graffiti,[1] written in black ink and recalling the famous one at Qaṣr Kharāna, which is dated 92 H. (710).[2]

The doorways opening from N (Plate 137 *e*) are constructed in the same way as the doorways of the rooms at Mshattā. At the top of the door-opening, here 1·21 cm. wide, was apparently a lintel which overlapped the opening considerably. These lintels, as at Mshattā, have all disappeared. Above was a stilted pointed arch, 10 cm. more in span than the opening below, composed of two rings of square bricks, the inner ring with the bricks placed face outwards and the outer ring with the bricks placed edgewise, exactly as at Mshattā. Jaussen and Savignac are inclined to believe that there were stone lintels, accompanied behind by a beam in which the spindle of the door was fixed,[3] but as every detail

1 First noticed by Jaussen and Savignac, *op. cit.*, p. 41. 2 See above, pp. 447–8. 3 *Op. cit.*, pp. 41–2.

that has been preserved is the same as at Mshattā, the missing part must be restored in the same way (see above, p. 589 and Fig. 649).

The two rooms P and P′ corresponding to O and O′ have almost exactly the same dimensions; their walls are complete to the springing of the vault, and, here and there, at the summit of the side walls, a few bricks, which have been placed so as to project 6 or 7 cm., correspond to the courses marking the springing of the vault in O and O′. Its construction does not appear to have advanced farther. The two rooms to the west of P and P′ are exactly the same in type, but their construction is still less advanced, and the two doorways are unfinished.

The rooms on the other side of the entrance passage, between it and tower D, correspond exactly to those just described and their measurements even are almost identical. There is first of all the narrow passage, closed at one end, then two chambers opening on to a court corresponding to N; beyond that another pair of rooms and then two slightly narrower rooms corresponding to those next the north-west corner. Here, however, the work is far less advanced; the first three courses of stone are the most that can have been built and this masonry has almost all crumbled away. The walls of the rooms have never reached the bonding stones left ready for them in the outer wall.

A wall starting from the centre of D runs right through to the southern side of the enclosure, and divides it into two almost equal and symmetrical parts, each being nearly square in plan. Jaussen and Savignac have marked a door in the centre of the wall, joining the corridors T and T′ and putting the two halves of the enclosure in communication. As they admit, it is impossible to say whether such a door existed, on account of the almost complete disappearance of this wall, but it is easy to accept the suggestion that there was such a door, for if there was not, the corridors T and T′, which break the perfect correspondence between the east and west sides of the two great courts, lose their *raison d'être*.

Although the space available to the east of court L is the same as that to the west, Jaussen and Savignac were of the opinion that there was a great difference in the arrangement,[1] for they did not notice the attachments of the wall shown in my Fig. 661 as continuing the west boundary wall of P and P′ right across the west side of M and M′. If we restore this wall the only difference between the two sides is caused by the fact that V, V′, X, and X′ are reduced a little by the passage T; T, X, and X′ were doubtless intended to be vaulted.

The right jamb of the doorway leading from L into M′ still exists;[2] it is of cut stone and must have been richly decorated. The doorway leading from M′ into R, although now ruined, must have had a richly decorated frame of carved stone, for one of its finely carved blocks is still lying on the ground.[3] That to the west of it was a plain doorway without a stone frame.

As there is no entrance on the south side it was inevitable that the chambers should be grouped differently; nevertheless their arrangement is regular and symmetrical. Behind the south wall of the great court are four rectangles practically square, flanked to east and west by oblong courts R and R′, on the south side of which are the two niches which I have suggested may be miḥrābs. Beyond these courts to east and west are two more rectangles, and then two narrow rooms corresponding to those in the north-west and north-east corners. Although this part of the enclosure is much ruined, enough remains to render the plan certain. The walls have fallen through the crumbling away of the three courses of masonry forming their lower part.[4] This part has never been finished, for the west walls never exceed from $2\frac{1}{2}$ to 3 m. in height and the others cannot have been more than a metre or a metre and a half. It would appear that all the rectangles on this side were unroofed except the two narrow chambers at each end, for R and R′ are obviously open courts like N, and it cannot have been intended to vault the enclosures, 8·30 m. square, which flank them, for the walls are not thick enough to provide adequate abutment for the great vaults which would be required to cover them. It is therefore probable that all the rectangles on this side, except the pair at either end, were merely enclosures (*ḥōsh*) open to the sky, with walls 3·50 to 4 m. in height, in which the prince's Bedawīn followers encamped.

THE EASTERN HALF. The eastern half of the enclosure, to which the great gateway F gives access, is in nearly all respects identical to the western half. With the exception of the north wall, which appears

1 *Op. cit.*, p. 44.

2 Now fallen; in 1912, when Jaussen and Savignac were there, it was in position; *op. cit.*, p. 44.

3 Jaussen and Savignac, *op. cit.*, pl. XVII_2.

4 The cause is exactly the same as at Qaṣr al-Ḥayr; see above, p. 530.

to have been completed to its full height, the rest has been merely marked out by one or more courses of stone. These stones have disintegrated, but their débris form white lines which give the plan quite clearly (Plate 137*d*). The great gateway is identical, and it is flanked to right and left first by a narrow corridor, then by two chambers opening on to a court, and beyond these courts are two more chambers of which the northern one is in communication with two narrower ones beyond. On the west side of the great court the arrangement corresponds to that on the east side of L; and on the south side we have the same arrangement as that found on the south side of the other enclosure. On the east side the two courts corresponding to M and M′ are also separated from the outer wall of the enclosure by two rooms nearly 4 m. in width, which no doubt were intended to be vaulted.

For the date, see below, pp. 623 ff.

XXIII

ARCHITECTURAL ORIGINS AND DATE

ARCHITECTURAL ORIGINS:—The triple-apsed hall—The *bayts*—The base moulding of the façade. The decoration of the façade.

THE DATE OF MSHATTĀ AND QAṢR AṬ-ṬŪBA:—Synopsis of discussion—Objections against the Lakhmid theory—Objections against the Ghassānid theory—Answers to objections against the Umayyad theory—Historical reasons for an Umayyad attribution—Architectural reasons for an Umayyad attribution.

QAṢR BĀYIR.

THE TRIPLE-APSED HALL. In spite of the amount of discussion that has taken place on this problem, as is indicated by the bibliography below,[1] the question of origin is still disputed. It is true that several archaeologists have employed their wide knowledge to accumulate all the available examples of this feature, but frequently without strict chronological arrangement, e.g. Rahtgens and Weigand. The latter cites an enormous number of examples with *scarcelye a date* from the beginning to the end of his memoir! As for Strzygowski, he is unable to cite any example on Persian soil, so he answers Vincent's sarcastic remarks[2] by citing Mshattā as 'iranisch aus dem III–IV. Jahrh.'[3] Even Vincent complicates the question by including Quṣayr 'Amra and Ḥammām aṣ-Ṣarakh as 'excellentes applications du tracé cruciforme et du plan nettement tréflé'.[4] If we are to treat two apses as the same as three, and include cruciform buildings as well, how can we expect to solve the problem?

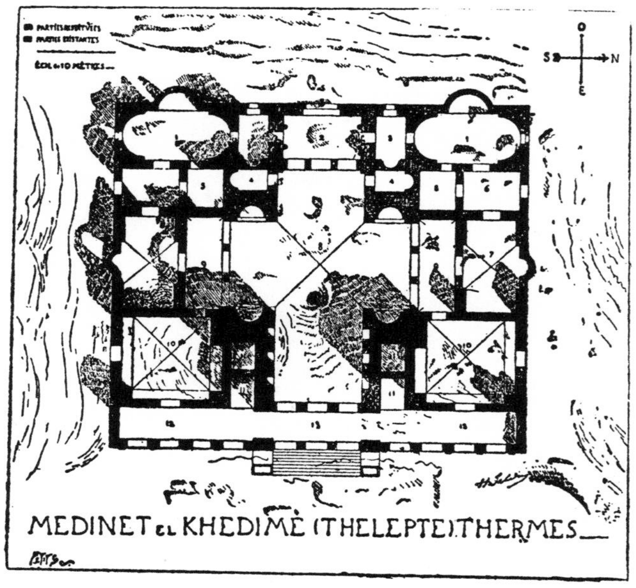

FIG. 664. THELEPTA: Roman Baths with two alleged triple-apsed rooms. (From Saladin, *loc. cit.*)

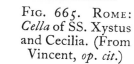

FIG. 665. ROME: *Cella* of SS. Xystus and Cecilia. (From Vincent, *op. cit.*)

Let us now endeavour to arrange the earliest examples in some sort of chronological order, leaving aside classical examples of open courts with exedrae on three of their sides (such as is found in the Villa of Hadrian at Tivoli), for they really have nothing to do with the present problem. I once thought it possible that the earliest examples of triple-apsed structures (Greek, τρίκογχος; Latin, *cella trichora*) were to be found in certain Roman baths, but the more I think about it, the more doubtful

[1] BIBLIOGRAPHY:—1902, Enlart (C.), *Manuel d'archéol. française*, I, *Architecture religieuse*, p. 147; 2me ed., I, pp. 160–61; — 1903, Strzygowski, *Kleinasien ein Neuland der Kunstgeschichte*, pp. 26–7, 111, 137, 186, 211, 219–20, and 233–4; and Strzygowski, *Ursprung und Sieg der altbyzantinischen Kunst* (*Byzantinische Denkmäler*, III), pp. xvi–xvii; — 1904, Strzygowski, *Mschatta*, in the *Jahrb. der Kgl. Preuszischen Kunstsammlungen*, XXV, pp. 232–7; — 1907, Dussaud (R.), *Les Arabes en Syrie*, pp. 41–3; — 1909, Blanchet, *Les Origines antiques du plan tréflé*, *Bulletin monumental*, LXXIII, pp. 450–60; and Sybel (L. von), *Christliche Antike*, II, pp. 307–8; — 1910, Diehl (C.), *Manuel d'Art byzantin*, pp. 45, 52, 58, 115, and 124; and Leclerq's article *Cella* in Cabrol's *Dict. d'archéologie chrétienne*, II₂, cols. 2894–2905; — 1912, Bell (G. L.), in Ramsay and Bell, *Thousand and One Churches*, pp. 347–8; and Strzygowski, in the *Byzantinische Zeitschrift*, XXI, p. 345; — 1913, Freshfield (E. H.), *Cellæ Trichoræ*, I, pp. v–xiii and II, pp. 31–3; and Rahtgens (H.), *Die Kirche S. Maria in Kapitol zu Köln*, pp. 127–82; — 1914, Rivoira, *Architettura musulmana*, pp. 282–3; English transl., pp. 277–8; Vincent and Abel, *Bethléem*, pp. 21–31; Weigand (E.), *Das Theodosioskloster* [*Dayr Dūsī*], *Byzantinische Zeitschrift*, XXIII, pp. 176–89; and Wulff (O.), *Altchristliche und byzantinische Kunst*, pp. 27–9; — 1915, Strzygowski, *Der Ursprung des trikonchen Kirchenbaues*, *Zeitschr. für christliche Kunst* XXVIII, pp. 181–5 and 189–90; — 1918, Diehl, Le Tourneau and Saladin, *Les Monuments chrétiens de Salonique*, pp. 208–10; — 1918, Strzygowski, *Die Baukunst der Armenier und Europa*, pp. 495–503; — 1920, Vincent (H.), *Le Plan tréflé dans l'architecture byzantine*, *Revue Archéologique*, 5me sér., t. XI, pp. 82–111; — 1921, Rivoira (G. T.), *Architettura romana*, pp. 173–5; English transl., pp. 135–6; — 1925, Dalton (O. M.), *East Christian Art*, pp. 87 and 108–10; Monneret de Villard (U.), *Les Couvents près de Sohâg*, I, pp. 47–60; — 1940, Lapeyre (P. G.), in *Atti del IVo Congresso Internazionale di Archeologia Cristiana*, I, pp. 183–96 (for the triconchos in Tunisia); — 1963, Lavin (S.), *The House of the Lord*, *Art Bulletin*, XLIV, pp. 1–27.

[2] 'Ceux qui se donneront désormais la tâche de soutenir que le plan tréflé de la basilique de Bethléem remonte à Constantin et dérive d'Anatolie, de Mésopotamie ou d'Égypte seront donc très bienvenus en produisant quelques nouveaux exemples précis et de date incontestablement antérieure à 326'; *Bethléem*, p. 31.

[3] *Der Ursprung des trikonchen Kirchenbaues*, *loc. cit.*, p. 190.

[4] *Revue Archéol.*, 5me sér., t. XI, p. 100. And is it not ridiculous to include also the crypt of the Church of the Samaritan at Nāblus? (*ibid.*, fig. 18).

it appears to be. For example, I cited the Palace of Diocletian at Spalato, A.D. 303–5, under reserve, for no trace of the part containing the trefoil shown on Adam's plan[1] exists to-day. Even[2] the basement beneath the main floor has disappeared at this point.[3] I believe that Adam may have restored it from insufficient indications, and I am supported in this by the fact that Clérisseau, who accompanied Adam and who also made a plan,[4] *only shows the central apse*.

Another example, Thelepta, which I cited in 1932, is equally suspect. I visited Thelepta about twenty-five years ago and was able to recognize most of the elements shown on Saladin's plan (Fig. 664), including the two oblong rooms on the west side, each with an apse at each end, but *not* the third

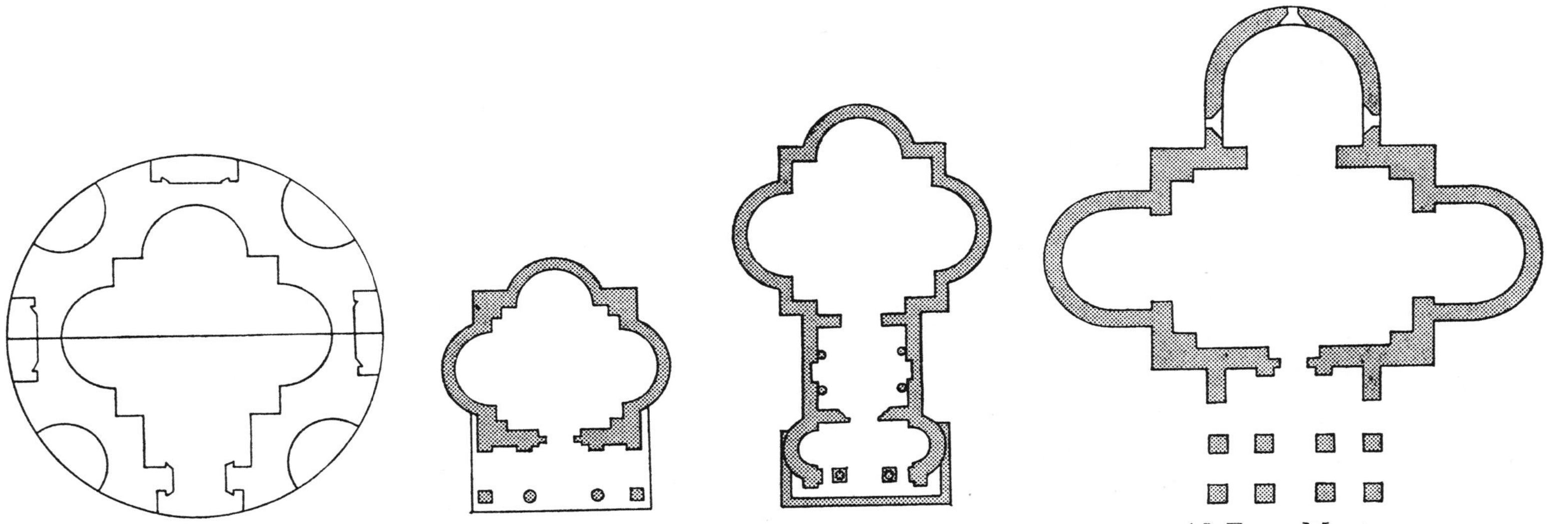

(*a*) (From Mongeri, *op. cit.*) (*b*) (From Montano, *Scielta.*) (*c*) From Montano, *Raccolta.*) (*d*) From Montano, *Raccolta.*)

FIG. 666. Plans of Roman three-lobed buildings.

apse shown projecting beyond the alignment of the west wall. The west wall had disappeared at the two places in question and there was nothing but bare ground. As Saladin does not speak of making excavations,[5] I can only conclude that the third apse is pure speculation. Another but less specific example occurs in the *calidarium* of the Roman baths at Lambessa.[6] Next in chronological order come the three little ruined structures in the Cemetery of Callixtus on the Via Appia Antica near Rome, viz.:

(1) SS. Xystus and Cecilia (Fig. 665).
(2) St. Soteris, believed by Wilpert to be the tomb of St. Zephyrinus.[7]
(3) A structure connected with St. Sinforosa, at the ninth milestone on the Via Tiburtina.

These little edifices, until recent times, have been regarded as of the third century, but it now appears that, in the first, the two side apses may have been inserted at a later date (Fig. 665).[8] And in addition to this Leclercq has expressed the opinion that St. Soteris is less ancient than SS. Xystus and Cecilia.[9] There remains St. Sinforosa.

This is not much, but to these may presumably be added the buildings shown in the drawings of Bramantino[10] and Montano,[11] to which Rivoira has drawn attention[12] (Fig. 666, *a–d*).

All these Roman examples were probably mausoleums, and the three early Christian examples were doubtless memorial chapels.

We have an example of a *cella trichora* of large size, but preceded by a narthex, in the Church of

1 *Ruins of the Palace of the Emperor Diocletian at Spalatro*, pl. V.
2 See Hébrard and Zeiller, *Le Palais de Dioclétien*, pl. III.
3 *Ibid.*, p. 129 and plan on p. 125.
4 Published by Joseph Lavallée, *Voyage pittoresque de l'Istrie et de la Dalmatie, rédigé d'après l'itinéraire de L. F. Cassas*, pl. 54 bis.
5 Saladin, *Rapport sur la mission faite en Tunisie*, in the *Archives des Missions Scientifiques*, 3me sér., t. XIII, pp. 116–19 and figs. 206–10.
6 Gsell, *Les Monuments antiques de l'Algérie*, I, pp. 218–19 and fig. 69. These baths have been attributed to Septimius Severus on account of an inscription (*C.I.L.*, VIII, No. 2706 and p. 1739), but there were at least three baths at Lambessa, and it is not certain to which one this inscription refers.
7 *Die Papstgräber und die Cäciliengruft in der Katakombe des hl. Kallistus*, pp. 91–104.
8 Marucchi, *Nuovo Bulletino di archeologia cristiana*, XVI (1910), pp. 220–21; quoted by Vincent and Abel, *Bethléem*, p. 26.
9 In Cabrol, *Dict. d'archéol. chrét.*, II_2, article *Cella*, col. 2903.
10 Published by Mongeri, *Le rovine di Roma*, tav. 21.
11 *Scielta d. varii tempietti antichi*, tav. 10, 12, 17, 27, 50, and 52, and *Raccolta de tempii*, tav. 8 and 33.
12 *Moslem Architecture*, p. 277.

St. John the Baptist at Jerusalem (Fig. 667), which was built by the Empress Eudoxia between A.D. 450 and 460.[1] This, according to Vincent, is probably the earliest example of its kind throughout the East; it is certainly the oldest in Syria.

But Vincent[2] has suggested, on the strength of a passage in Codinus,[3] according to which it was covered by a dome and had several apses, that the Church of St. John the Baptist, built by Theodosius the Great at Constantinople, was a cruciform building, and that when the Empress Eudoxia constructed the Church of St. John the Baptist at Jerusalem one can easily imagine that 'elle l'ait ordonné sur le même plan que celui dont s'enorgueillissait la cité impériale depuis un demi-siècle'. Several of the examples of *cellae trichorae* given here have a fourth arm well developed, whereas the Church of St. John, as the plan (Fig. 667) shows, has absolutely no trace of this feature; in other words it has less connexion with the cruciform plan than many examples. Moreover, seeing how scarce examples of the 'triconchos' are at Constantinople, and how late,[4] it is scarcely reasonable to suggest that Syria got this feature from that source. But what do we know of the church of Theodosius? Vincent himself has to admit that the details given by Codinus 'pourraient n'être applicables qu'à la restauration de Justinien' mentioned by Procopius.[5] Of course they must, for Codinus wrote *c.* A.D. 1100: so this church cannot be cited as evidence for a triple-apsed church at Constantinople in the fourth century.

A number of examples are also to be found in North Africa, e.g. Tebessa (Fig. 668),[6] Sīdī Muḥammad al-Gebīouī, Dugga, and Aguemmun Ubekkar,[7] but it is very doubtful if any go back before the middle of the fifth century.

But when and where was the trefoil plan first employed for a throne room? Apparently at Boṣrā in the Ḥaurān, where a perfect example occurs in the Episcopal Palace (Fig. 669)[8] which Butler believes to be contemporary with the Cathedral (A.D. 512–13).[9] I give Butler's section here (Fig. 670) because the central part appears to have been covered with a pyramidal roof, resting on a clerestory with three windows in each face, as was the *triconchos* in the Dayr al-Abyaḍ at Sohāg. This is a very important fact which must be borne in mind in all attempted restorations of the main hall of Mshattā. I do not feel at all convinced that the latter was covered by a dome as Brünnow[10] and Schulz[11] restore it; I think it is at least equally probable that there was a low, square tower rising above the roof, pierced with a row of windows in each face, and covered by a timber roof, perhaps pyramidal, but possibly flat like that over the three naves, for very little rain falls in this region.

The throne room of the Episcopal Palace seems to have been influenced by the throne room of an earlier palace of the Roman period[12] at the same place, the plan of which (Fig. 671), although it does not come within the strictest definition of a *triconchos*, is nevertheless remarkably near to it. Butler expresses the opinion that, in its style and construction, there is nothing to prevent us from assigning it to the beginning (A.D. 106) of the Roman period here.[13] Thanks to the kindness of Mr. Mougdad, the Inspector of Monuments, I was able to visit the remains of the Roman Governor's Palace, although occupied by families, on 23rd April 1963.

I found that the western apse was still intact with its three western doors, except that it had lost its semi-dome. The four corner piers of the square were also intact and the big windows on the north side, flanked externally by niches. The big rectangular bay opposite, although roofless, was easily recognizable with its three windows looking on to the street, likewise the square room on its east side, with its two windows and two doors, except that they are partly obstructed by the pilaster of a modern transverse arcade which carries the ceiling. The eastern apse, instead of its original semi-dome, is now

[1] Vincent in the *Revue Archéol.*, 5me sér., t. XI, pp. 82–4; Vincent and Abel, *Jérusalem*, II, pp. 642–68, figs. 263–9 and pls. LIII–LV.

[2] *Le Plan tréflé*, *loc. cit.*, pp. 104–5 and 109.

[3] *De edificiis Constantinopolis*, in Migne, *Patrologia*, *Series Græca*, CLVII, col. 592.

[4] The earliest example of which there is any record is the Church of the Theotokos of Blachernes, as altered by Justin II in A.M. 6064 = A.D. 564; see Theophanes, Bonn ed., p. 376. It may be asked: why is not the earlier τρίκογχος at Constantinople mentioned here? I omit to mention it because it is clear, from the fact that a procession took place in it (Theophanes, I, p. 159), that it was an open space with exedrae on three of its sides, and consequently quite different from the feature we are discussing here.

[5] I, 8; Bonn ed., III, p. 198.

[6] See Seriziat, *Pubn. of the Arch. Socy. of Constantine*, 2me sér., t. II (1868); Ballu, *Le Monastère byzantin de Tébessa*, pp. 27–8 and pl. II; Gsell, *op. cit.*, II, pp. 271–5, and fig. 134; and Freshfield, *Cellæ Trichoræ*, I, pp. 104–6 and pl. 55 (inscription).

[7] Gsell, *op. cit.*, II, pp. 157–9 and fig. 113.

[8] *Ancient Architecture in Syria, Sect. A: Southern Syria*, pp. 286–8 and Illus. 248 and 250–53.

[9] *Ibid.*, p. 286.

[10] *Op. cit.*, II, p. 126 and figs. 716–17.

[11] *Loc. cit.*, p. 218 and Taf. V–VI.

[12] Butler, *op. cit.*, pp. 255–60, pls. XI–XII and Illus. 227–9.

[13] *Ibid.*, p. 260. See above, pp. 515–16.

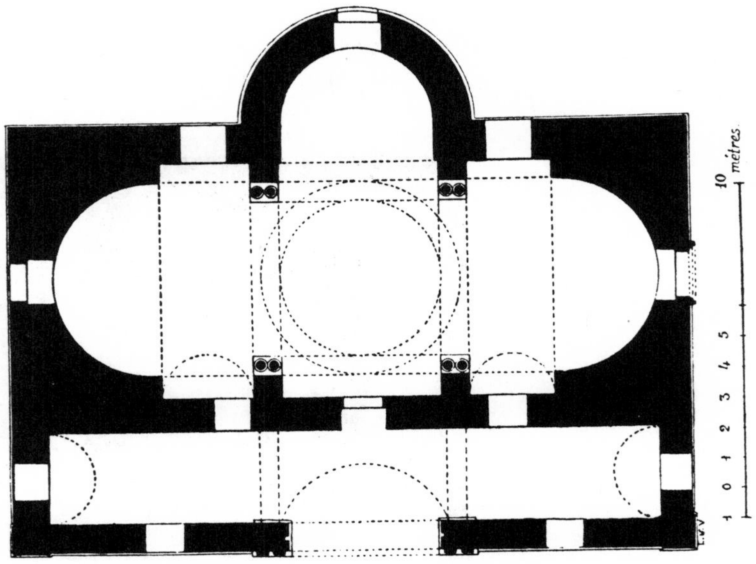

Fig. 667. Jerusalem: Church of St. John the Baptist, plan. (From Vincent and Abel, *Jerusalem*.)

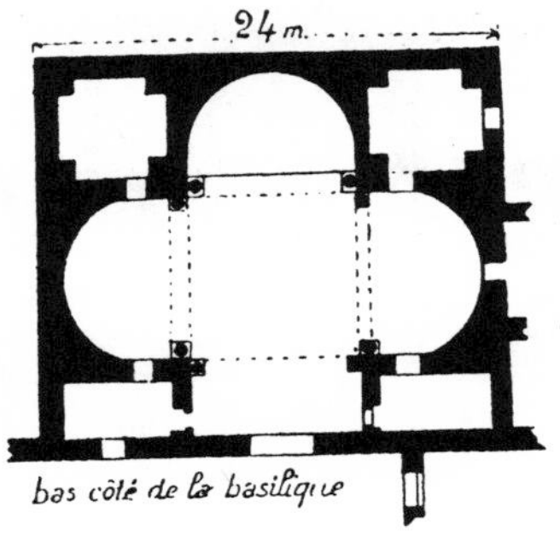

Fig. 668. Tebessa: Triple-apsed building attached to basilica. (From Ballu, *op. cit.*)

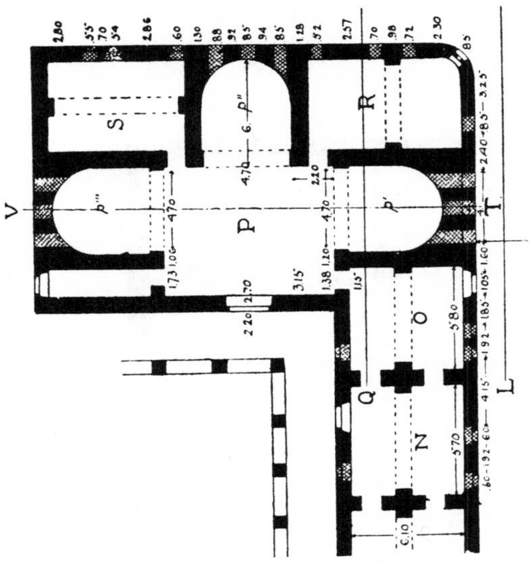

Fig. 669 Boṣrā: Episcopal Palace, plan of *triconchos*. (From Butler, *op. cit.*)

Fig. 670. Boṣrā: Episcopal Palace, section through V–T. (From Butler, *op. cit.*)

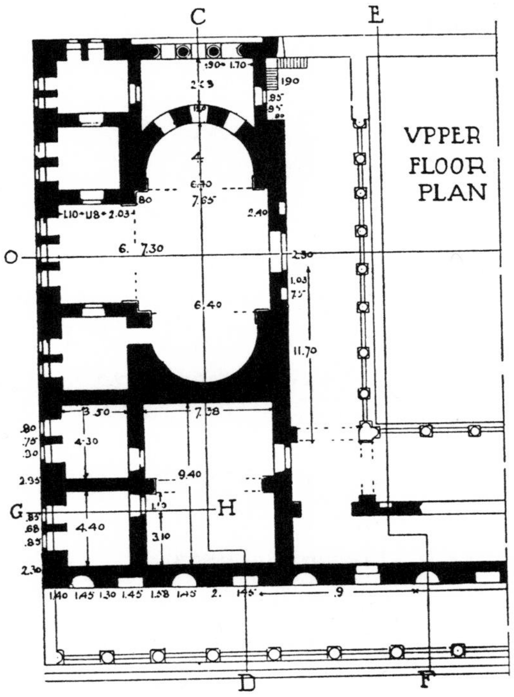

Fig. 671. Boṣrā: Roman Palace. Scale (From Butler, *op. cit.*)

covered by a flat ceiling resting on two modern transverse arches. If we descend to the street we can see the two windows of the south bay and the two of the south-east room, but all to the right of the latter has gone.

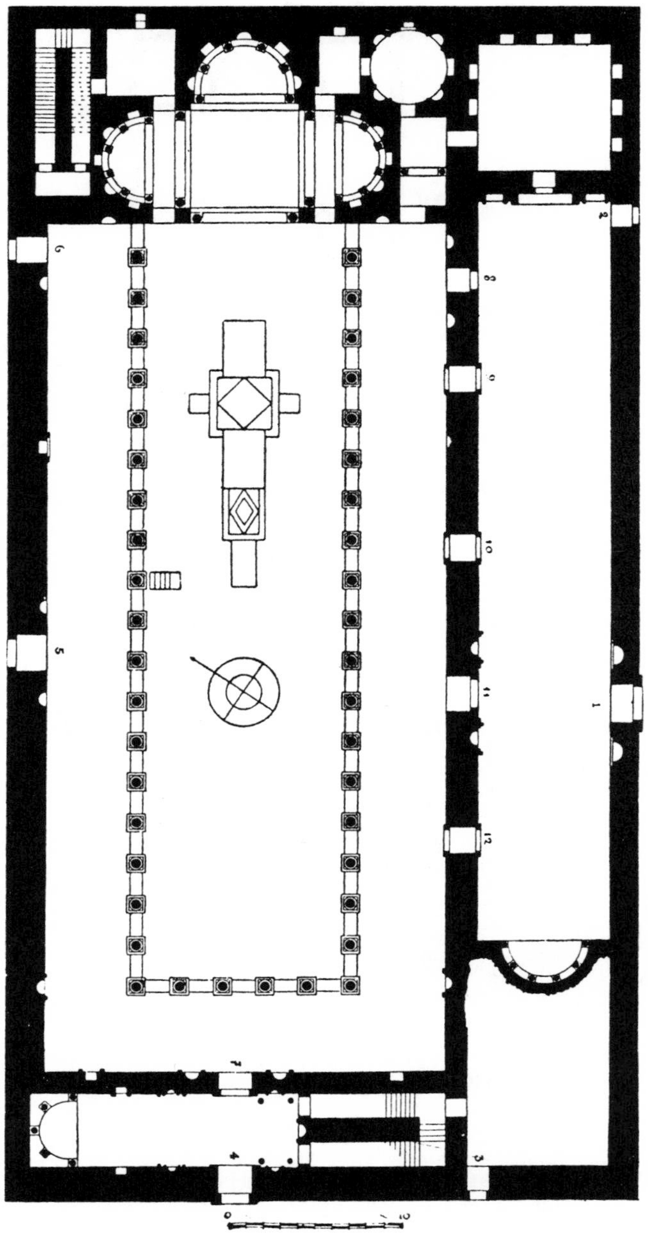

Fig. 672. Sohāg: Dayr al-Abyaḍ. (From Monneret, *op. cit.*)

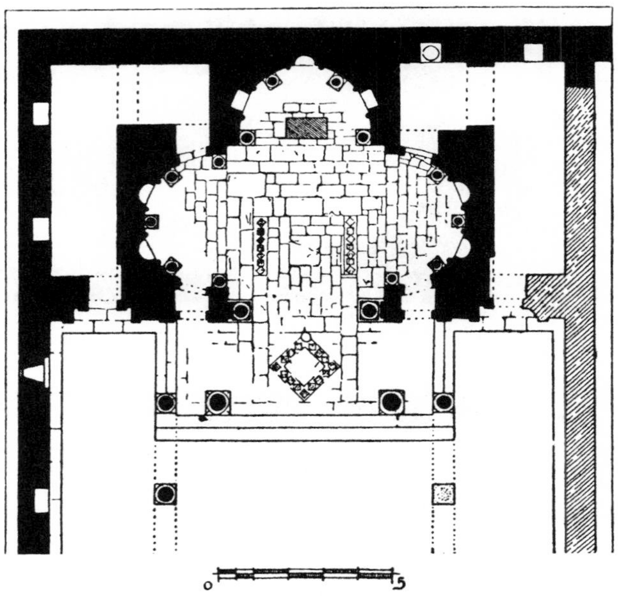

Fig. 673. Sohāg: Dayr al-Aḥmar, east end. (From Monneret, *op. cit.*)

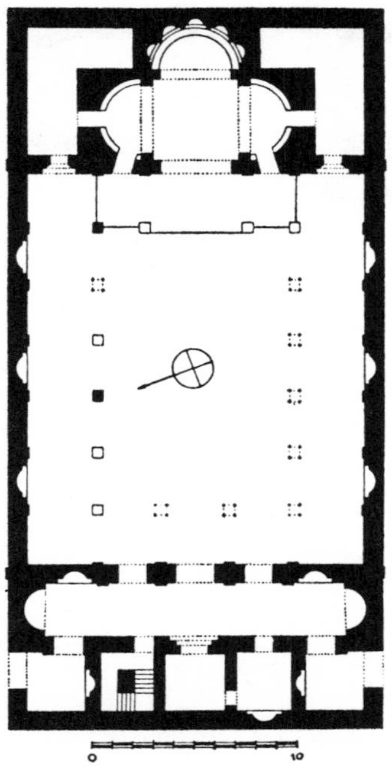

Fig. 674. Dendera: Basilica. (From Monneret, *op. cit.*)

Another Syrian building, the Palace at Qaṣr Ibn Wardān, built A.D. 564, has what may have been a *triconchos* on the first floor.[1] It may, of course, have had four apses, but the northern arm is completely ruined on the first floor and the corresponding part on the lower floor is buried under about 4 m. of débris. But in any case it is closely related to the Episcopal Palace at Boṣrā.

Examples of the use of a *triconchos* for a hall of audience do not appear to exist outside Syria until much later, the earliest examples known to me being:

(1) *Ravenna*: Palace of the Exarchate,[2] seventh–eighth century.
(2) *Aachen*: Aula Regis of Charlemagne.[3]
(3) *Rome*: Triclinium of Pope Leo III,[4] A.D. 795–800.[5]

[1] Butler, *op. cit.*, *Sect. B: Northern Syria*, pp. 34–40, pls. IV–VII and Illus. 31–7.

[2] Recently excavated; see *Kunstchronik*, XXI, neue Folge, col. 476.

[3] Thordeman, *Der Karölingerpalast in Aachen als Trikonchos*, in *Studien zur Kunst des Ostens* (Vienna), 1923, pp. 241–2.

[4] Lauer, *Le Palais de Latran*, pp. 105 and 121, and figs. 40–42, from manuscript drawings by Ugonio, and the plan in Rasponi, *De Basilica et Patriarchio Laterianensi*, p. 326. Pope Leo IV received Charlemagne here in A.D. 800.

[5] It must have been built after his election in 795, but before Charlemagne was crowned Emperor in 800, for his portrait in the mosaics is labelled *Rex*; Lavin in the *Art Bulletin*, XLIV, p. 13.

(4) *Constantinople*: τρίκογχος, built in the palace by the Emperor Theophilus in A.D. 839. It had three apses, north, east, and south, and on the west side were three doors.[1]

From the above it would appear that the custom of using the triple-apsed plan for a throne room arose in Syria.

We must now discuss the *combination* of a trefoil apse with a basilical hall. Which are the earliest examples of this combination? The answer, fortunately, is easy to give; the earliest existing examples are:

(1) *Nola*: Basilica of Paulinus, *c.* A.D. 401–3.[2]
(2) *Sohāg*: The Dayr al-Abyaḍ (Fig. 672), *c.* A.D. 440.[3]
(3) *Sohāg*: The Dayr al-Aḥmar (Fig. 673), *c.* A.D. 440.[3]
(4) *Dendera*: Basilica (Fig. 674), end of fifth century.[4]
(5) *Bethlehem*: Church of the Nativity, alteration of Justinian, i.e. before A.D. 565.[5]
(6) *aṭ-Ṭaiyibe* (in the Jordan Valley); Ruins of a church restored by the Crusaders. The masonry and style of the oldest part, according to Schneider, show that it was built 'not before the middle of the sixth century'.[6]

Thus, out of the five earliest examples of this feature, no less than three occur in Egypt. I therefore conclude:

(1) that the trefoil plan was first used at Rome for mausoleums;
(2) that the adoption of this feature for a throne room or audience hall first took place in Syria; and
(3) that the further development seen at Mshattā, in which the triple-apsed throne room is preceded by a basilical hall, was due to Egyptian influence.

THE MOULDINGS. The mouldings of Mshattā once stood in a class by themselves, but this is no longer the case thanks to an interesting set of profiles of mouldings, collected by Guyer in Urfa, Mayyāfāriqīn, Amida (Diyārbakr), and Jazīrat Ibn 'Umar (Fig. 675), which bear a striking family likeness those of Mshattā.[7] It is therefore practically certain that the latter were carved by masons from North-west Mesopotamia.

1 See the continuation of Theophanes, Bonn ed., III, p. 139 ff.; Symeon Magister, in the same volume, p. 640; Georgius Monachus, *ibid.*, p. 806; and Constantine Porphyrogennetos; Bonn ed., p. 297; all translated by Richter, *Quellen zur byzantinischen Kunstgeschichte*, pp. 342–6 and 348; also Leo Grammaticus, p. 225; Labarte, *Le Palais impérial de Constantinople*, pp. 148–9; Ebersolt, *Le Grand Palais de Constantinople*, pp. 110–26; and Paspates, *Τὰ Βυζαντινὰ Ἀνάκτορα*, Metcalfe's transl., pp. 204 ff.

2 As reconstructed from the description of Paulinus, by Holtzinger, *Die Basilika des Paulinus zu Nola*, in the *Zeitschrift für bildende Kunst*, XX, pp. 135–8 and fig. 1. The relative passages are: 'Intra apsidem trichorum videbatur altare in quo sacratae apostolorum et martyrum reliquiae reconditae erant, . . .'; and '. . . deindae cum duabus dextra laevaque conchulis intra spatiosum sui ambitum absis sinuata laxabatur'; *Prolegomena*, Cap. XLII, in Migne, *Patrologia, Series Latina*, LXI, cols. 98 and 99. Also '. . . reliquiis apostolorum et martyrum intra apsidem trichora sub altaria sacratis'; Migne, *ibid.*, col. 336; and Hartel's ed. (*Berlin Kirchenväter-Commission*, Bd. 29), p. 286; and '. . . tamen cum duabus dextra lævaque conchulis intra spatiosum sui ambitum apsis sinuata laxetur'; *Epistolae*, No. XXXII, in Migne, *ibid.*, col. 337, and Hartel's ed., p. 288.

3 For the date see Monneret, *Les Couvents près de Sohâg*, pp. 15–33.

4 Somers Clarke (*Christian Antiquities in the Nile Valley*, p. 140) compares the carved detail to that of the two monasteries at Sohāg, and Monneret (*op. cit.*, pp. 47–8) places it at the end of the fifth century.

5 Three different views have been held regarding this church: (1) that the whole structure is due to Constantine; (2) that the whole structure is due to Justinian; and (3) that it is a Constantinian building which Justinian has modified. The latter view is the only one now tenable, for Vincent and Abel (*Bethléem*, Chaps. II–IV) have conclusively shown that the transept, the three apses, and the narthex are due to Justinian. Wulzinger, in a review of the first edition of this work (*Orientalistische Literatur-Zeitung*, XXXVII, col. 623), maintains the first point of view and cites Wiegand's article in the *Z.D.P.V.*, XLVI (1923), p. 193 ff., as a decisive demonstration of it. However, the matter has been finally settled by Harvey's excavations in 1934, in which he not only laid bare a large extent of mosaic in the nave, but took up the pavement of the north-east apse and found the lower courses of a wall of the same thickness as the side walls and on the same alignment running almost right across the apse. It then turned at right angles to join the remains of an octagonal structure, centred on the cave, which formed the original east end of the church and which was probably covered by an octagonal cone of wood; see E. T. Richmond, *Basilica of the Nativity. Discovery of the Remains of an Earlier Church*, *Quarterly of the Department of Antiquities in Palestine*, V, pp. 75–81 and pls. XXXV–XLVIII; Richmond, *The Church of the Nativity. The Plan of the Constantinian Church*, *ibid.*, VI, pp. 63–6 and fig. 1; Vincent, *La Basilique de la Nativité à Bethléem d'après les fouilles récentes*, *Comptes rendus de l'Acad. des Inscriptions*, 1935, pp. 350–61; and his *Bethléem, la Sanctuaire de la Nativité d'après les fouilles récentes*, *Revue Biblique*, 1936, pp. 544–74, pls. I-XI and figs. 1–10, and 1937, pp. 93–121, pls. XII–XXI and figs. 11–20; and W. Harvey and J. H. Harvey, *Recent Discoveries in the Church of the Nativity, Bethlehem*, *Archaeologia*, LXXXVII, pp. 7–17 and pls. V–XV.

6 *Die Kirche von aṭ-Ṭaijibe*, *Oriens Christianus*, 3te serie, Bd. VI, pp. 15–22.

7 See Herzfeld, in the *Jahrb. der Preusz. Kunstsammlungen*, XLII, p. 140.

But there is another striking feature about these mouldings, viz. the manner in which those of the façade are bent at right angles at each end, and those of the triple-arched entrance turn at right angles so as to encircle all the openings, after which they turn up again at right angles at each end to form a rectangular frame (Fig. 639).

This peculiarity is a characteristic of the pre-Muhammadan architecture of Northern Syria in the sixth century, and striking examples of it are to be seen at Qal'at Sim'ān (Fig. 676, facing), at Bāqirḥā,[1] at Khirbet Tēzīn, with an inscription in Greek giving a date equivalent to A. D. 585,[2] at Kafr Lāb,[3] at Burj Ḥēdār,[4] etc.

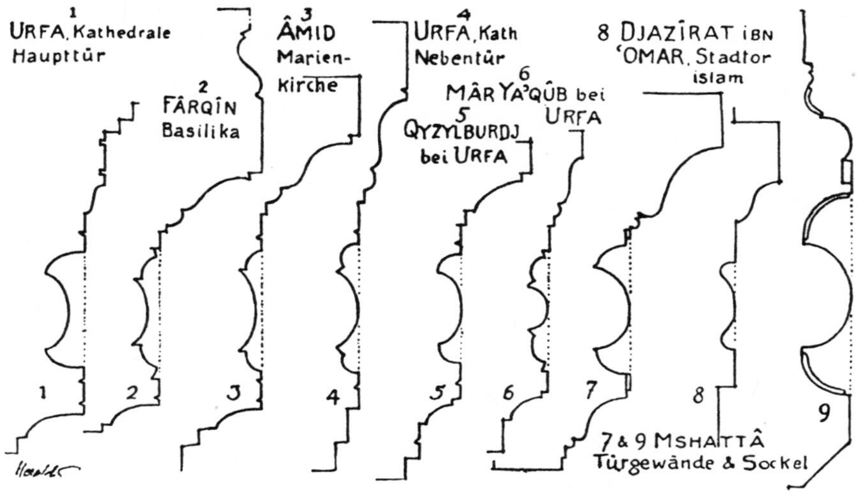

FIG. 675. Profiles of mouldings from North-west Mesopotamia. (From Herzfeld, *loc. cit.*)

THE DECORATION OF THE FAÇADE. The twenty upright triangles, and the two half-triangles flanking the entrance, may readily be divided into four groups, clearly distinguished by differences in style and composition, as Strzygowski[5] and Herzfeld[6] have pointed out. The inverted triangles, in so far as they have been executed, fall into the same grouping.

These four groups are as follows:

A–C (= 3 triangles). This group is distinguished by the following features: (1) The division of the field into two parts by a horizontal band, tangential to the lower edge of the rosette. (2) The living forms are limited to birds only, except for the human-headed feline at the apex of A. (3) In A and C the lower field is filled by four tangential and nine intersecting circles respectively, which are knotted together at their points of contact.

D–L (= 7 triangles and 2 half-triangles). In these triangles two animals (some mythical) are confronted, and in every case (except in J and K) they are placed on either side of a central chalice.

M–T (= 8 triangles). These triangles are dominated by vine scrolls and there are neither birds nor animals. The vine scrolls, however, are quite different from the naturalistic ones of A–L.

U–V (= 2 triangles). An extraordinary mixture of motifs: pine-cones, winged palmettes, etc.

One can therefore readily admit that four groups of craftsmen worked at this façade. From what countries did they come? Two elements at once present themselves as a basis for argument: (1) the circles connected by loops, and (2) the treatment of the vine.

The former feature, however, turns out to be so widely spread before Islam that it does not help us to answer the question. For example, it is found on Sasanian textiles,[7] on Byzantine textiles,[8] closure slabs,[9] and mosaic,[10] and in Coptic architecture[11] and textiles.[12] It is employed in the wall decoration of the Monastery of Bawīṭ in Upper Egypt (Fig. 682, facing p. 621); this is perhaps the most elaborate pre-Muslim example. This seems to me to be significant, more especially as the intersecting circles employed in triangle C are closely related in spirit to the ornament on certain pieces of carved woodwork, found in the cemetery of 'Ain aṣ-Ṣīra to the east of Fusṭāṭ and now preserved in the Museum of Islamic Art (Fig. 685, facing p. 621). But I only know of one solitary example in Syria, the Qaṣr al-Abyaḍ, which makes me doubt Herzfeld's attribution of triangles A–C to Syrian craftsmen.

THE VINE ORNAMENT. But when we come to examine the treatment of the vine, we find two remark-

[1] Butler (H. C.), *Architecture and Other Arts*, illus. on pp. 211–12.

[2] Prentice, *Greek Inscriptions*, Inscr. No. 54.

[3] Butler, *Ancient Architecture in Syria, Sect. B: Northern Syria*, illus. 309.

[4] *Ibid.*, illus. 316.

[5] *Loc. cit.*, pp. 307 ff.

[6] *Der Islam*, I, pp. 135 ff. Brünnow is almost, but not quite, so explicit; *op. cit.*, II, pp. 142–5.

[7] O. von Falke, *Orientalische Seidenweberei*, Abb. 96, 99, 100, and 107.

[8] *Ibid.*, Abb. 87, 88.

[9] At Ravenna: two in San Vitale, A. D. 536–47, and one in the Museum, see Colasanti, *Arte bizantina in Italia*, tav. 66; in the Cathedral and in San Apollinare Nuovo, *ibid.*, tav. 68; at Aquileia, in the Cathedral, *ibid.*, tav. 78; etc.

[10] In St. George at Salonika; see Diehl, Le Tourneau, and Saladin, *Les Monuments chrétiens de Salonique*, fig. 3.

[11] At Bawīt in Chapel XVIII; see Clédat, *La Monastère et la nécropole de Baouît*, pls. LXVI–LXX.

[12] O. von Falke, *op. cit.*, Abb. 25, 68, etc.

Fig. 676. Q̣al‘at Sim‘ān: Church of St. Simeon, north end. (From Butler, *op. cit.*)

Fig. 677. Coptic carved bone in the Egyptian Museum, Cairo

Fig. 678. Front and back of Coptic carved ivory in the Fouquet Collection. (From Strzygowski, *loc. cit.*)

Fig. 679. Coptic carved ivory in the Louvre. (From Strzygowski, *loc. cit.*)

Fig. 680. Coptic carved ivory in the Martino Collection (Cairo)

Fig. 681. Old Cairo. Door from the church of Sitt Burbāra

Department of Antiquities

Fig. 682. Bawīt: Wall decoration in monastery, now in the Museum of Antiquities, Cairo

Museum of Arab Art

Fig. 684. Cairo: Carved wooden panel from the cemetery of ʿAin as-Sīra

Fig. 683. Carved ivory in the Benaki Collection

Museum of Muslim Art

Fig. 685. Cairo: Carved wooden panel from the cemetery of ʿAin as-Sīra

able features, so rare in fact that their significance cannot be doubted: (1) the placing of one or three little grapes on many of the five-pointed vine leaves at the point of junction with the stalk. (2) The torus moulding on the socle and door-posts, and also on the inner arch of the basilical hall, is decorated with a pair of undulating vine stems which continually cross each other so as to form pointed ovals (Plate 116 *c*) the crossing points in the first and last being always marked by a little rosette. This peculiarity also occurs at Qaṣr aṭ-Ṭūba, on the frame of the door between M and N.[1]

As regards the former peculiarity, Strzygowski has pointed out that it is a characteristic of certain Coptic ivory carvings, of which he gives several examples, one from the Egyptian Museum (Fig. 677, facing p. 620), one from the Fouquet Collection, once in Cairo but now dispersed (Fig. 678, facing p. 620), and one from a piece in the Louvre (Fig. 679, facing p. 620).[2] On the piece in the Egyptian Museum a bird plucks at the fruit exactly as on the façade of Mshattā and the stalks are held together by a ring surmounted by a three-lobed leaf; both these features may be seen on the Benaki piece. I have found a similar piece in the collection of M. Fortuné Martino of Cairo, which he has kindly allowed me to reproduce here (Fig. 680, facing p. 620), in which a bird plucks at the fruit, although the five-pointed vine leaves are lacking. The finest example of all is the superb piece in the Benaki Collection (Fig. 683 facing).

As regards the rosettes at the crossing of two undulating stems, a parallel can now be produced thanks to the fortunate discovery of the walled-up door of the church of Sitt Burbāra at Old Cairo by Patricolo in 1918 (Fig. 681, facing p. 620). Here we see the upper panels at the back of the door. In the three vertical ones the two undulating vine stalks with three-lobed leaves are decorated at their points of crossing with six- and seven-lobed rosettes, exactly as at Mshattā. This door probably dates from the sixth century, so we may say that a Coptic decorative scheme was still full of vitality over a century later when it was used at Mshattā.[3]

The fact that *both* these peculiarities are found before Islam in Coptic work, and in Coptic work only, leaves little room for doubt that the vine decoration on the torus moulding of the socle, and door-posts, and on the inner arch of the basilical hall, as well as the vine-work and birds in triangles A–L, has been executed by Coptic craftsmen, conscripted by an all-powerful ruler, just as we have seen that they had already been conscripted for Damascus, Jerusalem, and Madīna.

Stern has recently suggested that these little plaques belong to the Umayyad period.[4] He admits that they have all been found in Egypt, but begs the question by adding 'on Moslem sites'.[5] This preposterous statement is without any foundation whatever.

Let us begin with (i) the piece carved on both sides in the Egyptian Museum. Strzygowski, who made the catalogue for the Service des Antiquités, says 'Achat zwischen 6–15. April, 1897'.[6] (ii) The piece from the Fouquet Collection. Fouquet was for many years a resident in Egypt and formed his collection there. (iii) The same applies to the piece in the Martino Collection. (iv) The piece in the Louvre. Stern says that it was bought by Benedite in Egypt at the end of the nineteenth century.[7] (v) The superb piece in the Benaki Museum. I was with Benaki in Alexandria in 1925 when he bought it from a dealer for £220.

As regards Stern's expression 'Moslem sites', the only Muslim site in Egypt that has been excavated is Fusṭāṭ, and the first four examples cited above were all known long before the excavation of Fusṭāṭ was begun in 1912.

And additional argument is provided by the door of Sitt Burbāra just mentioned (almost ignored by Stern) which is a basic document in our discussion, for its Coptic origin and pre-Muslim date cannot be contested.

1 Illustrated by Musil, *Ḳuṣejr 'Amra*, fig. 130; this block is now in the Staatliche Museen, Berlin.

2 *Mschatta*, *loc. cit.*, pp. 303–5.

3 See Patricolo and Monneret de Villard, *The Church of Sitt Burbâra in Old Cairo*, pp. 33–8, 45–52, figs. 20–21, 27–8, and 34–5. Monneret believes it to date from the fourth century; but, on iconographic grounds, e.g. the cruciform nimbus of Christ in the panel on the front, it seems to me that the sixth century is more probable. Unfortunately the group of Christ in the midst of the twelve apostles is so damaged that it is almost impossible to pick out the usual iconographic indications of date (e.g. bearded or unbearded apostles, the key in the hand of St. Peter, the number of apostles carrying rolls of the law, etc.).

4 *Quelques œuvres sculptées en bois, os et ivoire de style omeyyade*, *Ars Orientalis*, I, pp. 119–31; and *The Ivories on the ambo of the Cathedral of Aix-la-Chapelle*, *The Connoisseur*, vol. 153, pp. 166–71.

5 *Ibid.*, p. 166.

6 *Koptische Kunst*, p. 193 and Taf. XVI.

7 *The Connoisseur*, vol. 153, p. 171.

But the vine leaves of Sitt Burbāra are three-lobed only, whereas on the arch of the triconchos at Mshattā there are five-pointed vine leaves as well, with three grapes superimposed. If we regard this as a later development, then we must place our ivory carvings later than Sitt Burbāra, but not Umayyad (660–750) as Stern suggests, for not a single fragment of such ornament has been found at Minya, or Qaṣr al-Ḥayr al-Ghārbī, or Mafjar.[1] All this shows that this kind of vine-ornament was Coptic, and that it was only transported outside Egypt by the conscription of labour in late Umayyad times.

And here is a carved wooden panel (Fig. 684, facing p. 621) recently found (Feb. 1932) in the Muslim cemetery of ʻAin as-Sīra and now in the Museum of Islamic Art. It exhibits several features peculiar to Mshattā: (1) the six-lobed rosettes; (2) these rosettes, like the circles in triangle C, are joined by little loops; (3) the six leaves in the lower rosette are joined together as in rosettes D and I (Fig. 658); and (4) most remarkable of all, the curious motif like a pine-cone flanked by antennae, which occurs in rosette E–F and also in the rosettes of the façade of the basilical hall (Fig. 658), and for which no parallel has been found hitherto, occurs on our panel in the centre of the upper rosette.

I believe, therefore, that triangles A–C and D–L were executed, not as Herzfeld believes by Syrians and Copts respectively, but by two different groups, both of which were composed of Copts. Yet even here there is penetration of Persian influence, for in the midst of the vine tendrils are mythical animals taken from Sasanian art, just as the Sasanian tulip-like motif occurs in the mosaics of the Dome of the Rock (Plates XVIII *a* and XX *a*) in the midst of Hellenistic motifs. And, in addition to this, the wings of the birds are treated in the Sasanian fashion. We are witnessing that fusion from which Muslim art was born.

As regards triangles M–T and U–V, the occurrence of the winged palmette in several of them shows Persian influence, but whether from Persia and ʻIrāq, or from ʻIrāq only as Herzfeld suggests, I do not feel able to decide.

[1] *Der Islam*, I, pp. 137–9. However, he admits ʻIch bin mir der Schwierigkeit des Beweises bewußtʼ.

THE DATE OF MSHATTĀ AND QAṢR AṬ-ṬŪBA

I PROPOSE TO TREAT THIS QUESTION as one problem, for these two buildings resemble each other in so many respects that they must be of practically the same date;[1] whatever conclusions we arrive at as to the date of one must be equally valid for the date of the other.

The points of resemblance are as follows:

(1) Stone employed for the exterior walls, and brick for the interior walls on a finely dressed stone foundation grid three or four courses high.
(2) Slightly tapering form of stone-cutting.
(3) Bonding stones in enclosure wall for attachment of the brick walls of the interior.
(4) Size and texture of bricks.
(5) On the walls of the rooms in both buildings is a curious decoration; the joints between the bricks are marked by passing the finger over the mortar whilst still wet.
(6) Interior arranged in *bayts*.
(7) Brick vaults, with offset, *tas de charge*, and rings of bricks set Mesopotamian fashion.
(8) Pointed-arched section of vault.
(9) Bull's-eye windows in vaulted rooms.
(10) Doorways of interior, construction of (compare Plates 117 *d* and 137 *e*).
(11) Latrines in towers (e.g. central north tower at Qaṣr aṭ-Ṭūba).
(12) Vine stalks forming ovals with rosettes at their crossing point.
(13) Occurrence of winged motif on lintel of Qaṣr aṭ-Ṭūba; also tulip-like motif.
(14) Unfinished state of both.

SYNOPSIS OF DISCUSSION. But Mshattā, as van Berchem has pointed out, is a monument that 'has made more ink flow than any other in Syria',[2] so I cannot approach the controversial question of its date without giving a synopsis of the opinions of the numerous archaeologists who have already discussed this problem.

Tristram, the discoverer of Mshattā, left the question of the date to Fergusson, who discussed this problem in an Appendix to Tristram's work.[3] From the architectural point of view he points out that 'the full-bodied convex capitals . . . as contradistinguished from the hollow bell-shaped capitals of 'the Roman Corinthian order, are just such inventions which mark an epoch in the art, which admits 'of no question', by which, of course, he means that of Justinian. On the other hand, he points out that there is an equally certain limit, beyond which it cannot be brought down, viz. the Arab conquest. He then expresses the opinion (accepted by Tristram)[4] that it was built by Khusrau Parvēz in A. D. 614 during his Palestine campaign, when he wintered in Damascus. He points out that similar long, vaulted halls are found at Hatra, Ctesiphon, and Ṭāq-i-Bustān, and that the Byzantine features may be explained by the fact that Chosroes spent his youth at Hierapolis as the guest of the Emperor Maurice, and that he may thus have become imbued with the glories of the classical architecture of Asia Minor. Moreover, we are told that during his conquests he carried away many thousands of Greek and Syrian captives, whom he employed on his works. If Chosroes were the builder, the sudden abandonment of the work could be accounted for by the advance of Heraclius. Finally, he says that a Persian architect employing Byzantine workmen might be expected to produce just such a work as this.

Fergusson returned to the problem a year later in the second edition of his *History of Architecture*.[5] He points out that the 'capitals of the pillars are of that full-curved shape which are first found in the works of Justinian'; he suggests that the northern complex was built first and that Chosroes added the vast enclosure when he possessed all Asia from the Indus to the Nile, the previous modest scale not

1 This resemblance has already been emphasized by Brünnow (*Die Provincia Arabia*, II, p. 171), Musil (*Arabia Petraea*, I, pp. 201–2, and his *Kuṣejr 'Amra*, p. 32), van Berchem (*Journal des Savants*, 1909, pp. 300–301 and 402–8), Gertrude Bell (*Churches and Monasteries of the Ṭûr 'Abdîn*, p. 108), Herzfeld (in *Der Islam*, I, p. 128, and the *Jahrb. der Preusz. Kunstsammlungen*, XLII, p. 135), Jaussen and Savignac (*Les Châteaux arabes*, pp. 34, 121–2, and 126–7), and Diez (*Kunst der islamischen Völker*, pp. 32–3).

2 *Loc. cit.*, p. 402.

3 Tristram, *Land of Moab*, pp. 367–70.

4 *Ibid.*, pp. 208–15.

5 I, pp. 387–92; 3rd ed., I, pp. 401–2.

sufficing. He compares the ornament to that on the spandrels of the arches of Sancta Sophia at Constantinople. As for its unfinished state, he says that the workmen were probably called off in 627.

Rawlinson (1876) followed Fergusson in attributing Mshattā to Chosroes II (Parvēz), and placing it between 614 and 627.[1]

Merrill (1881) contested this view. He pointed out that there is no evidence that Chosroes himself ever went so far south as Damascus, and that his general Shahr Barāz was constantly occupied with his campaigns, and asks: Even if the latter built a palace, why should he choose a place in the desert beyond any other settlement? He expressed doubts as to its Persian origin and pointed out that many of the elements which form its decoration recall those found in Roman and Christian work of the second to fifth centuries. Finally, he suggested that Mshattā may have been a monastery and church built by a Byzantine emperor.[2]

Conder (1886) expressed doubts as to the possibility of Chosroes having built it, considering 'how short and how troubled was his rule over Western Asia'; and adds that it is not impossible that it may be Umayyad.[3] Dieulafoy (1887), however, accepted Fergusson's historical reasoning and placed it between Chosroes' invasion of Asia Minor in 611 and the first campaign of Heraclius in 623, expressing the opinion that the archaeological evidence did not oppose this conclusion.[4]

Layard (1887) merely quotes Fergusson's opinion in a footnote.[5] Gray Hill (1890) does not discuss the date, but he was the first to point out that the alleged Pahlavi inscriptions were merely *wasm* or tribal marks of the Bedawīn.[6] Phené Spiers (1890) accepted Fergusson's view without discussion.[7] Van Berchem (1891) was the second to doubt the Persian attribution, saying, 'l'origine persane ne me paraît pas encore prouvée'.[8] Merrill in 1891 again expressed doubts as to Chosroes ever having been in Palestine, or his general Shahr Barāz having had anything to do with Mshattā.[9] Riegl (1891) accepted Fergusson's dating.[10] Bliss (1895) did not attempt the problem of the date.[11]

Brünnow (1895) says that after Merrill's thorough demonstration one will scarcely take a Sasanian or Byzantine Emperor for the builder of Mshattā. This leaves the Ghassānids as the only possible alternative, a possibility thought of but rejected by Tristram (*op. cit.*, p. 213). He admits that it is nevertheless scarcely explicable how a prince dependent on Byzantium could have succeeded in bringing Byzantine architects to erect a palace for him in this region, which must have appeared comfortless desert to a Byzantine or Sasanian, although a Ghassānid would have regarded it as splendid grazing land. He says that, although this theory cannot be demonstrated with certainty, the following facts are in favour of it: (1) the chevron decoration on a large water-jug from the Jōlān, the very home of the Ghassānids, and (2) the resemblance of the lay-out of Mshattā to the Qaṣr al-Abyaḍ in the Ruḥba (square plan and round towers), as well as the animals and bunches of grapes.[12]

Gayet (1895) accepts the Sasanian theory.[13] Van Berchem, returning to this problem in 1896, points out that Chosroes can have had no leisure for building in a country which he passed through as a destroyer; nevertheless he admits certain incontestable Persian elements and suggests that they are the work of the Ghassānids without venturing to decide in which century.[14]

With Vailhé (1896) the Umayyad theory makes its first definite appearance. He points out that the basilical hall must be the audience hall of a palace, and attributes the building to 'Abd-al Malik.[15] Peters (1898) suggests 'that it might belong to the period when the Egyptian Sultans ruled Syria, and the road eastward of the Jordan, from Kerak to Damascus, was frequented and well fortified'.[16]

Von Oppenheim (1899) merely repeats Fergusson's opinions and mentions Brünnow's views.[17] Dussaud (1901) merely cites it in connexion with the ornament of the Qaṣr al-Abyaḍ.[18] Gautier (1901), whilst waiving any claim to competence, thinks it perhaps possible to accept the Ghassānid theory,

[1] *The Seventh Great Oriental Monarchy*, p. 594.
[2] *East of the Jordan*, pp. 256–63.
[3] *Syrian Stone-Lore*, pp. 354–5.
[4] *L'Art antique de la Perse*, V, p. 94.
[5] *Early Adventures in Persia, Susiana, and Babylonia*, p. 115, n. He had seen Mshattā in 1840.
[6] *P.E.F., Q.St.*, 1890, p. 173; and *With the Beduins*, pp. 58–9.
[7] *Sassanian Architecture*, in the *J.R.I.B.A.*, VII, pp. 58–9; reprinted his *Architecture: East and West*, pp. 83–4.
[8] *Notes d'archéologie arabe*, in the *Journal Asiatique*, 8me sér., t. XVII, p. 428, n. 1.
[9] *Visits to M'Shita*, in the *P.E.F., Q.St.*, 1891, p. 76.
[10] *Altorientalische Teppiche*, p. 134.
[11] *Narrative of a Mission to Moab*, *P.E.F., Q.St.*, 1895, pp. 230 ff.
[12] *Reisebericht*, in the *Mitth. und Nachr. der D. P. V.*, I, pp. 87–8.
[13] *L'Art persan*, p. 109.
[14] *Corpus Inscriptionum Arabicarum, I: Égypte*, pp. 266–7.
[15] *Dans les montagnes bleues*, in *Échos de Notre-Dame de France*, [Jerusalem], 1896, pp. 224–6.
[16] *Nippur*, II, p. 357.
[17] *Vom Mittelmeer zum Persischen Golf*, I, pp. 104 and 105.
[18] Dussaud and Macler, *Voyage archéologique au Ṣafâ*, p. 44.

and concludes: 'Whether one adopts it or not, Meschetta probably dates from the sixth or beginning of the seventh century.'[1] Nies (1901) suggests that it was built by one of the Umayyad or 'Abbāsid Khalifs, but as his guide called it a *khān*, he accepts it as a *khān* built for the pilgrims to Mekka.[2]

Musil (1902) says that these castles (Mshattā, Qaṣr aṭ-Ṭūba, etc.), lie in the midst of grazing lands regularly sought by the Bedawīn at certain times of the year. Ṭūba, for example, is the central point of the winter camping grounds of the Benī Ṣakhr and Mshattā is their summer camping place. He points out that the line of Roman and Byzantine frontier fortresses, running from Damascus to the Red Sea, lies as it were between the cultivated land and the desert, to the west of Mshattā and a long way to the west of Qaṣr aṭ-Ṭūba. He also emphasizes the fact that Mshattā and Qaṣr aṭ-Ṭūba are not, properly speaking, fortified, and he finally comes to the conclusion that they were built by princes of the Banū Ghassān who were in possession of a high culture and in constant relationship with Constantinople and Persia, but who could not do without the pure air of the desert.[3]

Borrmann (1904) is rather out of date in suggesting that the deciphering of the Pahlavi inscriptions will probably solve the problem.[4] Saladin (1904) vaguely suggests the Ghassānids.[5]

Brünnow, writing before the publication of the work of Schulz and Strzygowski, emphasizes the fact that Qaṣr aṭ-Ṭūba belongs to exactly the same style of architecture as Mshattā, both as regards the bricks used, the masonry, and the pointed tunnel-vaults. He also points out that it cannot have been Persians, but only true Arabs, who considered the desert their special home to which they always longed to return from civilized lands, who can have built their residences here, a conclusion to which Musil had already come. He expresses the conviction that Mshattā and Qaṣr aṭ-Ṭūba were built by Arabs with the help of architects and workmen from Byzantium, and says that as the latter were no longer to be had in Islamic times, a pre-Islamic and Ghassānid origin is thereby proved. He then quotes some verses from an Umayyad poet, Kuthayyir 'Azza (d. 723), in which mention is made of 'the two Qasṭals' and Muwaqqar (twelve miles east-north-east of Mshattā). He identifies one with Qasṭal, six kilometres west of Mshattā, and concludes that Mshattā, the outer walls and masonry of which closely resemble Qasṭal, must be the other. If correct, this would mean that Mshattā was already in existence before 723 and, as he claims that the expression 'Qasṭal' can scarcely have been employed for a contemporary building, he concludes that Mshattā, in the opinion of the poet, was pre-Islamic.

He then calls attention to the unfinished state of the building, e.g. the façade, the complex next the entrance, etc., and points out that this circumstance can only fit one Ghassānid for the following reasons. Great buildings, such as Mshattā and Qaṣr aṭ-Ṭūba, would only have been possible for a half-nomadic Phylarch when he was supported by Byzantium, as was the case with al-Ḥārith ibn Jabala (*c.* 529–69) and Abū Karib al-Mundhir (569–82). The former, an important prince, was the first to obtain the title of Patrician and Phylarch from the Emperor Justinian;[6] he stood in high favour and visited Constantinople in 563 and had important funds at his disposal. There is nothing, however, in his reign to explain the unfinished Mshattā. But his son and successor al-Mundhir (known to the Greeks as Ἀλαμούνδαρος) does fit the case. At the beginning of his reign he was in dispute with the Byzantine court and was in revolt for three years. He made peace, however, in 578 and two years later visited Constantinople, where he was received with great honour by the Emperor Tiberius, given magnificent gifts and presented with a crown, an honour never before granted to any Arab.

Brünnow believes that he may have expressed a desire to build a palace, and have brought back architects and workmen with him, and that he took Qasṭal as a model, for the enclosure walls of Mshattā are very similar. As for the nearly finished basilical hall and annexe, Brünnow believes that it may be an actual imitation of some building at Constantinople. At the beginning of 582 al-Mundhir fell into disgrace again, and Tiberius' successor banished him to Sicily. This would explain the unfinished state of Mshattā.[7]

Strzygowski (1904) says that the earliest investigators were led to attribute Mshattā to the time between Justinian and 'Umar, on account of erroneous ideas regarding the date at which capitals with a convex profile first appeared. He maintains that this form appeared much earlier, and that Mshattā

1 *Autour de la Mer Morte*, pp. 116–17.
2 *P.E.F.*, *Q.St.*, 1901, pp. 367–8.
3 *Sitzungsberichte*, CXLIV, pp. 46–7.
4 *Die Baukunst des Altertums und des Islam im Mittelalter*, p. 315.
5 *Les Palais de Machitta*, *Bull. archéologique du Comité*, 1904, p. 409, n. 1.
6 Procopius, *Wars*, I, xvii, 4–7.
7 *Die Provincia Arabia*, II, pp. 171–6.

was built between the fourth and sixth centuries, and probably before Justinian (527–65).[1] He considers that the enclosure wall fits the time of Diocletian and the dated Roman frontier forts of the fourth century. As for the 'triconchos', he says that it was known at least as early as Constantine.[2]

He comes to the conclusion that Mshattā must have been built by a man who was equally familiar with Mesopotamian brickwork and Syrian masonry, and who was in the service of a prince of the desert. He considers that this prince was probably a Ghassānid Phylarch of the fourth to sixth century, partly on chronological grounds and partly because their buildings, cited by Ḥamza al-Iṣfahānī, mostly lie in the region between Damascus and the Belqā.[3]

Rhodokanakis (1905), in his review of Strzygowski's work, gives a synopsis of the latter's arguments for a Ghassānid origin, which view he appears to accept.[4] He concludes with a number of examples of Persian influence in literature, art, court etiquette, etc., in support of Strzygowski's views on the predominant part played by Persian influence in the evolution of Mshattā.[5] Ameseder (1905), in his review of Strzygowski's work, gives a synopsis of the latter's views, with which he appears to agree.[6]

Van Berchem (1905), in reviewing Strzygowski's conclusions, says that having long since proposed to attribute Mshattā to the Ghassānids on historical grounds, it is interesting to observe that Strzygowski, solely on artistic grounds, is also led to place it in this period, but without venturing to name these princes. Finally, he expresses the conviction that Strzygowski's ideas as to the Mesopotamian inspiration of Mshattā will impose themselves more and more on science.[7]

Brünnow (1905), writing after the appearance of Strzygowski's *Mschatta*,[8] says that he and Strzygowski are in agreement in so far as both attribute Mshattā to a Ghassānid, but not on the question of date. He points out that one cannot rely on Ḥamza al-Iṣfahānī (*c.* A. D. 961), for his list of Ghassānid princes is demonstrably a compilation from several parallel lists. Also that the best list in his catalogue, that which he gives as running from A. D. 34 to 209, really goes from the fifth century to the Muslim conquest![9] The other Arabic sources are not much better, for they put the beginnings of the dynasty even farther back.

Our knowledge of the Ghassānids (based on Greek and Syriac sources) only begins with the end of the fifth century, and Nöldeke considers it very doubtful if there was a Ghassānid Phylarch before the time of Justinian.[10]

Brünnow therefore places Mshattā in the sixth century, saying that if an Arab prince had built it, he can only have been a Ghassānid and that none before al-Ḥārith and al-Mundhir had the means to do so. Moreover, a Ghassānid origin is only possible if the builder were in official relations with Byzantium, and could reckon on official support and the assistance of workmen from Byzantine controlled territory.

He disputes Strzygowski's statement that the masonry of Mshattā resembles that of the frontier forts built by Diocletian, and says that Qaṣr Bshayr, which an inscription states was built by him, is totally different throughout. He adds that the gradual encroachment of the East about the time of Severus corresponds to a gradual degeneration in masonry, and that it is not until the sixth century that masonry in this part of the world once more attains a level equal to that of Mshattā (e.g. the Cathedral of Boṣrā, built A. D. 512–13).[11]

Clermont-Ganneau (1906) suggests the possibility of attributing Mshattā to an Arab prince; not a Ghassānid, however, but a Lakhmid. He maintains that the decoration of the façade must be read from right to left, and interpreted as a kind of apotheosis of the vine; the vine is first of all represented in flower (?), then it develops through all the successive stages of maturity until it is invaded by all the beasts of creation which feed on its grapes. He suggests that the figure in the Phrygian bonnet (apex

[1] *Jahrb. der Kgl. Preusz. Kunstsammlungen*, XXV, p. 363. And this is the evidence he brings forward: (i) a detached capital in the Serai at Urfa, *undated* (p. 256); (ii) the capitals of Ṭāq-i-Bustān always attributed to Chosroes II (590–628), but which he roundly asserts must be fourth century (pp. 353–7); and (iii) the capitals found during the excavation of the Church of St. Gregory the Illuminator at Etshmiadzin, built A. D. 640–61 (p. 361). Could any argument be less convincing?

[2] He is referring to the Church of the Nativity at Bethlehem, but Harvey's excavations have proved that the two lateral apses are additions of Justinian; see above, p. 619, n. 5.

[3] *Loc. cit.*, p. 367.

[4] *W.Z.K.M.*, XIX, pp. 289–307.

[5] *Ibid.*, pp. 307–13.

[6] *Byzantinische Zeitschrift*, XIV, pp. 626–30.

[7] *Journal des Savants*, 1905, pp. 472–7.

[8] *Die Provincia Arabia*, II, p. 310.

[9] The first name in Ḥamza's list is Jafna, who was set up by the Emperor Anastasius (A. D. 491–518).

[10] *Die Ghassânischen Fürsten aus dem Hause Gafna's*, p. 12.

[11] *Op. cit.*, II, p. 311.

of first triangle, Plate 120) may have a Dionysiac interpretation. He doubts the interpretation put by Brünnow on the reference to the two qasṭals (*qasṭalain*), and doubts the possibility of its having any reference to Qasṭal. He thinks that it refers rather to a reservoir of water: 'one must not forget that the word *qasṭal*, borrowed from the Latin *castellum*, originally had, and long retained among the Arabs, the meaning of "châteaux d'eau", reservoir, a technical meaning which it frequently had in Latin'.[1]

Becker (1906), after resuming Strzygowski's ideas and conclusions, strongly emphasizes the view that, so far as our historical knowledge of the period (fourth to sixth century) chosen by Strzygowski goes, it is impossible to believe that a Ghassānid can have built Mshattā. He considers the monuments of this region enumerated by Musil to be neither Sasanian nor 'Abbāsid (what, he asks, would an 'Abbāsid be doing in Syria?) but Umayyad. If not, where must we seek their pleasure residences which admittedly lay in the desert? Moreover, if one places a building just before Islam, as Brünnow does, then one can also place it roughly a century later, for the Umayyads did not create a new art but took over piecemeal that which was there before them. Moreover, if we assume these buildings to be Umayyad, even the unfinished state of them (e.g. Mshattā and Qaṣr aṭ-Ṭūba) can be explained by the known vicissitudes of the dynasty. It is also known that their buildings were erected by imported workmen, and the direct borrowing of North Mesopotamian architects at a point so far to the south as Mshattā is more probable under this dynasty than at an earlier date. Without insisting on this view in opposition to Strzygowski, he mentions it in order to point out the possibility of an idea excluded by Strzygowski as *a priori* impossible.[2]

He concludes by pointing out how thoroughly the whole 'Abbāsid state was impregnated by Persian influences and how a Persianized Baghdād served as a pattern and model for the independent dynasties which arose on the territory of the weakened empire (e.g. Egypt under the Ṭūlūnids and North Africa under the Aghlabids).[3]

Reinach (1906) quotes a lecture given before the *Kunstgeschichtliche Gesellschaft* (Berlin), in which Poppelreuther called attention to some gold and silver filigree articles from the Rhine, published by Kisa in the *Bonner Jahrbücher* (1899, Taf. 1), apparently due to Oriental artisans of the fourth century. He suggests that they support Strzygowski's proposal to attribute Mshattā to that period. This view was contested by Sarre and Wulff (1) because of the difficulty of comparing a great work in stone to such small objects, and (2) because the same principle in decoration is maintained in Byzantine architecture down to the sixth century.[4]

Brünnow, returning to this problem in 1907, maintains that Mshattā and Qaṣr aṭ-Ṭūba were undoubtedly built in pre-Islamic times. That they are not Umayyad is shown by a comparison of their masonry with that of Quṣayr 'Amra. In addition to this the statues discovered at Mshattā can scarcely have been due to an Umayyad. But its position in almost waterless desert, far from any other settlement, shows that it can only have been erected for real Arabs and not by the Persians when they possessed Transjordan (A. D. 611–18).[5] He then points out that four building periods are to be distinguished clearly in Transjordan: (1) the oldest, represented by the *castra* of Odhroḥ, Lajjūn, and Qasṭal, and the finest buildings of Philadelphia ('Ammān) and Gerasa (Jerash) and certain temples in the Ḥaurān, of carefully executed ashlar with thoroughly classical ornament. This first period extends to the end of the second century, when Oriental influence begins to appear under the dynasty of Severus; (2) the second period is exemplified by the greater part of the buildings of Philippopolis (ash-Shuhba) which are due to the Emperor Philip (244–9), and the triumphal arch at Boṣrā dated in the second half of the third century; the masonry is still good, but not so carefully executed as in the first period, and the style, although still classical, shows degeneration; (3) the third period begins in the fourth century with the definite orientalizing of Syrian architecture, particularly in the ornament, and reaches its highest point in the course of the fifth century; (4) the fourth period corresponds with the sixth century, in which the heterogeneous elements of the earlier periods are blended in a harmonious style and the masonry, which had deteriorated during the last three centuries, almost reaches the quality of the first period once more. But, as Butler remarks, the later architecture of Transjordan does not rise

1 *Journal des Savants*, 1906, p. 52.
2 *Zeitschrift für Assyriologie*, XIX, pp. 425–6.
3 *Ibid.*, pp. 427–32.
4 *La Date de la façade de M'Schatta; Revue Archéologique*, 4me sér., t. VII, p. 485.
5 *W.Z.K.M.*, XXI, p. 286.

to the same level as that of Northern Syria. Mshattā and Qaṣr aṭ-Ṭūba, on account of their orientalizing ornament, can in no case be placed earlier than the fourth century; on the other hand, the fine execution of the masonry, recalling that of Odhroḥ and Qasṭal, makes it very improbable that they can be of the third period. Brünnow therefore places them in the sixth century.[1] But the façade, in his opinion, is older and he still holds to the opinion put forward in his *Provincia Arabia* that it came from Ḥira and was re-employed here.

Nöldeke (1907), in reviewing Musil's work, says that he thinks Mshattā is older than Islam in any case, and that many reasons point to a Ghassānid Phylarch of the sixth century; but he is not quite certain whether Ḥārith ibn Jabala himself (who died, after a long reign, in 569 or 570) was in a position to erect such a building.[2]

Dussaud (1907) appears to accept the fourth-century date suggested by Strzygowski but, in doing so, points out that this involves the surrender of the idea that it was built by the Ghassānids, for the earliest prince of this dynasty of certain date was Ḥārith ibn Jabala (Ἀρέθας τοῦ Γαβάλα) who gained a victory over al-Mundhir of Ḥīra in A. D. 528. On the other hand, the dynasty of the Lakhmids of Ḥīra to which al-Mundhir belonged goes back to the beginning of the fourth century,[3] and the famous inscription at Nemāra, on the eastern edge of the Ḥaurān, written in Nabataean characters on the tomb of Mar' al-Qais bar Imru', and dated 7 Keslūl 223 (of the Era of Boṣrā = 7th Dec. 329),[4] shows that the Lakhmid power at that time extended to the frontiers of Syria. Moreover, a Lakhmid origin, according to Dussaud, satisfactorily explains the Persian influences which he recognizes in the façade of Mshattā. He therefore accepts Strzygowski's suggested date—the fourth century—but attributes the construction of Mshattā to a Lakhmid, instead of to a Ghassānid prince.[5]

Herzfeld (1907) says that the offset of the vault is an indication that it is not earlier than the Umayyads.[6] Musil (1907) merely calls attention to the resemblance between Mshattā and Qaṣr aṭ-Ṭūba.[7]

Strzygowski, reviewing Dussaud's work in the same year, notes with satisfaction that the former places Mshattā in the same century as he does, but blames Dussaud for attributing it exclusively to Persian influence.[8]

Littmann (1908), reviewing Dussaud's work, says that Mshattā has always impressed him as belonging to the Umayyad period, during which a number of palaces are known to have been built in this region. He rejects the Ghassānid hypothesis, for the total lack of Christian symbols shows that it cannot have been built by these fanatical Jacobite Christians, nor had any of their princes the resources with which to undertake such an expensive work. Such an unusually magnificent palace can only have been undertaken by a Byzantine Emperor or an Umayyad Khalif. He also doubts that the crude statues found there can have had anything to do with the builder.[9]

Guthe (1908) merely says that it is supposed to be Umayyad.[10] Moritz (1908) places it in the Umayyad period because only the ruler of a mighty empire could dispose of the means necessary for the erection of such a magnificent building, the cost of which must have been enormously increased on account of the locality chosen for it. He then points out that Walīd II, who was of half Bedawīn origin, had lived in the Belqā when he was Crown Prince, that he had such a mania for building that his successor had to promise not to indulge in this direction, and that the *Kitāb al-Aghānī* expressly says that he built residences in this region, so that it is difficult to resist the conclusion that Mshattā is due to him.[11]

Rhodokanakis (1908), like Strzygowski, blames Dussaud for regarding Mshattā as entirely due to Persian inspiration and for not taking its classical and Hellenistic elements into consideration, but he does not dispute his dating.[12]

Lammens (1908) emphasizes the fact that the Umayyads made the Belqā their home and, seeking an

[1] *Loc. cit.*, pp. 286–9.

[2] *Z.D.M.G.*, LXI, pp. 228–9.

[3] *Les Arabes en Syrie avant l'Islam*, pp. 34–6. Dussaud has reconstructed the chronology of the kings of Ḥīra as follows:

(1)	'Amr (I) ibn 'Adī	?
(2)	Imru' al-Qais (I) ibn 'Amr	?–328
(3)	'Amr (II) ibn Imru' al-Qais	328–58
(4)	Aus ibn Qallām	358–63
(5)	Imru' al-Qais (II)	363–88
(6)	an-Nu'mān (I) ibn Imru' al-Qais	388–418

the rest as in Rothstein, *Dynastie der Laḫmiden*, pp. 69–87.

[4] For this inscription see below, p. 635.

[5] *Op. cit.*, pp. 48–54.

[6] *Samarra*, p. 18. But see below, p. 630, n. 1.

[7] *Arabia Petraea*, I, pp. 196–203; and his *Ḳuṣejr 'Amra*, pp. 30–32.

[8] *Byzantinische Zeitschrift*, XVI, pp. 721–2.

[9] *Göttingische gelehrte Anzeigen*, 170. Jahrg., pp. 150–51.

[10] *Palästina*, p. 159; 2te Aufl., p. 163.

[11] *Ausflüge*, in the *M.F.O.B.*, III, pp. 428–31.

[12] *W.Z.K.M.*, XXII, pp. 211–13.

explanation for the unfinished state of Mshattā, asks if the sudden death of Ḥabāba, the favourite of Yazīd II, followed almost immediately by the death of the latter himself (A. D. 724), is not the answer.[1]

Van Berchem (1909), returning again to the problem, resumes his previous views, and points out that scholars, in this discussion, have not sufficiently distinguished two points of view which, although connected with each other, must not be confused: the historical circumstances and the art period *Kunstkreis*). He says that he cannot accept the Umayyad attribution which, at this time, had been revived in Germany by Becker, Littmann, and Moritz as a result of the proof that Quṣayr ʿAmra was an Umayyad building. He then proceeds to develop his objections: (1st) the chronological, the style of Mshattā being incompatible with the eighth century; (2nd) the powerful influence of Persia and Mesopotamia on Muslim art is demonstrated by Becker, but none of the examples given by him goes back to the time of the Umayyads, in fact it is under them that Persian influence least shows itself. The Umayyad Khalifs built monuments in the Syrian style and Quṣayr ʿAmra is there to prove it. In plan, construction, materials, and paintings Quṣayr ʿAmra is purely Syrian and exhibits no connexion with Mshattā, which is a Mesopotamian building, adapted to the plan of the *castra* of the Roman *limes*.

And here is another difficulty: that the Romans, the Persians, or their Arab allies should have built *castra* on the frontier of their empire was quite natural, but why should the Umayyads, masters of Asia to beyond the borders of Persia, have perpetuated the type so close to their capital? Their *limes* were not in Moab, but in Transoxiana and beyond the Indus. Moreover, Quṣayr ʿAmra is not fortified, and why should it be, for an Umayyad had nothing to fear in the heart of his empire. Again, all Muslim monuments bear inscriptions which form one with the architecture and decoration, whereas Mshattā and Qaṣr aṭ-Ṭūba have none. On the other hand, the resemblance between Mshattā and Ṭūba is such that they must both be of about the same date. Supporters, therefore, of the scarcely tenable theory that Chosroes built Mshattā must now be prepared to believe that he built Ṭūba as well, so that the discovery of Ṭūba may be regarded as a fresh blow to the Sasanian theory. But the position of Qaṣr aṭ-Ṭūba, so far to the east of the Roman *limes*, but on the same longitude as the tomb of Imruʾ al-Qais at Nemāra, suits the Lakhmid hypothesis, which avoids nearly all our difficulties, and the entirely Oriental character of Mshattā and Ṭūba, the indications of Paganism (statues found at Mshattā), and the absence of Christian symbols, also suit a Lakhmid attribution, an attribution which permits us to go back to the fourth century.

However, he has to admit that it is surprising that ʿAmra is the only Umayyad palace yet found in this Belqā where several of them passed their lives, and he suggests that they probably transformed and used the buildings of their predecessors. This would explain why Qasṭal, a fort of the Roman *limes* attributed by Ḥamza al-Iṣfahānī to a Ghassānid, served as a residence for the children of Walīd I, that Muwaqqar, which appears to be earlier than the Umayyads, was inhabited by Yazīd II, and that Ṭūba in the Wādī Ghadaf, was one of the residences of Walīd II.[2]

Dalton (1910) is of the opinion that it is more likely to be of the sixth century at the earliest, and points out that the Persian elements seem to belong to the sixth or seventh century. One very characteristic feature, for instance, is a curious griffin with a peacock's tail; now this monster is so frequently found figured in Sasanian textiles and silver-work of the seventh century[3] that it would seem to be an indication of that epoch.[4] Diehl (1910) thinks, with Brünnow, that it is a little later than the fifth, perhaps sixth, century, and the work of a Ghassānid.[5] Lammens (1910) inclines to attribute it to Yazīd II (d. 724) who is known to have intended to build a palace to which he could retire with his beloved Ḥabāba.[6]

Herzfeld (1910) begins by emphasizing the following points: (1) that a mixture of brick and stone is foreign to the classical architecture of Syria; (2) that the bricks employed (21 and 27 cm. square) are smaller than Sasanian bricks (31½ cm. square, or more), and resemble those of the Muslim period in ʿIrāq, e.g. the Baghdād Gate of Raqqa (A. D. 772 or later); (3) that the offset vault is a feature that is

[1] *La Bâdia et la Ḥîra sous les Omaiyades, al-Machriq*, XI, pp. 772–3 (in Arabic); and in the *M.F.O.B.*, IV, pp. 109–11.

[2] *Au pays de Moab et d'Edom, Journal des Savants*, 1909, pp. 300–301 and 402–8.

[3] See two textiles in the Victoria and Albert Museum, and Smirnov's *Argenterie orientale*, pls. XLII, XLIX, and CXV, on Persian silver objects in the Hermitage Museum.

[4] Harvey, Lethaby, Dalton, etc., *The Church of the Nativity at Bethlehem*, p. 30.

[5] *Manuel d'art byzantin*, p. 48.

[6] *M.F.O.B.*, III, pp. 109–10.

not found in any Sasanian or classical building, but only in Muslim times;[1] (4) that the mouldings are quite different from the plain, simple mouldings of the Provincia Arabia (Transjordan); (5) that the Corinthian capital found in the basilical hall belongs to the second century; material was therefore used which had been taken from earlier buildings, a practice almost unknown in Syria before Islam; (6) that there is no example of an arch with a tie-beam in the pre-Muslim architecture of Syria; and (7) that the vaults have a pointed-arched section.[2]

As for its function, he points out that Mshattā (like Ukhaiḍir) is a *ḥīra*, i.e. a winter and desert residence, a *bādiya* of the most luxurious type that has been preserved to us, which only the will of an all-powerful Khalif could have created.[3]

He then analyses the whole structure and comes to the conclusion that craftsmen from four distinct regions must have worked at it: ʿIrāq, Diyārbakr, Syria, and Egypt.[4] This bringing together of workmen from all parts of the empire is one of the marked characteristics of early Muslim architecture.

All the indications, therefore, show that Mshattā must be regarded as a Muslim monument, i.e. Umayyad, for this region was the favourite place of residence of many of them. He then concludes from the historical facts concerning the Umayyads, brought forward by Lammens, that Mshattā was a *bādiya* of Yazīd II (A.D. 720–24) or Walīd II (A.D. 743–4), probably the former.[5]

Dalton (1911) places it between the fourth and seventh centuries without entering into a discussion.[6] Benoit (1912) merely classes it as pre-Islamic.[7]

Brünnow (1912) disputing Herzfeld's arguments (in *Der Islam*) begins by calling attention to the great difference in the architecture of Mshattā and Quṣayr ʿAmra, which he calls the strongest proof against an Umayyad attribution for the former. How explain, he asks, that two neighbouring palaces, erected for princes of the same dynasty within a period of a few years, bear not the slightest resemblance to each other, either in architecture, plan, or ornament?

To invalidate this objection, one must point out an Umayyad building of certain date, of which the style has at least some analogies with Mshattā. Until this is done one must absolutely reject the Umayyad theory. Against this consideration the reasons put forward by Herzfeld appear of small weight, e.g. the technique of the brickwork, the pointed arch, the wooden tie-beams, the re-use of material, etc. Mesopotamian brickwork is not found in Syria for the first time under Islam, pointed vaults occur already in the sixth century at Qaṣr Ibn Wardān, wooden tie-beams occur in Sancta Sophia, not hidden away in the side aisles as Herzfeld alleges, but in quite exposed places, and, as regards the re-use of material, it is not impossible that the Arabs already in the sixth century used looted material.[8]

He considers that its masonry is too good to have been built in the fourth or fifth century, which was a period of bad masonry, so he is led to place it in the sixth, and it is precisely in this century that brickwork first appears elsewhere in Syria, viz. at Qaṣr Ibn Wardān, A.D. 561–4. And just as he believes that the latter may have been built as an official residence for the *Dux Syriae*, so he suggests that Mshattā may have been built for the Ghassānid Phylarch as Warden of the Marches about the same period, and used later and added to by the Persian invaders of A.D. 613–28.[9] Finally, he summarizes his ideas as: 'Built with Byzantine gold under Byzantine rule, designed by a Ghassānid after a Lakhmid model, and restored under Persian rule. . . .'[10]

Brünnow's suggestion that Qaṣr Ibn Wardān may have been built for a Roman Governor, the *Dux Syriae*, is scarcely tenable for the date (564) is too late. By this time the Byzantine Government had handed over the guardianship of the eastern frontier to the Ghassānid Phylarchs, who ruled a sort of buffer state. The first of these was al-Ḥārith ibn Jabala (the Ἀρηθας του Γαβαλου of the Greek sources), who obtained the title of Patrician and Phylarch from the Emperor Justinian in 529. He stood high in favour and visited Constantinople in 563, and had important funds at his disposal.

We have seen that the palace of Qaṣr Ibn Wardān was built, according to a Greek inscription, in the following year and the church (the Ghassānids were Jacobite Christians), although without a dating

[1] This is not quite correct for several vaults at Hatra are offset; see fig. 484, facing p. 446.

[2] *Der Islam*, I, pp. 110–14 and 120–22.

[3] *Ibid.*, I, pp. 122–8.

[4] *Ibid.*, pp. 133–43.

[5] *Ibid.*, p. 143.

[6] *Byzantine Art and Archaeology*, p. 170.

[7] *L'Architecture: L'Orient, médiéval et moderne*, p. 105.

[8] *Zeitschrift für Assyriologie*, XXVII, pp. 129–30.

[9] *Ibid.*, pp. 134–7.

[10] *Ibid.*, p. 138.

inscription, being in exactly the same style and at a distance of only 6 m. from the palace, was doubtless built at about the same time.

I therefore venture to propose an entirely new attribution for Qaṣr IbnWardān, viz., that it was built by Justinian with Byzantine masons for al-Ḥārith ibn Jabala.

Herzfeld (1912) says that, after the excavations of Sāmarrā, it can no longer be disputed that Mshattā is a *ḥira* of Yazīd II (A. D. 720–24).[1]

Gertrude Bell in 1913 wrote: 'the castle of Ṭûba is certainly early Mohammadan; I do not doubt that Mshatta belongs to the same period'.[2] Dieulafoy (1913) says that it appears to date from the period when the country was a dependency of Sasanian Persia (i.e. A.D. 614–29).[3] Gertrude Bell, writing in 1914, follows Lammens in saying that it was perhaps built by Yazīd II and left unfinished at his death.[4] Rivoira (1914)[5] and Diez (1915) also accept Lammens' theory that it was built by Yazīd II (A.D. 720–24).[6]

Lammens (1915) says that formerly he had hesitated between Yazīd II and Walīd II (A. D. 743–4), but that the following passage from Severus ibn al-Muqaffa' renders the latter hypothesis more probable: 'Since, however, his people hated him, he began to build a city named after himself in the desert, for he 'gave his name to it; but the water was fifteen miles distant from it. He collected workmen from all 'quarters, and built that city by means of forced labour; and on account of the multitude many died 'every day from the scarcity of water; for though the water was carried thither by twelve hundred camels 'daily, yet this was not enough for them; the camels being divided into two convoys, six hundred carry-'ing water one day, and six hundred the next. Then al-Walīd was attacked by a man named Ibrāhīm,[7] 'who killed him, and seized the government instead of him. Ibrāhīm released the enslaved workmen, 'who departed each one to his own place.'[8] Lammens says that the geographical part suits Mshattā, and that fifteen miles is just about the distance to the Arnon (Mūjib). He also points out that this story explains why Yazīd III, on his accession, had to promise not to spend money on building.[9] Regarding this passage Sauvaget points out that the work of Severus ibn al-Muqaffa' was composed by a Copt, who was interested in Egyptian affairs only, and that no information about events in Syria or 'Irāq is to be found in it. Hence he concludes that an event in Transjordan would not have been recorded by him unless it had great importance for his community. He therefore suggests that 'he collected workmen from all quarters' must be taken to mean 'from all parts of Egypt', and he ends by remarking that this would explain the Egyptian influence I have recognized in the vine ornament and the design of the Throne-Room.[10]

Strzygowski (1919) says that the base moulding, the cornice, and the intermediate band of zigzag should be compared with those of Mesopotamia, where the oldest surviving example belongs to the year A.D. 359 (he is presumably referring to the Baptistery of Mār Ya'qūb at Naṣībīn), the rosettes with Armenian parallels, and the vine scroll with pilasters of Acre and Zwarthnotz (A.D. 650). He then asserts that Mshattā reveals that fusion of Iranian and Greek art which succeeded the displacement of the latter in late Roman times, and concludes that Mshattā may even be regarded 'as perhaps of Parthian rather than Sasanian origin'.[11]

Herzfeld (1921), in the course of a long memoir, calls attention, first to the fact that many of the Umayyad Khalifs resided in the desert, or on the edge of it, for a considerable part of the year (p. 130); then to their practice of conscripting labour from all parts of the empire, which would explain the mixture of influences in Mshattā (pp. 131–3); to the fact that the unfinished state of Mshattā perfectly suits the known facts of Walīd II's life (p. 145); and adds that the lack of any inscription is without

1 *Erster vorläufiger Bericht über die Ausgrabungen von Samarra*, p. 40.

2 *Churches and Monasteries of the Ṭûr 'Abdîn*, p. 108.

3 *Art in Spain and Portugal*, p. 15.

4 *Ukhaiḍir*, p. 117.

5 *Moslem Architecture*, p. 132.

6 *Kunst der islamischen Völker*, p. 33.

7 Presumably the brother of Yazīd III. He did not succeed Walīd II immediately, for Yazīd III did, but after the death of the latter he assumed the Government of Damascus and held it from 7 Dhu'l-qa'da 126 to 14 Ṣafar 127 (2nd Aug. to 25th Nov. 744). But no general homage was ever paid to him, and he was soon swept out of the way by Marwān II.

8 *Histoire des Patriarches d'Alexandrie* in the *Patrologia Orientalis*, V, pp. 114–15; the above is Evetts' translation.

9 *Journal Asiatique*, 11me sér., t. VI, pp. 258–9; reprinted in his *Études sur la siècle des Omayyades*, pp. 348–50. See also his article *al-Walīd ibn Yazīd*, in the *Encyclopaedia of Islām*, IV, p. 1112.

10 *Remarques sur les monuments omeyyades*, *Journal Asiatique*, CCXXXI, pp. 31–4.

11 *Origins of Christian Church Art*, pp. 113–14. The Parthian dynasty ended A. D. 226.

significance, for the construction of Mshattā was not sufficiently far advanced for the question of inscriptions to arise (pp. 145–6).[1] Finally, he attributes it to Walīd II in 126 H. (A.D. 743/4).

Lammens (1921) repeats the reasons, already expressed in 1915, which led him to believe that Mshattā must be attributed to Wālīd II.[2]

Jaussen and Savignac (1922) consider that the question has now been narrowed down to three possible hypotheses, the Ghassānid, the Lakhmid, and the Umayyad.

The Ghassānids, however, unlike the Lakhmids, do not appear to have had a fixed encampment; they were true nomads. Before Byzantium, by giving their chief the right to wear the crown (in A.D. 580; see above, p. 625), had confirmed their hegemony over the other Arabs of Syria, they were only a tribe which, although more powerful than the others, lived the same life and cared little about building. But with their elevation came a desire for building. Jafna, according to Abu'l-Fidā', created a number of establishments. His son and successor built Dayr Ḥālī, Dayr Ayyūb, and Dayr Hind. Tha'laba built the palace of al-Ghadīr, his son Jabala ibn Ḥārith those of al-Qanāṭir, Odhroḥ, and Qasṭal. Ḥārith ibn Jabala, who lived in the Belqā, built al-Ḥafīr; Dayr Dahm and Dayr al-Banawāt were due to al-Ayham, Nu'mān ibn 'Amr built the palace of Suwayda. Jabala ibn Ḥārith built Qaṣr Barqā' (? Burqa').

Jaussen and Savignac admit that the majority of the statements of the Arabic historians on pre-Islamic times are false, but it is evident that tradition considered the Ghassānids as great builders and it cannot be entirely false.

Nevertheless there is one most serious objection on stylistic grounds. How, they ask, could the Ghassānids, Arabs of Syria living expressly under the protection of Byzantium, have constructed edifices which bear such a strong mark of Persian and Mesopotamian influence, countries with which their relations were hostile, and to which they would certainly not have gone for their architects?

This difficulty is avoided by the Lakhmid theory. It is now known, thanks to the inscription of Nemāra, that, at the beginning of the fourth century, a Lakhmid king Imru' al-Qais, who calls himself 'King of all the Arabs', extended his power westward from the Euphrates as far as the Roman *limes*. Although invested by the Persians, he succeeded in becoming the ally of Rome, and in maintaining himself in equilibrium between the two great rival states. We do not know how long this state of affairs existed, but it may have lasted until the investiture of the Ghassānid al-Mundhir by the Byzantine Emperor in A.D. 580, an event which divided the desert into two sharply defined spheres.

According to the Lakhmid theory it was during this period that the Qaṣr al-Abyaḍ, Mshattā, and Qaṣr aṭ-Ṭūba were built by a Lakhmid prince. The former has usually been attributed to the fourth century. It is built of stone and its decoration is entirely confined to its lintels and door-posts, as in Qaṣr aṭ-Ṭūba.

The Lakhmid theory, they maintain, would perfectly explain the Mesopotamian and Persian influences in Mshattā, *if* it could be put back to such an early date, which it is difficult to do.

In favour of an Umayyad date for Qaṣr aṭ-Ṭūba (which they consider indissolubly interlocked with Mshattā) may be invoked the fact that it has served as a residence for Walīd II, if it be admitted that Ṭūba in the Wādī Ghadaf may be identified with Ghadaf or Aghdaf (see above, pp. 405–6) as seems quite probable. Moreover, there are early Arabic *graffiti* there, quite like those in Qaṣr Kharāna. But they admit that it may be urged that Walīd II reoccupied an unfinished Lakhmid or Ghassānid building, just as Walīd I occupied Qasṭal.

Finally, Jaussen and Savignac admit that although Qaṣr aṭ-Ṭūba and Mshattā must be contemporary with each other, it is difficult if not impossible to bring down the date of the latter to the eighth century, on account of the pagan character of the decoration and the presence of fragments of idols. Their final verdict is that although the question still remains in suspense, they feel that, of all the theories given above, the Umayyad hypothesis is the least probable.[3]

Brøndsted (1924) merely classes it as fourth–fifth century,[4] apparently after Strzygowski. Dalton (1925) merely quotes the opposing opinions of Strzygowski and Herzfeld.[5] Glück and Diez (1925) are non-committal, merely saying '4th–6th or 8th century?'.[6] Gröber (1925) merely classes it as Umay-

[1] *Mshattâ, Ḥîra und Bâdiya*, in the *Jahrb. der Preusz. Kunstsammlungen*, XLII, pp. 104–46.

[2] *La Syrie*, pp. 96–7.

[3] *Les Châteaux arabes*, pp. 122–6.

[4] *Early English Ornament*, p. 26.

[5] *East Christian Art*, pp. 109, n. 1, 118–19, 200, n. 2, and 368.

[6] *Die Kunst des Islam*, p. 531.

yad.[1] Monneret (1925) believes it to have been built in the sixth century.[2] Butler (1926) says that it is not Sasanian, but may date from the fifth to sixth century.[3] Jerphanion (1926) considers it contemporary with Syrian monuments of the sixth century or even later.[4] Dussaud (1927), in reviewing the second edition of Diehl's *Manuel d'Art byzantin*, compares it with Qaṣr Ibn Wardān and comes to the conclusion that the main structure, like the latter, is neither Ghassānid nor Umayyad but Byzantine work of the sixth century.[5] Pijoán (1927) leaves the reader wondering as to whom he actually attributes Mshattā.[6] Kühnel (1929) classes it as Umayyad.[7] Kammerer (1929/30) considers it to be Lakhmid of the fourth or the beginning of the fifth century.[8]

Diez (1932) supports the views of Becker, Herzfeld, and Lammens,[9] but he makes one extraordinary statement which must be corrected, namely, that Herzfeld finally crowned his work with the discovery of an inscription drawn up by Walīd II himself recording repairs made by him (p. 613). Diez must have read Herzfeld's *Mshattâ, Ḥîra und Bâdiya* very carelessly for the latter (p. 146) merely gives the text of an inscription which he suggests would have been carved on a slab above the entrance had Mshattā ever been finished!

Strzygowski, in a book published in 1936, but written in 1928, puts Mshattā farther back than ever. He actually asserts that it was constructed for the worship of fire, then used for an Aramaean cult (on account of the fragments of statues found there), and concludes that it must have been built in the Parthian period, i.e. before A.D. 242.[10]

On one of the blocks forming the broken masonry of the inner face of the south wall, behind the last two triangles to the east, Schulz had discovered a man's head with a Sasanian-like head-dress (reproduced here, Fig. 632*b*, lightly scratched by some mason in an idle moment, on the face of the block which was turned inwards and therefore not visible from the exterior.[11] This led to a new line of argument being started by von Bissing in 1948;[12] he maintained that the head was that of Khusrau II (590–628).

In the same year but independently Altheim took up the problem and insisted that the head was that of Bahrām II.[13] If accepted, this, according to him, would put Mshattā back to before 293, the year of Bahrām's death. But this conclusion cannot be accepted, for Sasanian coins circulated long after the conquest and a mason, wishing to draw a Sasanian head-dress, would not be limited to that of the reigning sovereign. That the insignia of the Persian kings was known right into Umayyad times is shown by the picture of the Persian king at Qusayr ʻAmra.

Erdmann, at the Congress of Orientalists held at Constantinople in 1951 (*Proceedings* not published until 1957[14]), exhibited a number of sketches of Sasanian royal head-dress, and he came to the conclusion that the head at Mshattā came nearest to Bahrām II. Altheim agreed with him,[15] but it is difficult to see any resemblance between the crude sketch at Mshattā and the head-dress of any Persian king, Bahrām II, Khusrau II, or any other.

Let us now tabulate these opinions:

1873	Fergusson and Tristram	Chosroes II (A.D. 614).
1874	Fergusson	,, (A.D. 614–27).
1876	Rawlinson	,, ,,
1878	Fergusson	,, ,,
1881	Merrill	Monastery and church due to a Byzantine emperor.
1886	Conder	Possibly Umayyad.
—	Thomson	Nil.
1887	Dieulafoy	Chosroes II (A.D. 611–23).
—	Layard	Merely quotes Fergusson's opinion.
1890	Hill	Nil.
—	Phené Spiers	Chosroes II.
1891	van Berchem	Persian origin does not appear proved.
—	Hill	Nil.
—	Merrill	Doubts Persian origin.
—	Riegl	Accepts Fergusson's dating.
1893	Séjourné	Chosroes II.
1895	Bliss	Nil.
—	Brünnow	Ghassānid.
—	Gayet	Chosroes II.

1 *Palästina, Arabien und Syrien*, p. xii.
2 *Les Couvents près de Sohâg*, p. 54.
3 *Islamic Pottery*, p. 112.
4 *Le Calice d'Antioche*, p. 124.
5 *Syria*, VIII, pp. 73–4.
6 *History of Art*, II, p. 207.
7 *Kunst des Ostens*, p. 22.
8 *Pétra et la Nabatène*, p. 338.
9 *Mshattā*, in the *Encyclopaedia of Islām*, III, pp. 613–14.
10 *L'Ancien art chrétien de Syrie*, pp. xlix, 149, and 171.
11 Schulz and Strzygowski, *loc. cit.*, p. 222 and Abb. 15.
12 *Äusserer Anhalt zur Datierung der Fassade des Schlösses von Mshatta, Forschungen und Fortschritte*, XXIV, pp. 124–5.
13 *Literature und Gesellschaft in ausgehenden Altertum*, pp. 254–63.
14 *Ein Betrag zur Datierung der Fassade von Mschatta. Proceedings of the Twenty-Second Congress of Orientalists, Istanbul*, 1951, pp. 614–19, with 13 figs. However, he published it independently in 1954 in *Forschungen und Fortschritte*, XXVIII, pp. 242–5, with 16 figs.
15 *Die Araber in den alten Welt*, I, p. 593.

1896	van Berchem	Ghassānid.
—	Vailhé	'Abd al-Malik.
1898	Lammens	Umayyad, Yazīd II (A. D. 720–24).
1899	Oppenheim	Merely mentions the opinions of Fergusson and Brünnow.
1901	Dussaud	Merely compares it to the Qaṣr al-Abyaḍ.
—	Gautier	Perhaps Ghassānid, sixth or beginning of seventh century.
—	Nies	A khān built by an Umayyad or 'Abbāsid for the Pilgrim route.
1902	Musil	Ghassānid.
1904	Borrmann	Nil.
—	Saladin	Vaguely suggests the Ghassānids.
—	Brünnow	Ghassānid, al-Mundhir (A. D. 580–82).
—	(Schulz) and Strzygowski	Fourth–fifth century.
1905	Rhodokanakis	Fourth–sixth century. Gives a synopsis of Strzygowski's views with which he appears to agree.
—	Ameseder	" " "
—	van Berchem	Ghassānid.
1906	Clermont-Ganneau	Lakhmid.
—	Becker	Umayyad.
—	Reinach	Fourth century.
1907	Dussaud	Lakhmid, fourth century.
—	Herzfeld	Umayyad.
—	Musil (*A. P.*)	Nil—but calls attention to resemblance between Mshattā and Qaṣr aṭ-Ṭūba.
—	Musil (*K. A.*)	Nil.
—	Brünnow	Ghassānid, sixth century.
—	Nöldeke	Ghassānid, sixth century.
—	Strzygowski	Fourth century.
1908	Littmann	Umayyad.
—	Guthe	Supposed to be Umayyad.
—	Moritz	Walīd II.
—	Rhodokanakis	Fourth century.
—	Lammens	Yazīd II (A. D. 720–24).
1909	van Berchem	Lakhmid, fourth century.
1910	Dalton	Sixth at the earliest, probably seventh century.
—	Diehl	Ghassānid, fifth or perhaps even sixth century.
—	Lammens	Umayyad, Yazīd II.
—	Herzfeld	Umayyad, Yazīd II (A. D. 720–24) or Walīd II (A. D. 743–4); probably Yazīd.
1911	Dalton	Fourth–seventh century. Accepts Strzygowski's views without discussion.
—	Rhodokanakis	Nil.
1912	Benoit	Classed as pre-Islamic. No discussion.
—	Brünnow	Sixth century.
—	Herzfeld	Yazīd II (A. D. 720–24).
1913	Bell	Early Muhammadan.
—	Dieulafoy	Sasanian.
1914	Bell	Yazīd II, quoting Lammens.
1915	Diez	Yazīd II, quoting Lammens.
1915	Lammens	Probably Walīd II, on account of a passage in Severus ibn al-Muqaffa'.
1916	Strzygowski	Classed as 'Scythian-Hellenistic'.
1916	Moritz	Walid II
1917	Strzygowski	Nil.
1918	Rivoira	Umayyad, perhaps Yazīd II.
1919	Strzygowski	Perhaps even Parthian (i.e. before A. D. 226) rather than Sasanian.
1920	Woermann	Agrees with Herzfeld.
1921	Herzfeld	Walīd II (A. D. 743/4).
—	Lammens	Walīd II (A. D. 743/4).
1922	Jaussen and Savignac	Pre-Muslim, but cannot decide between a Ghassānid or a Lakhmid attribution.
1923	Ahlenstiel-Engel	Early Muslim
1924	Brøndsted	Fourth–sixth century, apparently after Strzygowski.
1925	Dalton	Hesitates between Herzfeld and Strzygowski.
—	Glück and Diez	Offer no opinion.
—	Gröber	Classed as Umayyad.
—	Monneret	Sixth century.
1926	Butler (A. J.)	May be fifth–sixth century.
—	Jerphanion	Sixth century.
1927	Dussaud	Sixth century.
—	Migeon	Umayyad, perhaps Yazīd II.
—	Pijoán	Vague.
—	Kühnel	Classed as Umayyad.
1928	Musil	Nil.
1929	Cohn-Wiener	Probably Walid II
—	Kühnel	Umayyad
—	Munthe	Non-committal.
—	Wachtsmuth	Umayyad.
—	Strzygowski	'Mazdaique.'
1929/30	Kammerer	Lakhmid.
1930	Strzygowski	Nil.
1932	Diez	Umayyad.
—	Lammens	" (Walīd II).
—	Terrasse	"
1933	Berenson (Mary)	"
—	Kühnel	"
1936	Strzygowski	Second–third century (Parthian).
1937	Dimand	Umayyad, end of period.
1938	Sauvaget	Umayyad.
1939	"	Walīd II.
1947	Marçais	"
1948	von Bissing	Khusrau II
1948/9	Altheim	Bahrām II (276–93)
1949	Pijoán	Nil.
1952	Altheim	Bahrām II (A. D. 293 at latest).
1954	Erdmann	Umayyad
1955	Dussaud	Lakhmid (Imru'lqais, 363–88).
—	Bettino	Nil.
1956	Stern	Umayyad.
1960	Grabar	"
—	Field	" (Walīd II).
—	Harding	"
1962	Trümpelmann	First half eighth century.
1964	Altheim	Sasanian (A.D. 293 at latest).

OBJECTIONS AGAINST THE LAKHMID THEORY. Of all the theories put forward in connexion with the date of Mshattā, the Lakhmid appears to me to be the most fantastic. On the strength of the Nabataean-Arabic inscription of Nemāra,[1] recording the burial of a man calling himself Mar' al-Qais bar 'Imru, King of all the Arabs, on the 7th day of Keslūl, 223 (= 7th Dec. A. D. 328), on the outer edge of the Ṣafā,[2] it was suggested by Peiser[3] that this man was the Imru' al-Qais[4] ibn 'Amr whose name appears in the list of Lakhmid kings.[5] This suggestion has been generally accepted as probable. But there is nothing to show, as some have tacitly assumed, that the Lakhmids had already established themselves at Ḥīra at this early date, nor is there any proof that this Imru' al-Qais was a vassal of the Persian king. Had he been, it is scarcely likely that the era employed to express the date of his death would have been the Era of Boṣrā which began A. D. 106, the date of the creation of the Provincia Arabia by Cornelius Palma, the Roman Governor of Syria. Neither does the use of the Persian word *tāj* (he calls himself 'he who wears the *tāj*', or diadem) prove that he owed his investiture to the Persians, as Clermont-Ganneau has suggested,[6] for Lidzbarski[7] and Nöldeke[8] have pointed out that this word had already passed into Syriac. It is used in the Syriac translation of the New Testament, and also in the works of Hillel (first century B. C.).

I must emphasize that there is no mention of the Persians in the inscription, which merely says that Mar' al-Qais, King of all the Arabs, organized the tribes as cavalry corps for the Romans. Dussaud, later on, modified this reading and introduced the word 'Persians',[9] but this modified reading, contested by Lidzbarski,[10] and Rhodokanakis[11] has since been given up by Dussaud himself.[12]

Nöldeke believes that the simplest explanation is that Imru' al-Qais was a Lakhmid vassal of the Romans, as is evident from the inscription, that his tribe lived on the Roman border like the Ghassānid Phylarchs later on, and that his descendants, for some reason still obscure, crossed over to the Persian side of the desert, settled at Ḥīra, and became Persian vassals, not later than A. D. 420, for Nu'mān was then King of Ḥīra and a vassal of the Persian king, as we know from Simeon Stylites.[13]

But once established there, there is not a particle of evidence to show that the power of the kings of Ḥīra ever extended to the Ṣafā, still less to the Belqā (Transjordan) where Dussaud suggests that one of them may have built Mshattā as his residence.[14]

And even if it could be proved that their sphere of influence extended as far, is it conceivable that one of these princes, whose home was Ḥīra (only four miles from Kūfa), would construct a most magnificent residence at a distance of 500 miles (as the crow flies) from his capital and only four or five miles from the Roman *limes*, and exposed to immediate looting and burning in case of war?

No, it is unthinkable; when Roman rule was strong, such a thing would have been impossible, and in the sixth century, when the Roman hold on this region was weaker and its resources strained, it was

1 For this inscription, which was discovered by Dussaud in 1901, see Dussaud, *Comptes rendus de l'Acad. des Inscriptions et Belles-Lettres*, 1902, pp. 259–60; and his *Inscription nabatéo-arabe d'en-Nemâra*, *Revue Archéologique*, 3me sér., t. XLI, pp. 409–21, with two figs. (reprinted and revised in Dussaud and Macler, *Mission dans les régions désertiques de la Syrie Moyenne*, in the *Nouvelles Archives des Missions Scientifiques*, X, pp. 428–9 and pl. IV$_2$ and pp. 716–24); Halévy (J.), *L'Inscription nabatéo-arabe d'En-Némara*, *Revue Sémitique*, XI, pp. 58–62; Peiser, *Die arabische Inschrift von En-Nemâra*, *Orientalistische Literatur-Zeitung*, VI, cols. 277–81; Lidzbarski (M.), *Ephemeris für semitische Epigraphik*, II, pp. 34–7 and 375–9; Winckler, in the *Orientalistische Literatur-Zeitung*, VII, cols. 487–8; Clermont-Ganneau, *Le Roi de 'tous les Arabes'*, *Recueil d'archéologie orientale*, VI, pp. 305–10; and *Le tâdj dâr Imrou'l-Qais et la royauté générale des Arabes*, *ibid.*, VII, pp. 167–70; Hartmann, *Zur Inschrift von Nemāra*, *Orientalistische Literatur-Zeitung*, IX, cols. 573–84; Dussaud (R.), *Les Arabes en Syrie avant l'Islam*, pp. 34–8; Rhodokanakis, in the *W.Z.K.M.*, XXII, pp. 210–12; Lidzbarski (M.), *Ephemeris*, II, pp. 375–9; Brünnow and von Domaszewski, *Die Provincia Arabia*, III, pp. 285–6; Huart, *Histoire des Arabes*, I, pp. 63–4; Nöldeke, *Der Araberkönig von Namāra*, *Florilegium Melchior de Vogüé*, pp. 463–6; Abdel Fattah Ebada, *L'Écriture arabe*, pp. 6–7 and fig. 1; Jaussen and Savignac, *Les Châteaux arabes*, p. 124; Guidi, *L'Arabie antéislamique*, pp. 12–14; Dussaud, *Topographie historique de la Syrie*, p. 378; Kammerer, *Pétra et la Nabatène*, pp. 335–7; Wiet (G.), *Répertoire d'épigraphie arabe*, I, pp. 1–2; Nau, *Les Arabes chrétiens de Mésopotamie et de Syrie du VIIe au VIIIe siècle* (*Cahiers de la Société Asiatique*, I), pp. 32–3; and Abbott (Nabia), *The Rise of the North Arabic Script*, pp. 4–5 and 8–9, and pl. I$_{(2)}$.

2 The Ṣafā is the region of lava, east of the Ḥaurān and south-east of Damascus.

3 *Orientalistische Literatur-Zeitung*, VI, cols. 280–81.

4 The vocalization of this name is not certain; see Fischer, *Amra' al-qais oder Imra' alqais? Zeitschrift für Semistik*, I, pp. 196–9; Littmann's remarks, *ibid.*, II, pp. 199–200; and Nöldeke, *Zeitschrift für Assyriologie*, XXXIII, p. 5, n. 2.

5 See Rothstein (G.), *Die Dynastie der Laḫmiden in al-Ḥīra*, pp. 50 ff.

6 *Recueil d'archéol. orientale*, VI, p. 307; and Dussaud, *Les Arabes en Syrie*, pp. 35–6.

7 *Ephemeris*, II, p. 35.

8 *Florilegium Melchior de Vogüé*, pp. 465–6. See also Lidzbarski, *Ephemeris*, II, pp. 375–6.

9 *Les Arabes en Syrie*, p. 35.

10 *Ephemeris*, II, pp. 377–8.

11 *W.Z.K.M.*, XXII, p. 211, n. 3.

12 *Topographie historique*, p. 378, n. 7.

13 *Loc. cit.*, pp. 464–5, quoting the *Vita* of Simeon Stylites, *Acta Martyr. or.*, II, pp. 327 f.

14 *Les Arabes en Syrie*, pp. 53–4.

the Ghassānids (the deadliest enemies of the Lakhmids) who took their place and, as allies, protected the frontier here; they became, as it were, a sort of buffer state, with their capital or chief encampment at Jābiya.

But the most fatal of all objections against the Lakhmid theory, which has recently been revived by Altheim,[1] is the architectural, for it is impossible to put a building with a triple-apsed hall earlier than the middle of the fifth century A.D. (see above, pp. 614 ff.), and a building with pointed-arched vaults still later.

Objections against the Ghassānid Theory. This brings us to the Ghassānid theory, of which Brünnow was the principal champion (see above, pp. 624, 626, 628, and 630–31). From the historical point of view it is a much sounder theory than the Lakhmid, for the Ghassānids are actually known to have occupied the eastern frontier of Syria, from the Euphrates to the Ḥaurān and Transjordan, from at least as early as A.D. 500.[2] The Ghassānid state was probably destroyed by the Persians in A.D. 614, but the tribe and certain chiefs (e.g. Jabala ibn Ayham) are known to have existed down to the Arab conquest.

But there are three main objections to this theory: (1) the total lack of Christian symbols, as Littmann points out,[3] shows that Mshattā cannot have been constructed by these fanatical Jacobite Christians; (2) it is very doubtful if any of them, even the most famous, had the enormous resources required;[4] and (3) how could Arabs of Syria, expressly under the protection of Byzantium, have erected buildings with such a strong imprint of Persia and Mesopotamia?[5] Those who have been led to adopt the Lakhmid theory have done so to escape this very difficulty.

This last objection has now been strengthened; Ghassānid architecture is no longer an unknown quantity, as it once was, for four definitely Ghassānid buildings have now been identified and there is a possible fifth and sixth.

The first of these (going from north to south) is the building outside the north gate of Ruṣāfa, usually regarded as a church, but which is possibly a praetorium,[6] built by al-Mundhir himself (A.D. 569–82), with a Greek inscription in his name over the windows of the apse. It is built, including the vaults, of cut stone without any admixture of brickwork, and the pier capitals resemble some of those at Qalʿat Simʿān; in plan it is related to the Praetorium of Mismiya (see above, p. 454 and Figs. 495–6, facing).[7] In other words it is a completely Syrian building.

The second is the tower of a monastery built by the Ghassānid Phylarch, Ḥārīth ibn Jabala in 870 Sel. = A.D. 559, which was subsequently incorporated by the Khalif Hishām in his palace Qaṣr al-Ḥayr al-Gharbī (see above, p. 541).

The third is the great enclosure near Dumayr to the east of Damascus of which only a tower, known as al-Burj, now remains. This tower is 10 m. in diameter and 8 m. high;[8] and is built of very large masonry; according to Wetzstein (in 1858) the enclosure was oblong with walls 14 feet thick, but he says that the stones had been taken away for building purposes by the people of Dumayr and Jerūd.[9] The Greek inscription over the entrance[10] which recorded its construction by Ἀλαμούνδαρος (al-Mundhir) has recently been found on the ground by Dr. Brisch.

The fourth is the house at al-Hayāt[11] on the northernmost slopes of the Ḥaurān, erected by Flavios Seos (a Roman-Nabataean name) as *procurator* under the famous Alamoundaros (al-Mundhir), in the

[1] Altheim and Stiehl, *Die Araber in der alten Welt*, I, p. 394.

[2] A Ghassānid is mentioned in A.D. 498 under Anastasius (A.D. 491–518); see Theophanes, Bonn ed., p. 218; and Nöldeke, *Die Ghassānischen Fürsten aus dem Hause Gafna's* (*Abh. der Kgl. Preuss. Akad. der Wiss.*, 1887), pp. 6 and 10.

[3] *Göttingische gelehrte Anzeigen*, 170. Jahrg, p. 150.

[4] Becker, in the *Zeitschrift für Assyriologie*, XIX, p. 425; Nöldeke, in the *Z.D.M.G.*, LXI, p. 229; and Littmann, *loc. cit.*, pp. 150–51.

[5] Dussaud, *Les Arabes en Syrie*, p. 50; and Jaussen and Savignac, *Les Châteaux Arabes*, pp. 123–4.

[6] Sauvaget maintains that this building, on account of its resemblance to the Praetoriums of Mismiye and Canatha, was probably the audience hall of al-Mundhir; *Les Ghassanides et Sergiopolis*, *Byzantion*, XIV, pp. 115–30.

[7] For this building, see Guyer, in Sarre and Herzfeld, *Archäologische Reise*, II, pp. 39–43 and Abb. 151–6; Littmann, in the *Deutsche Literaturzeitung*, XLII (1921), col. 42 (for the inscription); Spanner and Guyer, *Rusafa*, pp. 42–4, 66–9, Abb. 11, 12, and 16, and Taf. 31–2; Musil, *Palmyrena*, pp. 163–5, 323–6, figs. 80–82 and 113–15; and Butler (H. C.), *Early Churches in Syria*, p. 170 and illus. 181–2.

[8] Brünnow and von Domaszewski, *Die Provincia Arabia*, III, p. 200 and fig. 1095.

[9] Wetzstein, *Ausgewählte griechische und lateinische Inschriften*, Inscr. No. 173.

[10] Waddington, *Inscriptions grecques et latines de la Syrie*, p. 585 (Inscr. 2562*c*).

[11] For this house, see Butler (H. C.), *Ancient Architecture in Syria, Sect. A: Southern Syria*, pp. 362–3 and illus. 322; and Herzfeld, *Mshattâ, Ḥîra und Bâdiya*, *loc. cit.*, pp. 115.

year A.D. 578. It is built in two storeys round a central court. In the latter are four piers carrying four great arches, which form a square and support an open gallery for the rooms of the upper storey. All the rooms have transverse arches carrying corbel-and-slab ceilings, exactly like the type described above (pp. 444–9) as typical of the Ḥaurān. The Ghassānids, therefore, when they did actually begin to erect buildings at the end of their dynasty, built *in the Syrian manner* without signs of Persian influence.

The possible fifth is the cruciform building in the Citadel at 'Ammān, published by Schulz and Strzygowski,[1] the plan of which is almost the same as the church (or praetorium) at Ruṣāfa, minus the apse.

The possible sixth is Qasṭal, only a few miles from Mshattā (see map on p. 404), which Hamza al-Iṣfahānī (10th cent.) says was built by Jabala ibn al-Ḥarīth.[2]

Answers to Objections Against the Umayyad Theory. Let us first attempt to answer the objections raised against the Umayyad theory. Van Berchem writes: 'Here is an objection taken from epigraphy: 'all Muslim monuments bear inscriptions, and these form one with the architecture or the decoration. 'This rule is so general that, in spite of their distant date, the Umayyad monuments do not form any 'exception to it. The beautiful band of inscription of 'Abd al-Malik in the Qubbat aṣ-Ṣakhra is well 'known; those of Walīd in the mosques of Damascus and Mekka have doubtless disappeared, but 'authors have preserved the memory of them. 'Amra presents the same peculiarity; moreover, a signi-'ficant fact that has not yet been grasped, the inscription which crowns the portrait of the sovereign is 'already treated as a decorative element. Nothing like that at Mshattā or in palaces of the same type.'[3]

Now if we go carefully into the matter and take the monuments, one by one in chronological order, we shall see that this objection is scarcely justified. It is true that there is a fine Kufic frieze, with the date, in the Dome of the Rock, and there is an inscription over two (and probably was over all four) doors (see above, pp. 81–2), but Mas'ūdī (*Prairies*, V. pp. 192–3) says that at Damascus the dating inscription of the Great Mosque was merely 'on a marble slab in the sanctuary, near the roof and next to the minaret'. Moreover, no inscriptions of al-Walīd are to be seen in the vast surface of mosaic recently laid bare. As for Mekka, the inscriptions seen by Muqaddasī were merely the signatures of the Christian mosaicists (above, p. 233).[4] In the Mosque of 'Amr at Fusṭāṭ the date (Ramadān 92 = June/July, 711) of Qurra ibn Sharīk's rebuilding was apparently recorded on green tablets on the façade of the sanctuary. At Quṣayr 'Amra and Ḥammām aṣ-Ṣarakh the exterior in both cases is without any inscription whatever, and in the former the inscriptions are merely painted on stucco. At Qaṣr al-Ḥayr ash-Sharqī there are no inscriptions on either enclosure, although the ornament at the summits of the gateway towers of the Lesser Enclosure is quite well preserved, nor are there any over the four entrances of the Greater Enclosure; as for the mosque, its masonry is quite plain, and the dating inscription was on a slab on one of the piers (above, p. 532). The well-preserved east façade of the sanctuary of the Great Mosque at Ḥarrān (Fig. 688, facing p. 646; preserved, be it especially noted, right up to the very eaves) is absolutely plain, and the only inscription is in the tympanum of the east entrance, which apparently dates from the twelfth century. At Raqqa there is no inscription on the well-preserved Baghdād Gate (A.D. 772?), nor are there any at Ukhaiḍir in spite of its remarkable preservation. At Cordova the two oldest periods in the Great Mosque are perfectly plain. At Qairawān there is no inscription on the early part, except a line on the capitals of the columns flanking the miḥrāb; the marvellous carved pulpit made in A.D. 861 bears no inscription whatever.

The first example of a dating inscription forming one with the architecture and the decoration is provided by the Mosque of Bū Fatātā at Sūsa, built between 223 and 226 H. (838–41); see Vol. II, 1st ed. The second example is the Great Mosque at Sūsa, 236 H. (850/51). The third is the doorway built by Muḥammad ibn 'Abd ar-Raḥmān in 241 H. (855/6) and now known as Postigo de San Esteban on the west side of the Great Mosque at Cordova.

In other words, we may say that in *really early* Muslim architecture, the exteriors seem to have been almost invariably without inscriptions, except perhaps over the entrance. As for the interiors, there were sometimes inscriptions forming part of the decoration, either executed in mosaic at the summit

[1] Mschatta, *Jahrbuch der Kgl. Preuszischen Kunstsammlungen*, XXV, pp. 350–3, Abb. 116 and pl. facing p. 352.

[2] Gottwaldt's ed., p. 117.

[3] *Journal des Savants*, 1909, p. 406.

[4] These inscriptions, by the way, were in work due to al-Mahdī (A.D. 775–85) and not to al-Walīd.

of the walls or painted on the stucco. The absence of an inscription on the exterior of Mshattā need not surprise us, and it is quite without significance; had there been one it would almost certainly have been over the entrance (as in the Qubbat aṣ-Ṣakhra), but the entrance, unfortunately, was only completed to about two-thirds of its height. As for the interior, the same remark applies; had there been inscriptions they would have been executed in mosaic or painted on the stucco coating of the walls, but the interior decoration was never even begun, except for the sawing up of some blocks of beautiful green stone for the dadoes (above, p. 590). Mshattā never reached the stage at which its embellishment with inscriptions became possible.

Van Berchem raises a second objection, viz. that Mshattā cannot be Umayyad because it is fortified, and the Umayyad *limes* were in Transoxiana and beyond the Indus, whereas the Belqā was the home of the Umayyads; there they were among their own people and had no need of fortifications.[1] This may have been true under a really powerful Khalif like Walīd I, but not under the later Umayyads when dynastic rivals and opposition parties were in the field, and Qaṣr al-Ḥayr is there to prove it.

And Qaṣr al-Ḥayr answers another objection of van Berchem's, viz. How can Mshattā be Umayyad in view of the fact that the Umayyad Khalifs built Syrian monuments?[2] Qaṣr al-Ḥayr proves that they built monuments in mixed style, and this mixing, as we have seen above, begins as early as A.D. 691 in the mosaics of the Dome of the Rock, especially in those on the outer face of the octagonal arcade; this mixing was of course the result of the conscription of labour from all parts of the Umayyad empire.

Brünnow formulates an objection based on the masonry. He points out (as we have seen above, p. 627) that four building periods are to be distinguished in Transjordan. In the first and oldest of these the masonry is of carefully executed ashlar, but in the second the masonry is not quite so good; it continues to deteriorate, and it is only in the fourth period (sixth century) that it almost reaches the quality of the first period (e.g. the Cathedral of Boṣrā, A.D. 512–13).[3] He therefore places Mshattā, the masonry of which recalls that of Odhroḥ and Qasṭal, in the sixth century. But the masonry of Mshattā is really not so good as it appears to be at first sight,[4] for the blocks are not properly squared but taper slightly inwards, so that the joints are only perfect at the surface of the wall. This is exactly what we find in the two enclosures of Qaṣr al-Ḥayr, one of which is dated 110 H. (A.D. 728/9), the masonry of which is exactly the same as that of Mshattā (above, p. 526). Brünnow's objection, formulated before the discovery of Qaṣr al-Ḥayr, therefore falls to the ground.

As for Clermont-Ganneau's remarks about the Dionysiac interpretation of the façade, etc., it can scarcely be alleged that the extensive use of the vine-motif is against a Muslim attribution, in view of the dominating part played by vine-motifs in the mosaics, and on the tie-beams, of the Dome of the Rock.

HISTORICAL REASONS FOR AN UMAYYAD ATTRIBUTION. I will now give the historical reasons which are definitely in favour of an Umayyad attribution, of which Herzfeld was the principal champion for over twenty years (see above, pp. 629–30 and 631–2). In the first place it is obvious that only a powerful ruler in possession of immense resources can have contemplated the creation of a structure like Mshattā. This at once suggests an Umayyad Khalif, whereas, as Nöldeke and Littmann have pointed out, it is very doubtful whether any Ghassānid ever had the necessary means.[5]

In further favour of an Umayyad date is the known fact that the Belqā was their favourite resort (see above, pp. 403–6), and the *Kitāb al-Aghānī* expressly says that Walīd II built in this region.[6]

Another historical fact of almost decisive importance is the known practice of the Umayyads in conscripting labour from all parts of the empire, as we have seen, e.g. for the Great Mosque at Madīna (above, pp. 142–3) and for the Great Mosque at Damascus (pp. 151–2) and as was done also for the Aqṣā Mosque at Jerusalem[7] and the sanctuary at Mekka under al-Mahdī.[8] The Ghassānids were not in a position to conscript labour from 'Irāq and Egypt, yet Mshattā shows signs of craftsmen from both these regions having worked on it.

[1] *Journal des Savants*, 1909, pp. 405–8.
[2] *Ibid.*, p. 405.
[3] *Die Provincia Arabia*, II, p. 311, and in the *W.Z.K.M.*, XXI, pp. 286–9.
[4] Except that of the piers of the triple-arched façade (p. 584).
[5] See above, p. 628.
[6] Moritz, *Ausflüge*, *M.F.O.B.*, III, pp. 430–31.
[7] Bell, *Translations of the Greek Aphrodito Papyri*, *Der Islam*, II, p. 383, III, p. 137, and IV, pp. 93 and 95.
[8] Muqaddasī, p. 73, l. 4.

Finally, the unfinished state of Mshattā would be adequately explained if we agree with Musil[1] that it is the building, referred to by Severus ibn al-Muqaffaʿ, which had been begun by Walīd II, who is known to have been a great builder,[2] and from which the workmen were called off at his death (see above, p. 631). The unfinished state of Qaṣr aṭ-Ṭūba would also be explained by the same event.

Architectural Reasons for an Umayyad Attribution. In considering this question we must bear in mind that ordinary criterions of dating do not apply in Syria, on account of the extraordinary vitality of Hellenistic art there. For example, the mosaic of Tyre, which de Rossi and Longpérier thought to be of the fourth century, bears a date equivalent to A.D. 576,[3] and Dalton remarks that the paintings of Quṣayr ʿAmra were at first thought by competent observers to be some centuries earlier than they are (above, p. 407). Let us now tabulate the reasons:

Fig. 686. Hippogriff on earthenware fragment. (From *Papyrus Erzherzog Rainer. Führer durch die Austellung.*)

(1) Brick, or a mixture of brick and stone, is foreign to the classical architecture of Syria. Brick is absolutely unknown before the second half of the sixth century, the first example being the *castrum* at Andārin, A.D. 558, followed by Qaṣr Ibn Wardān (palace, church, and barracks), A.D. 561–4.

These are the only examples, but Mshattā cannot be affiliated with them for technical reasons. In Byzantine brickwork the layers of mortar between the bricks are always equal in thickness to the bricks themselves, not only at Constantinople, but in Syria, in the examples just cited, and in Euphratesia, viz. in the Praetorium of Bālis (now known as Eski Meskene), whereas in early Muslim work they are thinner. In this respect the brickwork of Mshattā and Qaṣr aṭ-Ṭūba is exactly like that of Qaṣr al-Ḥayr (both enclosures and the dam), A.D. 728/9, and the Baghdād Gate of Raqqa, A.D. 772. The actual bricks of Mshattā (21 × 21 and 28 × 28 cm.) and Qaṣr aṭ-Ṭūba (25 cm. sq.) are smaller than the Sasanian bricks of Ctesiphon (31½ cm. sq.) and Dastajird (35½–37 cm. sq.), and the Byzantine bricks of Qaṣr Ibn Wardān (30 × 34 and 34 × 37 cm.) and Bālis (42 × 50 cm.), but they closely resemble those of the early Muslim period in ʿIrāq, e.g. the Baghdād Gate of Raqqa, A.D. 772 (see Vol. II, 1st ed.), in size (24 cm. sq.), colour, and quality.

(2) There is no example of an arch, braced with a tie-beam, in the pre-Muslim architecture of Syria; this feature appears for the first time in the Dome of the Rock, A.D. 691/2.

(3) The arches of the doorways are constructed like those of Ctesiphon and not like those of Qaṣr Ibn Wardān and are the first examples of their kind in Syria; nothing of the sort is to be found in any earlier Umayyad or pre-Muslim building.

(4) Vaults of a pointed-arched section such as those of Mshattā, where the separation of the centres is one-fifth of the span (see Plate 117 *e*), cannot be earlier than the eighth century, as may be seen from the tabulated list of pointed arches given above (pp. 443–4). Arches of such outline had not been evolved before that century.

(5) The style of the Corinthian capital found in the basilical hall shows that re-used material was used, and this practice, so typical of early Muslim work, was almost unknown in Syria before Islam.

(6) The griffin with a tail like a bunch of grapes (Plate 123), although a Sasanian motif (it occurs on Sasanian textiles and silver work),[4] is not incompatible with an Umayyad date, for this motif survived and was used under early Islam, as is proved by an example on a fragment of pottery accompanied by a Kufic inscription of very early type, which has been moulded with it before baking (Fig. 686). And more recently an example of it has been found at Qaṣr al-Ḥayr al-Gharbī; see Plate 86 *e*.

(7) To all the above may now be added the new evidence provided by the hitherto neglected ornament (on the tie-beams, in the mosaics, etc.) of the Dome of the Rock.

To begin with, the decoration of the great torus of the base-moulding (Fig. 655 *b*) of Mshattā, in which a vine tendril forms circular loops, each filled, as a rule, by one bunch of grapes and one five-

[1] Musil points out that Mshattā is only ten kilometres from a supply of spring water, whereas Qaṣr aṭ-Ṭība is twenty-three kilometres (or about fifteen miles) from the wells, now useless, of Ghadīr ad-Dīb (to the east-north-east of Ṭūba); *Palmyrena*, p. 285.

[2] His successor, Yazīd III, on his accession had to promise 'to lay neither stone on stone nor brick on brick'; see above, p. 406.

[3] Jerphanion, *Le Calice d'Antioche*, p. 129. See also Herzfeld's article *Arabesque*, in the *Encyclopaedia of Islām*, I, p. 366; and Mlle van Berchem's remarks (above, p. 321).

[4] See Smirnov, *Argenterie orientale*, pls. XLII, XLV, XLIX, LXX, LXXI, and CXV.

pointed vine-leaf, cannot be matched by any pre-Muslim work,[1] but is closely matched by the bronze covering of one of the tie-beams (S 2, see Plate 27 *a*) of the Dome of the Rock.

Then we have the pine-cones frequently employed in the rosettes of Mshattā (Fig. 645). The pine-cone, which is unknown, or at least extremely rare in Syria before Islam,[2] is frequently employed on the tie-beams of the Dome of the Rock, and pine-cones, set radially, as at Mshattā, also form rosettes in the mosaics at the top of the central window of the transept of the Great Mosque at Damascus (Plate 138 *a*).

Then let us take the motifs on the capitals of Qalʿa-i-Kuhna, early seventh century (Fig. 318), compare them with somewhat similar motifs (Figs. 319 and 320) in the mosaics of the Dome of the Rock, and then compare the latter with the almost identical motifs on the lintel at Qaṣr aṭ-Ṭūba (Plate 138 *a*). What do we find? We find that the latter are infinitely nearer to those in the Dome of the Rock than those in the Dome of the Rock are to those of Qalʿa-i-Kuhna! This can only mean that those of Qaṣr aṭ-Ṭūba are Umayyad. And this same motif occurs several times in the façade of Mshattā.

And let us take the half-palmettes at Qaṣr aṭ-Ṭūba (Fig. 647) and compare them with those on tie-beam N. 3 in the Dome of the Rock (Plate 28 *c*).

Thus the new 'Grammar of Early Umayyad Ornament' provided by the Dome of the Rock, and here made available to students, confirms in a striking fashion the Umayyad attribution of Mshattā and Qaṣr aṭ-Ṭūba.

(8) In the early ʿAbbāsid palace, Ukhaiḍir, about thirty miles from Kerbelā', we have four *bayts*, arranged to right and left of the Audience Hall group of rooms, which must have been intended for the self-contained households of the four legitimate wives of the Muslim prince who built it. Surely the four *bayts* which flank the Audience Hall at Mshattā and the four *bayts* in each of the two self-contained enclosures at Qaṣr aṭ-Ṭūba can only mean that these palaces were built for Muslim princes also.

(9) But there is another indication that Mshattā is a Muslim building. Let us turn again to Ukhaiḍir; here we find an entrance vestibule recalling what that of Mshattā was evidently intended to be, and on the right of it (the side of honour) is a mosque courtyard with a miḥrāb. At Mshattā also, to the right of the entrance, is a courtyard (ψ_2 in Fig. 623) and in the centre of its south (i.e. qibla) wall is a niche, with flanking recesses to take nook-shafts, which can only be a miḥrāb. I have given a measured drawing of it (Fig. 625) from which it should be prefectly clear that it forms one with the original structure. Schulz, after remarking that the fact that this niche faces the qibla might lead one to suppose that this room must have served as a mosque, nevertheless rejects the idea, because no attachments for arcades are to be seen on the east or west walls.[3] Diez, after having at one time accepted it as a miḥrāb,[4] has more recently rejected the idea for the following reasons: (i) because it projects 65 cm. from the inner face of the wall, and (ii) because of its size (1·62 m. wide and 1·48 deep), for, as he remarks: 'the breadth of the niche would be exceptional even in a very large mosque of late date (such a depth is hardly ever found anywhere)'.[5] This wild statement is all the more remarkable in that Diez is the author of the article *Miḥrāb* in the *Encyclopaedia of Islām*, so he ought to have been better informed. Here are fifteen examples of larger miḥrābs, the measurements given (width and depth), being for the semicircular part only, behind the nook-shafts:

Minya	Palace Mosque	709–15 A.D.	1·62 × 1·12 m.
Mafjar	Palace Mosque	c. 735–40 A.D.	2·05 × 1·02 m.
,,	Second Mosque	,,	2·05 × 1·02 m.
Ḥarrān	Great Mosque	126–32 H. (744–50)	2·23 × 1·95 m.
Qairawān	Great Mosque	248 H. (862/3)	1·98 × 1·58 m.
Cairo	Mosque of al-Ḥākim	380–403 H. (990–1013)	1·96 × 1·28 m.
	Mosque of aṣ-Ṣāliḥ Ṭalā'iʿ	555 H. (1160)	1·87 × 1·38 m.
	Mosque of Baybars I	665–7 H. (1266–9)	2·50 × 1·60 m.

[1] I see no reason for believing that the example in the Great Mosque at Diyārbakr (van Berchem and Strzygowski, *Amida*, Taf. IX–XI and XIV–XV), sometimes cited in this connexion, has come from a pre-Muslim church, alleged to have stood on the same site. I prefer to believe that it came from the earlier mosque, seen and described by Nāṣir-i-Khusrau (above, pp. 185–6), which was probably built in the Umayyad period.

[2] I believe the only example known is that shown in de Vogüé's *Syrie centrale*, pl. 13, reproduced above Fig. 56, facing p. 118.

[3] *Op. cit.*, p. 212.

[4] *Die Kunst der islamischen Völker*, p. 6.

[5] *Mshattā*, in the *Encyclopaedia of Islām*, III, p. 614. I did not refer to Diez's objection in the first edition of this volume, as I thought it captious, but as a reviewer (Shapiro, in the *Art Bulletin*, XVII, pp. 109–14) called attention to my silence, I now answer the objection in full.

CAIRO	Qalā'ūn, Mausoleum of,	683–4 H. (1284/5)	1·78 × 1·28 m.
	Qalā'ūn, Madrasa of,	684 H. (1285)	1·54 × 1·30 m.
	Madrasa of an-Nāṣir Muḥammad	695–703 H. (1295–1303)	1·59 × 1·34 m.
	Baybars II, Khānqā of,	706–9 H. (1306–9)	1·52 × 1·09 m.
	Baybars II, Mausoleum of,	„ „	1·55 × 1·24 m.
	Mausoleum of the Emīr Sunqur Sa'dī	715 H. (1315)	2·72 × 1·21 m.
	Madrasa of the Emīr Aqbughā	734–40 H. (1333–9)	1·50 × 1·05 m.
	Mosque of al-Māridanī	739–40 H. (1339–40)	1·65 × 1·46 m.
	Mosque of Aqsunqur	747–8 H. (1346–7)	1·88 × 1·44 m.
	Sultan Haṣan, Madrasa of,	757–64 H. (1356–62)	1·96 × 1·26 m.
	Sultan Haṣan, Mausoleum of,	„ „	1·94 × 1·25 m.

And here are two more large miḥrābs, of which the recess is rectangular:

Sāmarrā, Great Mosque,	234–7 H. (849–52)	2·57 × 2·05 m.
Sāmarrā, Mosque of Abū Dulaf,	245–7 H. (860–61)	1·94 × 1·04 m.

The existence in the same building of four *bayts* and a courtyard with a niche in the centre of the side facing Mekka ought to be convincing.

I am therefore convinced that Mshattā and Qaṣr aṭ-Ṭūba are Umayyad buildings, begun in all probability by Walīd II in A.D. 743–4, and left unfinished at his death.

QAṢR BĀYIR[1]

QAṢR BĀYIR is one of the most distant of all the Umayyad *qaṣrs*, being about fifty miles in a straight line south-east of Qaṭrānī and about sixty-eight miles north-east of Maʿān. It is first mentioned in modern times by Lammens (as Abā'ir) in 1910;[2] he classes it as Umayyad. It was seen by Musil in 1909[3] and Gertrude Bell in 1914; both believed it to be Umayyad but neither have given us a description of it. Schroeder planned it in 1928,[4] and three excellent air photographs in my possession, made by the R.A.F. in that year, show that his plan is an accurate one. When I was in

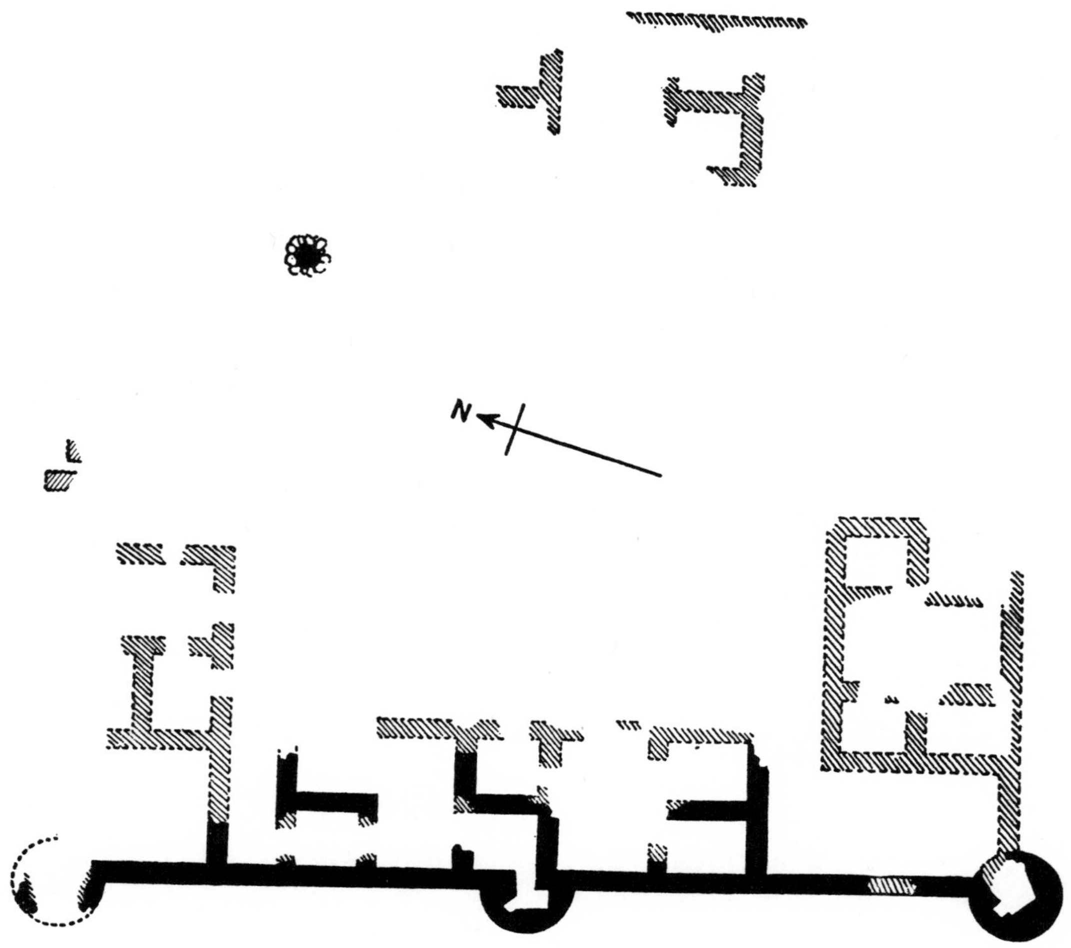

FIG. 687. QAṢR BĀYIR: Plan. (From H. Field, *North Arabian Desert Archaeological Survey.*)

ʿAmmān in May 1931 and was preparing to visit it, I learnt that Peake Pasha, only a few weeks previously, had used its masonry to build an outpost for the Arab Legion![5] In December of the following year Horsfield inspected what remained of it and produced a ridiculous plan,[6] in which he shows a half-round tower on the south side and a round tower at the east corner which my air photographs show did not exist in August 1928.

Unfortunately the underline to Schroeder's plan reads 'Scale 1 : 200', according to which it would only measure 26 m. a side internally, whereas Horsfield's plan, which does bear a scale, shows that the internal diameter must have been about 72 m., that is to say the standard size of an Umayyad *qaṣr* (above, p. 382). I take it that Schroeder's plan was drawn out to a scale of 1 : 200; it has obviously been

[1] BIBLIOGRAPHY:— 1910, Lammens (Henri), *La Bâdia et la Ḥîra sous les Omaiyades. Mélanges de la Faculté Orientale, Beyrouth*, IV, p. 109; reprinted in his *Études sur le siècle des Omayyades*, p. 345; — 1927, Hogarth (D. G.), *Gertrude Bell's Journey to Hayil, Journ. Roy. Geographical Socy.*, LXX, p. 6, with 1 illus.; and her *Letters*, I, p. 327; and Musil (A.), *Arabia Deserta*, p. 324, n. 76; — 1934, Glueck (N.), *Explorations in Eastern Palestine, Annual of the American Schools of Oriental Research*, XIV, p. 73 and pl. XXXIX (Horsfield's plan); — 1939, Sauvaget (Jean), *Remarques sur les Monuments Omeyyades, Journ. Asiatique*, CCXXXI, pp. 39–40; — 1940, Glueck (Nelson), *The other side of the Jordan*, pp. 42–3; — 1960, Field (Henry), *North Arabian Desert Archaeological Survey, 1925–50*, pp. 99–101 and figs. 29, 29*a*, and 54–5.

[2] *Bâdia*, *loc. cit.* IV, p. 106.

[3] *Loc. cit.*

[4] In Field, *op. cit.*, pp. 99–100 and fig. 29.

[5] For a photograph of it see *American Journal of Archaeology*, XXXVII, pl. XXXIX$_3$.

[6] In Glueck, *Explorations*, *loc. cit.*, pp. 72–3 and pl. 19.

reduced by the printer so as to exactly fit the width of the letterpress, and that the scale 1 : 200, presumably written on the drawing, has been stupidly repeated in the underline of the reduced reproduction.

Here is Schroeder's account:

'A short description suffices for the existing ruins of Bayir. They stand on a gravel bank above the 'bed of the wadi, and consist of a wall with round towers at either extremity, with a round [tower] of 'like circumference in the center. The remains of a few chambers abutting on the wall exist to a height 'of 4 or 5 courses, and the lower courses of some other walls are barely recognizable elsewhere. The 'whole is nearly 70·0 m. in length.

'A single course, itself broken, connects the southern corner tower on the east with the foundations 'of a chamber complex. In the thickness of the tower was built an irregular 4-sided chamber, appar-'ently a latrine, of which two obtuse-angle corners remain, near the most westerly of which is a small 'recess in the tower wall, of rectangular plan. The threshold of this chamber remains, but both jambs 'are broken. Both chambers and recess are at varying irregular angles with the plan.

'Halfway between the above and the semicircular [?] room in the center, a partition joins the outer 'wall, which together with neighbouring walls and foundations formed a group of 3 rooms looking on 'a small open court, a "bayt" or suite, therefore, of the same type as those in Meshetta (Mshatta).

'The central semicircular room contains a small rectangular latrine chamber in alignment with the 'general plan of the ruins, with a similar recess to the one described above let into the right-hand corner 'at an irregular angle. The doorway to this recess leads from a room which again is part of a third 'chamber-complex, with either 2 or 3 rooms opening onto a court, and a room or wide corridor along 'its northern side. The northern corner tower exists only in fragments, and a few foundations can be 'made out to the east of it.

'At 55 m. east of the existing wall a few scraps of foundation remain; these probably mark the 'eastern wall of the building. The entire area here is littered with large blocks of the same sandstone 'as the ruins, and some have been gathered into graves for chieftains of the Huwaitat tribe.' [This suggests that Qaṣr Bāyir was once much more complete, nevertheless it is probable that, like Mshattā and Qaṣr aṭ-Ṭūba it was never finished on account of the murder of Walīd II after he had reigned less than 14 months.] 'One of the wells now in use is dug within the bounds of the building's original plan, and another lies 30 paces north of it.'[1]

THE DATE. The only archaeologists to have seen Qaṣr Bāyir before its destruction in 1931, viz. Musil, Gertrude Bell, and Schroeder,[2] classed it as Umayyad. The latrines, which are identical to those of Mshattā, and the *bayts* of which the one to the east of the south tower is identical to those of Mshattā, and the pair in the centre of the south side, which resemble it except that each appears to have lost a room, all these elements, which were still recognizable in 1928, justify us in grouping it with Mshattā, that is to say, in attributing it to Walīd II (743–4) as Musil had already done.

1 In Field, *loc. cit.*, pp. 99–100.
2 He does not say so in so many words, but we have seen above that he compares its *bayts* to those of Mshattā.

XXIV

THE GREAT MOSQUE AT ḤARRĀN[1]

Description — The sanctuary — The excavations — The date — Architectural Origins
THE GREAT MOSQUE OF DER'A

DESCRIPTION. The Great Mosque at Ḥarrān is a rectangle about 100 m. square (Fig. 688), built of fine ashlar in courses averaging 37 cm. in height. The best-preserved part is the east wall (Plate 139 *a–b* and Fig. 688, facing p. 646) of which the southern half is nearly intact, except for a gap of about 6 m. in the middle.[2] The last 9·42 m. are deflected 60 cm. to the west. There is an imposing entrance, 2·85 m. wide, immediately to the north of the façade of the sanctuary, as at Damascus. It is spanned by a fine lintel of a light buff stone, above which is a pointed horse-shoe relieving arch with a cusped inner border. The tympanum which it frames is filled with nine courses of masonry, of which the upper seven are occupied by a Naskhī inscription. Farther to the south is a small door only 1·01 m. wide, opening into the second aisle of the sanctuary.[3]

The eastern part of the south wall is preserved to a height of nearly 4 m.; its top now corresponds to the ground level at this point. At 6·17 m. from the south-east corner is the lower part of a window, 83 cm. wide and slightly splayed inwards. This is the only splayed window to be seen, with the possible exception of the two to the north of the east entrance, which I omitted to examine. The west wall has almost disappeared and what remains is covered by débris, the outer ground level on this side now being higher than the floor of the mosque. But I believe that there was an entrance on this side,[4] corresponding to the great eastern entrance, for a pair of parallel walls, about 2·75 m. apart, can still be traced outside the limit of the mosque and leading up to it at this point.

The west half of the north wall has almost gone, but several courses of the other half are still visible, likewise the opening of the northern entrance, which is approximately in the centre.

On this side rises the tall, square shaft of the minaret, its east side being 19·75 m. from the inner north-east corner. It averages 5·30 m. a side externally and 3·83 internally. According to Preusser's drawing it must have been 26 m. in height, but the last 8 m. are of brick. The masonry is perfectly plain except for a cyma reversa moulding at a height of 16 m., and a number of small slits on each side, measuring about 50 × 15 cm., for light (Plate 140 *a*). The staircase begins on the side opposite the entrance, the first flight, which is 80 cm. wide, resting on an arch with a stepped extrados. Beyond this first flight nothing remains except a number of splay-faced corbels, 77 cm. wide, set at alternate levels, thirteen on the north, and fourteen on the south, wall.

In the north-east corner of the ṣaḥn is what looks like the remains of an angle pier, 7·42 m. and 9·10 m. distant from the north and east walls respectively. The presence of a great column of pink stone at F indicates that the east riwāq must have been two aisles deep. In the ṣaḥn, immediately to the east of the main axis, is an octagonal basin, measuring 6·10 m. over all.

[1] BIBLIOGRAPHY:— 1184, Ibn Jubayr, Wright's ed., pp. 247–8; de Goeje's ed., p. 246, ll. 8–21; Schiaparelli's transl., pp. 236–7; Broadhurst's transl., p. 256; — *d.* 1285, Ibn Shaddād, *al-A'lāq al-Khaṭīra*, Bodleian MS. (Marsh 333), fol. 20*a*; passage translated by D. S. Rice in *Bull. Sch. Oriental Studies*, XVII, p. 447; — 1358, Mufaḍḍal ibn Abi'l-Faḍā'il, Blochet's ed., *Patrologia Orientalis*, XII, p. 548; — 1851, Walpole (F.), *The Ansayrii*, I, pp. 309–10; — 1852, Badger (G. P.), *The Nestorians and their Ritual*, I, pp. 341–2; — 1883, Sachau (E.), *Reise in Syrien und Mesopotamien*, pp. 220–21, with figure; — 1910, Strzygowski (J.), in van Berchem and Strzygowski, *Amida*, pp. 321–3, 330–31, and 332–3, and Abb. 269–70, 277, and 281; — 1911, Preusser (C.), *Nordmesopotamische Baudenkmäler*, pp. 59–62, Abb. 19–22, and Taf. 73–6; and Herzfeld, in the *Orientalistische Literaturzeitung*, 1911, cols. 421–3; — 1914, Bell (Gertrude L.), *Palace and Mosque at Ukhaiḍir*, pp. 152–3 and 158; — 1922, Wiet (G.), *Les Inscriptions de Saladin*, in *Syria*, III, pp. 308–9; — 1947, Sauvaget (J.), *La Mosquée Omeyyade de Médine*, pp. 97–100 and fig. 6; — 1951, Lloyd (Seton), and William Brice, *Harran*, in *Anatolian Studies*, I, pp. 78–9 and pl. X_1; — 1952, Rice (D. S.), *Medieval Harran: Studies on its Topography and Monuments. I. Anatolian Studies*, II, pp. 36–84, with 8 plates and 19 figs.; — 1953, Lloyd (Seton), *Seeking the Temple of Sin, Moon-God of Harran, The Illustrated London News*, CCXXII, 21st Feb., pp. 288–9, and figs. 3, 11, 12, and 14; — 1957, Rice (D. S.), *From Sin to Saladin: Excavations in Harran's Great Mosque, The Illustrated London News*, CCXXXI, 21st Sept., pp. 466–9, with 16 illus.

[2] Walpole (*op. cit.*, I, p. 310) describes the 'whole of the north-east wall', by which he clearly means this wall, as standing.

[3] As regards the other door on this side, shown by Preusser (*op. cit.*, Taf. 73), I do not remember seeing any trace of it either in 1919 or 1930.

[4] Walpole (*op. cit.*, I, p. 310) describes the east entrance, and then mentions 'the ruins of two others ornamented with richness and tolerable skilfulness of execution'.

Preusser says that the outer octagonal border of this basin bears clear marks of the bases of columns,[1] and that several fragments of shafts, 40 cm. in diameter, which doubtless served to support a dome, are lying near. This is fully confirmed by Ibn Jubayr who, speaking of the Great Mosque, says: 'It is of 'great beauty and provided with a large ṣaḥn in which are three lofty domes (*qubba*) on columns of 'marble; under each is a well of good water, and in the ṣaḥn there is also a fourth dome of large size 'supported by ten columns of marble, each nine spans in circumference; in the centre of it is a massive 'marble column fifteen spans in circumference. This dome (*qubba*) was built by the *Rūm*; the upper 'part of it is hollowed out in the form of a lofty tower. They say that it served as a depôt for military 'equipment.'[2] The remark that it served as a depôt proves that it was not merely a dome on an open circle of columns, but a domed chamber on columns, a treasury (*Bayt al-Māl*) in fact, like that at Damascus (above, pp. 179-80 and Plate 45 *b*). A good deal of the stone paving of the ṣaḥn is visible in the immediate neighbourhood of this basin.

THE SANCTUARY. It is clear from an examination of the inner face of the east wall (Plate 139 *c*) that the sanctuary consisted of four aisles, 8·17, 7·59, 9·15, and 9·18 m. wide respectively, going from north to south, but all that now remains are a number of piers and two columns still standing, and dozens of columns lying on the ground. In most cases the stumps of the piers, which were very broad, are incomplete, one side having fallen away. The only arch still standing is the great central arch of the arcade next the ṣaḥn, which Ibn Jubayr compares to the gate of some large city.

This arcade can be reconstructed thanks to the key given to us by his description. He says: 'This 'blessed mosque is roofed with wooden beams and arches. Its beams are massive and long on account 'of the width of the aisles, which is fifteen paces, and it has five aisles [this must be an error, see Plate '139 *c*]. Nowhere have I seen a mosque with arches of greater span. The wall of the mosque next the 'ṣaḥn, through which entry is made into the mosque itself, is pierced with doorways. Their number is 'nineteen, nine right and nine left, and the nineteenth is a lofty door in the middle of these, of which the 'arch occupies the whole height of the façade, of very beautiful aspect, and well executed, like the gate 'of some large city. All these openings are closed with wooden doors of fine workmanship, covered 'with carved ornament which makes them resemble the doors of the audience hall of a palace. We have 'been astonished at the quality of the workmanship of this mosque.'[3]

Its ruin dates from the following century, for Mufaḍḍal ibn Abi'l-Faḍā'il tells us that 'on the 15th 'Ramaḍān 670 (15th April 1271) a body of Tatars arrived at Ḥarrān; they destroyed its enclosure wall, 'and sacked most of the bazaars and houses; they destroyed its Great Mosque, and took away its timber; 'then they captured all the men who had remained in the city. It was thus completely depopulated and 'has remained in ruins until the present day.'[4]

Let us now try to reconstruct the façade. The great central arch is of a pointed form and the voussoirs are cut so as to give it a stepped extrados. It rests on two great piers (B and C) 8·32 m. apart, and to the west of it is a smaller pier D; attached to the upper part of the latter is a capital, somewhat like a Corinthian one, decorated with arabesque, but the attached column belonging to it is lying on the ground. It is 3·15 m. in length and about 50 cm. in diameter. The rear face of this pier is in exact alignment with the rear face of the great arch, and also with the south face of the wall which runs forward next the east entrance. To the west of D is the stump of a column (E) of pink limestone clearly *in situ*. From the west side of D to the centre of this column measures 7·32 m., which gives 8·02 m. as the distance from centre to centre. The rear face of this column is in a line with the front face of D, so it doubtless belonged to a similar pier which has disappeared. It is obvious, however, that there must have been another such support between it and D, for the interval is more than twice what it should be. The columns are 8·02 m. from centre to centre; this gives 8·02 − 1·40 = 6·62 m. as the space between the piers. If we insert another pier of 1·40 m., this gives two intervals of 2·61 m., which is just what we require. If we mark off the piers accordingly (see plan, Fig. 688) we find that there is just room for

[1] *Op. cit.*, p. 61; see Abb. 21 for a detail drawing of this basin. Walpole (*op. cit.*, I, p. 310) says: 'In the centre of the court is a large handsome fountain in perfect preservation' which might be taken to mean that the dome was still standing about 1848, but strictly speaking it may only refer to the basin.

[2] De Goeje's ed., p. 246, ll. 9–14; Schiaparelli's transl., p. 236.

[3] De Goeje's ed., p. 246, ll. 14–21.

[4] Blochet's ed., *Patrologia Orientalis*, XII, p. 548. Maqrīzī says that Baybars, on 4 Rabīʿ II, 670 (9th Nov. 1271) sent troops from Aleppo, who massacred these Tatars; *Sūlūk*, Ziāda's ed., I, p. 600, l. 14; Quatremères transl., *Sultans Mamlouks*, p. 101.

nine arches between the great arch, and the junction with the west *riwāq*, supposing it to have been of the same width as the east *riwāq* appears to have been, judging from the remains in the north-eastern corner.

If we now repeat this process on the east side of the great arch, we find that it works well until we arrive at A, after which the arches must have been narrower, owing to want of space, always assuming that my measurements here are accurate.

These eighteen flanking openings were each spanned by two arches, one resting on the piers and a larger one springing from the columns; the latter must have formed a frame to the former. The latter were of a horse-shoe form,[1] for the return of the first to the west of the great arch still exists, recessed in the side of C. The same thing may be observed on the east side of B, and in both cases it may clearly be seen that the pier arch has a slight return also.

I have attempted to plan the interior of the sanctuary, but it is impossible to suggest a reconstruction, for the irregularities are so curious and so inexplicable. For example, the supports of the various arcades do not appear to have corresponded with each other, nor do there appear to have been the same number of columns between the various piers. In addition to this, the axis of the miḥrāb in the south wall is some 5 m. to the west of the axis of the central arch of the southernmost arcade.

Nor was the central aisle wider than the rest; although the central arch of the ṣaḥn has a span of 8·32 m. the one behind it can only have been about 6 m. wide, and the central arch of the back row had a span of 3·30 m. only.[2] The back row was of very massive construction, as may be seen from the springing of the arch shown in Plate 130 *e*, where the great depth of the voussoirs can be seen. Here again they are cut so as to give a stepped extrados. The main axis was slightly askew.[3] Only excavation can settle the true plan of the sanctuary.[4]

THE EXCAVATIONS. Consequently I was delighted when an Expedition headed by the late D. S. Rice started excavations, and I hoped that many curious features would be explained. The expedition did actually excavate the Great Mosque and thanks to Dr. Fehérvéri I am able to publish its plan but, owing to the tragic death of Dr. Rice, we still await a full report.

Two new entrances were discovered, one on the east side, the other on the west but slightly farther north. The east *riwāq* was two aisles deep, the outer on piers, the inner on columns; the northern and western were of one aisle only on piers.

It was found that the rectangle, roughly 100 m. square, occupied by the mosque was encroached upon on its west side, northern half, as shown. This perhaps is the reason why the west *riwāq* is only one aisle deep.

As regards the sanctuary it presents nothing but problems. For example, there are 28 supports (columns and piers) in the back row, 33 in the next, and then 23, consequently the supports in one row do not correspond with the supports of the other rows.

In the centre of the back row was an arch on massive piers, of which one still stands (Plate 139 *e*). Then going west we have 2 col., 1 pier, 2 cols., and then the base of an arch on massive piers like the central one. To the east we have 2 cols., 1 pier, 2 cols. then the massive pier of an arch, then 2 cols., and 3 piers. The second and third rows are much more uniform.

It will be noticed that the excavators' plan does not provide sufficient space for the nine arches mentioned by Ibn Jubayr to right and left of the great central arch.[5]

[1] Probably of a pointed horse-shoe form like the arch of the east entrance.

[2] The west pier of this arch, seen by me in 1919, had gone when I revisited Ḥarrān in 1930.

[3] The axis of the central arch on the ṣaḥn is 49·66 m. from the inner face of the east wall, whereas the axis of the central bay of the south arcade is 50·40 m. from the same wall face: difference 76 cm.

[4] It is very much to be hoped that this interesting task will be undertaken in the near future. There is the necessary labour on the spot, for in the old enclosure of the town is a village of bee-hive huts inhabited by Arabs of the Jemayl tribe with their Sheykh ʿĪsā. The excavators would not need tents, for, with camp-beds, they would be very comfortable in the vacant bee-hive guest-hut, where I passed four days in 1919.

[5] I was very glad to get this new plan, showing parts of the mosque that were not visible before, although it differs seriously from mine in a number of places. These differences can only be checked on the spot, except one—the depth of the back aisle of the sanctuary—which according to my plan is 8·17 m. but which, when scaled off the excavators' plan, comes to 10·30. In this case, fortunately, my plan can be checked. The sum of the width of the four aisles of the sanctuary, the walls between them, and the left door jamb agrees, within a few centimetres, with the distance (40·55), on my elevation, from the south-east corner of the mosque to the same door jamb.

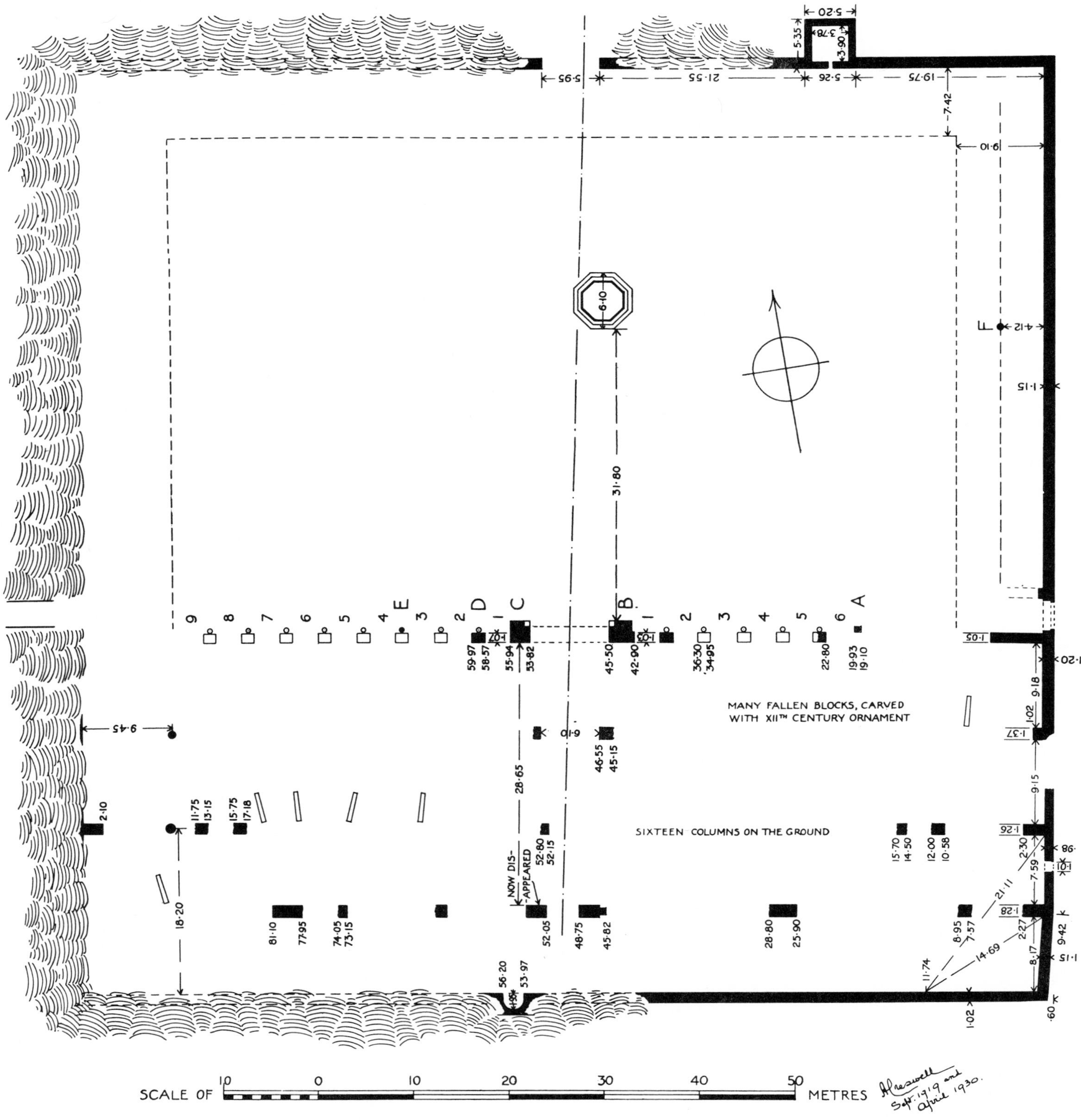

FIG. 688. HARRAN: Great Mosque, author's and excavator's plans, (left and right, above) and elevation of east side, (below). Measured by K. A. C. Creswell and drawn by M. Lyon

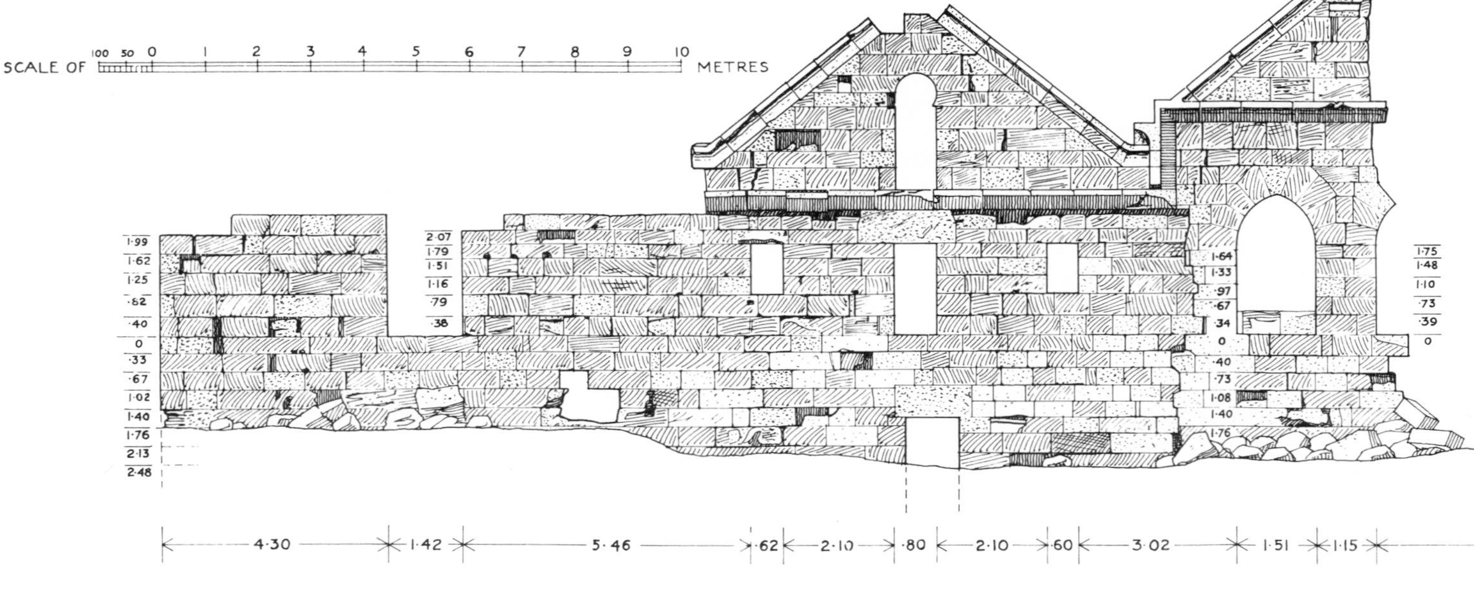

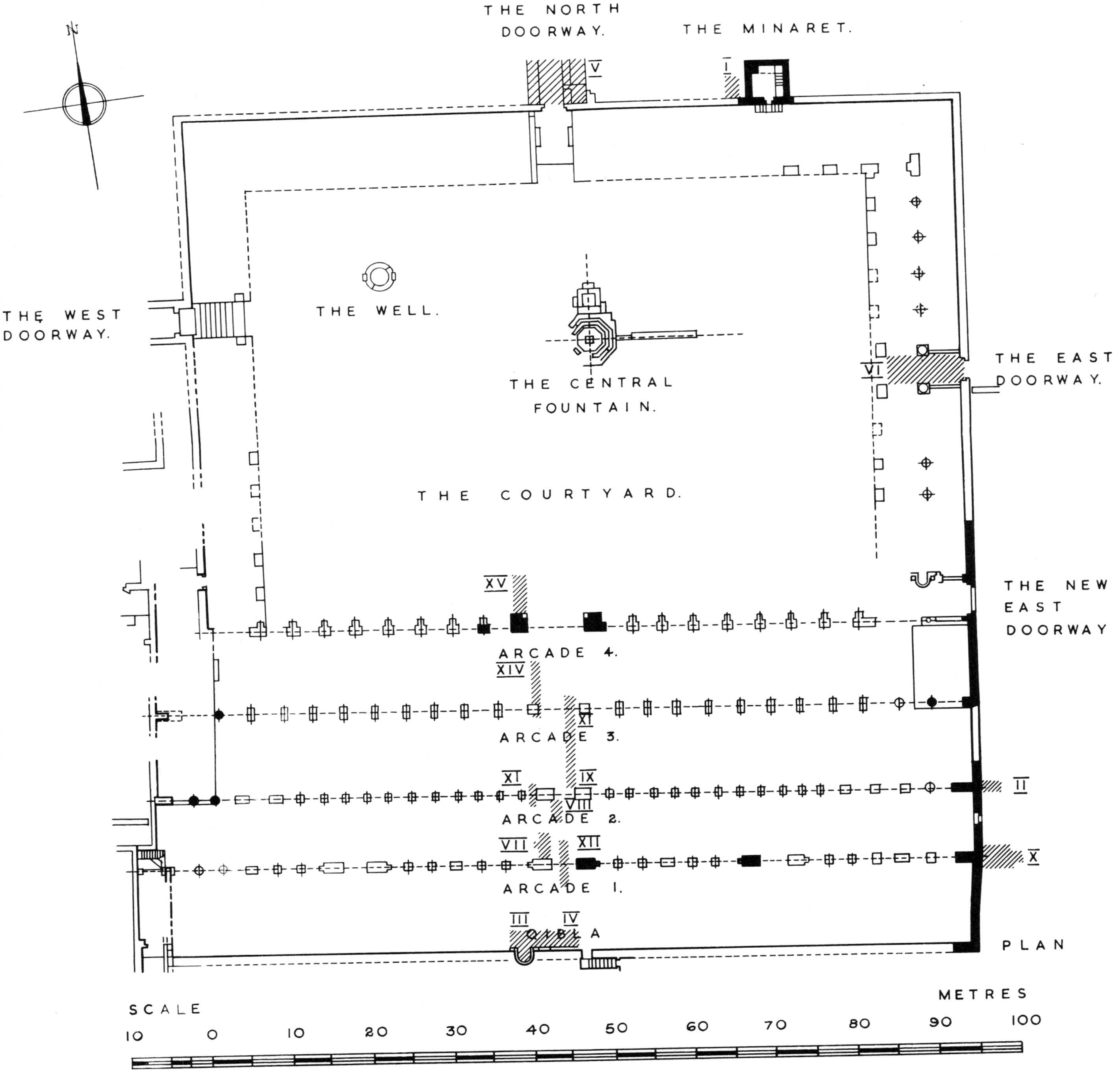
N
THE NORTH DOORWAY.
THE MINARET.
I
V
THE WEST DOORWAY.
THE WELL.
THE CENTRAL FOUNTAIN.
THE EAST DOORWAY.
VI
THE COURTYARD.
THE NEW EAST DOORWAY
XV
ARCADE 4.
XIV
XI
ARCADE 3.
XI
IX
II
VIII
ARCADE 2.
VII
XII
X
ARCADE 1.
III
IV
QIBLA
PLAN
SCALE
METRES
10 0 10 20 30 40 50 60 70 80 90 100

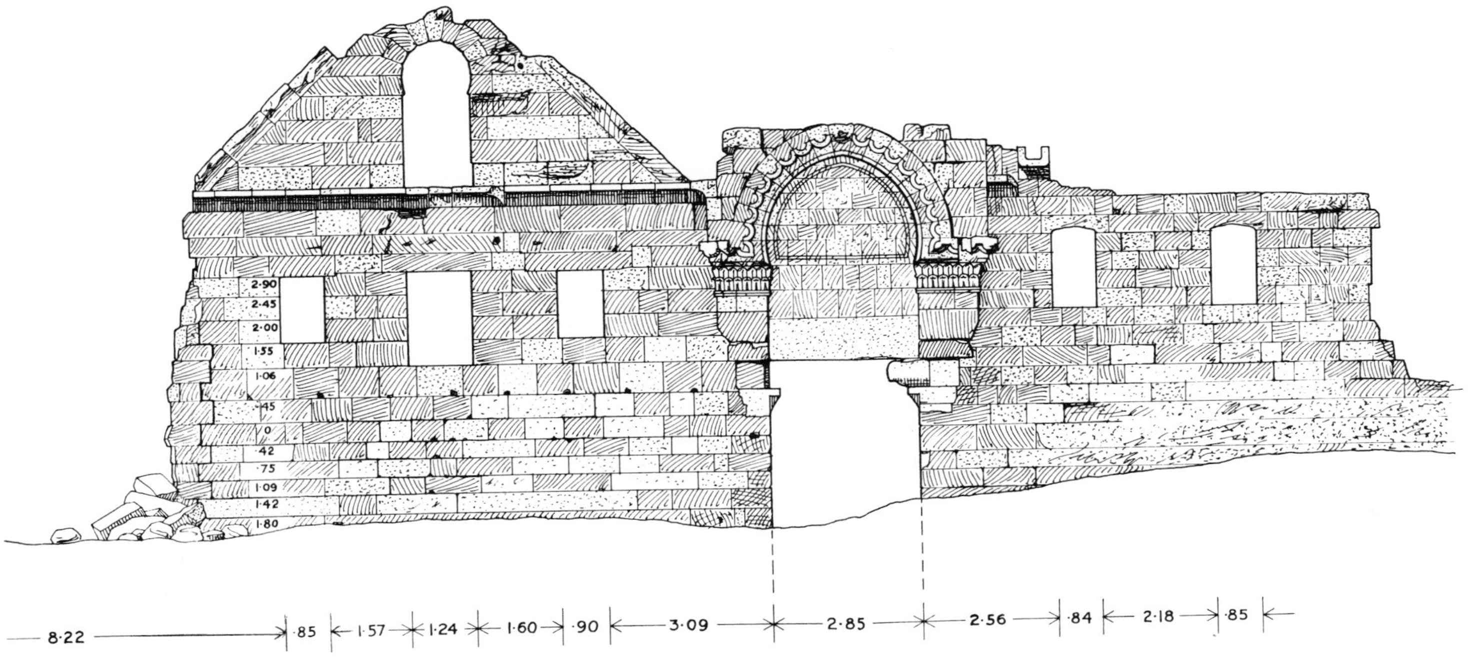
2·90
2·45
2·00
1·55
1·06
·45
0
·42
·75
1·09
1·42
1·80
8·22
·85
1·57
1·24
1·60
·90
3·09
2·85
2·56
·84
2·18
·85

THE DATE. An examination of the east façade makes one thing perfectly clear; we have to do with at least two periods, for there is a complete break in bond between the second and third bays (Fig. 688 and Plate 139 *a–b*), and the height of the ceiling level to the right of the break is 1·70 m. more than it is to the left. There appears to be a second break between the third and fourth bays, but on examination this turns out to be without significance; what appears to be a break is merely due to a settlement of the masonry, for all the courses correspond up to the lower window level, above which there is one irregularity. Moreover, the six lowest courses correspond, within a centimetre or two, to those on the left of the gap.

But here is a peculiarity: the third bay has sharply pointed window arches, whereas the fourth bay, which is equal to it in height, appears to be an enlarged copy of No. 2, for the three lower windows are rectangular and the window in the gable has a horse-shoe arch.

If we examine the inner face of this wall we have further confirmation that the two halves are of different date, for the first two wall piers from the south are plain, whereas that dividing the third aisle from the fourth has an elaborate Corinthian capital (Plate 139 *d*). Secondly, the arches which once formed the façade of the sanctuary are lying, in two cases exactly as they fell, face forward on the ground. In some cases, however, the stones are on their sides, and the ornament is such that it cannot be earlier than the twelfth century. In the aisle next the ṣaḥn there are many blocks with parts of an inscription in large Naskhī characters, surmounted by a guilloche border, which can scarcely be earlier than the twelfth century, for only one Naskhī inscription is known before A. D. 1100.[1]

Then again the double row of curious turned-over leaves with a stiff central rib, on the cornice of the pier to the west of the great central arch (which is repeated on the side of the piers of the latter and which is also used for the capitals of the door-posts of the east entrance, Plate 139 *b*) is absolutely identical to those on the door-posts of the west gate of the town (the Bāb Ḥalab) which is dated 588 H. (1192).[2]

Finally, Sachau in 1879 saw an inscription, on the wall above the two windows to the right of the east entrance,[3] in the name of Ṣalāḥ ad-Dīn (A. D. 1171–93).[4] Ṣalāḥ ad-Dīn was at Ḥarrān for about three months at the beginning of 1183.[5] He was also there for short periods in 1185 and 1186,[6] but as the work was seen by Ibn Jubayr in 1184 one must conclude that Ṣalāḥ ad-Dīn probably ordered it during his visit in 1183.

I therefore fully agree with Herzfeld's verdict that we have here an Umayyad mosque, partly rebuilt by Ṣalāḥ ad-Dīn,[7] but I would go further and point out that we have to do with three periods, for the following reason. We have seen that the northern half of the east wall of the sanctuary is of a later date than that to the south of it, yet it can scarcely belong to the time of Ṣalāḥ ad-Dīn, for the pier with the Corinthian capital (Plate 139 *d*) is completely bonded into it, and all its courses correspond to those of the wall. We are therefore in the presence of work of three periods.

Ḥarrān was famous as the city of the Sābians, and its inhabitants were regarded as pagans by the early Muslims. I very much doubt if Walīd I, or any other Khalif before Marwān II, ever thought of building a mosque there. But the latter, who was the last Umayyad Khalif (A. D. 744–50) made Ḥarrān his capital,[8] and the need for a congregational mosque must then have made itself felt. I therefore attribute the oldest part to him. The second, on account of the Corinthian pier capital, cannot be very much later; to whom can we attribute it? It is well known that the Khalif al-Ma'mūn, when he passed through Ḥarrān in A. D. 830 on his expedition against the Byzantine Emperor, was irritated by the

[1] On the minaret of the Great Mosque at Aleppo, begun by the Qāḍī Abu'l-Ḥasan ibn Khashshāb in 482 H. (1089/90) and finished in 487–8 H. (1094–5); Abu'l-Fidā, III, p. 268; Herzfeld in *Encyc. of Islām*, II, pp. 235–6; and his *Mshattâ, Ḥîra und Bâdiya*, in the *Jahrb. der Preusz. Kunstsammlungen*, XLII, p. 141; and the *C.I.A.*, *Syrie du Nord*, *Inscriptions et Monuments d'Alep*, pp. 151–64 and pls. LIV and LXI–LXIII.

[2] Van Berchem, *Inschriften aus Syrien, Mesopotamien und Kleinasien*, pp. 57–8.

[3] This part of the wall has disappeared since Sachau's day; see Plate 139 *b*.

[4] Sachau, *op. cit.*, p. 221. I should add, however, that a certain reserve is necessary here, for Wiet has shown (*Syria*, III, pp. 307–28) that in all the known inscriptions of Ṣalāḥ ad-Dīn, with one exception which is suspect, he never calls himself *al-Malik as-Sulṭān al-Malik an-Nāṣir* as here. Unfortunately, he has not been able to read more than a few words of the long inscription over the east entrance, of which I showed him two photographs, as the surface of the stone is in such a bad state. Sachau apparently experienced the same difficulty, for he mentions this inscription but does not give the complete text of it.

[5] Maqrīzī, *Sulūk*, VIII, 556; Blochet's transl., *R.O.L.*, VIII, 550.

[6] *Ibid.*, IX, 15 and 17 transl., pp. 165 and 166–9.

[7] *Orientalistische Literature-Zeiting*, 1911, col. 422.

[8] Abu'l-Fidā', *Ta'rīkh*, Reiske's ed., I, pp. 463 and 488.

long hair and outlandish costumes of its inhabitants, and offered them the choice between Islam, the adoption of one of the tolerated religions, and extermination.[1] Many became Christians, and many Muslims, which would well explain the enlargement of the mosque. As for the third period, that is to say the east entrance and the façade on the ṣaḥn, it must be due to Ṣalāḥ ad-Dīn between A. D. 1171 and 1193. But we can fix it still more closely and say between A. D. 1171 and 1184, for Ibn Jubayr's description of the mosque, which he saw in that year, clearly corresponds to the present structure (e.g. he expressly mentions the great central arch of the façade of the sanctuary flanked by nine smaller ones to right and left).

ARCHITECTURAL ORIGINS. Like all Umayyad monuments the Great Mosque at Ḥarrān exhibits a mixture of influences; its masonry is North Mesopotamian, which forms one with that of Northern Syria, as we have seen above (pp. 25–6), its arches with the stepped extrados continue the tradition of pre-Muslim Syria, but its square plan is derived from Mesopotamia. As for the façade on the ṣaḥn, with columns attached to the front faces of the piers, it at once recalls the work of the Īnālides in the Great Mosque of Diyārbakr between 510 and 559 H. (1116 and 1164).[2]

[1] an-Nadīm al-Baghdādī (A. D. 988), *al-Fihrist*, text and transl. in Chwolsohn, *Die Ssabier und der Ssabismus*, II, pp. 14–17; see also I, pp. 140–42.

[2] See van Berchem and Strzygowski, *Amida*, pp. 52–3 and pls. IX–XI and XII–XV.

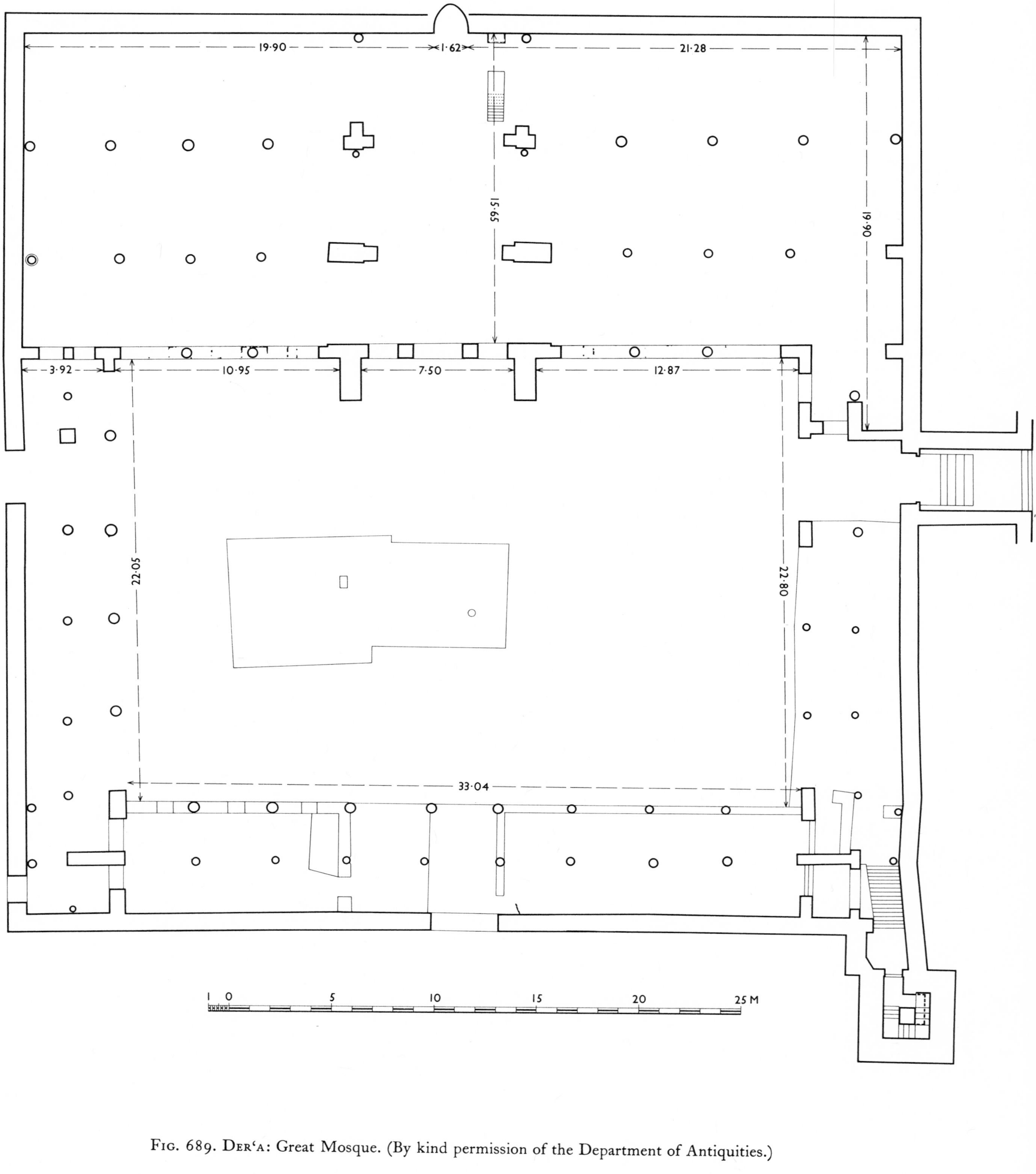

Fig. 689. Der'a: Great Mosque. (By kind permission of the Department of Antiquities.)

THE GREAT MOSQUE OF DER'A[1]

I PLACE THIS MOSQUE here under reserve, for although it is built in Umayyad style, the crude execution and the material employed—re-used black basalt—make a hideous impression. Moreover, the very pointed arch at the north end of the transept and the two pointed arches which cross it, in my opinion can scarcely be Umayyad.

The mosque is nearly square, measuring 42·20 m. internally from east to west and 44·17 from north to south. There are three axial entrances,[2] plus one in the north-east corner.

The ṣaḥn measures 33·36 m. wide and 22·05 deep; it is surrounded by *riwāqs*, of which the east and west open on to it by five arches and the northern by nine. These *riwāqs* all have an outer and inner row of stumpy columns supporting a flat stone roof. On the south side there are three arches to right and left of the transept (Plate 140 *b*). As for the north end of the latter, it has a high arched opening in the centre, very pointed, and two low openings to right and left with segmental arches. Between these and the rest of the façade are two massive rectangular buttresses which take the thrust of the transept.

The sanctuary is 42·20 m. long and 15·87 deep. It consists of three aisles running from east and west, which are cut through their centre by a transept 6·30 m. wide, leaving four arches in each half (Plate 140 *c–e*). These arcades rest on stumpy columns less than 2 m. high, but the arcades of the transept rest on piers, the northern pair being quite different from the southern. Two high and boldly pointed arches cross this transept (Plate 140 *c*). There are two windows to right and left in each bay of the transept, and one high up above the miḥrāb. In addition to this there are four windows in each half of the back wall[3] and one at each end of the three aisles of the sanctuary, making 27 in all. The miḥrāb has a semicircular frontal arch with a semi-dome behind it.

The roofing system is typical of the Haurān, a corbel course being set above the arcades so as to reduce the space between them; flat stone slabs were then laid across, exactly as at Boṣrā (above, pp. 486-7). However, the distance must have proved too great for, at some unknown date, three supporting arcades were built between the original ones, thus reducing the space to be spanned to half. These arcades existed when I first saw the mosque towards the end of 1919, but they were removed by Écochard when he restored the mosque in 1935, and replaced by a reinforced concrete roof over the aisles and the transept.

At the north-west corner of the mosque, standing almost free, is a square minaret measuring 2·40 m. a side, of which the first storey has a fine classical moulding. The lower part of this minaret may be really old.

The only inscription in this mosque is on a slab in the façade of the east *riwāq* (Plate 140 *b*). It records 'the restoration of this *riwāq* in 651 H.' (1253).[4]

[1] BIBLIOGRAPHY:—1947, Sauvaget (Jean), *La Mosquée Omeyyade de Médine*, pp. 107–8;—1965, Wiet (G.), *Deux inscriptions arabes de la Syrie méridionale*, in *Syria*, XLII, pp. 87–90, with 1 illus.

[2] The northern is not quite in the exact centre, but a little to the west of it.

[3] The ground behind the back wall has risen to within three courses of these window sills.

[4] Wiet, *loc. cit.*, pp. 88–90.

GENERAL CONCLUSIONS CONCERNING UMAYYAD ARCHITECTURE

WE HAVE SEEN (above, p. 64) that the Arabs, for two generations, remained so untouched by any architectural ambitions that they showed not the slightest desire to make use of the developed architectural talent of the conquered peoples. In Syria, at first they used divided or converted churches as mosques, and in 'Irāq, where they founded new cities on bare ground, the first mosques were primitive in the extreme. When they did begin to feel such ambitions it was chiefly for political reasons, and to the desire of 'Abd al-Malik and al-Walīd to show that Muslim civilization was capable of as much splendour as Christian civilization; hence the Dome of the Rock, etc. At first they turned to the conquered people for craftsmen, e.g. Ziyād ibn Abīhī, when about to rebuild the Great Mosque at Kūfa, employed a man who had been an architect of the Persian kings (above, p. 46), Ibn az-Zubayr employed Persian masons when rebuilding the Ka'ba in 684, and al-Walīd employed Copts from Egypt and Greeks from Syria when rebuilding the Mosque of Madīna in 707–9, the Aqṣā Mosque at Jerusalem and also for his mosque at Damascus. He also employed imported quarry-men for 'Anjar.

When we survey the architecture of this period we find that all the surviving monuments (with one exception) are in Syria, which is not surprising, for Syria was the seat of the dynasty.

Most of them are really splendid structures of cut stone (some of ashlar in courses 90 cm. high) with arcades resting on marble columns and splendidly decorated internally, but none had monumental entrances. Except in the Ḥaurān, the mosques are nearly always covered with a gable roof (*jamalūn*) of timber, for the enormous timber resources of the Lebanon (the great timber reserve of the ancient world) had not yet been exhausted. The minarets, of which the oldest is at Boṣrā, were tall square towers, derived from the church towers of pre-Muslim Syria, and the triple-aisled sanctuaries were due to the same influence. And these splendid structures were not limited to those described here; others which have disappeared, e.g. the first Great Mosque at Ramla and the first Great Mosque at Aleppo, appear to have been as splendid as that of Damascus.

Although the influence of the Christian architecture of pre-Muslim Syria dominated, as might be expected, another influence is apparent even in the earliest monument—the Dome of the Rock—where late Sasanian motifs appear in the mosaic decoration, alongside well-known classical forms. This was due to a remarkable factor, the conscription of labour on a large scale, by the all-powerful Khalifs, from all parts of the Muslim Empire. For this reason all existing Umayyad monuments exhibit a mixture of influences, Syria occupying the first place and Persia the second, and Coptic influence is definitely demonstrable towards the end of this period (Mshattā).

But there was another new factor also—the half-Bedawīn instincts of all the Umayyad Khalifs (except Mu'āwiya) and their love of the desert life—which led to the erection of a number of desert residences, such as Quṣayr 'Amra, Qaṣr al-Ḥayr al-Gharbī, Qaṣr al-Ḥayr ash-Sharqī, Mshattā, and Qaṣr aṭ-Ṭūba. In constructing these residences, which were generally about 70 m. square, or multiples of that dimension, the fortresses of the great block-house line that ran from the Gulf of 'Aqaba to Damascus and from Damascus to Palmyra, were taken for models as far as their outer fortified enclosure walls were concerned, but the interior was divided up differently into *bayts*. These *bayts*, usually of five rooms each, were arranged round the interior of the enclosure so that a court was left over in the centre.

Thanks to the discoveries of the last forty years we now have a clear idea of these Umayyad palaces, e.g. Minya, Jabal Says, Qaṣr al-Ḥayr al-Gharbī, Qaṣr al-Ḥayr ash-Sharqī, and Mafjar. Externally these palaces, with their flanking towers, look like fortified enclosures, but this is a mistaken impression, for they lack arrow-slits and flanking defences, and Qaṣr al-Ḥayr ash-Sharqī alone has a mâchicoulis. As for their interiors, they consist of groups of rooms (*bayts*), usually five, set round the interior in two storeys so that a square court is left over in the centre. This court is surrounded by a colonnaded portico, likewise in two storeys. This type is clearly derived from the second-century palace of the Roman governor at Boṣrā in the Ḥaurān. These new discoveries leave Mshatta and Qaṣr aṭ-Tūba in a separate class, for they can never have had either two storeys or a colonnaded portico.

It was during the later Umayyad period that brick walls and brick vaults, hitherto almost unknown in Syria, again make their appearance, but it must be especially noted that the technique (joints thinner than the bricks) shows that this innovation did not come, as previously, from Byzantium, but from ʿIrāq.

Umayyad architecture employed the following constructive devices: the semicircular arch, the round horse-shoe arch, the pointed arch, flat arches or lintels with a semicircular relieving arch above, arches braced with tie-beams, joggled voussoirs, tunnel-vaults in stone and brick, the latter constructed without centering, the system of roofing in which transverse arches support parallel tunnel-vaults (Fr. *arcs doubleaux et formerets*), wooden domes, and also domes of stone on true spherical-triangle pendentives. The squinch does not appear to have been employed and the intersection of tunnel-vaults was avoided. In fortification, half-round flanking towers were employed, likewise the mâchicoulis, but the bent entrance does not appear to have been known.

In planning, a geometrical network, derived from earlier Syrian practice, was employed for the laying-out of the Dome of the Rock, and a curious system of successive, symmetrical subdivisions into three, not yet noted elsewhere, is found at Mshattā.

The decoration was of the most splendid kind; marble was used for panelling, the slabs being cut in half and opened like a book, so that the wavy grain ran from opposite sides towards the joint. The upper part of the interior and exterior walls were sometimes decorated with glass mosaic (*fusaifisāʾ*), vaster surfaces being covered than had ever been known before. But the most surprising fact is that figure subjects were painted in fresco, at Quṣayr ʿAmra and Ḥammām aṣ-Ṣarakh, for the hostility against painting had not yet taken a decisive theological form, and two large paintings have survived from Qaṣr al-Ḥayr al-Gharbī.

And just as the Muslims in Syria were influenced by the Hellenistic traditions and Christian art of their environment, so those who found themselves in ʿIrāq or Persia, as a result of the fan-wise invasion of the Arab armies, were influenced by the Sasanian traditions of their environment.

As regards ʿIrāq and Persia, we know from the descriptions of early authors and recent excavations that a type of mosque prevailed there quite different from the stone-walled, gable-roofed mosques of Syria. This Persian type of mosque, which was constructed at Baṣra and Kūfa, and later on at Wāsiṭ, and Baghdād, was square in plan (the result of the first mosques in this region having been marked out with arrow-casts), had walls of brick (sometimes of mud-brick), and its flat timber roof rested directly on the columns *without the intermediary of arches*. In this type of mosque we have a direct link between the ancient Persian *apadāna*, or hypostyle audience-hall of the Achaemenian kings, and the *tālār* or flat-roofed portico of more recent Persian palaces. It was usually 200 cubits square and was placed back to back with a Dār al-Imāra 400 cubits square (e.g. Kūfa, Wāsiṭ, and Baghdād).

In Persia, materials such as Persepolitan columns with bull-headed capitals, were taken from older buildings, just as Corinthian columns from older buildings were used in Syria.

2 H. (623) MADĪNA: Muhammad arrives at Madīna 12 Rabīʿ I (24th Sept. 622) and shortly after begins the construction of his *dār*, the courtyard of which became the first Congregational Mosque in Islam. Finished Ṣafar 2 (= Aug. 623).

See above, pp. 6–10.

2 H. (624) MADĪNA: direction of qibla changed from Jerusalem to Mekka, 15 Shaʿbān 2 (11th Jan. 624).

See above, pp. 12–13.

14 H. (635) BAṢRA: First mosque marked out (*ikhtaṭṭa*).

See above, p. 22.

15 H. (636) ZANGIYĀN: 'In the neighbourhood is the Bridge of Khudā Āfarīn, over the Aras river, which was built in the year 15 by Bakr ibn ʿAbd Allāh, one of the Companions of the Prophet.'

Mustawfī, *Nuzhat al-Qulūb*, Le Strange's ed., p. 88; transl., p. 89; and Pope, *Survey of Persian Art*, p. 1227 and figs. 434–5.

16 H. (637) AL-MADĀ'IN (Ctesiphon) captured and the Friday prayer held in the Great Īwān.

See above, pp. 22–3.

17 H. BAṢRA: Great Mosque reconstructed.

See above, p. 22.

—— (638) KŪFA founded and Great Mosque marked out.

See above, pp. 22–6.

—— MEKKA: The Khalif ʿUmar demolishes houses, so as to enlarge the limited area round the Kaʿba. A wall, the height of a man, is put round the enlarged area.

See above, p. 27.

—— MADĪNA: Mosque restored and enlarged.

See above, pp. 27–8.

18 or 21 H. (639 or 641/2) JERUSALEM: First mosque in Temple Area.

See above, pp. 29–34.

19 H. (640) SYRIA: Muʿāwiya fortifies the Syrian coast and constructs watch-towers.

Balādhurī, p. 128; Hitti's transl., p. 196; Caetani, *Annali*, IV, pp. 164–5.

21 H. (640/41) FUSṬĀṬ: Foundation of the Mosque of ʿAmr.

See above, pp. 36–8.

21–2 H. (642–3) JĪZA: fortress (*ḥiṣn*) begun by ʿAmr on his return from Alexandria in 21 H. and finished in 22 H.

Yaʿqūbī, *Geography*, p. 331; Wiet's transl., p. 181; Abū Ṣāliḥ, Evetts' ed., p. 74; transl., p. 173; Ibn Duqmāq, IV, p. 125, l. 27–p. 126, l. 13; Maqrīzī, *Khiṭaṭ*, I, p. 206, ll. 10 and 22–3; Bouriant's transl., pp. 605–7; as-Suyūṭī, *Ḥusn*, I, p. 81, ll. 18–19; Hassan el-Hawary, in the *J.R.A.S.*, 1930, pp. 331–2.

24 H. (644) MADĪNA: ʿUthmān, on his election (1 Muḥarram 24 = 7th Nov. 644) is asked to enlarge the mosque, and proceeds to do so.

See above, p. 40.

26 H. (646/7) MEKKA: ʿUthmān enlarges the Ḥaram.

See above, p. 40.

28 H. (648/9) MADĪNA: ʿUthmān builds himself a house called az-Zawrā'.

Yaʿqūbī, *Taʾrīkh*, II, p. 191, l. 15; Ṭabarī, I, p. 2827, l. 14; Ibn al-Athīr, III, p. 76, l. 2; Caetani, *Annali*, VII, p. 232.

24–35 H. (644–56) DAMASCUS: Muʿāwiya builds a residence known as the Qubbat al-Khaḍrā.

See above, pp. 40–41.

31 H. (650/51) NĪSHĀPŪR captured and first mosque built.

Yāqūt, IV, p. 858, ll. 3–6; Barbier de Meynard's transl., p. 579; Herzfeld, *Khorasan*, in *Der Islam*, XI, p. 163.

38 H. (658) FUSṬĀṬ: Masjid Zimām built by the eunuch Zimām, for the body of the Emīr Muḥammad ibn Abū Bakr, who was killed on 14 Ṣafar 38 (22nd June 658). Outside the town of Fusṭāṭ. Still existed in the time of Ibn Iyās.

Ibn Iyās, *Taʾrīkh*, I, p. 27, ll. 5–6 and 8–10.

38 H. (658/9) IṢṬAKHR: Ziyād ibn Abīhi builds a fortress known as Qalʿat Ziyād and afterwards as Qalʿat Manṣūr, between Iṣṭakhr and the village of Baiḍā.

Ṭabarī, I, 3450, ll. 6–9; Ṭabarī-Zotenberg, III, p. 699; Ibn al-Athīr, III, p. 321, ll. 15–17; Caetani, *Chronographia*, p. 441.

45 H. (665) BAṢRA: Great Mosque rebuilt by Ziyād ibn Abīhi.

See above, pp. 44–5.

Before 50 H. (670) BAṢRA: ʿAbd ar-Raḥmān (Governor of Sīstān for Muʿāwiya, until Ziyād came to Baṣra) employs slaves captured at Kābul to build a mosque in his *qaṣr* at Baṣra, in the Kābul style.

Balādhurī, p. 397; Murgotten's transl., p. 147.

50 H. (670) KŪFA: Great Mosque rebuilt by Ziyād ibn Abīhi.

See above, pp. 46–8.

—— QAIRAWĀN founded and first mosque built by 'Uqba ibn Nāfi'.

See above, p. 61.

53 H. (673) FUSṬĀṬ: Mosque of 'Amr enlarged and given four minarets by Maslama. Minarets added to all the *masjids* except those of Khaulān and Tujīb.

See above, pp. 58–61.

55 H. (675) QAIRAWĀN: Palaces, houses, and lesser mosques finished.

an-Nuwayrī, de Slane's transl., *Journal Asiatique*, 3me sér., t. XI, p. 120.

Before 60 H. (680) MEKKA: Mu'āwiya's house named ar-Ruqṭ built by Persian masons from 'Irāq, with burnt brick (*ājurr*) and gypsum (*jiṣṣ*).

Kitāb al-Aghānī, III, p. 86, ll. 10–20; Lammens, *Études sur le règne du calife Mo'âwia Ier*, *M.F.O.B.*, II, p. 137; Rivoira, *Moslem Architecture*, p. 96.

62 H. (681/2) NEFĪS: 'Uqba ibn Nāfi' takes Nefīs and builds the mosque 'which one still sees there' (i.e. A.D. 1068).

al-Bakrī, p. 160; de Slane's transl., p. [353] 303; *Kitāb al-Istibṣār*, Paris MS., Bibl. Nat., No. 2225, fol. 79 *b*; Fagnan's transl., p. 178.

63 H. (683) MADĪNA given a wall for the first time.

Mas'ūdī, *Tanbīh*, p. 305, l. 4; Carra de Vaux, transl., pp. 395–6.

64 H. (684) SHĪRĀZ laid out by Muḥammad ibn al-Qāṣim ibn Abī 'Aqīl, cousin of Ḥajjāj.

Yāqūt, III, p. 349, ll. 1–2; Barbier de Meynard's transl., p. 364; Le Strange, *Lands of the Eastern Caliphate*, p. 249; Herzfeld, *Khorasan*, in *Der Islam*, XI, p. 163.

64–5 H. (684) MEKKA: The Ka'ba having been ruined by the mangonels of the Syrian army, is demolished by Ibn az-Zubayr on news of Yazīd's death (reached Mekka 27th Nov. 683) and reconstructed 7 cubits longer and 9 cubits higher than before (i.e. 27 cubits long and 27 cubits high), with two doors. Decorated with mosaics from a church at Ṣana'ā', built by Abraha the Abyssinian. Persian masons employed. Area round it enlarged, houses being demolished for this purpose.

See above, pp. 62–4.

67 H. (686/7) FUSṬĀṬ: 'Abd al-'Azīz ibn Marwān, Governor of Egypt, builds a great house, known as the Golden House on account of its gilded dome (until then the Governors of Egypt had lived in their own private houses.) Marwān II, the last Umayyad Khalif, when he fled to Egypt, stayed in this house until the arrival of his pursuers, whereupon he set fire to it (132 H. = 750).

al-Kindī, Guest's ed., p. 49, ll. 1–3; Qalqashandī, III, p. 335; Wüstenfeld's transl., p. 55. For burning, see Maqrīzī, *Khiṭaṭ*, I, p. 304, l. 8; Casanova's transl., *M.I.F.A.O.*, III, pp. 173–4; and Abu'l-Maḥāsin, p. 351, ll. 14–15.

69 H. (688) 'ASQALĀN, which had been destroyed by the Greeks in the time of Ibn az-Zubayr, is rebuilt and fortified by 'Abd al-Malik.

Balādhurī, p. 143; Hitti's transl., pp. 219–20.

—— CAESAREA, which had been devastated by the Greeks in the time of Ibn az-Zubayr, is restored by 'Abd al-Malik, together with its mosque.

Balādhurī, p. 143; Hitti's transl., pp. 219–20.

—— FUSṬĀṬ: Bridge on the Grand Canal built by Sa'd Abū 'Uthmān for 'Abd al-'Azīz ibn Marwān, Governor of Egypt, Ṣafar 69 (Aug. 688), with inscription in his name.

Abū Ṣāliḥ, Evetts' ed., p. 67; transl., p. 155; Ibn Duqmāq, IV, p. 120, ll. 16–19; Maqrīzī, *Khiṭaṭ*, II, p. 113, ll. 32–6, and p. 146, ll. 9–14; as-Suyūṭī, II, p. 271, ll. 18–19; Guest, in the *J.R.A.S.*, 1907, p. 68; Caetani, *Chronographia*, p. 814; Wiet, *C.I.A.—Égypte*, II, pp. 17–19.

70 H. (689/90) ḤELWĀN: The plague appears in Egypt in 70 H., so 'Abd al-'Azīz goes to Ḥelwān and builds houses and mosques there. According to Abū Ṣāliḥ he wished to depopulate Fusṭāṭ and make Ḥelwān the capital.

al-Kindī, p. 49, ll. 16–19; Eutychius, Pococke's ed., II, pp. 368–9; Ibn Khallikān, de Slane's transl., III, pp. 453–4; Abū Ṣāliḥ, Evetts' ed., p. 67; transl., p. 155; Maqrīzī, I, p. 209, ll. 4 and 17–25 (Bouriant's transl., p. 618); p. 302, ll. 4–6 (Casanova's transl., *M.I.F.A.O.*, III, p. 165); Wüstenfeld, *Statthalter*, pp. 34–5; Lane-Poole (S.), *History of Egypt in the Middle Ages*, p. 26.

72 H. (691/2) JERUSALEM: Qubbat aṣ-Ṣakhra built by the Khalif 'Abd al-Malik. Finished in 72 H.

See above, pp. 65–129.

74 H. (693) MEKKA: al-Ḥajjāj having damaged the Ka'ba during his siege of Mekka, demolishes the entire structure and rebuilds it, 7 cubits less in length than the edifice of Ibn az-

Zubayr, and with one door only. Black stone placed in the interior.

Ibn Qutayba, *Kitāb al-Ma'ārif*, p. 277, ll. 19–20; Ibn Rusta, p. 30, ll. 7–16; Ṭabarī, II, p. 854, ll. 11–13; Mas'ūdī, *Prairies*, V, p. 193; Michael the Syrian, Chabot's text, II, p. 446; transl., II, p. 470; Abu'l-Fidā', *Ta'rīkh*, Reiske's ed., I, p. 420; Ibn Baṭṭūṭā, I, pp. 384–5; as-Suyūṭī, *Khalifs*, Jarrett's transl., p. 219; Snouck Hurgronje, *Mekka*, I, p. 3; Périer, *Vie d'al-Ḥadjdjâdj*, p. 62; Caetani, *Chronographia*, pp. 881–2.

——MEKKA: al-Ḥajjāj constructs a mosque in the quarter of the Banī Salima. Still existed in the time of Ṭabarī (i.e. A. D. 915).

Ṭabarī, II, p. 854, l. 15; Périer, *Vie d'al-Ḥadjdjâdj*, p. 61; Caetani, *Chronographia*, p. 881.

79 H. (698/9) FUSṬĀṬ: Mosque of 'Amr rebuilt by 'Abd al-'Azīz ibn Marwān.

See above, p. 131.

65–86 H. (685–705) ARRAJĀN: Mosque built by al-Ḥākam ibn Nahīk al-Hujaimī, Governor under al-Ḥajjāj.

Balādhurī, p. 392; Murgotten's transl., p. 138; Muqaddasī, p. 425, l. 2; Herzfeld, *Khorasan*, in *Der Islam*, XI, p. 163.

—— ARRAJĀN: Bridge with an arch of 80 paces, known as Qanṭarat ad-Daylamī, built over the Ṭāb by ad-Daylamī, doctor of al-Ḥajjāj. 'Four much decayed piers' still exist.

Ibn Khurdādba, p. 43, l. 10; Ibn Rusta, p. 189, l. 14; Ibn al-Faqīh, p. 199, l. 11; Iṣṭakhrī, p. 152, ll. 2–6; Ibn Ḥauqal, p. 212, l. 14; Ṭabarī, transl. by Nöldeke, *Geschichte der Perser und Araber zur Zeit der Sassaniden*, p. 146; Dimishqī, p. 177; Le Strange, *Lands of the Eastern Caliphate*, pp. 268–9; Schwarz, *Iran im Mittelalter*, pp. 117–18; Herzfeld, *loc. cit.*, XI, p. 163; and Stein (Sir Aurel), *Old Routes in Western Asia*, pp. 81–6 and figs. 22–3.

—— 'ASKAR MUKRAM laid out by Mukram ibn Mi'zā' al-Ḥārith, slave of al-Ḥajjāj.

Yāqūt, III, p. 676, ll. 9–19; Barbier de Meynard's transl., p. 403; Herzfeld, *loc. cit.*, XI, p. 163.

81 H. (700) TRANSJORDAN: al-Walīd, before becoming Khalif, erects a building in Transjordan. Foundation inscription runs: 'In the name of God—This is what he hath built, the Emīr al-Walīd, the son of the Commander of the Faithful . . . year one and eighty.' The stone on which this inscription is carved now forms the lintel of the entrance of Qaṣr al-Burqu', on the easternmost edge of the Ḥaurān. Qaṣr al-Burqu', although large, is very irregular and so crudely constructed of rough blocks of basalt that I cannot help thinking that the stone with the inscription must have been re-used. Although it forms the lintel, it does not even overlap both door-jambs properly.

Field, *Early Man in North Arabia*, *Natural History*, XXIX, p. 44 and illus. on pp. 37 and 43; Hassan el-Hawary, in the *J.R.A.S.*, 1930, pp. 327 and 329 and Plate IV (*c*); Wiet, *Répertoire*, I, p. 12.

c. 81 H. (700) QAZVĪN: when al-Ḥajjāj sent his son Muḥammad into the province of Daylam (*c.* 81 H. = 700) to suppress a revolt, the latter, during his stay at Qazvīn, built a mosque called Masjid ath-Thawr (Bull Mosque), near the gate of the palace of the Banī Junayd, on which he inscribed his name.

Ibn al-Faqīh, p. 283, ll. 19–22; Yāqūt, IV, p. 89, ll. 20–22; Barbier de Meynard's transl., p. 444; Mustawfī, *Ta'rīkh-i-Guzīda*, Barbier de Meynard's transl., in the *Journal Asiat.*, 5me sér., t. X, pp. 269–70; Le Strange, *Lands of the Eastern Caliphate*, p. 219; Herzfeld, *Khorasan*, in *Der Islam*, XI, p. 163; and in the *Jahrb. der Preuszischen Kunstsammlungen*, XLII, p. 146, n. 3.

83 H. (702) QŪMM laid out by Ḥajjāj ibn Yūsuf.

Yāqūt, IV, p. 175, ll. 17–18; Barbier de Meynard's transl., p. 459; Abu'l-Fidā', *Taqwīm*, pp. 409–10 and 421; Guyard's transl., II₂, pp. 159–60 and 168; Herzfeld, *Khorasan*, in *Der Islam*, XI, p. 163.

84–5 H. (703/4) MAṢṢĪṢA (Mopsuestia): 'Abd Allāh, the son of 'Abd al-Malik, rebuilds the fortress and constructs a mosque on the citadel hill. No Muslims had lived there before.

Anon. Syriac Chronicle of A. D. 846, Brooks's ed., in the *Z.D.M.G.*, LI, p. 581 (under 1015 of the Era of the Greeks = 704); Balādhurī, p. 165; Hitti's transl., p. 255 (begun 84 H., finished 85 H.); Ya'qūbī, *Ta'rīkh*, II, p. 466; Ṭabarī, II, p. 1127, ll. 11–12 (conquest only under 84 H.); Elias bar Shīnāyā of Nisibis, in Baethgen, *Fragmente*, pp. 38–9; transl., p. 120; Delaporte's transl., p. 97 (under 84 H.); Samuel of Ani (Vagharshapat ed., 1893), p. 57 (under A. D. 692); Michael the Syrian, Chabot's ed., II, p. 451; transl., II, p. 478 (under 1017 = 706); Ibn al-Athīr, IV, pp. 398–9 (under 84 H.); Bar Hebraeus, *Chronography*, Bedjan's ed., p. 114; Budge's transl., p. 105 (under 1017 = 706); Ibn as-Shiḥna (Beyrut ed.), p. 179, ll. 9–10 (under 84 H.); Le Strange, *Lands of the Eastern Caliphate*, p. 130; Honigmann's art. *Miṣṣīṣ*, in the *Encyc. of Islām*, III, pp. 521–2.

84 H. (703) QAIRAWĀN: Great Mosque rebuilt by Ḥassān ibn an-Nu'mān, and inaugurated Ramaḍān 84 (Sept./Oct. 703).

See above, pp. 139–41.

84–6 H. (703–5) WĀSIṬ founded by al-Ḥajjāj ibn Yūsuf. Five iron gates taken from Zandaward, Dauqara, Dārūsāt, Dayr Mār Sarjīs, and Sharābīṭ. Palace, known as Qubbat al-Khadrā', and Great Mosque built. Palace measured 400×400 cubits, mosque 200×200. Cost 43,000,000 dirhems. Seen by Mas'ūdī in 332 H. (943/4).

See above, pp. 133–8.

88 H. (707) DAMASCUS: al-Walīd begins the construction of the Great Mosque.

See above, pp. 151 ff.

—— DAMASCUS: al-Walīd builds a hospital (*māristān*).

Qalqashandī, *Subḥ al-'Asha*, I, p. 431; Maqrīzī, *Khiṭaṭ*, II, p. 405, ll. 18–19. Ṭabarī, however (II, p. 1271), merely says that he gave pensions to lepers.

—— FUSṬĀṬ: 'Abd Allāh ibn 'Abd al-Malik builds the mosque known as Mosque of 'Abd Allāh. Demolished by Ṣāliḥ ibn 'Alī.

al-Kindī, Guest's ed., p. 59, ll. 3–4, and p. 406, ll. 7–15.

89 H. (708) FUSṬĀṬ: 'Abd Allāh ibn 'Abd al-Malik raises the roof of the Mosque of 'Amr.

See above, p. 149.

88–90 H. (707–9) MADĪNA: Great Mosque pulled down and rebuilt by 'Umar ibn 'Abd al-'Azīz.

See above, pp. 142–9.

90 H. (708/9) NA'ŪRĀ (8 miles east of Aleppo): Maslama constructs a little palace (*qaṣr*) of black stone, and a fort (*ḥiṣn*) of which a tower still existed when Kemāl ad-Dīn wrote (i.e. in 641 H.).

Kemāl ad-Dīn, in Freytag, *Selecta ex historia Halebi*, p. 8, ll. 7–8; Ibn ash-Shiḥna, ed. of Sarkis, p. 18, l. 6; Sauvaget's transl., p. 10.

—— DAIBOL (Sind): Mosque constructed by Muḥammad ibn al-Qāsim.

Balādhurī, p. 437; Murgotten's transl., p. 218; Périer, *Vie d'al-Ḥadjdjādj*, p. 247.

—— FUSṬĀṬ: Erection of Masjid al-Qal'a, or al-Ghafla, near the Bāb Rayḥān near Qaṣr ash-Sham'.

Ibn 'Abd al-Ḥakam, Torrey's ed., p. 132, ll. 6–9; as-Suyūṭī, *Ḥusn*, II, p. 9, ll. 11–13; Wüstenfeld, *Statthalter*, I, p. 39; Caetani, *Chronographia*, p. 1091.

91 H. (709/10) MEKKA: Ka'ba restored, and Mosque reconstructed with marble columns, glass mosaic (*fuṣūṣ*), marble panelling, gilt spouts (*mīzāb*), and crenellations (*shurrāfāt*). Glass mosaic employed at Mekka for first time. Cost 36,000 dīnārs.

Azraqī, in Wüstenfeld, *Chroniken*, I, p. 146, l. 17–p. 147, l. 19, and p. 309, l. 16–p. 310, l. 2; Ya'qūbī, *Ta'rīkh*, II, p. 340, ll. 9–15; Quṭb ad-Dīn, in Wüstenfeld, *op. cit.*, III, p. 53, ll. 15–19, and p. 86, ll. 4–14; Wüstenfeld, *ibid.*, IV, p. 151.

92 H. (710/11) FUSṬĀṬ: First Nilometer erected on Rōḍa Island by 'Usāma.

See II (first ed.), p. 296.

92–3 H. (710–12) FUSṬĀṬ: Mosque of 'Amr pulled down, rebuilt and enlarged by Qurra ibn Sharīk.

See above, pp. 149–51.

93 H. (712) SAMARQAND: Qutayba ibn Muslim compels the inhabitants to construct a mosque; Qutayba prays in it with 4,000 men.

Balādhurī, p. 421; Murgotten's transl., p. 188; Ṭabarī, II, p. 1245, ll. 11–16; Caetani, *Chronographia*, p. 1132.

93–6 H. (712–15) MINYA: Palace of al-Walīd on Lake Tiberias.

See above, pp. 381–9.

93–6 H. (712–15) TRANSJORDAN: Quṣayr 'Amra built in the Wadī Buṭm.

See above, pp. 390 ff.

94 H. (713) BUKHĀRĀ: First mosque built by Qutayba ibn Muslim, on the site of a temple of idolaters (probably Buddhists).

Narshakhī, pp. 47–51, quoted by Barthold, *Turkestan*, Gibb's transl., p. 108.

Before 95 H. (714) Near BAṢRA: Ḥassān the Nabataean, who had been employed by al-Ḥajjāj to drain the lagoons, builds a tower called Manāra Ḥassān, on the great lagoon called Hawr al-Muḥammadīya.

Ibn Serapion, Le Strange's text, *J.R.A.S.*, 1895, p. 28; transl., p. 297; Le Strange, *Lands of the Eastern Caliphate*, p. 42.

Before 96 H. (715) RAMLA founded, and construction of Great Mosque begun.

See above, pp. 482–3.

c. 96 H. (714) SHIYĀN (in district of Askīmasht in Sīstān): Mosque built by Qutayba ibn Muslim.

Muqaddasī, p. 303, ll. 8–9; Le Strange, *Lands of the Eastern Caliphate*, p. 350; Herzfeld, *Khorasan*, in *Der Islam*, XI, p. 163.

96 H. (715) DAMASCUS: Great Mosque finished.

See above, pp. 153–4.

97 H. (715) BAṢRA: the Khalif Sulaymān, on his accession, orders Ṣāliḥ ibn 'Abd ar-Raḥmān to reconstruct the Dār al-Imāra, which had been destroyed by al-Ḥajjāj. He did so on the old foundations, using baked bricks and gypsum, and increased the height of the roof.

Balādhurī, p. 349, ll. 7–9; Murgotten's transl., p. 64.

97 H. (715/16) FUSṬĀṬ: Second Nilometer erected on Rōḍa Island by Usāma, by order of the Khalif Sulaymān.

See II (first ed.), p. 296.

96–9 H. (715–17) BAṢRA: Ṣāliḥ ibn 'Abd ar-Raḥmān, when in charge of the *Kharāj* of 'Irāq for the Khalif Sulaymān, rebuilds the mosque of Ziyād with burnt bricks and gypsum.

Balādhurī, p. 348; Murgotten's transl., p. 62.

—— ALEPPO: the Khalif Sulaymān builds the Great Mosque of Aleppo on the site of the cemetery of the principal church.

See above, p. 483.

—— AL-MAḤFŪZA (Sind) built as a city of refuge.

Balādhurī, p. 444; Murgotten's transl., p. 229.

99 H (717/18) FUSṬĀṬ: *Bayt al-Māl* built under *riwāqs* of the Mosque of 'Amr.

See pp. 483–4.

Before 100 H. (718) SARAGOSSA: 'In 100 H. died Ḥanash ibn 'Abd Allāh aṣ-Ṣan'ānī. It was he who first marked out the plan of the Great Mosque of Saragossa.'

Ibn al-Athīr, V, p. 41; Fagnan's transl., in *Annales du Maghreb*, p. 56; al-Ḥimyarī, Lévi-Provençal's text, p. 97; transl., p. 119.

JABAL SAYS: Buildings of al-Walīd.

See above, pp. 472–7.

Before 100 H. (718) ELVIRA: Mosque built by Ḥanash ibn 'Abd Allāh aṣ-Ṣan'ānī.

al-Ḥimyarī, p. 29; transl., p. 37.

100 H. (718/19) MAṢṢĪṢA: The Khalif 'Umar II constructs the Great Mosque.

Balādhurī, p. 165; Hitti's transl., p. 256.

—— LATAKIA: Fortifications restored after the attack of the Greeks.

Balādhurī, p. 133; Hitti's transl., p. 204.

99–101 H. (717–20) BARDASĪR (Kirmān): Mosque of 'Umar ibn 'Abd al-'Azīz built.

Nāṣir ad-Dīn, *Simṭ al-'Ulā*, quoted by Ḥamd Allāh Mustawfī, *Nuzhat al-Qulūb*, Le Strange's ed., p. 140; transl., p. 139; Herzfeld, *Khorasan*, in *Der Islam*, XI, p. 163.

—— RAMLA: 'Umar II finishes the construction of the Great Mosque, begun by Sulaymān.

See above, p. 482.

—— RAS AL-'AIN (N. Mesopotamia): Great Mosque built by 'Umar II.

Ibn Jubayr, de Goeje's ed., p. 244, ll. 4–7; Schiaparelli's transl., p. 234.

102 H. (720/21) BOṢRĀ: the so-called 'Umar Mosque' built by Yazīd II.

See above, pp. 489–90.

—— CORDOVA: Bridge reconstructed on the old piers, with stones taken from the town wall, by the Governor as-Samḥ by order of the Emīr 'Abd ar-Raḥmān.

See II (first ed.), p. 138.

—— KŪFA: 'Umar ibn Hubayra, Governor of Kūfa, builds the bridge (*qanṭarat al-Kūfa*).

Balādhurī, p. 286; Hitti's transl., p. 445 (without date); Caetani, *Chronographia*, p. 1282 (puts it under 102 H.).

104 H. (722/3) MADĪNA: the Governor, 'Abd al-Wāḥid, restores the roof of the mosque and provides it with crenellations (*shurrāfāt*).

Ibn Rusta, p. 70, ll. 15–16; Wiet's transl., p. 70; Samhūdī, p. 140, ll. 18–20; Wüstenfeld, *Geschichte de Stadt Medina*, pp. 74–5; Caetani, *Chronographia*, p. 1309.

105 H. (724) AL-MUTHAQQAB: Ḥassān ibn Māhawayh al-Anṭākī constructs the fortress of this name (near Maṣṣīṣa) by order of the Khalif Hishām.

Balādhurī, pp. 166–7; Hitti's transl., pp. 257–8 (without date); Le Strange, *Lands of the Eastern Caliphate*, p. 130; Caetani, *Chronographia*, p. 1323 (under 105 H.).

—— QAṬARGHĀSH: 'Abd al-'Azīz ibn Ḥayyān al-Anṭākī constructs the fortress of this name, by order of the Khalif Hishām.

Balādhurī, p. 167; Hitti's transl., p. 258 (without date); Caetani, *Chronographia*, p. 1323 (under 105 H.).

—— MŪRA, BŪQĀ, and BAGHRĀS (fortresses) constructed by order of the Khalif Hishām; the former was built by a man from Antioch.

Balādhurī, p. 167; Hitti's transl., p. 258 (without date); Caetani, *Chronographia*, p. 1323 (puts it under 105 H.).

106 H. (724/5) MOSUL: Dār al-Manqūsha constructed by the Governor al-Ḥurr ibn Yūsuf. Panelled with teak-wood (*sāj*), marble, and mosaic (*fuṣūṣ*).

Ibn al-Athīr, V, p. 99, ll. 17–19; an-Nuwayrī, Vatican MS., No. 740, fols. 115 *b*–116 *a*, quoted by Caetani, *Chronographia*, p. 1338.

105–9 H. (724–727/8) QAIRAWĀN: Great Mosque rebuilt by Bishr ibn Ṣafwān, by order of the Khalif Hishām.

See above, p. 518.

107–8 H. (725/6) FUSṬĀṬ: the Qaysarīya Hishām constructed near the bridge known as al-Jisr by the Governor, al-Ḥurr. Begun Rajab 107 (Nov./Dec. 725) and finished in 108 H.

al-Kindī, Guest's ed., p. 74, ll. 6–10; Caetani, *Chronographia*, p. 1352.

c. A. D. 725–30 TRANSJORDAN : Ḥammām aṣ-Ṣarakh constructed.

See above, pp. 498–502.

—— TRANSJORDAN : Mosque at Quṣayr al-Ḥallābāt.

See above, pp. 502–3.

105–109 H. (724–7) QAṢR AL-ḤAYR AL-GHARBĪ constructed by the Khalif Hishām.

See above, pp. 507–14.

109 H. (727) QAṢR AL-MILḤ (between Qaryatain and Palmyra) : Gateway (of *khān*) with inscription of the Khalif Hishām.

Mordtmann, in the *Sitzungsberichte der Bayerischen Acad. der Wiss., Philos.-philolog. und hist. Classe*, 1875, II, Supp., p. 287; Sachau, *Reise in Syrien*, p. 49; Moritz, *Zur antiken Topographie der Palmyrene, Abh. der Kgl. Akad., Berlin, Phil.-hist. Abh.*, 1889, p. 12; Wiet, *Répertoire*, I, p. 23; Krenker, Puchstein, Schulz, &c., *Palmyra*, pp. 6–8, Abb. 7–10 and 13–14, and Taf. 3, and above pp. 506–7.

110 H. (728/9) QAṢR AL-ḤAYR ASH-SHARQĪ constructed by the Khalif Hishām.

See above, pp. 522–38.

114 H. (732/3) TUNIS : first Great Mosque and Arsenal constructed by 'Ubayd Allāh ibn al-Ḥabḥāb.

See II (first ed.), p. 321.

117 H. (735) MADĪNA (Upper Egypt) : House discovered by Somers Clarke in 1900. Six lines of simple Kufic, written on the wall with a *qalam* : '. . . and Malik son of Kathīr has written [it] in Rajab of the year 117' (Aug. 735).

Van Berchem, *C.I.A.—Égypte*, I, pp. 693–7; Creswell, *Brief Chronology*, *B.I.F.A.O.*, XVI, p. 62, n. 2; Wiet, *Répertoire*, I, p. 25.

120 H. (737/8) BRAHMĀNĀBĀD-MANṢŪRA (Sind) founded by 'Amr ibn Muḥammad ibn al-Qāsim.

Balādhurī, p. 444; Murgotten's transl., p. 229; Ya'qūbī, *Ta'rīkh*, II, p. 389, ll. 9–10; Caetani, *Chronographia*, pp. 1507–9.

124 H. (743/4) DIYĀRBAKR : The bridge across the Tigris is destroyed by a mass of timber and great trees, brought down by a flood. The Khalif Hishām assembles masons and workmen and all the necessary material, but dies and leaves the work unfinished.

Dionysius of Tell Maḥrē, p. 32; Chabot's transl., p. 29.

125 H. (743) JISR AL-WALĪD : Bridge built on road between Adhana and Maṣṣīṣa (9 miles from latter); called Jisr al-Walīd after al-Walīd II.

Balādhurī, p. 168; Hitti's transl., pp. 259–60; Yāqūt, II, p. 82, ll. 15–17; Honigmann's article *Miṣṣīṣ*, in the *Encyc. of Islām*, III, p. 522.

Before 125 H. (743) QUṬAIYIFA : Palace of the Khalif Hishām.

Ya'qūbī, *Geography*, p. 325; Wiet's transl., p. 172.

126 H. (744) MSHATTĀ : Probably begun by al-Walīd II and left unfinished at his death on 27 Jumādā II, 126 (16th April 744).

See above, pp. 623–41.

—— QAṢR AT-ṬŪBA : Probably begun by al-Walīd II and left unfinished at his death on 27 Jumādā II, 126 (16th April 744).

See above, pp. 623–41.

127 H. (744/5) ḤOMṢ and BA'ALBEK : Walls destroyed by Marwān II.

Agapius of Manbij, Vasiliev's ed., in the *Patrologia Orientalis*, VIII, p. 520.

126–30 H. (744–8) MOSUL : Marwān II builds what afterwards came to be known as the Old Mosque. According to Muqaddasī it was covered by domes resting on alabaster piers, and the façade of the covered part had no doors (i.e. the arches were open).

Muqaddasī, p. 138; Ranking's transl., p. 225; Ibn Jubayr, Wright's ed., p. 237; de Goeje's ed., p. 235; Shiaparelli's transl., p. 224; Yāqūt, IV, p. 684, ll. 8–9; *Marāṣid*, III, p. 174, ll. 2–3; Le Strange, *Lands of the Eastern Caliphate*, p. 87; Sarre and Herzfeld, *Archäologische Reise*, II, p. 232.

126–32 H. (744–50) ḤARRĀN : Great Mosque built by Marwān II, probably soon after his accession.

See above, pp. 647–8.

128 H. (745/6) BAṢRĀ : the so-called 'Umar Mosque' repaired.

See above, p. 490.

130 H. (747/8) JERUSALEM : earthquake destroys part of the Aqṣā Mosque.

See above, p. 374.

—— MAR'ASH : al-Walīd ibn Hishām reconstructs the Citadel.

Ṭabarī, II, p. 2016, ll. 1–2; Ibn al-Athīr, V, p. 301, ll. 11–12; an-Nuwayrī, Vatican MS., No. 740, fol. 143 *a*, quoted by Caetani, *Chronographia*, p. 1665.

APPENDIX

TO MAKE AN ACCURATE PLAN of the Dome of the Rock is a matter of considerable difficulty, for it is impossible to get a clear measurement from side to side owing to the piers, screens, etc. (see Fig. 21).

I therefore measured the sides of the triangles shown (Fig. 690) with a new 25-metre Chesterman tape, and asked Mr. F. S. Richards of the Survey of Egypt if he could compute the results for me. Mr. Richards was struck by the novelty of the problem, all the data obtained by me for the various triangles being sides, instead of angles as is usually the case in a survey.

The sole object of the computation was to make the smallest possible adjustments to get the network to close, and, at the same time, to arrive at a self-consistent system of co-ordinates.

The computation was divided into two parts. The twenty-four measured distances comprising the sides of the outer octagon and the lengths joining the four inner points, 17, 18, 19, and 20, were first adjusted to self-consistency, putting the least possible adjustment into any one measured length. The maximum adjustment applied amounted to 11 millimetres, which was quite satisfactory. This computation (Table A) fixed the true shape of the outer octagon.

TABLE A. LIST SHOWING LENGTHS OF LINES COMPUTED AND MEASURED

Line	*Lengths* Computed metres	Measured metres	*Difference* Comp.-Meas. millimetres	Line	*Lengths* Computed metres	Measured metres	*Difference* Comp.-Meas. millimetres
1–17	14·391	14·39	+1	1–20	22·900	22·90	0
3–17	13·895	13·90	−5	11–20	23·600	23·60	0
5–17	22·694	22·69	+4	13–20	14·509	14·51	−1
15–17	23·734	23·73	+4	15–20	14·172	14·17	+2
3–18	23·691	23·68	+11				
5–18	14·578	14·57	+8	1–3	19·028	19·03	−2
7–18	14·015	14·01	+5	3–5	18·862	18·87	−8
9–18	22·751	22·74	+11	5–7	19·241	19·25	−9
				7–9	19·200	19·21	−10
7–19	23·341	23·33	+11	9–11	19·071	19·08	−9
9–19	14·296	14·30	−4	11–13	19·156	19·16	−4
11–19	14·328	14·32	+8	13–15	19·223	19·22	+3
13–19	23·291	23·28	+11	15–1	19·134	19·13	+4

The inner octagon was then fitted into this fixed frame so that the smallest adjustments possible were applied to any given measurement. The greatest adjustment applied in this computation (Table B) was 17 millimetres.

TABLE B. LIST SHOWING LENGTHS OF LINES COMPUTED AND MEASURED

Line	*Lengths* Computed metres	Measured metres	*Difference* Comp.-Meas. millimetres	Line	*Lengths* Computed metres	Measured metres	*Difference* Comp.-Meas. millimetres
2–4	15·608	15·61	−2	9–12	17·858	17·86	−2
4–6	15·547	15·55	−3	10–11	17·852	17·84	+12
6–8	15·792	15·79	+2	11–14	17·922	17·92	+2
8–10	15·749	15·74	+9	12–13	17·924	17·94	−16
10–12	15·676	15·69	−14	13–16	17·922	17·91	+12
12–14	15·736	15·74	−4	14–15	18·008	18·00	+8
14–16	15·741	15·75	−9	15–2	17·912	17·90	+12
16–2	15·686	15·69	−4	16–1	17·893	17·88	+13
1–4	17·776	17·78	−4	1–2	4·490	4·49	0
2–3	17·837	17·83	+7	3–4	4·470	4·47	0
3–6	17·710	17·71	0	5–6	4·440	4·44	0
4–5	17·679	17·68	−1	7–8	4·480	4·48	0
5–8	17·977	17·96	+17	9–10	4·460	4·46	0
6–7	18·008	18·01	−2	11–12	4·450	4·45	0
7–10	17·993	18·00	−7	13–14	4·450	4·45	0
8–9	17·917	17·90	+17	15–16	4·531	4·53	+1

Mr. Richards remarks that the adjustments applied in these computations are so small that no appreciable violence has been done to any of my measurements.

The eight corners of the outer and the eight corners of the inner octagon being thus fixed, their co-ordinates were calculated so as to permit of these sixteen points being plotted on a scale of $\frac{1}{50}$th, by the Coradi Co-ordinatograph, after which the whole drawing was completed as shown in Fig. 21. This instrument works to a tenth part of a millimetre, and, as this drawing has been reduced to a quarter, it

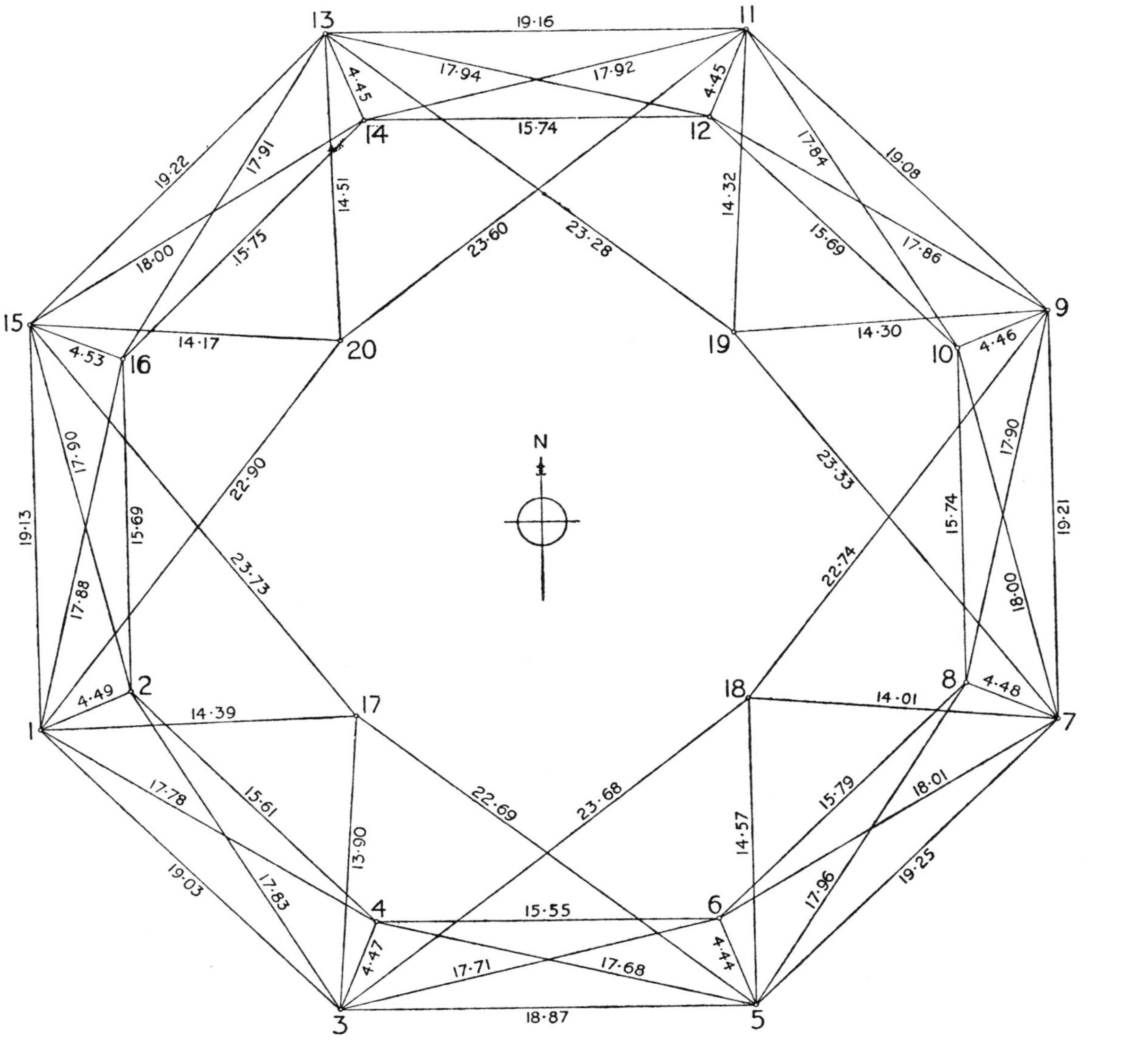

FIG. 690. JERUSALEM: Dome of the Rock, diagram showing measurements taken to fix the true shape of the two concentric octagons.

follows that the exact shape of the two octagons appears in Fig. 21, no point being more than a fortieth part of a millimetre (one-hundredth part of an inch) out of position.

LIST OF CO-ORDINATES

No. of point	X Metres	Y Metres	No. of point	X Metres	Y Metres
1	20·000	20·000	6	10·312	50·589
3	6·407	33·315	8	21·205	62·022
5	6·165	52·175	10	36·954	62·116
7	19·414	66·128	12	48·184	51·179
9	38·614	66·256	14	48·396	35·444
11	52·269	52·943	16	37·396	24·184
13	52·527	33·789			
15	39·134	20·000	17	20·260	34·389
			18	20·743	52·176
2	21·710	24·152	19	37·974	51·974
4	10·529	35·043	20	38·022	34·128

The distances apart of the following points were then computed as shown:

No. of point	Metres	No. of point	Metres
1–7	46·132 } (46·240 measured)	1–11	46·114
15–9	46·259 }	3–9	46·070
3–13	46·122	7–13	46·285
5–11	46·110	5–15	46·067

from which it follows that the opposite sides of the outer octagon are not truly parallel to the following degree:

North and south	1 cm.	difference	in *c.*19	metres
North-east and south-west	4	,,	,,	,,
East and west	13	,,	,,	,,
South-east and north-west	22	,,	,,	,,

I must again express my thanks to Mr. Richards and his assistants for all the trouble they have taken on my behalf.

INDEX

a. Remains of the mosque of al-Walīd: arcades to east of dome, looking east

b. Remains of the mosque of al-Walīd: arcades to east of dome, looking north-east

THE AQṢĀ MOSQUE, JERUSALEM

(by kind permission of the Department of Antiquities)

a. South-east tower, from the south

b. South-east tower with take-off of south wall

c. Entrance, from the north-east

d. Entrance, half-round niches in northern recess

e. Entrance vestibule, niche on south side

f. Entrance vestibule, niche on north side

MINYA ON LAKE TIBERIAS: PALACE OF AL-WALĪD
(by kind permission of the Staatliche Museen, Berlin)

a

b

c

d

e

f

a–f. Rosettes of dome

g. Cornice under entrance dome

h. Frieze of opening in dome

i and *j*. Blocks found in entrance

j

MINYA ON LAKE TIBERIAS: PALACE OF AL-WALĪD

(by kind permission of the Staatliche Museen, Berlin)

a. Exit from vestibule

b. Passage leading from vestibule

c. Interior, looking south-east: on left entrance passage and ramp

d. Interior, east side looking south

e. The mosque, looking north

f. The mosque, looking south

MINYA ON LAKE TIBERIAS: PALACE OF AL-WALĪD

(by kind permission of the Staatliche Museen, Berlin)

a. Mosque, guide stone for pavement

b. Mosque, the miḥrāb

c. Mosque, from the north-west

d. South side of palace, from the north-east

e. Room with central arcade

f. South side of state-room; wall pitted for the attachment of marble panelling

MINYA ON LAKE TIBERIAS: PALACE OF AL-WALĪD

(by kind permission of the Staatliche Museen, Berlin)

a. Jamb of door between Long room and Throne-room

b. Mosaic floors of state-rooms

c. Room in south-west corner

d. West side, northern staircase

e. Window of south-west staircase

f. North side, latrine tower

MINYA ON LAKE TIBERIAS: PALACE OF AL-WALĪD

(by kind permission of the Staatliche Museen, Berlin)

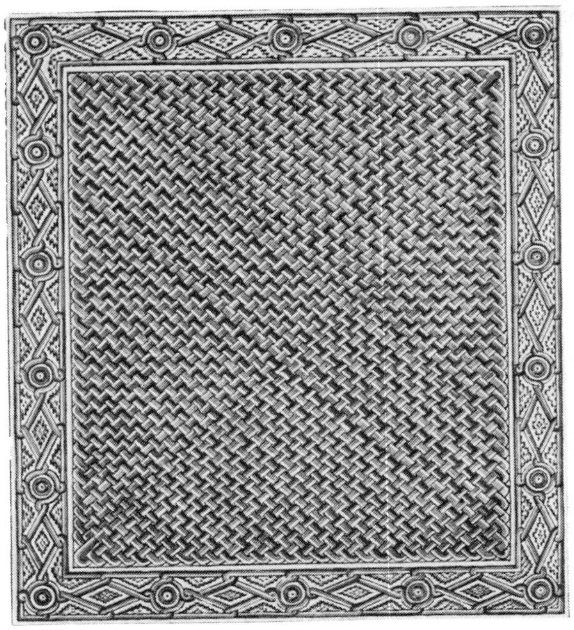

a. South-eastern room

b. South-western room

c. Five-roomed *bayt*

MINYA: PALACE OF AL-WALID

Floor mosaics in five-roomed *bayt*

a. Quṣayr ʿAmra and the Wādī Buṭum from the air, looking south-east

b. From the south

c. General view from the north-west

QUṢAYR ʿAMRA

A.D. 712–715

a. Ḥammām from the north-west

b. Entrance to the audience-hall

c. Audience-hall

d. Audience-hall: slightly pointed transverse arch

e. Painting on west wall of audience-hall, showing the enemies of Islām defeated by the Umayyads. (From Musil, *Ḳuṣejr ʿAmrā*)

QUṢAYR ʿAMRA

A.D. 712–715

Savignac

a. Painting on east side of room D, to left of window

Savignac

b. Painting on east side of room D, to right of window

c. Painting over door on west side of room D

Savignac

QUṢAYR ʿAMRA

A.D. 712–715

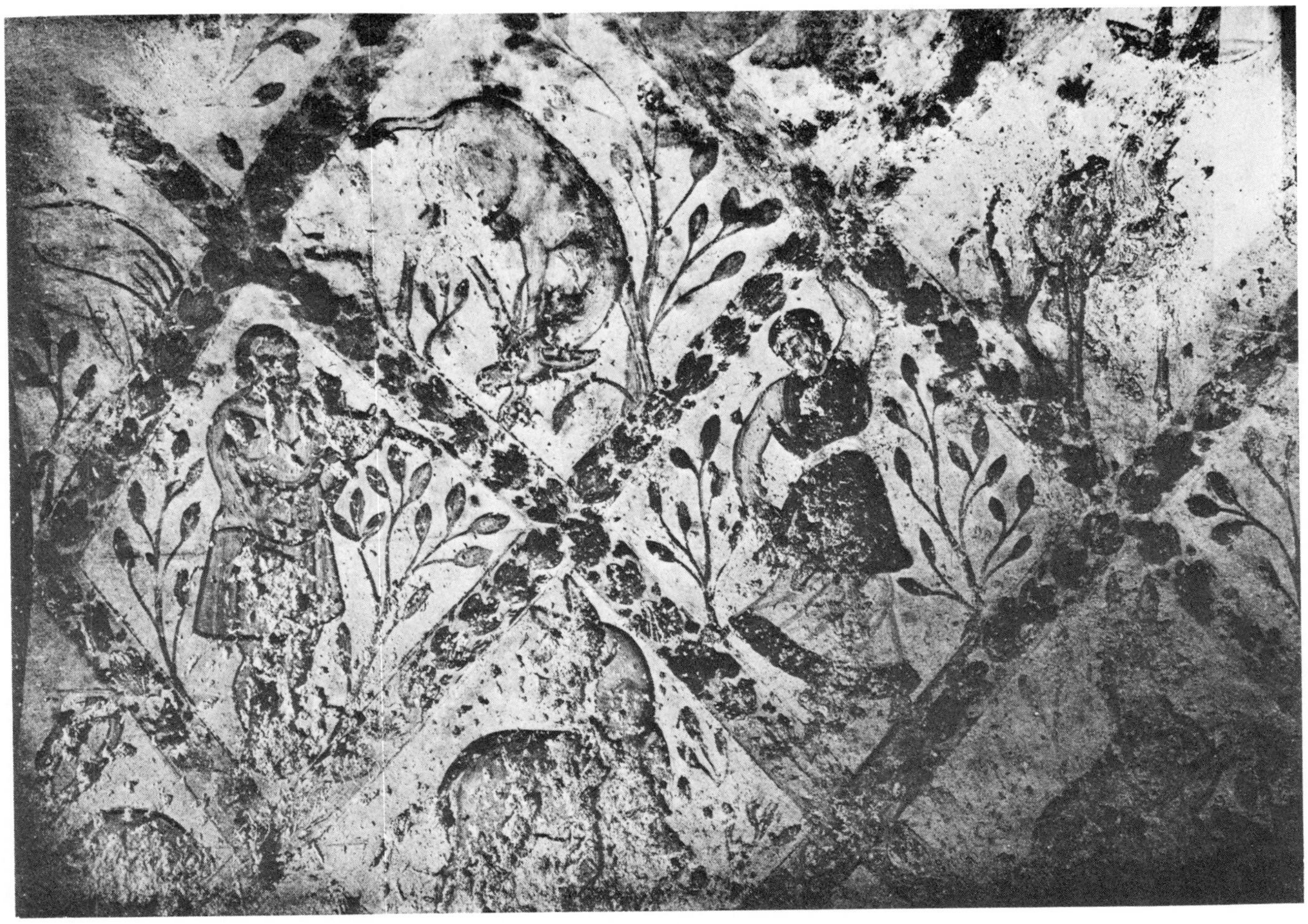

a. Painting on vault of *apodyterium*, northern half

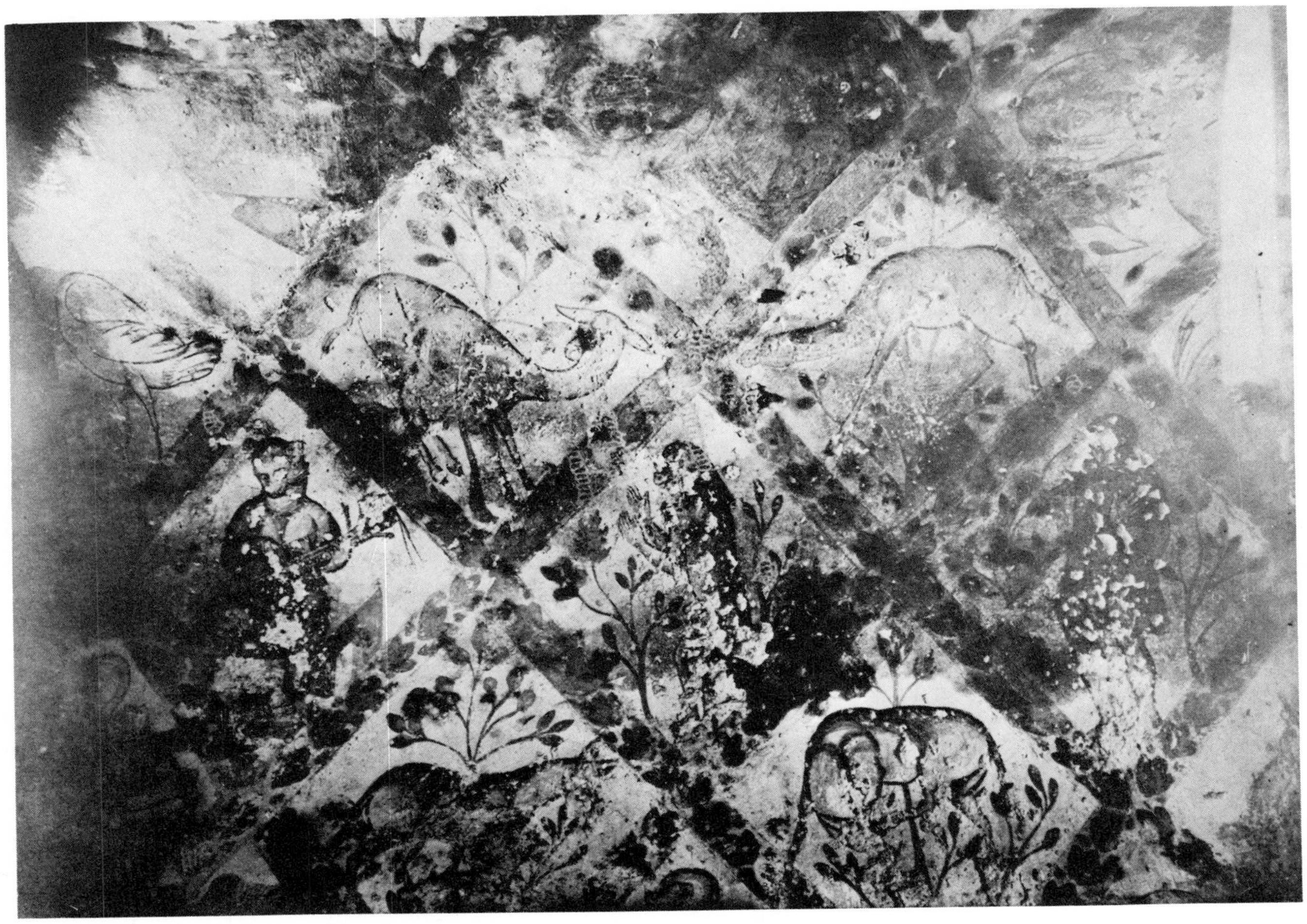

b. Painting on vault of *apodyterium*, southern half

QUṢAYR ʻAMRA

A.D. 712–715

a. Painting on south side of *tepidarium*

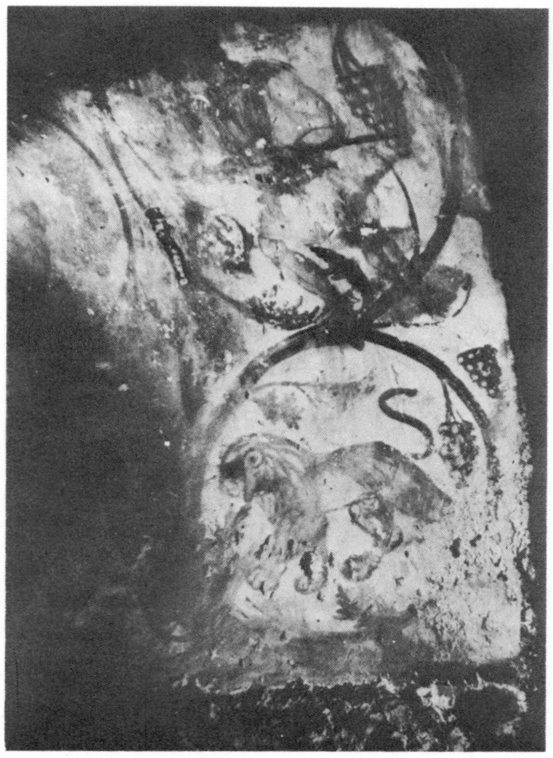

b. Painting in window recess of *tepidarium*

c. Painting on south side of *tepidarium*, detail of right-hand part of *a*

Skira

QUṢAYR ʻAMRA

A.D. 712–715

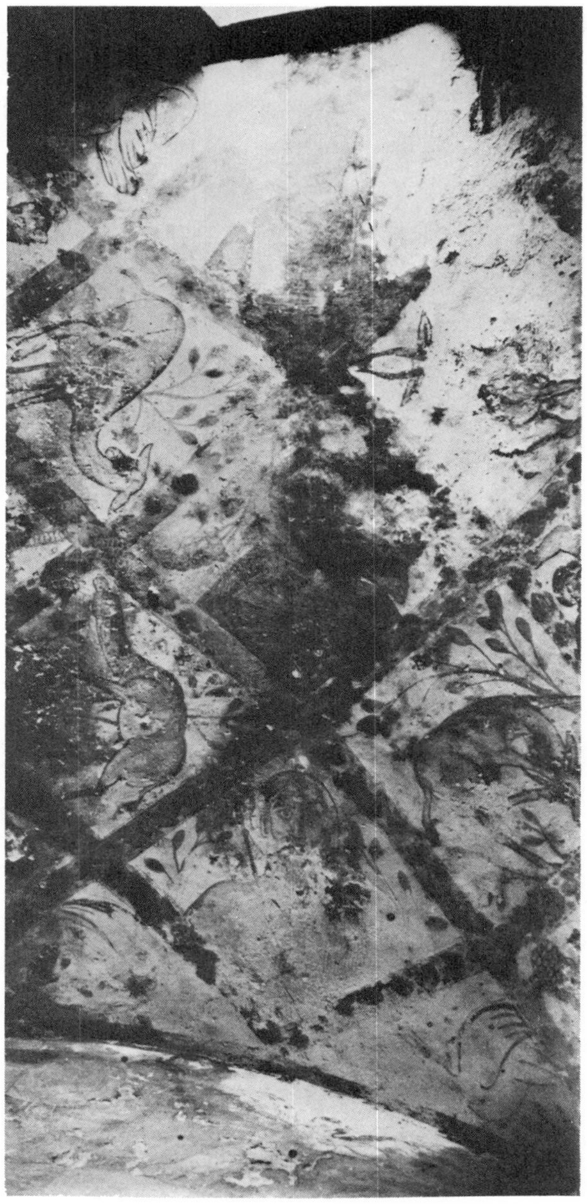

a. Apodyterium: painting on apex of vault, the three ages of man

b. Calidarium *Department of Antiquities*

c. Dome setting in *Calidarium*: Sagittarius between windows

d. Calidarium: detail of Zodiac

QUṢAYR ʿAMRA

A.D. 712–715

a. Painting showing Signs of the Zodiac, etc., on dome of *Calidarium*

b. Zodiac, seen centrally from below, a correction made from above. Drawn by Magdalena Stein

QUṢAYR 'AMRA

A.D. 712–715

a. General view of the *qasr*, from the north-east

b. Entrance, before excavation

c. Entrance after Dr. Brisch's excavations

d. The mosque, from the north

f. The mosque, remains of miḥrāb

e. The mosque, from the north-east

AL-WALĪD'S *QAṢR* AT JABAL SAYS

a. Remains of audience-hall and door to *ḥammām*

b. Remains of audience-hall

c. Remains of two small rooms at end of audience-hall opposite apse

d. Balustrade of upper floor

e. Remains of apse of audience-hall

AL-WALĪD'S *QAṢR* AT JABAL SAYS

a. Main N–S street: four arches re-erected

b. Main N–S street, looking north

'ANJAR

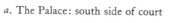

a. The Palace: south side of court

b. The Palace: fifth window from left

c. Hood of panel

‘ANJAR

a. The Tetrapylon, partly re-erected

b. The *Hammām*: remains of mosaic floor

'ANJAR

a. East side with portico, in 1962

b. West side in 1919

d. East *riwāq* in 1919

c. Interior, south-eastern corner in 1919

e. Sanctuary in 1919

BOṢRĀ: THE SO-CALLED ‘‘UMAR MOSQUE’
102 H. (721/2)

a. Interior, south-west corner in 1919

b. Interior, east *riwāq* with stone ceiling almost intact (before 1904) (From Kondakov, *op. cit.*)

c. Interior, north-eastern corner and minaret in 1962

BOṢRĀ: THE SO-CALLED ʻʻUMAR MOSQUEʼ

a

b

c

d

e

f

g

h

i

j

k

l

m

n

o

MUWAQQAR: CAPITALS FROM THE PALACE
104 H. (722/3)

a

b

c

d

e

f

g

h

i

j

k

l

MUWAQQAR: *a-f.* CAPITALS FROM THE PALACE, *g-l.* WATER GAUGE
104 H. (722/3)

a. General view from the north

b. From the north

c. *Calidarium*: interior

d. General view from the north-west

e. *Calidarium*: semi-domed recess

ḤAMMĀM AṢ-ṢARAKH

c. A.D. 725–30

a. Ḥammām aṣ-Ṣarakh, from the west

c. Mosque at Quṣayr al-Ḥallābāt, west façade

b. Ḥammām aṣ-Ṣarakh: *Calidarium*, dome on pendentives

d. Mosque at Quṣayr al-Ḥallābāt: interior looking west

a and *b.* ḤAMMĀM AṢ-ṢARAKH *c* and *d.* MOSQUE AT QUṢAYR AL–ḤALLĀBĀT

(1st half, VIIIth century)

a. QAIRAWĀN: Minaret of Great Mosque

b. Entrance to minaret

c. QAṢR AL-ḤAYR AL-GHARBĪ: Inscription over entrance to Khān

a. East side, after the clearance

b. Model of the *Qaṣr* restored

d. The Khalif Hishām?

c. The entrance, from within

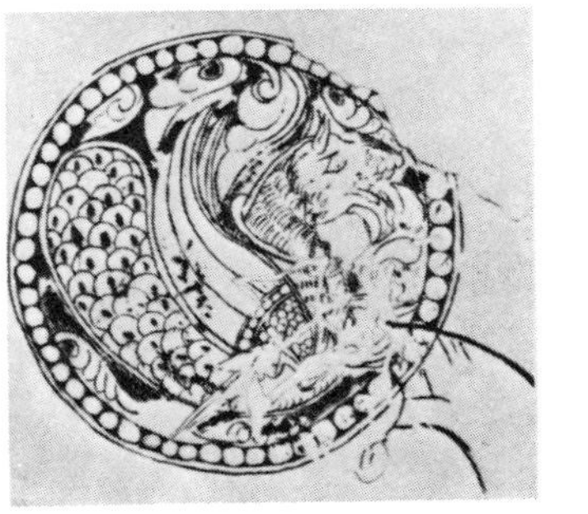

e. Hippogriff in stucco found in one of the rooms

QAṢR AL-ḤAYR AL-GHARBĪ

105–9 H. (A.D. 724–7)

a. Panel farthest from entrance

d. The entrance, as reconstructed

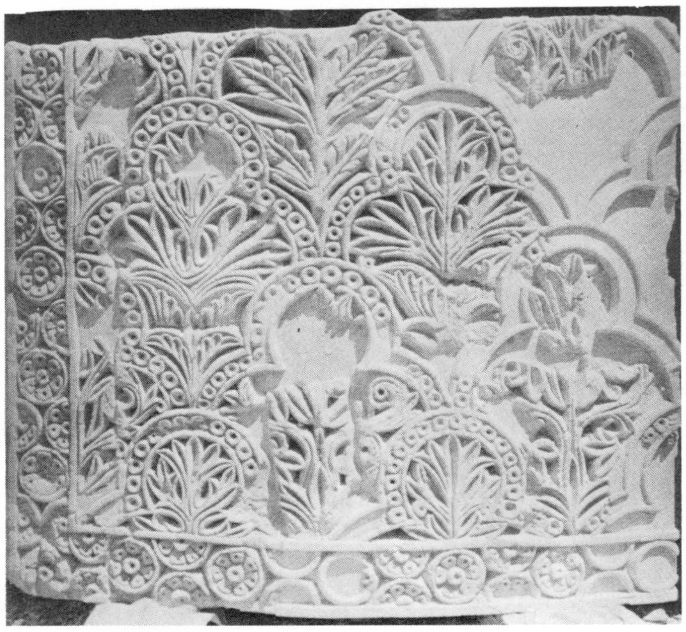

b. Central panel of left tower

e. String course

c. Right panel of left tower

f. The lowest band of ornament

QAṢR AL-ḤAYR AL-GHARBĪ
105–9 H. (A.D. 724–7)

a. Entrance passage, south side

b. The courtyard, south-east corner

c. Entrance passage, north side

d. Drain pipe from latrine on upper floor

e. Grille from a lunette above a doorway

f. Grille from a lunette above a doorway

QAṢR AL-ḤAYR AL-GHARBĪ
105–9 H. (A.D. 724–7)

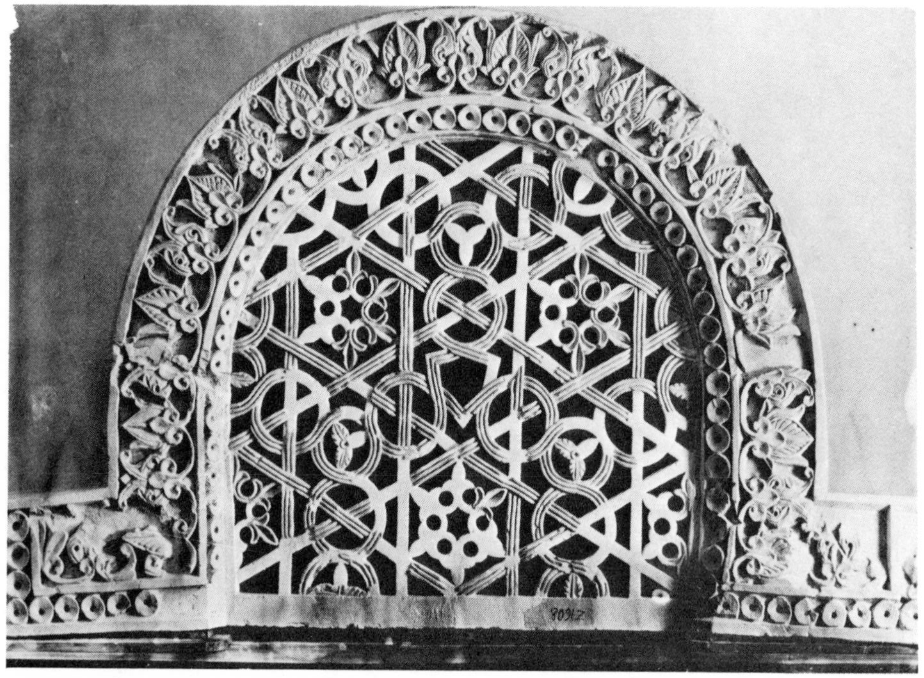

a. Grille of a lunette above a doorway

c. Reconstructed window grille

b. Grille of a lunette above a doorway

d. Closure slab from upper gallery

QAṢR AL-ḤAYR AL-GHARBĪ

105–9 H. (A.D. 724–7)

QAṢR AL-ḤAYR AL-GHARBĪ:
Painting on floor of Room XIV

QAṢR AL-ḤAYR AL-GHARBĪ: Painting on floor of Room XIX

a. General view from the south

b. Lesser enclosure, from the south-west

c. Lesser enclosure: entrance in centre of west side

QAṢR AL-ḤAYR ASH-SHARQĪ
110 H. (728/9)

a. Summit of left entrance tower

b. Blind arcading and decorative panels in dark stucco

c. Entrance, showing details

d. Interior, south-western corner, showing brick tunnel vaults

QAṢR AL-ḤAYR ASH-SHARQĪ. Lesser enclosure (*c*. A.D. 728)

a. Entrance in centre of north side

b. Details of mâchicoulis

c. Remains of mosque. Pier to right once bore inscription dated 110 H. (728)

QAṢR AL-ḤAYR ASH-SHARQĪ. Greater enclosure (A.D. 728)

a. Mosque, looking east at side of transept

b. Mosque, north façade of sanctuary

QAṢR AL-ḤAYR ASH-SHARQĪ. Greater enclosure (A.D. 728)

a. Inner face of west side

c. North-western corner tower

b. Interio·, north-east corner

d. Inner face of south side

QAṢR AL-ḤAYR ASH-SHARQĪ. Lesser enclosure (*c.* A.D. 728)

a. Entrance and postern gate in east side

b. Entrance in centre of south side

c. Entrance in centre of west side

d. Entrance in centre of north side

QAṢR AL-ḤAYR ASH-SHARQĪ. Greater enclosure (A.D. 728)

a. Posts from balustrades of gallery of forecourt

b. Balustrade from gallery of forecourt, reassembled from fragments

d. One of the crenellations of Palace

c. Detail of border in *b*

e. Acanthus cornice in stone

a. Lintel of entrance to Palace

b. Entrance hall of Palace, looking inwards

d. Entrance to Palace, right jamb

c. Entrance hall, north side, first bay from left

e. Entrance hall, detail of stucco wall-panel, south wall, west bay

a. Remains of mosque, arch at extreme left of façade and pilaster for take-off of east *riwāq*

b. Tower (minaret?) between the two enclosures

c. Dam with sluice-gates

QAṢR AL-ḤAYR ASH-SHARQĪ (A.D. 728)

a. Front of Palace, partly reconstructed (from the south-east)

b. The aqueduct

c. Palace gateway, archivolt

d. Rosette from gate tower

e. Niche-head from portico of palace

KHIRBAT AL-MAFJAR

a. Balustrade panel 14A(1)

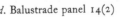

b. Balustrade panel 14A(2)

c. Balustrade panel 14(1)

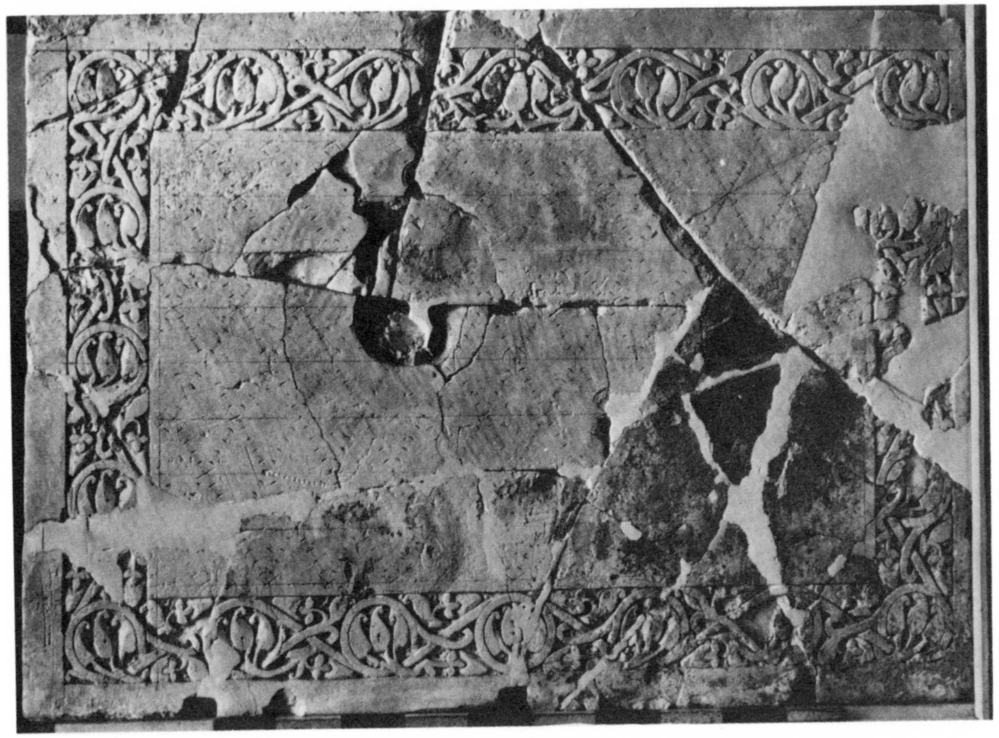

d. Balustrade panel 14(2)

KHIRBAT AL-MAFJAR: Balustrade panels from the Palace

a. The pool and octagonal pavilion

b. Pavilion balustrade

c. The Bath, lintel of porch

d. The Khalif

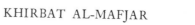

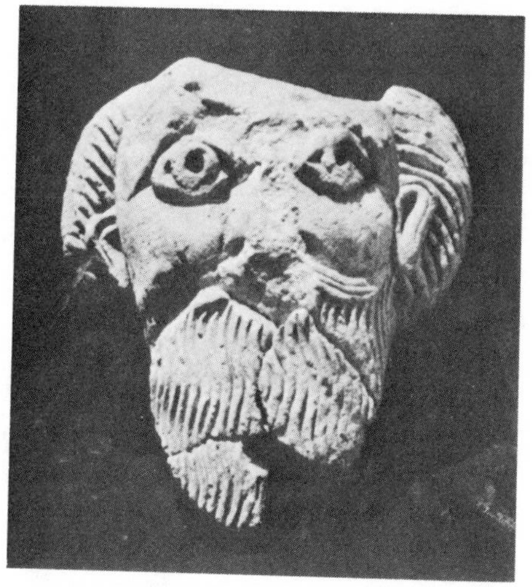
e. The Khalif's head

f. Dancing girl

KHIRBAT AL-MAFJAR

a. Entrance hall, panel 5

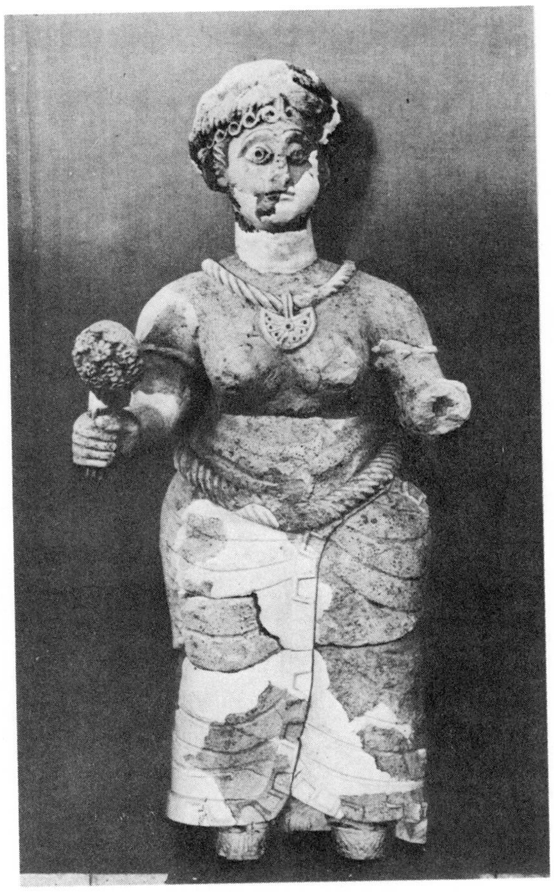

c. Dancing girl

b. Entrance hall, south side, decoration of third bay from left

d. Palace mosque, with miḥrāb

e. Entrance hall, south side, decoration of second bay from left

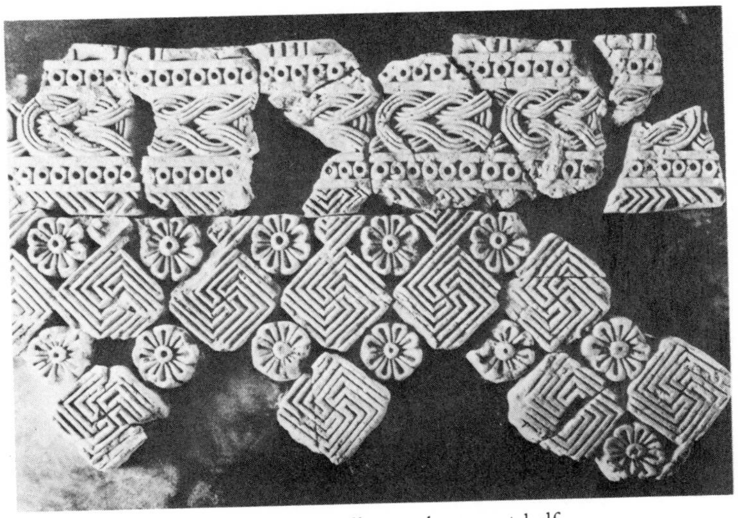

f. Decoration of panel in south wall, west bay, west half

KHIRBAT AL-MAFJAR

a. The courtyard, from entrance hall

b. The Palace, east side northern half, from entrance hall

c. Stone window grille

d. The *Sirdāb*

e. Miḥrāb of public mosque

f. Stone chain which hung from semi-dome of exedra in bath

KHIRBAT AL-MAFJAR

a. The *Dīwān*: general view of mosaic floor

b. The *Dīwān*: mosaic floor

c. The *Dīwān*: mosaic floor of throne recess (Skira)

KHIRBAT AL-MAFJAR

a. The *Dīwān*: one of the windows in drum

b. The *Dīwān*: stucco decoration of throne recess, western side

c. The *Dīwān*: stucco decoration of throne recess, eastern side

KHIRBAT AL-MAFJAR

a. The Bath porch, human pendentive

b. The Bath, swimming pool with three exedrae

c. The Bath, corner of exedra VIII

d. The Bath, niche-head

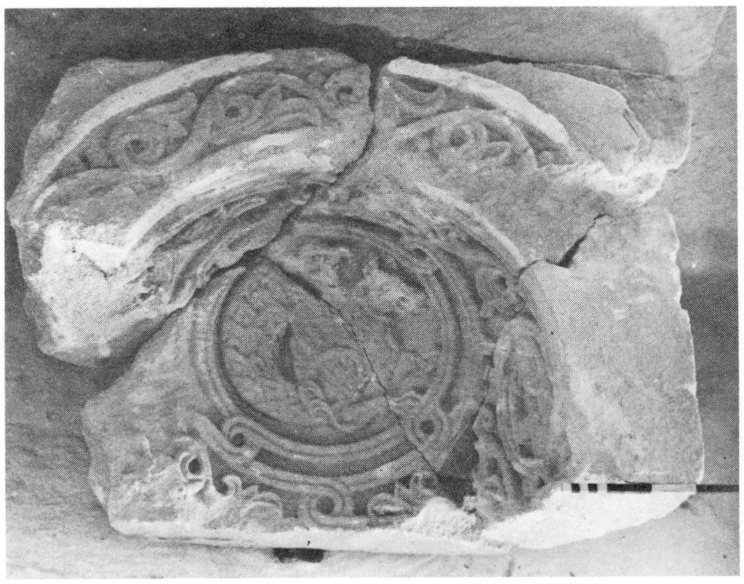

e. The Bath, niche-head with hippogriff

KHIRBAT AL-MAFJAR

a. The Bath hall, mosaic floor from the west

b. The Bath hall, mosaic floor from the north-west

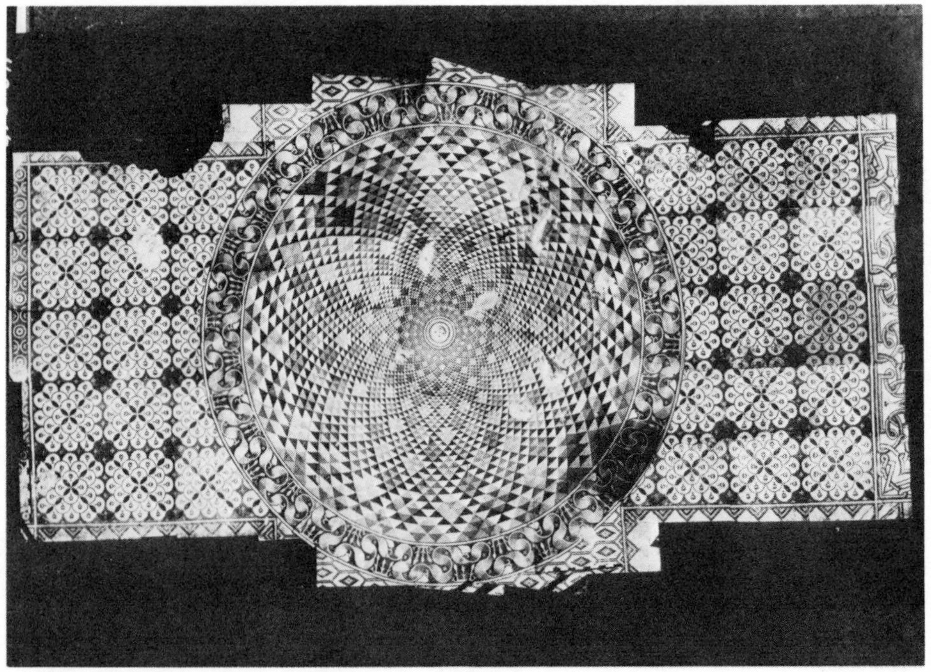

c. The Bath hall, mosaic floor, the central medallion

d. The Bath hall, mosaic floor of exedra V

KHIRBAT AL-MAFJAR

a. General view from the south-east

Deutscher Palästina-Verein

b. South façade: decorated portion before removal to Berlin

c. South façade: all that is left of decoration to east of entrance

MSHATTĀ

a. Part to west of entrance, in 1873

Palestine Exploration Fund, New York (1875)

b. The entrance, in 1873

Palestine Exploration Fund, New York (1875)

MSHATTĀ

a. The *Dīwān*: dome cap

b. The *Dīwān*: dome cap, central part

c. The Bath: hot room D, looking north

d. The Bath: hot room C, looking east

KHIRBAT AL-MAFJAR

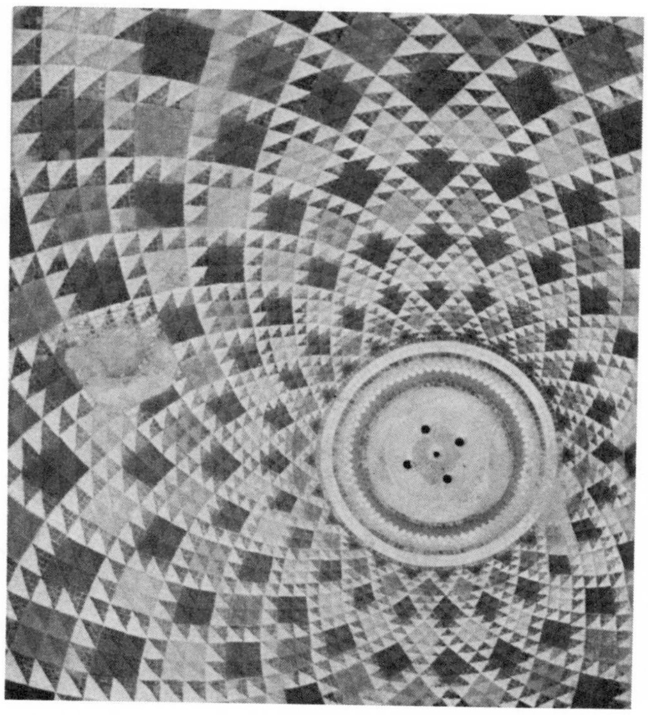

a. Panel 17

b. Exedra V

c. Exedra X

d. Exedra VIII

e. Panel 17

f. Panel 11

g. Exedra VIII

Schulz?

a. Basilical hall and triple apse before clearance

c. Part of arch of triple apse, now in Berlin

b. Basilical hall and triple apse after clearance

d. Capital of wall-pier to right in *b* (above), from the west

e. Capital of wall-pier to left in *a* (above)

MSHATTĀ

a. Triple apse, or 'triconchos' terminating basilical hall

b. Triple apse, or 'triconchos' terminating basilical hall

c. Latrine in tower to west of entrance

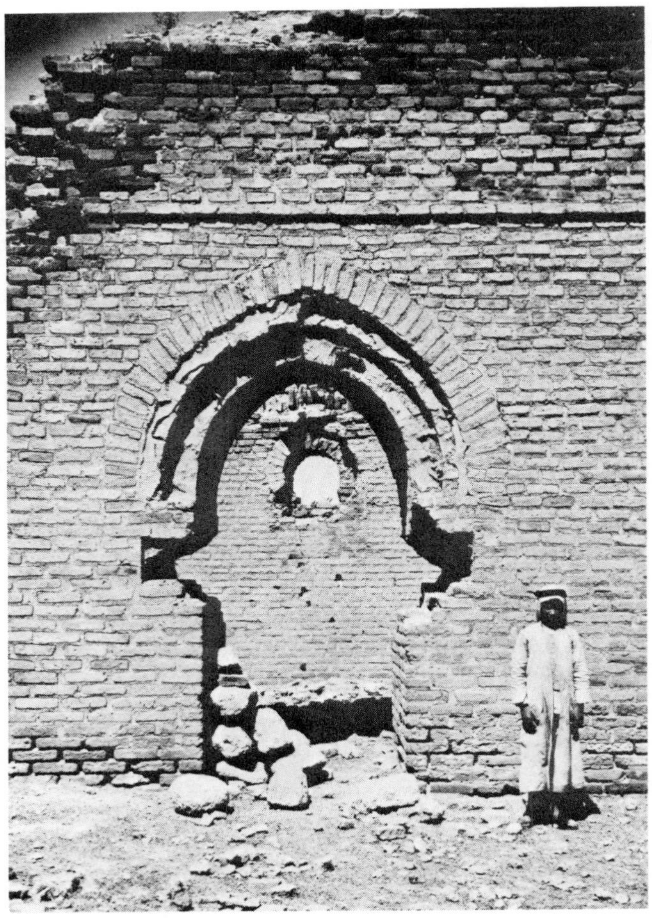

d. Doorway leading into p_1

e. Outline of vault in room e_1

MSHATTĀ

a. Basilical audience hall and living quarters, from the south

b. Basilical audience hall, terminating in triple apse

c. Capital of pier 1 above

e. A photograph taken in 1872 when the voussoirs of the arches lay as they had fallen

d. Capital of pier 2 above

MSHATTĀ

a. The miḥrāb before the clearance

c. Inner side of triple-arched façade of basilical hall

b. The miḥrāb after the clearance

d. The basilical hall, looking south-west

MSHATTĀ

a. Main Building, from the north

b. Vault in room d_1

c. Detail showing construction of vault at X above

d. From the air

MSHATTĀ

a. Interior, west side: detail of masonry, showing attachments for brick partition walls

b. The façade as erected in Berlin

MSHATTĀ

Staatliche Museen

MSHATTĀ

Façade to west of entrance: 1st triangle (A)

Scale $\frac{1}{12}$

Staatliche Museen

MSHATTĀ

Façade to west of entrance: 2nd triangle (B)

Scale $\frac{1}{12}$

Staatliche Museen

MSHATTĀ

Façade to west of entrance: 3rd triangle (C)

Scale $\frac{1}{12}$

Staatliche Museen

MSHATTĀ

Façade to west of entrance: 4th triangle (D)

Scale $\frac{1}{12}$

Staatliche Museen

MSHATTĀ

Façade to west of entrance: 5th triangle (E)

Scale $\frac{1}{12}$

Staatliche Museen

MSHATTĀ

Flanking tower on west side of entrance: 1st triangle (F)

Scale $\frac{1}{12}$

Staatliche Museen

MSHATTĀ

Flanking tower on west side of entrance: 2nd triangle (G)

Scale $\frac{1}{12}$

Staatliche Museen

MSHATTĀ

Flanking tower on west side of entrance: 3rd triangle (H)

Scale $\frac{1}{12}$

Staatliche Museen

MSHATTĀ

Flanking tower on west side of entrance: 4th triangle (I)

Scale $\frac{1}{12}$

Staatliche Museen

MSHATTĀ

Flanking tower on west side of entrance: 5th triangle (J)

Scale $\frac{1}{12}$

Staatliche Museen

MSHATTĀ

West side of entrance (K)

Scale $\frac{1}{12}$

Staatliche Museen

MSHATTĀ

East side of entrance (L)

Scale $\frac{1}{12}$

Staatliche Museen

a. Flanking tower on east side of entrance: 1st triangle (M)

Staatliche Museen

b. Flanking tower on east side of entrance: 2nd triangle (N)

MSHATTĀ

Scale $\frac{1}{12}$

a. Flanking tower on east side of entrance: 3rd triangle (O)

Staatliche Museen

b. Flanking tower on east side of entrance: 4th triangle (P)

Staatliche Museen

MSHATTĀ

Scale $\frac{1}{12}$

Staatliche Museen

a. Flanking tower on east side of entrance: 5th triangle (Q)

Germer-Durand

b. Façade to east of entrance: 1st triangle (R)

c. Façade to east of entrance: 1st triangle, present state (*c*. 1940)

MSHATTĀ

a. Façade to east of entrance, 2nd triangle (S) *Germer-Durand*

b. Half rosette embedded over a doorway in courtyard of same house

c. Rosette from triangle T embedded over a doorway in Zīza village

d. Façade to east of entrance: 2nd, 3rd, and 4th triangles (S, T, and U) *Germer-Durand*

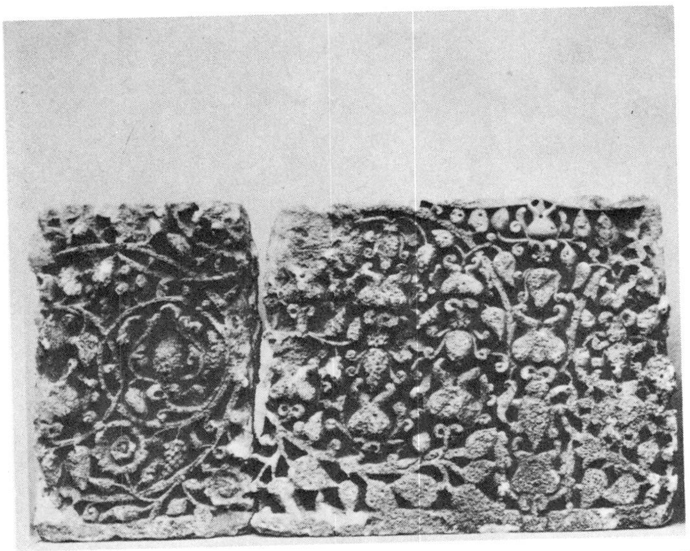

a. Background of last triangle?

Germer-Durand

b. Rosette, placed in last triangle at Berlin, but which apparently came from triple-arched façade

c. Façade to east of entrance: 5th and last triangle (V), before removal to Berlin

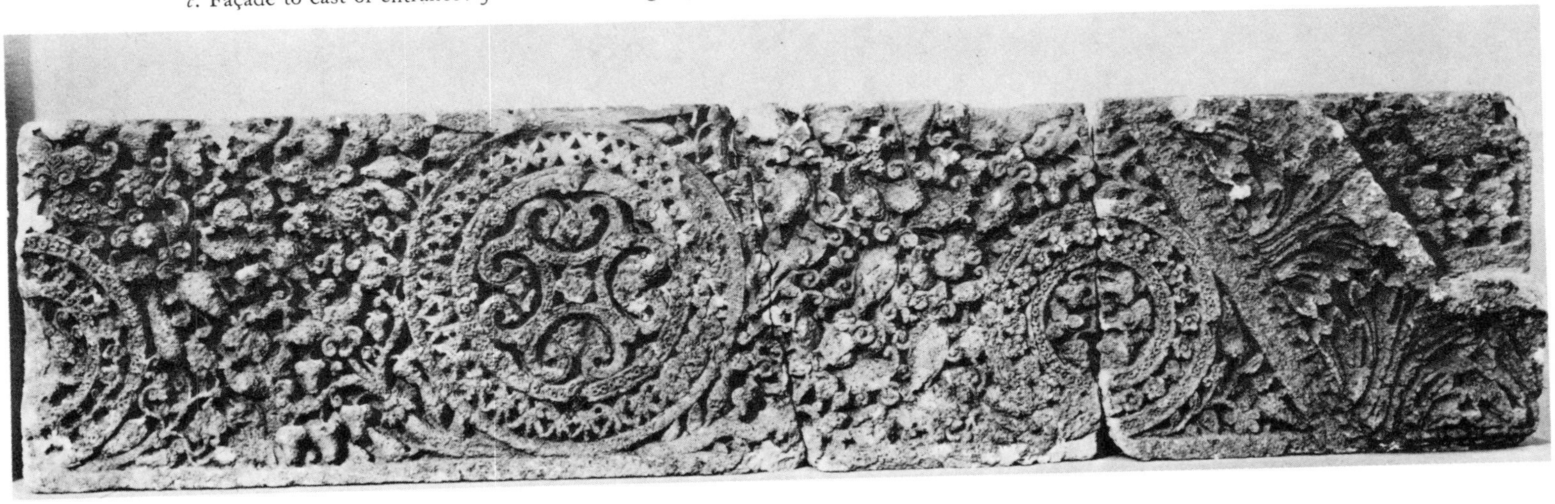

d. Last triangle, lowest course

a. From the north

b. North façade, west end

d. From the air *R.A.F., 'Ammān*

c. Entrance into room B

e. Doorway into room P

QAṢR AṬ-ṬŪBA

a. Lintel of doorway into room B

b. East side of rooms O and O′, and main entrance

d. Windows in room O, looking into O′

e. East side of rooms O and O′, showing how rings of vault lean against end wall

QAṢR AṬ-ṬŪBA

a

b

a and *b*. East façade of sanctuary showing breaks in masonry. The space between these two photographs has been adjusted to give the correct distance

c. East façade, inner face

d. Wall-pier (see *c* for position)

e. Pier of central arch of back arcade of sanctuary

ḤARRĀN: THE GREAT MOSQUE

b. The *ṣaḥn*, looking south-east

d. The transept

a. ḤARRĀN: minaret of Great Mosque

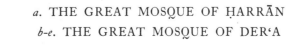

c. The transept

e. The transept and side aisles

a. THE GREAT MOSQUE OF ḤARRĀN

b–e. THE GREAT MOSQUE OF DERʿA